Methodological Advancements in Intelligent Information Technologies:
Evolutionary Trends

Vijayan Sugumaran
Oakland University, USA

 **INFORMATION SCIENCE REFERENCE**

Hershey · New York

Director of Editorial Content:	Kristin Klinger
Senior Managing Editor:	Jamie Snavely
Assistant Managing Editor:	Michael Brehm
Publishing Assistant:	Sean Woznicki
Typesetter:	Kurt Smith, Sean Woznicki
Cover Design:	Lisa Tosheff
Printed at:	Yurchak Printing Inc.

Published in the United States of America by
Information Science Reference (an imprint of IGI Global)
701 E. Chocolate Avenue
Hershey PA 17033
Tel: 717-533-8845
Fax: 717-533-8661
E-mail: cust@igi-global.com
Web site: http://www.igi-global.com/reference

Library of Congress Cataloging-in-Publication Data

Methodological advancements in intelligent information technologies : evolutionary trends / Vijayan Sugumaran, editor.
    p. cm.

Includes bibliographical references and index.
Summary: "This book provides various aspects of intelligent information technologies as they are applied to organizations to assist in improving productivity through the use of autonomous decision-making systems"--Provided by publisher.

ISBN 978-1-60566-970-0 (hbk.) -- ISBN 978-1-60566-971-7 (ebook) 1.
Information technology. 2. Expert systems (Computer science) 3. Intelligent
agents (Computer software) I. Sugumaran, Vijayan, 1960-
T58.5.M448 2010
004--dc22
                        2009035472

British Cataloguing in Publication Data
A Cataloguing in Publication record for this book is available from the British Library.

Advances in Intelligent Information Technologies Series (AIIT)

ISBN: 1935-3375

Editor-in-Chief: Vijayan Sugumaran, Oakland University, USA

Application of Agents and Intelligent Information Technologies

IGI Publishing • copyright 2007 • 377 pp • H/C (ISBN: 1-59904-265-7) • E-Book (ISBN: 1-59904-267-3)

Intelligent agent technology is emerging as one of the most important and rapidly advancing areas. Researchers are developing a number of agent-based applications and multi-agent systems in a variety of fields, such as: electronic commerce, supply chain management, resource allocation, intelligent manufacturing, mass customization, industrial control, information retrieval and filtering, collaborative work, mobile commerce, decision support, and computer games. Application of Agents and Intelligent Information Technologies presents an outstanding collection of the latest research associated with intelligent agents and information technologies. Application of Agents and Intelligent Information Technologies provides a comprehensive analysis of issues related to agent design, implementation, integration, deployment, evaluation, and business value. This book presents research results and application of agents and other intelligent information technologies in various domains. Application of Agents and Intelligent Information Technologies offers the intelligent information technologies that will potentially revolutionize the work environment as well as social computing.

Intelligent Information Technologies and Applications

IGI Publishing • copyright 2007 • 300+ pp • H/C (ISBN: 978-1-59904-958-8)

With the inundation of emergent online- and Web-centered technologies, there has been an increased focus on intelligent information technologies that are designed to enable users to accomplish complex tasks with relative ease. Intelligent Information Technologies and Applications provides cutting-edge research on the modeling; implementation; and financial, environmental, and organizational implications of this dynamic topic to researchers and practitioners in fields such as information systems, intelligent agents, artificial intelligence, and Web engineering.

The Advances in Intelligent Information Technologies (AIIT) Book Series endeavors to bring together researchers in related fields such as information systems, distributed Artificial Intelligence, intelligent agents, and collaborative work, to explore and discuss various aspects of design and development of intelligent technologies. Intelligent information technologies are being used by a large number of organizations for improving productivity in many roles such as assistants to human operators and autonomous decision-making components of complex systems. While a number of intelligent applications have been developed in various domains, there are still a number of research issues that have to be explored in terms of their design, implementation, integration, and deployment over the Internet or a corporate Intranet. The Advances in Intelligent Information Technologies (AIIT) Book Series aims to create a catalyst for emerging research in this field of growing importance through developing and delivering comprehensive publications for the betterment of intelligent information technologies and their applications. Through the availability of high-quality resources, the series hopes to further the development of this field and build upon the foundation of future implications.

Hershey • New York
Order online at www.igi-global.com or call 717-533-8845 x100 –
Mon-Fri 8:30 am - 5:00 pm (est) or fax 24 hours a day 717-533-8661

Table of Contents

Section 1
Intelligent Agent and Multiagent Systems

Section 2
Semantic Technologies and Applications

Section 3
Decision Support and Modeling

Detailed Table of Contents

Section 1
Intelligent Agent and Multiagent Systems

Chapter 1

Manuel Kolp, Université catholique de Louvain, Belgium

Yves Wautelet, Université catholique de Louvain, Belgium

Sodany Kiv, Université catholique de Louvain, Belgium

Vi Tran, Université catholique de Louvain, Belgium

Multi-Agent Systems (MAS) architectures are gaining popularity over traditional ones for building open, distributed, and evolving software required by today's corporate IT applications such as e-business systems, Web services or enterprise knowledge bases. Since the fundamental concepts of multi-agent systems are social and intentional rather than object, functional, or implementation-oriented, the design of MAS architectures can be eased by using social-driven templates. They are detailed agent-oriented design idioms to describe MAS architectures as composed of autonomous agents that interact and coordinate to achieve their intentions, like actors in human organizations. This chapter presents social patterns, as well as organizational styles, and focuses on a framework aimed to gain insight into these templates. The framework can be integrated into agent-oriented software engineering methodologies used to build MAS. The authors consider the Broker social pattern to illustrate the framework. The mapping from system architectural design (through organizational architectural styles), to system detailed design (through social patterns), is overviewed with a data integration case study. The automation of patterns design is also overviewed.

Chapter 2

Faheema Maghrabi, Ain Shams University, Egypt

Hossam M. Faheem, Ain Shams University, Egypt

Taysir Soliman, Asuit University, Egypt

Zaki Taha Fayed, Ain Shams University, Egypt

Biological data has been rapidly increasing in volume in different Web data sources. To query multiple data sources manually on the internet is time consuming for biologists. Therefore, systems and tools that facilitate searching multiple biological data sources are needed. Traditional approaches to build distributed or federated systems do not scale well to the large, diverse, and the growing number of biological data sources. Internet search engines allow users to search through large numbers of data sources, but provide very limited capabilities for locating, combining, processing, and organizing information. A promising approach to this problem is to provide access to the large number of biological data sources through a multiagent-based framework where a set of agents can cooperate with each other to retrieve relevant information from different biological Web databases. The proposed system uses a mediator-based integration approach with domain ontology, which uses as a global schema. This chapter proposes a multiagent-based framework that responds to biological queries according to its biological domain ontology.

Chapter 3

Yves Wautelet, Université catholique de Louvain, Belgium
Christophe Schinckus, Facultés Universitaires St-Louis, Belgium
Manuel Kolp, Université catholique de Louvain, Belgium

This chapter presents a modern epistemological validation of the process of agent oriented software development. Agent orientation has been widely presented in recent years as a novel modeling, design and programming paradigm for building systems using features such as openness, dynamics, sociality and intentionality. These will be put into perspective through a Lakatosian epistemological approach. The contribution of this chapter is to get researchers acquainted with the epistemological basis of the agent research domain and the context of the emergence of object and agent-orientation. This chapter advocates the use of the Lakatosian research programme concept as an epistemological basis for object and agent orientation. This is done on the basis of how these frameworks operationalize relevant theoretical concepts of the Kuhnian and Lakatosian theories.

Chapter 4

T. Chithralekha, Pondicherry University, India
S. Kuppuswami, Pondicherry University, India

Language ability is an inevitable aspect of delegation in agents to provide for collaborative natural language interaction (CNLI) during task delegation. To cater to users of different languages, the CNLI is required to be multilingual. When multilingual CNLI has to be provided in a manner characteristic of agents, it leads to realizing two types of autonomies viz. behavior autonomy - to provide CNLI in every language and management autonomy for managing the multiple language competencies. Thereby, the language ability of an agent evolves into a language faculty which encompasses behavior and behavior management autonomies. The existing paradigms for the internal state of agents are only behavior-oriented and cannot accommodate the behavior and behavior management autonomies. In this chapter, a new paradigm for the internal state of the language faculty of agents consisting of the belief, task and behavior (BTB) abstractions has been proposed, defined and illustrated.

Learning is a process to acquire new knowledge. Ideally, this process is the result of an active interaction of key cognitive processes, such as perception, imagery, organization, and elaboration. Quality learning has emphasized on designing a course curriculum or learning process, which can elicit the cognitive processing of learners. However, most e-learning systems nowadays are resources-oriented instead of process-oriented. These systems were designed without adequate support of pedagogical principles to guide the learning process. They have not explained the sequence of how the knowledge was acquired, which, in fact, is extremely important to the quality of learning. This study aims to develop an e-learning environment that enables students to get engaged in their learning process by guiding and customizing their learning process in an adaptive way. The expected performance of the Agent-based e-learning Process model is also evaluated by comparing with traditional e-learning models.

Dynamic and active information fusion processes select the best sensor based on expected utility calculation in order to integrate the evidences acquires both accurately and timely. However, inference degradation happens when the same/similar sensors are selected repeatedly over time if the selection strategy is not well designed that considers the history of sensor engagement. This phenomenon decreases fusion accuracy and efficiency, in direct conflict to the objective of information integration with multiple sensors. This chapter tries to provide a mathematical scrutiny of this problem in the myopia planning popularly utilized in active information fusion. In evaluation it first introduces the common active information fusion context using security surveillance applications. It then examines the generic dynamic Bayesian network model for a mental state recognition task and analyzes experimentation results for the inference degradation. It also discusses the candidate solutions with some preliminary results. The inference degradation problem is not limited to the discussed task and may emerge in variants of sensor planning strategies even with more global optimization approach. This study provides common guidelines in information integration applications for information awareness and intelligent decision.

Section 2
Semantic Technologies and Applications

This chapter proposes a multi-agent based framework that allows multiple data sources and models to be semantically integrated for spatial modeling in business processing. The authors introduce a multi-agent system (OSIRIS – Ontology-based Spatial Information and Resource Integration Services) to semantically interoperate complex spatial services and integrate them in a meaningful composition. The advantage of using multi-agent collaboration in OSIRIS is that it obviates the need for end-user analysts to be able to decompose a problem domain to subproblems or to map different models according to what they actually mean. The authors also illustrate a multi-agent interaction scenario for collaborative modeling of spatial applications using the proposed custom feature of OSIRIS using Description Logics. The system illustrates an application of domain ontology of urban environmental hydrology and evaluation of decision maker's consequences of land use changes. In e-government context, the proposed OSIRIS framework works as semantic layer for one stop geospatial portal.

Chapter 8

Nwe Ni Tun, National University of Singapore, Singapore
Satoshi Tojo, Japan Advanced Institute of Science and Technology, Japan

Ontologies are intended to facilitate semantic interoperability among distributed and intelligent information systems where diverse software components, computing devices, knowledge, and data, are involved. Since a single global ontology is no longer sufficient to support a variety of tasks performed on differently conceptualized knowledge, ontologies have proliferated in multiple forms of heterogeneity even for the same domain, and such ontologies are called heterogeneous ontologies. For interoperating among information systems through heterogeneous ontologies, an important step in handling semantic heterogeneity should be the attempt to enrich (and clarify) the semantics of concepts in ontologies. In this chapter, a conceptual model (called EnOntoModel) of semantically-enriched ontologies is proposed by applying three philosophical notions: identity, rigidity, and dependency. As for the advantages of EnOntoModel, the conceptual analysis of enriched ontologies and efficient matching between them are presented.

Chapter 9

H. Arafat Ali, Mansoura University, Egypt
Ali I. El Desouky, Mansoura University, Egypt
Ahmed I. Saleh, Mansoura University, Egypt

Search engines are the most important search tools for finding useful and recent information on the Web today. They rely on crawlers that continually crawl the Web for new pages. Meanwhile, focused crawlers have become an attractive area for research in recent years. They suggest a better solution for general purpose search engine limitations and lead to a new generation of search engines called vertical-search engines. Searching the Web vertically is to divide the Web into smaller regions; each region is related to a specific domain. In addition, one crawler is allowed to search in each domain. The innovation of this chapter is adding intelligence and adaptation ability to focused crawlers. Such added features will certainly guide the crawler perfectly to retrieve more relevant pages while crawling the Web. The proposed crawler has the ability to estimate the rank of the page before visiting it and adapts itself to any changes in its domain using.

Chapter 10

Information overload on the World Wide Web is a well recognized problem. Research to subdue this problem and extract maximum benefit from the Internet is still in its infancy. Managing information overload on the Web is a challenge and the need for more precise techniques for assisting the user in finding the most relevant and most useful information is obvious. Search engines are very effective at filtering pages that match explicit queries. Search engines, however, require massive memory resources (to store an index of the Web) and tremendous network bandwidth (to create and continually refresh the index). These systems receive millions of queries per day, and as a result, the CPU cycles devoted to satisfying each individual query are sharply curtailed. There is no time for intelligence which is mandatory for offering ways to combat information overload. What is needed are systems, often referred to as information customization systems, that act on the user's behalf and that can rely on existing information services like search engines that do the resource-intensive part of the work. These systems will be sufficiently lightweight to run on an average PC and serve as personal assistants. Since such an assistant has relatively modest resource requirements it can reside on an individual user's machine. If the assistant resides on the user's machine, there is no need to turn down intelligence. The system can have substantial local intelligence. In an attempt to circumvent the problems of search engines and contribute to resolving the problem of information overload over the Web, this chapter proposes SOMSE, a system that improves the quality of Web search by combining meta-search and unsupervised learning.

Increasingly information systems log historic information in a systematic way. Workflow management systems, but also ERP, CRM, SCM, and B2B systems often provide a so-called "event log" (i.e., a log recording the execution of activities). Thus far, process mining has been mainly focusing on structured event logs resulting in powerful analysis techniques and tools for discovering process, control, data, organizational, and social structures from event logs. Unfortunately, many work processes are not supported by systems providing structured logs. Instead very basic tools such as text editors, spreadsheets, and e-mail are used. This chapter explores the application of process mining to e-mail, (i.e., unstructured or semi-structured e-mail messages) are converted into event logs suitable for application of process mining tools. This chapter presents the tool EMailAnalyzer, embedded in the ProM process mining framework, which analyzes and transforms e-mail messages to a format that allows for analysis using our process mining techniques. The main innovative aspect of this work is that, unlike most other work in this area, the current analysis is not restricted to social network analysis. Based on e-mail logs, the authors can also discover interaction patterns and processes.

Section 3
Decision Support and Modeling

Chapter 12

A. F. Salam, University of North Carolina at Greensboro, USA

This research is motivated by the critical problem of stark incompatibility between the contractual clauses (typically buried in legal documents) and the myriad of performance measures used to evaluate and reward (or penalize) supply participants in the extended enterprise. This difference between what is contractually expected and what is actually performed in addition to the lack of transparency of what is measured and how those measures relate to the contractual obligations make it difficult, error prone and confusing for different partner organizations. To address this critical issue, this chapter presents a supplier performance contract monitoring and execution decision support architecture and its prototype implementation using a business case study. The author uses the SWRL extension of OWL-DL to represent contract conditions and rules as part of the ontology and then use the Jess Rule Reasoner to execute the contract rules integrating with Service Oriented Computing to provide decision support to managers in the extended enterprise.

Chapter 13

Harold J. Lagroue III, University of Louisiana - Lafayette, USA

This chapter addresses an area which holds considerable promise for enhancing the effective utilization of advanced information technologies: the feasibility of using system-directed multi-modal user support for facilitating users of advanced information technologies. An application for automating the information technology facilitation process is used to compare group decision-making effectiveness of human-facilitated groups with groups using virtual facilitation in an experiment employing auditors, accountants, and IT security professionals as participants. The results of the experiment are presented and possible avenues for future research studies are suggested.

Chapter 14

Mirjam Minor, University of Trier, Germany
Alexander Tartakovski, University of Trier, Germany
Daniel Schmalen, University of Trier, Germany
Ralph Bergmann, University of Trier, Germany

The increasing dynamics of today's work impacts the business processes. Agile workflow technology is a means for the automation of adaptable processes. However, the modification of workflows is a difficult task that is performed by human experts. This chapter discusses the novel approach of agile workflow technology for dynamic, long-term scenarios and on change reuse. First, it introduces new concepts for a workflow modelling language and enactment service, which enable an interlocked modelling and execution of workflows by means of a sophisticated suspension mechanism. Second, it provides new process-oriented methods of case-based reasoning in order to support the reuse of change experience. The results from an experimental evaluation in a real-world scenario highlight the usefulness and the practical impact of this work.

Raoudha Ben Djemaa, MIRACL, Tunisie
Ikram Amous, MIRACL, Tunisie
Abdelmajid Ben Hamadou, MIRACL, Tunisie

The complexity of adaptive Web applications (AWA) is increasing almost every day. Besides impacting the implementation phase, this complexity must also be suitably managed while modeling the application. To this end, this chapter proposes an approach for AWA called GIWA based on WA-UML (Web Adaptive Unified Modeling Language). This extension defines a set of stereotypes and constraints, which make possible the modeling of AWA. GIWA's target is to facilitate the automatic execution of the design and the automatic generation of adaptable web interface. The GIWA methodology is based on different step: requirement analysis, conceptual design, adaptation design and generation. Using GIWA, designers can specify, at a requirement analysis, the features of Web application to be generated. These features are represented, at the conceptual level using WA-UML. At the adaptation level, GIWA acquires all information about users' preferences and their access condition to be used at the generation level. The last level is based on java swing interface to instantiate models which are translated in XML files. GIWA uses then XSL files (user preferences) and RDF files (devices' capability) to generate the HTML page corresponding to the user.

Sandeep Kumar, Banaras Hindu University (IT-BHU), India
Kuldeep Kumar, Kurukshetra University, India

Semantic Web service selection is considered as the one of the most important aspects of semantic Web service composition process. The Quality of Service (QoS) and cognitive parameters can be a good basis for this selection process. This chapter presents a hybrid selection model for the selection of semantic Web services based on their QoS and cognitive parameters. The presented model provides a new approach of measuring the QoS parameters in an accurate way and provides a completely novel and formalized measurement of different cognitive parameters.

Preface

In the highly inter-connected world we live in today, a variety of intelligent information technologies are enabling the exchange of information and knowledge to solve problems. Communication technologies and social computing are emerging as the backbone to gather information and execute various tasks from any place at any time. While it is putting significant pressure on the bandwidth that carries much of this communication, it is also pushing the frontiers of innovation on the capabilities of handheld devices. Continued innovations are needed to ensure that mobile intelligent information technologies can continue to meet our needs in an environment, where our ability to make decisions depends on our ability to access a reliable source of information that is real time — something that can be facilitated by tapping into the collective wisdom of a network of people in a community and the knowledge coming together on-demand.

Community networks exist in several disciplines; however, they are generally limited in scope. The content and knowledge created in a community network typically stays within its boundary. One of the main reasons why there is not much connectivity or interaction between various community networks is that each community has its own data and knowledge representation and the content repositories are heterogeneous. Moreover, there are no common standards that facilitate data interoperability between the applications in disparate community networks. Several research efforts attempt to fill this gap through the use of semantic technologies. They focus on developing interoperability mechanisms to support knowledge and data exchange through semantic mediation. For each community, a local ontology and metadata can be created that capture the syntactic and semantic aspects of the content that is part of the network. The community network interface will enable users to participate in this metadata and ontology creation process. The ontologies and the metadata from each of the networks can then be integrated to create a global ontology and meta schema. This can be used to provide interoperability between multiple community networks and facilitate broader collaboration.

A community network supports both individual interactions and multiple collaborations within a group. Users can create and contribute content, discover services, use resources, and leverage the power of the community. The community network can provide a range of opportunities for users to access various knowledge repositories, database servers and source documents. The infrastructure provided by the community network enables multiple channels of accessibility and enhanced opportunities for collaboration. One of the goals of this stream of research is to create a community infrastructure with appropriate services, protocols, and collaboration mechanisms that will support information integration and interoperability.

Human Computation refers to the application of human intelligence to solve complex difficult problems that cannot be solved by computers alone. Humans can see patterns and semantics (context, content, and relationships) more quickly, accurately, and meaningfully than machines. Human Computation therefore applies to the problem of annotating, labeling, and classifying voluminous data streams. Of course, the application of autonomous machine intelligence (data mining and machine learning) to the annotation, labeling, and classification of data granules is also valid and efficacious. Machine learning and data mining techniques are needed to cope with the ever-increasing amounts of data being collected by scientific instruments. They are particularly suited to identify near-real-time events and to track the evolution of those events. Thus, a real challenge for scientific communities is the categorization, storage and reuse of very large data sets to produce knowledge. There is a great need for developing services for the semantic annotation of data using human and computer-based techniques.

The best annotation service in the world is useless if the markups (tags) are not scientifically meaningful (i.e., if the tags do not enable data reuse and understanding). Therefore, it is incumbent upon science disciplines and research communities to develop common data models, common terminology, taxonomies, and ontologies. These semantic annotations are often expressed in XML form, either as RDF (Resource Description Framework) triples or in OWL (Web Ontology Language).

Consequently, in order for the data to be reusable, several traditional conditions must be met, except that these must be satisfied now through non-traditional approaches. For example, data reusability typically depends on: (1) data discovery (all relevant data must be found in order for a research project to be meaningful); (2) data understanding (data must be understood in order to be useful); (3) data interoperability (data must work with legacy data and with current data from multiple sources in order to maximize their value); and (4) data integration (data must work with current analysis tools in order to yield results). Non-traditional approaches are needed to meet these conditions as the enormous growth in scientific data volumes render it impractical for humans alone to classify and index the incoming data flood. These new approaches include intelligent techniques such as machine learning, data mining, annotation, informatics, and semantic technologies. To address these needs, one needs to design and implement a semantic annotation service based on current and emerging standards that incorporate tags in loosely-structured folksonomies and ontologies. This could be offered as a service similar to other data services provided by intelligent agent and multiagent systems.

BOOK ORGANIZATION

Section 1: Intelligent Agent and Multiagent Systems

This book is organized in three sections. The first section discusses issues related to intelligent agent and multiagent systems, the second section introduces semantic technologies and their applications and the third section delves into decision support and modeling. In the first section, there are six chapters related to intelligent agents. The first chapter is titled "*Engineering Software Systems with Social-Driven Templates*," by Manuel Kolp, Yves Wautelet, Sodany Kiv, and Vi Tran. They contend that Multi-Agent Systems (MAS) architectures are gaining popularity over traditional ones for building open, distributed, and evolving software required by today's corporate IT applications such as e-business systems, web services or enterprise knowledge bases. Since the fundamental concepts of multi-agent systems are social and intentional rather than object, functional, or implementation-oriented, the design of MAS architectures can be eased by using social patterns. They are detailed agent-oriented design idioms to describe MAS architectures composed of autonomous agents that interact and coordinate to achieve their intentions, like actors in human organizations. This chapter presents social patterns and focuses on a framework aimed to gain insight into these patterns. The framework can be integrated into agent-oriented software engineering methodologies used to build MAS. An overview of the mapping from system architectural design (through organizational architectural styles), to system detailed design (through social patterns), is presented with a data integration case study.

The second chapter is titled "*A Multiagent-Based Framework for Integrating Biological Data*," authored by Faheema Maghrabi, Hossam M. Faheem, Taysir Soliman, and Zaki Taha Fayed. Biological data has been rapidly increasing in volume in different web data sources. To query multiple data sources manually on the internet is time consuming for the biologists. Therefore, systems and tools that facilitate searching multiple biological data sources are needed. Traditional approaches to build distributed or federated systems do not scale well to the large, diverse, and growing number of biological data sources. Internet search engines allow users to search through large numbers of data sources, but provide very limited capabilities for locating, combining, processing, and organizing information. A promising approach to this problem is to provide access to the large number of biological data sources through a multiagent-based framework where a set of agents can cooperate with each other to retrieve relevant information from different biological web databases. The proposed system uses a mediator based integration approach with domain ontology, which uses as a global schema. This chapter proposes a multiagent-based framework that responds to biological queries according to its biological domain ontology.

The third chapter is titled "*A Modern Epistemological Reading of Agent Orientation*," by Yves Wautelet, Christophe Schinckus, and Manuel Kolp. This chapter presents a modern epistemological validation of the process of agent oriented software development. Agent orientation has been widely presented in recent years as a novel modeling, design and programming paradigm for building systems using features such as openness, dynamics, sociality and intentionality. These will be put into perspective through a Lakatosian epistemological approach. The contribution of this chapter is to get researchers acquainted with the epistemological basis of the agent research domain and the context of the emergence of object and agent-orientation. The chapter advocates the use of the Lakatosian research programme concept as an epistemological basis for object and agent orientation. This is done on the basis of how these frameworks operationalize relevant theoretical concepts of the Kuhnian and Lakatosian theories.

The fourth chapter is titled "*A Generic Internal State Paradigm for the Language Faculty of Agents for Task Delegation*," by T. Chithralekha, and S. Kuppuswami. Language ability is an inevitable aspect of delegation in agents to provide for collaborative natural language interaction which is very much essential for delegation. In order that the agent is able to provide its services to users of multiple languages, this collaborative natural language interaction is required to be multilingual. When these two language ability requirements have to be provided in a manner characteristic of agents, it leads to realizing two types of autonomies viz. behavior autonomy to provide collaborative natural language interaction in every language and language ability management autonomy for managing the multiple language competencies. Thus, the language ability of an agent evolves into a language faculty by possessing behavior and behavior management autonomies. The existing paradigms for the internal state of agents are only behavior-oriented and do not suffice to represent the internal state of the language faculty. Hence, in this chapter a new paradigm for the internal state of the language faculty of agents consisting of the belief, task and behavior (BTB) abstractions has been proposed. Its semantics and dynamism have been explained. The application of this paradigm has also been illustrated with examples.

The fifth chapter is titled "*An Agent-Based Approach to Process Management in E-Learning Environments*," by Hokyin Lai, Minhong Wang, Jingwen He, and Huaiqing Wang. Learning is a process to acquire new knowledge. Ideally, this process is the result of an active interaction of key cognitive processes, such as perception, imagery, organization, and elaboration. Quality learning has emphasized on designing a course curriculum or learning process, which can elicit the cognitive processing of learners. However, most e-Learning systems nowadays are resources-oriented instead of process-oriented. These systems were designed without adequate support of pedagogical principles to guide the learning process. They have not explained the sequence of how the knowledge was acquired, which, in fact, is extremely important to the quality of learning. This study aims to develop an e-Learning environment that enables students to get engaged in their learning process by guiding and customizing their learning process in an adaptive way. The expected performance of the Agent-based e-Learning Process model is also evaluated by comparing with traditional e-Learning models.

The sixth chapter is titled "*Inference Degradation in Information Fusion: A Bayesian Network Case,*" by Xiangyang Li. Bayesian networks have been extensively used in active information fusion that selects the best sensor based on expected utility calculation. However, inference degradation happens when the same sensors are selected repeatedly over time if the applied strategy is not well designed to consider the history of sensor engagement. This phenomenon decreases fusion accuracy and efficiency, in direct conflict to the objective of information integration with multiple sensors. This chapter provides mathematical scrutiny of the inference degradation problem in the popular myopia planning. It examines the generic dynamic Bayesian network models and shows experimentation results for mental state recognition tasks. It also discusses the candidate solutions with initial results. The inference degradation problem is not limited to the discussed fusion tasks and may emerge in variants of sensor planning strategies with more global optimization approach. This study provides common guidelines in information integration applications for information awareness and intelligent decision.

Section 2: Semantic Technologies and Applications

The second section contains five chapters dealing with semantic technologies and applications. The seventh chapter titled "*Agent-Based Semantic Interoperability of Geo-Services,*" is authored by Iftikhar U. Sikder and Santosh K. Misra. This chapter proposes a multi-agent based framework that allows multiple data sources and models to be semantically integrated for spatial modeling in business processing. The chapter reviews the feasibility of ontology-based spatial resource integration options to combine the core spatial reasoning with domain-specific application models. The authors propose an ontology-based framework for semantic level communication of spatial objects and application models. A multi-agent system (OSIRIS – Ontology-based Spatial Information and Resource Integration Services) is introduced, which semantically interoperates complex spatial services and integrates them in a meaningful composition. The advantage of using multi-agent collaboration in OSIRIS is that it obviates the need for end-user analysts to be able to decompose a problem domain to subproblems or to map different models according to what they actually mean. A multi-agent interaction scenario for collaborative modeling of spatial applications using the proposed custom feature of OSIRIS is illustrated. The framework is then applied in the use case scenario in e-Government by developing a prototype system. The system illustrates an application of domain ontology of urban environmental hydrology and evaluation of decision maker's consequences of land use changes. In e-Government context, the proposed OSIRIS framework works as semantic layer for one stop geospatial portal.

The eighth chapter is titled "*EnOntoModel: A Semantically-Enriched Model for Ontologies,*" written by Nwe Ni Tun and Satoshi Tojo. Ontologies are intended to facilitate semantic interoperability among distributed and intelligent information systems where diverse software components, computing devices, knowledge, and data, are involved. Since a single global ontology is no longer sufficient to support a variety of tasks performed on differently conceptualized knowledge, ontologies have proliferated in multiple forms of heterogeneity even for the same domain, and such ontologies are called *heterogeneous ontologies*. For interoperating among information systems through heterogeneous ontologies, an important step in handling semantic heterogeneity should be the attempt to enrich (and clarify) the semantics of concepts in ontologies. In this chapter, the authors propose a conceptual model (called EnOntoModel) of semantically-enriched ontologies by applying three philosophical notions: *identity*, *rigidity*, and *dependency*. As for the advantages of EnOntoModel, the conceptual analysis of enriched ontologies and efficient matching between them are presented.

The ninth chapter is titled "*A New Approach for Building a Scalable and Adaptive Vertical Search Engine*," authored by H. Arafat Ali, Ali I. El Desouky, and Ahmed I. Saleh. Search engines are the most important search tools for finding useful and recent information on the web, which rely on crawlers that continually crawl the web for new pages. They suggest a better solution for general-purpose search engine limitations that lead to a new generation of search engines called vertical-search engines. Searching the web vertically is to divide the web into smaller regions; each region is related to a specific domain. In addition, one crawler is allowed to search in each domain. The innovation of this work is adding intelligence and adaptation ability to focused crawlers. Such added features guide the crawler perfectly to retrieve more relevant pages while crawling the web. The proposed crawler has the ability to estimate the rank of the page before visiting it and adapts itself to any changes in its domain using. It also uses novel techniques for rating the extracted links so that it can decide which page to be visited next with high accuracy. The proposed approach integrates evidence from both content and linkage. It is unique in two aspects. First, it simplifies the focused crawling and improves the crawling performance by maximizing both crawler intelligence and adaptively. Second, it tries to overcome drawbacks of traditional crawling approaches by combining a number of different disciplines like; information retrieval, machine learning, link context and linking structure of the web. Hence, it can simply achieve; tunneling, better accuracy, simple implementation, and self-dependency. Experimental results have shown that the proposed strategy demonstrates significant performance improvement over traditional crawling techniques.

The tenth chapter titled "*Information Customization using SOMSE: A Self-Organizing Map Based Approach*," is written by Mohamed Salah Hamdi. Conventional Web search engines return long lists of ranked documents that users are forced to sift through to find relevant documents. The notoriously low precision of Web search engines coupled with the ranked list presentation make it hard for users to find the information they are looking for. One of the fundamental issues of information retrieval is searching for compromises between precision and recall. It is generally desirable to have high precision and high recall, although in reality, increasing precision often means decreasing recall and vice versa. Developing retrieval techniques that will yield high recall and high precision is desirable. Unfortunately, such techniques would impose additional resource demands on the search engines. Search engines are under severe resource constraints and dedicating enough CPU time to each query might not be feasible. A more productive approach, however, seems to enhance post-processing of the retrieved set, such as providing links and semantic maps to retrieved results of a query. If such value-adding processes allow the user to easily identify relevant documents from a large retrieved set, queries that produce low precision/high recall results will become more acceptable. This chapter attempts to improve the quality of Web search by combining meta-search and self-organizing maps. This can help users both in locating interesting documents more easily and in getting an overview of the retrieved document set.

The eleventh chapter is titled "*Mining E-Mail Messages: Uncovering Interaction Patterns and Processes Using E-Mail Logs,*" by Wil M.P. van der Aalst and Andriy Nikolov. Increasingly information systems log historic information in a systematic way. Workflow management systems, as well as ERP, CRM, SCM, and B2B systems often provide a so-called "event log", i.e., a log recording the execution of activities. Thus far, process mining has been mainly focusing on structured event logs resulting in powerful analysis techniques and tools for discovering process, control, data, organizational, and social structures from event logs. Unfortunately, many work processes are not supported by systems providing structured logs. Instead very basic tools such as text editors, spreadsheets, and e-mail are used. This chapter explores the application of process mining to e-mail, i.e., unstructured or semi-structured e-mail messages are converted into event logs suitable for application of process mining tools. This chapter presents the tool *EMailAnalyzer,* embedded in the ProM process mining framework, which analyzes and transforms e-mail messages to a format that allows for analysis using process mining techniques. The main innovative aspect of this work is that, unlike most other work in this area, the analysis is not restricted to social network analysis. Based on e-mail logs the proposed approach can also discover interaction patterns and processes.

Section 3: Decision Support and Modeling

The third section of the book deals with decision support and modeling and contains five chapters. The twelfth chapter titled "*Semantic Supplier Contract Monitoring and Execution DSS Architecture,*" by A. F. Salam is motivated by the critical problem of stark *incompatibility* between the contractual clauses (typically buried in legal documents) and the myriad of performance measures used to evaluate and reward (or penalize) supply participants in the extended enterprise. This difference between what is *contractually* expected and what is *actually* performed in addition to the lack of transparency of what is measured and how those measures relate to the contractual obligations make it difficult, error prone and confusing for different partner organizations. To address this critical issue, this chapter presents a supplier performance contract monitoring and execution decision support architecture and its prototype implementation using a business case study. This work uses the SWRL extension of OWL-DL to represent contract conditions and rules as part of the ontology and then uses the Jess Rule Reasoner to execute the contract rules integrating with Service Oriented Computing to provide decision support to managers in the extended enterprise.

Chapter thirteen titled "*Supporting Structured Group Decision Making through System-Directed User Guidance: An Experimental Study,*" is contributed by Harold J. Lagroue III. This chapter addresses an area which holds considerable promise for enhancing the effective utilization of advanced information technologies: the feasibility of using system-directed multi-modal user support for facilitating users of advanced information technologies. An application for automating the information technology facilitation process is used to compare group decision-making effectiveness of human-facilitated groups with groups using virtual facilitation in an experiment employing auditors, accountants, and IT security professionals as participants. The results of the experiment are presented and possible avenues for future research studies are suggested.

The fourteenth chapter is titled "*Agile Workflow Technology for Long-Term Processes: Enhanced by Case-Based Change Reuse,*" presented by Mirjam Minor, Alexander Tartakovski, Daniel Schmalen, and Ralph Bergmann. The increasing dynamics of today's work impacts the business processes. Agile workflow technology is a means for the automation of adaptable processes. However, the modification of workflows is a difficult task that is performed by human experts. This chapter discusses the novel approach of agile workflow technology for dynamic, long-term scenarios and on change reuse. First, it introduces new concepts for a workflow modelling language and enactment service, which enable an interlocked modelling and execution of workflows by means of a sophisticated suspension mechanism. Second, it provides new process-oriented methods of case-based reasoning in order to support the reuse of change experience. The results from an experimental evaluation in a real-world scenario highlight the usefulness and the practical impact of this work.

Raoudha Ben Djemaa, Ikram Amous, and Abdelmajid Ben Hamadou have contributed chapter fifteen titled *"Extending a Conceptual Modeling Language for Adaptive Web Applications."* The complexity of Adaptive Web Applications (AWA) is increasing almost every day. Besides impacting the implementation phase, this complexity must also be suitably managed while modeling the application. In fact, personalization is a critical aspect in many popular domains such as e-commerce. It is so important that it should be dealt with through a design view, rather than only an implementation view (which discusses mechanisms, rather than design options). To this end, this chapter proposes an approach for AWA called GIWA based on WA-UML (Web Adaptive Unified Modeling Language). In fact, the acceptance of UML as a standard for the design of object-oriented systems, together with the explosive growth of the World Wide Web have raised the need for UML extensions to model hypermedia applications running on the Internet. GIWA's objective is to facilitate the automatic execution of the design and the automatic generation of adaptable web interface. The GIWA methodology is based on different steps: requirement analysis, conceptual design, adaptation design and generation. Using GIWA, designers can specify, at the requirement analysis stage, the features of web application to be generated. These features are represented, at the conceptual level using WA-UML; an UML extension for Adaptive Web Applications. It increases the expressivity of UML while adding labels and graphic annotations to UML diagrams. This extension defines a set of stereotypes and constraints, which facilitates the modeling of AWA.

The sixteenth chapter titled " " is written by Sandeep Kumar and Kuldeep Kumar. One of the most important aspects of semantic web service composition process is the selection of most appropriate semantic web service. The Quality of Service (QoS) and cognitive parameters can be a good basis for this selection process. This chapter presents a hybrid selection model for the selection of semantic web services based on their QoS and cognitive parameters. The presented model provides a new approach of measuring the QoS parameters in an accurate way and provides a completely novel and formalized measurement of different cognitive parameters.

Considerable advancements are being made in intelligent information technologies and novel methodologies and applications are emerging as these technologies mature. Efficient use of intelligent systems is becoming a necessary goal for all, and an outstanding collection of latest research associated with advancements in intelligent agent applications, semantic technologies, and decision support and modelling is presented in this book. Use of intelligent applications will greatly improve productivity in the social computing arena.

Vijayan Sugumaran
Editor-in-Chief
Methodological Advancements in Intelligent Information Technologies: Evolutionary Trends

Section 1
Intelligent Agent and Multiagent Systems

Chapter 1
Engineering Software Systems with Social-Driven Templates

Manuel Kolp
Université catholique de Louvain, Belgium

Yves Wautelet
Université catholique de Louvain, Belgium

Sodany Kiv
Université catholique de Louvain, Belgium

Vi Tran
Université catholique de Louvain, Belgium

ABSTRACT

Multi-Agent Systems (MAS) architectures are gaining popularity over traditional ones for building open, distributed, and evolving software required by today's corporate IT applications such as e-business systems, Web services or enterprise knowledge bases. Since the fundamental concepts of multi-agent systems are social and intentional rather than object, functional, or implementation-oriented, the design of MAS architectures can be eased by using social-driven templates. They are detailed agent-oriented design idioms to describe MAS architectures as composed of autonomous agents that interact and coordinate to achieve their intentions, like actors in human organizations. This paper presents social patterns, as well as organizational styles, and focuses on a framework aimed to gain insight into these templates. The framework can be integrated into agent-oriented software engineering methodologies used to build MAS. We consider the Broker social pattern to illustrate the framework. The mapping from system architectural design (through organizational architectural styles), to system detailed design (through social patterns), is overviewed with a data integration case study. The automation of patterns design is also overviewed.

DOI: 10.4018/978-1-60566-970-0.ch001

INTRODUCTION

This section introduces and motivates the research. We describe the advantages of using multi-agent systems over traditional systems. We then present the importance of *social templates* for designing information systems. We formulate our research proposal and introduce elements for work validation. The context of the research and an overview of the state of the art are then given. Finally, we present the organization of the paper.

Advantages of Multi-Agent Systems

The meteoric rise of Internet and World-Wide Web technologies has created overnight new application areas for enterprise software, including e-business, Web services, ubiquitous computing, knowledge management and peer-to-peer networks. These areas demand software that is robust, can operate within a wide range of environments, and can evolve over time to cope with changing requirements. Moreover, such software has to be highly customizable to meet the needs of a wide range of users, and sufficiently secure to protect personal data and other assets on behalf of its stakeholders.

Not surprisingly, researchers are looking for new software designs that can cope with such requirements. One promising source of ideas for designing such business software is the area of multi-agent systems. Multi-agent system architectures appear to be more flexible, modular and robust than traditional including object-oriented ones. They tend to be open and dynamic in the sense they exist in a changing organizational and operational environment where new components can be added, modified or removed at any time.

Multi-agent systems are based on the concept of agent which is defined as "a software component situated in some environment that is capable of flexible autonomous action in order to meet its design objective" (Aridor & Lange, 1998). An agent exhibits the following characteristics:

- Autonomy: an agent has its own internal thread of execution, typically oriented to the achievement of a specific task, and it decides for itself what actions it should perform at what time.
- Situateness: agents perform their actions in the context of being situated in a particular environment. This environment may be a computational one (e.g., a Web site) or a physical one (e.g., a manufacturing pipeline). The agent can sense and affect some portion of that environment.
- Flexibility: in order to accomplish its design objectives in a dynamic and unpredictable environment, the agent may need to act to ensure that its goals are achieved (by realizing alternative plan). This property is enabled by the fact that the agent is autonomous in its problem solving.

An agent can be useful as a stand-alone entity that delegates particular tasks on behalf of a user (e.g., a personal digital assistant and e-mail filter (Bauer, Muller & Odell, 2001), or a goal-driven office delivery mobile device (Castro, Kolp & Mylopoulos, 2002)). However, in the overwhelming majority of cases, agents exist in an environment that contains other agents. Such environment is a multi-agent system (MAS).

In MAS, the global behavior derives from the interaction among the constituent agents: they cooperate, coordinate or negotiate with one another. A multi-agent system is then conceived as a society of autonomous, collaborative, and goal-driven software components (agents), much like a social organization. Each role an agent can play has a well defined set of responsibilities (goals) achieved by means of an agent's own abilities, as well as its interaction capabilities.

This *sociality* of MAS is well suited to tackling the complexity of today's organization software systems for a number of reasons:

- It permits a better match between system architectures and its organizational operational environment for example a public organization, a corporation, a non-profit association, a local community, …
- The autonomy of an agent (i.e., the ability an agent has to decide what actions it should take at what time (Aridor & Lange, 1998)) reflects the social and decentralized nature of modern enterprise systems (Bauer, Muller & Odell, 2001) that are operated by different stakeholders (Parunak, 1997).
- The flexible way in which agents operate to accomplish its goals is suited to the dynamic and unpredictable situations in which business software is now expected to run (see Zambonelli, Jennings, Omicini & Wooldridge, 2000, Zambonelli, Jennings & Wooldridge, 2000).

MAS architectures become rapidly complicated due to the ever-increasing complexity of these new business domains and their human or organizational actors. As the expectations of the stakeholders change day after day, as the complexity of the systems, communication technologies and organizations continually increases in today's dynamic environments, developers are expected to produce architectures that must handle more difficult and intricate requirements that were not taken into account ten years ago, making thus architectural design a central engineering issue in modern enterprise information system life-cycle (Aridor & Lange, 1998).

Templates for Designing Systems

An important technique that helps to manage this complexity when constructing and documenting such architectures is the reuse of development experience and know-how. Over the past few years, *design patterns* have significantly contributed to the reuse of design expertise, improvement application documentation and more flexible and adaptable designs (Gamma, Helm, Johnson & Vlissides, 1995, Buschmann, Meunier, Rohnert, Sommerlad & Stal, 1996, Bosch, 1998). The idea behind a pattern (or a template) is to record the essence of a solution to a design problem so as to facilitate its reuse when similar problems are encountered (Cockburn, 1996, Pree 1994, Riehle & Züllighoven, 1996).

Considerable work has been done in software engineering on defining design patterns (Gamma, Helm, Johnson & Vlissides, 1995, Buschmann, Meunier, Rohnert, Sommerlad & Stal, 1996, Bosch, 1998). Unfortunately, they focus on object-oriented (Fernandez & Pan, 2001) rather than agent-oriented systems. In the area of MASs, little emphasis has been put on social and intentional aspects. Moreover, the proposals of agent patterns that could address those aspects (see e.g., Aridor & Lange, 1998, Deugo, Oppacher, Kuester & Otte, 1999, Hayden, Carrick & Yang, 1999) are not aimed at the design level, but rather at the implementation of lower-level issues like agent communication, information gathering, or connection setup. For instance, the Foundation for Intelligent Physical Agents (FIPA, 2007) identified and defined a set of agent's interaction protocols that are only restricted to communication. This research fills this gap by propping a series of social templates for the detailed design phases of software engineering methodologies so that pattern-oriented development can be fully integrated at higher level development stages.

A Framework for MAS Detailed Design

Since there is a fundamental mismatch between the concepts used by the object-oriented paradigm (and other traditional mainstream software engineering approaches) and the agent-oriented approach (Jennings & Wooldridge, 2001), there is a need to develop high level templates that are specifically tailored to the development of (multi-) agent systems using agent-oriented primitives.

Research objective is to take the principles of a social organization-based approach that contributes to reduce the distance between the system and the real world together with the important role of design patterns to help to reuse design experience. This research proposes a design framework and develops a catalogue of social templates for making MAS design more efficient. Research contributions include:

- A framework composed of a set of complementary dimension for designing MAS. The concepts and notions used for each dimension are introduced and illustrated;
- A catalogue of social patterns to help the designer's tasks so that development time is reduced. Each social pattern in the catalogue will be designed in detail through this framework;
- A tool for designing MAS. It allows the designer to: (i) design the components of a MAS to-be constructed in a graphical way, (ii) reuse the catalogue of patterns to construct the MAS, and (iii) generate the code for automating the programmer task.

The research also brings secondary contributions:

- A set of predefined predicates integrated for formalizing each pattern;
- The illustration of concepts introduced in our framework through a case study.

Validation

The social templates for developing a business data integration application have been applied to multiple case studies. The reusability of these patterns and the code generation help to reduce the development tasks of the application on both designer and programmer sides.

Furthermore, an empirical experience to evaluate the benefits of pattern-oriented development should be to achieve similar case studies with and without the use of patterns and to evaluate the results on the basis of software metrics. To focus on the contribution of the design-patterns we point to structural complexity evaluation. Indeed, structural complexity focuses on MAS architecture and agent relationships, features that should be enriched using patterns.

Due to the poorness of literature concerning agent-oriented software metrics evaluating structural complexity, we point to the use of existing object-oriented ones. As a preliminary tests suite, we claim for the use of the metrics proposed by Chidamber and Kemerer (1994). Those include:

- The Depth of Inheritance Tree (DIT). This metric measures the maximum level of the inheritance hierarchy of a class. The root of the inheritance tree inherits from no class and has a DIT count of 0. Chidamber and Kemerer suggest that DIT can be used to indicate the complexity of the design, potential for reuse;
- The Number Of Children (NOC). This metric counts the number of immediate subclasses belonging to a class. NOC was intended to indicate the level of reuse in a system and a possible indicator of the level of testing required;
- The Lack of Cohesion in Methods (LCOM). This metric is intended to measure the lack of cohesion in the methods of a class. It is based on the principle that different attributes occurring in different methods of a class causes that class to be less cohesive than one where the same attribute is used in few methods of the class. It is viewed that a lack of cohesiveness as undesirable as it is against encapsulation. Lack of cohesion could imply that the class should probably be split into two or more subclasses;
- The Weighted Methods per Class (WMC). The sum of the complexities of the methods in a class;

- The Coupling between objects (CBO). The number of other classes whose methods or instance attribute(s) are used by methods of this class;
- The Response for a Class (RFC). The sum of the number of methods in the class and the number of methods called by each of these methods, where each called method is counted once.

Context of the Research and Limitations

Design patterns are generally used during the *detailed design* phase while organizational styles are unsed during the *architectural* design phase of software methodologies. Agent-oriented methodologies such as TROPOS (Castro, Kolp & Mylopoulos, 2002), GAIA (Woodridge, Jennings & Kinny, 2000), MASE (Wood, DeLoach & Sparkman, 2001) and MESSAGE (Caire & al., 2002) span the following steps of software engineering:

- Early requirements, concerned with the understanding of a problem by studying an organizational setting; the output is an organizational model which includes relevant actors, their goals and their interdependencies.
- Late requirements, where the system-to-be is described within its operational environment, along with relevant functions and qualities.
- Architectural design, where the system architecture is defined in terms of subsystems, interconnected through data, control, and dependencies.
- Detailed design, where the behavior of each architectural components is defined in detail.

The catalogue of social patterns proposed in (Kolp, Giorgini, & Mylopoulos, 2002) constitutes

a contribution to the definition of agent-oriented design patterns. This paper focuses on these patterns, conceptualizes a framework to explore them and facilitate the building of MAS during detailed design as well as the generation of code for agent implementation. It models and introspects the patterns along different complementary dimensions.

As pointed out above, the patterns proposed into this paper take place at the detailed design step. The process described hereafter is part of a broader methodology called I-Tropos (Wautelet, Kolp & Achbany, 2006) based on Tropos, driven by i* diagrams and organized following an iterative software development life cycle. This methodology is conceived to bring Agent-Oriented development to be adopted into real life development of huge enterprise information systems. Due to lack of space we only present the detailed design discipline in the form of a workflow, more details can be found in (Kolp, Faulkner & Wautelet, 2007). Figure 1 describes the workflow of the detailed design discipline using the *Software Process Engineering Metamodel* (*SPEM*) notation (see OMG, 2005). The Software Architect selects the most appropriate Social Patterns for the components under development from the catalogue overviewed in the paper. New goals are included to the Strategic Dependency Model (Social Dimension) according to the semantics of the pattern. The Agent Designer identifies services provided by each agent to achieve the goal dependencies. Each service belongs to an agent and is represented with an NFR goal analysis to refine the Strategic Rationale Diagram (Intentional Dimension). The structure of each agent and its components such as Plans, Events and Beliefs are then specified with an agent UML class diagram (Structural Dimension). Agents communicate through events exchanged in the system and modeled in a temporal manner with extended Agent UML sequence diagrams (Communicational Dimension). The synchronization and the relationships between plans and events are

Figure 1. The detailed design workflow

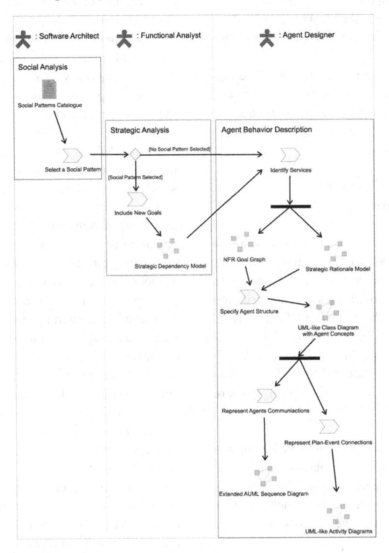

designed through agent oriented activity diagrams (Dynamic Dimension).

We nevertheless point out some important limitations of our research:

- We only consider the design of cooperative MASs. Indeed, MAS may be either cooperative or competitive. In a cooperative MAS, the agents cooperate together in order to achieve common goals. Inversely, a competitive MAS is composed of agents that pursue personal goals and defend their own interests. The design of competitive MAS is left for future developments;

- The patterns need to gain experience with their use. In this dissertation, we have applied them on a case study. By doing so, we have explored the applicability of patterns and shown how our framework can help the design of MAS. However, it should be tested on more case studies;

- The work only considers a MAS composed of more than one pattern as an "addition" of them. However, the combination of multiple patterns in a MAS is more complicated than that, and the emergence of conflicts remains possible. This issue needs further investigation.

- We extend the consideration of the concept of social templates to organizational styles that will be presented later. These styles intervene at the *architectural design* phase and propose macroscopic structures to organize socially a MAS architecture.

Paper Organization

The paper is organized as follows. We describe the social templates called patterns. We propose a framework and illustrate its different modeling dimensions through the Broker pattern while the next section overviews organizational styles for architectural design. A *data integrator* case study that illustrates the mapping from organizational styles (architectural design phase) to social patterns (detailed design phase), is then presented. The automation of social patterns is overviewed while the next section overviews related work on software patterns. Finally, we point to some conclusions.

SOCIAL DESIGN TEMPLATES: SOCIAL PATTERNS

Social patterns can be classified in two categories. The *Pair* patterns describe direct interactions

between negotiating agents. The *Mediation* patterns feature intermediate agents that help other agents to reach agreement about an exchange of services.

In the following, we briefly model patterns using i* (Do, Kolp, Hang Hoang & Pirotte, 2003) and AUML (Bauer, Muller & Odell, 2001) sequence diagrams respectively to represent the social and communicational dimensions of each pattern. In i*, agents are drawn as circles and their intentional dependencies as ovals. An agent (the *depender*) depends upon another agent (the *dependee*) for an intention to be fulfilled (the *dependum*). Dependencies have the form *depender→dependum→dependee*. Note that i* also allows to model other kind of dependencies such as resource, task or strategic ones respectively represented as rectangles, hexagons and clouds as we will see in Figure 13. AUML extends classical sequence diagrams for agent oriented modeling. For instance, the diamond symbol indicates alternative events.

The broker, as well as the subscription and call-for-proposal patterns that are both part of the broker pattern, will be modeled in detail to explain the framework in the next section.

Pair Patterns

The **Booking** pattern (Figure 2) involves a client and a number of service providers. The client issues a request to book some resource from a service provider. The provider can accept the request, deny

Figure 2. Social and communicational diagrams for the Booking pattern

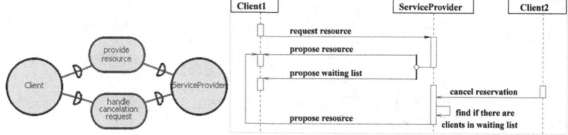

Figure 3. Social and communicational diagrams for the Bidding pattern

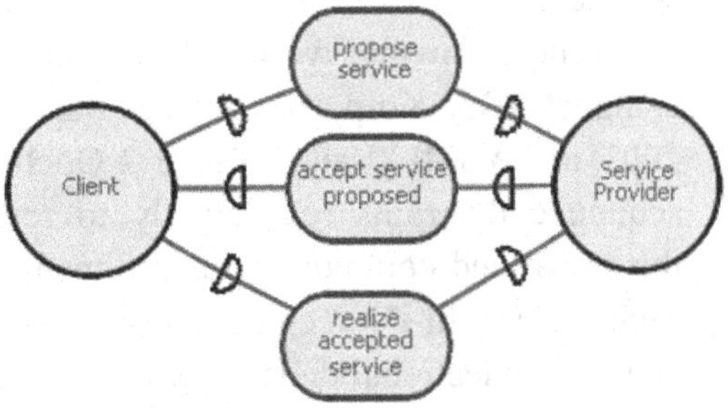

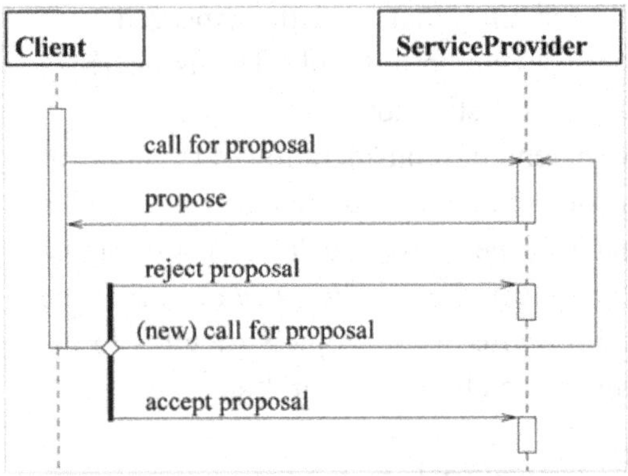

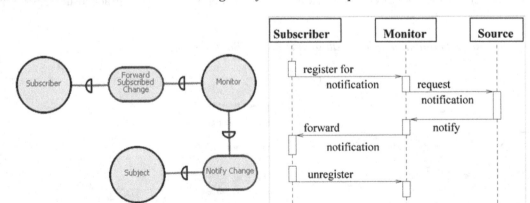

it, or propose to place the client on a waiting list, until the requested resource becomes available when some other client cancels a reservation.

The **Subscription** pattern involves a yellow-page agent and a number of service providers. The providers advertise their services by subscribing to the yellow pages. A provider that no longer wishes to be advertised can request to be unsubscribed.

The **Call-For-Proposals** pattern involves an initiator and a number of participants. The initiator issues a call for proposals for a service to all participants and then accepts proposals that offer the service for a specified cost. The initiator selects one participant to supply the service.

The **Bidding** (Figure 3) pattern involves a client and a number of service providers. The client organizes and leads the bidding process, and receives proposals. At each iteration, the client publishes the current bid; it can accept an offer, raise the bid, or cancel the process.

Mediation Patterns

In the **Monitor** pattern (Figure 4), subscribers register for receiving, from a monitor agent, notifications of changes of state in some subjects of their interest. The monitor accepts subscriptions, requests information from the subjects of interest, and alerts subscribers accordingly.

In the **Broker** pattern, the broker agent is an arbiter and intermediary that requests ser-

Figure 4. Social and communicational diagrams for the Monitor pattern

Figure 5. Social and communicational diagrams for the Matchmaker pattern

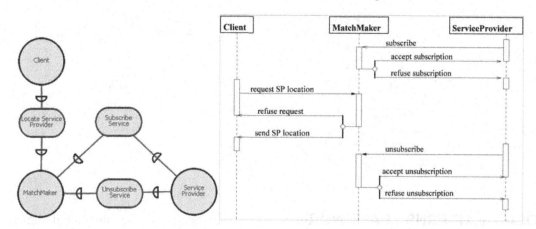

vices from providers to satisfy the request of clients.

In the **Matchmaker** pattern (Figure 5), a matchmaker agent locates a provider for a given service requested by a client, and then lets the client interact directly with the provider, unlike brokers, who handle all interactions between clients and providers.

In the **Mediator** pattern (Figure 6), a mediator agent coordinates the cooperation of service provider agents to satisfy the request of a client agent. While a matchmaker simply matches providers with clients, a mediator encapsulates interactions and maintains models of the capabilities of clients and providers over time.

In the **Embassy** pattern, an embassy agent routes a service requested by an external agent to a local agent. If the request is granted, the external agent can submit messages to the embassy for translation in accordance with a standard ontology. Translated messages are forwarded to the requested local agent and the result of the query is passed back out through the embassy to the external agent.

The **Wrapper** pattern (Figure 7) incorporates a legacy system into a multi-agent system. A wrapper agent interfaces system agents with the legacy system by acting as a translator. This ensures that communication protocols are respected and the legacy system remains decoupled from the rest of the agent system.

Figure 6. Social and Communicational diagrams for the Mediator pattern

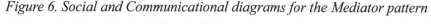

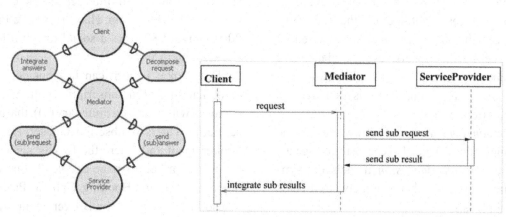

Figure 7. Social and Communicational diagrams for the Wrapper pattern

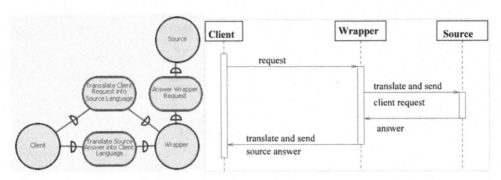

A SOCIAL PATTERNS FRAMEWORK

This section describes a conceptual framework based on five complementary modeling dimensions, to investigate social patterns. The framework has been applied in the context of the Tropos development methodology (Castro, Kolp & Mylopoulos, 2002). Each dimension reflects a particular aspect of a MAS architecture, as follows.

- The *social dimension* identifies the relevant agents in the system and their intentional interdependencies.
- The *intentional dimension* identifies and formalizes services provided by agents to realize the intentions identified by the social dimension, independently of the plans that implement those services. This dimension answers the question: "What does each service do?"
- The *structural dimension* operationalizes the services identified by the intentional dimension in terms of agent-oriented concepts like beliefs, events, plans, and their relationships. This dimension answers the question: "How is each service operationalized?"
- The *communicational dimension* models the temporal exchange of events between agents.
- The *dynamic dimension* models the synchronization mechanisms between events and plans.

The social and the intentional dimensions are specific to MAS. The last three dimensions (structural, communicational, and dynamic) of the architecture are also relevant for traditional (non-agent) systems, but we have adapted and extended them with agent-oriented concepts. They are for instance the modeling dimensions used in object-oriented visual modeling languages such as UML.

The rest of this section details the five dimensions of the framework and illustrates them through the Broker pattern (Yu, 1995).

This pattern involves an arbiter intermediary that requests services from providers to satisfy the request of clients. It is designed through the framework as follows.

Social Dimension

The social dimension specifies a number of agents and their intentional interdependencies using the i* model (Do, Kolp, Hang Hoang & Pirotte, 2003). Figure 8 shows a social diagram for the Broker pattern.

The Broker pattern can be considered as a combination of (1) a Subscription pattern (shown enclosed within dashed boundary (a)), that allows service providers to subscribe their services to the Broker agent and where the Broker agent plays the role of a yellow-page agent, (2) one of the other pair patterns - Booking, Call-for-Proposals, or Bidding - whereby the Broker agent requests

Figure 8. Social diagram for the Broker pattern

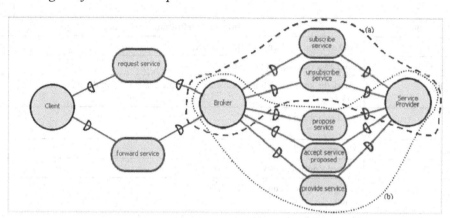

and receives services from service providers (in Figure 13, it is a Call-for-Proposals pattern, shown enclosed within dotted boundary (b)), and (3) interaction between the broker and the client: the Broker depends on the client for sending a service request and the client depends on the Broker agent to forward the service.

To formalize intentional interdependencies, we use Formal Tropos (Fuxman, Pistore, Mylopoulos, & Traverso, 2001), a first-order temporal-logic language providing a textual notation for i* models and allows to describe constraints. A *forward service* dependency is defined in Formal Tropos as follows.

Dependum Forward Service
Mode: Achieve
Depender: Client *cl*
Dependee: Broker *br*
Fulfillment:
    ($\forall$ *sr*: ServiceRequest, *st*: ServiceType)
        request(*cl, br, sr*) $\wedge$ provide(*br, st*) $\wedge$
        ofType(*sr, st*)
        $\rightarrow \Diamond$ received(*cl, br, st*)
[Broker *br* successfully provides its service to client *cl* if all requests *sr* from *cl* to *br*, that are of a type *st* that *br* can handle, are eventually satisfied]

Intentional Dimension

While the social dimension focuses on interdependencies between agents, the intentional dimension aims at modeling agent rationale. It is concerned with the identification of *services* provided by agents and made available to achieve the intentions identified in the social dimension. Each service belongs to one agent. Service definitions can be formalized by its fulfillment condition.

Table 1 lists several services of the Broker pattern with an informal definition. With the FindBroker service, a client finds a broker that can handle a given service request. The request is then sent to the broker through the SendServiceRequest service. The broker can query its belief knowledge with the QuerySPAvailability service and answer the client through the SendServiceRequestDecision service. If the answer is negative, the client records it with its RecordBRRefusal service. If the answer is positive, the broker records the request (RecordClientServiceRequest service) and then broadcasts a call (CallForProposals service) to potential service providers. The client records acceptance by the broker with the RecordBRAcceptance service.

The Call-For-Proposals pattern could be used here, but this presentation omits it for brevity.

The broker then selects one of the service providers among those that offer the requested

Table 1. Some services of the Broker pattern

Service Name	Informal Definition	Agent
FindBroker	Find a broker that can provide a service	Client
SendServiceRequest	Send a service request to a broker	Client
QuerySPAvailability	Query the knowledge for information about the availability of the requested service	Broker
SendService RequestDecision	Send an answer to the client	Broker
RecordBRRefusal	Record a negative answer from a broker	Client
RecordBRAcceptance	Record a positive answer from a broker	Client
RecordClient ServiceRequest	Record a service request received from a Client	Broker
CallForProposals	Send a call for proposals to service providers	Broker
RecordAndSend SPInformDone	Record a service received from a service provider	Broker

service. If the selected provider successfully returns the requested service, it informs the broker, that records the information and forwards it to the client (RecordAndSendSPInformDone service).

Service FindBroker (*sr*: ServiceRequest)
Mode: Achieve
Agent: Client *cl*
Fulfillment:

$$(\exists \; br: \text{Broker}, \; st: \text{ServiceType})$$
$$\text{provide}(br, st) \land \text{ofType } (sr, st)$$
$$\rightarrow \Diamond \; \text{known}(cl, br)$$

[*FindBroker* is fulfilled when client *cl* has found (*known* predicate) *Broker br* that is able to perform (*provide* predicate) the service requested.]

Structural Dimension

While the intentional dimension answers the question "What does each service do?", the structural dimension answers the question "How is each service operationalized?". Services are operationalized as *plans*, that is, sequences of actions.

The knowledge that an agent has (about itself or its environment) is stored in its *beliefs*. An agent can act in response to the *events* that it handles through its plans. A plan, in turn, is used by the agent to read or modify its beliefs, and send events to other agents or post events to itself.

The structural dimension is modeled using a UML style class diagram extended for MAS engineering.

The required agent concepts extending the class diagram model are defined below.

Structural Concepts

Figure 9 depicts the concepts and their relationships needed to build the structural dimension. Each concept defines a common template for classes of concrete MAS (for example, Agent in Figure 9 is a template for the Broker agent class of Figure 10).

A **Belief** describes a piece of the knowledge that an agent has about itself and its environment. Beliefs are represented as tuples composed of a key and value fields.

Events describe stimuli, emitted by agents or automatically generated, in response to which the agents must take action. As shown in Figure 9, the structure of an event is composed of three parts: declaration of the attributes of the event, declaration of the methods to create the event,

Figure 9. Structural diagram template

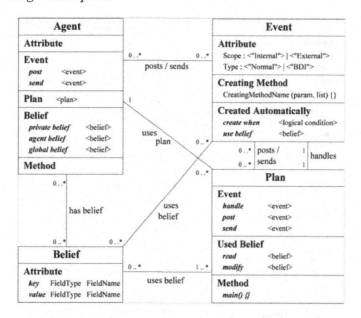

declaration of the beliefs and the condition used for an automatic event. The third part only appears for automatic events. Events can be described along three dimensions:

- *External or internal* event: external events are sent to other agents while internal events are posted by an agent to itself. This property is captured by the *scope* attribute.
- *Normal or BDI* event: an agent has a number of alternative plans to respond to a BDI (Belief-Desire-Intention) event and only one plan in response to a normal event. Whenever an event occurs, the agent initiates a plan to handle it. If the plan execution fails and if the event is a normal event, then the event is said to have failed. If the event is a BDI event, a set of plans can be selected for execution and these are attempted in turn. If all selected plans fail, the event is also said to have failed. The event type is captured by the *type* attribute.
- *Automatic or nonautomatic* event: an automatic event is automatically created when certain belief states arise. The *create when*

statement specifies the logical condition which must arise for the event to be automatically created. The states of the beliefs that are defined by *use belief* are monitored to determine when to automatically create events.

A **Plan** describes a sequence of actions that an agent can take when an event occurs. As shown by Figure 9, plans are structured in three parts: the Event part, the Belief part, and the Method part. The Event part declares events that the plan handles (i.e., events that trigger the execution of the plan) and events that the plan produces. The latter can be either posted (i.e., sent by an agent only to itself) or sent (i.e., sent to other agents). The Belief part declares beliefs that the plan reads and those that it modifies. The Method part describes the plan itself, that is, the actions performed when the plan is executed.

The **Agent** concept defines the behavior of an agent, as composed of five parts: the declaration of its attributes, of the events that it can post or send explicitly (i.e., without using its plans), of the plans that it uses to respond to events, of the

Figure 10. Structural diagram - some components of the Broker pattern

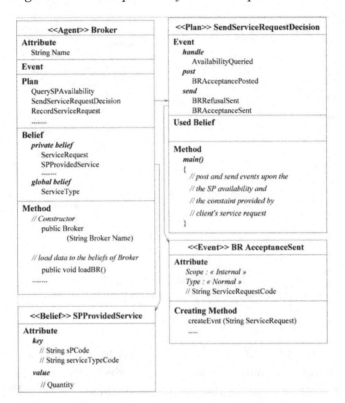

beliefs that make up its knowledge, and of its methods.

The beliefs of an agent can be of type *private*, *agent*, or *global*. A *private* access is restricted to the agent to which the belief belongs. *Agent* access is shared with other agents of the same class, while *global* access is unrestricted.

Structural Model for the Broker Pattern

Figure 10 depicts the Broker pattern components. For brevity, each construct described earlier is illustrated only through one component. Each component can be considered as an instantiation of the (corresponding) template in Figure 9.

Broker is one of the three agents composing the Broker pattern. It has plans such as QueryS-PAvailability, SendServiceRequestDecision, etc. When there is no ambiguity, by convention, the plan name is the same as the as the name of the service that it operationalizes. The private belief SPProvidedService stores the service type that each service provider can provide. This belief is declared as private since the broker is the only agent that can manipulate it. The ServiceType belief stores the information about types of service provided by service providers and is declared as global since its must be known both by the service provider and the broker agent.

The constructor *method* allows to give a name to a broker agent when created. This method may call other methods, for example loadBR(), to initialize agent beliefs.

SendServiceRequestDecision is one of the plans that the broker uses to answer the client: the BRRefusalSent event is sent when the answer is negative, BRAcceptanceSent when the broker has found service provider(s) that may provide the requested service. In the latter case, the plan also posts the BRAcceptancePosted event to invoke the process of recording the service request and the 'call for proposals' process between the broker and services providers. The SendServiceRequest-Decision plan is executed when the Availability-Queried event (containing the information about the availability of the service provider to realize the client's request) occurs.

SPProvidedService is one of the broker's beliefs used to store the services provided by the service providers. The service provider code sP-Code and the service type code serviceTypeCode form the belief key. The corresponding quantity attribute is declared as value field.

BRAcceptanceSent is an event that is sent to inform the client that its request is accepted.

At a lower level, each plan could also be modeled by an activity diagram for further detail if necessary.

Communication Dimension

Agents interact with each other by exchanging events. The communicational dimension models, in a temporal manner, events exchanged in the system. We adopt the sequence diagram model proposed in AUML (Bauer, Muller & Odell, 2001) and extend it: *agent_name/role:pattern_name* expresses the role (*role*) of the agent (*agent_name*) in the pattern; the arrows are labeled with the name of the exchanged events.

Figure 11 shows a sequence diagram for the Broker pattern. The client (customer1) sends a service request (ServiceRequestSent) containing the characteristics of the service it wishes to obtain from the broker. The broker may alternatively answer with a denial (BRRefusalSent) or a acceptance (BRAcceptanceSent).

In the case of an acceptance, the broker sends a call for proposal to the registered service providers (CallForProposalSent). The call for proposal (CFP) pattern is then applied to model the interaction between the broker and the service providers. The service provider either fails or achieves the requested service. The broker then informs the client about this result by sending a InformFailureServiceRequestSent or a ServiceForwarded, respectively.

The communication dimension of the subscription pattern (SB) is given at the top-right

Figure 11. Communication diagram - Broker

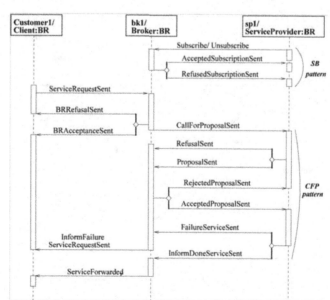

and the communication dimension of the call-for-proposals pattern (CFP) is given at the bottom-right part of Figure 11. The communication specific for the broker pattern is given in the left part of the figure.

Dynamic Dimension

As described earlier, a plan can be invoked by an event that it handles and it can create new events. Relationships between plans and events can rapidly become complex. To cope with this problem, we propose to model the synchronization and the relationships between plans and events with activity diagrams extended for agent-oriented systems. These diagrams specify the events that are created in parallel, the conditions under which events are created, which plans handle which events, and so on.

An internal event is represented by a dashed arrow and an external event by a solid arrow. As

mentioned earlier, a BDI event may be handled by alternative plans. They are enclosed in a round-corner box. Synchronization and branching are represented as usual.

We omit the dynamic dimension of the Subscription and the CFP patterns, and only present in Figure 12 the activity diagram specific to the Broker pattern. It models the flow of control from the emission of a service request sent by the client to the reception by the same client of the realized service result sent by the broker. Three swimlanes, one for each agent of the Broker pattern, compose the diagram. In this pattern, the FindBroker service described earlier, is either operationalized by the FindBR or the FindBRWithMM plans (the client finds a broker based on its own knowledge or via a matchmaker).

Figure 12. Dynamic diagram – Broker

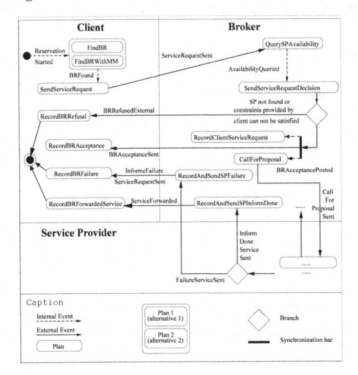

SOCIAL ARCHITECTURAL TEMPLATES: ORGANIZATIONAL STYLES

Software architectures describe a software system at a macroscopic level in terms of a manageable number of subsystems, components and modules inter-related through data and control dependencies (Bass et al. 1998). System architectural design has been the focus of considerable research during the last fifteen years that has produced well-established architectural styles and frameworks for evaluating their effectiveness with respect to particular software qualities. Examples of styles are pipes-and-filters, event-based, layered, control loops and the like (Shaw and Garland 1996).

A key aspect to conduct MAS architectural design is the specification and use of *organizational styles* (Castro, Kolp & Mylopoulos, 2002, Kolp, Giorgini & Mylopoulos, 2002, Do, Faulkner, & Kolp, 2003) that are socially-based architectural designs inspired from models and concepts from organization theory (e.g., Mintzberg, 1992, Scott, 1998, Yoshino & Srinivasa Rangan, 1995) and strategic alliances (e.g., Dussauge & Garrette, 1999, Morabito, Sack & Bhate, 1999, Segil, 1996) that analyze the structure and design of real-world human organization. Both disciplines aim to identify and study organizational patterns that describe a system at a macroscopic level in terms of a manageable number of subsystems, components and modules inter-related through dependencies.

We are interested, in this section to identify, formalize and apply, for MAS design, templates that have been already well-understood and precisely defined in organizational theories. Our purpose is not to categorize them exhaustively nor to study them on a managerial point of view. The following sections will thus only insist on patterns that have been found, due to their nature, interesting candidates also considering the fact that they have been studied in great detail in the organizational literature and presented as fully formed templates.

Organization Theory

"An organization is a consciously coordinated social entity, with a relatively identifiable boundary, that functions on a relatively continuous basis to achieve a common goal or a set of goals" (Morabito et al. 1999).

Organization theory is the discipline that studies both structure and design in such social entities. Structure deals with the descriptive aspects while design refers to the prescriptive aspects of a social entity. Organization theory describes how practical organizations are actually structured, offers suggestions on how new ones can be constructed, and how old ones can change to improve effectiveness. To this end, since Adam Smith, schools of organization theory have proposed models and patterns to try to find and formalize recurring organizational structures and behaviors.

In the following, we briefly present organizational patterns identified in Organization Theory.

The Structure-in-5. An organization can be considered an aggregate of five substructures, as proposed by Minztberg (Mintzberg 1992). At the base level sits the *Operational Core* which carries out the basic tasks and procedures directly linked to the production of products and services (acquisition of inputs, transformation of inputs into outputs, distribution of outputs). At the top lies the *Strategic Apex* which makes executive decisions ensuring that the organization fulfils its mission in an effective way and defines the overall strategy of the organization in its environment. The *Middle Line* establishes a hierarchy of authority between the Strategic Apex and the Operational Core. It consists of managers responsible for supervising and coordinating the activities of the Operational Core. The *Technostructure* and the *Support* are separated from the main line of authority and influence the operating core only indirectly. The Technostructure serves the organization by making the work of others more effective, typically by standardizing work processes, outputs, and skills. It is also in charge of applying analytical procedures to adapt the organization to its operational environment. The Support provides specialized services, at various levels of the hierarchy, outside the basic operating workflow (e.g., legal counsel, R&D, payroll, cafeteria).

Figure 13 models in *i** the Structure-in-5 as a social template composed of five actors.

A number of constraints supplement the basic template:

- the dependencies between the *Strategic Apex* as depender and the *Technostructure, Middle Line* and *Support* as dependees must be of type goal
- a softgoal dependency models the strategic dependence of the *Technostructure, Middle Line* and *Support* on the *Strategic Apex*
- the relationships between the *Middle Line* and *Technostructure* and *Support* must be of goal dependencies

- the *Operational Core* relies on the *Technostructure* and *Support* through task and resource dependencies
- only task dependencies are permitted between the *Middle Line* (as depender or dependee) and the *Operational Core* (as dependee or depender).

The pyramid style is the well-know hierarchical authority structure. Actors at lower levels depend on those at higher levels. The crucial mechanism is the direct supervision from the Apex. Managers and supervisors at intermediate levels only route strategic decisions and authority from the Apex to the operating (low) level. They can coordinate behaviors or take decisions by their own, but only at a local level.

The chain of values merges, backward or forward, several actors engaged in achieving or realizing related goals or tasks at different stages of a supply or production process. Participants who act as intermediaries, add value at each step of the chain. For instance, for the domain of goods dis-

Figure 13. The structure-in-5 organizational style

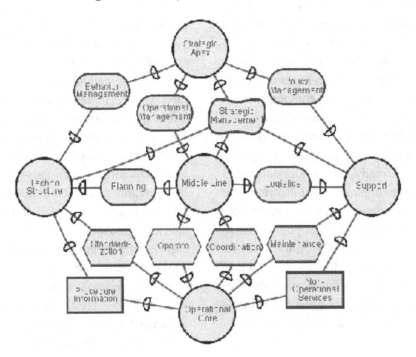

tribution, providers are expected to supply quality products, wholesalers are responsible for ensuring their massive exposure, while retailers take care of the direct delivery to the consumers.

The matrix proposes a multiple command structure: vertical and horizontal channels of information and authority operate simultaneously. The principle of unity of command is set aside, and competing bases of authority are allowed to jointly govern the workflow. The vertical lines are typically those of functional departments that operate as "home bases" for all participants, the horizontal lines represents project groups or geographical areas where managers combine and coordinate the services of the functional specialists around particular projects or areas.

The bidding style involves competitivity mechanisms, and actors behave as if they were taking part in an auction. An auctioneer actor runs the show, advertises the auction issued by the auction issuer, receives bids from bidder actors and ensures communication and feedback with the auction issuer who is responsible for issuing the bidding.

Strategic Alliances

A strategic alliance links specific facets of two or more organizations. At its core, this structure is a trading partnership that enhances the effectiveness of the competitive strategies of the participant organizations by providing for the mutually beneficial trade of technologies, skills, or products based upon them. An alliance can take a variety of forms, ranging from arm's-length contracts to joint ventures, from multinational corporations to university spin-offs, from franchises to equity arrangements. Varied interpretations of the term exist, but a strategic alliance can be defined as possessing simultaneously the following three necessary and sufficient characteristics:

- The two or more organizations that unite to pursue a set of agreed upon goals remain

independent subsequent to the formation of the alliance.
- The partner organizations share the benefits of the alliances and control over the performance of assigned tasks.
- The partner organizations contribute on a continuing basis in one or more key strategic areas, e.g., technology, products, and so forth.

In the following, we briefly present organizational style identified in Strategic Alliances.

The joint venture style involves agreement between two or more intra-industry partners to obtain the benefits of larger scale, partial investment and lower maintenance costs. A specific joint management actor coordinates tasks and manages the sharing of resources between partner actors. Each partner can manage and control itself on a local dimension and interact directly with other partners to exchange resources, such as data and knowledge. However, the strategic operation and coordination of such an organization, and its actors on a global dimension, are only ensured by the joint management actor in which the original actors possess equity participations.

Figure 14 models in *i** the joint-venture as a social template.

A number of constraints supplement the basic template:

- Partners depend on each other for providing and receiving resources.
- Operation coordination is ensured by the joint manager actor which depends on partners for the accomplishment of these assigned tasks.
- The joint manager actor must assume two roles: a private interface role to coordinate partners of the alliance and a public interface role to take strategic decisions, define policy for the private interface and represents the interests of the whole partnership with respect to external stakeholders.

Figure 14. The joint venture organizational style

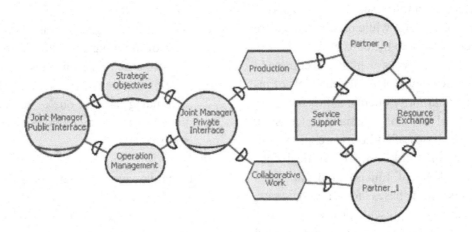

The **arm's-length style** implies agreements between independent and competitive, but partner actors. Partners keep their autonomy and independence but act and put their resources and knowledge together to accomplish precise common goals. No authority is lost, or delegated from one collaborator to another.

The **hierarchical contracting style** identifies coordinating mechanisms that combine arm's-length agreement features with aspects of pyramidal authority. Coordination mechanisms developed for arm's-length (independent) characteristics involve a variety of negotiators, mediators and observers at different levels handling conditional clauses to monitor and manage possible contingencies, negotiate and resolve conflicts and finally deliberate and take decisions. Hierarchical relationships, from the executive apex to the arm's-length contractors restrict autonomy and underlie a cooperative venture between the parties.

The **co-optation style** involves the incorporation of representatives of external systems into the decision-making or advisory structure and behavior of an initiating organization. By co-opting representatives of external systems, organizations are, in effect, trading confidentiality and authority for resource, knowledge assets and support. The initiating system has to come to terms with the contractors for what is being done on its behalf; and each co-opted actor has to reconcile and adjust its own views with the policy of the system it has to communicate.

As already said, organizational styles are used during the architectural design phase. Figure 15 describes the workflow for this phase taking such social templates into account. The Software Architect uses a non-functional requirements analysis to select the most appropriate The architectural style for the module to-be from the Architectural Styles Catalogue. If such a style has been selected, new actors and their identified intentions are added to the Strategic Dependency and Strategic Rationale Models according to the semantics of the selected style. Finally, the System Architecture is formally specified with an ADL (Architectural Description Language).

FROM ORGANIZATIONAL ARCHITECTURAL STYLES TO SOCIAL DESIGN PATTERNS

As described in (Castro, Kolp & Mylopoulos, 2002, Zambonelli, Jennings & Wooldridge, 2000), in MAS architectural design, organizational styles are used to give information about the system

Figure 15. Architectural design workflow

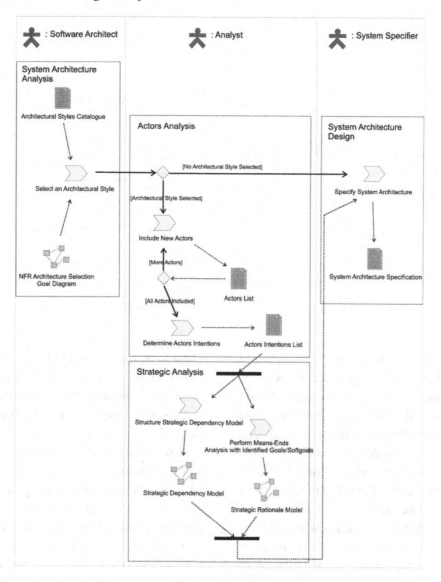

architecture to be: every time an organizational style is applied, it allows to easily point up, to the designer, the required organizational actors and roles. Then the next step needs to detail and relate such (organizational) actors and roles to more specific agents in order to proceed with the agent behavior characterization. Namely, each actor in an organization-based architecture is much closer to the real world system actor behavior that we consequently aim to have in software agents. As a consequence, once the organizational

architectural reflection has figured out the MAS global structure in terms of actors, roles, and their intentional relationships, a deepener analysis is required to detail the agent behaviors and their interdependencies necessary to accomplish their roles in the software organization. To effectively deal with such a purpose, developers can be guided by social patterns proposed in this paper.

Social patterns offer a microscopic view of the MAS at the *detailed design* phase to express in deeper detail organizational styles during the

Figure 16. A joint-venture MAS architecture expressed in terms of social patterns - a data integration example

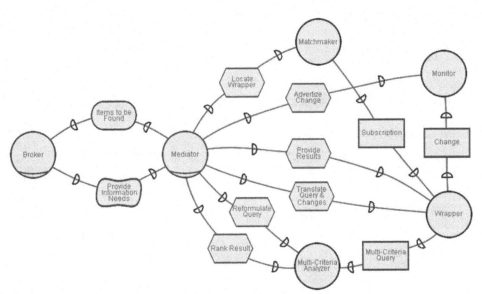

architectural design. To explain the necessary relationship between *styles* and *patterns* we consider an original *data integrator* case study and overview how a MAS designed from some style at the architectural level is decomposed into social patterns at the detailed design level.

The **data integrator** allows users to obtain information that come from different heterogeneous and distributed sources. Sources range from text file systems agent knowledge bases. Information from each source that may be of interest is extracted, translated and filtered as appropriate, merged with relevant information from other sources to provide the answer to the users' queries (Widom, 1995).

Figure 16 shows a MAS architecture in i* for the data integrator that applies the *joint-venture* style (Castro, Kolp & Mylopoulos, 2002, Do, Faulkner, & Kolp, 2003) at the architectural design level.

Joint-venture's roles at the architectural design level are expressed in the detailed design level in terms of patterns, namely the broker, the matchmaker, the monitor, the mediator and the wrapper.

The *joint management private interface* is assumed by a mediator, the joint-venture partners are the *wrapper*, the *monitor*, the *multi-criteria analyzer* and the *matchmaker*. The *public interface* is assumed by the *broker*.

The system works as follows. When a user wishes to send a request, she contacts the *broker* agent which is an intermediary to select one or many *mediator(s)* that can satisfy the user information needs. Then, the selected mediator(s) decomposes the user's query into one or more subqueries to the sources, synthesizes the source answers and return the answers to the broker.

If the mediator identifies a recurrent user information request, the information that may be of interest is extracted from each source, merged with relevant information from other sources, and stored as knowledge by the mediator. This stored information constitutes a materialized view that the mediator will have to maintain up-to-date.

A *wrapper* and a *monitor* agents are connected to each information source. The *wrapper* is responsible for translating the subquery issued by the mediator into the native format of the source and translating the source response in the data model used by the mediator.

The *monitor* is responsible for detecting changes of interest (e.g., change which affects a matcrializcd vicw) in the information source and reporting them to the mediator. Changes are then translated by the wrapper and sent to the mediator.

It may be also necessary for the mediator to obtain the information concerning the localization of a source and its connected wrapper that are able to provide current or future relevant information. This kind of information is provided by the *match-maker* agent which then lets the mediator interacts directly with the correspondant wrapper.

Finally, the *multi-criteria analyzer* can reformulate a subquery (sent by a mediator to a wrapper) through a set of criteria in order to express the user preferences in a more detailed way, and refine the possible domain of results.

AUTOMATION

The main motivation behind organizational styles and design patterns is the possibility of reusing them during system detailed design and implementation. Numerous CASE tools such as Rational Software Architect (IBM Rational Software Architect, 2008) and Together (Borland Together, 2008) include code generators for object-oriented design patterns. Programmers identify and parameterize, during system detailed design, the patterns that they use in their applications. The code skeleton for the patterns is then automatically generated and programming is thus made easier.

For agent-oriented programming, SKwyRL (Do, Kolp, Hang Hoang & Pirotte, 2003), for instance, proposes a code generator to automate the use of social patterns introduced earlier. Figure 17 shows the main window of the tool. It has been developed in Java and produces code for JACK (JACK Intelligent Agents, 2006), an agent-oriented development environment built on top of Java. JACK extends Java with specific

Figure 17. JACK code generation

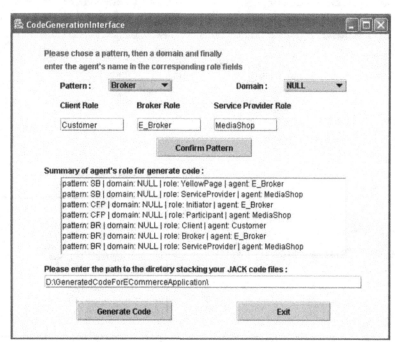

capabilities to implement agent behaviors. On a conceptual point of view, the relationship of JACK to Java is analogous to that between C++ and C. On a technical point of view, JACK source code is first compiled into regular Java code before being executed.

In SKwyRL's code generator, the programmer first chooses which social pattern to use, then the roles for each agent in the selected pattern (e.g. the E_Broker agent plays the *broker* role for the Broker pattern but can also play the *initiator* role for the CallForProposals pattern and the *yellow page* role for the Subscription pattern in the same application). The process is repeated until all relevant patterns have been identified. The code generator then produces the generic code for the patterns (.agent, .event, .plan, .bel JACK files).

The programmer has to add the particular JACK code for each generated files and implement the graphical interface if necessary.

Figure 18 shows an example of the (e-business) broker for the data integrator presented earlier. It was developed with JACK and the code skeleton was generated with SKwyRL's code generator using the Broker pattern explained in the paper. The bottom half of the figure shows the interface between the customer and the broker. The customer sends a service request to the broker asking for buying or sending DVDs. He chooses which DVDs to sell or buy, selects the corresponding DVD titles, the quantity and the deadline (the time-out before which the broker has to realizes the requested service). When receiving the customer's request, the broker interacts with the media shops to obtain the DVDs. The interactions between the broker and the media shops are shown on the bottom-right corner of this figure. The top half of the figure shows the items that are provided by each media shop.

Figure 18. An e-business broker

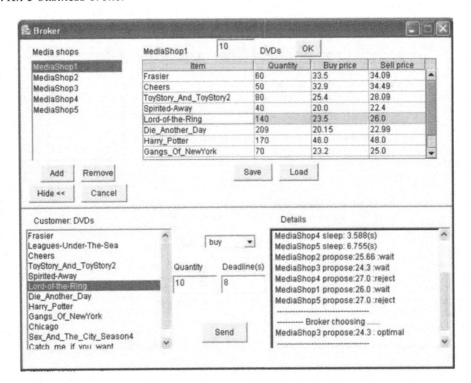

RELATED WORK

As already said, a lot of work has been devoted to software patterns and styles these last fifteen years. Patterns for software development are one of software engineering problem-solving discipline that has its roots in a design movement in contemporary architecture and the documentation of best practices and lessons learned in all vocations. The goal of patterns is to create a body of literature to help software developers resolve recurring problems encountered throughout all of software development. Patterns help create a shared language for communicating insight and experience about these problems and their solutions.

Ward Cunningham and Kent Beck developed a small set of five patterns (Beck & Cunningham, 1987), for guiding Smalltalk programmers to design user interface. Jim Coplien introduced a catalog of for C++ patterns, called *idioms* (Coplien, 1991). Software patterns then became popular with the wide acceptance of the Gang of Four or GoF (Erich Gamma, Richard Helm, Ralph Johnson, and John Vlissides) book (Gamma, Helm, Johnson, & Vlissides, 1995).

However, the patterns in the GoF book are only one kind of pattern – the object-oriented *design patterns*. There are many other kinds of patterns. For example, Martin Fowler's "*Analysis Patterns*" (Fowler, 1997) describe the models of business processes that occur repeatedly in the analysis phase of software development; *organizational patterns* (Coplien & Schmidt, 1995) are about software-development organizations and about people who work in such organizations. *Process patterns* (Ambler, 1998) relate to the strategies that software professionals employ to solve problems that recur across organizations. Frank Buschmann, Regine Meunier, Hans Rohnert, Peter Sommerlad, and Michael Stal, helped popularize these kinds of patterns (organizational and process patterns) (Buschmann, Meunier, Rohnert, Sommerlad & Stal, 1996).

Contrary to pattern, that represents a "best practice", an *anti-pattern* represents a "lesson learned". There are two kinds of "anti-patterns": those that describe a bad solution to a problem which resulted in a bad situation and those that describe how to get out of a bad situation and how to proceed from there to a good solution. Anti-pattern is initially proposed by Andrew Koenig. Anti-patterns extend the field of software patterns research into exciting new areas and issues, including: refactoring, reengineering, system extension, and system migration (Opdyke, 1992, Webster, 1995, Brown, Malveau, Hays, McCormick Iii & Mowbray, 1998, Love, 1997).

Recent popularity of autonomous agents and agent-oriented software engineering has led to the discovery of agent patterns (Aridor & Lange, 1998, Deugo, Oppacher, Kuester, & Otte, 1999, Hayden, Carrick & Yang, 1999, Do, Faulkner & Kolp, 2003, Mouratidis, Giorgini & Manson, 2003), that capture good solutions to common problems in agent design in many aspect such as security, architecture, organization, etc. However, as pointed out earlier, little focus has been put on social and intentional considerations and these agent patterns rather aim at the implementation level. The framework presented in the chapter should add more detail to the design process of agent oriented software engineering (Do, Kolp, Hang Hoang & Pirotte, 2003, Do, Faulkner & Kolp, 2003).

Over the last years, a number of agent-oriented software development methodologies have been proposed. Most agent-oriented software development and requirements-driven methodologies only use a waterfall system development life cycle or advice their users to proceed iteratively without offering a strong project management framework to support that way of proceeding. Consequently they are not suited for the development of huge and complex user-intensive applications. I-Tropos is based on the work described in this chapter. It fills the project and product life cycle gaps of agent-oriented methodologies and offers a goal-oriented project management perspective to support project stakeholders. The I-Tropos project management framework covers several dimensions including risk, quality, time and process management. Contributions include, among others, taking threats and quality factors' evaluation directly in account for planning the goals realization over multiple iterations.

I-Tropos is an adequate project management for building large-scale enterprise systems from scratch. However, many firms have turned to the reuse of existing software or using commercial off-the-shelf (COTS) software as an option due to lower cost and time of development. Work for enlarging its scope including COTS software customization onto specific case and adequate project management is in progress. The basic adaptation of I-Tropos to support this paradigm of software development is described in (Wautelet, Achbany, Kiv, & Kolp, 2009).

CONCLUSION

Nowadays, software engineering for new enterprise application domains such as e-business, knowledge management, peer-to-peer computing or Web services is forced to build up open systems able to cope with distributed, heterogeneous, and dynamic information issues. Most of these software systems exist in a changing organizational and operational environment where new components can be added, modified or removed at any time. For these reasons and more, Multi-Agent Systems (MAS) architectures are gaining popularity in that they do allow dynamic and evolving structures which can change at run-time.

An important technique that helps to manage the complexity of such architectures is the reuse of development experience and know-how. Like any architect, software architects use patterns to guide system development. Over the years, patterns have become an attractive approach to reusing architectural design knowledge in software

engineering. Templates such as patterns and styles describe a problem commonly found in software designs and prescribe a flexible solution for the problem, so as to ease the reuse of that solution.

As explored in this paper, MAS architectures can be considered social structures composed of autonomous and proactive agents that interact and cooperate with each other to achieve common or private goals. Since the fundamental concepts of multi-agent systems are intentional and social, rather than implementation-oriented, social abstractions could provide inspiration and insights to define patterns for designing MAS architectures.

This paper has focused on social templates such as social patterns and organizational styles. With real-world social behaviors as a metaphor, social patterns are agent-oriented design patterns that describe MAS as composed of autonomous agents that interact and coordinate to achieve their intentions, like actors in human organizations while organizational styles focus on architectural templates inspired by organization theory.

The paper has described such templates, a design framework to introspect them and formalize their "code of ethics", answering the question: what can one expect from a broker, mediator, embassy, etc. It aims to be used during the detail design phase of any agent-oriented methodology detailing the patterns following different point of views.

REFERENCES

Ambler, S. (1998). *Process patterns: Building large-scale systems using object technology.* Cambridge University Press.

Aridor, Y., & Lange, D. B. (1998). Agent design patterns: Elements of agent application design. In *Proc. of the 2nd Int. Conf. on Autonomous Agents, Agents'98, Minneapolis, USA* (pp.108-115).

Bauer, B., Muller, J. P., & Odell, J. (2001). Agent UML: A formalism for specifying multiagent interaction. In *Proc. of the 1st Int. Workshop on Agent-Oriented Software Engineering, AOSE'00, Limerick, Ireland* (pp. 91-103).

Beck, K., & Cunningham, W. (1987). Using pattern languages for object-oriented programs. *Workshop on the Specification and Design for Object-Oriented Programming (OOPSLA'87).*

Borland Together (2007). Retrieved August 16, 2007 from http://www.borland.com/downloads/download_together.html

Bosch, J. (1998). Design patterns as language constructs. *JOOP Journal of Object-Oriented Programming, 11*(2), 18–32.

Brown, W. J., Malveau, R. C., Hays, W., McCormick Iii, H., & Mowbray, T. J. (1998). *AntiPatterns: refactoring software, architectures, and projects in crisis.* John Wiley & Sons.

Buschmann, F., Meunier, R., Rohnert, H., Sommerlad, P., & Stal, M. (1996). *Pattern-oriented software architecture - A system of patterns.* John Wiley & Sons.

Caire, J. & al. (2002). Agent-oriented analysis using MESSAGE/UML. In *Proceedings of the 2nd Int. Workshop on Agent-Oriented Software Engineering* (LNCS 2222, pp. 119-135).

Castro, J., Kolp, M., & Mylopoulos, J. (2002). Towards requirements-driven information systems engineering: The Tropos project. *Information Systems, 27*(6), 365–389. doi:10.1016/S0306-4379(02)00012-1

Chidamber, & S.R, Kemerer, C.F. (1994). A metrics suite for object-oriented design. *IEEE Transactions on Software Engineering, 20*(6), 476-493.

Cockburn, A. (1996). The interaction of social issues and software architecture. *Communications of the ACM, 39*(10), 40–49. doi:10.1145/236156.236165

Coplien, J., & Schmidt, D. (1995). *Pattern languages of program design.* Addison-Wesley.

Coplien, O. (1991). *Advanced C++ programming styles and idioms.* Addison-Wesley International.

Deugo, D., Oppacher, F., Kuester, J., & Otte, I. V. (1999). Patterns as a means for intelligent software engineering. In *Proceedings of the Int. Conf. on Artificial Intelligence, IC-AI'99, Las Vegas, Nevada, USA* (pp. 605-611).

Do, T. T., Faulkner, S., & Kolp, M. (2003). organizational multi-agent architectures for information systems. In *Proceedings of the 5th International Conference on Enterprise Information Systems, ICEIS 2003* (pp. 89-96).

Do, T. T., Kolp, M., Hang Hoang, T. T., & Pirotte, A. (2003). A framework for design patterns for Tropos. In *Proceedings of the 17th Brazilian Symposium on Software Engineering, SBES 2003.*

Dussauge, P., & Garrette, B. (1999). *Cooperative strategy: Competing successfully through strategic alliances.* Wiley and Sons.

Fernandez, E. B., & Pan, R. (2001). A pattern language for security models. In *Proceedings of the 8th Conference on Pattern Language of Programs, PLoP 2001.*

FIPA. (2007). *The Foundation for Intelligent Physical Agent (FIPA).* Retrieved from http://www.fipa.org

Fowler, M. (1997). *Analysis patterns: Reusable object models.* Addison-Wesley.

Fuxman, A., Pistore, M., Mylopoulos, J., & Traverso, P. (2001). Model checking early requirements specifications in Tropos. In *Proc. of the 5th IEEE Int. Symposium on Requirements Engineering, RE'01* (pp. 174-181).

Gamma, E., Helm, R., Johnson, R., & Vlissides, J. (1995). *Design patterns: Elements of reusable object-oriented software*. Addison-Wesley.

Hayden, S., Carrick, C., & Yang, Q. (1999). Architectural design patterns for multiagent coordination. In *Proceedings of the 3rd Int. Conf. on Agent Systems, Agents'99, Seattle, USA*.

Intelligent Agents, J. A. C. K. (2006). Retrieved August 16, 2007 from http://www.agent-software.com

Jennings, N. R., & Wooldridge, M. (2001). Agent-oriented software engineering. In *Handbook of Agent Technology*. AAAI/ MIT Press.

Kolp, M., Faulkner, S., & Wautelet, Y. (2007). Social-centric design of multi-agent architectures. In P. Giorgini, N. Maiden, J. Mylopoulos, E. Yu (Eds.), *Social modeling for requirements engineering*. MIT Press.

Kolp, M., Giorgini, P., & Mylopoulos, J. (2002). Information systems development through social structures. In *Proceedings of the 14th Int. Conference on Software Engineering and Knowledge Engineering, SEKE'02, 27* (pp. 183-190).

Love, T. (1997). *Object lessons*. Cambridge University Press.

Mintzberg, H. (1992). Structure in fives: Designing effective organizations. Prentice-Hall.

Morabito, J., Sack, I., & Bhate, A. (1999). Organization modeling: Innovative architectures for the 21st century. Prentice Hall.

Mouratidis, H., Giorgini, P., & Manson, G. (2003). Modelling secure multiagent systems. In *Proceedings of the 2nd International Joint Conference on Autonomous Agents and Multiagent Systems* (pp. 859-866). ACM Press.

OMG, 2005. *The software process engineering metamodel specification*. Version 1.1.

Opdyke, W. F. (1992). *Refactoring object-oriented frameworks*. PhD Thesis, University of Illinois at Urbana-Champaign.

Parunak, V. (1997). Go to the ant: Engineering principles from natural agent systems. *Annals of Operations Research, 75*, 69–101. doi:10.1023/A:1018980001403

Pree, W. (1994). *Design patterns for object oriented development*. Addison Wesley.

Rational Rose, I. B. M. (2007). Retrieved August 16, 2007 from http://www-306.ibm.com/software/rational

Riehle, D., & Züllighoven, H. (1996). Understanding and using patterns in software development. *Theory and Practice of Object Systems, 2*(1), 3–13. doi:10.1002/(SICI)1096-9942(1996)2:1<3::AID-TAPO1>3.0.CO;2-#

Scott, W. R. (1998). *Organizations: Rational, natural, and open systems*. Prentice Hall.

Segil, L. (1996). Intelligent business alliances: How to profit using today's most important strategic tool. *Times Business*.

Wautelet, Y., Achbany, Y., Kiv, S., & Kolp, M. (2009). A service-oriented framework for component-based software development: An i* driven approach. In *Proceedings of the 11th International Conference on Enterprise Information Systems, ICEIS '09, Milan*.

Wautelet, Y., Kolp, M., & Achbany, Y. (2006). *I-Tropos: An iterative SPEM-centric software project management process* (Technical Report IAG Working paper 06/01). IAG/ISYS Information Systems Research Unit, Catholic University of Louvain, Belgium. Retrieved from http://www.iag.ucl.ac.be/wp

Webster, B. F. (1995). *Pitfalls of object oriented development*. John Wiley & Sons Inc.

Widom, J. (1995). Research problems in data warehousing. In *Proceedings of the Fourth Int. Conf. on Information and Knowledge Management* (pp. 25-30). ACM Press.

Wood, M., DeLoach, S. A., & Sparkman, C. (2001). Multi-agent system engineering. *International Journal of Software Engineering and Knowledge Engineering, 11*(3), 231–258. doi:10.1142/S0218194001000542

Woodridge, M., Jennings, N. R., & Kinny, D. (2000). The Gaia methodology for agent-oriented analysis and design. *Autonomous Agents and Multi-Agent Systems, 3*(3), 285–312. doi:10.1023/A:1010071910869

Yoshino, M. Y., & Srinivasa Rangan, U. (1995). *Strategic alliances: An entrepreneurial approach to globalization*. Harvard Business School Press.

Yu, E. (1995). *Modeling strategic relationships for process reengineering*. PhD thesis, University of Toronto, Department of Computer Science.

Zambonelli, F., Jennings, N. R., Omicini, A., & Wooldridge, M. (2000). Agent-oriented software engineering for Internet applications. In *Coordination of Internet Agents: Models, Technologies and Applications* (pp. 326-346). Springer Verlag.

Zambonelli, F., Jennings, N. R., & Wooldridge, M. (2000). Organizational abstractions for the analysis and design of multi-agent systems. In *Proceedings of the 1ˢᵗ International Workshop on Agent-Oriented Software Engineering* (pp. 243-252).

Chapter 2
A Multiagent–Based Framework for Integrating Biological Data

Faheema Maghrabi
Ain Shams University, Egypt

Hossam M. Faheem
Ain Shams University, Egypt

Taysir Soliman
Asuit University, Egypt

Zaki Taha Fayed
Ain Shams University, Egypt

ABSTRACT

Biological data has been rapidly increasing in volume in different Web data sources. To query multiple data sources manually on the internet is time consuming for biologists. Therefore, systems and tools that facilitate searching multiple biological data sources are needed. Traditional approaches to build distributed or federated systems do not scale well to the large, diverse, and the growing number of biological data sources. Internet search engines allow users to search through large numbers of data sources, but provide very limited capabilities for locating, combining, processing, and organizing information. A promising approach to this problem is to provide access to the large number of biological data sources through a multiagent-based framework where a set of agents can cooperate with each other to retrieve relevant information from different biological Web databases. The proposed system uses a mediator-based integration approach with domain ontology, which uses as a global schema. In this paper we propose a multiagent-based framework that responds to biological queries according to its biological domain ontology.

INTRODUCTION

Recent advances in laboratory technology have resulted in massive amounts of biological data that are often deposited in Web databases. Clearly, access to this data is very important to biological researchers. However, heterogeneity among biological databases due to the incompatibilities in data formats, data representations, and data source schema has impeded the accessibility to such databases. Three fundamental approaches have been used to address the challenges associated with the incompatibilities among biological databases: (a) data warehouse integration, (b) information linkage integration, and (c) mediator-based integration.

Data warehousing consists of materializing the data from multiple data sources into a local warehouse and executing all queries on the data contained in the warehouse rather than in the actual sources. Data warehousing suffers from a lack of scalability, when considering the exponential growth of biological databases. The information linkage integration, motivated by the fact that many of data sources on the Web are browsed instead of queried, the integration happens through links and applies to any collection of data sources which can be seen as a set of pages with their interconnections and specific entry point. Information linkage takes advantage of distributed resources. However, maintaining and updating the static links between the various databases is a challenge. Furthermore, the only queries that can be answered by information linkage based systems are those that are within the scope of the pre-existing static links (Hernandez & Kambhampati, 2004; Miled, Webster, & Liu, 2003).

The proposed framework is based on the third approach, namely, mediator-based integration. It establishes a transparent access to heterogeneous data sources without physically copying them into a single data repository. Database integration systems which use mediator-based integration consisting of three elements: wrappers, an integration layer, and a query interface. The wrappers provide uniform access to the heterogeneous data sources. The integration layer decomposes user queries, sends them to the relevant wrappers, and finally integrates the query results before the final result is returned to the user via the query interface (Köhler, Philippi, & Lange, 2003).

This class of integration systems can be divided into two subclasses: local as view (LAV) and global as view (GAV). In LAV, there is no global schema, and the user needs to specify the component databases in the query by using a multi-database query language. One of the disadvantages of LAV is that the component databases are not transparent to the user. This approach is used by BioKleisli (Davidson, Overton, Tannen, & Wong, 1997). In GAV, a global data schema is constructed, and the queries are expressed on this unified schema. The global schema integrates all the component schemas. Therefore, the component databases are transparent to the user. TAMBIS (Baker, Brass, Bechhoferb, et al., 1998) and BACIIS (Miled, Li, & Bukhres, 2005) are examples of GAV, where they use ontology as a conceptual model to integrate multiple biological Web databases.

Domain ontology and mapping schema are the two main components of the proposed system. The domain ontology can be used to define a common controlled vocabulary and to semantically define databases. It is designed with hierarchal structure describing the biological concepts and the relationship between them. When integrating heterogeneous databases, some issues have to be addressed, namely, semantic and syntactic variability. Resolving semantic variability consists of adequately interpreting and cross relating information stored in different databases. Syntactic variability arises from the heterogeneity of the database schema, data models, and query processing approaches. Domain ontology has been used successfully as a domain model in several general-purpose information integration systems. The domain ontology in this architecture serves as a global schema and plays a major role in resolving both semantic and syntactic variability. Domain ontology can be used for guiding the user through query formulation. Also, it is used in data source selection utilizing mapping schema, and in rewriting the user query into smaller subqueries.

The mapping schema is used to describe each database participating in the integration. In each mapping schema, a mapping between data schema of Web database and domain ontology is made, where it includes concepts and terms from domain ontology that are relevant to specific database. These concepts are organized according to the hierarchal structure of domain ontology. Also, it contains metadata of how to query and extract data from the Web interface of a specific Web database. Each mapping schema consists of the metadata which includes general information about the Web database such as database name, the input data types accepted, and the output data types generated by the corresponding Web database. These data types are expressed by using ontology terms. The mapping schema is also used to select the component database that can respond to the given subquery.

The proposed framework employs a mediator-based integration approach with domain ontology. Agent technology can significantly improve the design and the development of Internet applications due to their characteristics of autonomy and adaptability to open and distributed environment. In this article we propose a multiagent-based framework that responds to biological queries according to its biological domain ontology.

This article is organized as follows: we first discuss the importance of biological data integration and introduce some existing biological domain ontology. We then discuss ontology-based biological data integration. After that we provide an overview of agent technology, agent communication language, and planning in multiagent-based system. Next, we introduce agent program types and discuss why we use agent technology in integrating biological data. We then provide

the proposed multiagent-based framework and describe an example of integrating biological data using the proposed framework. Finally, we highlight our research contributions and provide some concluding remarks.

BIOLOGICAL DATA INTEGRATION

The integration of biological data is just one aspect of the entire molecular biology research. Until recently, molecular biologists managed to perform their research without any type of automated integration. The integration of their repositories and other information sources was done when researchers needed it, without specifically automating the process, thereby consuming most of a molecular biologist's typical workday. However, now that relevant data is widely distributed over the Internet and made available in different formats, manual integration has become practically infeasible, and the amount of data stored in biological databases has indeed grown exponentially over the past decade. In fact, for these reasons bioinformatics sources are difficult—if not simply time-consuming—for biologists to use in combination with one another. So, a flexible and efficient way to integrate information from multiple bioinformatics data sources are needed (Hernandez & Kambhampati, 2004).

The need for effective integration of various bioinformatics sources is justified by the characteristics of these sources, which store a variety of data, and suffer from representational heterogeneity. These sources are also autonomous and Web-based, and provide different querying capabilities.

Variety of data. The data exported by the available sources cover several biological and genomic research fields. Typical data that can be stored includes gene expressions and sequences, disease characteristics, molecular structures, microarray data, protein interactions, and so forth. Depending on how large or small domain-specific the sources are, they can store different types of data. Furthermore, bioinformatics data can be characterized by many relationships between objects and concepts, which are difficult to identify formally (either because they are abstract concepts or simply because they span across several research topics). Finally, not only can the quantity of data available in a source be quite large, but also the size of each datum or record can itself be extremely large (i.e., DNA sequences, 3-D protein structures, etc.).

Representational heterogeneity. The collection of bioinformatics sources has the property that similar data can be contained in several sources but represented in a variety of ways depending on the source. This representational heterogeneity encompasses structural, naming, semantic, and content differences. In other words, not only are they very large but they also have their own schema complexity (i.e., structural differences). Furthermore, each source may refer to the same semantic concept or field with its own term or identifier, which can lead to a semantic discrepancy between many sources (i.e., naming and semantic differences). The opposite can also occur, as some sources may use the same term to refer to different semantic objects. Finally, the content differences involve sources that contain different data for the same semantic object, or that simply have some missing data, thus creating possible inconsistencies between sources.

Autonomous and Web-based sources. Sources operate autonomously, which means that they are free to modify their design and/or schema, remove some data without any prior "public" notification, or occasionally block access to the source for maintenance or other purposes. Moreover, they may not always be aware of or concerned by other sources referencing them or integration systems accessing them. This instability and unpredictability is further affected by the simple fact that nearly all sources are Web-based and are therefore dependent on network traffic and overall availability. An important consequence of the sources being autonomous is that the data

is dynamic: new discoveries or experiments will continually modify the source content to reflect the new hypotheses or findings.

In fact, the only way for an integration system to be certain that it will return the latest data is to actually access the sources at query time.

Different querying capabilities. Individual sources provide their own user-access interface, all of which a user must learn in order to retrieve information that is likely spread across several sources. Additionally, the sources often allow for only certain types of queries to be asked, thereby protecting and preventing direct access to their data. These intentional access restrictions force end-users and external systems to adapt and limit their queries to a certain form (Hernandez & Kambhampati, 2004).

ONTOLOGY IN BIOINFORMATICS

Ontology is a formal way of representing knowledge in which concepts are described both by their meaning and their relationship to each other. There is a large variety of biological ontology they differ in the type of biological knowledge they describe, their intended use, the adopted level of abstraction and the knowledge representation language. Examples of biological domain ontologies are TAMBIS and BACIIS ontologies.

The TAMBIS ontology (TAO) is an ontology covering a wide range of biological concepts and is used as a unified schema to support queries over multiple data sources. The TAMBIS ontology is expressed using the description logic (DL) (Borgida, 1995) called GRAIL, which is a type of knowledge representation language. One of the key features for TAMBIS is that these representations offer reasoning services about concepts and their relationships to their clients. In addition to the traditional "is a kind of" relationship (a protein is a kind of biopolymer), there are partitive, locative, and nominative relationships that are supported. This means that the TAMBIS ontology can describe relationships such as: 'Motifs are parts of proteins;' 'Organelles are located inside cells' and a 'gene has a name gene name.' The ontology initially holds only asserted concepts, but these can be joined together, via relationships to form new, compositional concepts. For example, motif can be joined to protein using the relationship "is component of" to form a new concept protein motif (Stevens, Goble, Paton, et al., 1999).

Another example of biological ontology is the BACIIS ontology (BAO). The ontology developed in BAO has three dimensions: object, property, and relation. In the ontology of BAO, the properties of an object are defined as a property class, which occupies a position in the property hierarchy tree. A relation refers to the association between two concepts. In BAO, classes under the object and property dimensions are arranged into a hierarchy, based on the relation "is-a-subclass-of." For example, GENE is a subclass of the class NUCLEIC-ACID in the object hierarchy. Similarly, "base-count" is a subclass of "NUCLEIC-ACID-SEQ-INFO" in the property hierarchy. The relation "has property" is used for the object classes and property classes, as in the case of the class NUCLEIC-ACID in the object hierarchy and the class "NUCLEIC-ACID-INFO" in the property hierarchy. The relation "is-a-subsetof" is used for property classes or object classes with parent-descendant relationships. The relations "regulate" and "source-of" are used for object classes that are neither parents nor descendants of each other (Miled et al., 2005). BACIIS ontology is less complex compared to the concepts in TAMBIS ontology. Moreover, BACIIS concepts are easier to understand and could be modified easily.

ONTOLOGY BASED BIOLOGICAL DATA INTEGRATION

Some of the important steps in querying over multiple data sources are user query formulation, data sources selection together with the query rewriting into subqueries over the selected data sources, and identification of relevant data items on which results from different subqueries can be joined. In this section, we describe how the biological domain ontology can be used to support these steps.

Query formulation. Domain ontology can be used for guiding users through query formulation. The proposed framework can provide domain ontology as a query formulation interface or can support inclusion of ontology terms into a query. Domain ontology enables the selection of relevant types of biological knowledge, while specialized ontology can be useful for the precise specification of properties for data items of interest. Also, relationships between concepts in domain ontology can lead to the retrieval of more relevant results

Data source selection and query rewriting. The domain ontology is important for describing data sources uniformly from the domain perspective. When user queries include ontological terms, they provide support for data source selection and the user query rewriting into subqueries over these data sources. Terms from domain ontology can specify types of biological data stored in data sources. At the same time, relationships between data items in a data source could be derived by the available relationships between ontological terms. Also, ontological terms can be used to refine the description of the content of a data source. Often, not all data are stored explicitly in a biological data source. In addition, mapping rules between data source and ontology terms should be used to specify the data source schema. Also, it provides a basis for translating query constraints expressed over ontologies to data source specific terms.

Result integration. When results for the subqueries are retrieved from different data sources, the next step is to combine them into an integrated result set. The result data are integrated according to the structure of the domain ontology (Jakoniene & Lambrix, 2005).

AGENT TECHNOLOGY

An agent may exhibit three important general characteristics: autonomy, adaptation, and co-operation. By "autonomy" we mean that agents have their own agenda of goals and exhibit goal-directed behavior. They are not simply reactive, but can be proactive and take initiatives as they deem appropriate. Adaptation implies that agents are capable of adapting to the environment, which includes other agents and human users, and can learn from the experience in order to improve in a changing environment. Cooperation and coordination between agents is probably the most important feature of multi-agent systems. Unlike those stand-alone agents, agents in a multi-agent system collaborate with each other to achieve common goals. In other words, these agents share information, knowledge, and tasks among themselves.

The intelligence of a multiagent-based system is not only reflected by the expertise of individual agents but also exhibited by the emergence of collective behavior beyond individual agents. The approach of multiagent-based system is also proven to be an effective way to develop large distributed systems. Since agents are relatively independent pieces of software interacting with each other only through message-based inter-agent communication, system development, integration, and maintenance become easier and less costly. Cooperation and coordination of agents in multiagent-based system requires agents to be able to understand each other and to communicate effectively with each other through agent communication language (Peng, Finin, Labrou et al., 1998).

Agent Communication Language

Communication between agents is modeled as the exchange of declarative statements, typically based on first-order predicate logic. Continuing the parallelism that a multiagent-based system simulates a society for agents, we can go further by examining the language. Linguists describe certain characteristics (Yule, 1996) of natural languages, which can be considered as the different parts needed to properly describe a language. These characteristics are phonetics, phonology, morphology, lexis (words), semantics, syntax, and pragmatics. The first three describe the oral aspects of communication and thus we can ignore for our purposes. The last four need to be retained. By including lexis in the semantics we can use this sub-set of natural language characteristics to describe a language for agents. To be more precise, it can be partitioned into three layers:

Pragmatics. Specifies the way that an entity will express its needs and/or the effect that it wants to convey to the receiver. This layer can be thought of as the specification for information exchange. It specifies the way that two (or more) entities—agents—will communicate and it comprises of, among other things, sender, recipient, and the content of the message. Pragmatics is referred to as the agent communication language or ACL. In natural languages, pragmatics is implicit—the intent of the speaker is inferred by his or her intonation and choice of words. An example of such a specification is KQML (Finin, Weber, Wiederhold et al., 1993) in which speech acts are called performatives.

Syntax. Used to structure the information that will be sent (i.e., message content). The content of the message contains words that are arranged according to a structure, defined by the syntax of the language. Examples of such languages include KIF (Genesereth & Fikes, 1992) or PROLOG (Sterling & Shapiro, 1986).

Semantics. A correctly structured message content consists of a number of words (lexis). However, these words do not mean anything to computational entities such as agents. They are just strings that make up a larger string, the message. Semantics is used to give meaning to these words. It ensures that the word is associated with the correct concept. By doing this we can avoid inconsistencies such as having different words for the same concept or one word for different concepts. A group of concept definitions describing a specific domain is called ontology. Semantics for ACLs can comprise of multiple ontologies (Karasavvas, Baldock, & Burgera, 2004).

PLANNING IN MULTIAGENT SYSTEMS

Traditional centralized planning (Weld, 1994, 1999) is not enough for a system that is naturally distributed. In this section we will briefly describe the most common strategies in distributed problem-solving. One of the most classic and popular techniques to distribute problem-solving is by task sharing, also called task passing. The idea is straightforward. Each agent tries to solve the given problem and when it reaches a task that it does not know how to handle it requests help from other agents. The basic steps in task sharing are task decomposition, task allocation, and result synthesis.

Task decomposition. Generates a set of tasks to be passed to other agents. This could generally involve decomposing large tasks into sub-tasks that could be tackled by different agents.

Task allocation. Requests from the appropriate agents to handle the sub-tasks. In task accomplishment, the appropriate agents accomplish their sub-tasks, which may require further task decomposition and allocation.

Result synthesis. When an agent completes a sub-task that it was responsible for, it sends the result back to the requesting agent. The requesting agent will then synthesize the results into a solution, which could be a sub-solution and thus, in turn, needs to return the result to its requesting agent. This process is repeated until we reach the initial (root) agent that will compose an overall solution.

Notice how similar these steps are to the typical integration process—a query is one type of task.

Multi-agent task sharing is naturally capable of dealing with mediator-like integration problems. In task sharing, each agent makes a local plan (centralized planning) and then requests, in a way, other agents to continue part of the planning—by solving subtasks of the same problem. Hence, globally, the planning process—and execution—is distributed and potentially in parallel (Karasavvas et al., 2004).

Agent Types

Agents have four major types, which are: simple reflex agents, agents that keep track of the world, goal-based agents, and utility-based agents. A simple reflex agent works by finding a rule whose condition matches the current situation (as defined by the percept) and then doing the action associated with that rule. An agent that keeps track of the world works by finding a rule whose condition matches the current situation (as defined by the percept and the stored internal state) and then doing the action associated with that rule. A goal-based agent selects any action (from a set of actions) that can achieve the goal. Utility-based agent selects the best action (from a set of actions that can achieve the goal) to achieve the goal in order to maximize the happiness (Russel & Norvig, 1995).

AGENT TECHNOLOGY AND BIOLOGICAL DATA INTEGRATION

The three important aspects of biological data integration are distribution, autonomy, and heterogeneity. Distribution—in most cases data sources are distributed. The user need not know the location and other details of each available data resource. Autonomy—it is very often the case that integrated resources belong to different organizations or research groups. While most people are willing to share their data, they do not want to lose control over decisions related to their data source. Thus, developers of an integrated system do not usually have any control over the underlying systems, which are autonomous. Heterogeneity—in an open and diverse environment it is very common that some or all of the data sources are different from each other. Integrating heterogeneous databases involves extra work so as to ensure the correct relationship of data between the information systems.

Agents have been designed with the intention of information exchange between data sources. Sharing information is a major part of system integration, and thus agents naturally cover the fundamental aspects of data integration. With respect to distribution, multiagent-based systems are naturally distributed. They offer location transparency by providing facilities for service discovery and brokering. In addition, a high-level communication language enables flexible and advanced communication between distributed agents. Regarding autonomy, agents are designed

with the assumption that software entities are autonomous. To deal with heterogeneity, agents communicate only via ACL. A common communication language and a common message content language that deals with technical heterogeneity while sharing an ontology handles the semantic differences (Karasavvas et al., 2004).

Proposed Multiagent Framework

The multi-agent based framework shown in Figure 1 is comprised of a network of cooperating agents communicating by means of the ACL. The user interface agent (UIA) guides users to construct ontology based query, and then sends this query to the query planner agent (QPA). The QPA decomposes this query into a list of subqueries, and then sends these subqueries to the mapping agent (MA). The MA prepares a list of appropriate databases using mapping schema, and then sends this list of databases to the QPA. The QPA

Figure 1. Multiagent-based framework

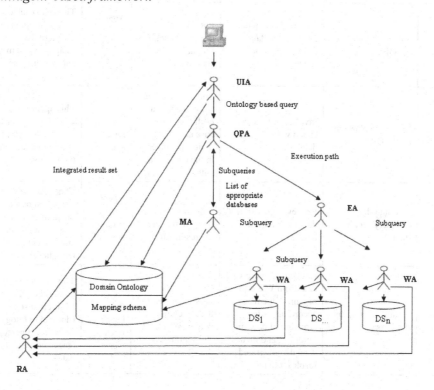

constructs the execution path for this query (selects the best execution path), and then sends this execution path to the execution agent (EA). The EA invokes the wrapper agent (WA) associated with each Web database that corresponds to a given subquery. The WA retrieves the result data from remote databases using the mapping schema of the database, and then sends the resulting data to the result agent (RA). The RA collects query results data from WAs and organizes it according to the structure of domain ontology, and then sends the integrated result set to the UIA to display results. Table 1 shows a brief description for each agent, percepts, actions, goals, and type.

The proposed system is being developed using JADE (Java agent development framework) which is a software development framework aimed at developing multi-agent systems and applications conforming to FIPA (Foundation for of Intelligent Physical Agent) standards for intelligent agents (Bellifemine, Poggi, & Rimassa, 2001). The goal of the proposed system is to hide the large variety

Table 1. Agent description

Agent Name	Percepts	Actions	Goals	Type	Explanation
UIA	Input query from the user and the integrated result set sent by the RA	Guide user to construct ontology-based query and output the integrated result set to user	Construct ontology-based query, output the integrated result set to the user	Simple reflex agent	This agent selects actions on the basis of current percept (input query) only
QPA	Ontology based query from the UIA	Decompose input query into smaller subqueries	Construct the execution path	Utility-based agent	This agent selects the best action (best execution path) that achieves the goal.
MA	Subqueries sent by the QPA	Map each subquery to a specific data source using mapping schema	Find list of appropriate data sources for subqueries submitted.	Agent that keeps track of world	This agent selects action based on an internal state (mapping schema) and current percept (subquery).
EA	Execution plan sent by the QPA	Invoke the Was associated with each Web database.	Invoking the Was associated with each Web database according to dependencies in the execution path.	Simple reflex agent	This agent selects actions on the basis of current percept (selected execution path) only.
WA	Ontology-based subquery sent by the EA	Retrieves the result data from remote databases.	Submit the subquery and retrieve the result data	Agent that keeps track of world	This agent selects the action based on an internal state (mapping schema) and current percept (subquery).
RA	Result data sent by the WAs	Collects query results data from Was and organizes them according to the structure of domain ontology, and then send the integrated result set to the UIA.	Organizing result data according to the structure of domain ontology and sending it to the UIA.	Agent that keeps track of world	This agent selects actions based on an internal state (domain ontology) and current percept (received results data).

of local or remote biological databases and the disparity in their interfaces. A user should see only one interface and be able to query the system by specifying what he or she wants to know without a detailed knowledge of where relevant information is located, what its representation is like, and how the biological databases' interfaces must be handled. The system includes three parts:

1. A multi-agent system, which contains a set of agents interacting with each other to get results (as shown in the framework).The multi-agent system is being developed using JADE.

2. The biological ontology, which is being developed using Protégé-2000. It is an extensible, platform independent ontology and knowledge-base editor, developed by Stanford Medical Informatics at the Stanford University School of Medicine. Protégé is available as free software. The biological ontology is converted to JADE compatible java classes using the JadeJessProtege tool (plugin for protégé).

3. The mapping schema, we initially use two biological databases SWISSPROT (protein) and GENBANK (gene). We map each term in the database to biological ontology concepts. Through this mapping operation we solve the heterogeneity problem between databases. The ontology is used to map all the different terms used by the remote databases to a single term. Each database has its own mapping schema. We can easily add other biological databases by creating a mapping schema and a wrapper agent for this database.

EXAMPLE

The proposed framework retrieves relevant biological data from different data sources. The "new," biological data is integrated using

multiagent-based approach which will add more benefits. For example, multiagent systems can offer a high level of encapsulation, abstraction, modularity, and autonomy. Because agents are independent, every agent can decide what the best strategy is for solving its particular problem. The agents can be built by different developers; as long as they understand the communication, they can work together. Other important benefits are that multi-agent systems offer distributed and open platform architecture. Agents can support a dynamically changing system without the necessity of knowing each part in advance.

In order to clarify the idea, consider the following example query: find nucleic acid sequences for "SHH" gene in "Homo sapiens" organism, also find amino acid sequences and protein 3D structure for the proteins that are encoded by this gene. For this example, the inputs of the query are the gene "SHH" and organism "Homo sapiens." The outputs of the query are the nucleic acid sequences of the gene, amino acid sequences, and protein 3D structure for the proteins that are encoded by this gene. In this example query we use BAO as the biological domain ontology. Each input element consists of a biological term and its type. The input type is a subset of the biological domain ontology. For example, the "SHH" gene is of input type GENE_NAME and "Homo sapiens" is of input type ORGANISM-NAME. The properties PROTEIN-3D-STRUCTURE and AMINO-ACID-SEQ-INFO of the Object Sub-Class NORMAL-PROTEIN, and the property NUCLEIC-ACID-SEQ-INFO of the Object Class NUCLEIC-ACID are chosen as the query output (Miled et al., 2003).

The proposed framework executes this query as follows: UIA provides an intelligent interface; it guides the user in constructing the query by navigating ontology concepts and relations extracted from domain ontology. In this example the biological terms are GENE_NAME "SHH" and ORGANISM-NAME "Homo sapiens." As part of input query, PROTEIN-3D-STRUCTURE, AMINO-ACID-SEQ-INFO are added and NU-CLEIC-ACID-SEQ-INFO is added as part of the output query. Then the UIA sends the ontology based query to QPA. The QPA constructs the best execution path by decomposing the query into a list of subqueries based on the query output properties, domain ontology and mapping schema. An example of the subquery is select GENBANK-ACCESS-NUMBER when ORGANISM-NAME is "Homo sapiens" and GENE-NAME is "SHH." The QPA sends these subqueries to the MA which maps the ontology properties in each subquery to specific Web databases using the mapping schema. In the previous example subquery, the MA finds GENBANK database is the most appropriate one. The MA then sends a list of appropriate databases to the QPA that constructs the best execution path for this query as shown in Figure 2.

The execution path generated by the QPA is forwarded to the EA and the EA invokes the WAs associated with each database that correspond to a given subquery. The WA executes the subquery and retrieves the result data. The result data extracted by the WAs are tagged by the corresponding biological domain ontology properties according to hierarchal structure of domain ontology. The RA collects the query results from the WAs and combines them into an integrated result set also according to biological domain ontology.

Research Contribution

Some biological integration systems exist such as TAMBIS, BACIIS and SEMADA (Köhler et al., 2003) which support querying different biological data sources based on domain ontology. Our framework also supports different biological queries based on domain ontology, however, the novelty in our approach is that the framework is based on agent oriented programming (AOO) which is an extension to object oriented programming (OOP). AOO relies on the assumption that a complex distributed software system can be programmed as a set of communicating, interacting and knowledge base entities called (software) agents. Object-oriented modeling of social systems requires the integration of new concepts related to cognitive processes such as learning, planning, knowledge representation, and communication. If one defines an agent as an object that combines a mental state to perceive its environment and achieve some goals, a knowledge base to hold its memory and an interface for communicating with other entities, then all the above properties could be fulfilled. Agent technology is an attempt to accommodate basic OO concepts (e.g., abstraction, modularity) and advanced artificial intelligence techniques (e.g., reasoning, learning). The promise is that they will provide the programmer with a basic unit of design (the agent), which enhances software modularity, maintainability, and reusability (Brugali & Sycara, 2000).

Figure 2. Execution path

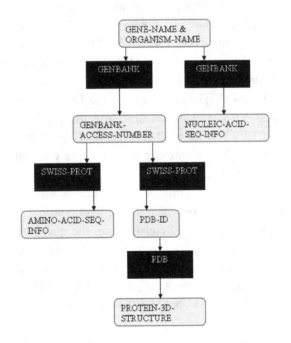

CONCLUSION

Agent-oriented techniques are being increasingly used in several applications. They are ideally suited for developing complex, distributed software systems. Also, they enhance software modularity, maintainability, and reusability. In this article, we proposed a multiagent-based framework that responds to biological queries according to its biological domain ontology. A set of agents can cooperate with each other to retrieve relevant information from different biological Web databases. The proposed framework resolves the incompatibilities that exist in data formats, data representations, and mapping schema of biological Web databases. Also, it reduces the overhead associated with changing the existing data sources or adding different data sources. We use a mediator-based integration approach with domain ontology. One of the main advantages of this approach is not requiring that component databases to be physically combined into one database. The domain ontology serves as a global schema and plays a major role in resolving both semantic and syntactic variability of biological Web databases. The proposed framework can be easily implemented using existing agent development environments such as JADE (Bellifemine et al., 2001) that support building a multi-agent based system.

REFERENCES

Baker, P.G., Brass, A., Bechhoferb, S., Goble, C., Paton, N., & Stevens, R. (1998). TAMBIS-Transparent Access to Multiple Bioinformatics Information Sources. In *Proceedings of the 6th International Conference on Intelligent Systems for Molecular Biology, AAAI Press*, (pp. 25-34).

Bellifemine, F., Poggi A., Rimassa, G. Developing multi-agent systems with a FIPA-compliant agent framework. *Software Pract Experience 2001, 31*(2),103–28.

Borgida, A. (1995). Description logics in data management. *IEEE Trans Knowledge and Data Engineering, 7*(5), 671–782.

Brugali, D., & Sycara, K. (2000). Towards agent-oriented application frameworks. ACM Computing Surveys (CSUR), *ACM Press 32*(21).

Davidson , S.B., Overton ,C., Tannen, V., & Wong, L.(1997). BioKleisli: a. digital library for biomedical researchers. *International Journal on Digital Libraries, 1*(1), 36-53.

Finin, T., Weber, J., Wiederhold, G., Genesereth, M., Fritzson, R., & McGuire, J. (1993). *Specification of the KQML agent communication language.* Technical Report, DARPA knowledge sharing initiative, External Interfaces Working Group.

Genesereth, M., & Fikes, R. (1992). Knowledge Interchange Format, *Version 3.0 Reference Manual.* Technical Report 92-1. Computer Science Department. Stanford University.

Hernandez, T., & Kambhampati, S. (2004). Integration of biological sources: current systems and challenges ahead. ACM SIGMOD Record, *ACM Press, 33*(3), 51 – 60.

Jakoniene, V., & Lambrix. (2005). Ontology-based integration for bioinformatics. Proceedings of the VLDB Workshop on Ontologies-based techniques for DataBases and Information Systems—ODBIS, (pp. 55-58).

Karasavvas, K. A., Baldock, R., & Burgera, A. (2004). Bioinformatics integration and agent technology. Journal of Biomedical Informatics, *Elsevier Science, 37*(3), 205 – 219.

Köhler, J., Philippi, S., Lange, M.(2003). SEMEDA: ontology based semantic integration of biological databases. *Bioinformatics, 19*(18), 2420-2427.

Miled, Z. B., Webster, Y.W., & Liu,Y. (2003). An ontology for semantic integration of life science web Databases. *International Journal of Cooperative Information Systems, 12*(2), 275-294.

Miled, Z.B., Li, N., & Bukhres, O. (2005). BACIIS: Biological and chemical information integration system. *Journal of Database Management, 16*(3), 72-85.

Peng, Y., Finin, T., Labrou, Y., Chu, B., Long, J., Tolone, W. J. et al. (1998). A multi-agent system for enterprise integration. International Journal of Agile Manufacturing, *UMBC eBiquity, 1*(2), 213-229.

Russel, S., & Norvig, P. (1995). *Artificial intelligence: A modern approach.* New Jersey: Printice Hall Inc.

Sterling, L., & Shapiro, E. (1986). *The art of prolog.* Cambridge, MA: MIT Press

Stevens, R., Goble, C.A., Paton, N.W., Bechhofer, S., Ng, G., Baker, P. et al. (1999). Complex Query Formulation Over Diverse Information Sources Using an Ontology. Workshop on Computation of Biochemical Pathways and Genetic Networks, European Media Lab (EML), (pp. 83–88).

Weld, D. (1994). An introduction to least commitment planning. *AI Mag, 15*(4), 27–61.

Weld, D. (1999). Recent advances in AI planning. *AI Mag, 20*(2), 93- 123.

Yule, G. (1996). The study of language. Cambridge: Cambridge University Press.

This work was previously published in the International Journal of Intelligent Information Technologies, Vol. 4, Issue 2, edited by V. Sugumaran, pp. 24-36, copyright 2008 by IGI Publishing (an imprint of IGI Global).

Chapter 3
A Modern Epistemological Reading of Agent Orientation

Yves Wautelet
Université catholique de Louvain, Belgium

Christophe Schinckus
Facultés Universitaires St-Louis, Belgium

Manuel Kolp
Université catholique de Louvain, Belgium

ABSTRACT

This article presents a modern epistemological validation of the process of agent oriented software development. Agent orientation has been widely presented in recent years as a novel modeling, design and programming paradigm for building systems using features such as openness, dynamics, sociality and intentionality. These will be put into perspective through a Lakatosian epistemological approach. The contribution of this article is to get researchers acquainted with the epistemological basis of the agent research domain and the context of the emergence of object and agent-orientation. This article advocates the use of the Lakatosian research programme concept as an epistemological basis for object and agent orientation. This is done on the basis of how these frameworks operationalize relevant theoretical concepts of the Kuhnian and Lakatosian theories.

INTRODUCTION

Information systems are deeply linked to human activities. Unfortunately, development methodologies have been traditionally inspired by programming concepts and not by organizational and human ones. This leads to ontological and semantic gaps between the systems and their environments. The adoption of agent orientation and Multi-Agent Systems (MAS) helps to reduce these gaps by offering modeling tools based on organizational concepts (actors, agents, goals, objectives, responsibilities, social dependencies, etc.) as fundamentals to conceive systems through all the development processes. Moreover, software development is becoming increasingly complex. Stakeholders' expectations are growing higher while the development agendas have to be as short as possible. Project managers, business analysts and software developers need adequate processes and models to specify the organizational context, capture requirements and build efficient and flexible systems.

We propose, in this article, a modern epistemological validation of the emergence of Object-Orientation (OO) and Agent-Orientation (AO). The latter will be put into perspective through the Lakatosian approach. Related work and contributions to the epistemological position of OO and AO will first be explicated. The emerging context of the conceptual frameworks of OO and AO, the software crisis, is then briefly described. The validation of our epistemological reading will be done on the basis of OO and AO operationalization of some critical theoretical concepts derived from the Kuhnian and Lakatosian theories. We finally discuss the adoption of the Lakatosian research programme concept to characterize both OO and AO. Implications of this epistemological position on everyday work have been distinguished both for software engineering researchers and practitioners. For researchers, it mostly has an implication on how agent ontologies are built and for practitioners it has an implication on how software problems are envisaged.

This article is organized as follows. Section two (State of the Art) presents the contributions as well as the research context. We point out the emergence of OO and AO as a consequence of the software crisis. That is why the software crisis is briefly reviewed. Section three (Epistemological Approach) focuses on our epistemological approach: AO is successively considered as a paradigm and a research programme. On the basis of

how some relevant concepts of the Kuhnian and Lakatosian frameworks are operationalized by OO and AO, we provide a Lakatosian reading of those modeling concepts. Conclusions are summarized in Section four.

STATE OF THE ART

This section presents the contributions of an epistemological reading for the computer science researcher as well as the software crisis and AO; we consider this framework and many others as consequences of the crisis.

Related Work and Contributions

Basili (1992) defines Software Engineering (SE) as, "The disciplined development and evolution of software systems based upon a set of principles, technologies and processes." These theoretical frameworks are expected to solve practical problems by proposing software solutions. SE is a practice-oriented field (where empiricism often plays an important role) and is constantly evolving; however, one must dispose of a framework to build common (and preferably best) practices improvement. Kaisler (2005) points out that, "We develop more experience, we not only continue to learn new practices, but we refine and hone the practices that we have already learned." SE is the genuine discipline that emerged from this interconnection between practices and software solutions. Today's software development has become a very complex task and no one has the required skills or time to resolve a sophisticated problem on his or her own. Software development phases need the input from lots of people having to use concepts and ideas for which they share a common understanding. This can be referred as SE's key role: providing some common theoretical entities to allow specialists to develop software solutions.

Few papers in specialized literature point to an in depth questioning of SE knowledge evolution. As Kaisler (2005) emphasizes, the literature is mainly technical or practical and focused on the software design processes. Research methodologies, however, need to be conscientiously built to favour the development and improvement of software solutions. To this end, an epistemological analysis is of primary importance as pointed out by Basili (1992):

The goal is to develop the conceptual scientific foundations of SE upon which future researchers can build.

In this article, we mostly focus on a specific aspect of SE: OO and AO, which are modeling and programming ontologies rather than development processes. A few papers have discussed the evolution of knowledge in SE but encompass a broader range of aspects of this discipline than the current article.

In the book titled Software Paradigms (Kaisler, 2005) published in 2005, Kaisler uses the notion of a paradigm to characterize the way of solving problems in software development. Though Kaisler explicitly quotes Kuhn's work to define the concept of paradigm, Kaisler explains that included in this definition are the, "Concepts of law, theory, application and instrumentation: in, effect, both the theoretical and the practical." The practical dimension being a key issue in computer science, it must be integrated into the paradigm when this concept is used in engineering software. Kaisler's work is based on an empirical process: "We are going to apply the notion of paradigm to the investigation of programming languages and software architectures to determine how well we can solve different types of problems." On the basis of this study, Kaisler proposes a problem typology which would determine the programming approach: "For a given problem class, we'd like to be able to create software that solves the problem or parts of it efficiently. There are two

aspects to creating such software: the software's architecture and the choice of programming language." Kaisler uses the term paradigm in a very large sense since applying the concept to the whole "top-down analysis." The problem typology defines a software typology, which finally determines a specific implementation.

Even if we do not assign the same meaning as Kaisler to the "paradigm" concept, our analysis can be related to his work. By proposing an epistemological reading of the evolution toward AO, we only focus on the last step of Kaisler's view. Indeed, the emergence of AO can be seen as a broadening of the unit of implementation and consequently to the amount of problems that can be solved. This is in line with the vision developed in Jennings and Wooldridge (2001). AO is the best suited to solve complex problems because it refers to a higher abstraction level and it provides some advantages for solution programming. Jennings and Wooldridge (2001) use the term "paradigm" to characterize the evolution from OO to AO. They paradoxically emphasize the continuity between these two paradigms. Indeed, as far as the Kuhnian discussion is concerned, if two theoretical frameworks can be compared they cannot be quoted as paradigms; this will be explained in the following sections.

Finally, Göktürk and Akkok (2004) points out that, "One of the most recent (and widely accepted) examples to a 'rescuer new paradigm' in software engineering is the object-orientation paradigm..." and recalls that the evolution from OO toward AO is often presented in terms of paradigm shift (Basili, 1992; Jennings & Wooldridge, 2001; Woodridge & Jennings, 1995). A very important point discussed by Göktürk and Akkok (2004), is that the choice of a paradigm is similar to the choice of a conceptualization/communication language; consequently mixing two different paradigms could be counter productive. What Göktürk and Akkok (2004) emphasize indirectly is what epistemologists call the "incommensurability thesis." Following this line of argument, two paradigms are totally incomparable since they represent two different set of knowledge.

Based on these related works, our contribution is multiple:

- We emphasize on the epistemological reasons why the paradigm concept is inappropriate to explain the differences between OO and AO. To be considered as paradigm, two theoretical frameworks need to be incomparable and "incommensurable;"
- We propose a new epistemological analysis of the evolution toward AO by using a Lakatosian framework, which can explain and justify the effectiveness of this framework. In this article, AO will be presented as a new research programme widening and improving the knowledge in SE. This improvement cannot be seen as discontinuity of knowledge but rather as continuity since AO could encapsulate object technology;
- By proposing an epistemological reading of the emergence of the AO, we try to reduce what Jennings and Wooldridge (2001) call the "gap" between knowledge and applications. We prove that this evolution can be explained in line with the conventional standards to justify the scientific status of the SE discipline. The paradigm-concept cannot justify the scientific status whereas the research programme-concept can.

The Software Crisis

Although constant progress is being made in software development, complex information systems often imperfectly match users' requirements. A "software engineering crisis" diagnosis was first made in the late sixties. Considerable work has been done in conceptual modeling and other engineering methodologies and processes so that the crisis can be mitigated. However, the diagnosis still remains partially to date. Indeed, structured

methods are not systematically used in software projects and computers expect responsible users, but most of the time the problems encountered are the result of human decisions or methodological insufficiencies.

Software engineering can be defined as the methodological processes and the relevant artifacts used for the development of software on a large scale. The SE crisis has different reasons:

- The increasing complexity of modern software: continuous technological progress allows us to develop larger and larger applications while the increasing demand exceeds the productivity gains obtained by methodological, techniques and tool improvements;
- The common under-estimation of the difficulty and consequently the software development cost (the methods, widely empiric, of individual programming are not applicable to the development of large and complex systems), conflicting software development process and inadequate software products;
- Lack of reliability and maturity of software compared to hardware and its relative importance in the realization of the complex system functions;
- Substantial delay in the diffusion of best practices within the software industry (Davis, 1995; Meyer, 1997; Sommerville, 1992) due to the complexity and cost of education of software developers in a constantly evolving discipline;
- Inherent complexity:
- The problems that a software has to deal with can be arbitrarily complex; for example, the limits of system functionalities are often much less clear than those of tangible products;
- The sequential decomposition of the development phases is not so natural for SE than it is for other engineering disciplines (mechanical engineering for example).

We argue that advances in SE conceptual modeling such as OO and AO are part of the effort to address the crisis; this point becomes important in the context of the epistemological reading, as discussed in the section Epistemological Approach.

Towards Agent Orientation

The meteoric rise of the Internet and World-Wide Web technologies has created new application areas for enterprise software, including eBusiness, web services, ubiquitous computing, knowledge management and peer-to-peer networks. These areas demand software design that is robust, can operate within a wide range of environments, and can evolve over time to cope with changing requirements. Moreover, such software has to be highly customizable to meet the needs of a wide range of users, and sufficiently secure to protect personal data and other assets on behalf of its stakeholders.

Not surprisingly, researchers are looking for new software designs that can cope with such requirements. One promising source of ideas for designing such business software is the area of MAS. They appear to be more flexible, modular and robust than traditional systems including object-oriented ones. They tend to be open and dynamic in the sense that they exist in a changing organizational and operational environment where new components can be added, modified or removed at any time.

MAS are based on the concept of agent and are defined as, "A computer system, situated in some environment that is capable of flexible autonomous action in order to meet its design objective" (Woodridge & Jennings, 1995). An agent exhibits the following characteristics:

- Autonomy: an agent has its own internal thread of execution, typically oriented to the achievement of a specific task, and it decides for itself what actions it should perform at what time.

- Situateness: agents perform their actions in the context of being situated in a particular environment. This environment may be a computational one (e.g., a Web site) or a physical one (e.g., a manufacturing pipeline). The agent can sense and affect some portion of that environment.

- Flexibility: in order to accomplish its design objectives in a dynamic and unpredictable environment, the agent may need to act to ensure that its goals are achieved (by realizing alternative plan). This property is enabled by the fact that the agent is autonomous in its problem solving.

Agents can be useful as stand-alone entities that delegate particular tasks on behalf of a user (e.g., personal digital assistants and e-mail filters (Maes, 1994), or goal-driven office delivery mobile devices (Mataric, 1992). However, in the overwhelming majority of cases, agents exist in an environment that contains other agents. Such an environment is called a multi-agent system.

In MAS, the global behavior is derived from the interaction among the constituent agents: they cooperate, coordinate or negotiate with one another. A MAS is conceived as a society of autonomous, collaborative, and goal-driven software components (agents), much like a social organization. Each role an agent can play has a well-defined set of responsibilities (goals) achieved by means of an agent's own abilities, as well as its interaction capabilities.

This sociality of MAS is well suited to tackle the complexity of an organization's software systems for a number of reasons:

- It permits a better match between system architectures and their operational environment (e.g., a public organization, a corporation, a non-profit association, a local

- The autonomy of an agent (i.e., the ability an agent has to decide what actions it should take at what time (Woodridge & Jennings, 1995)) reflects the social and decentralized nature of modern enterprise systems (Tennenhouse, 2000) that are operated by different stakeholders (Parunak, 1997);
- The flexible way in which agents operate to accomplish their goals is suited to the dynamic and unpredictable situations in which business software is now expected to run (Zambonelli, Jennings, Omicini, & Wooldridge, 2000; Zambonelli, Jennings, & Wooldridge, 2000).

EPISTEMOLOGICAL APPROACH

We argue that a Lakatosian vision should be adapted for an epistemological reading of the emergence of AO. To develop our argumentation, we first consider its use in the literature dealing with the "paradigm" concept to characterize the evolution from OO to AO. We then explain why the Lakatosian "research programme" concept is more adequate than the Kuhnian "paradigm" concept to illustrate the evolution of modeling and programming concepts.

The Traditional Kuhnian Perspective of Software Engineering

The Paradigm-Concept: A Definition

The word "paradigm" comes directly from philosophy where its meaning remains surprisingly rather vague. Plato and Aristotle were the first authors to introduce this concept. According to them, the paradigm is a kind of explanatory model, which allows people to understand, in terms of causality, the changes imposed by Nature. However, the paradigm is not, strictly speaking, a logic. For Aristotle, the "paradigm" was, "different from both deduction, which goes from universal to particular, and induction, which goes from particular to universal, in the sense that the paradigm goes from particular to particular" (Göktürk & Akkok, 2004).

The term "paradigm" has not really been used before the 20th century when Thomas Kuhn developed a specific epistemology based on this concept. The paradigm is defined as, "A constellation of concepts, values, perceptions and practices shared by a community and which forms a particular vision of reality that is the basis of the way a community organizes itself" (Kuhn, 1996). Nevertheless, Kuhn himself admits that the use of the word remains rather vague: it is possible to identify twenty-two different meanings of the "paradigm" concept used in Kuhnian epistemology (Masterman, 1970). In the last edition of his book, Kuhn even recognized that the "paradigm" concept is vague but explained that it is close to what Kuhn calls a "disciplinary matrix."

This leads us to consider in this article the "paradigm" as a way of representing the world, which necessarily includes conceptual tools and methods (the conjunction of these two elements forming what Kuhn called a disciplinary matrix), such that an observer can create models. Each paradigm refers to a particular ontology and represents a subset of "what is representable." The representation abilities of a paradigm are basically related to the conceptual tools, to the modeling methodology and the use of these two elements by theoreticians.

Paradigms and Software Engineering

The first paradigm to be introduced in SE was the procedural paradigm (Göktürk & Akkok, 2004). It was based on the use of algorithms to execute particular tasks. The second paradigm was the data-hiding paradigm, which focused on the data's organization and introduced the concept of modules (to hide the data's). This paradigm was followed by the data-abstraction paradigm, which concentrated on the types and on the operations defined on these types. Next was the object-oriented paradigm, "built upon the data-abstraction" paradigm but introducing new concepts like inheritance and polymorphism. Finally, using the flexibility of the component-oriented logic, the agent-oriented paradigm has divided software into independent and communicating entities called "agents" (Woodridge & Jennings, 1995). This last paradigm has been described in detail in the section Towards Agent Orientation.

Programming languages and modeling paradigms are interdependent. The "chicken and egg" metaphor could be used to characterize their reciprocal relationship (Göktürk & Akkok, 2004); sometimes, specific needs for a programming language lead to a better implementation of a modeling paradigm and sometimes, the evolution of the modeling paradigm influences and improves the development of a specific programming language. However, even if programming languages and modeling paradigms are interdependent, the agent-oriented paradigm differs in the sense that it is not formally related to specific programming languages. The concepts used in AO have been inspired from the organizational structures found in the real world. In the beginning, agent-oriented models were implemented in object-oriented languages but further evolutions allow to support and directly implement MAS in terms of full-fledged agent concepts such as Beliefs, Desires and Intentions (BDI) (JACK Intelligent Agents, 2006; JADEX BDI Agent System, 2007).

A Lakatosian Perspective of Software Engineering

In the following sections, we will propose to review the Kuhnian vision of OO and AO to demonstrate that it is not best suited to describe the evolution in SE. With respect to the research programme concept developed by Lakatos, we will explain why a Lakatosian understanding of the evolution to AO is more appropriate than a Kuhnian one.

"Research programme" Concept: A Definition

In the continuity of the Popperian philosophy (which will be briefly presented in the following section), Imre Lakatos has developed in 1974 an original approach of science. Lakatos considers scientific theories as general structures called "research programmes." A Lakatosian research programme is a kind of scientific construction, a theoretical framework, which guides future research (in a specific field) in a positive or negative way. Each research programme is constituted by a hard core, a protective belt of auxiliary hypotheses, and a positive and a negative heuristic.

The hard core is composed of general theoretical assumptions, which constitute the basic knowledge for the program development. In other words, these axioms are the assumptions the theorists will not challenge in their research. This hard core is surrounded with a protective belt composed of the auxiliary hypotheses, which complete the hard core and with assumptions related to the description of the initial conditions of a specific problem. These auxiliary hypotheses will be thoroughly studied again, widened and completed by theorists in their further studies within the program. This widening of the protective belt hypotheses contributes to the evolution of the research programme without calling into question the basic knowledge shared by a scientific community.

The positive heuristic represents the agreement among the theoreticians over the scientific evolution of the research programme. It is a kind of "problem solving machinery" composed by proposals and indications on the way to widen and enrich the research programme. The negative heuristic is the opposite of the positive one. Within each research programme, it is important to maintain the basic assumptions unchanged. It means that all the questions or methodologies that are not in accordance with the basic knowledge must be rejected. All doubts appearing about the basic knowledge of the main theoretical framework become a kind of negative heuristic of the research programme. When the negative heuristic becomes more and more important, a research programme can become "degenerative" (i.e., it has more and more empirical anomalies). This means that theoreticians have to reconsider the basic knowledge of the program, which can lead to the creation of another research programme. Let us mention that this revision is always a very slow process.

According to Lakatos, we can characterize the evolution of knowledge as a series of "problems shifts" which allow the scientific theories to evolve without rejecting the basic axioms shared by theorists within a specific research programme. The concept of "research programme" represents a descriptive and minimal unit of knowledge, which allows for a rational reconstruction of the history of science.

At first glance, the "research programme" concept seems rather close to the "paradigm" concept. Indeed, it is, in both cases, a matter of "disciplinary matrix" used to describe a particular ontology of the external world. However, differences exist between these two concepts especially in the evolution of science and knowledge in a large sense.

According to Kuhn, the evolution of science does not follow a straight line and does not converge towards something, which would be the "truth." In the Kuhnian vision, the evolution of science could be represented by a broken line where discontinuity would mark the passage from one paradigm to another. From this point of view, different paradigms cannot be compared. Moreover, Kuhn specifies that a paradigm always emerges within a discipline facing a methodological crisis (characterized by the absence of a dominating theoretical framework) (Kuhn, 1996). Following a crisis undergone by a previously dominating paradigm, a new paradigm emerges with a new language and a new rationality. This new way of thinking does not allow a comparison between the old and the new paradigm. Given that a new paradigm is a new way of thinking about the world, there is no basis for comparison. The "paradigms incommensurability" thesis has become a very well known issue in the philosophy of sciences (Sankey, 1994).

Lakatos decomposes the evolution of science into successive methodological and epistemological steps. These steps form a kind of vertical structure built with a multitude of "layers of knowledge" and where each layer represents a particular research programme. In the Lakatosian vision, the emergence of a new research programme is induced by an empirical degeneration of a previously dominating research programme. The new research programme will constitute a superior layer of knowledge, which will integrate the same conceptual tools as the former but which would be able to solve its empirical anomalies through what Lakatos calls a "problem shift." The latter is characterized by an extension or a redefinition of the protective belt of the preceding program. In this vision, research programmes remain comparable to each other (in both conceptual and empirical terms). The language and rationality of the new research programme result from a progressive evolution of knowledge and from the resolution of the empirical anomalies of the previous research programme. In contrast to the Kuhnian vision, Lakatos explains that there is no discontinuity between the different research programmes.

Agent-Orientation: Paradigm vs Research Programme

In this section, we present three main arguments for the use of the Lakatosian research programme to understand the shift from OO to AO.

Kuhnian Crisis or Lakatosian Problem Shift?

As discussed in the first part of this article, a SE-crisis has been observed due to the fact that few software projects successfully manage to fully satisfy users' requirements. In the Kuhnian vision, this crisis could be considered as a favourable argument for the emergence of a new paradigm. In this perspective, a crucial question raises: "Does the current crisis characterize the end of a dominating paradigm or is it simply the result of a pre-paradigmatic step specific to young sciences which have not found a dominating paradigm yet?" Using the Kuhnian rhetoric to analyse this crisis, we can consider the situation as a paradigm evolution. Indeed, the pre-paradigmatic step was rather characterized by the procedural framework (which was defined by an algorithmic and sequential (i.e., a strictly computer/mathematical logic) as well as the data-hiding and the data-abstraction frameworks. This pre-paradigmatic period was essential to the evolution process towards OO. However, the crisis situation observed in SE must be carefully analysed. Even if the "SE-crisis" diagnosis has been noted for several years, we think that the context in which AO has emerged cannot be considered as a crisis in the Kuhnian sense. Indeed, most of the methodological rules existed before AO and the current software development process does not seem to be so chaotic: IT specialists dispose of analysis methods and methodological tools with a high level of abstraction (Castro, Kolp, & Mylopoulos, 2002; Kruchten, 2003). These elements tend to show that what looks like a crisis is rather an (animated but normal) evolution of knowledge in SE (Odell, 2002; Skarmeas, 1999), which could be interpreted as a "problem shift" in the Lakatosian vision.

Kuhnian Discontinuity or Lakatosian Continuity?

We consider that the Kuhnian discontinuity between paradigms is not appropriate to explain the emergence of AO because there is no real "fracture" between OO and AO. Indeed, in some software solutions, communicating objects are used and are completely relevant and sufficient. In software problems where no learning skills are valuable, the use of agents would not bring crucial advantages: they would just transfer messages and would not behave like learning and collaborating agents pursuing goals (Odell, 2002). In this special case, there is no contribution of the agent concept to the software solution in comparison to object technology. We can see that the cohabitation within the same application between modules exploiting object technology and others exploiting agent technology can thus be an "optimal" solution (Odell, 2002). In a Lakatosian vision, this cohabitation represents a progressive evolution of knowledge in SE. Indeed, the Lakatosian epistemology implies that the transition between research programmes is not clear and depends on the specific aspects of the experiment conducted (the software solution is the experiment in our case). A hybrid solution between modules developed on the basis of objects and others on the basis of agents can thus be explained by the continuity between research programmes inherent to the Lakatosian vision of knowledge applied to SE.

Kuhnian Incommensurability or Lakatosian Commensurability?

Another drawback of the adoption of the Kuhnian epistemology in SE is the incommensurability between paradigms. OO and AO can be compared since collaborating agents can be used as communicating objects and, more important, agents can be implemented using object-oriented languages (see for example (Bigus & Bigus, 1997; Bellifemine, Poggi, & Rimassa, 2000). In this perspective, agents can be considered as "super objects" (i.e. objects possessing skills as collaboration, intentionality, learning, autonomy, reasoning, etc.) If we consider SE development as a history of "raising the level of abstraction,"

AO can be seen as an evolution of OO because it raises that level a little higher (Skarmeas, 1999). In this perspective, research programmes preceding OO can also be considered as lower layered than the later. This vision perfectly matches with the Lakatosian concept of layers of knowledge introduced earlier. Indeed, considering SE evolution, each new research programme raises the abstraction level and constitutes a higher layer of knowledge. These layers are comparable so that OO and AO are said to be commensurable.

Lessons Learned

AO is based on the basic knowledge that existed before its emergence. We could say that agent-oriented modeling and programming has a hard core composed of the concepts defined in the previous research programmes (procedural, data hiding and data abstraction) on the one hand, and the artificial intelligence field (Woodridge & Jennings, 1995) on the other hand. The protective belt of the AO research programme would be characterized by the evolution towards a widely used SE methodology allowing the development of large projects.

Table 1 summarizes the contrast between the Kuhnian and Lakatosian epistemologies applied to the evolution from OO to AO. The lessons learned are:

- The context in which AO has emerged cannot

be considered as a Kuhnian crisis because of the existence of strong methodological rules that emerged within OO preceding the emergence of AO. We claim there is a problem shift;
- AO seems to be based on the evolution of the previous methodological rules so that we point to continuity between OO and AO;
- OO and AO are directly commensurable since the latter can be conceptualized as a knowledge layer upon the first.

In the light of the arguments presented above, we contend that the Kuhnian epistemology often referred to in the literature is not appropriate to provide a correct epistemological analysis of the knowledge in SE. We rather propose to use the Lakatosian epistemology to characterize the emergence of AO.

We argue that the Lakatosian epistemology is directly in line with the idea of computer knowledge depicted as a "structure in layers." We have represented this architecture in Figure 2.

Implications

In this section, we briefly discuss the implications of using the concept of research programme rather than paradigm to characterize OO and AO for both SE researchers and practitioners.

Our work provides SE researchers a complementary view and the specific nature of the

Table 1. Kuhnian and Lakatosian visions of AO emergence

		Kuhnian paradigm	Lakatosian research programme
Evolution Steps	**Knowledge Emergence**	Crisis	Problem shift
	Knowledge Evolution	Discontinuity	Continuity
	Knowledge Maturity	Incommensurability	Commensurability

research area they are working on. Moreover, the impact of this nuance is important due to the fact that, as we have pointed out, no fundamental departure was observed when evolving from OO to AO. Therefore, concepts developed in OO and other related research areas can be adapted to AO with some consequence on the process of building agent ontologies.

Managers and other SE practitioners will learn that AO should be envisaged as a natural evolution rather than as a complete revolution. AO can be seen as complementary to OO and leads to the fact that the modularity of software solutions resulting from several techniques can be utilized when developing new systems. Software modeling techniques can then be considered as problem oriented (i.e., modeling, design and implementation techniques are driven by the problem specificities), rather than solution oriented (where those should be driven by an ex ante methodological/ technical choice). This conclusion can be taken at different levels:

- At the analysis stage where organizational modeling can be better performed using models representing collaborative agents (Yu, 1995) while purely functional require-

ments can be simply modeled using object modeling languages such as UML use cases;

- At the design stage, entities required to collaborate and learn can be designed as agents while others requiring less sophisticated behavior can be designed as objects;
- At the implementation level, modules can be implemented using agent technologies that facilitate communication with modules implemented in object technology.

Finally, our new conceptualization has a profound impact on the SE development life cycles. Indeed, the literature on the evolution of SE life cycles is rich and the adoption of mature development life cycles such as the spiral model, the Rational Unified Process, or agile methodologies traditionally operationalized by OO technologies can be adapted to AO development without revising the fundamental concepts.

CONCLUSION

User requirements that have been poorly taken into account as well as modeling and development

Figure 2. Evolution of Knowledge in SE

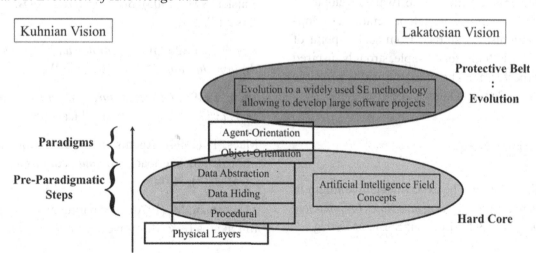

languages inspired by programming concepts as opposed to organization and enterprise has led to a software crisis. Solutions can be found at different levels, and among those, OO at the first level and AO at the second level constituted definite progress. AO furnishes concepts to model the organization more precisely, thus enabling analysts to create more accurate models.

This article has presented an epistemological analysis of these improvements. AO is a promising innovation in tools allowing analysts to model the organization and user requirements. We have shown in this article that the emergence of this innovation can be better studied using Lakatosian ideas rather than Kuhnian ones. In this vision, AO would be considered as a research programme rather than a paradigm. Even if it seems to be just a matter of terminology, the difference between these two epistemological concepts is clear and profound so that they should not be confused. This article also advocates that the approaches taken by both researchers and practitioners to software problems and their possible solutions is influenced by the vision of OO and AO as a research programme.

More work should be carried out in SE fundamentals by studying other methodological frameworks and epistemological foundations to provide the computer science researcher a more accurate conscience of the research field that the researcher is working on. Software development life cycles such as waterfall or iterative development can also be studied from such a point of view. The latter is, for example, strongly inspired by Herbert Simon's bounded rationality principle as well as Popper's knowledge growth theory.

REFERENCES

Basili, V. (1992). The experimental paradigm in software engineering. *Lecture Notes In Computer Science, 706*, 3-12. London: Springer-Verlag.

Bellifemine, F., Poggi, A., & Rimassa, G. (2000). *Developing multi-agent systems with JADE*. Proceedings of the Seventh International Workshop on Agent Theories, Architectures and Languages (ATAL 2000), Boston, MA.

Bigus, J. P., & Bigus, J. (1997). *Constructing intelligent agents with Java: A programmer's guide to smarter applications*. New Jersey: Wiley.

Castro, J., Kolp, M., & Mylopoulos, J. (2002). Towards requirements-driven information systems engineering: The *Tropos* project. *Information Systems, 27*(6), 365-389.

Davis, A. (1995). *201 principles of software development*. McGraw-Hill.

Göktürk, E. & Akkok, N. (2004). Paradigm and software engineering. *Proceedings of Impact of Software Process on Quality*.

JACK Intelligent Agents (2006). Retrieved on January, 1st, 2008 from http://www.agent-software.com.

JADEX BDI Agent System (2007). Retrieved on January, 1st, 2008 from http://vsis-www.informatik.uni-hamburg.de/projects/jadex/

Jennings, N. R., & Wooldridge, M. (2001). Agent-oriented software engineering. *Handbook of Agent Technology*, AAAI/ MIT Press.

Kaisler, S.H. (2005). *Software paradigms*. New Jersey: Wiley.

Kruchten, P. (2003). *The rational unified process: An introduction (3rd Ed.)*. Addison-Wesley.

Kuhn, T. (1996). *The structure of scientific revolutions (3rd Ed.)*. University of Chicago Press.

Maes, P. (1994). Agents that reduce work and information overload. *Communications of the ACM, 37*(7), 30-40.

Masterman, M. (1970). The nature of paradigm. In Lakatos I., & Musgrave A., *Criticism and the*

Growth of Knowledge, Cambridge University Press.

Mataric, M. (1992). Integration of representation into goal-driven behavior-based robots. *IEEE Transactions on Robotics and Automation, 8*(3), 304-312.

Meyer, B. (1997). *Object-oriented software construction (2nd Ed.).* Prentice Hall.

Odell, J. J. (2002). Objects and agents compared. *Journal of Object Technology, 1*(1), 41-53.

Parunak, V. (1997). Go to the ant: Engineering principles from natural agent systems. *Annals of Operations Research, 75,* 69-101.

Sankey, H. (1994). *The incommensurability thesis.* Ashgate.

Skarmeas, N. (1999). *Agents as objects with knowledge base state.* Imperial College Press.

Sommerville, I. (1992). *Software engineering (4th Ed.).* Addison-Wesley.

Tennenhouse, D. (2000). Embedding the Internet: Proactive computing. Communications of the ACM, 43(5).

Woodridge, M., & Jennings, N. R. (1995). Intelligent agents: Theory and practice. *The Knowledge Engineering Review, 10*(2), 115-152.

Yu, E. (1995). *Modeling strategic relationships for process reengineering.* (PhD thesis). Toronto, Canada: University of Toronto, Department of Computer Science.

Zambonelli, F., Jennings, N. R., Omicini, A., & Wooldridge, M. (2000). Agent-Oriented Software Engineering for Internet Applications. In *Coordination of Internet agents: Models, technologies and applications.* (pp. 326-346). Springer-Verlag.

Zambonelli, F., Jennings, N.R., & Wooldridge, M. (2000). Organizational abstractions for the analysis and design of multi-agent systems. In *Proceedings of the 1st international workshop on agent-oriented software engineering,* (pp. 243-252).

This work was previously published in the International Journal of Intelligent Information Technologies, Vol. 4, Issue 3, edited by V. Sugumaran, pp. 46-57, copyright 2008 by IGI Publishing (an imprint of IGI Global).

Chapter 4
A Generic Internal State Paradigm for the Language Faculty of Agents for Task Delegation

T. Chithralekha
Pondicherry University, India

S. Kuppuswami
Pondicherry University, India

ABSTRACT

Language ability is an inevitable aspect of delegation in agents to provide for collaborative natural language interaction (CNLI) during task delegation. To cater to users of different languages, the CNLI is required to be multilingual. When multilingual CNLI has to be provided in a manner characteristic of agents, it leads to realizing two types of autonomies viz. behavior autonomy - to provide CNLI in every language and management autonomy for managing the multiple language competencies. Thereby, the language ability of an agent evolves into a language faculty which encompasses behavior and behavior management autonomies. The existing paradigms for the internal state of agents are only behavior-oriented and cannot accommodate the behavior and behavior management autonomies. In this paper, a new paradigm for the internal state of the language faculty of agents consisting of the belief, task and behavior (BTB) abstractions has been proposed, defined and illustrated.

INTRODUCTION

A software agent is one which acts on behalf of someone to carry out a particular task which has been delegated to it (Bradshaw, 1997). Delegation of a task to an agent is possible only if the agent possesses the expertise to perform the particular task in a manner required by the user. That is, the agent should be able to blend the task expertise with the knowledge of the user (Bradshaw, 1997). While delegating a task to an agent, the people have to interact with the agent for which the agents have to provide for a natural form of interaction (Norman, 1997). Thereby, to work on delegation the agent needs the following expertise:

- Task – to perform the delegated task
- user-modeling – to model user preferences and perform the task in a customized manner
- Language – to provide interaction in natural language

The language aspect of delegation unfolds into the following language abilities to support delegation effectively:

- Collaborative natural language interaction (CNLI) (Jurafsky & Martin, 2000; McTear, 2002)
- Dynamic multilingualism

The former is required to interact with the user in a more comprehensive manner to assist the user to carry out the requested task. This includes the ability to collaborate with the user to explicate an incomplete, ambiguous or erroneous request, providing alternative suggestions proactively. Dynamic multilingualism is required to enable the agent to cater its services to users of various languages. This is achieved by supporting multiple languages and dynamically configuring to the required language to provide its service.

Since the language faculty is realized as a combination of two different autonomies, its internal state and its dynamism cannot be captured by the internal state definitions of existing agents (Brooks 1986; Muller & Pischel, 1994; Muller, Pischel & Thiel 1994; Rao & Georgeff, 1991; Wooldridge, 2000, 1999) as their focus is only towards action/behavior and does not encompass the management aspect. The definition of the internal state should help to accommodate both the management context and the behavior contexts. In addition, it should enable the agent to be internally aware that it supports multiple languages so that dynamic multilingualism and knowledge discovery across languages is possible. This has also not been taken care of in the existing approaches of achieving multilingualism in agents (Connell, 2000; Huang, Haft & Hsu, 2000; Pazienza, Stellato, Henriksen, Paggio & Zanzotto, 2005; Ritter, Meier, Yang & Waibel, 1999; Ren & Shi, 2000; Turunen & Hakulinen, 2000; Ws2). Hence, a new paradigm consisting of the **Belief, Task and Behavior (BTB)** abstractions has been proposed. Each of these abstractions has been defined, and the dynamism with respect to these abstractions is also described. This paradigm is a generic paradigm as it is applicable to any agent which has to support multiple facets of a particular task. This generality is illustrated by applying the paradigm to two examples of multi-faceted task agents.

Thus, the objectives of this chapter are:

- Deriving the language ability requirements of task delegation and defining their characteristics
- Hypothesizing the language ability management autonomy for managing multiple languages
- Conceptualizing the language ability of an agent as a Language Faculty which is attributed with language ability management autonomy and language behavior autonomy

- Developing a new internal state paradigm for the Language Faculty based on the BTB abstractions and defining their semantics and dynamism
- Generalizing and applying the paradigm for a multi-faceted task agent

The remainder of the chapter is organized as follows. The second section, Identification of Language Ability Requirements of Task Delegation, describes the process of deriving and characterizing the language ability requirements of task delegation. The third section, Hypothesis of Language Faculty with Language Ability Management Autonomy, provides the hypothesis of the language ability management autonomy as a combination of four autonomies and proceeds to defining the language faculty. The existing works in the internal state definitions of agents and multilingualism in agents is outlined in the fourth section, Existing Works. The limitations in these works help to elicit the need for the proposed paradigm. The fifth section, Proposed Belief Task and Behavior (BTB) paradigm for the Internal State of Language Faculty of Agents, describes the proposed BTB paradigm. Application of the paradigm to a multi-faceted task agent is given in the sixth section, Application of the Paradigm for a Multi-faceted Task Agent. The seventh section, Advantages and Limitations of the new BTB paradigm, provides an overview of the advantages and limitations of the paradigm. Conclusion is given in the last section.

IDENTIFICATION OF LANGUAGE ABILITY REQUIREMENTS OF TASK DELEGATION

Software Agents are entities that work on delegation. They are able to carry out a task autonomously on behalf of the user who has entrusted the task with it. The ability to work on delegation is a characteristic which is unique of agents (Brad-

shaw, 1997). In fact, the conceptualization of an agent is based on delegation. In this section, the language ability requirements of task delegation have been derived by considering the various aspects of delegation.

Negroponte's work on *Agents: From direct manipulation to delegation* (Negroponte, 1997) gives his view of how an agent would be able to provide for delegation by acting as intelligent interfaces such as digital butlers, personal filters and digital sister-in-law. From this, the core competencies required of an agent to work on delegation has been identified as given:

- Language
- User-modeling
- Task

The language ability enables a natural form of interaction, whereby the agent can comprehend and interact with the user in natural language. The user-modeling ability helps to provide a customized behavior in performing the delegated task. The task ability is constituted by the task expertise required to carry out the task on behalf of the user. Since language ability is the ultimate focus of this chapter, the subsequent discussions progresses towards identifying the language requirements of delegation.

Considering from a language perspective, the request for task delegation is found to be characterized with the following attributes:

- Natural language
- Impreciseness, ambiguity, incompleteness
- Multilingual

The following example illustrates the same. If an agent is embedded in the interface of a flight information system, which is installed in an airport, then when a person asks for the details of the flights, distances, and other flight information, it should be able to provide the user with the required information. Suppose the user's request is not complete, ambiguous or there is no flight available at the time which the user asks for, then it can collaborate with the user to obtain the required details and suggest other flights which may be suitable for travel. Since the flight information system would be used by people of various languages, especially in a country like India, known for its language diversity, it should be able to support at least a subset of languages. Depending upon the language required by the user, the agent should configure itself to the corresponding language.

In order to cater to the three attributes specific to language as specified previously, the following language abilities are identified to be essentially required of an agent:

- Collaborative Natural Language Interaction (CNLI) (Jurafsky & Martin, 2000; McTear, 2002; Ws3; Ws4)
- Dynamic Multilingualism

In order that these two language abilities are attributed characteristic of agents, the requirements of these abilities are analyzed with respect to agent properties are shown in Table 1.

Thus, the language abilities and their characterization needed to support effective form of task delegation have been identified.

HYPOTHESIS OF LANGUAGE FACULTY WITH LANGUAGE ABILITY MANAGEMENT AUTONOMY

When the agent has to exhibit the properties found in Table 1 from monolingual and multilingual perspectives, two dimensions of autonomy are required to be made available for the agent. First is the behavior autonomy, which any conventional agent is conceived to possess. This autonomy would help the agent to provide CNLI behavior in a particular language. But, to provide for dynamic multilingualism, the agent needs a higher level of

autonomy, which helps it to manage the various languages. For this, the individual behavior level autonomy would not suffice because the behavior level autonomy has the view of only a single language. Thereby, the need for the hypothesis of a new language ability management autonomy that can control and manage the language ability in multiple languages is realized. The language ability management autonomy is pictorially depicted in Figure 1.

Language ability management involves:

- Managing competence in the languages supported
- Managing knowledge in the languages supported
- Configuring to the required language based on preference or need
- Acquiring new languages to increase the degree of multilingualism

Each of the functions of language ability management has a different function and scope. Thereby, they contribute for the various dimensions of language ability management. Hence, language ability management cannot be realized as a single monolithic autonomy, but, needs to be realized as a cooperation of individual autonomies pertaining to each of the dimensions of language ability management. Thus, language ability management is hypothesized to be composed of the following autonomies.

- **Language Competence Management Autonomy:** This autonomy enables the agent to manage the language competencies it holds in the various languages. It can also update its competence in the required language using this autonomy.
- **Language Knowledge Management Autonomy:** This autonomy enables the agent to manage the language knowledge corresponding to the various languages it supports. In addition, it can update the

Table 1. Agent properties and their semantics from monolingual and multilingual perspectives

Agent Property (Etzioni & Weld, 1995; Franklin & Graesser, 1996; Wooldridge, 1999; Wooldridge & Jennings, 1995)	CNLI	Dynamic Multilingualism
Autonomy	Control of internal state and behavior with respect to language so that it is able to carry out CNLI with the user independently.	Independent control of the language knowledge and competence available in the languages supported.
Reactivity	Reacting to a request that is expressed in natural language and provide for the appropriate response again in natural language.	Dynamically configuring to the required language depending upon the user's need.
Proactivity	Exhibiting goal-directed behavior by carrying out a collaborative dialogue in natural language to enable the user to complete his job. It proactively suggests alternatives if the user's request cannot be fulfilled exactly as per his specifications.	Decide which of the languages to provide the agent's service based on user's preferences. Dynamically configure to the language decided upon.
Social Ability	Communicating with the user in natural language.	Ability to support multiple languages and communicate with the user in the required language.
Adaptation	Adapting the interaction process according to the user's reply during a conversation.	Adapt new languages easily so as to extend the services to new languages.
Learning	Learning new words pertaining to the task domain and update its vocabulary. The agent is able to update its language competence so that it uses the most appropriate technique for collaborative interaction.	Discovering new knowledge from the available language knowledge. When the agent supports multiple languages, the agent should be able to discover new knowledge by comparing and contrasting the knowledge pertaining to the various languages. Should be able to update knowledge and competence in the required language.

Figure 1. Abstract model of an agent with language ability management autonomy to support multiple languages

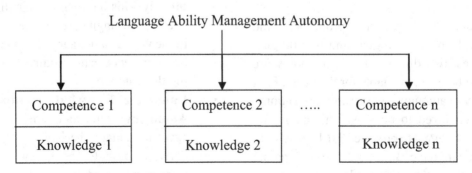

language knowledge like that of vocabulary individually without the necessity for the competence module to intervene. Also, this autonomy enables the agent to discover new knowledge from the existing knowledge, whereby, it can for example construct multilingual vocabularies from the existing language-specific ones.

- **Language Configuration Management Autonomy**: This autonomy enables the agent to configure its competence and knowledge to the required language. When the agent supports multiple languages, the users have the option of choosing the language of interaction. Even better, the agent can try to infer the language preferences of the user by observing the user's language use and automatically configure to that language when the corresponding user logs in. These operations require that the agent has the competence to dynamically configure itself to the required language.
- **Language Acquisition Autonomy:** This autonomy enables the agent to acquire new languages with minimum human intervention and implement the new language, so as to extend its services to the new language also. This requirement is realized because, when the agent has to be put to use for a new language environment, it should not reiterate the development process of a new language agent, which is the existing case.

This helps to realize a new level of abstraction in autonomy whereby the autonomy has evolved from the behavior level to the management level. Thus, the agent would now possess behavior level autonomy for providing CNLI in the languages supported and management level autonomy to provide for dynamic multilingualism. The language ability of an agent that possesses both the forms of autonomies is termed as a **Language Faculty**.

The structure of the language faculty is as depicted in Figure 2. The four management autonomies are depicted as tasks as they correspond to the fours aspects of the language ability management task which the agent should perform. Under every management task, behaviors corresponding to the management task in all the supported languages are available. For example, under the language competence management task, the CNLI behaviors corresponding to all the languages supported by the agent are available.

EXISTING WORKS

The previous two sections described the language ability requirements that have been identified as inevitable for task delegation, the properties required to be fulfilled by the language ability requirements of task delegation and the hypothesis of the language ability management autonomy that would help to fulfill the requirements. This section gives an overview of the existing works in the internal state definitions of agents and multilingualism of agents and how they shortfall in accommodating the internal state requirements of the hypothesized Language Faculty. The limitations have been the motivation for proceeding to define the new internal state paradigm.

Internal State Definition of Agents

In this section, an overview of the existing works in the internal state definitions of agents is given. The discussion which follows describes the limitations in these definitions and why a new internal state definition for the language faculty of agents is required.

An example of a simple state-based agent (Wooldridge, 1999) is given as:

See: $S \rightarrow P$

Figure 2. Structure of the language faculty

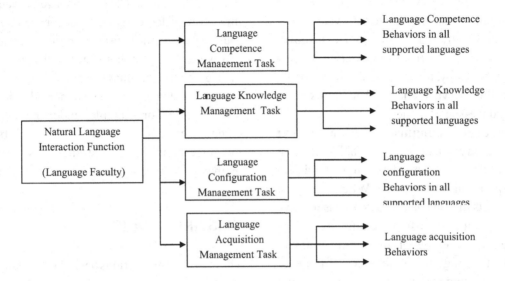

Where S is the set of all environment states (s_1, s_2, s_3... s_n) and P is a non-empty set of percepts. The function "See" maps environment states to percept.

The percept is compared with that of the internal state of the agent and the most appropriate action is carried out. For example:

Next: I X P → I

I is the set of all internal states of the agent. The function "Next" maps the internal state of the agent to a new internal state based on the percept, which is received. Based on this current internal state the required action is initiated. This is given as:

Action: I → A

Where A is the set of all actions the agent can perform.

This is a very abstract definition of an internal state. The four existing types of agents namely the logic-based agents, reactive agents, belief-desire-intention agents, and layered agents are considered and their internal state definitions are analyzed.

Logic-Based Agents

In the case of logic-based agents (Wooldridge, 1999), the internal state definition is as follows. Let L be the set of sentences of classical first-order logic, and let D = ρ(L) be the set of L databases (i.e., the set of sets of L-formulae). The internal state of an agent is an element of D. The logic-based agent is defined as follows:

See: S→P
Next: D X P → D
Action: D → A

The action selection function is defined in terms of deduction rules.

Reactive Agents

In reactive agents (Brooks, 1986; Wooldridge, 1999), the agent's decision-making is realized through a set of task accomplishing behaviors, where each behavior is an individual action function. These behaviors are implemented as rules of the form:

Situation→ Action

Thus, similar to the logic agents, the internal state of a reactive agent corresponds to a situation which becomes true because of the percept received. But here, the "Situation" is directly mapped to "Action" unlike the logic-based agents where the action is derived through deduction. The actions are related by means of an inhibition relation, which specifies which action inhibits another action. This helps to establish a priority among the actions so that the action of highest priority gets activated when multiple situations becomes true for a particular percept.

Belief-Desire-Intention (BDI) Agents

The internal state of a BDI agent (Rao & Georgeff, 1991; Wooldridge, 1999) is composed of the belief, desire and intention components:

- Belief represents the information the agent has about its current environment
- Desire represents the set of current options–possible courses of actions available for the agent corresponding to the current set of beliefs
- Intentions represent the agent's current focus–those state of affairs that it has committed to trying to bring about

To revision the beliefs based on the percept received, the agent uses a belief revision function (BRF). To determine the possible courses of actions available, it uses an option generation function (options). To determine the intentions on the basis of its current beliefs and desires, it uses a filter function (filter). Using these functions, the agent transitions between the internal state components and determines the action to perform. This process is known as deliberation and hence these agents are also known as deliberative agents.

Layered Agents

In these agents, its various subsystems are arranged into a hierarchy of interacting layers (Muller & Pischel, 1994; Muller et al, 1994). At every layer, the subsystem is built using either reactive and BDI concepts described previously. Thus, the internal state of these agents is in turn composed of the reactive and BDI states.

Limitations

Table 2 gives a summary of the internal state definitions of the different types of agents, how they select an action to perform and the focus of their action.

The internal states of the various agents act as a staging component before the selection of the action. Also, the internal state definitions and how the agent transitions between these states to determine the action(s) to perform define the architecture of the agent. This shows that the internal state definitions can only help to exhibit the functional/behavior autonomy for selecting and executing the action to be performed. They would be suitable only for the behavior layer of the language faculty shown in Figure 2. Thus, they cannot help the agent to exhibit the management level autonomy which focuses on the management aspect of the agent. Therefore, there is a need for a new internal state definition of an agent which accommodates the management task context and behavior task context.

Multilingualism in Agents

The necessity to address the language diversity that exists globally was also realized in the agent domain. A single agent supporting multiple languages has not received much focus in the literature. Thus, multilingualism was achieved by either multilingual agent-based dialoguing systems or using multiple language agents each of

Table 2. Summary of internal state of different types of agents

Type of Agent	Internal State	Process of Action Selection	Focus
Logic-Based Agent	An element of the set of L-formulae	Logical Deduction	Action
Reactive Agent	Situation	Inhibition	Immediate Action
BDI Agent	Belief, Desire, Intention	Deliberation	Rational Action

which supports a single language. This is obvious in the following discussion that describes the various ways by which multilingualism is achieved.

- Using parallel language agents

Turunen and Hakulinen (2000) propose Jaspis, which is an agent-based adaptive multilingual speech application development framework. To handle multilingual dialogues, input agents and presentation agents that are specialized in the required languages are used. The input agent of a particular language processes the inputs received in the corresponding language. To deliver response, the required presentation agent that generates messages in the required language is chosen by the presentation evaluator.

- Using Internationalization and Localization

Internationalization is the process of designing and developing software so that it can be adapted to various locales and regions without further engineering changes (Connell, 2000; Huang et al, 2000). Microsoft agents (Ws2) support for multi-localization by providing individual localization modules for the various languages supported by it.

- Using Translation

Here, the agent supports for multiple language by using a translator that translates one language to another. M. Ritter et al (1999) propose a trans-lation agent that translates a spoken utterance to another language.

- Using Ontology

The use of ontology has brought about a major break through in handling multilingualism. This is because unlike the other approaches of handling multilingualism, ontology helps to abstract domain concepts from language expressions. Thus, it naturally helps to achieve language independence amidst the presence of multiple languages. Ren & Shi (2000) and Pazienza et al (2005) describe using ontology-based approach for achieving multilingualism.

Limitations

When the agent supports multiple languages, it should be internally aware that it supports multiple languages so as to enable the following:

- To independently control the various language knowledge and competencies
- To discover new knowledge from the existing knowledge. Only if the agent is aware that it possesses knowledge corresponding to various languages, the agent would be able to relate conceptual level ontological abstractions to the language-specific knowledge to discover new knowledge.
- The dynamic multilingualism requires that the agent is able to configure dynamically to the required language. Only if the agent is internally aware of the multiple languages,

will the agent be able to configure to the required language.

When multiple language agents are used for supporting multiple languages, every agent is internally aware of a single language only. Similar is the case of the agent which is localized to a particular language. Since the localized agent supports a single language only, it is internally aware about this language only. When translators are used to support multiple languages, the agent is externally aware of the multiple languages as the translator has to handle all the language translation to the language which the agent comprehends. Internally, the agent is aware of this single language only. In the ontology-based approach, the awareness of multiple languages is possible to achieve, but because the existing internal state definitions of agents are not suitable for accommodating the management and behavior autonomy as described previously, the necessity for a new internal state for the language faculty of agents arises.

Thus, the discussion clearly delineates the necessity for a new internal state for the language faculty of agents. The subsequent section describes the newly proposed internal state paradigm for the language faculty of agents.

PROPOSED BTB PARADIGM FOR THE INTERNAL STATE OF LANGUAGE FACULTY OF AGENTS

In defining the new internal state paradigm, the following activities have been performed:

- Identification of the components
- Definition of the components
- State definition of the components
- Control Loop of the components

After the description of the activities, a discussion on how the BTB paradigm helps to fulfill the requirements arising from the multilingual perspective as identified in the previous subsection is also given.

Identification of the Components

The language faculty of an agent has to work in four different task contexts pertaining to the four different management level autonomies, which the agent has to exhibit. These tasks correspond to language competence management, language knowledge management, and language acquisition management. Similarly, every task context has a set of behaviors in all the supported languages corresponding to the task. Figure 2 depicts this. These behaviors operate in the behavior context. Therefore, the internal state of the language faculty should encompass task as well as behavior contexts. In addition, the internal state comprises of the beliefs of the language faculty which is revised on every percept received to determine which of the task contexts and hence the behavior context to activate.

Hence, internal state of the language faculty is proposed based on the following abstractions:

- Beliefs
- Task Context
- Behavior Context

These abstractions constitute for the **BTB** paradigm. These abstractions are also conceived to be mentalistic abstractions because it would help to discern how the language faculty and its various tasks accommodate language internally and reason with it.

Definition of the Components

This section defines each of the components of the internal state in terms of the first order logic.

Beliefs

The primary constituent of the internal state is that of the beliefs. This is because the agent does not work simply by mapping situations to actions, but has an internal state which it reflects upon during every percept before deciding the task and hence the action to perform. This implies that the internal state necessarily has beliefs which it revisions during every percept that is received. The concept of beliefs is borrowed from that of the BDI logic (Wooldridge, 2000) and hence the same semantics are retained.

The beliefs at the language faculty level are the general beliefs that the language faculty holds about language. These are given in Table 3.

Task Context

The following contribute for the composition of the task context:

a. Task context beliefs
b. Percept
c. References to various behaviors supported
d. Currently active behavior

The task context is primarily composed of beliefs pertaining to the task performed. Thus, each of the tasks has task contexts that vary or is populated with relevant beliefs pertaining to the task. These beliefs correspond to the internal beliefs of the task context, or in other words, the beliefs corresponding to the agency. In addition, the task context also holds beliefs about the other task contexts or other agencies so that it can interact with the corresponding task context, if required. These beliefs correspond to the external beliefs. These external beliefs are also required because an agency's belief set is composed not only of the internal personal beliefs but also of environmental and relational beliefs pertaining to other entities in the environments (Ferber, 1999).

The percept received at the language faculty level that triggered this task is also part of the task context. This is because the percept is used in the task context to revision the beliefs pertaining to the task context level and choose the appropriate behavior. When a particular behavior is chosen it becomes the currently active behavior pertaining to the task context. The context also holds references to the various behaviors so that it can activate them whenever required.

a. *Task Context Beliefs*: The beliefs of the task context is explored further to explicate the various internal and external beliefs.

The competence management task TC_{co} is driven by the belief - (Bel TC_{co} languagecompetence (l_k, DO)) where

(Bel TC_{co} languagecompetence(l_k, DO)) $\rightarrow$ (Bel TC_{co} perceive(l_k))

Table 3. Beliefs of the language faculty and first order logic description of beliefs

Beliefs of language faculty	First order logic description of beliefs
Beliefs of generic language ontology	(Bel i language(l)) $\rightarrow$ languageontology(LO)
Beliefs about the languages it supports	$\forall l_1, l_2, \ldots l_n$. language(l_i) $\wedge$ (Bel i language(lj, DO)) $\Rightarrow$ (Bel i, l_i) where $l_1, l_2, \ldots l_n \subseteq L$ and L is the set of all languages and DO is the functional domain of the agent
Beliefs about the current language of the agent	(Bel i, currentlanguage(l_j)) $\Rightarrow$ (Bel i language(lj, DO))

$\wedge$ (Bel TC_{co} languagecomprehension(l_k, DO))
$\wedge$ (Bel TC_{co} dialoguing (l_k)) where $k = 1..n$ where n is equal to the no. of languages in the belief set of language faculty

That is, to be able to independently control its language functional behavior in a language l_k, the language competence task context should have beliefs that it can perform the functions of perception, comprehension and dialoguing in the corresponding languages. DO corresponds to the functional domain ontology which defines the scope of the language competence of the agent. This task requires the services of the language knowledge management task for its knowledge services. Hence, the external beliefs correspond to the beliefs about the knowledge management task TC_{km}, which is:

(Bel TC_{co} TC_{km})

The language knowledge management task TC_{km} has beliefs pertaining to the various language knowledge resources, language knowledge (grammar and vocabulary) that it supports and its abilities in servicing the knowledge requests for all the supported languages.

(Bel TC_{km} language knowledge (l_k, DO) $\rightarrow$ (Bel TC_{km} language resources(l_k)
$\wedge$ (Bel TC_{km} grammar rules(l_k, DO)
$\wedge$ (Bel TC_{km}, vocabulary(l_k, DO))
$\wedge$ (Bel TC_{km}, knowledgeservices(l_k)

The beliefs of **the language configuration management task** could be characterized in terms of a set of possible worlds (Divers, 2002; Wooldridge, 2000) in the following way. Every possible world corresponds to a language supported by the agent. In other words, the agent has many possible worlds (l, b), where $l \subseteq L$ and L is the set of languages supported by the agent and $b \subseteq B$ where B is set of all language beliefs. At any time, the agent has beliefs pertaining to

any of these language worlds. The beliefs of the language faculty keeps moving from one world to another, depending upon the language to which it is configured. This can be represented as:

$W = \{ (l, b) \mid l \subseteq L \text{ and } b \subseteq B\}$

The configuration task makes true the following beliefs:

(Bel TC_{co} language(l_i, DO)) $\wedge$ (Bel TC_{km} language knowledge (l_i, DO) where l_i is one of the languages supported by the language faculty.

The language acquisition management task TC_{aq} has internal beliefs pertaining only to the task ontology and language ontology. The language ontology gives details about the resources, knowledge and competences to acquire in order to realize a new language in the agent and the task ontology constrains the domain of the language details to be acquired. This belief is given as:

(Bel TC_{aq} LO, DO)

If the language acquisition task performs acquisition of a new language 'l_{new}' then its belief set about languages is updated with the beliefs about the new language. This could be represented as follows:

o(Bel i language (l_{new}, DO))

Where l_{new} is the new language acquired. The semantics of 'o' is the same as that in first order logic.

The external beliefs about this task context corresponds to that of the language competence task where it implements the acquired competences and language knowledge management task where it stores the acquired resources and knowledge.

(Bel TC_{aq}, TC_{co}) $\wedge$ (Bel TC_{aq}, TC_{co})

b. *Percept:* The percept which is received by the language faculty causes the required task context and hence the behavior context to be activated. The same percept is interpreted differently at the task context level and in the behavior context level. For example, if the user gives a natural language request in a particular language, then at the task context level, it is interpreted and the need for the language competence context is realized and activated accordingly. When the percept travels down to the behavior context, the behavior context that helps to perform NLP in the corresponding language is activated. Thus, the same percept is interpreted differently at different levels of the language faculty.

c. & d. References to various behavior contexts and the currently active behaviors: These are atomic entities which are self-explanatory. Hence, these are not explored further. The section Behavior Context describes the behavior context.

Behavior Context

Corresponding to every task context there are multiple behavior contexts, one for every language supported as depicted in Figure 2. When the language faculty is executing a particular behavior, then it is said to be in the particular behavior context BC. The behavior context is composed of the percept which the behavior is to act upon in order to provide the required action response. Also, beliefs about language capabilities in the particular language whose behavior is activated is also true. This is represented as:

(Bel BC (languagebehavior(lj, DO), P))

P represents the percept that activated this task context.

It is only at this behavior level that the already defined BDI abstractions may be used, if the NLP is to be recognized as a rational decision making behavior. Thus, the BDI abstractions could be considered as a part or a subset of the newly defined paradigm.

Thus, a new paradigm for the language faculty of agents comprising of beliefs, task context and behavior context abstractions has been formulated. Each of these abstractions has been explained individually to explicate the semantics of the paradigm. In order to explicate the further intricacies of the abstractions of the paradigm the following aspects are considered.

State Definitions of the BTB Paradigm

Using the definitions of the BTB paradigm, the definitions of the Faculty State, Task Context state and the behavior context state are defined. The formal definitions of each of these are as follows:

Faculty State F_s is defined as a tuple consisting of the following parameters:

$F_s = (P, F_{sB}, \cup TC_i, TC_{active})$ Where,

P = percept received

F_{sB}, = Beliefs of the faculty. The beliefs of the language faculty correspond to those given in Table 2.

$\cup TC_i$ = Union of the set of all task contexts supported by the functional faculty, where i = 1..n where n is equal to the number of task contexts supported. In case of the language faculty, it corresponds to the task context of the four tasks described above.

$TC_{active} = TC_i$, which is the currently active task context.

The Task Context state TC_i again is a tuple consisting of:

$TC_i = P, TC_{iB}, \cup BC_i, BC_{active}$ where,

P = percept

TC_{iB} = Internal and External beliefs corresponding to the task context. In case of the task contexts corresponding to the language faculty, the beliefs are as defined individually for each of the task contexts.

$\cup\ BC_i$ = Union of the set of all belief contexts supported by the behavior faculty where i = 1..n, and n is equal to the number of behaviors supported. In case of the language faculty, it corresponds to the behavior contexts of the language behaviors and the number of language behaviors corresponds to the number of languages supported.

BC_{active} = BC_i, which is the currently active behavior state where BC_{iB} = true. In case of the language faculty, it corresponds to the language behavior corresponding to either competence, or knowledge management or configuration tasks in a particular language.

Control Loop of the BTB Agent

This section describes the details with respect to the newly defined abstractions.

- Itinerary across the paradigm abstractions:
  Initially, all the task contexts are initialized. When the agent receives a percept, it maps the percept to the required task context. This corresponding task context is activated. This mapping requires no extensive reasoning. The task context corresponds to the nature of the task to be performed by the agent. It may be reasoning about how to perform an action in order to deliver an externally visible natural language interaction behavior or performing some knowledge related behavior which is internal, or performing configuration of knowledge and behavior which is both internal and external or performing language acquisition which at present influences the faculty internally and

later helps to exhibit behavior in the new language externally. While the agent is in the particular task context, it chooses the particular language behavior and hence the behavior context based upon the currently active language.

- Altering between the task context and behavior context:
  The task context and the behavior context could be considered analogous to the process context and thread context of the operating system respectively. Similar to the thread working within the confines of a process, so is the behavior working within the confines of the task. The process regains control after the completion of the execution of the thread. Similarly, after the language behavior finishes execution, the task context regains control.

- Visibility of the task context:
  While describing the various task contexts, some of the task contexts like the language competence task context and the language acquisition task context have external beliefs corresponding to that of other task contexts. This puts forth the question of the visibility or the accessibility of a task context from within other task contexts. While a behavior context is active, it may require the services provided by a particular behavior available in other task contexts. The other context belongs to that of another agency. Hence, its services could be obtained by sending a request. This is made possible by the external beliefs that an agency context maintains about the other task contexts.

With all the definitions of the BTB paradigm, the control loop of the agent is described in Box 1.

The control loop begins by checking whether the faculty state is true. That is, the agent holds initial beliefs about the faculty functions and all its task contexts are initialized. Also, the task and behavior are initialized to the default task and the corresponding behavior context. For example, for the language faculty the default task context corresponds to that of the language competence context whereby the agent is ready to receive natural language requests and process it to comprehend the request. The behavior context corresponds to that of the language behavior for performing NLU in the language which is set as the default language.

If the incoming percept changes the functional faculty beliefs, then task context switch has to be performed. The task context whose beliefs becomes true (TC_{iB} = true) is chosen as the current active context. In this context the required behavior has to be activated. The behavior context whose belief context is true (BC_{iB} = true) is chosen. Then this behavior execution is invoked. This execution works on the percept P to produce the required response behavior. This also indicates that whenever there is a task context switch, it is always followed by a behavior context switch. This is because when the context changes, the most appropriate behavior in that context has to be chosen based on the percept and the current beliefs. If the percept does not bring about any change in the faculty state, then the same behavior context is continued.

Sometimes, during the execution of the behavior in context BC_j, the behavior corresponding to another task context may be required. In this case, it sends a request to the corresponding task context using the external beliefs that it holds about this task context. This task context then activates the required behavior and performs the required function. Incorporating this change, the refined control loop is seen in Box 2.

The function Requestexecution(TC_j, BC_j, req) requests the behavior BC_j corresponding to the task context TC_j. The parameter 'req' is a structure that contains the input parameters required to carry out the behavior BC_j.

Fulfillment of Requirements Arising from Multilingual Perspective

The proposed paradigm helps to fulfill the requirements identified from the multilingual perspective as given in the need for the internal state sub-section, in the following ways:

- The paradigm helps the agent to be aware of the multilingual support as the language faculty beliefs as well as the task context is aware of all the behavior contexts sup-

Box 1.

```
While F_s is true
        TC_active = default task context
        BC_active = default behavior context within default task context
        While true
        Get next percept P
        If P changes F_sB then
        TC_active = TC_i where TC_iB = true   (Switch task context)
        BC_active = BC_i where BC_iB = true (switch behavior context)
        End if
        Invoke behavior execution (TC_active , BC_active, P)
        End while
End while
```

Box 2.

```
TC_active = default task context
BC_active default behavior context within default task context
While F_s is true
   Get next percept P
   If P changes F_sB then
      TC_active = TC_i where TC_iB = true   (Switch task context)
      BC_active = BC_i  where BC_iB = true (switch behavior context)
   End if
   Invoke behavior execution (TC_active , BC_active, P)
End while

   Invoke behavior execution(TC_active , BC_active, P)
      Perform (BC_active, P)
      If BC_active requires BC_j then
         Requestexecution(TC_j, BC_j, req)
      End if
   return
```

ported and hence the number of languages supported

- Dynamic configuration to required language is made possible by switching to the appropriate language behavior context by configuration.

- Since the language knowledge management context has knowledge about the various languages supported, it can discover new knowledge based on the knowledge it possesses. For example, it can compare the no. of characters, character types between languages. It can also construct a multilingual dictionary by mapping the ontological concept to the words in the various languages. This is explained as follows

The domain ontology corresponds to the functional domain of the agent.

$$Ontology(DO) \rightarrow concept(c, DO) \wedge \exists\ co_1, co_2\ .$$
$$concept(co_1, DO) \wedge$$
$$concept(co_2, DO) \wedge Rel(co_1, co_2)^+$$

That is, an ontology is composed of declaration of domain concepts and their relationships. Thus concept(c, DO) implies that c is a concept in domain ontology DO.

$Rel(i, j)$ is a relational structure where Rel specifies the relationship between any co_i and co_j, for (e.g., 'is a', 'has a', 'part of' etc.). Therefore, every ontological concept(s) has its representation in all the languages supported by the agent. This implies that if an agent knows a domain concept co_j, then it believes that it is true in all the languages it supports. That is, it believes that it has language representation corresponding to concept co_j in all the languages supported as:

$$\forall\ co_j \in DO(Bel\ i\ concept(co_j, DO))$$

$$concept(co_j, DO) \rightarrow \exists\ w_1, w_2, \ldots w_n \in l_j\ |word(w_j, l_j, DO)$$

Since every concept is ultimately represented using word(s), the concept co_j is mapped to word w_j in language l_j.

The agent holds similar beliefs about the existing words in all the languages (l_1, l_2,.. l_n), supported by it. Hence, corresponding to concept co_j, the equivalent words are the words

word(w_j, l_j, DO) in language j
word(w_k, l_k, DO) in language k
…. word(w_n, l_n, DO)in language n

Therefore, the agent is able to correspond between the languages using the language-independent domain concepts. This is because it is these domain concepts that are instantiated in the various languages. This helps the agent not only to have a global view of all the language knowledge but also relate or perform comparison between entities of different languages. For example, the agent can infer that a concept 'c' is represented by a word(s) 'w11, w12..' in language 1 and words 'w21, w22' in language 2.

The discussion clearly evinces that the BTB paradigm not only helps to represent the internal state of a two-dimensional autonomous agent, but also helps to fulfill the requirements identified from a multilingual perspective, which the language capabilities in the existing agents fail to do.

APPLICATION OF THE PARADIGM FOR A MULTI-FACETED TASK AGENT

This section describes how this paradigm defined for the language faculty contributes for a generalized paradigm which is applicable to any multi-faceted task agent. First, a multi-faceted task is defined and illustrated with example. Subsequently, how the paradigm is suitable for the multi-faceted task is described.

Multi-Faceted Task Agent

A task is defined as an activity the task doer performs in order to accomplish a goal (Vakkari, 2003). A task can have multiple facets as follows, as described by Li (2004):

- Source of the task
- Task Doer
- Time
- Action
- Product
- Goal
- Task Characteristic and
- User's perception of task

A multi-faceted task agent is one which supports multiple facets of the same task. For example, in the case of language faculty, the various languages contribute for the multiple facets of the same CNLI task. Though the task performed is the same CNLI task, the procedure or the action required to perform CNLI is different in the various language facets. This is further explained by considering the following two examples of agents and describing their multiple facets as follows:

- Travel Planning Agent
- Ontology Services Agent

A Travel Planning Agent is one which can perform travel planning for the user based on the travel requirements given by him or her (Sobia & Nirmala, 2007). It would suggest the various modes of travel possible and other alternatives available for making the travel based on climatic conditions, cost willing to spend for the travel, traveler's preferences so as to provide a customized travel plan.

The multiple facets of the task of travel planning correspond to the various countries for which the agent performs the travel planning. Every country has got its own modes of transport, climate, types of terrain, taste of people for travel, and more. Hence, for performing the same traveling planning task, different knowledge and competencies are required. Thus, each of them contributes for the different facets of the travel planning task. Here, the various facets are differentiated by the 'action' required to perform travel planning for the various countries.

An ontology services agent is one which helps the two communicating agents to communicate and interoperate without using implicit ontology (Ws1). Usually, when two agents have to communicate with each other, they should be using a communication protocol and an implicit pre-shared ontology. This would not facilitate dynamic communication, which is very much required in open software environments of today. Hence, in order to overcome this limitation, an ontology service agent has been conceived. This agent would hold the ontologies pertaining to various domains and help two communicating agents to comprehend each others' messages in terms of their own ontologies by providing the appropriate mapping or translation of terms or concepts.

Ontologies are different for different task domains. If an ontology-services agent provides ontology service for n task domains, then for each of these, the competence and knowledge required are different. Thus, here the multiple facets correspond to the various domains for which the ontology service is being performed. In this case also the facets are differentiated by means of the action performed in the various facets.

Application of the BTB Paradigm

This section describes how this paradigm defined for the language faculty contributes for a generalized paradigm which is applicable to any agent. The four tasks of the language faculty of the agent are

- Language Competence Management
- Language Knowledge Management
- Language Configuration Management
- Language Acquisition Management

These four tasks are required so that the agent is able to manage multiple language facets of the CNLI task. Considering generically, the agent needs all the tasks for managing its competence and knowledge in the multiple facets of any task it supports, configuring to the required task facet and acquiring new facets, if required.

For a Travel Planning Agent, the travel planning is the function performed by it. The competence management aspect of the task focuses on managing its travel planning competencies for the various countries, it supports. The knowledge management task corresponds to managing the knowledge required for travel planning for the various countries. The knowledge base could also be augmented with new places and other details pertaining to travel planning. It can configure itself dynamically for performing travel planning corresponding to a country with the required knowledge and competence for that country. Acquisition management would help the agent to acquire competence and knowledge for travel planning for places pertaining to new countries.

The Travel Planning faculty level beliefs correspond to that of the travel ontology, beliefs about the number of countries for which it supports travel planning, beliefs about its competencies and knowledge in the corresponding countries and beliefs about the country for which it is currently configured to perform travel planning.

The various *Management Task Context beliefs* are as follows.

- *Competence Management task*: Beliefs about the traveling planning competence modules in the countries supported.
- *Knowledge Management task*: Beliefs about the knowledge and resources required to facilitate the travel planning task corresponding

to the various countries for which it supports travel planning.

- *Configuration Management task*: Beliefs about competence and knowledge of the country to which the agent is currently configured.
- *Acquisition Management task*: Beliefs about the travel ontology and the generic competence and knowledge ontologies required to perform travel planning in a particular country. The acquisition of knowledge and competence for performing travel planning for a new country is carried out according to these beliefs.

The *Behavior Context Beliefs* correspond to the beliefs about the competence and knowledge required to perform planning for a particular country.

The control loop defined describes how the internal state of the agent transitions between these beliefs, task context and behavior context.

Similarly, in the ontology-services agent, ontology service is the function of the agent. The competence management would help the agent to manage its ontology-service competence for the various domains its supports. The knowledge management would help the agent to add new terms or concepts pertaining to the ontology domains. Configuration would help the agent to configure itself to the required domain when an ontology service request is to be serviced. Acquisition would help the agent to acquire ontologies and ontology service competence pertaining to new domains. Thus, the BTB paradigm is applicable to this agent also.

These examples indicate that the proposed BTB paradigm and the abstractions are suitable for any multi-faceted task performed by an agent. The proposed abstraction is not only generic but also multi-perspective in nature whereby it focuses on all aspects of the agent functionality namely, its functional competence, knowledge competence, knowledge configuration and functionality aug-

mentation. This is in contrast with the existing agents, where, only the competence aspect is focused upon and the abstractions like that of BDI have been proposed to explicate how the agent should be capable of rational decision making in order to exhibit its functional behavior efficiently.

ADVANTAGES AND LIMITATIONS OF THE NEW BTB PARADIGM

This section briefly describes the consequences of the newly defined BTB paradigm in terms of its advantages and disadvantages.

Advantages

The following list highlights the advantages of the proposed BTB paradigm:

- The BTB paradigm helps to discern how the language ability of an agent should be designed for facilitating effective task delegation. This is because the definition of the paradigm has been performed by first deriving the language ability requirements of task delegation and identifying their characteristic properties.
- The paradigm exactly fits the requirements of the language faculty helping to accommodate the various task contexts, behavior contexts and behaviors in the most appropriate manner.
- The paradigm is a generic paradigm in that it is not only applicable for language faculty but also helps to realize any function of an agent in the form of a faculty. This is because it encompasses behavior contexts and management contexts to manage the behavior contexts. The generality of the paradigm has been illustrated by the examples described. This is unlike the existing paradigm such as BDI which focuses only on the agent behavior and cannot accommodate management aspects.

- The architecture of an agent depends upon the internal state definition and how the agent manipulates its internal state to perform a suitable action. Since this paradigm is a newly proposed one, it paves way for exploring new architectures that help to accommodate the paradigm, as the existing architectures focus only on the behavior.
- The paradigm provides for a mature and evolved conceptualization of the internal state of an agent. This conceptualization of an agent is very much essential while considering the requirements of the agents that have to work in open, dynamic and smart environments. This is because when agents work in these environments, they have to bring into play the aspects of self-management before providing an action. For example, in a smart ubiquitous environment, the agent embedded in any device in the environment has to configure itself to provide a customized behavior according to the preferences of the user. Hence, their internal state should accommodate for managerial decision-making and behavioral decision-making, which are taken care of by the proposed paradigm.
- Helps to realize a new class of agent called as the multi-faceted task agent as the definition of the internal state paradigm is most appropriate when the agent supports multiple facets of the same task. Only then the agent requires the aspects of management to manage the multiple facets of the task.

Limitation

The only limitation of the paradigm is that it is useful for agents which support multiple facets of the same task. For example, as in the case of providing CNLI behavior in multiple languages, travel planning for different countries, ontology services for different task domains. Only these agents need to manage themselves as they support multiple competencies, knowledge, and need to configure them dynamically to provide the required behavior. If the agent supports only a single facet of a task, then based on the percept, it can proceed to determine the action to perform without the intervention of any management tasks. Hence, the application of the paradigm is focused only for multi-faceted task agents.

CONCLUSION

The language ability requirements of delegation are collaborative natural language interaction to interact comprehensively with the user to enable the user to complete the task successfully and dynamic multilingualism to support multiple languages of interaction and dynamically configuring to the required language depending upon the language required by the user. This leads to realizing the language ability of an agent as a language faculty attributed with behavior autonomy for CNLI and language ability management autonomy for supporting dynamic multilingualism. Since the existing internal state BDI paradigm is only behavior-oriented, it cannot cater to representing the internal state of the language faculty which is behavior and behavior management oriented. Hence, a new paradigm comprising of belief, task and behavior abstractions has been defined to represent the internal state of agents. Their semantics and dynamism have been explained. This paradigm is a generic paradigm as it helps to represent the internal state of any agent that supports multiple facets of the same task. This generality is illustrated with examples.

REFERENCES

Bradshaw, J. M. (1997). An Introduction to Software Agents. In Bradshaw J. M., *Software Agents*, Cambridge, MA: MIT Press, 3- 46.

Brooks, R. A. (1986). A robust layered control system for a mobile robot. *IEEE Journal of Robotics and Automation, 2*(1), 14-23.

Connell, T. A. (2000). A simplistic approach to internationalization: Design considerations for an autonomous intelligent agent. In *Proceedings of the 6th ERCIM Workshop on User Interfaces for All*, Italy.

Etzioni, O., & Weld, D. S. (1995). Intelligent agents on the Internet: Fact, fiction, and forecast. *IEEE Expert, 104(4)*, 44-49.

Ferber, J. (1999). *Multi-agent systems: An introduction to distributed artificial intelligence.* Addison Wesley.

Franklin, S., & Graesser, A. (1996). Is it an agent or just a program? A taxonomy for autonomous agents. In *Proceedings of the Third International Workshop on Agent Theories, Architectures, and Languages*, New York: Springer Verlag.

Huang, E., Haft, R., & Hsu, J. (2000). Developing a roadmap for software internationalization. Retrieved from www.symbio-group.com/knowledge_center.html

Jurafsky, D., & Martin, J. H. (2000). Dialogue and conversational agents. In *Speech and language processing: An introduction to natural language processing, computational linguistics, and speech recognition*, Prentice Hall.

Li, Y. (2004). Task type and a faceted classification of tasks. In Schamber, L., & Barry, C. L. (Eds.), *ASIST 2004: proceedings of the 67th ASIS&T Annual Meeting, volume 41 of Proceedings of the ASIST Annual Meeting*, Medford, NJ: Information Today.

McTear, M. F. (2002). Spoken dialogue technology: Enabling the conversational user interface. *ACM Computing Surveys (CSUR), 34*(1).

Muller, J. P., & Pischel, M. (1994). Modeling interacting agents. In Dynamic environments, in

Proceedings of the Eleventh European Conference on Artificial Intelligence (ECAI-94), (pp. 709-713), The Netherlands.

Muller, J. P., Pischel, M., & Thiel, M. (1994). A pragmatic approach to modeling autonomous interacting systems. In Wooldridge, M., & Jennings, N. R. (Eds.), *Pre-proceedings of the 1994 Workshop on Agent Theories, Architectures, and Languages*, Netherlands, 226-240.

Negroponte, N. (1997). Agents: From direct manipulation to delegation. In J. M. Bradshaw (Ed.), *Software Agents*, Cambridge: MIT Press, 57-66.

Norman, D. A. (1997). How might people interact with agents. In J. M. Bradshaw, (Ed.), *Software Agents*, Cambridge: MIT Press, 49-55.

Pazienza, M. T., Stellato, A., Henriksen, L., Paggio, P., & Zanzotto F. M. (2005). Ontology mapping to support multilingual ontology-based question answering. In *Proceedings of the 4th International Semantic Web Conference*, Galway, Ireland.

Ren, F. & Shi, H. (2000). A general ontology based multilingual multi-function multi-media intelligent system. In *Proceedings of the IEEE International Conference on Systems, Cybernetics,* (pp. 2362-2368), Nashville.

Ritter, M., Meier, U., Yang, J., & Waibel, A. (1999). Face translation: A multimodal translation agent. In *Proceedings of Auditory Visual Speech Processing.*

Rao, A. S., & Georgeff, M. P. (1991). Modeling rational agents within a BDI architecture. In Fikes, R. & Sandewall, E. (Eds.), *Proceedings of knowledge representation and reasoning (KR&R 91)*, San Mateo, CA: Morgan Kaufmann Publihsers.

Sobia, S., & Nirmala, P. (2007), Context-based travel planning agent. (Tech. Rpt. No.) Pondicherry: Pondicherry University, Department of Computer Science.

Turunen, M., & Hakulinen, J. (2000). Jaspis: A framework for multilingual adaptive speech applications. In *Proceedings of the 6th International Conference of Spoken Language Processing.*

Vakkari, P. (2003). Task-based information searching. *Annual Review of Information Science and Technology, 37,* 13-464.

Wooldridge, M. (2000). *Reasoning about rational agents.* MIT Press.

Wooldridge, M. (1999). Intelligent agents. In Weiss, G. (Ed.), *Multiagent systems: A modern approach to distributed artificial intelligence,* MIT Press, 27-77.

Wooldridge, M., & Jennings, N. R. (1995). Intelligent agents, theory and practice. *Knowledge Engineering Review, 10*(2).

Websites

Ws1. www.fipa.org

Ws2. http://www.microsoft.com/msagent/downloads/user.asp

Ws3. http://www.cs.cmu.edu/~dbohus/SDS/index.html

Ws4. www.ling.gu.se/~sl/dialogue_links.html

This work was previously published in the International Journal of Intelligent Information Technologies, Vol. 4, Issue 3, edited by V. Sugumaran, pp. 58-78, copyright 2008 by IGI Publishing (an imprint of IGI Global).

Chapter 5
An Agent-Based Approach to Process Management in E-Learning Environments

Hokyin Lai
City University of Hong Kong, Hong Kong

Minhong Wang
The University of Hong Kong, Hong Kong

Jingwen He
City University of Hong Kong, Hong Kong

Huaiqing Wang
City University of Hong Kong, Hong Kong

ABSTRACT

Learning is a process to acquire new knowledge. Ideally, this process is the result of an active interaction of key cognitive processes, such as perception, imagery, organization, and elaboration. Quality learning has emphasized on designing a course curriculum or learning process, which can elicit the cognitive processing of learners. However, most e-learning systems nowadays are resources-oriented instead of process-oriented. These systems were designed without adequate support of pedagogical principles to guide the learning process. They have not explained the sequence of how the knowledge was acquired, which, in fact, is extremely important to the quality of learning. This study aims to develop an e-learning environment that enables students to get engaged in their learning process by guiding and customizing their learning process in an adaptive way. The expected performance of the Agent-based e-learning Process model is also evaluated by comparing with traditional e-learning models.

INTRODUCTION

Learning is a complex interactive process that involves environmental, social, motivational, emotional, and cognitive facts. Most people view learning as a systematic process through which students could gain and output processed knowledge. Based on this assumption, cognitive models of learning can be adopted to describe the learning process.

According to Bloom's Taxonomy of the Cognitive Domain (Bloom, et al., 1956), educational objectives can be built on a hierarchy from the lowest level of intellectual activities to more complex and abstract mental levels. Vygotsky (1978) mentioned that most students are only willing to take a challenge with their current level of development or slightly above. By experiencing the successful completion of challenging tasks, learners gain confidence and motivation to embark on more complex challenges. Furthermore, according to Von Glasersfeld (1989), sustaining motivation to learn is strongly dependent on the student's confidence in his or her potential for learning. These feelings of competence and belief in potential to solve new challenges are derived from their past experience in solving similar problems rather than any external acknowledgement and motivation (Prawat & Floden, 1994). These imply that teachers should design the learning process with an appropriate level to students in order to motivate students to learn as well as to strengthen their confidence. In order to deliver good quality of learning, motivation to learn and support of cognitive processing are the major pedagogical concerns. However, most current e-learning systems are designed without these concerns.

Nowadays, both academic and business institutions support learning with technology, such that e-learning has evolved into any learning activity that highly involves technology for its presentation (Shute & Towle, 2003). E-learning can also be defined as activities which take place in front of one or more computers that are connected to the Internet. Since e-learning is maturing in technology-wise—even to the point that more artificial intelligence can be integrated into the e-learning systems—its focus is at the same time shifting from simply providing an infrastructure and delivering information online to supporting pedagogical principles (Shute & Towle, 2003).

It is a fact that recent e-learning research has focused mostly on process-oriented educational technology, i.e., the technology that supports sequencing of learning activities and learning content. Currently, it has two different types of sequencing technologies: SCORM-based and workflow-based learning systems (Marjanovic, 2007). In addition, many adaptive e-learning systems are also available, like Arthur (Gilbert & Han, 1999), iWeaver (Wolf, 2002), CS383 (Carver et al., 1999), and EDUCE (Kelly & Tangney, 2002).

Furthermore, IS researchers have begun investigating an emerging, technology-enabled innovation that involves the use of intelligent software agents in e-learning. The presence of these agents stimulates the human aspects of instruction in a more natural and valid way than other computer-based methods. The representation of knowledge in the agent-based architecture can support students' learning activities adaptively (Xu & Wang, 2006). Agent-based infrastructure possess reasoning power, such that it can make dynamic decisions on which content and style should be delivered to a particular learner based on the pedagogical practices and the learner's profile. Such complicated knowledge exchange can then be done in a more efficient and effective way with the support of intelligent agents, rather than manually.

The objective of this study is to develop an e-learning environment that is able to motivate students to learn and make students well engaged in their learning process by guiding and customizing their learning processes in an adaptive way.

In this study, an Agent-based e-learning Process model has been developed using agent technology approach. Intelligent agents were utilized to deliver the appropriate course content, to monitor the student performance, and to refine their learning process if necessary. Students may get instant feedback from the model over time in order to engage them into the learning process. In order to maintain its extendibility, the model was designed based on certain common standardized technologies like the workflow technique.

The contribution of this study is the design of an e-learning model which can motivate students to learn, as well as provide support for the cognitive processing.

LITERATURE REVIEW

Learning is a Process

Learning is a process of acquiring new knowledge (Reynolds, et al, 2002). The process is active and complete and involves active interaction of key cognitive processes, such as perception, imagery, organization, and elaboration. These processes facilitate the construction of conceptual relations (Glynn, et al., 1991). The learning process also involves environmental, social, motivational, emotional, and cognitive facts through which students gain knowledge and apply the processed knowledge in appropriate ways. Recent educational research has adopted the cognitive models of learning to describe the learning process.

Aligned with Bloom's Taxonomy, it can be argued that students can learn better through a well-designed learning process. The Bloom's Taxonomy is a classification of different levels of the learning objectives and skills which educators had set for learners. Benjamin Bloom organized the taxonomy in a hierarchical framework, such that learning at higher levels requires attained pre-requisite knowledge and skills at lower levels (Orlich, et al., 2004). This implies that the conceptual organization of skills at lower levels is contributing to the success in learning the

skills at higher levels, where a learning process is embedded.

Besides, students are concerned about the level and source of motivation for learning. According to Von Glasersfeld (1989), sustaining motivation to learn is strongly dependent on student's confidence in his or her potential for learning. These feelings of competence and belief in potential to solve new challenges are derived from their past experience in solving similar problems rather than any external acknowledgement and motivation (Prawat & Floden, 1994). This links up with Vygotsky's viewpoint (Vygotsky, 1978) that learners are only willing to take a challenge with their current level of development or slightly above. By experiencing the successful completion of challenging tasks, learners gain confidence and motivation to embark on more complex challenges. Therefore, educators should have understood the learning capability of students before they design the course with an appropriate level of difficulty. Furthermore, students who study in the same class sometimes vary in learning capabilities and confidence, hence, learning pace should be adjusted as well.

In addition, according to the constructive view of learning science, Shawn et al. (1991) mention that educators should emphasize the quality of learning rather than the quantity because of the ever-changing technology and knowledge. Conceptual understanding is more important than rote memorization. Students are encouraged to actively organize, elaborate, and interpret knowledge, rather than just repeat it and memorize it. This approach aims at training students to be a self-learner. Teachers, as facilitators, have to closely monitor the learning progress of their students and to provide appropriate support at the right time. However, it is difficult for teachers to keep track of individual students' learning progress without the support of technology.

It should be kept in mind that learning is not just a straight-through process but a cyclic one. The learning cycle has three phases (Champagne

& Bruce, 1991) and each phase is named according to the stage in the learning process: engagement, elaboration, and assessment. A student would first engage in a learning task, and then elaborate the task and finally assess his or her performance on the task. If the performance is acceptable, then he or she would begin a new learning task and repeat the three phases again. Since the learning cycle could be enriched through interactions with peers or teachers, an instructional cycle can be used to complement the learning cycle. With teachers setting the learning tasks, monitoring interactions among students and evaluating the students' progress, this learning task is goal-directed and is designed to induce cognitive change in the student, i.e., teachers can monitor the students' progress and their interactions, and intervene when needed.

Observation of student discussion provides the teacher with valuable information about all aspects of student achievement, especially in their development of cognitive skills. The information helps teachers to modify their instructional planning flexibly when it is not closely linked to the students' previous learning. The results of the learning task assessment and teacher evaluations would shape the subsequent steps in the learning process.

Technology Development in E-Learning Applications

The applications on the Internet are pull in nature. To some extent, Internet users are irregular in their actions and may not return once they leave (Chang et al., 2001). If the course provided in the e-learning environment is not interesting and could not motivate students to learn, the students are not likely to stay with e-learning environment unless it is mandatory.

As learning is a cyclic process, the e-learning model should be designed in a process-oriented approach, such that the cognitive learning goals can be achieved through better management in

each phase. However, most e-learning models are designed without taking into account the pedagogical practice, just like a learning resources repository. Only few of them are constructed using process-oriented educational technology. Currently, there are two types of sequencing e-learning technologies, which are SCORM-based and workflow-based systems respectively (Marjanovic, 2007). The design objective of SCORM-based approach is mainly for learning object reuse, while that of the workflow-based systems is for sequencing of learning objects. However, neither of them has taken into account the cognitive process of students, which is the most important element in the learning process.

Recently, IS researchers have begun investigating an emerging, technology-enabled innovation that involves the use of intelligent software agents in e-learning. Wooldridge and Jennings (1995) define an intelligent agent as a computer system that work in an autonomous way and can work in a dynamic environment in order to achieve the goals defined by the system designer. Furthermore, they also claim that agents can work interactively with each other without human intervention. The interactivity of the agents opens a communication channel for the participants (both instructors and students) to deal with the e-learning system and interact with other participants. The presence of agents stimulates the human aspect of instruction in a more natural and valid way than other computer-based methods, and it has been shown that the representation of knowledge in the agent-based architecture can support students' learning activities adaptively (Xu & Wang 2006).

In the past, agents were mostly designed as personal assistants or human-system mediators. Agent-based infrastructure provides reasoning power such that dynamic decisions based on the instructional planning could be made by the agents. Responsiveness of a system affects the adoption rate obviously. With the support of intelligent agents, the response time is not a big concern as agents are able to perform complicated knowledge exchange in an effective and efficient manner without too much intervention from human.

LEARNING PROCESS DESIGN

Referring to the centered approach derived by Marjanovic (2005), a typical e-learning Process is modeled (Figure 1). The model is formed using five basic steps: (1) to identify the pedagogical goals and pedagogical objectives of the course; (2) to identify some learning activities that can guide students to achieve the goals. This step can be further divided into a few sub-steps: selecting individual learning tasks; grouping related tasks into one learning process with an order; mapping available learning resources to each individual task; and selecting appropriate system functions to

support them. In addition, in order to maintain the interoperability between tasks, some extra tasks, like social interactions, can be added as well; (3) to execute the learning activities according to the predefined sequence; (4) to closely monitor the execution of the learning activities; and (5) to review the existing model based on the learning progress of students. Amendments on the existing learning activities are crucial to support the adaptive learning feature. Since adaptive learning is a recursive process, steps (2) to (5) should be repeated until the course is about to end or no further improvement can be done.

As an example, an adaptive e-learning process for a 4-week introductory course on Information Systems is shown in Figure 2. The process is the expected outcome of the second step (Design Learning activities) in Figure 1. The learning tasks of the process are interrelated. Each learning

Figure 1. A typical e-learning process

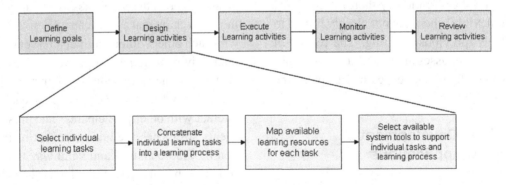

Figure 2. A sample e-learning process for a 4-week introductory course

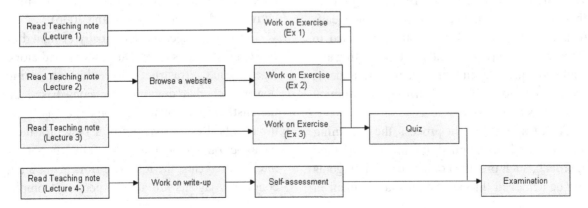

task links with corresponding learning resources and system functions. Once the process is set, a student can start learning from the most preceding task.

AGENT-ORIENTED E-LEARNING PROCESS MODEL

Design Philosophy

The design philosophy of the model is shown in Table 1. Basic elements in the model include: a

communication channel between users and the e-learning environment, learning process management mechanism, assessment steps to evaluate students' performance etc. All are derived from the educational theories.

The Model

A conceptual agent-oriented e-learning Process model has been developed, as shown in Figure 3. In the model, there are three core agents: Learning Process Management Agent, Student Activity Monitoring Agent, and Assessment Agent respectively.

Table 1. Agents in the e-learning process model

Agent	Properties	Design philosophy
Learning Process Management Agent	• Acts as an interface between teachers, students, and the e-learning environment	• Constructivism stresses the importance of social interaction (Gredler, 1997; Wertsch, 1985) • A facilitator (i.e., teacher) needs to interact with the learners in order to help learners create value (Rhodes & Bellamy, 1999) • In collaboration with capable peers, learner can develop a faster learning capability which may even beyond their existing level. In addition, learners can avoid lagging behind the learning process (Vygotsky, 1978)
	• Manages the learning process, e.g, determines the next available learning task and then retrieve the required learning resources for individual students	• Constructive alignment is a method to achieve meaningful and effective teaching and learning activities (Biggs, 1996) • Teachers, especially science teachers, view instruction as a process of helping students acquire theories and concepts progressively (Glynn, et al., 1991)
	• Reports the students' performance to teacher	• Personal and social influences can create a feedback loop that can influence a student's self-regulated learning (Zimmerman, 1989) • Teacher can counteract misconceptions of students and facilitate conceptual change if he can identify the misconceptions of students (Glynn, et al., 1991)
Student Activity Monitoring Agent	•Monitors the learning progress of each individual student throughout learning process •Monitors the performance of individual student by learning task	• People have different learning styles so that they process the same piece of information differently (Felder, 1996) • By applying the Workflow Management concept, the execution of the learning activities should be closely monitored (Marjanovic, 2005)
Assessment Agent	•Evaluates the learning performance of students	• Assessments can act as basic diagnostic tools to access the effectiveness of instruction (Shute & Towle, 2003) • Assessment is the process of gathering evidence of student learning, reviewing the evidence to determine if students are learning what they are expected to learn, and using this evidence to enhance the direction of course (Anderson and Krathwohl, 2001)

The Learning Process Management Agent works as a major interface between the agent-based framework and users. Possible users include teachers and students and this agent has the ability to identify the user's role, pick the appropriate learning task for individual students, and assemble the corresponding learning resources for the selected learning task. Before the course begins, teachers should input the learning process, learning resources, assessment answers, and minimum threshold for each assessment task for the course to the e-learning model through interacting with this agent. When all the settings are completed, students can start learning.

Once the Learning Process Management Agent receives a learning request from student, it will retrieve the appropriate learning task based on the learning process, as well as the learning progress log, of the student. For example, if the learning progress log shows that the students have completed the learning task #5, but not yet started task #6, the Learning Process Management Agent will then assemble the learning resources for task #6 and advise the students to begin their learning starting from task #6. In case of having more than one preceding task, the Learning Process Management Agent will list out all possible preceding tasks for the students to choose.

The Assessment Agent is used to evaluate the performance of students by the end of each stage in the learning process. Since the educational goal is to deliver learning quality rather than learning quantity in this study, if individual student's performance is lower than the minimum threshold, he or she would be requested to review the learning tasks in the same level and retake the assessment task. Once they have passed the threshold (Figure 4), they would then be able to advance to the next learning level. Basically, the assessment questions are generated dynamically by the Assessment Agent each time to avoid students' rote memorization. All the assessment results are stored in a log file called Learning Progress Log.

Teachers can have a rough understanding on the learning performance of students by browsing the records in the log file via an agent called Student Activity Monitoring Agent. This Agent would actively request the Learning Process Management Agent to send an email to the teachers in case of any abnormal situation, say for instance, over 50% of students have lagged behind the expected pace, within the e-learning system. Different kinds of abnormal situations are supposed to be defined by the teachers. As they would have more understanding of the competence of their students' progress, such feedback mechanism is

Figure 3. The agent-based e-learning process model

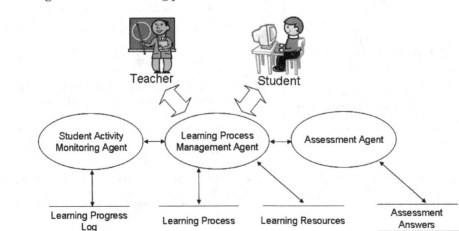

84

Figure 4. Assessment before going to next level

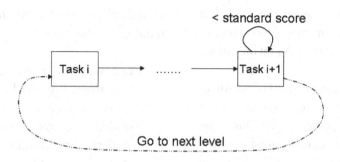

crucial to the teachers for making the appropriate adjustments accordingly.

A sample workflow for the learning process in Figure 2 is illustrated in Figure 7. Learning tasks are sequenced according to the level of difficulty. Before getting to the next level, an assessment task, for example task no. 2, 5, 7, 9, 10, 11, or 12 in Figure 7, is given to the student in order to evaluate his or her learning performance. This design is used to reflect the psychological feeling of students. Students are only willing to take a challenge with their current level of development or slightly above (Vygotsky, 1978).

To cope with the need that was addressed by constructivism that students can develop a faster learning capability through collaborating with other peers (Vygotsky, 1978), a discussion forum has been developed to facilitate knowledge exchange between students. Students can access the forum via the Learning Process Management Agent. When there are new posts in the forum, teachers are informed by emails by the Learning Process Management Agent once or twice a day, so that they are able to provide on-time teaching support to avoid any misconceptions of the course content among students themselves.

Teachers, as facilitators, can monitor students' performance by reading the learning log via Student Activity Monitoring Agent. Teachers would "intervene" the learning process only if the predefined learning process does not fit the

class or when there are some common conceptual mistakes in class, such that they can rectify the misconceptions of students.

Roles of Agents

1. *Learning Process Management Agent*

This agent provides the user interface for teachers and students to access the e-learning system. It also works as a central hub in the model. Its roles are mainly to manage the learning process of each individual student.

After a student has logged into the system, it will determine and retrieve the next available learning task as well as the required learning resources for the student. In order to better monitor the learning progress of each individual student, the Learning Process Management Agent works closely with the Student Activity Monitoring Agent and the Assessment Agent correspondingly.

2. *Student Activity Monitoring Agent*

The main responsibility of this agent is to keep track of the learning performance of each individual student in the model. It does not have any direct contact, i.e., it will not interface with the users directly, but the users, including teachers and students, can use its services through interacting with the Learning Process Management Agent. For any requests regarding managing and tracking students' performance, the Learning Process Management Agent would pass them to the Student Activity Monitoring Agent for further processing.

In fact, the Student Activity Monitoring Agent is able to fulfill two types of requests sent by the Learning Process Management Agent. First, the Learning Process Management Agent is eager to know which learning task should be retrieved for the individual student. Second, the Learning Process Management Agent wants to report the students' performance, especially the assessed outcomes, to the teacher.

The Learning Progress Log can only be accessed by the Student Activity Monitoring Agent. This agent helps record the students' activities as well as their assessment outcomes. Furthermore, the agent helps keep track of students' performance through a proactive mechanism. Teachers can set their own definitions of certain cases which the agent needs to report once discovered. For example, if one student cannot pass the same assessment test after he or she has tried for over three times, it should be reported.

3. *Assessment Agent*

Only this agent has permission to access the answers of those assessment tasks. The main duty of the assessment agent is to deal with the assessment-related tasks, such as updating the assessment sample answers, and marking the assessment task for teachers.

All the assessed results are kept as a record in the Learning Progress Log. Since this log is not maintained by the assessment agent, the assessment agent itself needs to pass the calculated results to the Student Activity Monitoring Agent, which manages this log, via the Learning Process Management Agent, as shown in Figure 3.

Data Storage

Four database tables are used to manage the data required by the model.

1. **Learning Progress Log:** Referring to Figure 5, Learning Progress Log is a log that records the tasks that have been completed by each student. Each record in this log contains the student ID, task number, and the assessment result if the task is an assessment task.

2. **Learning Process:** As shown in Figure 6, all the learning tasks for a course are assembled with task dependency in this database table.

Figure 5. The learning progress log

Table - dbo.L...g_Progress_Log	Summary	
Student_ID	Task_No	Score
50001111	1	0
50001111	2	30
50001111	3	0
50001112	1	0
50001112	2	60
50001112	3	0
50001112	4	0
50001113	1	0
50001113	2	50
50001113	3	0
50001113	4	0
50001113	5	60

Figure 6. The learning process

Table - dbo.Learning_Process	Summary			
Task_No	Task_Description	Task_Level	Standard	Preceding_Task
1	Read Teaching Note 1	1	0	
2	Work on Exercise 1	1	40	0
3	Read Teaching Note 2	2	0	2
4	Browse a website	2	0	3
5	Work on Exercise 2	2	50	4
6	Read Teaching Note 3	3	0	5
7	Work on Exercise 3	3	60	6
8	Read Teaching Note 4	4	0	7
9	Work on Write up	4	50	8
10	Self-assessment	4	50	9
11	Quiz	5	50	2, 5, 7
12	Examination	6	50	10, 11

Each task is stored as one record. The task number, task description, task level, task dependency and relevant learning resources are included in the record. In case of an assessment task, a standardized threshold is included as well.

3. **Learning Resources:** Attributes such as resources ID, its availability, and its physical location are included.

4. **Assessment Answers:** Before any student attempts to work on the assessment task, answers are needed to be input by the teacher and stored in this table. All the assessment questions in this model are in multiple choice format, so that it is more convenient to come up with assessment result by comparing the answers given by students to the sample answer set.

Case Scenario

Students are required to log into the e-Learning model via the Learning Process Management Agent. After being successfully logged in, the Learning Process Management Agent will retrieve the latest learning history of this student through interacting with the Student Activity Monitoring

Agent. It will then determine the next learning task for this student. In this case, let's assume the student is a first-time user to the model.

By referring to the workflow for the sample course in Figure 7, the first task in the learning process is task 1. Task 1 requires the student to read through a teaching note (Figure 6) so the Learning Process Management Agent will retrieve the relevant learning resources and make it available to the student. After the student has completed task 1, the Learning Process Management Agent then informs the Student Activity Monitoring Agent to add a new record in the Learning Progress Log to indicate the completion of task 1. According to the task dependency, task 2 would be available to the student only after the student has completed task 1.

Task 2 is an assessment task to evaluate the student's performance. The student can only move onto task 3 if he or she is able to get a score which is higher than 40 marks in task 2. In order to enhance the responsiveness of the model, the Assessment Agent takes up the responsibility to compare the answers given by the student to the ones stored in the Assessment Answers table and then calculate the assessment score that supposed to be done by teachers manually. The

Figure 7. The sample learning workflows

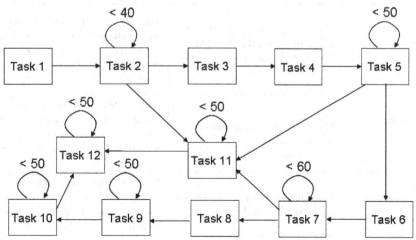

assessment result is then passed to the Learning Process Management Agent as well as the Student Activity Monitoring Agent. The Student Activity Monitoring Agent then adds a new record in the Learning Progress Log, but the status may or may not be "completion". If the assessment result is greater than or equal to the threshold set in the Learning Process record, then the status will be a "completion". Otherwise, the status is still kept as "incomplete". Since task 2 is an assessment task, the assessment result is stored in the record of the Learning Progress log as well.

If the student has passed the thresholds of task 2 and 5 simultaneously, then the Learning Process Management Agent would suggest the student to study either task 6 or 11. The student will then be given an opportunity to pick one on his or her own.

The involved agents work with the same mechanism until the student logs out.

EVALUATION AND DISCUSSION

In Table 2, a comparison between the features of the proposed Agent-based e-learning Process model and that of the traditional e-learning model without process-oriented support is provided. The Agent-based e-learning Process model is more flexible and more compatible with the pedagogical theory when compared to the traditional one.

CONCLUSION AND FUTURE WORK

Learning is a complex interactive process that involves various aspects of facts. According to

Table 2. Comparison between the features of the proposed agent-based e-learning Process model and that of the traditional e-learning model without process-oriented support

Features	Traditional e-learning models without agent and process management support	Agent-based e-learning Process Model
Learning process management	Like Blackboard and WebCT, it has no task management feature. It just provides content management support.	The tasks have been arranged in sequence. Students can learn based on a process that has been defined by the teachers. There is a higher chance to achieve good quality of learning.
Manipulation of pedagogical rules	No linkage with the pedagogical rules. Inconsistency between the pedagogical rules and the course content may happen.	The learning process is generated with reference to the pedagogical rules. Teachers can even change the pedagogical rules when the course is running.
Customization to individuals	Most of them are unable to support personalization.	Agent technology with logical reasoning function enables dynamic customization feature. Agent provides a clear guideline for students to learn in an appropriate level of difficulty.
Support of interactive learning tasks	They are quite passive. All requests are initiated by students.	The learning is more interactive. After the student has completed one task, then the agent suggests the next task proactively.

Bloom's Taxonomy, educational objectives have been arranged in a hierarchy from less to more complex. It has also been shown that students are only eager to study within their current competency level or slightly above. By experiencing the successful completion of challenging tasks, learners gain confidence and motivation to embark on more complex challenges. These imply that teachers should design the learning process with an appropriate level to students in order to motivate students to learn as well as to strengthen their confidence. However, currently available e-learning models mainly act as a learning resources repository.

In fact, e-learning is getting more mature in technology such that the design focus should be shifted from simply providing an infrastructure to supporting pedagogical principles (Shute & Towle, 2003). Technology is now more advanced to the point that more artificial intelligence can be integrated into the e-learning systems. In order to deliver good quality of learning, motivation to learn and support of cognitive processing are the major pedagogical concerns. Unfortunately, most current e-learning systems are designed without these concerns.

An intelligent agent is a software agent that works in an autonomous way and can communicate with each other in order to complete the goals defined by the system designer. The interactivity of the agents opens a communication channel for the participants, such as teachers and students, to deal with the e-learning system in a more interactively way. The presence of agents stimulates the human aspect of instruction in a natural and valid way than other computer-based methods.

In this study, an agent-based e-learning Process model has been developed using the agent technology approach. To maintain its extendibility, the model is designed with some common standardized technologies like the workflow technique. The intelligent agents are able to provide learning guidance to students, monitor the learning progress of students, assess the competence of students, and reflect the learning progress of students to teachers, etc. The design philosophy is mainly based on those mainstream educational theories such as Bloom's taxonomy and constructivism.

By evaluating the performance of both the traditional e-learning model and the proposed one, it was found that the proposed model can supplement the lack of manipulation of pedagogical rules in the traditional approach, and can provide better learning process management and customization for individual students respectively. This study has practical implications to the e-learning system researchers, developers and users.

In the proposed model, we have simplified the steps by using multiple choice questions to evaluate the students' performance. If the teachers request their students to describe a concept in text, the proposed model is unable to assess the answers. In addition, the content on the discussion forum is now manually processed by the teachers. Some previous research suggested using concept map approach to solve this problem. However, the accuracy is still very low. Therefore, in future research, we will further investigate how to automate the knowledge processing steps.

REFERENCES

Anderson, L. W., & Krathwohl, D. R. (2001). A Taxonomy for Learning, Teaching, and Assessing: A Revision of Bloom's Taxonomy of Educational Objectives. New York: Longman.

Baddeley, A. (1990). Human memory. Boston: Allyn & Bacon.

Biggs, J. (1996). Enhancing Teaching through Constructive Alignment, Higher Education, 32, 347-364.

Bloom, B., Englehart, M. Furst, E., Hill, W., & Krathwohl, D. (1956). Taxonomy of educational objectives: The classification of educational goals.

Handbook I: Cognitive domain. New York, Toronto: Longmans, Green.

Carver, C.A., Howard, R.A., & Lane, W.D. (1999). Enhancing Student Learning Through Hypermedia Courseware and Incorporation of Student Learning Styles, IEEE Transactions on Education, 42(1), pp. 33-38.

Champagne, A. & Bunce, D (1991). Learning-theory-based science teaching. In The Psychology of learning science, (Eds.) S.M. Glynn, R.H. Yeany, B.K. Britton, Hillsdale, NJ, Lawrence Erlbaum Associates.

Chang, M.K., & Cheung, W. (2001). Determinants of the intention to use Internet/WWW at work: a confirmatory study. Information & Management 29(1) 1-4.

Felder, R. M. (1996). Matters of Styles. ASEE Prism, 6(4), 18-23.

Gilbert, J.E. & Han, C.Y. (1999). Adapting Instruction in Search of "A Significance Difference". Journal of Networking and Computing Applications, 22, 3.

Gredler, M. E. (1997). Learning and instruction: Theory into practice (3rd ed). Upper Saddle River, NJ: Prentice-Hall. Kelly, D., & Tangney, B. (2002), Incorporating Learning Characteristics into an Intelligent Tutor, Proceedings of the 6th International Conference on Intelligent Tutoring Systems, p.729-738, June 02-07.

Hokyin Lai, Huaiqing Wang, & Minhong Wang (2007). Agent-oriented e-learning Process Modeling, Proceedings of Americas Conference on Information Systems (AMCIS 2007), Colorado, USA, August 2007.

Marjanovic, O. (2005). Towards A Web-Based Handbook of Generic, Process-Oriented Learning Designs, Educational Technology and Society, 8(2), 66-82.

Marjanovic, O. (2007). Using Process-oriented, Sequencing Educational Technologies: Some Important Pedagogical Issues, Computers in Human Behavior, 23, 2742-2759.

Orlich, D.C., Harder, R.J., Callahan, R.C., Trevisan, M.S., & Brown, A.B. (2004). Teaching Strategies, a guide to effective instruction. (7th Ed.), Boston: Houghton Mifflin Company.

Prawat, R.S., & Floden, R.E. (1994). Philosophical-perspectives on Constructivist Views of Learning, Educational Psychologist 29(1): 37-48, WIN 1994.

Reynolds, R., Caley, L., & Mason, R. (2002). How do People Learn? London: CIPD.

Rhodes, L.K., & Bellamy, G.T. (1999). Choices and Consequences in the Renewal of Teacher Education. Journal of Teacher Education, 50(1), 17.

Shawn M. Glynn, Russell H. Yeany, & Bruce K. Britton.A Constructive View of learning Science. The Psychology of learning science. LEA Publishers, 1991

Shute, Valerie & Towle, Brendon (2003). Adaptive E-Learning, Educational Psychologist, 38(2), 105-114.

Von Glasersfeld, E.(1989) Constructvism in education. 162-163. In Husen, T., & Postlethwaite, T.N(eds). The international encyclopedia of education, \AS;supplementary volume one\AS;, Pergamon Press plc.

Vygotsky, L. S. (1978). Mind in society: The development of higher psychological processes. Cambridge, MA: Harvard University Press. Published originally in Russian in 1930.

Wang, M. H., & Wang, H. Q. (2006). From Process Logic to Business Logic – A Cognitive Approach to Business Process Management, Information and Management, 43, 179-193.

Wertsch, J.V. (1985). Vygotsky and the social formation of mind. Cambridge, Mass.: Harvard University Press.

Wolf, C. (2002). iWeaver: Towards an interactive web-based adaptive learning environment to address individual learning styles. European Journal of Open and Distance Learning.

Wooldridge, M. & Jennings, N.R. (1995). Agent theories, architectures and languages: a survey. In: Wooldridge, M. and Jennings, N.R. (eds) Intelligent Agents, Lecture Notes in AI, Vol. 890, pp. 1-39, Springer-Verlag.

Xu, D. M., & Wang, H. Q. (2006). Intelligent Agent Supported Personalization for Virtual Learning Environments, Decision Support Systems, 42(2), 825-843.

Zimmerman, B. J. (1989). A social cognitive view of self-regulated academic learning. Journal of educational psychology, 81(3), 329-339.

This work was previously published in the International Journal of Intelligent Information Technologies, Vol. 4, Issue 4, edited by V. Sugumaran, pp. 18-30, copyright 2008 by IGI Publishing (an imprint of IGI Global).

Chapter 6
Inference Degradation in Information Fusion:
A Bayesian Network Case

Xiangyang Li
University of Michigan – Dearborn, USA

ABSTRACT

Dynamic and active information fusion processes select the best sensor based on expected utility calculation in order to integrate the evidences acquires both accurately and timely. However, inference degradation happens when the same/similar sensors are selected repeatedly over time if the selection strategy is not well designed that considers the history of sensor engagement. This phenomenon decreases fusion accuracy and efficiency, in direct conflict to the objective of information integration with multiple sensors. This chapter tries to provide a mathematical scrutiny of this problem in the myopia planning popularly utilized in active information fusion. In evaluation it first introduces the common active information fusion context using security surveillance applications. It then examines the generic dynamic Bayesian network model for a mental state recognition task and analyzes experimentation results for the inference degradation. It also discusses the candidate solutions with some preliminary results. The inference degradation problem is not limited to the discussed task and may emerge in variants of sensor planning strategies even with more global optimization approach. This study provides common guidelines in information integration applications for information awareness and intelligent decision.

INTRODUCTION

Data and information becomes very rich if not overwhelming in many modern applications, such as real-time driving assistance systems that integrate information from the sensors installed at different locations of a vehicle, or military C3I systems that make critical decisions based on efficient command and intelligence processing in complex battlefield. The 911 tragedy asks for essential security applications such as event surveillance and detection, intelligence monitoring and analysis, intrusion and deception detection, as well as their implementations in terrorism tracking, analysis, and response.

DOI: 10.4018/978-1-60566-970-0.ch003

Within various research fields, knowledge discovery and integration algorithms can lead to efficient solutions to assist model integration and decision making in complex and distributed environment. With so much information in hand in such applications, a suitable strategy that must apply intelligent and active information fusion is the key enabling technique.

Information fusion/integration aims at combining multiple evidences, which normally contain overlapping (correlating) information relating to the underlying hypothesis due to the generating mechanism of these evidences, in order to gain better accuracy or higher confidence on information of interest (Hall & McMullen, 2004; Klein, 2004). Thus any algorithm that takes multiple inputs to evaluate a target output can be candidates for information fusion. The main challenges in information fusion include uncertainty and incompleteness in evidence, requirement on processing speed and cost, etc.

In this article, we set the knowledge discovery and integration task used in discussion and experimentation to be human subject modeling. Such a model integrates video and acoustic information of human subjects as well as other related contextual information, and infer about the internal status about the subject's mental and emotional aspects. This internal status can provide information of significant safety and security interests. Moreover the model could be about not only individuals but also a crowd of people. Through certain active strategy, it generates in a timely manner important indicators such as anxiety and stability of an individual or a crowd, which are useful measures of danger level of a special event involving human participants. Based on the given information, further analysis could be done with the help of other information such as the interacting machinery like a car or a fighter aircraft, or identification of the subject and report about possible terrorist plot, leading to proactive procedures of warning and countermeasures. Therefore such a human subject model can in fact function as a core component of intelligent assistance in battlefields, or scene surveillance and analysis in homeland security settings, providing real-time support for efficient decision making in emergency response and control.

Machine learning, artificial intelligence and psychological models have been extensively used in the information fusion in user modeling or human mental state detection (Cohen et al, 2000; Duric et al, 2002; Horvitz et al, 1998; Hudlicka & McHeese, 2002; Jameson, 1996; Picard, 1997; Salvucci et al, 2001). Of them, Bayesian network (BN) models have been applied in many user modeling and information fusion applications because of the capability to handle uncertainty and the analogy to human reasoning process, exemplified in a set of studies of intelligent office software assistants in the Lumiere Project other studies by Microsoft (Horvitz et al, 1998; Horvitz & Paek, 1999, 2000) and studies in affective state detection (Ball & Breese, 2000; Conti, 2002). In addition there are a range of information fusion applications for Bayesian networks, such as security modeling for service and health enterprise (Li et al, 2009; Li & Chandra, 2008).

Although the computing power increases with the development of new computer technology, the complexity and rapid growth of the size of problem space often require a supervised selective sensory strategy to acquire and integrate the most significant evidence. Therefore active fusion strategies based on information entropy and utility theories have been proposed to respond to the challenge of constraints in terms of Bayesian inference in information processing and sensory cost in information acquisition (Horvitz et al, 1998; Li & Ji, 2005). However, if not carefully designed and implemented, as we will discuss here and show in the experimentation, such active strategy is prone to select the same set of sensors again an again. This can lead to the reduction in inference capability for accurate and timely belief updating. This is in direct conflict to the objective of multiple sensor fusion. We call the phenomenon of reduction in inference capability due to that the fusion algorithm is presented repeatedly with the same sensor the "Bayesian inference degradation."

We discuss here the inference degradation in active fusion using Bayesian network models. The next section is devoted to the introduction of Bayesian network models and the formalization of a general myopia active fusion strategy based on value of information and expected utility calculation. The following section defines and discusses in detail the inference degradation and the mathematical proof. Then we describe a generic human mental state recognition model, which applies the above framework of modeling and active information integration. Some experimentation results are shown for the inference degradation phenomenon thereafter using this model. After that we propose the possible solutions to alleviate the degradation problem and some initial result is given for the same mental state recognition model. At the conclusion we discuss the implication of this research and future research issues.

ACTIVE INFORMATION FUSION IN BAYESIAN NETWORK MODELS

A typical information fusion task is to infer the belief or confidence about the hypothesis that is difficult to observe directly, based on the information that can be observed from some sensory channels. We generally choose a set of relevant sensors in order that we could get a more accurate and robust estimate of such belief. However due to other constraints on available computation or physical resources such as time, storage space, and the cost to turn on and off sensors, sometimes we could not always use all sensors and update the hypothesis beliefs at a very high frequency. Therefore we use "active information fusion" to selectively control the sensory information acquisition.

Bayesian Networks

Bayesian networks are probabilistic dependency models representing joint probabilities of a set of random variables and their conditional independence relations in a physical system (Jensen 2001; Pearl, 1988). The nodes characterize the hypothesis/goal variables, the hidden state variables, and the evidence/observation variables in the physical system, while the acyclic arcs linking these nodes represent the causal dependency among these variables. Hypothesis nodes represent what we want to infer while the observation nodes represent sensory evidence that could be observed. The intermediate hidden nodes are necessary to model the state generation process although in some cases they do not have explicit counterparts in the physical system. Nodes are often arranged hierarchically at different levels, representing information at different levels of abstraction. The probabilities of the node states represent the belief about the possible status that node currently is. We often use discrete states while continuous values can also be assigned to nodes with limitation on inference capability. The conditional probabilities represent the dependency between the states of a node and its parent nodes. The universal Bayesian theorem guides the inference in the process called belief propagation (Mackay, 2003). The propagation can be from evidence to hypothesis or in the other way, depending on the available knowledge and the interests.

Static Bayesian Networks (SBNs) work with evidence and belief from a single time instant. As a result, SBNs are not particularly suited to modeling systems that evolve over time. Dynamic Bayesian Networks (DBNs) have been developed to overcome this limitation, made up of interconnected time slices of SBNs. The relationships between two neighboring time slices are modeled by a Markov model, i.e., random variables at time t are affected by the corresponding random variables at time $t-1$ only, as well as by other variables at time t. The slice at the previous time provides prediction sup-

Figure 1. A general dynamic Bayesian network structure, where H represents a collection of hypothesis nodes, Ss hidden nodes, Es observation nodes, and t represents time; prior and conditional probabilities model the dependency among them

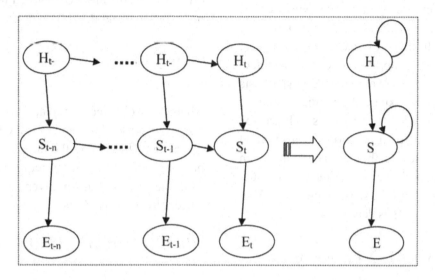

port for current slice through its temporal links, and it is used in conjunction with current evidence to infer the current hypothesis. DBNs represent a generalization of the conventional systems such as Kalman filtering and Hidden Markov Models for modeling dynamic events. A general DBN structure is shown in figure 1.

Bayesian networks have several advantages for modeling and inferring in dynamic and complex system. Firstly, BNs provide a hierarchical framework to systematically represent information from different locations and at different abstraction levels and systematically account for their uncertainties. Furthermore, with the dependencies coded in the graphical dependency model, Bayesian networks can handle situations where some data entries are missing. Secondly, the system's dynamically changing state and the surrounding situations call for a framework that not only captures the beliefs of current events, but also predicts the evolution of future scenarios. DBNs provide a very powerful tool for addressing this problem by providing a coherent and unified hierarchical probabilistic framework for sensory information representation, integration, and inference over

time. Given the evidence, DBNs could work in either prediction mode or diagnosis mode.

Active Information Fusion

Like any control mechanism, this active strategy is based on an objective function, representing the trade-off between benefit and cost. The benefit and cost are closely coupled with the current state of the system, especially the distribution of hypothesis and state beliefs and the causal relations among hypotheses and sensors. Thus this active fusion realizes in a dynamic and stately control process.

Mathematically, inference in fusion tasks may be viewed as a hypothesis testing problem, with hypothesis, $H=\{h_1, h_2,...,h_n\}$, representing the possible mental states in the later mental state recognition example. The sensory observation E is from m diverse sensors, i.e., $E=\{E_1, E_2,...,E_m\}$. The goal is to estimate the posterior probability that $H=h_i$ is true given E, i.e., $P(H=h_i|E)$. According to the Shannon's measure of entropy, the entropy over the hypothesis variable H is:

$$ENT(H) = -\sum_i P(h_i) \log P(h_i) \tag{1}$$

ENT(H) measures the uncertainty associated with *H*. It is zero when *H* is unambiguous, i.e., when one state has a probability 1; it has the highest value when the probability is evenly distributed. The benefit of a piece of evidence to a hypothesis is measured by its expected potential to reduce the uncertainty with the hypothesis. It can be quantified by mutual information, the differential entropy before and after the sensory action. Given the beliefs in hypothesis of last time slice H^{t-1}, the mutual information of a sensory evidence E_j to current hypothesis H^t is denoted as $I(H^t; E_j)$.

$$I(H^t; E_j) = ENT(H^t) - \sum_j P(e_j) ENT(H^t \mid e_j)$$
$$= -\sum_i P(h_i^t \mid H^{t-1}) \log P(h_i^t \mid H^{t-1})$$
$$+ \sum_j [P(e_j) \sum_i P(h_i^t \mid H^{t-1}, e_j) \log P(h_i^t \mid H^{t-1}, e_j)] \tag{2}$$

We could easily extend it to consider the case that multiple sensors, $E = \{E_1, ..., E_n\} \subseteq \mathbf{E}$, are instantiated simultaneously.

$$I(H^t; E_1, ..., E_n) = -\sum_i P(h_i^t \mid H^{t-1}) \log P(h_i^t \mid H^{t-1})$$
$$+ \sum_{e_1} ... \sum_{e_n} [P(e_1, ..., e_n) \sum_i P(h_i^t \mid H^{t-1}, e_1, ..., e_n)$$
$$\log P(h_i^t \mid H^{t-1}, e_1, ..., e_n)] \tag{3}$$

However if the number of censors is large, we meet the combinatorial exploration when we consider all sensor subsets. Here we use a so-called myopia strategy that takes into consideration sensors individually. If we want to turn on more than one sensors, we can cut off the top ones from the calculation.

Acquiring information incurs cost. The cost may include the cost of information retrieval, the time to include the information from source into the fusion system, the computation time for sensory data processing, and the hardware execution time.

We consider the sensor cost *C* of selecting *E*, a set of *n* sensors, where we assume that the costs for different sensors are incorporated with the same importance, using the following formula:

$$C(E) = \sum_{i=1}^{n} C_i \Big/ \sum_{j=1}^{m} C_j \tag{4}$$

where C_i or C_j is the cost to acquire the information from sensor *i* or *j* and *m* is the total number of sensors. Combining the uncertainty reducing potential and information acquisition cost, we form the expected utility given sensor set *E* for current hypothesis H^t as:

$$EU(H^t, E) = \alpha I(H^t; E) - (1 - \alpha)C(E) \tag{5}$$

where α is the balance coefficient between the two terms. The optimal sensor action can be found by using the following decision rule:

$$E^* = \arg \max_E EU(H^t, E) \tag{6}$$

We search for the best sensory action by examining the utilities for all configurations of sensors. Equation (6) is the fundamental equation for our dynamic and active sensing strategy. Though we can ignore the cost of sensors (i.e. $\alpha = 1$) in order to simply the parameterization consideration in experimentation.

INFORMATION DEGRADATION IN THE ACTIVE FUSION STRATEGY

We have to keep in mind the aim of information fusion. Better accuracy and robustness are the most important performance measures and thus the core target for any fusion system. From experimentation, the above active strategy could do better job to drive the beliefs of hypothesis - the mental state here - in the right direction for more certainty, in a pace faster than randomly or deterministically selecting sensors. But we also observed that certain sensor or certain sensor sequence repeatedly occurs in applying this expected utility calculation. This is at first glance reasonable because the above calculation tends to yield the same utility values over time for the sensors when the underlying hypothesis converge to certain unchanged beliefs. However such situation is suspicious since it compromises the advantage of multiple sensors if only a small set of sensors dominate the selection process.

Definition of Inference Degradation

A "degradation" effect is observed from the repeated selection of same sensors. We first give the definition of the "Inference Degradation," and then in this article as the first step we analyze the case of choosing only one sensor each time in fusion.

Definition 1: When repeated sensor sequence appears in inferring the hypothesis belief in dynamic Bayesian network, the belief of the hypothesis tends to converge to certain value. Consequently this leads to the same sensor to be selected again in the future. This situation is called '*inference degradation* of repeated sensor sequence.'

To explain such degradation in active information fusion applying expected utility calculation, we need notice in most situations the physical system does not always change under disturbance. In another words, the true hypothesis state, say the anxiety at certain level in our work of mental state assessment, may remain unchanged over a period of time. Obviously the formulas of calculating expected sensor utilities largely depend on the whole model with fixed structure and parameters, and now combined with unchanged hypothesis beliefs. Together this easily leads to that the change in the calculated utility score of the same sensor becomes less and less over time. Consequently this results in the tendency that the same sensor yields the highest utility value

consecutively. In one case, the sensor gives us the same state (discrete sensor states) each time we turn on this sensor. In another case, if this sensor were not a very good indicator for current true hypothesis status, it would provide readings more randomly. We will consider both cases in the following discussion.

The impact of inference degradation could be illustrated in two scenarios. Firstly the convergence in hypothesis beliefs could lead to a lower or higher belief than the "truth," which unfortunately is not as accurate as the belief when all the sensors are turned on. Then this degradation compromises the ability of multiple evidence combination for a better inference performance. Secondly another problem is the resistance in such fusion process to the change of underlying hypothesis status. Because of the tendency of choosing the same sensor, even though the underlying state is changed, such active fusion strategy has the inertia to choose the sensor currently engaged, although it may not be the really significant one to distinguish the new state. Moreover if the evidence (the yielded state) from the chosen sensor remains the same somehow, i.e. this sensor is not sensitive to the change of the underlying state because it is not the best any more, the utility calculation faces the risk to choose the same sensor in the next and further decision cycles. In this situation there is a higher possibility that the selection even fails to choose the "correct" sensor at all. This means the active fusion strategy could be trapped into generating a set of "false" decisions.

Bayesian Proof

We use the DBN model in Figure 2 to analyze the inference degradation. In this model, we simplify by using only one hypothesis node. There are two observation/evidence nodes, *A* and *B*, representing two different sensory channels. The figure represents two consecutive time slices, *t* and *t*+1. Here we further simplify this model by setting all nodes as binary ones, with states 0 and 1. The

Figure 2. The simplified Bayesian model in analyzing inference degradation, where there are two binary evidence nodes and one binary hypothesis node

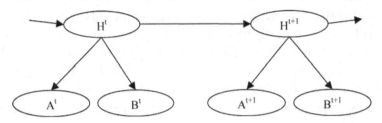

analysis can be extended to more general cases. In the following we discuss different fusion scenarios in terms of the evidence provided by the chosen sensor.

(1) *The Chosen Sensor Provides the Same State as Evidence in the Fusion Cycles.* We assume that sensor A is selected in both time slices t and $t+1$. The state given by A is 1, i.e. a_1. We want to infer the belief for H to take state 1, i.e. h_1^{t+1}. We could get this value as follows:

$$P(h_1^{t+1}, a_1^{t+1}) = \sum_{H^t} P(h_1^{t+1}, a_1^{t+1} \mid H^t)P(H^t)$$

$$= \sum_{H^t} P(h_1^{t+1}, a_1^{t+1}, H^t)$$

$$= \sum_{H^t} P(a_1^{t+1} \mid h_1^{t+1})P(h_1^{t+1} \mid H^t)P(H^t)$$

$$= P(a_1^{t+1} \mid h_1^{t+1})P(h_1^{t+1} \mid h_1^t)P(h_1^t)$$

$$+ P(a_1^{t+1} \mid h_1^{t+1})P(h_1^{t+1} \mid h_0^t)P(h_0^t) \quad (7)$$

We need to transform a joint probability of node states to the product of a set of conditional probabilities. These conditional probabilities are fixed once the DBN structure is chosen and configured. Here we represent those conditional probabilities as:

$$P(a_1^{t+1} \mid h_1^{t+1}) = r$$
$$P(h_1^{t+1} \mid h_1^t) = u \quad (8)$$
$$P(h_1^{t+1} \mid h_0^t) = v$$

and then:

$$P(h_1^{t+1}, a_1^{t+1}) = urP(h_1^t) + vrP(h_0^t) \quad (9)$$

We are interested in the change of this belief in consecutive time slices. We calculate the ratio of the beliefs for the same hypothesis state in two consecutive time slices.

$$\frac{P(h_1^{t+1}, a_1^{t+1})}{P(h_1^t, a_1^t)} = \frac{urP(h_1^t) + vrP(h_0^t)}{urP(h_1^{t-1}) + vrP(h_0^{t-1})}$$

$$= \frac{uP(h_1^t) + vP(h_0^t)}{uP(h_1^{t-1}) + vP(h_0^{t-1})} \quad (10)$$

Since we have the equation $P(h_1^t) + P(h_0^t) = 1$, after replacing $P(h_0^t)$ by $P(h_1^t)$, we get:

$$\frac{P(h_1^{t+1}, a_1^{t+1})}{P(h_1^t, a_1^t)} = \frac{(u-v)P(h_1^t) + v}{(u-v)P(h_1^{t-1}) + v} \quad (11)$$

Also we notice that in DBN, the posterior belief in last time slice is used as the prior belief in current slice, i.e. we can replace $P(h_1^t)$ by $P(h_1^t, a_1^t)$ and $P(h_1^{t-1})$ by $P(h_1^{t-1}, a_1^{t-1})$ in the above equation. Finally we get this equation:

$$\frac{P(h_1^{t+1}, a_1^{t+1})}{P(h_1^t, a_1^t)} = \frac{(u-v)P(h_1^t, a_1^t) + v}{(u-v)P(h_1^{t-1}, a_1^{t-1}) + v} \quad (12)$$

In DBN model, the transitional probability in two consecutive time slices between the same states is often greater than that between different states, i.e. we have $u > v$. This is from the consideration of slow evolution of hypothesis state, e.g. the probability of maintaining anxiety is bigger than a sudden change to another mental state. (In fact, it can lead to interesting discussion on use of DBN to model temporal aspect of physical systems if this is not held true.) With this assumption, when we examine the equation (12), we can find the conditions to satisfy it:

- The beliefs in consecutive time slices could be equal, i.e. $P(h_1^{t+1}, a_1^{t+1}) = P(h_1^t, a_1^t)$. Or
- If they are not equal, then the change of such beliefs is monotonous, i.e. if $P(h_1^t, a_1^t) < P(h_1^{t-1}, a_1^{t-1})$, then there must be $P(h_1^{t+1}, a_1^{t+1}) < P(h_1^t, a_1^t)$; vice versa. And when we consider the case of $Ph_1^t, a_1^t) < P(h_1^{t-1}, a_1^{t-1})$, we could also find that:

$$\frac{P(h_1^{t+1}, a_1^{t+1})}{P(h_1^t, a_1^t)}$$
$$= \frac{(u-v)P(h_1^t, a_1^t) + v}{(u-v)P(h_1^{t-1}, a_1^{t-1}) + v} > \frac{P(h_1^t, a_1^t)}{P(h_1^{t-1}, a_1^{t-1})}$$

The difference of the probabilities between the two time slices becomes smaller. Or

- In the extreme case when $u = v$, the belief $P(h_1^t, a_1^t)$ does not change from the beginning.

In any possible case, the belief for the hypothesis states will converge to a certain value. In the second case, since probability is in the range of (0, 1), this $P(h_1^t, a_1^t)$ has either an upper boundary or a lower boundary. This convergence means that the inference process eventually ceases to change the related beliefs. Experimentation shows that this convergence can be very quick. If we are lucky, we could get a converged belief near the truth. However since we only use one sensor, it is normally not good enough to reach the acceptable closeness to the truth.

(2) *The Binary Sensor Node Provides Alternating States.* Use the same induction we get:

$$\begin{cases} P(h_1^{t+1}, a_1^{t+1}) = \\ \quad P(a_1^{t+1} \mid h_1^{t+1})P(h_1^{t+1} \mid h_{t1}^t)P(h_1^t) \\ \quad + P(a_1^{t+1} \mid h_1^{t+1})P(h_1^{t+1} \mid h_0^t)P(h_0^t) \\ P(h_1^t, a_0^t) = \\ \quad P(a_0^t \mid h_1^t)P(h_1^t \mid h_1^{t-1})P(h_1^{t-1}) \\ \quad + P(a_0^t \mid h_1^t)P(h_1^t \mid h_0^{t-1})P(h_0^{t-1}) \end{cases} \quad (13)$$

Use the same notation, we get:

$$\frac{P(h_1^{t+1}, a_1^{t+1})}{P(h_1^t, a_0^t)} = \frac{urP(h_1^t) + vrP(h_0^t)}{u(1-r)P(h_1^{t-1}) + v(1-r)P(h_0^{t-1})}$$
$$= \frac{uP(h_1^t) + vP(h_0^t)}{uP(h_1^{t-1}) + vP(h_0^{t-1})} \frac{r}{1-r} \quad (14)$$

Use the same replacement, finally we have:

$$\frac{P(h_1^{t+1}, a_1^{t+1})}{P(h_1^t, a_0^t)} = \frac{(u-v)P(h_1^t, a_0^t) + v}{(u-v)P(h_1^{t-1}, a_1^{t-1}) + v} \frac{r}{1-r} \quad (15)$$

The above equation tells about more complicated relation of the hypothesis beliefs between two time slices. This belief tends to fluctuate around a certain value. If r is big (higher than 0.5), which means the conditional $P(a_1^{t+1} \mid h_1^{t+1})$ is big, the belief $P(h_1^{t+1}, a_1^{t+1})$ very likely becomes higher. But in the meanwhile, $P(h_1^t, a_0^t)$ becomes lower. In a more general sense, this equation shows that the change of this belief is largely dependent on a small set of parameters u, v and r.

In fact, when we think about the physical meaning of a sensor demonstrating alternating states, turning on a sensor giving confusing indications for a relatively stable hypothesis indicates obvious defect of choosing this sensor.

INFORMATION FUSION APPLICATIONS

Many modern information fusion applications as in homeland security or vehicle safety are centered on human subjects; no matter it is protecting people or deterring enemies. Uncertainty involved in human behaviors and mental states demands powerful inferential ability and efficient information integration capability in any kind of computing systems involving human subjects in implementation. Such event detection and scene surveillance is necessary to incorporate a human modeling component that collects information and automatically analyze and integrate such information to assist the decision-making.

Mental State Recognition Model

Challenges to human subject modeling are obvious in implementation for intelligent decision-making systems: (1) human subject's states and behaviors often show uncertainty that constantly changes over circumstance and time; (2) sensory observations of the human subject's behavior are often incomplete, uncertain, and from different modalities; (3) decisions about the human subject's need and the assistance must be rendered appropriately and efficiently under various constraints. BN and DBN models have been popular candidates for human subject modeling and fault diagnosis because of the capability in modeling causal and temporal dependency and in handling uncertainty in complex systems. A set of literature is also available for automatic troubleshooting (Heckerman et al, 1996; Langseth & Jensen, 2003).

We have proposed a generic modeling framework called "Context-Affective State-Profile-Observation" model to apply dynamic Bayesian networks in mental state recognition. It is used to infer the user's mental state from their observations (visual and other modalities if available). *Context component* represents information about the specific environmental factors that can influence the human subject's mental state, such as noise and time of the day. *Profile component* models user's physical/personality character, ability and competitiveness in finishing the operations. This provides the adaptation capability of the model to individual users. *Affective state component* represents the human subject's mental status. Typical states include but not limited to anxiety, frustration, fear, and anger. *Observation component* includes sensory observations of different modalities describing user behaviors that are influenced by mental states. More details of this model and the active fusion strategy discussed in the next section are in (Li & Ji, 2005).

Event Detection and Scene Surveillance

Let us consider important homeland security tasks of event detection and scene surveillance. In traditional surveillance systems, video information is collected from different locations of a target system or an activity scene, generally displayed on a set of screens. Human operators are in charge of monitoring and analyzing these screens to alarm any anomaly occurrences. However such working mechanism is not sufficient any more in the context of homeland security where the relative events could be distributed into a large geographical domain with huge information collected and required to be integrated in real-time. The target event is coordinated by activities in different locations and in different stages. Thus a computing system able of automatic analysis and detection of any abnormal events from heterogeneous data is necessary and a must for the next generation of security surveillance. Such systems are based on advanced information modeling and fusion technology using all available information, visual, acoustic, and contextual. They are especially vital in mission critical applications such as key infrastructure protection and border-crossing screening.

Figure 3. A higher-level security assessment model to incorporate individual models, where each evidence node represents the hypothesis belief in an individual human subject model

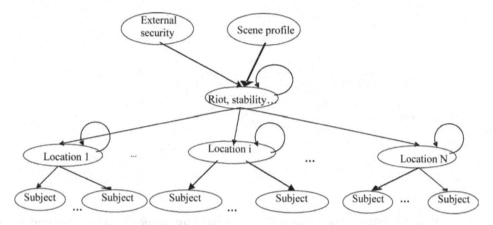

Compared with the applications in intelligent assistance systems and troubleshooting, security surveillance and event detection tasks have different features. Firstly, in the evidence collection, the sensor nodes are turned on and the belief is updated constantly. This continues until the confidence about certain hypothesis is strong enough and response needs to be taken for the confirmed hypothesis. Secondly due to the constant updating and monitoring mechanism, in many cases, the constraints limit all sensors from being fully engaged and thus an active strategy has to be sought. The active strategy selectively turns on the sensor that has the potential to provide the most significant evidence regarding the hypothesis.

BN and DBN models are competent for prediction of future development based on current system status and inference about causes and reasons from observable information. Both of them are the generic tasks required by the surveillance applications in homeland security. In such security applications, the hypothesis could be about different safety and security event types. Therefore, a higher-level model could be built up that incorporates the beliefs about individual subjects at different locations, and other information such as the current external security level and the classification of monitored scene or facility. It is

illustrated in Figure 3. The high level hypothesis in this model could be the danger or stability that leads to more or specific hypotheses like riot, explosion events, "mole" activity, and so on. Thus the models at individual and aggregate layers can create a hierarchical structure. Each individual subject node can be a "Context-Affective State-Profile-Observation" model as mentioned previously. One interesting issue in this higher-level model is how to configure the model to accommodate the varied number of individual nodes.

EXPERIMENTATION

We have evaluated the mental state detection model using both simulated and real data. For this study on inference degradation, the simulated experimentation detects whether a computer operator is among three mental states: "fatigue," "nervousness" and "confusion", using various visual cues. Figure 4 shows the DBN model we used. Table 1 summarizes the discrete variables and their states used in the experimentation. We use three separate hypothesis nodes for the three mental states because we do not require that these states are exclusive from each other in presence. The implementation of DBN is in MATLAB using

Figure 4. The DBN network structure used in experimentation, which uses five visual cues and direct query to assess three mental states

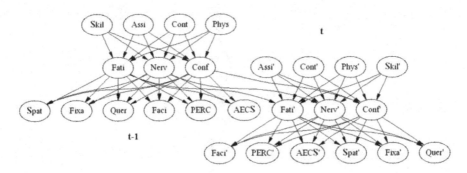

the BNT toolkit (Murphy, 2001). The inference algorithm we use is the junction tree engine.

Most probability parameters in the DBN were specified subjectively in the experimentation here while it shows similar results in other experiments that apply randomly generated parameters. In particular, the prior probabilities of all the three mental state nodes are set to (0.5, 0.5). The transitional probabilities between mental states in two consecutive time slices are specified accordingly. For example, the transitional probability between the same states of two slices, e.g., "positive" to "positive" for fatigue, is high, if we consider a user's mental state remain relatively stable. For transient mental states such as "confusion", which may come and go quickly, the transitional probability may be lower. The transitional probability between opposite states, "positive" to "negative"

Table 1. Variables and their states used in the evaluation model

Component	Variables	States	Description
Assistance	Assistance	null/warning/emphasis/simplification	
Context	Context	complex/simple	The surrounding environment of the subject.
Profile	Physical condition	strong/weak	Physical condition of the subject.
	Skill	strong/weak	Computer skill of the subject.
Mental states	Fatigue	positive/negative	
	Nervous	positive/negative	
	Confusion	positive/negative	
Sensor	Facial expression	neutral, happiness, sadness, anger, surprise, disgust, fear	Expressions from the FACS system. (1)
	Eyelid PERCLOS	high/normal/low	Percentage of eyelid closure over time. (2)
	Eyelid AECS	fast/normal/slow	Average eye closure/open speed over time. (3)
	Gaze spatial distribution	high/even/low	The ratio of gaze fixations on computer to gaze fixations outside computer over time. (4)
	Gaze fixation ratio	high/even/low	The ratio of gaze fixation to saccade eye movement over time. (5)
	Query	fatigued/confused/no	Answers to direct questioning in the form "are you __?" among "fatigued, confused, comfortable." (6)

or "negative" to "positive," is much lower correspondingly for a mental state node. In our experimentation, the transitional probability between the same states of "fatigue" is 0.9, while it is 0.85 for the other two mental states. Other conditional probability values are obtained subjectively in a similar fashion.

Experimental Scenarios, Settings and Data

In active fusion, the sensor costs are initially set to zero in active fusion, i.e., α is 1 in equation 5. Data for different mental state scenarios ("fatigue," "nervousness," "confusion" and "normal") were synthetically generated. For scenario, we first configure the corresponding mental hypothesis node to its desired state with certain probability. And then we perform a forward propagation to determine the probability distribution for each sensor in this model. For example, for the scenario where the subject is fatigued, the "fatigue" node is instantiated with a 99% probability for the positive state and 1% for its negative state; in the meanwhile the probabilities for the positive states of "nervousness" and "confusion" are set to 1% and negative states 99% respectively. After the forward propagation of beliefs from the mental state nodes to the sensor nodes, each sensor has

a probability distribution over its states. Then in the generated data of each scenario, each sensor turns out the state of the highest probability, the state most indicative of the underlying mental status. In other words, such sensory channel could always catch the most likely expression from the underlying mental status.

Experiment Results Analysis

We use the active fusion strategy choosing one or two sensors for the three "mental" scenarios, i.e., "fatigue," "nervousness" and "confusion," and the "normal" scenario, fed with the data generated as in the above to instantiate the selected sensor in each time slice. When we choose two sensors, the top two sensors in utility ranking are selected. The posterior probability for the positive state of each affect variable in each time slice is recorded. Thereafter, we call this probability the belief of the corresponding affective state, e.g., the belief of "fatigue." This belief and the information entropy associated with the probability distribution are the measures in evaluating various settings.

The performance comparison of active and passive fusions is in Figure 5 and Figure 6. The sensors are selected randomly or fixed sensors are selected in passive fusion. As the curves show, active fusion detects the underlying status of the

Figure 5. Passive fusion with random sensor selection versus active fusion, with two sensors activated

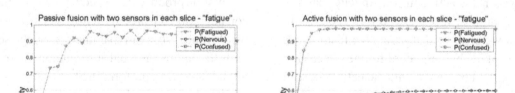

Figure 6. Active fusion versus passive fusion, with one sensor activated, where the passive fusion selects a fixed sensor of visual sensors 1 to 5 respectively for the five curves

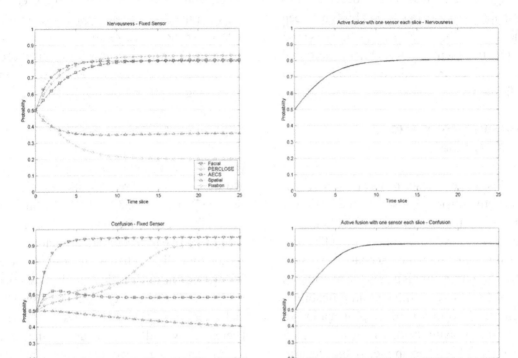

subject more quickly. From other results, we can generalize that the active information fusion can produce better performance in terms of fusion accuracy and the speed to distinguish out the underlying affective state. Please refer to (Li & Ji, 2005) for more detailed discussion on this.

However this active fusion strategy may not generate the best inference performance. From Figure 6 we observe that the active fusion does not give out the highest belief for the underlying mental state compared with selecting certain sensor in passive fusion. We could examine this more clearly in Figure 7 for the active fusion with/out sensor costs. Because of the different sensor costs, the belief curves differ from each other when different sensor sequences are chosen. The result with different sensor cost is better, yielding higher 'fatigue' beliefs. And when we

compare the results of using one sensor in Figure 6 and Figure 7, and two sensors in Figure 5, we can easily see that the result of two sensors outperforms that of one sensor. This means that the active fusion may converge to a belief value not the best. Simply to put it, the mutual information calculation produces an expected score taking into consideration the probability of evidence and the whole model structure/parameters. So the sensor with the highest mutual information score may not be the one to perform the best.

We observe clearly the degradation problem by examining the sensor sequence in active fusion with and without sensor costs, as shown in table 2. Active fusion selects the sensor with the highest utility in each time slice. Because the way we assign the initial beliefs in the hypothesis nodes, the first sensor selected for all scenarios are all

Figure 7. The belief curves for "fatigue" scenario, where different sensor costs change the sensor selection sequence in active fusion

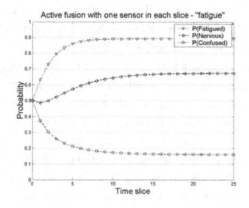
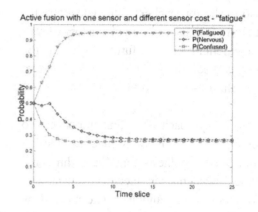

the same, i.e. "AECS" (sensor 3). Subsequently, with the change of mental hypothesis beliefs after different sensor evidence input is fed into the Bayesian model, different sensors may be selected, based on the new calculated utility values. However, we notice that not all sensors are used in the whole fusion process. Specifically only sensors 2 (PERCLOS), 3 (AECS) and 5 (gaze fixation ratio) are ever selected in all scenarios. We also notice that in the late fusion stage, the sensor sequence is fixed, with certain sensors selected repeatedly. Therefore, the inferred belief converges quickly to certain value, which may not be the best that we can achieve.

IMPROVE THE ACTIVE FUSION STRATEGY

The active fusion strategy discussed in this article tends to favor certain sensors especially at the late stage of the fusion process. From the way calculating the expected sensor utility, it is determined by the structure and parameter of the model. Especially if the conditional probability table has very uneven entries for configurations of parent node states for certain sensors, some sensors tend to yield higher mutual information scores than others. The stabilization of the hypothesis state beliefs over the fusion can further deteriorate this problem. To counter the effect of

Table 2. Sensor sequences in active fusion, where one sensor is selected in each time slice, with (a) no sensor cost and (b) higher cost for sensors with higher mutual information value

Time slice	Fatigued (a)	Fatigued (b)	Nervous (a)	Nervous (b)	Confused (a)	Confused (b)	Normal (a)	Normal (b)
1	3	3	3	3	3	3	3	3
2	3	3	3	3	2	2	2	2
3	3	5	3	3	2	2	5	5
...	...	...	...	...	...	...	...	...
13	3	5	3	3	2	2	5	5
14	3	5	3	2	2	2	2	2
...	...	...	...	...	...	...	...	...
25	3	5	3	2	2	2	5	5

degradation due to repeated sensor sequence, we could incorporate different approaches in choosing sensors. The approaches to alleviate inference degradation are to incorporate the history of sensor engagement in selecting future sensors, in the following two solutions. We briefly discuss two possible solutions in the following.

- "Forget" approach - The first approach is to forget the previous knowledge, i.e. the accumulated hypothesis belief here, through a "reset" mechanism in selection management. We could use a calibration-like method by requiring, at some time instance, all sensors should be activated together or sequentially to incorporate as much as possible heterogeneous information that the system can yield.
- "Remember" approach - In the second approach, we record and utilize the knowledge about selection history of the active fusion process, to penalize those sensors that have been recently selected intensively. For example, the utility of a sensor can decrease over time when it is more often selected than the others. Such history information can be incorporated into the utility calculation in the form of certain decay function.

In this study we apply a simple "remember" approach by maintaining a "taboo" list that contains the sensors that should be excluded from current selection. This taboo list has only one parameter, i.e., the length or the number of entries. A list length of 1 means that this taboo list contains only one entry at any time, which is the sensor selected in the most recent time slice. We examine the effect of such taboo list in experimentation.

In Figure 8, we compare the information entropy of hypothesis state belief distribution during active fusion using a taboo list of length 1 and in the setting without the taboo list. We plot the difference of them by subtracting the information entropy with taboo list from that without taboo list of the underlying mental state for the three "mental" scenarios. We observe that such taboo list improves the performance of "fatigue" and "nervousness" scenarios in late fusion stages. The entropy of active fusion with taboo list is less than the active fusion without it, resulting in data points with positive difference values. This means that the hypothesis state is clearer with this taboo list. However, this figure also shows higher uncertainty for "confusion" scenario from the beginning. Thus, rather than we conclude the effect of such a way using utilization history of

Figure 8. The difference between information entropies of the underlying affect in each "mental" scenario, for active fusion settings with and without taboo list

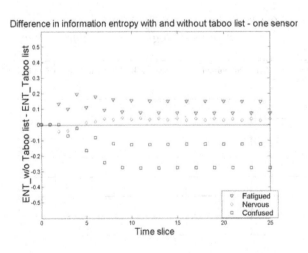

sensors, an advice of delicate deployment is more important for this method to alleviate the inference degradation.

FURTHER DISCUSSION AND CONCLUSION

Inference degradation shows in a special situation the conflict between active fusion and use of multiple sensor channels. In active fusion, due to the chosen mutual information definition, and if the conditional probability table has very uneven entries for configurations of parent node states in the Bayesian model, some sensors tend to yield higher mutual information scores than others. Then the fusion favors a particular set of sensors. This tendency intensifies as time passes by because the change in the hypothesis state beliefs becomes less and less, as observed from the implementation. This is on one hand understandable since our objective in active fusion is to seek the sensor, which could most efficiently distinguish the various hypotheses to support faster decision making. On the other hand, the situation that a small set of sensors dominate the selection depresses the advantage of fusing multi-modal information from multiple sensors for better accuracy and robustness. Furthermore, the superiority of these sensors in mutual information scores comes partially from using the expected potential. In expected potential (utility) calculation, all possible states of a sensor are inspected and the whole network structure and parameters impacts the utility value largely. In this sense, such criterion has bias to certain sensors in the selection process. To reduce the inference degradation effect, mutual information should not be the only factor in determining the benefit of sensor engagement.

The fundamental question regarding inference degradation is about the confliction between the active selection of sensors and the ultimate goal of multi-sensor fusion. The root cause of this phenomenon stays with the expected utility calculation and the convergence of beliefs in a DBN over time. This is a universal issue in active information fusion although "long term" optimization strategy might do better than a "myopia" strategy analyzed here. We use dynamic Bayesian networks but other models such as POMDP (partially observable Markov decision process) model can move into the same dilemma if the root cause is not correctly handled. In future study, the analysis of sensor noise and correlation will also contribute to the analysis.

Inference degradation may plague active fusion in many information integration applications. This study is just a wake-up call to such problems when applying active selection strategy. As the starting point, we try to tackle this problem with a simple setting and analytic and experimental analysis, as well as potential counter measures. Further investigation into the cause and mechanism of this problem and better strategy that dynamically adapts to the fusion process will greatly contribute to relevant research areas.

REFERENCES

Ball, G., & Breese, J. (2000). Emotion and personality in a conversational agent. *Embodied Conversational Agents* (pp. 189-218). Cambridge, MA: MIT Press.

Cohen, I., Garg, A., & Huang, T. S. (2000). *Emotion recognition from facial expressions using multilevel-HMM*. Paper presented at the 2000 NIPS Workshop on Affective Computing. Denver, Colorado.

Conati, C. (2002). Probabilistic assessment of user's emotions in educational games. *Applied Artificial Intelligence, 16*(7-8), 555–575. doi:10.1080/08839510290030390

Duric, Z., Gray, W., Heishman, R., Li, F., Rosenfield, A., & Schoelles, M. J. (2002). Integrating perceptual and cognitive modeling for adaptive and intelligent human-computer interaction. *Proceedings of the IEEE, 90*(7), 1272–1289. doi:10.1109/JPROC.2002.801449

Hall, D. L., & McMullen, A. H. (2004). *Mathematical techniques in multisensor data fusion.* Norwood, MA: Artech House.

Heckerman, D., Breese, J., & Rommels, K. (1996). Decision-theoretic: Troubleshooting. *Communications of the ACM, 38*(3), 49–57. doi:10.1145/203330.203341

Horvitz, E., Breese, J., Heckerman, D., Hovel, D., & Rommelse, K. (1998). The Lumiere Project: Bayesian user modeling for inferring the goals and needs of software users. In *Proceedings of the Fourteenth Conference on Uncertainty in Artificial Intelligence* (pp. 256-265). San Francisco: Morgan Kaufmann.

Horvitz, E., & Paek, T. (1999). A computational architecture for conversation. In *Proc. of the Seventh International Conference on User Modeling* (pp. 201-210). New York: Springer-Verlag.

Horvitz, E., & Paek, T. (2000). *DeepListener: Harnessing expected utility to guide clarification dialog in spoken language systems.* Paper presented at the 6th International Conference on Spoken Language Processing, Beijing.

Hudlicka, E., & McNeese, M. D. (2002). Assessment of user affective and belief states for interface adaptation: Application to an Air Force pilot task. *User Modeling and User-Adapted Interaction, 12,* 1–47. doi:10.1023/A:1013337427135

Jameson, A. (1996). Numerical uncertainty management in user and student modeling: An overview of systems and issues. *User Modeling and User-Adapted Interaction, 5,* 193–251. doi:10.1007/BF01126111

Jensen, F. V. (2001). *Bayesian networks and decision graphs.* New York: Springer.

Klein, L.A. (2004). *Sensor and data fusion: A tool for information assessment and decision making.* SPIE Press Monograph, PM138.

Langseth, H., & Jensen, F. V. (2003). Decision theoretic troubleshooting of coherent systems. *Reliability Engineering & System Safety, 80*(1), 49–61. doi:10.1016/S0951-8320(02)00202-8

Li, X., & Chandra, C. (2008). Toward a secure supply chain: A system's perspective. *Human Systems Management, 27*(1), 73–86.

Li, X., Chandra, C., & Shiau, J.-Y. (2009). Developing security taxonomy and model for security centric supply chain management. *International Journal of Manufacturing Technology and Management, 17*(1/2), 184–212. doi:10.1504/IJMTM.2009.023785

Li, X., & Ji, Q. (2005). Active affective state detection and user assistance with dynamic Bayesian networks. *IEEE Transactions on Systems, Man, and Cybernetics-Part A, 35*(1), 93–105. doi:10.1109/TSMCA.2004.838454

Mackay, D. (2003). *Information theory, inference, and learning algorithms.* Cambridge, UK: Cambridge University Press.

Murphy, K. (2001) The Bayes Net Toolbox for Matlab. *Computing Science and Statistics, 33.*

Pearl, J. (1988). *Probabilistic reasoning in intelligent systems: Networks of plausible inference.* San Mateo, CA: Morgan Kaufmann.

Picard, R. (1997). *Affective computing.* Cambridge, MA: MIT Press.

Salvucci, D. D., Boer, E. R., & Liu, A. (2001). Toward an integrated model of driver behavior in a cognitive architecture. *Transportation Research Record,* 1779.

Section 2
Semantic Technologies
and Applications

Chapter 7
Agent–Based Semantic Interoperability of Geo–Services

Iftikhar U. Sikder
Cleveland State University, USA

Santosh K. Misra
Cleveland State University, USA

ABSTRACT

This chapter proposes a multi-agent based framework that allows multiple data sources and models to be semantically integrated for spatial modeling in business processing. The authros introduce a multi-agent system (OSIRIS – Ontology-based Spatial Information and Resource Integration Services) to semantically interoperate complex spatial services and integrate them in a meaningful composition. The advantage of using multi-agent collaboration in OSIRIS is that it obviates the need for end-user analysts to be able to decompose a problem domain to subproblems or to map different models according to what they actually mean. The authors also illustrate a multi-agent interaction scenario for collaborative modeling of spatial applications using the proposed custom feature of OSIRIS using Description Logics. The system illustrates an application of domain ontology of urban environmental hydrology and evaluation of decision maker's consequences of land use changes. In e-government context, the proposed OSIRIS framework works as semantic layer for one stop geospatial portal.

INTRODUCTION

With the growth of Internet, there is an increasing demand for location specific data and analytical solutions requiring Geographic Information System (GIS), to locate and integrate multiple databases. This, in turn, requires federal, state and local government agencies to develop capabilities so that their data can interoperate. For example, a real estate entrepreneur, looking for a suitable location for a new business, would require data that combines GIS data with that of the local government's zoning and tax incentive areas. Home owners and home buyers, looking for information about environmental hazards, can use E-MAPS that combine data from several sources including the EPA's environmental data, and the HUD's (Department of Housing and Urban Development) housing community programs

DOI: 10.4018/978-1-60566-970-0.ch013

(GAO, 2003). Similarly, a water/sewer storm water utility company evaluating the feasibility of a new project to expand the existing infrastructures in mountain areas may need information about geomorphologic formations and associated potential landslide risk from the local and federal government databases.

In an e-Government environment, simple transactions can require interactions among multiple resources possibly from different entities within the government, and meaningful understanding of system architectures and the service compositions. Interagency transactions become simple if the agencies involved in a transaction have homogeneous representation structures as well as the same discourse domain (Malucelli, Palzer, & Oliveira, 2006). A geospatial application can use business services with relative ease if it can understand another application' service descriptions and representations of workflows and information flows within and across organizations. However, these representations become complicated when one needs to embed complex data structures and models into an application. For instance, suppose we are interested in a mobile commerce application that would provide geospatial information as a prelude to completing a business transaction. The transaction protocol for such an application would require access to and representation of geographic data and models. These models themselves may require chaining of multiple services that depend on service level description of geo-processing models, spatial geometries, spatial analysis and implementation logic. Typical query such as "Find the nearest Italian restaurant along the highway" could possibly be answered by chaining multiple services such as geocoding points of interest, integrating transport networks, creating dynamic segmentation of network, providing routing network, rendering cartographic information and possibly converting text to voice. It is possible to envision integration and chaining of services to provide higher levels of functionality if such services are distributed all over the enterprise

and are accessible in a uniform standard manner. (Peng & Tsou, 2003).

This paper proposes a framework for a semantic-level communication between geo-spatial services in business processes and application models. The paper presents an overview of interoperability efforts with specific reference to geo-spatial databases and application models and reviews the feasibility of an ontology-based spatial resource integration to combine the core spatial reasoning with domain-specific application models. Existing industry standards and practices in geo-spatial interoperability are identified. This is followed by a discussion of the role of ontology in explicating the implicit semantics of spatial data models and the need for formalism in descriptions of spatial categories. Use of markup languages for spatial resource description and the tagging of spatial ontology are illustrated. Finally, a multi-agent based architecture (OSIRIS-Ontology-Based Spatial Information and Resource Integration Services) for semantic interoperability of spatial data sets and models is proposed. The architecture is illustrated using an application model that uses domain ontology of urban environmental hydrology

GIS SERVICES IN THE FRAMEWORK OF E-GOVERNMENT

The National Spatial Data Infrastructure (NSDI) seeks to build an organizational and virtual network to promote the sharing of spatial data among federal, state, regional, and local government agencies and the private sector. The Federal Geographic Data Committee (FGDC) (FGDC, 2009) is tasked to develop a spatial data and metadata standard as well as to create data clearinghouse. FGDC is also responsible for coordinating the development of a "framework" data (Wayne, 2005). Similar initiatives have been taken by European communities for developing a spatial Data Infrastructure (SDI) (Craglla & Signoretta, 2000). In Europe, an infrastructure for spatial information in Europe (INSPIRE) has been established, which is built on built on top of national spatial information infrastructures(Annoni et al.,2008). The U.S. Department of Homeland Security (DHS) Geospatial Data Model also covers a broad number of themes, and spatial data-model. Parts of the DHS are based on the FGDC Framework Data Content Standard, which depends on the ISO TC211 feature model upper-level ontology (DHS, 2009).

The application of Web services in geospatial service management offers an opportunity towards the local autonomy of databases. Web services can be used to dynamically query various GIS layers while maintaining local agency level independence in a distributed environment. From an organizational point of view, this may be very appealing. Local governments, such as counties can independently collect and manage data and still integrate information and services using Web services. A client of the local government entity, for example a transportation company, can directly access the government's base map without maintaining its own dataset. With appropriate permissions, a client can also update the government's dataset from the client's own record. An extended collaboration and partnership between multiple agencies and clients using Web Services can provide opportunity to interoperate through open interfaces and communication protocols. Typical geo-processing services may include data management tools like projection and transformation, topology manipulation, indexing and spatial join.

The interoperability issue in the context of e-Government services is not limited to technical issues such as linking computer networks. There is a fundamental requirement to share and re-use knowledge networks and reorganize administrative processes to better support the services themselves. The key areas of interoperability in need of consideration when implementing e-Government services include the organizational, semantic and technical issues(CEC, 2003, 2006).

At the semantic level, there is an imperative that the meaning of the information exchanged is not lost in the process of acquiring e-Government services from all levels of government. Thus semantic interoperability entails seamless integration of information and services from agencies at different levels whether they are local, regional, or national. This ensures organizational or local autonomy as well as global integration.

ONTOLOGY FOR SEMANTIC INTEROPERABILITY

The objective of semantic interoperability is to be able to attach meaning to information entities or services and thereby draw inferences from the semantic annotation. In spatial semantic interoperability, the integration goes beyond the process of data translation or the conversion of geometric primitives (Fallahia et al., 2008; Kuhn, 2005). The semantic interoperability eventually boils down to the problem of the identification of semantically similar objects that belong to different databases and the resolution of their semantic differences (Kashyap & Sheth, 1996; Tanasescu, 2007). The use of an ontology (Guarino & Giaretta, 1995) as a framework for defining similarity among objects has the benefit of a formal definition for concepts in different metadata, a definition that could be used to define axioms for semantic translation between ontologies. The term "Ontology" has its root in the philosophical literature as the study of being. In the domain of information systems and AI, ontology has a somewhat different connotation as an "explicit specification of a conceptualization" (Gruber, 1993) (Farquhar, Fikes, & Rice, 1996) and provides a more pragmatic definition: Ontologies are explicit specifications of domain conceptualization names and describe the entities that may exist in that domain and relationships among those entities. In other words, the tacit and implicit knowledge hidden in a particular domain is explicitly conceptualized in ontology (Guarino,

1997). Ontology is considered as a logical theory accounting for the intended meaning of a formal vocabulary, while conceptualizations are the formal structures of reality as perceived and organized by an agent. In spatial ontology, although agents may have a shared vocabulary capable of establishing relationships, or mapping between corresponding instances, the conceptualization of space as "object-based" and "field-based" may be still implicit among agents.

Although spatial ontology is an established concept, and is capable of providing a naturalistic representation of spatial objects, in the sense of "Naive Geography"(Egenhofer & Mark, 1995), it is still a complex specification to be realized. Spatial semantic interoperability goes beyond simple data translation or the conversion of geometric primitives based on a-priori ontology. Classical ontology, offering limited expression of spatial relations to simulate spatial processes can be used to express spatially complex phenomena, is not well understood. Specifically, such explication requires an understanding of Mereology and Mereotopology (Smith, 1996). The study of parts and boundaries of the whole is an important aspect of representing the multiple constituents of a complex spatial object in relation to adjacency, containment, selection, or the separateness of constituent parts. Ontology in this sense needs also to be viewed as a mediator for knowledge exchange, to build a business application that can enable data integration and avoid problems such as inconsistency between ad-hoc ontologies which might be built into the system (Fonseca & Egenhofer, 1999). This approach to ontology in geo-spatial service management would address issues concerning knowledge sharing by creating components from ontology in an object-oriented fashion, using classical object-oriented concepts such as multiple inheritances. Thus, spatial ontology should allow overcoming the implicit semantics of apparently disparate spatial data models by providing a higher-level description to prepare a cognitive correspondence among multiple com-ponents. Such ontology is relevant not only for spatial data models to unravel the representational scheme of topological part-and-whole dichotomy but also for the application models of GIS where certain spatial operators (e.g., overlay, buffer or interpolation etc.) must be executed in specific sequences to reach a goal. Spatial application developers should be able to combine classes from diverse ontologies and create new classes that represent the user needs. For example, a class that represents a land parcel for a specific city can be built from land parcel components specified in urban ontology, from polygons specified in geometry ontology and from crisp boundary specifications in boundary ontology (Fonseca & Egenhofer, 1999).

ONTOLOGY-BASED SPATIAL RESOURCES INTEGRATION SERVICES (OSIRIS)

So far, we have discussed the feasibility of an ontology-based spatial resource integration that combines the core spatial reasoning with spatial data models and domain specific application models. We have noted that the application of ontology-based semantic mediation can lead to model integration. In this section, we describe our proposed OSIRIS architecture that involves different levels of ontology to create meta-models, especially for spatial services. In addition, we demonstrate a specialized prototype for decision making in spatial planning in a multi-agent environment. Later, we use the OSIRIS framework to illustrate the collaborative aspect of multi-agent interaction to solve complex spatial problems. The advantage of using multi-agent collaboration in OSIRIS is that it obviates the need for end-user analysts to be able to decompose a problem to subproblems or to map different models according to what they actually mean. The proposed approach provides a means for communicating different models in a common semantic framework without the loss of native autonomy. Having a comprehensive source description of different modeling representation has a unique advantage in understanding how the models are organized in terms of interconnection of schema and scope.

Multi-Agent Agent Architecture of OSIRIS

The OSIRIS architecture (figure 1) is composed of several integrated components. The model manager is in charge of providing the overall coordination of the agents by acting as a mediator for instantiating an appropriate model through the Ontology Agent. It also maintains a catalog of models and ontological semantics with the help of ontology agents. The model manager exposes the model schema to the ontology agent to be used in response to specific user request. Using the encapsulated description of the model from the ontology agent, the model manager creates appropriate instances. The integration of data and corresponding models is coordinated by the model manager which ensures a proper correspondence through the ontology agent and resolves any disagreements between data and models. Through the interaction of ontology agent and user interface agent, the model manager composes services or custom models from discrete services to produce a meaningful interconnection among them.

OSIRIS architecture incorporates spatial and non-spatial databases as well as a collection of application models (GIS resources). A wrapper is used to encapsulate application models as well as the database. The wrapper provides a comprehensive description of model parameters, scope, input/ output options, limitations, context, method of use, and other necessary semantics. Encapsulation agents encapsulate models and data to create meta-models and created interfaces necessary for the wrapper object. Meta-models may include legacy models, domain models, generic procedures or high-level schema of interconnected data. Encapsulation agents process queries originating from ontology agents and retrieve information back to

the system. In addition, these agents translate query to the local query language, process the query in a local system and then forward query results to the ontology agent. These descriptions could be encoded in the extended RDF or OWL-enabled ontology. Such descriptions promote consistency, exchangeability and reuse of modules through the shared repositories in a distributed environment. Above the communication layer of the OSIRIS are two components which ensure the consistent construction of the agent platform. The Internal Platform Message Transport (IPMT) provides a message routing service for agents in this particular platform. The IPMT can use either OMG's IIOP (Internet Inter-ORB Protocol) or HTTP protocol. The Agent Platform Security Manager (APSM) is responsible for managing the agent's transport level security by creating an audit log.

Models and Databases

The OSIRIS framework relies on a repository of models and databases. The choice of models and data set would depend on the type of system being considered in a particular case. For example, a system for studying land slide hazard may need composite of several application models, algorithms including geoprocessing algorithms, discrete event simulation models and non-linear dynamic models for estimating rainfall runoff. In an e-Government system, the set of models and algorithms may include land use policies, zoning regulations, and economic development priorities. Encapsulation agent is responsible to provide appropriate wrapper around such models and make them available to an ontology agent for semantic annotation and thereby help create a meta model ontology. The creation of wrapper involves interaction with the Ontology Repository through the Ontology Agent to determine if an existing ontological specification is adequate; otherwise a new specification and taxonomy is created by the encapsulation agent and the specification is deposited in the Ontology Repository.

Figure 1. Multi-agent OSIRIS architecture

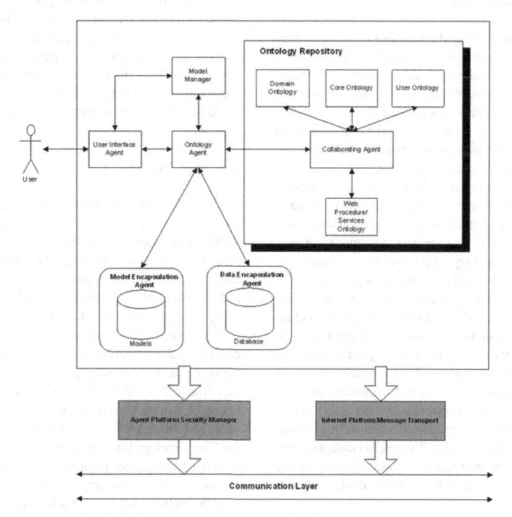

OSIRIS Model Manager

The model manager provides the overall coordination of the agents by acting as a mediator for instantiating an appropriate model corresponding to the meta-model ontology. It also maintains a catalog of models. The export model schema to be used in response to specific user request is exposed to model manager by an ontology agent. The integration of data and corresponding models is coordinated by the model manager which ensures a proper correspondence through the ontology agent and resolves any disagreements between data and models. The model manager composes services or custom models from discrete services to produce a meaningful interconnection among them.

A model manager can be divided into two-core components: a) Custom model manager and, b) Generic model manager. A custom model manager is designed to create and manage modules dynamically from core ontology and extended domain ontology while a generic model manager is used to integrate legacy models through encapsulated interfaces by maintaining reusable libraries of models. Generic model managers offer services to custom model managers as encapsulated methods and services of a particular class module and embed them in the model hierarchy.

Ontology Agent

An Ontology agent establishes correspondences and interrelations among different domain knowledge and data models and relations. It defines a common semantic framework and formalism to share data and models and identifies a set of modeling approaches and corresponding data sources to resolve semantic ambiguities. An ontology agent is responsible for ensuring the class consistency and implicit relationships of application models and data. It exposes higher level model schema of legacy models and native data structure to model manager and help generate meta-model catalog.

An ontology agent provides standardized descriptions of model constructs in conformity with ontological specifications. Its responsibility also includes ontology deployment, validation of specification leading to creation of new wrapper objects in the database, and updating the Ontology Repository. For example, consider an e-Government system that maintains databases regarding water/sewer stormwater utility. A network infrastructure provider company may need access to the existing Water Sewer database. This client's request can be realized by dynamically populating a template schema of water utilities data model.

The Ontology Agent populates the template schema from existing databases for which it receives the necessary request from the model manager or the User Interface Agent (UIA) of the OSIRIS. The template schema can be created if there exists a User Ontology matching the specific client's request. In case such a match is not available, the Ontology Agent can create a User Ontology through an interactive process between itself, the client, and the UIA. The Ontology Agent invokes the Model Manager to service the client request.

In the case of complex requests, the Ontology Agent invokes the services of Collaborative Agent to resolve ambiguities or semantic disagreement between domain ontologies and user ontologies.

Embedded within the Ontology Agent is a reasoning support engine. At the implementation level, it may include a reasoning engine like FaCT (I. Horrocks, 1998) system that can translate ontology into $\Sigma H I \Theta (\Delta)$ DL to indicate inconsistencies and implicit subsumptions. In addition, axioms could be added to make implicit subsumptions explicit.

Ontology Repository

The Ontology repository consists of i) Core ontology, ii) Domain ontology, iii) User ontology, and iv) Web procedure/services ontology. In general, these repositories contain a set of axioms (e.g., assertion of class subsumptions / equivalence), and taxonomic class hierarchies. All of these ontologies are strongly related to one another. The Core Ontology contains immutable and generic concepts and top-level categorical abstractions of physical relationships and corresponding semantic descriptions and axioms. For example, in the case of complex spatial data required for representing water and sewer network, it will be necessary to use Core Ontology that contain high-level definitions of spatial entities and geometric primitives. Domain Ontologies are generally associated with specific application domains such as Geographic Information Metadata-ISO 19115 (Islam, Bermudez, Beran, Fellah, & Piasecki, 2006) and Infrastructure Product Ontology (Osman & El-Diraby, 2006) . A domain model is incorporated into the Domain Ontology following the semantic structure of the core ontology.

In OSIRIS, Core ontology is related to the Domain Ontology to specify appropriate semantic characterization of the domain model. An example would be the relationship between the classes of core ontology and the classes of domain ontology that can be expressed using an user-defined semantics such as: equivalentClassOf (DomainClass, CoreClass) or aggregateClassOf (DomainClass, CoreClass). In specific cases, Core Ontology may include reusable UpperCyc

(OpenCyc, 2006) ontology which covers most of the top concepts applicable to the domain of e-Government. The class relationships allow generating ontology in a hierarchy with the child class having explicit attributes to specialize the parent classes. Thus the orthogonal property of ontology can be maintained by decomposing compound concepts into constituent parts. An Ontology Agent relies on web services and generic procedures to discover new services and modules. Web Procedure/Services Ontology manages this function by defining the levels of abstractions of external services and fitting them with the repository structure. At an implementation level, web services can be expressed with a Web Service Description Language (WSDL).

Ontology Collaboration Agent (OCA)

OCA is designed to assert inter-ontology relationships within ontology repository and compute class hierarchy/consistency. It merges multiple ontologies by mapping domain classes with core ontology and provides semantic agreement of user ontology with domain ontology. For example, a road network classification by water/sewer network authorities may not match with a specific domain of a user's ontologies. In such cases, the collaboration agent first tries to match the disparate schema by mapping individual road network classes with classes from core ontology. If the mapping does not result in consistent well-formed class hierarchy, the collaboration agent may proceed to modify user ontology through mediation of user interface agent and ontology agent. It also integrates specialized Web Procedure Services Ontology (WPSO) and provides web resources for custom model formulation. WPSO also includes a set of triggers that gets activated in the event of any change of web-service composition or changes in domain ontology. OCA also reacts to these changes and carries out necessary updates to user ontology.

User Interface Agent (UIA)

This component of OSIRIS is the primary intermediary between the system user and OSIRIS. It resolves ambiguities in the user expression in formulating structured requests through an interactive session using the user profile. The Ontology Agent collaborates with the UIA to develop modeling profiles of the user following user needs and strategies. Some of the tasks achieved through the interaction between the Ontology Agent and the UIA include the user modeling (Cali, Calvanese, Colucci, Noia, & Donini, 2004; Rich, 1989), identification of trends in user requests and extreme or unusual requests. Embedded within the UIA is a query formulation engine that has access to native data semantics of user profiles via Ontology Agent. Once the UIA completes the query formulation, the resultant query is parsed by the Model Manager for the identification of specific model or service as requested by the UIA, and finally validated by the user. The User Ontology in the Ontology Repository is updated through the interaction among UIA, Ontology Agent, and the Collaborating Agent. In the absence of the requested service in the OSIRIS' meta-model catalog, custom model is composed dynamically and validated by an interactive session involving the UIA and multiple agents in OSIRIS. The UIA also includes a set of triggers to respond to events such as changes of user ontology in ontology repository, and meta-model catalog updates. As a practical implementation issue, at the end of an interactive session, the UIA generates and updates log files of frequently requested services and creates corresponding index structure to facilitate faster retrieval of future request.

Agent Platform Security Manager

The Agent Platform Security Manager verifies inputs from ontology agents, and enforces compliance with underlying system security protocol. The nature of the compliance may differ based on the application domain. For example, the security standards specified by FIPA (FIPA, 2006) would be enforced by the security manager in an application involving landslide hazards.

Internet Platform Message Transport

The Internet Platform Message Transport is designed to transfer a message from one system to another. Such a transfer may involve technologies such as web services or CORBA. The intention of the OSIRIS model is to be a high level protocol that interacts with the underlying system's network.

Multi-Agent Collaboration: an Event Flow Scenario

In this section, we illustrate two different scenarios for processing user requests: composition of services using generic models, and custom models. A generic model can be created by means of searching the model catalog (see the description of Model Manager). Model Manager maintains reusable libraries of geo-processing models that can be integrated with legacy models through the

wrapper objects in the database. For example, in order to extend an existing water utility infrastructure, the local government agency would need to identify the optimum location and network of services matching those of its customers' locations. A user request for identifying location for the proposed water utility infrastructure would result in a service request to OSIRIS. The resolution of this request may consist of searching geocoded customer location (geocoding combines map information with street addresses to locate a point uniquely) and combining the search results with the gravity model (Haynes & Fotheringham, 1984) for location allocation. The OSIRIS can accomplish this task by initiating a series of message transports through inter-agent communication. Figure 2 illustrates a scenario where a generic model is formulated from the user's declarative request. A request for geocoding customer location is initiated by a series of message transports and the creation of the request object. While the Model Manager (MM) provides access to meta-model of geo-processing catalogue, the Ontology Agent (OA) and the Ontology Collaboration Agent (OCA) provide semantic sup-

Figure 2. Message sequence of agent interactions for composing generic procedures

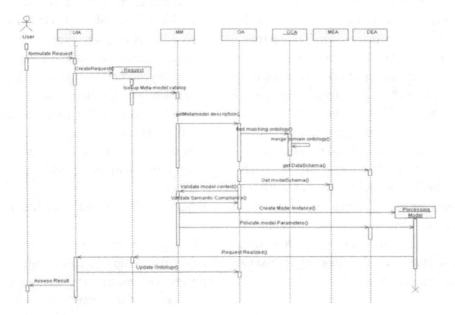

port to resolve semantic mismatch between user request and domain ontology. Additionally, the Data Encapsulation Agent (DEA) interprets the schema of existing spatial data and corresponding meta-data, and populates the instances in the parameters of processing model.

Unlike the generic model formulation, custom models are composed dynamically from core ontology and extended domain ontology. The composition process involves logical inferences from core ontology to generate generic procedures from domain ontology and WPSO (figure 3). The derivation of the logical inference is iterative and requires user feedback for semantic refinement of the model design. In the next section, we describe an example of custom model composition from axiomatic proposition in core ontology.

Composing Custom Models by Collaborative Modeling: Example of Logical Inference

The interaction of multi-agents in collaborative environments can lead to the solution of complex problems not otherwise amenable to analysis in a stand-alone system [43]. The custom model manager feature of OSIRIS exploits the interaction of multi-agents in a collaborative environment in modeling spatial applications. A simplified application scenario of OSIRIS for custom model management can be visualized in a spatial planning problem. Consider, for instance, an insurance company is interested in finding out the regions that are prone to landslides in the proposed extended water/sewer utility network. This problem can be addressed in two different ways. First, the domain expert model for the landslide hazard zone modeling (a domain model developed by Geomorphologists) can be identified by OSIRIS model manager as the candidate model to address the issue of landslide hazard. The model parameters, requirements, constraints, and schema can be described using Description Logics. This description would constitute a meta-model of the actual landslide model that eventually becomes the domain ontology for this particular problem. The model may require different input classes, e.g., 3D Digital Elevation Model (DEM), soil map,

Figure 3. Composing custom procedure through logical inference in OSIRIS agent interactions

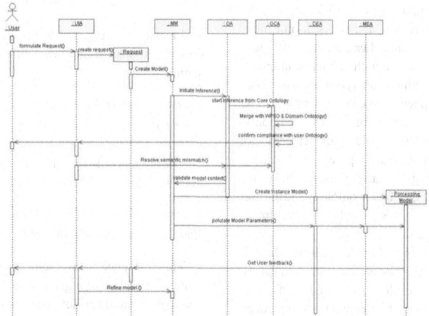

moisture index map, and satellite images. Once the processing of the available input is completed, output such as landslide risks and zonation can be produced.

Suppose the model server does not have access to the domain model for the landslide hazard zonation model. This scenario would invoke the custom modeling abilities of OSIRIS which then proceeds to answer the landslide query indirectly in some less rigorous way by using core ontology and user templates. Let us assume that the user input is only a DEM class. The system should be able to reason that the DEM class can be used to create a slope map class that would eventually identify the locations of highly steep areas that are likely to be landslide-prone. Creating a slope map from the DEM is a standard and simple GIS procedure and the system should have no problem converting the map to a slope map using standard functions from domain ontology. The core ontology should be able to infer that higher the slope, the greater is the probability of landslide and specifies to the model manager the requirements for generating the slope map. The common sense understandings are encoded and inferred from the knowledge of core ontology agent. This knowledge includes generic axioms and contexts such as rocks fall downward under gravity; rocks move faster as the slope increases; and rocks do not move in flat plains. The model can progressively lead to more sophistication with enhanced inference and reasoning. Since soil types are associated with landslide phenomena, the system may infer that it needs to create a soil class in addition to DEM and therefore, would begin searching for soil data before it actually processes the query. While developing the "custom" model, the system might "consult" the domain ontology and the user ontology to gain further "insight" to solve similar complex problem.

In the following example, consider the following 4 axioms: a plot is sameClassAs a parcel; landslide is the result of (or subClassOf) steep slope and high moisture content; and the slope

can be derived from DEM. Given a set of well-formed axioms, the semantics can be defined via a translation into an expressive Description Logic (DL) which is equivalent to *SHIQ* (**D**) DL (Ian Horrocks, Patel-Schneider, & Harmelen, 2003).

$$Plot \doteq Parcel$$

$$Landslide \sqsubseteq steepSlope \cap highMoisture$$
$$Slope \sqsubseteq \exists hasSlopefunction.DEM$$

Using multiple equality/inclusion axioms, one can derive following assertion.

$$steepPlot \doteq Plot \cap \exists hasHighval.Slope$$

$$moistPlot \doteq Plot \cap \exists hasHighval.Moisture$$

$$steepPlot \cap moistPlot$$

$$\doteq Plot \cap \exists hasHighval.Moisture$$
$$\cap \exists hasHighval.Slope$$

Transitive role of classes or causality can be captured as:

$$HeavyRain \sqsubseteq \exists causes.Moisture$$
$$Moisure \sqsubseteq \exists causes.Landslide$$
$$\Rightarrow HeavyRain \sqsubseteq \exists causes.Landslide$$

Inverse roles e.g., causes/causedBy relation provides similar to the power of abductive reasoning.

$$Moisture \cap \exists causedBy.HeavyRain \sqsubseteq Landslide$$
$$\Rightarrow HeavyRain \sqsubseteq \exists causes.Landslide$$

The inference also provides cardinality restrictions and adds consistency constraints.

$$RiskIndex \sqsubseteq \exists hasValue.(High \cap Low) \wedge \leq 1hasValue)$$
$$High \sqsubseteq \neg Low \Rightarrow HighLowRiskindex \sqsubseteq \bot$$

The inference allows one to express risk score of landslide of a given area from the core ontology. It should be noted that causal inference can be derived from the core as well as domain ontology of OSIRIS.

SEMANTIC MATCHING OF SPATIAL FEATURES IN OSIRIS

The relationship between domain ontology and core ontology in OSIRIS corresponds to the relationship between the concepts of specialization and generalization. Just as the RDF schemas allow the creation of subtypes using multiple inheritance properties like subClassOf or subPropertyOf, the domain classes can be derived from core classes or ontology. In a spatial context, by using GML's core schema, one can develop fundamental building blocks for features and feature geometry, and define application or domain schemas following RDF/DAML constraints. For example, we can define new feature types or collection types from gml:AbstractFeatureType or gml:AbstractFeatureCollection which could be real world categories such as "roads", or "bridges". A user-defined complex geometric feature can consist of many other geometric elements. Such schema can be enriched by DAML+OIL constraints. The DAML+OIL enabled spatial agent is capable of new classifications by inference and reasoning. Using GML's spatial primitives within RDF, a domain specific application schema can be expressed to describe the different associative, causal and functional relationships of the domain.

Suppose the water/sewer authority in an e-Government system defines a namespace <myDef:River> using GML's namespace and type hierarchy.

```
< -- xmlns:myDef="http://www.xyzcorp/ex-
ample.rdf -->
<myDef:River>
<gml:description> T1</gml:description>
<myDef:classification>water body</
myDef:classification>
```

```
<gml:CenterLineOf>
<gml:LineString srsName="GFD:987"/>
<gml:coordinate>0.00, 1000.0 1000.0,
0.0</gml:coordinate>
</gml:LineString>
</gml:CenterLineOf>
</myDef:River>
```

It is possible that there exists other definitions for the river class, say <usgs:River>, defied by some other agency such as USGS. The use of a namespace prefix <myDef:River> allows the user to specify the agent's domain, or to scale specific vocabularies which essentially differentiate other namespace of similar categories such as <usgs:River>. DAML allows constructs such as daml:equivalentTo or daml:samePropertyAs that can be used to inherit specific properties from existing type definitions and associated descriptions. Thus it is possible to have two distinct spatial objects, having two different application schemas, sharing the common geometric primitive of GML and the semantics of the two data sets from two different agencies. At the implementation level, this approach can be used to identify spatial features and objects in different web pages and to initiate spatial reasoning among disparate data sources. The serialized and machine-readable semantic descriptions, as supported by DAML, GML and other, provide a means for ontology agents to exchange spatial models and schema on the Web.

Domain Ontology for Spatial Application: An Example

Using features of the OSIRIS framework, we have developed domain ontology for urban environmental hydrology tightly coupled with a Web-based "What-if" scenario generator. The ontology expresses the widely used specification of a "non-point pollution model" or what is commonly known as "Simple Method" [41] for estimating surface runoff or pollutant load. The first step in markup of the domain components is to describe each constituent component of the pollution model. It consists of a declarative description of the model's properties. The objective is to model pollutant loads originating from different changes of land use category. Depending on the land use category, the planning authority classifies a certain number of zones. Zones are spatial as well as administrative features managed by an environmental agency in accordance with the environmental regulations. The definition of the organization (in this case-Environment and Conservation-and-Wildlife-Organizations) relevant to zonal planning is derived from another top level ontology namespace to ensure the semantic correspondence. Land use classes have essentially spatial features. A specific land use category can result in several "pollutant" types which are expressed as enumeration types - daml:one of element as a closed lists of the daml:collection parse type. Since the ontology is extensible, any new ontology component can be added to describe wider algorithm of the domain. An excerpt from an example of an urban hydrology developed using DAML is shown below.

```
<rdf:RDF
  xmlns:rdf ="http://www.
w3.org/1999/02/22-rdf-syntax-ns#"
  xmlns:daml="http://www.daml.
org/2001/03/daml+oil#"
  xmlns:rdfs="http://www.w3.org/TR/1999/
PR-rdf-schema-19990303#">
  xmlns="http://cis.csuohio.edu/daml/on-
tologies/Non-point-pollution#"
>
<daml:Ontology rdf:about="http://opengis.
net/gml/gml.rdfs#">
        <daml:versionInfo>$1.0</
daml:versionInfo>
        <rdfs:comment>An ontology for Non-
point Pollution modelling</rdfs:comment>
        <daml:imports rdf:resource="http://
www.daml.org/2001/03/daml+oil#"/>
        <daml:imports rdf:resource="http://
```

```
opengis.net/gml/gml.rdfs#"/>

</daml:Ontology>
<daml:Class rdf:ID="ManagementAgency">
  <rdfs:subClassOf rdf:resource="http://
www.daml.org/cgi-bin/hyperdaml?http://
opencyc.sourceforge.net/daml/
naics#Environment,-Conservation-and-Wild-
life-Organizations;813312"/>
    <rdfs:label>Urban Land Land management
Agency</rdfs:label>
  </daml:Class>
<rdfs:Class rdf:ID="Zone">
  <rdfs:subClassOf rdf:resource="http://
opengis.net/gml/gml.rdfs#Polygon"/>
    <rdfs:subClassOf>
    <daml:Restriction>
      <daml:onProperty
rdf:resource="#zoneID"/>
      <daml:toClass rdf:resource="http://
www.w3.org/2000/10/XMLSchema#string"/>
      <daml:maxcardinality>1</
daml:maxcardinality>
    </daml:Restriction>
    </rdfs:subClassOf>
  <rdfs:subclassOf>
  <daml:Restriction>
    <daml:onProperty rdf:resource="#envir
onmentalRegulation"/>
    <daml:toCalss rdf:resource="#Manageme
ntAgency"/>
  </daml:Restriction>
  </rdfs:subClassOf>
  <daml:DataProperty rdf:ID="environmental
Regulation">
<daml:DataProperty rdf:ID="#zoneID">
<rdfs:Class rdf:ID="LandUse">
  <rdfs:subClassOf rdf:resource="Zone">
    <rdfs:subClassOf>
    <daml:Restriction>
    <rdfs:domain rdf:resource="#LandUse"/>
  <daml:onProperty rdf:resource="#name">
<daml:toClass rdf:resource="http://www.
w3.org/2000/10/XMLSchema#string"/>
    <daml:maxcardinality>1</
```

```
daml:maxcardinality>
  </rdfs:subClassOf>
 </daml:Restriction>
<rdfs:subClassOf>
    <daml:Restriction>
      <daml:onProperty
rdf:resource="#pollutant"/>
        <daml:toClass
rdf:resource="#Pollutant"/>
    <daml:Maxcardinality>1</
daml:Maxcardinality>
      </daml:Restriction>
  </rdfs:subClassOf>
<daml:DatatypeProperty
rdf:ID="LandUseID">
<daml:toClass rdf:resource="http://www.
w3.org/2000/10/XMLSchema#string"/>
<rdfs:range rdf:resource="http://
www.w3.org/2000/10/
XMLSchema#nonNegativeInteger"/>
<rdf:type rdf:resource="http://www.
w3.org/2001/10/daml+oil#UniqueProperty"/>
</daml:DatatypeProperty>
<rdfs:Class rdf:ID="Pollutant">
  <daml:unionOf rdf:parseType="daml:coll
ection">
    <Pollutant rdf:ID="BOD"/>
    <Pollutant rdf:ID="TotalNitrogen"/>
    <Pollutant
rdf:ID="TotalPhosphorous"/>
  </daml:unionOf>
</rdfs:Class>
<daml:DatatypeProperty
rdf:ID="pollutant">
<.....X.......>
```

The full XML serialization is not shown here due to space limitations. In the above example, the daml:collection represents a DAML+OIL extension of RDF to provide a "shorthand" representation of structured list that defines triples. It should be noted that the daml:Class rdf:ID="ManagementAgency" is derived from an external URI of Opencyc (OpenCyc, 2006) to

illustrate inheritance from a generic class. Using the set of axioms provided by DAML+OIL, one can assert class subsumption, equivalence of class or property, and various constructors such as intersectionOf, and Maxcardinality to create complex semantic constraints. An intelligent agent with an inference engine can easily deduce new knowledge about the environment from the ontology.

Explorative Land Use Change Analysis: Simulations of Multi-agent Interaction

Given ontology, multiple agents can interact meaningfully. The following example illustrates an agent's understanding of the domain model that can be used to simulate different disicion scenarios visualized by map rendering. We have developed a "what-if" type of pollution simulation model in response to the decision of changing land use from one category to another category (see figure 4). This model can be used to simulate the consequence of an agent's decision, when for example; an agent changes a certain category of land use from "vacant" to "landfill". The result is a corresponding increase or decrease in pollution content. Every request to change in land use type results in recalculation of the mass export of pollutant and corresponding statistics. The resulting pollution map can be visualized with multiple theme overlay. The system logs individual user's preferences to input into mediating algorithm to resolve conflict among user preferences of land use choice. Built on top of the ESRI's ArcIMS, the system uses ArcXML (native XML encoding of spatial object) to communicate between the custom middleware and the Web mapping server. The services offered by the Web Mapping Server are similar to the requirements of OGC's implementation specification for a Web map service (WMS).

The map server contains registered model components which are instantiated following a request from an agent. The server side application processes the agent's request and makes necessary updates in the database to reflect the corresponding changes of the pollutant coefficients. Every request to change in land use type results in recalculation of the mass export of pollutants and corresponding statistics. The processed result is then sent back to the Web server and then to the client agents. For a given planning zone the environmental regulation of land use constraints is stipulated by the management agency. The domain ontology includes several such constraints:

Zone (low_density_residential) →PermittedLandUseCategory(multifamily_dwelling)

$\forall x,y \exists d$ HighDensityResZone$(x)^{\wedge}$PreservationZone$(y)\rightarrow$MinDistApart$((x,y),d)$

Similarly, other spatial contiguity constraints or topologic constraints can be expressed in domain ontology in relation to the neighboring zone or land use. The system provides cartographic rendering options for typical mapping manipulation procedures such as selecting and identifying a feature, visual queries, rendering legends corresponding to feature types (classification for both continuous and unique data type), multiple themes, and overlays. The solution space of the explorative scenario generated by the simulation process can be further resolved using different a mediation algorithm in an evolutionary process. For instance, we can use genetic algorithms to construct links between an agent's template and a possible solution space and let the system evolve until a mutually acceptable solution converges.

CONCLUSION

In this paper, we have demonstrated how the use of semantic reasoning can be used to aggregate and reason over geographic features taken from multiple sources. Using a multi-agent paradigm, we have demonstrated a promising direction to solve complex spatial problems that would be otherwise difficult to solve. The OSIRIS framework

Figure 4. Implementing map service for simulation of land use change

holds that the description of the infrastructure of spatial data is essential for ontology-assisted interoperability of heterogeneous sources. We have demonstrated that ontology can be used to provide a common context for the semantic grounding for spatial application models which agents can relate to their native terminologies and thereby enable access to multiple services. Spatial services can be composed or manipulated along with other type of services, including Web services. The implementation of the sample prototype of OSIRIS framework indicates that a scaleable Web based spatial ontology can be developed using ontology modeling language to enable real world spatial decision-making. However, further research is needed to understand the requirements of ontology language to represent the semantic structure for complex spatial and temporal objects. This is especially important for ontology matching and merging of complex spatial systems. In particular, the implication of imprecision related to the finite resolution observation of an agent is not well addressed in current ontology research. We still need a robust specification for expressing topology and mereological aspect of spatial reasoning in a semantic language. Further research is necessary to identify the mechanism by which spatial representation and different level of explicitness at multiple scales affects an agent's logical reasoning and comprehension of spatial processes.

REFERENCES

Annoni, A., Friis-Christensen, A., Lucchi, R., & Lutz, M. (2008). Requirements and challenges for building a European spatial information infrastructure: INSPIRE. In P. v. Oosterom & S. Zlatanova (Eds.), *Creating spatial information infrastructures: Towards the spatial Semantic Web* (pp. 216). CRC.

Cali, A., Calvanese, D., Colucci, S., Noia, T. D., & Donini, F. M. (2004). *A description logic based approach for matching user profiles*. Unpublished manuscript.

CEC. (2003). *Linking up Europe: The Importance of interoperability for e-government services- Commission of the European communities- Commission staff working paper* (No. 801): Commission of the European Communities & Interchange of Data between Administrations (IDA).

CEC. (2006). *European interoperability framework for pan-European e-government services- communication from the commission to the council and the European parliament*. Brussels: Commission of the European Communities.

Craglla, M., & Signoretta, P. (2000). From global to local: The development of local geographic information strategies in the United Kingdom. *Environment and Planning, B*(27), 777–788.

DHS. (2009). DHS Geospatial Data Model, version 2.7 [Electronic Version]. Retrieved March, 2009 from http://www.fgdc.gov/participation/working-groups-subcommittees/hswg/dhs-gdm/

Egenhofer, M., & Mark, D. (1995). *Naive geography*. Paper presented at the International Conference COSIT '95 (LNCS).

Fallahia, G. R., Frankb, A. U., Mesgaria, M. S., & Rajabifardc, A. (2008). An ontological structure for semantic interoperability of GIS and environmental modeling. *International Journal of Applied Earth Observation and Geoinformation, 10*(3), 342–357. doi:10.1016/j.jag.2008.01.001

Farquhar, A., Fikes, R., & Rice, J. (1996). *The Ontolingua Server: A Tool for collaborative ontology construction*. Stanford, CA: Knowledge Systems Laboratory- Stanford University.

FGDC. (2009). Content Standard for Digital Geospatial Metadata (CSDGM), Vers. 2 (FGDC-STD-001-1998) Retrieved March 2009 from http://www.fgdc.gov/metadata/geospatial-metadata-standards

FIPA. (2006). The foundation for intelligent physical agents. Retrieved May, 2006, from http://www.fipa.org/

Fonseca, F., & Egenhofer, M. (1999). Ontology-driven geographic information systems. In C. B. Medeiros (Ed.), *7th ACM Symposium on Advances in Geographic Information Systems* (pp. 14-19). Kansas City: ACM Press.

GAO. (2003). *Geographic information systems: Challenges to effective data sharing* (Testimony Before the Subcommittee on Technology, Information Policy, Intergovernmental Relations and the Census, Committee on Government Reform, House of Representatives No. GAO-03-874T): United States General Accounting Office.

Gruber, T. R. (1993). A translation approach to portable ontology specifications. *Knowledge Acquisition, 5*(2). doi:10.1006/knac.1993.1008

Guarino, N. (1997). Semantic matching: Formal Ontological distinctions for information organization, extraction, and integration. In M. Pazienza (Ed.), *Information extraction: A multidisciplinary approach to an emerging information technology* (pp. 139-170). Frascati, Italy: International Summer School.

Guarino, N., & Giaretta, P. (1995). Ontologies and knowledge bases: Towards a terminological clarification. In N. Mars (Ed.), *Towards Very large knowledge bases: Knowledge building and knowledge sharing* (pp. 25-32).

Haynes, K. A., & Fotheringham, A. S. (1984). *Gravity and spatial interaction models.* Beverly Hills, CA: Sage Publications.

Horrocks, I. (1998, May 5-8). *The FaCT system.* Paper presented at the TABLEAUX '98, In Automated Reasoning with Analytic Tableaux and Related Method, International Conference Proceedings, Oisterwijk, The Netherlands.

Horrocks, I., Patel-Schneider, P. F., & Harmelen, F. v. (2003). From SHIQ and RDF to OWL: The making of a Web ontology language. *Journal of Web Semantics, 1*(1), 7–26. doi:10.1016/j.websem.2003.07.001

Islam, A. S., Bermudez, L., Beran, B., Fellah, S., & Piasecki, M. (2006). Ontology for geographic information - Metadata (ISO 19115:2003). Retrieved May 2006, from http://loki.cae.drexel.edu/~wbs/ontology/iso-19115.htm

Kashyap, V., & Sheth, A. (1996). Semantic heterogeneity in global information system: The role of metadata, context and ontologies. In M. Papazoglou & G. Schlageter (Eds.), *Cooperative information systems: Current trends and directions* (Vol. London, pp. 139-178). Academic Press.

Kuhn, W. (2005). Geospatial semantics: Why, of what, and how. *Journal on Data Semantics, 2*, 1–24.

Lassila, O., & Swick, R. (2004). Resource description framework (RDF) model and syntax specification. *W3C (World-Wide Web Consortium).* Retrieved from http://www.w3.org/TR/REC-rdf-syntax/

Malucelli, A., Palzer, D., & Oliveira, E. (2006). Ontology-based Services to help solving the heterogeneity problem in e-commerce negotiations. *Electronic Commerce Research and Applications, 5*, 29–43. doi:10.1016/j.elerap.2005.08.002

Nedovic-Budic, Z., & Pinto, J. K. (1999). Interorganizational GIS: Issues and prospects. *The Annals of Regional Science, 33*, 183–195. doi:10.1007/s001680050100

OpenCyc. (2006). OpenCyc 1.0. Retrieved May 2006, from http://www.cyc.com/cyc/opencyc/

Osman, H., & El-Diraby, T. E. (2006, June 14-16). *Interoperable decision support model for routing buried urban infrastructure*. Paper presented at the Joint International Conference on Computing & Decision Making in Civil and Building Engineering, Montreal.

Peng, Z. R., & Tsou, M. H. (2003). *Internet GIS: Distributed Geographic information services for the Internet and wireless networks*. John Wiley.

Rich, E. (1989). Stereotypes and user modeling. In A. Kobsa & W. Wahlster (Eds.), *User models in dialog systems*. Springer.

Smith, B. (1996). Mereotopology: A theory of parts and boundaries. *Data & Knowledge Engineering, 20*, 287–303. doi:10.1016/S0169-023X(96)00015-8

Tanasescu, V. (2007). Spatial semantics in difference spaces. In *Spatial Information Theory* (Vol. 4736/2007, pp. 96-115). Berlin / Heidelberg: Springer.

Warnecke, L., Beattie, J., Cheryl, K., & Lyday, W. (1998). *Geographic information technology in cities and counties: A nationwide assessment*. Washington, DC: American Forests.

Wayne, L. (2005). *Metadata in action: Expanding the utility of geospatial metadata*. Federal Geographic Data Committee.

Chapter 8
EnOntoModel:
A Semantically–Enriched Model for Ontologies

Nwe Ni Tun
National University of Singapore, Singapore

Satoshi Tojo
Japan Advanced Institute of Science and Technology, Japan

ABSTRACT

Ontologies are intended to facilitate semantic interoperability among distributed and intelligent information systems where diverse software components, computing devices, knowledge, and data, are involved. Since a single global ontology is no longer sufficient to support a variety of tasks performed on differently conceptualized knowledge, ontologies have proliferated in multiple forms of heterogeneity even for the same domain, and such ontologies are called heterogeneous ontologies. For interoperating among information systems through heterogeneous ontologies, an important step in handling semantic heterogeneity should be the attempt to enrich (and clarify) the semantics of concepts in ontologies. In this article, a conceptual model (called EnOntoModel) of semantically-enriched ontologies is proposed by applying three philosophical notions: identity, rigidity, and dependency. As for the advantages of EnOntoModel, the conceptual analysis of enriched ontologies and efficient matching between them are presented.

INTRODUCTION

Today, ontologies have become a silver bullet not only in the development of the semantic Web, but also in several collaborative application areas such as intelligent environments (or smart spaces), e-commerce, life sciences, social networks, multi-agent systems, and so forth, because they are respected as a means of consensus for intelligent reasoning and sharing capabilities. Since a single global ontology is no longer enough to support the variety of tasks pursued in distributed environments, the Web involves a proliferation of ontologies, and faces a trade off between interoperability and heterogeneity.

In order to keep a balance between heterogeneity and interoperability, ontology matching has become a plausible solution in various tasks, such as ontology merging, query answering, information retrieval, exchange, and integration. Heterogeneity is generally distinguished in terms of syntactic heterogeneity and semantic heterogeneity. *Syntactic heterogeneity* is caused by using different ontology modeling paradigms (e.g., RDF-based model or frame-based model) and different ontology languages (e.g., DAML or OWL), while *semantic heterogeneity* is created by conceptualization divergence in describing the semantics of ontological classes. Research on resolving syntactic heterogeneity has been undertaken by many researchers so far (Bowers & Declambre, 2000; Chalupsky, 2000). In this article, semantic heterogeneity between ontologies is focused on. Dealing with semantic heterogeneity is a recurrent issue for ontologies, like the problems related to information integration of heterogeneous databases and systems (Batini et al., 1986; March, 1990). Ceri and Widom (1993) listed four categories of semantic conflicts concerning schema matching: naming conflicts, domain conflicts, meta-data (or datatype) conflicts, and structural conflicts. Visser, Jones, Bench-Capon, and Shave (1997) classified ontology mismatches into two levels: conceptualization mismatches (class mismatches and property mismatches) and explication mismatches (abstraction level mismatches and categorization mismatches). According to the works, semantic heterogeneity in ontologies is classified into four categories. For two semantically similar or equivalent classes, there is (a) *terminological* heterogeneity if they have different names or labels; (b) *taxonomical* heterogeneity if they have different subsumption structures; (c) *schematic* heterogeneity if they have

different sets of properties and constraints; and (d) *instantiation* heterogeneity if they are interpreted using different sets of instances.

The main aim of this article is *to deal with wide-scale semantic heterogeneity in ontology matching.* Although several efforts in ontology mapping have already been contributed, they have different focuses, assumptions, and limitations. A common point among existing methods is that possible correspondences between two ontologies are determined by the similarity of entity names; this is known as *name-based matching.* In order to decide semantic correspondences between concepts, those methods need to analyze the similarities between all related properties and instances; this is known as *content-based matching.* In the case of wide-scale semantic heterogeneity, content-based matching becomes complex and user's approval or expert-interaction needs to verify mapping results.

In the research, two issues are focused on. The first issue is that the chance of correspondence between two terminologically quite different concepts is very less or not obtainable through name-based matching, because the name of a concept cannot express the precise semantics of the concept. In practice, two concepts with the same name may have different semantics, or two differently-naming concepts may have the same semantics. Thus, what is an alternative approach besides name-based matching, to find the possible correspondences between terminologically heterogeneous ontologies? The second issue is how to reduce complexity, concerning wide-scale semantic heterogeneity in content-based matching.

To accomplish the major aim and focuses, the underlying assumption is *the more explicit semantics is specified in ontologies, the feasibility of matching will be greater.* In order to improve the accuracy and automation of mapping processes, it is necessary that ontologies be well conceptualized with adequate semantics. Hence, an important step in handling semantic heterogeneity should be the attempt to enrich (and clarify) the semantics of concepts in ontologies.

Therefore, a semantically-enriched model of ontologies (called EnOntoModel) is proposed, in which every domain concept is treated as a sort—an entity type that carries criteria for determining the individuation, persistence, and identity of its instances—regarding every individual defined in a universe of discourse is countable and identifiable. In the philosophical literature, ontological concepts can be classified into four disjoint sort categories: type, quasi-type, role, and phase. A logic-based formal system was set up to classify domain concepts into these sort categories, using three philosophical notions: identity, existential rigidity, and external dependency. In the research, this classification knowledge is intuitively represented as concept-level properties that are different from ordinary properties (called individual-level properties) which are used to specify individuals. Then, EnOntoModel was defined, in which the semantics of domain concepts are described by using individual-level properties, as well as concept-level properties; this is the approach of *semantic enrichment*.

The innovation behind EnOntoModel is to supply an identifiable link between two heterogeneous descriptions of a concept, regarding that if two concepts are semantically equivalent, then they must be classified within the same sort category. For the usability of EnOntoModel, sortal meta-class ontology was implemented as an open source interface in enrichment process as well as conceptual analysis of enriched ontologies. By the aim of this research, a matching method between enriched ontologies was designed.

A novel idea of EnOntoModel-based ontology matching method is that direct concept matching is driven between the same categories of sorts instead of exhaustive search among all sorts, because domain concepts are systematically classified into four disjoint sort categories. Moreover, it is examined that EnOntoModel can support not only determining the scope of possible correspondences, but also determining the most relevant properties which can certainly indicate a correspondence between two similar concepts. This means that semantic correspondences between highly heterogeneous concepts can be achieved without taking an exhaustive search in taxonomies and an analysis among all related properties. Consequently, the approach of semantic enrichment supports a content-based matching in a less complexity.

The method is implemented in Java for matching between OWL ontologies by utilizing Jena OWL API and Protégé OWL API. The efficiency of EOM is evaluated in terms of mathematical complexity and proved that this method could reduce the complexity of the matching process by comparing it with other methods, particularly GLUE's content learners. Moreover, an experiment is done in two real data sets and the effectiveness of EOM is shown in terms of precision and recall.

Semantic Enrichment in Ontologies

Semantic enrichment is a process that renders adequate and precise semantics for domain concepts in the form of structured and consistent taxonomies.

A First-Order Quantified Modal Language L^E

Quantified modal logic (QML) is a philosophical logic that develops formal systems for the analysis of ontological concepts using philosophical notions such as essence, existence, actualism, individualism, possibilism, identity, part-whole, dependency, and so forth. QML comprises modal logic and first-order predicate logic grammatically, axiomatically, and semantically.

There are three circumstances for this research to employ QML.

- The basic influence is by the former works (Guarino & Welty, 2001; Welty & Andersen, 2005) in which philosophical notions (called meta-properties in OntoClean) were formalized in $S5$ QML with the Barcan formula $(BF)^1$, which gives us a *constant domain* and *universal accessibility*.
- The second condition is a need to claim of *varying actual domains* among possible worlds, because in practice, it cannot expected that the same set of individuals actually exists in each arbitrary accessible world. Actual existence is opposed to logical existence; that indicates some objects actually exist in the possible worlds (Miller, 1987; Cresswell, 2001). For example, "God exists" is a kind of logical existence, however "Mars exists" is an actual existence because it can be proven that a planet called Mars actually exists in our universe.
- The third condition is that QML amounts to *trans-world identity* that is the identity of two incomplete descriptions of an individual can be detected across multiple possible worlds.

Syntax

Let L^E be a first-order modal language which consists of **alphabet** $A^E = \{X,C,P_n,F_n,E,=\}$ for countable infinite sets of individual variables, individual constants, n-ary predicate symbols, n-ary function symbols, the actual existential predicate symbol, and an identity symbol, where n is a finite natural number. Terms of L^E are either constants, variables or constructed terms $f_n(t_1,...,t_n) \in F_n$ where $t_1,...,t_n$ are terms.

Definition 1 (Atomic Formula): *If p_n is an n-ary predicate symbol and $(t_1,...,t_n)$ is an n-tuple of terms, then $p_n(t_1,...,t_n)$ is an atomic formula.*

Definition 2 (Atomic Identity Formula): *If t_1 and t_2 are any terms, then $t_1 = t_2$ is an atomic identity formula, that is, t_1 is identical to t_2.*

Definition 3 (Atomic Actual Existence Formula): *If t is any term, then $E(t)$ is an atomic actual existence formula, that is, an individual belongs to term t actually exists in a possible world.*

Definition 4 (Formulas of L^E) *A set of formulas $\phi,\psi,...$ in alphabet A^E (called Δ_A^E) is defined as follows:*

- All atomic formulas are formulas of Δ_A^E.
- If ϕ is a formula, then so is $\neg\phi$.
- If ϕ,ψ are formulas, then so is $\phi \rightarrow \psi$.
- If ϕ is a formula and x is a variable, then $\forall x\phi$ is a formula of Δ_A^E.
- If ϕ is a formula, then so is $\Box\phi$.

Falsehood $\bot$, propositional connectives $\wedge$, $\vee$, $\leftrightarrow$, existential quantifier $\exists$, and modal operator $\Diamond$, are defined in the usual way of first-order predicate logic and modal logic (Hughes & Cresswell, 2003). Then, complex formulas can be constructed using these connectives such as $\phi\wedge\psi =_{def} \neg(\phi\rightarrow\neg\psi)$, $\phi\leftrightarrow\psi =_{def} (\phi\rightarrow\psi)\wedge(\psi\rightarrow\phi)$, $\exists x\phi =_{def} \neg x\forall\neg\phi$, and $\Diamond\phi =_{def} \neg\Box\neg\phi$.

Semantics

The semantics of languages L^E are given in terms of Kripke semantics. A **kripke frame** is $F = \langle W,R \rangle$ where W is a non-empty set, and R is a binary relation on W. Set W is intuitively interpreted as a set of *possible worlds*, whereas R is the *accessibility relation* between worlds (Cresswell, 2001). **Universe** U includes a set of individuals U_{ind} and a set of datatype values U_{dtp}, such that $U = U_{ind} \cup U_{dtp}$, regarding owl:ObjectProperty and owl:DatatypeProperty[2].

The key insight in Kripke's QML is instead of a single domain common to all worlds, domains are permitted to vary from world to world. Regarding an *S*5 Kripke frame, domains of possible worlds become constant. However, if the actual existence of individuals is respected and there is no individual that actually exists forever in a world, for example, a person can die in someday, and then each world has two nested domains: a possible domain and an actual domain. Therefore, such nested domains are defined in each possible world, constant outer domain and varying inner domain, by distinguishing the actual domain of a possible world from its possible domain using existential predicate E.

Definition 5 (Kripke Model): *A Kripke model given in universe U, is a quintuple* $M = \langle F, \Vdash, D, d, I \rangle$ *where*

- F is a Kripke frame,
- $\Vdash$ is a satisfaction relation between $w \in W$ and formulas of Δ_A^E,
- D is a function that assigns a non-empty outer domain $D(w) = U$ to every $w \in W$,
- d is a function that assigns a non-empty inner domain to every $w \in W$ such that $d(w) \subseteq D(w)$, and
    - $I = \langle U, ^I \rangle$ is the interpretation in frame F such that
    - $I(p_n^I, w) \subseteq D(w)^n$ for any n-ary predicate $p_n \in P_n$,
    - $I(f_n^I, w): D(w)^n \rightarrow D(w)$ for any n-ary function $f_n \in F_n$,
    - $I(c^I, w) \in D(w)$ for any individual constant $c \in C$, and
    - $I(E^I, w) = d(w)$ for existential predicate E.

Definition 6 (w-assignment): *To define truth conditions for atomic and quantified formulas with variables* $x \in X$, **w-assignment function** ∂ *into interpretation I in world w is defined as* $I(x^I, w) = \partial(x, w)$. *There is also a variant of w-assignment,* $\partial^{x,a}$, *which assigns individual element* $a \in D(w)$ *to x.*

Definition 7 (Satisfaction): *For any world* $w \in W$ *given in Kripke model M, the satisfaction relation*

of the formulas of Δ_A^E *with respect to* I^∂ *is as follows:*

- $(I^\partial, w) \Vdash p_n(t_1, ..., t_n)$ iff $\langle I^\partial(t_1^I, w), ..., I^\partial(t_n^I, w) \rangle \in I^\partial(p_n^I, w)$
- $(I^\partial, w) \Vdash t_1 = t_2$ iff $I^\partial(t_1^I, w) = I^\partial(t_2^I, w)$
- $(I^\partial, w) \Vdash \neg\phi$ iff not $(I^\partial, w) \Vdash \phi$
- $(I^\partial, w) \Vdash \phi \rightarrow \psi$ iff $(I^\partial, w) \Vdash \neg\phi$ or $(I^\partial, w) \Vdash \psi$
- $(I^\partial, w) \Vdash \Box\phi$ iff for every $w' \in W$ such that wRw', $(I^\partial, w') \Vdash \phi$
- $(I^\partial, w) \Vdash \forall x\phi$ iff for every individual $a \in D(w)$, $(I^{\partial x,a}, w) \Vdash \phi$
- $(I^\partial, w) \Vdash E(t)$ iff $I^\partial(t^I, w) \subseteq d(w)$

In particular $(I^\partial, w) \Vdash \bot$ never holds. A formula is true in Kripke model M if and only if it is true in every possible world $w \in W$ of M. Similarly, a formula is *valid* (denoted by $\vdash$) in Kripke frame F if and only if it is true in every Kripke model M given on F. For obtaining an *S*5 frame F, four axioms: K, T, 4, and 5[3], must be satisfied in any Kripke model M given in the frame.

Figure 1 illustrates the state of outer and inner domains of possible worlds given in an *S*5 Kripke model M which also satisfies the *inclusion requirement*, that is, if wRw' then $D(w) \subseteq D(w')$. In an *S*5 Kripke model, every world is accessible not only to itself, but also to any other possible worlds. This is called universal accessibility, and by that every possible world has a constant outer domain whilst the inner domains differ from each other according to the actual existence of individuals in the worlds.

Philosophical Foundations for Ontological Conceptualization

Conceptual modeling is a fundamental discipline in computer science, playing an essential role in areas such as software and domain engineering, knowledge-based and intelligent systems, information integration, and semantic interoperability. Modeling a set of concepts used to articulate abstractions of the state of affairs in a given do-

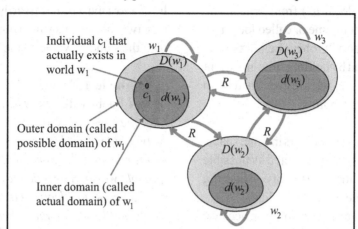

Figure 1. The outer and inner domains of possible worlds in an S5 Kripke model

main is named as *ontological conceptualization.* Therefore, domain ontology is a kind of conceptual specification and, hence, ontology modeling is a specific type of conceptual modeling.

Having a precise representation of a given conceptualization becomes more critical when it is wanted to integrate independently-developed models (or systems based on those models). In order for these systems to function properly together, it must be guaranteed that they ascribe compatible meanings to real world entities of their shared subject domain. The ability of systems to interoperate, with compatible real-world semantics, is known as *semantic interoperatibility.* In order to support semantic interoperability through heterogeneous ontologies, a theory of conceptual modeling is applied based on some philosophical notions and an enrichment framework is proposed.

In the philosophical literature, ontological concepts are generally divided into two categories: sortal concepts (called sorts) and non-sortal concepts. **Sort** is an entity type[4] that carries the criteria for determining the individuation,[5] persistence, and identity[6] of its instances (Corazzon, 1729).[7] In this article, treat the most fundamental ontological classes as sorts, and non-sortals as the attribute values or properties of sorts. Some examples of sorts are person, planet, dog, house,

student, wine, book, and car, where individuals (or instances) are countable and identifiable. Unlike sorts, red, happy, and beautiful, are non-sortals, which do not supply identity for their individuals. However, whether a concept is a sort or not should rely on the possession of identity criteria, rather than the common sense of concept's name.

Identity is the logical relation of sameness, in which an individual identifies only to it globally. Guarino and Welty think of IC as *diachronic IC*—a stable IC at different time points (Guarino & Welty, 2001). Their formalization of diachronic IC is as follows:

$$\Box(E(x,t) \wedge p\phi(x,t) \wedge E(y,t') \wedge p\phi(y,t') \wedge x=y \rightarrow \Sigma(x,y,t,t')) \qquad (1)$$

$$\Box(E(x,t) \wedge p\phi(x,t) \wedge E(y,t') \wedge p\phi(y,t') \wedge \Sigma(x,y,t,t') \rightarrow x=y) \qquad (2)$$

where the predicate E is for actual existance, t and t' are time parameters, and Σ is the sameness formula (for example, fingerprint (x,t)=fingerprint (y,t') for a diachronic identity between two individual persons). An IC is *necessary* if it satisfies Equation 1 and *sufficient* if it satisfies Equation 2. In OntoClean, Guarino and Welty used a non-modal time parameter 't' to mention a time line in each possible world in order to distinguish diachronic IC (it may be called global IC) from synchronic IC (IC at a single point in time or called local IC). Basically, the definition of IC obeys Leibniz's rule[8] with no exceptions and by holding time-invarient identity. Equations 1 and 2 are redefined with respect to the following points:

- Every state of possible affairs in time, space, or any possibility, is interpreted as possible worlds in modalities instead of considering a time line inside possible worlds.
- IC is assumed as a property of sorts because only sortal concepts carry or supply ICs.
- IC is considered as a unary function of language L^E (denoted by ι) in order to represent it as an OWL datatype property (owl:DatatypeProperty). And IC values are considered as datatype values.
- The sameness formula Σ is reformulated in terms of equality between the IC values of two common individuals of a sort, and the identity of an individual is entailed by this.

Note that if temporal aspect for some tense-intensive domains is considered, it is necessary to fuse temporal logic into language L^E.

Definition 8 (Identity Condition): *Identity condition (IC) of a sort is a datatype property, which provides a unique IC value to each individual of the sort. Formally, if ι is an IC of sort s (denoted by p_s), then it satisfies one of the following conditions:*

$$\Box \forall x,y[p_s(x) \wedge E(x) \wedge p_s(y) \wedge E(y) \wedge x=y \rightarrow \iota(x)=\iota(y)] \tag{3}$$

$$\Box \forall x,y[p_s(x) \wedge E(x) \wedge p_s(y) \wedge E(y) \wedge \iota(x)=\iota(y) \rightarrow x=y] \tag{4}$$

Equation (3) states that "The IC of a sort must *necessarily* provide the same IC value for the same individual of the sort." Equation (4) states that "The IC of a sort must be necessarily *sufficient* to recognize two individuals which both actually exist and own the same IC value as the same individual."

Example 1 *Suppose that hasISBN is the IC of sort* PublishedBook. *Then, it is necessary to have the same ISBN for the same published book, or two individual books with the same ISBN can be identified as the same published book in every possible world. Someone may use a global product bar-code to identify each copy of the same PublishedBook (say an individual of PublishedBookCopy). For other examples, hasFingerprint, hasURI, and hasLatitudeLongitude can be used as the ICs of* Person, WebResource, *and* Location, *respectively. Note that ICs should be globally identifiable for individuals. For example,* Student *possesses property 'hasStudentID,' however it is world-variant and can not be used as an IC. It is called local IC, and is used to identify individuals inside a possible world.*

In Definition 8, unary predicates of language L^E are used, by adding predicated names corresponding to sort names, such as $p_s \in P_n$. Then, the fundamental semantics of a **subsumption relationship** $<$ between two sorts s_1 and s_2, can be interpreted in the form of implication relation, that is, if $s_2 <_1$ then $\forall x[p_{s2}(x) \rightarrow p_{s1}(x)]$ (Beierle, 1992; Kaneiwa, 2001). This is read as "If sort s_2 is subsumed by sort s_1 then every individual of s_2 is an individual of s_1." In this case, s_1 is a *super-sort* and s_2 is a *sub-sort*. The IC of a sort allows inheritance through subsumption relationships.

Definition 9 (OwnIC and CarriedIC): *If sort s originates an IC, then the IC is called the ownIC of s, denoted by ι_s. If a sort inherits an IC from a super-sort through subsumption relationship, then the IC is called "carriedIC" denoted by ι.*

Example 2 *Suppose that hasFingerPrint is the ownIC of sort* Person *because every person* is identifiable by such fingerprint. According to Student < Person and ι_{Person}=hasFingerPrint, hasFingerprint is a carriedIC for Student. In this case, it is said that Person supplies its ownIC to Student and Student carries the IC of Person.

Rigidity provides the modality of a sort. In general, the rigid designation in modal context is "*it designates the same thing in all possible worlds.*" However, Kai-Yee Wong (2003) mentioned that what Saul Kripke (1971) likes to say about rigidness is with existence conception: "...a designator rigidly designates a certain object if it designates that object wherever the object exists." Regarding this quoted reference, the actual existence of rigidity is applied (Welty & Andersen, 2005).

Definition 10 (Existential Rigidity): *Sort s is existentially* **rigid** *iff*

$$\forall x[\Diamond p_s(x) \rightarrow \Box(E(x) \rightarrow p_s(x))], \qquad (5)$$

otherwise, s is existentially **anti-rigid** *iff*

$$\forall x[\Diamond p_s(x) \rightarrow \Diamond(E(x) \wedge \neg p_s(x))]. \qquad (6)$$

In the rigid case, if every individual of a sort in world w exists in every world w' such that wRw', the individual is always a member of the sort. In the case of anti-rigid sort, this is not so.

Example 3 Person *can be defined as a rigid sort and* Student *as an anti-rigid sort, by expecting every person is a person in every possible world if s/he exists there, and a person is not always a student.*

Dependency expresses the external and existential dependent relation of a certain sort to another disjoint sort whose individuals are neither a part nor a constituent[9] of any individual of the sort.

Definition 11 (Existential Dependency): *Sort s is existentially dependent on sort s' iff, as a matter of necessity, some individuals of sort*

s' exist whenever an individual of sort s exists, formally:

$$\Box\forall x[p_s(x) \wedge E(x) \rightarrow \exists y[P_{s'}(y) \wedge E(y)].$$

For example, if a student exists in a world then there is at least one school for that student.

Definition 12 (Externally Dependent) *Sort s is externally dependent on another sort s' if, for all individuals x of s, necessarily some individual y of s' exist, which is neither a part nor a constituent of x:*

$$\forall x\Box[p_s(x) \wedge E(x) \rightarrow \exists y(p_{s'}(y) \wedge E(y) \wedge p_d(x,y)] \qquad (7)$$

where s and s' are disjoint.

The original dependent definition[10] is modified by defining existential dependency and by adding an external dependency relationship (EDR) denoted by p_d, so that Equation 7 states the external dependency of s to s' explicitly.

Example 4 Student *is externally dependent on* School *with "EnrollIn" relationship. This means a person who does not enroll in a school is not defined as a student. Thus, EnrollIn is called the EDR of* Student *on* School. *Similarly, parent, child, customer, and supplier are externally dependent sorts.*

Modeling Semantically-Enriched Ontologies

The objective of modeling semantically-enriched ontologies is to provide a well-structured taxonomy and adequate semantics for ontologies concerning the issue of semantic heterogeneity in ontology matching.

Description of a Sort

Taxonomies are a central part of ontologies. A hierarchy of sorts with subsumption relationships is called a sortal taxonomy, denoted by $\langle S, \leq \rangle$ where S is a set of sorts and $\leq$ is a collection of subsumption relationships between any two sorts of S. A set of properties that constitutes the intentional semantics of a sort are called *individual-level* properties, because the semantics of a certain individual is described in terms of these properties. For a sort $s \in S$, there is a set of individual-level properties $P^D(s)$. For example,

$P^D(PublishedBook)=\{hasTitle, hasAuthor, hasPublisher,$
$hasPublishedYear, hasISBN\}.$

Among the given properties, let us assume that hasISBN is defined as the IC of PublishedBook. By the definition of IC (Definition 8), every individual instantiated to PublishedBook must possess a unique ISBN value.

For every $p \in P^D(s)$, there is a specific domain D_s and range R_p such that $p:D_s \Rightarrow R_p$. I divide $P^D(s)$ into two kinds.

- **Object properties:** $P_j(s) \subseteq P^D(s)$ are the properties that relate two individuals, that is, $p_j:D_s \Rightarrow R_j$ for every $p_j \in P_j(s)$. For example, $P_j(PublishedBook)=\{hasAuthor, hasPublisher\}$

- **Datatype properties:** $P_t(s) \subseteq P^D(s)$ are the properties that relate an individual to a data value defined in a standard or user-defined datatype such as string, integer, boolean, date, year, ISBN, URI, and so forth, that is, $p_t: D_s \Rightarrow R_j$ for every $p_t \in P_t(s)$. For example,

$P_t(PublishedBook)=\{hasTitle, hasPublishedYear, hasISBN\}$

Thus, the individual-level properties of sort s consists of object properties as well as datatype properties, that is $P^D(s)=P_j(s) \cup P_t(s)$. IC denoted by ι is a kind of datatype property. Then, the IC of PublishedBook can be described as $\iota_{PublishedBook}=$ hasISBN. The value

returned by an IC for an individual is called *"IC value"* and a set of identity conditions for sort s *"IC set"* denoted by $I(s)$, such that $I(s) \subseteq P_t(s)$. $I(s) \neq \varnothing$ for every sort s because every sort originates or carries at least one IC. For every $\iota \in I(s)$, $\iota: D_s \Rightarrow R_\iota$ and ι is restricted to be functional. Moreover, every IC ι has an inverse functional property such that $\iota*: R_\iota \Rightarrow D_s$. By Definition 8, one-to-one relation is fixed between the domain and range of an IC. This characteristic differentiates ICs from other properties.

One of the major concerns in this research is if ontological concepts are considered as sorts, then how to represent them in terms of OWL. It was intuitively found that a sort can be represented as an OWL class (owl:Class) with the restriction having at least one IC (ownIC or carriedIC). Also, owl:Datatypeproperty can be used to represent IC with the restriction of owl:FunctionalProperty and owl:InverseFunctionalProperty regarding its characteristic of one-to-one functional. In addition, =1 cardinality is set up to restrict every individual possesses at least one IC value. The description of sort PublishedBook is presented in the form of OWL-Full syntax in Figure 2.

A Classification System of Sorts

Based on the classifications of sorts in OntoClean and by Guizzardi (2004), four categories of sort are defined: type, quasi-type, role, and phase. Before defining each category of sort, some critical properties need to be clarified. They are identity condition (IC), common value attribute (CVA), external dependency relation (EDR), and common constraint (CC). For IC, Definition 8 is referred to.

- **Common value attribute (CVA):** A datatype property is defined as a CVA for a sort, if the property provides a common attribute value for all individuals belonging to the

Figure 2. A representation of sort and IC in OWL-full

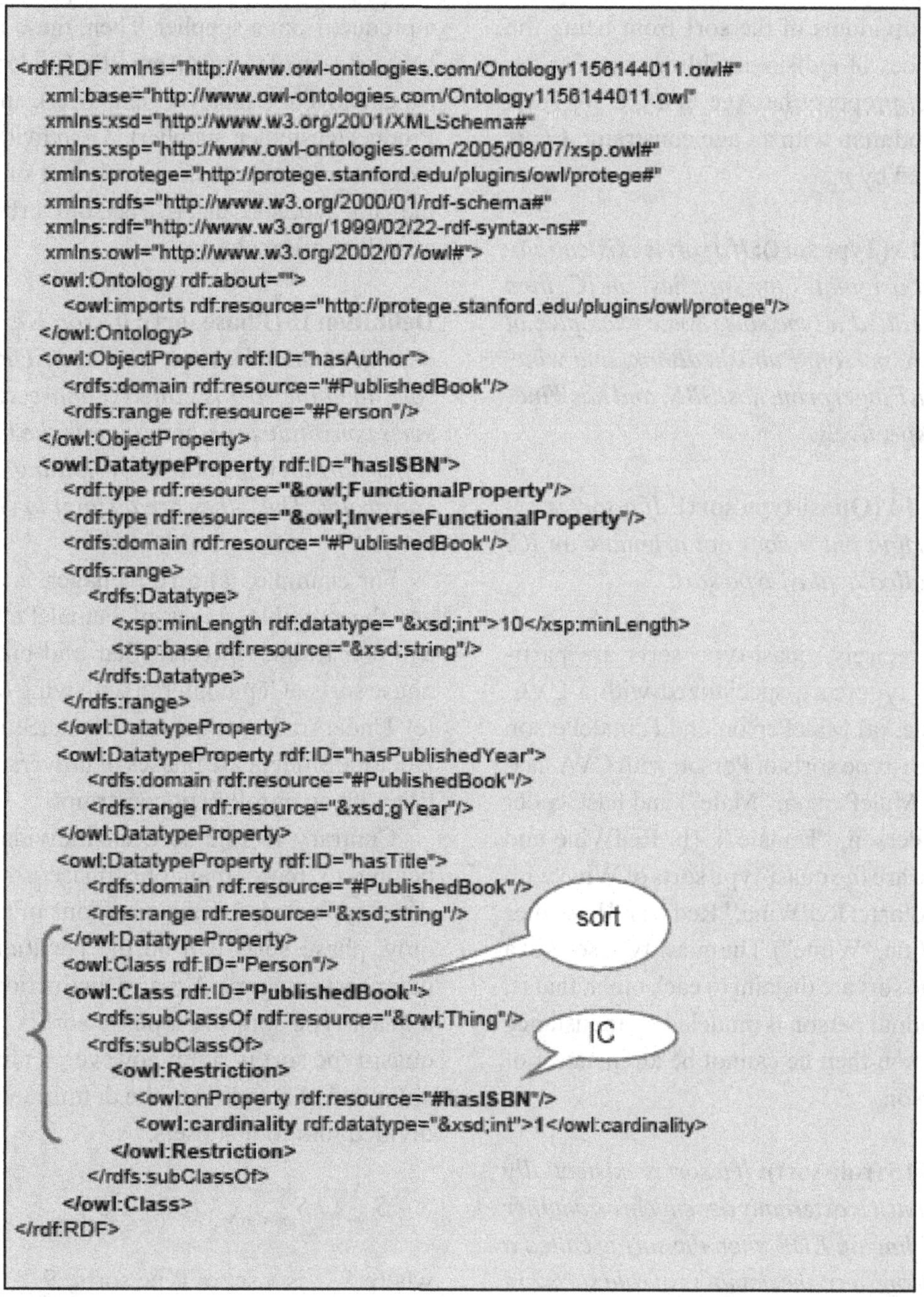

```
<rdf:RDF xmlns="http://www.owl-ontologies.com/Ontology1156144011.owl#"
    xml:base="http://www.owl-ontologies.com/Ontology1156144011.owl"
    xmlns:xsd="http://www.w3.org/2001/XMLSchema#"
    xmlns:xsp="http://www.owl-ontologies.com/2005/08/07/xsp.owl#"
    xmlns:protege="http://protege.stanford.edu/plugins/owl/protege#"
    xmlns:rdfs="http://www.w3.org/2000/01/rdf-schema#"
    xmlns:rdf="http://www.w3.org/1999/02/22-rdf-syntax-ns#"
    xmlns:owl="http://www.w3.org/2002/07/owl#">
  <owl:Ontology rdf:about="">
    <owl:imports rdf:resource="http://protege.stanford.edu/plugins/owl/protege"/>
  </owl:Ontology>
  <owl:ObjectProperty rdf:ID="hasAuthor">
    <rdfs:domain rdf:resource="#PublishedBook"/>
    <rdfs:range rdf:resource="#Person"/>
  </owl:ObjectProperty>
  <owl:DatatypeProperty rdf:ID="hasISBN">
    <rdf:type rdf:resource="&owl;FunctionalProperty"/>
    <rdf:type rdf:resource="&owl;InverseFunctionalProperty"/>
    <rdfs:domain rdf:resource="#PublishedBook"/>
    <rdfs:range>
      <rdfs:Datatype>
        <xsp:minLength rdf:datatype="&xsd;int">10</xsp:minLength>
        <xsp:base rdf:resource="&xsd;string"/>
      </rdfs:Datatype>
    </rdfs:range>
  </owl:DatatypeProperty>
  <owl:DatatypeProperty rdf:ID="hasPublishedYear">
    <rdfs:domain rdf:resource="#PublishedBook"/>
    <rdfs:range rdf:resource="&xsd;gYear"/>
  </owl:DatatypeProperty>
  <owl:DatatypeProperty rdf:ID="hasTitle">
    <rdfs:domain rdf:resource="#PublishedBook"/>
    <rdfs:range rdf:resource="&xsd;string"/>
  </owl:DatatypeProperty>                      sort
  <owl:Class rdf:ID="Person"/>
  <owl:Class rdf:ID="PublishedBook">
    <rdfs:subClassOf rdf:resource="&owl;Thing"/>
    <rdfs:subClassOf>                          IC
      <owl:Restriction>
        <owl:onProperty rdf:resource="#hasISBN"/>
        <owl:cardinality rdf:datatype="&xsd;int">1</owl:cardinality>
      </owl:Restriction>
    </rdfs:subClassOf>
  </owl:Class>
</rdf:RDF>
```

sort. For example, property hasColor is a CVA for sort WhiteWine because it provides a common color value "White" for every individual of WhiteWine. CVA is denoted by p_a. For example, property EmployFor is an EDR for sort employee because there at least one employer (firm or organization) exists for any employee. EDR is denoted by $p_{d'}$

- **Common constraint (CC):** A datatype property is defined as a CC for a sort, if the property provides a common constraint such as the same boolean value, data value range, or qualification, that can distinguish the individuals of the sort from being the instances of a disjoint sibling sort. For example, property hasAge is a CC for sorts boy and man with an age constraint. CC is denoted by p_C.

Definition 13 (Type sort): *If a sort is existentially rigid and it originates (or supplies) an IC, then the sort is called a type sort. Some examples of type sort are person, PublishedBook, and wine, with ICs hasFingerprint, hasISBN, and hasWine-Name,[11] respectively.*

Definition 14 (Quasi-type sort): *If a sort is existentially rigid but it does not originate an IC, then it is called a quasi-type sort.*

More precisely, quasi-type sorts are partitions[12] of a type sort, specialized with a CVA. For example, (a) MalePerson and FemalePerson are the quasi-type sorts of Person with CVA has-Gender (c: MalePerson, "Male") and hasGender (c: FemalePerson, "Female"), (b) RedWine and WhiteWine are the quasi-type sorts of Wine with CVA hasColor (c: RedWine, "Red") and hasColor (c: WhiteWine, "White"). The quasi-type sorts of a certain type sort are disjoint to each other, that is, if an individual person is modeled as an instance of MalePerson then he cannot be an instance of FemalePerson.

Definition 15 (role sort): *If a sort is existentially anti-rigid and it is externally dependent on another sort by holding an EDR, then the sort is called a role sort. Moreover, the domains of role sorts are not necessarily disjoint.*

Student, employee, and customer are some examples of role sorts, that is (a) a student is a person who enrolls in a school or university, (b) an employee is a person who is hired by an organization to perform a job, and (c) a customer is a person who buys a product from a supplier. Then, these EDRs will hold for each of them: (a) enrollIn (student, school), (b) employFor (employee, employer), and (c) BuyProduct (customer, supplier). An individual can be a member of more than one role sort subsumed by the same type sort, that is, a person can be a student as well as an employee.

Definition 16 (Phase sort): *If a sort is existentially anti-rigid and does not need an EDR like role sort, then the sort is called a phase sort. Phase sorts constitute possible stages in the history of a super-sort they specialize, by holding a common constraint. Thus, they are disjoint to each other.*

For example, (a) girl, teenager, and woman, are the possible stages of FemalePerson, with age constraint; (b) caterpillar and butterfly are phase sorts of lepidopteran with wing constraint; (c) UndergraduateStudent, MasterStudent, and DoctoralStudent are phases of university student life with an enrollment constraint.

Contrary to role sort, an individual cannot belong to more than one phase sort. Whilst quasi-type sorts are the partitions of a type sort only, phase sorts can be the partitions of any other sort category. A major distinction between a quasi-type sort and a phase sort is rigidity. A quasi-type sort is rigid; however, a phase sort is anti-rigid. According to the definitions, S can be divided into four subsets:

$$S = S_{type} \cup S_{quasi\text{-}type} \cup S_{role} \cup S_{phase}$$

where S_{type} is a set of type sorts, $S_{quasi\text{-}type}$ is a set of quasi-type sorts, S_{role} is a set of role sorts, and S_{phase} is a set of phase sorts. It is claimed that each subset of S is disjoint to the others, because their modality and identifiable characteristics are different.

Concept-Level Properties of Sorts

In order to apply the classification of sorts into the formal conceptual model, a modeling component is created, that is, concept-level properties of sorts. This is the novel idea of embedding the sort classification into formal ontology model. Here, it is liked to distinguish between concept-level properties and individual-level properties. For an ontological concept/class, a set of individual-level properties are defined for the precise semantics (or meaning) of the concept. They are abstracted from the specification of individuals of the concept. Inheritance is allowed among individual-level properties along subsumption relationships. For sort s, $P^D(s)$ is a set of individual-level properties. When $s_2 < s_1$, not $P^D(s_2) \supseteq P^D(s_1)$. Concept-level properties are different from individual-level properties. They are defined only for the conceptual knowledge of a sort such as it is a type sort and it has an ownIC, and so forth. Inheritance is restricted among concept-level properties along subsumption relationships. Let $P^C(s)$ be a set of concept-level properties for sort s. For any $s_2 < s_1$, $P^C(s_2) \supseteq P^C(s_1)$.

At the current state, two concept-level properties based on the sort classification are defined. They are the category and classification constraint of a sort. More clearly, the category of a sort describe a particular sort is classified under which sort category such as type, quasi-type, role, or phase. When a sort is classified under a specific category, there is a specific constraint that forces

Table 1. Two kinds of concept-level properties by sort classification

Sort Category	Constraint
type	ownIC: $\iota_s \in P^D(s)$
quasi-type	CVA: $p_a \in P^D(s)$
role	EDR: $p_d \in P^D(s)$
phase	CC: $p_c \in P^D(s)$

individual-level properties defined for the sort to be semantically adequate. Table 1 describes sort categories and their specific constraints.

The concept-level properties of a sort controls not only subsumption relationship of the sort, but also what kinds of individual-level properties should be explicitly defined for a precise semantics of the sort. Suppose that sort s_1 is going to be defined as a role sort. Then, the conceptual modeler has to think of the following questions:

- What are the property EDR and dependent sort, of s_1 that prove s_1 to be a role?
- Is there a type sort s_2 such that $s_1 < s_2$?
- What is the ownIC of s_2 which can globally identify every individual of s_1?

Expressed another way, concept-level properties enrich the semantics of sorts.

EnOntoModel: A Conceptual Model of Semantically-enriched Ontologies

Ontologies are the conceptualized models of a domain. A source ontology can be modeled as a quadruple $O = \langle S, \leq, P^D, A \rangle$ where S is a set of concepts, $\langle S, \leq \rangle$ is a taxonomy of subsumption relationships between any two concepts, P^D is a set of individual-level properties, and A is a set of ontological axioms and constraints. The formalization of each modeling component of O is assumed to be the same as OWL-DL ontologies (Badder, 2003). Following by the theoretical foundations discussed in the previous sections, mainly the classification of sorts, now a formal semantically-enriched model of ontologies is defined. The model is called EnOntoModel, in which concept-level properties are additionally embedded in O to enrich the semantics of concepts.

Definition 17 (EnOntoModel) *EnOntoModel is a quintuple $O^E = \langle S, \leq, P^C, P^D, A \rangle$ where S is a non-empty set of sorts, $\langle S, \leq \rangle$ is a taxonomic structure of S with subsumption relationship $<$, P^C is* *a set of concept-level properties such that $P^C(s)$ for each sort $s \in S$, P^D is a set of individual-level properties such that $P^D = \{P^D(s) | s \in S\}$, and A is a set of ontological axioms and constraints.*

The following axioms and constraints are defined as standards for any EnOntoModel-based ontology:

$A = \{$

[a1] For any $s_1, s_2, s_3 \in S_{type}$, if s_1 and s_2 are disjoint (denoted by $s_1 <> s_2$) then not $s_3 < s_1$ and not $s_3 < s_2$

[a2] For any $s_1 \in S_{type}, s_2, s_3 \in S_{quasi-type}$, if $s_2 < s_1$ and $s_3 < s_1$ then $s_2 <> s_3$

[a3] For any $s_1 \in S, s_2, s_3 \in S_{phase}$, if $s_2 < s_1$ and $s_3 < s_1$ then $s_2 <> s_3$

[c1] For any $s \in S_{type}$, $\iota_s \in P^D(s)$ and '=1' cardinality for ι_s

[c2] For any $s \in S_{quasi-type}$, $p_a \in P^D(s)$

[c3] For any $s \in S_{role}$, $p_d \in P^D(s)$

[c4] For any $s \in S_{phase}$, $p_c \in P^D(s)$

$\}$

Moreover, other domain-dependent constraints can be defined in ontologies. A simple domain ontology named Research-Community.owl is presented as an example of EnOntoModel.

Example 5 (Research-Community.owl) *Domain concepts defined in the ontology are listed according to their sort categories, as follows:*

S_{type} = {ResearchProject, SoftwareTool, Research-Publication, Event, Person, LegalOrganization}

$S_{quasi-type}$ = {CommercialProject, AcademicProject, OntologyEditor, Reasoner, NLParser, JournalPaper, ProceedingsPaper, Conference, Workshop, Seminar, Enterprise, Association, ResearchInstitute, University}

S_{role} = {Employee, Researcher, FacultyMember, AdminMember, Author, ResearchStudent, Secretary, Manager, President}

S_{phase} = {AssociateProfessor, Professor, MasterStudent, PhdStudent, ScholarshipEligible, ScholarshipNon-eligible}

The taxonomic structure of Research-Community.owl is described in Figure 4 which follows the standard axioms and constraints of EnOntoModel. Moreover, other domain-dependent constraints such as FacultyMember <> Student, Staff ≡ Employee, and so forth, are also defined.

Let the classification system of given concepts be explained. The root of any sub-taxonomy is restricted as a type sort. Also, an IC must be defined for each type sort and by such IC; the individuals of each type sort are identifiable. ICs are defined not only by using single property but also by using a tuple of individual-level properties. For example, the IC value of each ResearchProject individual is a couple of research project name and organizer name, such as "The 21st Century COE Program" + "Japan Advanced Institute of Science and Technology." It is similar that each event has a unique event title such as "AAAI-06: Twenty-First National Conference on Artificial Intelligence" is an instance of conference. The quasi-type sorts of a specific type sort is distinguished from each other by a common CVA with distinctive attribute values such as "conference," "workshop," "seminar" of CVA hasEType. For role sorts, modelers need to define appropriate EDRs such as EmployIn (FacultyMember, University), EnrollIn (Student, University). It is similar that CCs are necessary to define to distinguish between phase sorts. For example, hasFacultyPosition is for different faculty members.

Recall that deciding whether a sort is a type sort or another kind of sort does not fully depend on the common sense of its name. More precisely, a sort is classified according to the properties and constraints defined for it. It is claimed that if two sorts belong to different kinds of sort category, then they cannot be the same sort. Suppose that Figure 5 is the sub-taxonomy of another ontology which is conceptualized for a similar domain

Figure 3. The taxonomy of Research-Community.owl

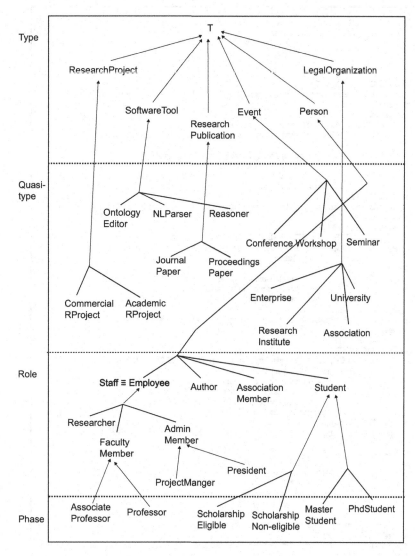

Figure 4. An example of the similar domain ontology

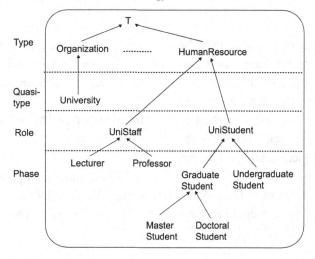

Figure 5. Five PAL constraints in sortal meta-class ontology "sort.owl"

```
<protege:PAL-CONSTRAINT rdf:ID="PAL-CONSTRAINT_1">
<protege:PAL-STATEMENT rdf:datatype="http://www.w3.org/2001/XMLSchema#string">
        (forall ?sub (forall ?super
                (=> (and ('sort-category' ?super "role"
                (subclass-of ?sub ?super)
                (own-slot-not-null 'sort-category' ?sub))
        (not ('sort-category' ?sub "type")))))
</protege:PAL-STATEMENT>
<protege:PAL-NAME rdf:datatype="http://www.w3.org/2001/XMLSchema#string">notRoleToType
</protege:PAL-NAME>
</protege:PAL-CONSTRAINT>
<protege:PAL-CONSTRAINT rdf:ID="PAL-CONSTRAINT_2">
<protege:PAL-STATEMENT rdf:datatype="http://www.w3.org/2001/XMLSchema#string">
        (forall ?sub (forall ?super
                (=> (and ('sort-category' ?super "quasi-type"
                (subclass-of ?sub ?super)
                (own-slot-not-null 'sort-category' ?sub))
        (not ('sort-category' ?sub "type")))))
</protege:PAL-STATEMENT>
<protege:PAL-NAME rdf:datatype="http://www.w3.org/2001/XMLSchema#string">notQuasi-typeToType
</protege:PAL-NAME>
</protege:PAL-CONSTRAINT>
<protege:PAL-CONSTRAINT rdf:ID="PAL-CONSTRAINT_3">
<protege:PAL-STATEMENT rdf:datatype="http://www.w3.org/2001/XMLSchema#string">
        (forall ?sub (forall ?super
                (=> (and ('sort-category' ?super "phase"
                (subclass-of ?sub ?super)
                (own-slot-not-null 'sort-category' ?sub))
        (not ('sort-category' ?sub "type")))))
</protege:PAL-STATEMENT>
<protege:PAL-NAME rdf:datatype="http://www.w3.org/2001/XMLSchema#string">notPhaseToType
</protege:PAL-NAME>
</protege:PAL-CONSTRAINT>
<protege:PAL-CONSTRAINT rdf:ID="PAL-CONSTRAINT_4">
<protege:PAL-STATEMENT rdf:datatype="http://www.w3.org/2001/XMLSchema#string">
        (forall ?sub (forall ?super
                (=> (and ('sort-category' ?super "role"
                (subclass-of ?sub ?super)
                (own-slot-not-null 'sort-category' ?sub))
        (not ('sort-category' ?sub "quasi-type")))))
</protege:PAL-STATEMENT>
<protege:PAL-NAME rdf:datatype="http://www.w3.org/2001/XMLSchema#string">notRoleToQuasi-type
</protege:PAL-NAME>
</protege:PAL-CONSTRAINT>
<protege:PAL-CONSTRAINT rdf:ID="PAL-CONSTRAINT_5">
<protege:PAL-STATEMENT rdf:datatype="http://www.w3.org/2001/XMLSchema#string">
        (forall ?sub (forall ?super
                (=> (and ('sort-category' ?super "phase"
                (subclass-of ?sub ?super)
                (own-slot-not-null 'sort-category' ?sub))
        (not ('sort-category' ?sub "quasi-type")))))
</protege:PAL-STATEMENT>
<protege:PAL-NAME rdf:datatype="http://www.w3.org/2001/XMLSchema#string">notPhaseToQuasi-type
</protege:PAL-NAME>
</protege:PAL-CONSTRAINT>
```

like Research-Community.owl. There may be some corresponding sorts between those two ontologies. For example, DoctoralStudent can be a correspondence of PhdStudent from Research-Community.owl because they are classified in the same sort category. However, it is visible that both sorts have terminological heterogeneity and taxonomical heterogeneity.

In summary, the main idea of EnOntoModel is that domain concepts are represented as sorts and classified into four groups according to the philosophical notions. Then, concept-level properties make the sorts enriched semantically.

Implementation of Sortal Meta-Class Ontology

In this section, the implementation framework of sortal meta-class ontology using Protégé OWL API is explained. There are two purposes in implementing sortal meta-class ontology named "sort.owl": (1) to support for the usability of EnOntoModel and (2) to provide conceptual analysis of the enriched ontologies. Sortal meta-class ontology consists of two major parts as follows:

a. **Specification of sortal meta-classes**

There are four sortal meta-classes. Their specification is described in Table 2. Each meta-class has two concept-level properties: sort-category and conceptual constraint. For example, an ownIC must be explicitly defined for any instance class of TypeSort meta-class.

b. **Axiomatization for Conceptual Analysis**

Five PAL constraints in the meta-class ontology are defined for the purpose of conceptual analysis. These constraints are written based on (a) ontological assumption "anti-rigid sort never subsumes rigid sorts," and (b) the disjointness between rigid sorts and between anti-rigid sorts. The names and meanings of these PAL constraints are:

1. notRoleToType: a role sort never subsumes a type sort;
2. notQuasi-typeToType: a quasi-type sort never subsumes a type sort;
3. notPhaseToType: a phase sort never subsumes a type sort;
4. notRoleToQuasi-type: a role sort never subsumes a quasi-type sort; and
5. notPhaseToQuasi-type: a phase sort never subsumes a quasi-type sort.

Figure 6 describes these five constraints. sort.owl is uploaded in Protégé ontology library[13] as an open source.

Table 2. Meta-classes and their properties

Meta-class	Properties
TypeSort	sort-category has "type"
	nameofOwnIC
Quasi-typeSort	sort-category has "quasi-type"
	nameOfCVA
RoleSort	sort-category has "role"
	nameOfEDR
PhaseSort	sort-category has "phase"
	nameOfCC

Development of EnOntoModel-Based Ontologies

The major steps of semantic enrichment process are illustrated in Figure 7.

1. First, users need to open a new project in Protégé for a source ontology called *O*. After opening a new project with ontology *O*, the classes and properties (both object and datatype properties) can be viewed via a click on OWL classes and properties respectively. Object tab is for individual properties and datatype tab is for datatype properties.

2. Second, it is necessary to import sort.owl into the opened project via the import service of Protégé.

3. Third, the meta-class of each ontological class needs to be changed from standard class, owl:class, to one of the sortal meta-classes via change metaclass option of Protégé. For this selection, users need the background knowledge of sort classification. By the selection of meta-class, the sort category value of each ontological class will be assigned automatically. Then, the user needs to assert necessary concept-level properties together with individual-level properties, according to the constraints given in Table 2.

Figure 6. Major steps of semantic enrichment process

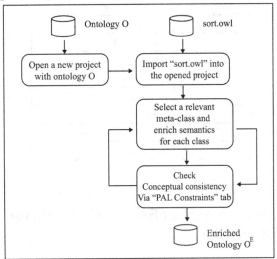

4. Fourth, the conceptual consistency of semantic enrichment can be evaluated by invoking the PAL constraints defined in sort.owl, via the PAL constraints tab of Protégé. For this verification, users need to run a DIG reasoner: Racer[14] or Pellet.[15] The steps of conceptual analysis through PAL constraints tab are listed.

   a. Add all constraints to the list (click on third button from choose constraints menu bar).

   b. Select the constraints you want to verify, by clicking a checkbox for each constraint.

   c. Select taxonomies and sorts to be evaluated for the selected constraints, via a click on attachments for selected constraints. If users intend to verify all defined sorts, this step will not be needed.

   d. Then, execute the selected PAL constraints via a click on evaluate selected constraints.

If there are some sorts that violate some PAL constraints, a list of the sorts will be displayed on the right-hand side. Then, users can view and correct them until they are consistent. An iterated process may need between Steps 3 and 4. Finally, the semantically-enriched ontology, O^E, can be successfully generated in OWL via Show RDF/XML source code option from code menu. A part of enriched ontology Research-Community. owl in OWL source code is shown in Figure 10, where each sort $s \in S$ is represented as an instance class of a certain sortal meta-class. The complete source code of Research-Community.owl is also uploaded in Protégé ontology library.[16]

ENRICHMENT-BASED ONTOLOGY MATCHING

The approach of ontology matching is based on an enrichment process as depicted in Figure 11. As the focal point of this ontology matching is for semantic heterogeneity, an enrichment process prior to matching process intends to clarify the semantics of concepts and their taxonomic structures.

There are several purposes for performing ontology matching. They can be divided into two general cases: *query answering* for information exchange, retrieval, or integration, and *ontology merging*. For query answering, a matching process is executed only for desired concepts (or candidate sorts). In the case of merging, the process needs to discover all possible correspondences between two ontologies. Then, some articulation rules are needed to integrate corresponding concepts in a balanced way. The objective of ontology merging is particularly for knowledge reuse in ontology management. For either purpose, ontology matching comprises how a class of ontology can be semantically matched to a class of the next ontology in an automatic or semi-automatic way. In this article, EnOntoModel-based ontology matching will be mainly discussed from the perspective of query answering.

Figure 7. An example of enriched concepts in OWL-full

```
<rdf:RDF xml:base="http://www.owl-ontologies.com/Research-Community.owl">
<owl:Ontology rdf:about=""><owl:importsrdf:resource="http://protege.stanford.edu/plugins/owl/protege"/>
</owl:Ontology>
-----------------------------------------------
<m-c:TypeSort rdf:ID="ResearchProject">
<m-c:sort-category rdf:datatype="http://www.w3.org/2001/XMLSchema#string">type</m-c:sort-category>
      <m-c:nameOfOwnIC rdf:datatype="http://www.w3.org/2001/XMLSchema#string">hasRProjName
</m-c:nameOfOwnIC>
<m-c:nameOfOwnIC rdf:datatype="http://www.w3.org/2001/XMLSchema#string">hasRProjOrganizer
</m-c:nameOfOwnIC>
<rdfs:subClassOf>
      <owl:Restriction>
          <owl:onProperty><owl:DatatypeProperty rdf:ID="hasRProjName"/></owl:onProperty>
          <owl:cardinality rdf:datatype="http://www.w3.org/2001/XMLSchema#int">1</owl:cardinality>
      </owl:Restriction>
</rdfs:subClassOf>
<owl:disjointWith rdf:resource="#Event"/><owl:disjointWith rdf:resource="#Person"/>..................

<m-c:Quasi-typeSort rdf:ID="Enterprise">
<m-c:sort-category rdf:datatype="http://www.w3.org/2001/XMLSchema#string">quasi-type</m-c:sort-category>
<m-c:nameOfCVA rdf:datatype="http://www.w3.org/2001/XMLSchema#string">hasOrgGroup</m-c:nameOfCVA>
<rdfs:subClassOf rdf:resource="#LegalOrganization"/>
      <owl:Restriction>
          <owl:onProperty><owl:DatatypeProperty rdf:about="#hasOrgGroup"/></owl:onProperty>
          <owl:hasValue rdf:datatype="http://www.w3.org/2001/XMLSchema#string">enterprise</owl:hasValue>
      </owl:Restriction>
</rdfs:subClassOf>
<owl:disjointWith rdf:resource="#University"/><owl:disjointWith rdf:resource="#Association"/>.............

<m-c:RoleSort rdf:ID="Employee">
      <owl:equivalentClass><m-c:RoleSort rdf:ID="Staff">
      <rdfs:subClassOf rdf:resource="#Person"/>
<m-c:sort-category rdf:datatype="http://www.w3.org/2001/XMLSchema#string">role</m-c:sort-category>
<m-c:nameOfEDR rdf:datatype="http://www.w3.org/2001/XMLSchema#string">employIn</m-c:nameOfOwnIC>
<owl:ObjectProperty rdf:ID="employIn">
      <rdfs:domain rdf:resource="#Employee"/>
      <rdfs:range rdf:resource="#LegalOrganization"/>
</owl:ObjectProperty>

<m-c:PhaseSort rdf:ID="Professor">
<rdfs:subClassOf rdf:resource="#FacultyMember"/>
<m-c:sort-category rdf:datatype="http://www.w3.org/2001/XMLSchema#string">phase</m-c:sort-category>
<m-c:nameOfCC rdf:datatype="http://www.w3.org/2001/XMLSchema#string">hasFacultyPosition
</m-c:nameOfOwnIC>
<rdfs:subClassOf>
      <owl:Restriction>
          <owl:hasValue rdf:datatype="http://www.w3.org/2001/XMLSchema#string">professor</owl:hasValue>
          <owl:onProperty rdf:resource="#hasFacultyPosition"/>
      </owl:Restriction>
</rdfs:subClassOf>
<owl:disjointWith rdf:resource="#AssociateProfessor"/>
.............................................
```

Design of EnOntoModel-Based Matching Method

A general architecture of EnOntoModel-based ontology matching is given in Figure 12. Suppose that there are two information systems driven in a common or overlapped domain. The systems are constructed using two heterogeneous ontologies: O and O'. A requirement of this mapping architecture is ontologies need to enrich their semantics in terms of EnOntoModel. The major characteristics of enriched ontologies are:

- Domain concepts are divided into four disjoint sort categories and conceptual consistency among the sorts is verified by using some philosophical constraints.
- The semantics of each sort, $s \in S$, is defined by a set of individual-level properties ($P^D(s)$), as well as a set of concept-level properties ($P^C(s)$).

For the purpose of information sharing and integration, semantic interoperability is required between the systems. In order to achieve this

Figure 8. An overview of enrichment-based matching

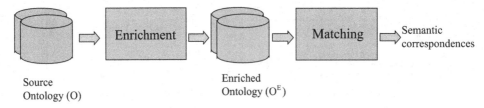

Figure 9. A general architecture of EnOntoModel-based ontology matching

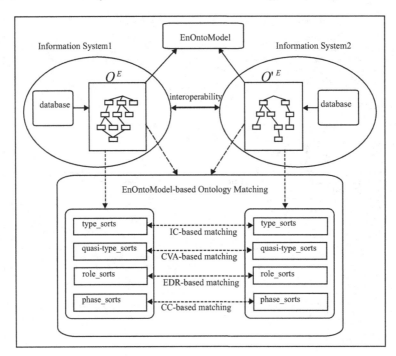

Figure 10. A view of roleMatching through divide-and-conquer approach

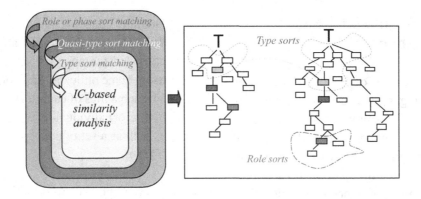

semantic interoperability, the responsibility of ontology matching is to find semantically similar sorts between two ontologies. Two enriched ontologies, O_E and O'_E together with related databases, are the input of EnOntoModel-based ontology matching process. Since sorts defined in each enriched-ontology are systematically divided into four groups, the taxonomy of ontology can be viewed as four-layered sort categories, as shown in Figure 12.

A novel idea of this matching architecture is, for a query, direct matching can be driven between sorts defined in the same classification group, instead of matching to all sorts by traversing taxonomies completely. *For ontology matching, it is claimed that there is no semantic correspondence between rigid sorts and anti-rigid sorts, nor between rigid sorts (type sorts and quasi-type sort) nor between anti-rigid sorts (role sorts and phase sorts), because their modality and classification constraints are different from each other.* This is an advantage over other existing mapping methods. Consequently, it can flatten iterations of a matching process and possibly reduce complexity. A detailed technique of EnOntoModel-based matching method is explained.

Let $O^E = \langle S,\leq,P^C,P^D,A \rangle$ and $O'^E = \langle S',\leq',P'^C, P'^D,A' \rangle$ be the logical view of two enriched heterogeneous ontologies. In the matching method, a mapping function $f : s \in S \to s' \in S'$ is considered where f performs a matching process to find a semantically corresponding sort s' for s. f is further divided into four sub-functions: (1) type sort matching f_{type}, (2) quasi-type sort matching $f_{quasi-type}$, (c) role sort matching f_{role}, and (4) phase sort matching f_{phase}.

- *typeMatching* is a mapping function that finds correspondence of a type_sort $s \in S_{type}$ in S'_{type}. Since each type_sort originates an IC, the main idea in determining correspondence between type_sorts is analyzing whether the ownICs of two type_sorts can export and import interchangeably or not (Tun & Tojo, 2005).

Exportability: If the ownIC of sort $s \in S_{type}$, ι_s, can identify and distinguish all the individuals of another sort $s' \in S'_{type}$, then the IC is called *exportable* to s', formally, $\forall x,y[p_{s'}(x) \wedge p_{s'}(y) \wedge x = y \to \iota_s(x) = \iota_s(y))]$.

Importability: If the ownIC of a sort $s' \in S'_{type}$, $\iota_{s'}$, can identify and distinguish all the individuals defined for sort $s \in S_{type}$, then the IC is called *importable* to s, formally, $\forall x,y[p_s(x) \wedge p_s(y) \wedge x = y \to \iota_{s'}(x) = \iota_{s'}(y))]$.

Correspondence (or semantic equality) between two type_sorts is determined by mutuality or sameness relation between their ownICs. The *mutuality* between two ownICs is decided when they are both exportable and importable, that is,

Figure 11. Experimental results in two domains

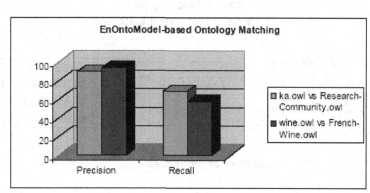

the IC values provided by the ownICs for each individual are different but they are unique. In the case of *sameness*, both ownICs must provide the *same IC value* for the same individual, in addition to being exportable and importable.

Example 6 *Suppose that 'hasFingerPrint' and 'hasIrisPattern'*[17] *are defined as the ICs of* Person, *and 'hasOrgName' and 'TitleOfOrganization' for the ICs of* organization. *Then, 'hasFingerPrint' and 'IrisPatternOf' have mutuality relation, while 'hasOrgName' and 'TitleOfOrganization' have sameness relation.*

The procedure of IC-based type_sort mapping is summarized. A bottom-up searching approach is applied because ICs are inherited from top to bottom:

1. Choose a sort s'_i from S'_{type}.
2. Test whether the own IC of sort s, ι_s, is exportable to s'_i.
3. If yes, find s'_j such that $s'_j > s'_i$, and test the top-most exportable sort s'_j for ι_s, then test whether the ownIC of sort s', $\iota_{s'}$, is importable to s or not.
   a. If yes, there is mutuality, then test for sameness.
      i. If yes, there is sort equality by sameness between s and s'_j.
      ii. Otherwise, there is sort equality by mutuality between s and s'_j.
   - Otherwise, try such $s'_j < s'_i$ on other branches for mutuality.
   - Otherwise, go to (1) to select a next possible sort s'_i.

The reason the mapping is contended by ICs is advantageous instead of comparing all properties and individuals is two-fold: (a) picking up only ownIC among properties, all the properties nor the property values need to be compared; (b) even the IC names do not need to be identical in different ontologies as far as they return same values:

- **quasi-typeMatching** is a mapping function that finds the correspondence of quasi-type_sort $s \in S_{quasi\text{-}type}$ in $S'_{quasi\text{-}type}$. First, the scope of possible matches in $S'_{quasi\text{-}type}$ is decided by finding type_sort $s'_1 \in S'_{type}$ which has a matched type_sort $s_1 \in S_{type}$ such that $s < s_1$. After that, the correspondence of s is determined by a similar CVA in both $P^D(s)$ and $P^D(s')$.
- **roleMatching** is a mapping function that finds the correspondence of role_sort $s \in$

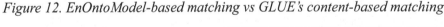

Figure 12. EnOntoModel-based matching vs GLUE's content-based matching

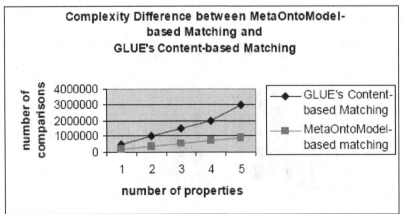

S_{role} in S'_{role}. There are three steps in the roleMatching function.

- First, select sort $s_1 \in S$ such that $s < s_1$, to find a corresponding type_sort $s'_1 \in S'_{type}$ through typeMatching.

- Second, if typeMatching successfully returns a corresponding type_sort s'_1, then determine the scope of possible matches by searching a corresponding quasi-type sort $s'_2 \in S'_{quasi-type}$.

- Third, according to s'_2, examine the scope of possible matches among role_sorts again, by selecting role_sorts s' such that $s' < s'_2$, and then determine the correspondence of s by a common EDR in both $P^D(s)$ and $P^D(s')$.

A general view of roleMatching through divide-and-conquer approach is illustrated in Figure 15.

- ***phaseMatching*** is a mapping function that finds the correspondence of phase_sort $s \in S_{phase}$ in S'_{phase}. The process of phaseMatching is almost similar to roleMatching, in analyzing a common CC except for EDR.

Evaluation

In this section, the EnOntoModel-based matching method is evaluated by calculating the mathematical complexity of matching function f.

Suppose that the maximum number of sorts in O^E and O'^E are N. Let m and n be the number of individuals for sorts s and s'. The retrieval of IC value for an individual takes a constant time. Also, the computation for the equality between two IC values takes a constant time. Therefore, the complexity to check whether two ICs supply the same IC value for an individual or not, will cost $O(1)$. Consequently, the tests for exportable IC and importable IC would take $O(m)$ and $O(n)$ respectively. For the convenience of estimation, if

a binary tree for taxonomies is regarded, then the average depth would be $\log N$, and the approximate number of leaves would be $N/2$.

The mathematical complexity of matching function f, denoted by T_f, is calculated based on the complexity of four sub-functions: f_{type}, $f_{quasi-type}$, f_{role}, and f_{phase}. Since type sorts are necessary for EnOntoModel-based ontologies concerning the identity of individuals, the number of type sorts in both ontologies is not zero. Let the maximum number of type sorts be k, $1 \leq k \leq N$. Then, the maximum number of quasi-type sorts, role sorts, and phase sorts, in each of ontologies will be $N-k$.

Let T_{type} be the worse case complexity of type sort matching. T_{type} can be calculated based on the cost of exportable IC in maximum plus the cost of importable IC. The maximum steps to achieve a top-most exportable sort in O'^E would be $k/2 + \log k$. Then, the worse case complexity of type sort matching will be as follows:

$$T_{type} = (k/2 + \log k) \times m + n$$

where $(k/2 + \log k/2) \times m$ for the maximum number of comparisons in export test, and n for the maximum number of comparisons in import test. Let $T_{quasi-type}$, T_{role}, and T_{phase}, are the worse case complexities of $f_{quasi-type}$, f_{role}, and f_{phase}, respectively. Then, the complexities of these sub-functions are as follows:

$$T_{quasi-type} = T_{type} + (N-k) \times O(1)$$
$$T_{role} = T_{quasi-type} + (N-k) \times (m+n)$$
$$T_{phase} = T_{quasi-type} + (N-k) \times O(1)$$

Note that the complexity of CVA or CC, is assumed to be $O(1)$ because of direct attribute value or constraint checking. In the case of role sort matching, matching between two EDRs will cost $O(m+n)$, due to checking whether two EDRs are semantically similar. Finally, T_f in the worse case will be as follows:

$$T_f = T_{type} + T_{quasi\text{-}type} + T_{role} + T_{phase}$$
$$= (((k/2 + \log k) \times m + n) + ((N-k) \times m) + ((N-k) \times n))$$
$$= O(N \times m)$$

Although the mathematical complexity of f_{type} is $O(N \times m)$, in practical cases, we can expect that $(k/2 + \log k) < N$.

If T_f is applied for the complete ontology matching, T_c, of all available sorts between O_c and O^{rc}, then T_c would be $N \times T_{type} = O(N^2 \times m)$. However, it can be reduced to $O(N \log N \times m)$, because the matching functions need not be executed for the sub-sorts of every un-matched type sort.

EXPERIMENTAL RESULTS

In this section, the experimental results of EOM and the experience of ontology mapping is presented. The major objective is to evaluate the matching accuracy of EOM using real data sets. The implementation of EOM is coded in Java by utilizing Jena OWL API and Protégé OWL API.

In the experiments, evaluations were conducted in terms of two measurements: *precision* and *recall*. In general, precision and recall measures are designed to compare the set of correct correspondences in the program generated correspondences with expert-defined correspondences. Three sets are denoted: (a) C_e for expert-defined correct correspondences, (b) C_f for program-generated correspondences by using EOM function f, and (c) C_{fe} for the correctness of C_f in C_e such that $C_{fe} = C_f \cap C_e$. Then, the correctness of Precision and recall are defined as follows:

- Precision (P) is the percentage of correctness in the program generated correspondences. P is calculated by $|C_{fe}|/|C_f|$.
- Recall (R) is the percentage of the correctness of program generated correspondences,

comparing with expert-defined correct correspondences. R is calculated by $|C_{fe}|/|C_e|$.

In order to get real data sets for this experiment, a number of OWL ontology libraries were analyzed on the Web, in particular Protégé OWL library.[18] Even though a large number of ontologies are available, most of them are domain-dependent such as bio-medical, chemical, geographic, micro-electronic, space & earth, PSM-problem solving method, country, travel, wine, and so forth. Thus, it is not easy to choose some of them as mapping candidates without adequate background knowledge of each domain. Here, we selected two domains: academic research and wine. Then, we chose two ontologies for each domain as follow and prepared two data sets:

1. **Ontologies in academic research:** Ontologies describe concepts in academic research such as research areas, activities, publications, institutions, and kinds of community people. Namely, they are ka.owl[19] and Research-Community.owl. In ka.owl,[20] the developer focuses on the concepts of academic research particularly in knowledge acquisition. Research-Community.owl is general rather than ka.owl. However, both ontologies are partially overlapped with some kinds of heterogeneity.

2. **Ontologies in wine:** Wine ontologies describe concepts in wine domain that consist of winery, wine region, wine grape, wine categories, and recommended food of fine wines, and so forth. wine.owl[21] covers most of famous wineries and vineyards around the world. French-Wine.owl is developed by the author and it is specialized only for wines in France regions. The significant difference between two wine ontologies is the approach of conceptualization, that is, wine.owl is mainly focused on wine regions while wine categories in French-Wine.owl are based on wine grapes particularly grown

in France regions. Thus, heterogeneity is highly involved between two similar concepts.

Note that the enriched versions of ka.owl and wine.owl are generated in the form of EnOnto-Model. Table 3 shows the statistics of data sets given for enriched ontologies. Ninety percent common individuals for both wine ontologies were assigned. However, the percentage of overlapped individuals between two academic research ontologies is about 40%. Table 4 shows the precision and recall of two mapping experiments. Then, Figure 16 illustrates the experimental results in a bar chart style.

What was learnt from this experiment is the precision of EOM method is sufficient, that is, the concept correspondences found by the program is mostly correct. It is contended to say this correctness is affected from enrichment because concepts and individuals are consistently defined in terms of specific properties such as ICs, EDR, CVA, and CC. It was observed that there is a little tricky in comparing two IC values—mostly string values in different orders and phrases—which are given in terms of compound ICs. It is better to use an appropriate text analyzer instead of conventional string matching. Also, an issue with these measures is that the correctness of expert-defined correspondences is a subjective measure, which can be slightly varied by expert to expert according to their knowledge. A better way is to let appropriate domain experts evaluate the method through ontologies used in real information systems, and then compare the results with other methods.

RELATED WORK

As for related work, it will be discussed in two divisions. The first division is a comparative discussion with existing mapping methods. The next division is difference between OntoClean and the research.

Ontology Matching

Here, a brief summary of some matching methods are described, such as MAFRA, ONION, PROMPT, IF-Map, COMA++, QOM, and GLUE, as related work to EnOntoModel-based matching.

In *MAFRA* (Maedche, Motik, Silva, & Volz, 2003), similarity between two concepts is calculated mainly using lexical analysis via WordNet, domain glossaries, bi-lingual dictionaries, and corpuses. There is no explicit deterministic heuristics other than lexical heuristics (or synonyms), in the semantic bridge construction.

ONION (Mitra & Wiederhold, 2002) is an heuristic-based ontology mapping system to resolve terminological heterogeneity using two matching approaches: linguistic matching via WordNet[22] and instance-based matching via databases. ONION provided algorithms for how to calculate a similarity score between a little complex names of ontological concepts such as 'Department of Defense' and 'Defense Ministry'.

Table 3. Statistics of data sets

Ontology	$|S|$	$|S_{Type}|$	$|S_{Quasi\text{-}type}|$	$|S_{Role}|$	$|S_{Phase}|$	P^D	Individual
ka.owl	82	10	60	8	4	137	250
ReasearchCommunity.owl	35	6	14	9	6	59	80
wine.owl	105	26	79	0	0	67	186
FrenchWine.owl	73	15	58	0	0	43	142

PROMPT (Noy & Musen, 2003) is a semi-automatic and interactive tool suit for performing ontology merging, based on the frame paradigm. For concept matching, AnchorPROMPT firstly detects linguistic similarity matches (called anchors) between domain concepts. It is a usual way of fixing the scope of possible correspondences. Secondly, AnchorPROMPT analyzes the paths of the input ontologies delimited by the anchors in order to determine concepts frequently appearing in similar positions on similar paths. Thirdly, PROMPT proposes some correspondences determined by analyzing the structural knowledge—both schematic and taxonomical knowledge—of terminologically similar concepts. The limitation of PROMPT is that the two ontologies in the merging process should be different versions of the same ontology. This limitation intends to reduce the complexity of mapping and merging between heterogeneous ontologies.

IF-Map (Kalfoglou & Schorlemmer, 2002) is a channel-theory-based ontology mapping technique. In IF-Map, there are two assumptions: (1) using a common reference ontology for all local ontologies and (2) considering an equal set of instances for the decision of concept mapping. Kalfoglou and Schorlemmer claim that IF-Map could provide fully automation for a matching process. However, the second assumption is a big restriction for the applicability of IF-Map concerning instantiation heterogeneity.

COMA++ (Aumueller & Massmann, 2005) supports higher-level strategies to address complex match problems, in particular fragment-based matching and the reuse of previous match results. Following the divide-and-conquer idea, it decomposes a large match problem into smaller sub-problems by matching at the level of schema fragments. COMA++ encompasses two matching phases: (a) identifying similar fragments, and (b) matching fragments.

QOM (Ehrig & Stabb, 2004) focuses on less run-time complexity for mapping efficiency of large-size, light-weight ontologies. However, QOM mostly constitutes a straightforward name-based similarity computation via RDFS syntax in order to determine correspondences between two ontologies.

GLUE (Doan, Madhavan, Domingos, & Halevy, 2002) is a system that employs a multi-strategy machine learning technique with joint probability distribution. Firstly, GLUE identifies the similarities of instances. Secondly, it compares between relations, based on the similarity results of instances. GLUE uses two kinds of base learners: a name learner to encounter possible correspondences through a linguistic approach and a number of content learners to predict the similarity between instances and between properties according to the types of properties. Finally, meta-learner combines the predictions of all base learners and determines concept correspondences.

Among the mapping tools, the matching methods of PROMPT, COMA++, and GLUE are similar even though PROMPT and COMA++ do not apply instance-based analysis. The same point among them is that the scope of possible matches is predicted using name-based matching. EnOntoModel-based matching method uses concept-level properties together with intentional

Table 4. Precision (P) and recall (R) on data sets

Ontology Mapping	$|C_e|$	$|C_j|$	$|C_{fe}|$	P	R
ka.owl and Reasearch-Community.owl	26 = 6+11+5+4	20=5+7+4+4	18	90.00	69.23
wine.owl and French-Wine.owl	29=11+18+0+0	18=6+12+0+0	17	90.44	58.62

and extensional knowledge of domain concepts. This usage is a distinctive feature of our method from the others. Each mapping method has its own advantages with different focuses, assumptions, and limitations.

In general, two advantages for EnOntoModel-based matching are contended over other mapping methods. The first advantage is a more reliable approach of predicting possible correspondences. As has been discussed, two concepts with the same name may have different semantics. Suppose that ontology developed by a certain university, where only graduate courses are available, uses concept name Student for a set of graduate students. Another ontology developed by a different university, where only undergraduate courses are available, may use the same name for different semantics. In the opposite case, two concepts might have different names. Because the meaning of concept names cannot completely express the semantics of concepts, a chance of correspondence between two terminologically quite different concepts is very less or not obtainable. In the method, domain concepts are systematically classified into sort categories according to EnOntoModel. Therefore, the scope of possible correspondences is already fixed. Moreover, the method can trim impossible correspondences mainly by analyzing the equalities of type sorts. The second advantage is less complexity that is achieved by the following points:

- The complexity is initially reduced by a direct matching between the same sort groups.
- The complexity is reduced by trimming impossible correspondences via type sorts.
- The method can determine sort correspondences by analyzing only a specific property, ownIC, CVR, EDR, or CC, while other methods need to analyze all defined properties.

In order to prove for less complexity, the similarity analysis by the content learners of GLUE in terms of mathematical complexity is examined. In GLUE, the similarity between two nodes (classes) is determined by the similarity of their attributes and relations with their neighbor nodes. Then, the similarity between two attributes is calculated by the similarity between their corresponding instances. Suppose that Nc, Np, and Ni are the maximum number of nodes, properties (attributes & relations), and instances. Let us assume that the complexity of comparing two attribute values between two instances is $O(1)$. Then, the complexity of calculating similarity between two instances will be $O(N_p)$. And, $O(N_p^2 \times N_i)$ will be the complexity for the similarity between two nodes. Finally, the matching between two ontologies will take $O(\log N_c \times N_p^2 \times N_i)$, by assuming the cost of meta-learner is constant. In order to compare GLUE with our matching method, let us substitute N for every parameter; the cost of GLUE will become $O(N^3 \log N)$, while the matching method costs $O(N^2 \log N)$ because the method does not require comparing all properties belonging to each class.

Figure 17 illustrates the complexity difference between EnOntoModel-based matching and GLUE's content-based matching in a line chart style. The chart states that the complexity difference is especially by number of properties, assuming that number of sorts and instances are equal in each case. Whenever the number of properties specified for sorts increases, then the complexity difference will increase proportionally. In this comparison, IC is considered as a compound property, that is, the number of individual-level properties compiled for an IC is ≥ 1.

Ontological Analysis

Welty and Guarino provided a methodology called OntoClean to perform ontological analysis—cleaning the taxonomic structure of ontologies by validating subsumption relationships. The methodology is based on some ontological notions drawn from philosophy. The foundation of Onto-Clean was started in 1994. Then, the OntoClean methodology was first introduced in a series of papers (Welty & Guarino, 2000b, 2000a; Kaplan, 2001; Guarino & Welty, 2001; Welty & Andersen, 2005). All references can be found at the home page of OntoClean[23] .

OntoClean methodology consists of three main contributions: (a) defining four fundamental meta-properties: identity (**I**), rigidity (**R**), unity (**U**)[24] , and dependency (**D**) for ontological concepts, (b) classifying ontological concepts into sortal and non-sortal concepts given by a quadruple of certain values[25] based on the meta-properties, and (c) providing some subsumption constraints to clean taxonomic structures of ontologies.

It was observed that the philosophical notions behind OntoClean are useful not only for onto-logical analysis but also for conceptual modeling of ontologies. Therefore, three[26] of OntoClean's meta-properties are applied for ontology mapping in order to deal with semantic heterogeneity. Concerning the philosophical notions, the add-ons are described over OntoClean as follows:

- The formalizations of OntoClean's meta-properties are confusing without a precise semantics by a formal logic language. Thus, a first-order quantified modal language L^E was provided and each notion explicitly redefined.

- In OntoClean, IC is formalized as a characteristic relation which is not precise to apply in computer systems. An explicit formalization of IC was provided using a unary function of language L^E. In additon, it was shown that ICs can be written in the form of owl:DatatypeProperty with restrictions of owl:FunctionalProper- ty, owl:InverseFunctionalProperty, and =1 cardinality. Relatively, domain concepts/classes can be represented as sorts and sorts can be

written in the form of owl:Class which is restricted by an IC.

- A semantically-enriched model of ontologies (named EnOntoModel) could be provided, in which the philosophical notions are explicitly embedded into domain ontologies as concept-level properties.

- Also, how to enrich domain ontologies in the form of EnOntoModel through Protégé OWL API was demonstrated, and an idea similar to OntoClean's analysis in the meta-class ontology was applied to check conceptual consistency of enriched ontologies.

In summary, the philosophical notions are applied for ontological analysis in the work of OntoClean. Then, they are employed in the research for an efficient matching between heterogeneous ontologies through a semantic enrichment process.

BENEFIT AND COST OF ENONTOMODEL

The fundamental objective of semantic enrichment is to provide adequate and precise semantics for domain concepts by fertilizing additional knowledge in the descriptions of concepts. In this research, the motivation of semantic enrichment is derived from matching between heterogeneous ontologies. In order to deal with wide-scale semantic heterogeneity, philosophy-based concept classification theory and EnOntoModel were proposed. Though some advantages particularly time cost and accuracy, are significant in EOM method, the cost of enrichment for this is admitted. Thus, what is the development cost of EnOntoModel-based ontology and how to calculate it, is raised as an issue.

There are two ways in the development of enriched ontologies. The first choice is the development of enriched version for an existing OWL ontology. The second choice is the direct development of ontologies in the form of EnOntoModel. In the case of second choice, a conceptually consistent and structured ontology, O^E, is first built. Then, developers can reformat O^E version to O by reformatting the meta-class of each domain concept to standard OWL class, and then removing the imported link of sortal meta-class ontology sort.owl via *remove* option of Protégé import. Note that the import link should not be moved out before reformatting concepts; otherwise concepts can be lost together with import withdrawal. Taxonomies and concept descriptions between O^E and O are almost the same except concept-level properties. By the first way, there may be different between two versions not only in taxonomies but also in concept descriptions, because enrichment process might affect to original version in order to clarify and enrich the semantics of concepts.

In order to deal with semantic heterogeneity, most matching methods need either a preprocessing before mapping or pruning off mapping results via expert-interaction, or both. For example, a mapping approach called risk minimization-based ontology matching (RiMOM) (RiMOM06) is recently contributed concerning both name-based matching and instance-based matching. In RiMOM, the developers use pre-pruning as well as post-pruning processes in their experiment. In EOM, it can be said that enrichment framework is a kind of pre-pruning process. However, this enrichment can improve not only mapping results between heterogeneous ontologies, but also conceptual consistency of ontologies.

Currently, there is no idea to estimate the cost of enrichment in mathmetical formula. However, the discussion would be useful to judge the benefit and cost of EnOntoModel.

CONCLUSION

In this article, finding semantic correspondences between two heterogeneous ontologies is approached with focus on a matching method between classified concepts using the most relevant properties which can certainly determine a correspondence between two semantically equivalent concepts. The whole approach can be partitioned into two phases: (1) the semantic enrichment phase and (2) the mapping phase. The former phase consists of modeling and implementing semantically-enriched ontologies. The later phase is for a matching method between enriched ontologies.

The advantages of the EnOntoModel-based matching method over other mapping methods are as follows:

- Direct concept matching is initiated between the same sort categories, instead of a blind or exhaustive matching among all sorts.
- The scope of possible correspondences can be determined according to IC inheritance via type sorts. This approach is more rigorous than natural language approaches in the case of highly terminological heterogeneity.
- Semantic correspondence between two sorts is decided by direct matching between the properties, ownICs, CVA, EDR, and CC, instead of comparing all the properties belonging to the sorts. Consequently, the time complexity of EnOntoModel-based matching is less than others.
- Moreover, expert-interaction is not necessarily required to verify the matching results.

Also, some philosophical foundations are successfully added into formal ontologies to support semantic interoperability among information systems. Guarino and Welty first introduced these philosophical notions for ontological analysis. After them, Guizzardi introduced the same notions for the foundations of conceptual models, particularly UML diagrams, as a meta-model. These ideas were originally applied for ontology matching. EnOntoModel is an integrated research work of philosophy, conceptualization, formal ontologies, mathematical logic, and knowledge representation.

The limitation of this work is that domain ontologies need to be enriched in the form of EnOntoModel, in order to use the matching method. It is also admitted that users need sufficient knowledge to classify domain concepts into sort categories. Although it was proved that the matching has an advantage in finding correspondences, the user effort required for the enrichment phase will be the cost of this enrichment-based matching method. This matching will be particularly attractive for information exchange in identity intensive domains such as e-commerce, social security, and trust-worthy services.

It is hoped to implement the matching method as a Java plug-in, and do empirical evaluation by uploading as a protégé plug-in and let domain experts to evaluate it by using some ontologies developed for real information systems and operations. However, the implementation work for a plug-in is not yet complete. This implementation will be continured as a part of future work.

REFERENCES

Beierle, C. (1992). An Order-sorted logic for knowledge representation systems. *Artificial Intelligence, 55,* 149–191.

Belardinelli, F. (2006). *Quantified modal logic and ontology of physical objects.* PhD Thesis, Scuola Normale Superiore (SNS) in Pisa.

Bowers, S., & Delcambre, L. (2000). *Representing and transforming model-based information.* Paper presented at the Workshop on the Semantic Web at the Fourth European Conference on Digital Libraries.

Ceri, S., & Widom, J. (1993). Managing semantic heterogeneity with production rules and persistent queues. In *Proceedings of the 19th VLDB Conference* (pp. 108–119). Dublin, Ireland.

Chalupsky, H. (2000). A translation system for symbolic logic. In Proceedings of the *Principles of Knowledge Representation and Reasoning (KR2000)* (pp. 471–482).

Corsi, G. (2002). A unified completeness theorem for quantified modal logics. *Journal of Symbolic Logic, 67,* 1483-1510.

Cresswell, M. J. (2001). *A Blackwell guide to philosophical logic.*

Doan, A., Madhavan, J., Domingos, P., & Halevy, A. (2002). Learning to map between ontologies on the semantic Web. In *Proceedings of the World Wide Web Consortium 2002,* ACM.

Ehrig, M., & Stabb, S. (2004). *Qom-quick ontology mapping.* Technical report, University of Karlsruhe, Institute of AIFB.

Fitting, M., & Mendelsohn, R. L. (1998). *First-order modal logic.*

Guarino, N., & Welty, C. (2001), Supporting ontological analysis of taxonomic relationships. *Data and Knowledge Engineering, 39,* 51–74.

Guizzardi, G., Wagner, G., & Sinderen, M. (2004). A formal theory of conceptual modeling universals. In *Proceedings of the Workshop on Philosophy and Informatics (WSPI).*

Hughes, G. E., & Cresswell, M. J. (2003). *A new introduction to modal logic* (3rd ed.). Routledge.

Kalfoglou, Y., & Schorlemmer, M. (2002), If-map: An ontology mapping method based on information-flow theory. In *Proceedings of* the *1st International Conference on Ontologies, Databases and Applications of Semantics (ODBASE'02).*

Kalfoglou, Y., & Schorlemmer, M. (2005). Ontology mapping: The state of the art. *Journal of Semantic Interoperability and Integration,*

Kaneiwa, K., & Mizoguchi, R. (2005). An order-sorted quantified modal logic for meta-ontology. In *Proceedings of the International Conference on Automated Reasoning with Analytic Tableaux* and Related Methods (TABLEAUX 2005), LNCS 3702.

Kaplan, A. N. (2001). Towards a consistent logical framework for ontological analysis. In *Proceedings of the International Conference on Formal Ontology in Information Systems* (pp. 244–255). ACM Press.

Kripke, S. (1971). Identity and necessity. In M. Munitz (Ed.), *Identity and individuation* (pp. 135–164).

Maedche, A., Motik, B., Silva, N., & Volz, R. (2003). *MAFRA—an ontology mapping framework in the context of the semantic Web.*

March, S. T. (1990). Heterogeneous databases [Special issue]. *ACM Computing Surveys*, 22(3).

Miller, B. (1987). "Exists" and existence. *Review of Metaphysics*, 40, 237–270.

Mitra, P., & Wiederhold, G. (2002). Resolving terminology heterogeneity in ontologies. In *Proceedings of ECAI'02 Workshop on Ontologies and Semantic Interoperability.*

Noy, N. F., & Musen, M. A. (2002). Evaluating ontology-mapping tools: Requirements and experience. In *Proceedings of the Workshop on Evaluation of Ontology Tools at EKAW'02.*

Noy, N. F., & Musen, M. A. (2003). The prompt suite: Interactive tools for ontology merging and mapping. *International Journal of Human-Computer Studies*, 59, 983–1024.

Tang, J., Li, J., Liang, B., Huang, X., Li, Y., & Wang, K. (2006). Using Bayesian decision for ontology mapping. *Journal of Web Semantics*,

Tun, N. N., & Tojo, S. (2005). IC-based ontology expansion in devouring accessibility. In *Proceedings of the Australian Ontology Workshop (AOW 2005)* (Vol. 58, pp. 99–106). Australian Computer Society.

Visser, P. R. S., Jones, D. M. R., Bench-Capon, T. J. M., & Shave, M. J. R. (1997). Assessing heterogeneity by classifying ontology mismatches. In *Proceedings of AAAI'97 Spring Symposium on Ontological Engineering*, Stanford University, USA.

Welty, C., & Guarino, N. (2000a). A formal ontology of properties. In *Proceedings of EKAW-2000: The Conference on Conceptual Modeling.*

Welty, C., & Guarino, N. (2000b). Identity, unity and individuality: Towards a formal toolkit for ontological analysis. In *Proceedings of ECAI-2000.*

Welty, N., & Andersen, W. (2005). Towards OntoClean 2.0: A framework for rigidity. *Journal of Applied Ontology*,

Wong, K. (2003). *Rigid designation, existence and semantics for quantified modal logic* (Tech. Rep.), Department of Philosophy, The Chinese University of Hong Kong.

ENDNOTES

1    $\forall x \Box \phi \rightarrow \Box \forall x \phi$ [Barcan formula]

2   owl:ObjectProperty relates two individuals, but owl:DatatypeProperty relates an individual and a datatype value (see http://www.w3.org/TR/owl-guide/).

3    $K: \Box(\phi \rightarrow \psi) \rightarrow (\Box \phi \rightarrow \Box \psi)$, $T: \Box \phi \rightarrow \phi$, $4: \Box \phi \rightarrow \Box \Box \phi$, and $5: \phi \rightarrow \Box \Diamond \phi$

4   Entity type has an extension (instances) and an intension which includes an applicability criteria for determining whether an entity is an instance of it.

5   An individual means an entity which is countable as a whole (Welty & Guarino, 2000).

6   An identity criteria (also called identity condition) supports the judgment of whether two particulars describe the same entity or not.

7 http://www.formalontology.it/index.htm

8 $(x=y)\rightarrow(p_\phi\rightarrow p_\phi[x/y])$ where p_ϕ denotes a first-order unary predicate for ontological property ϕ.

9 Part-of relation states the component relation between two individuals such as PC and processor, and constituent states the composition relation between individuals such as mother board and chips.

10 $\forall x \;\Box[p_\phi(x)\rightarrow\exists y(p_\psi(y)\wedge\neg Part(y,x)\wedge\neg Constituent(y,x))]$ (Guarino00c)

11 hasWineName includes winery, appellation, and a vintage. For example, "Joseph Drouhin 2004 Chablis Premier Cru" is the name of a wine produced from 'Joseph Drouhin', appellation is 'Chablis Premier Cru', and vintage year is '2004'.

12 The partions of a type sort form a complete generalization and they are disjoint from each other.

13 http://Protégé.cim3.net/cgi-bin/wiki.pl?ProtégéOntologiesLibrary

14 http://www.sts.tu-harburg.de/ r.f.moeller/racer/

15 http://www.mindswap.org/2003/pellet/

16 http://Protégé.cim3.net/cgi-bin/wiki.pl?ProtégéOntologiesLibrary

17 It is admitted that a type_sort can originate more than one IC (say multiple ownICs), for example, Person has three ownICs: hasFingerPrint, IrisPatternOf, and hasPalmVeinPattern.

18 http://Protégé.cim3.net/cgi-bin/wiki.pl?ProtégéOntologiesLibrary

19 ka.owl is developed by Ian Horrocks who is a professor in the School of Computer Science at the University of Manchester, also a member of Information Management Group for Formal Methods and Bio and Health Informatics (see http://www.cs.man.ac.uk/%7Ehorrocks/).

20 http://Protégé.cim3.net/file/pub/ontologies/ka/ka.owl

21 wine.owl is developed from Stanford University (see http://Protégé.cim3.net/file/pub/ontologies/wine/wine.owl). The original version is in DAML and it is substantially changed to OWL version.

22 http://wordnet.princeton.edu/

23 http://www.ontoclean.org/

24 Unity is the notion of whole for each individual of a concept. Something is a *whole* if all of its parts are connected to each other and to nothing else (Guarino & Welty, 2000). The unity considers an internal relation between an instance and its parts, such as the parts of a human body are tightly connected to each other as a whole body of a human.

25 A combination of meta-property values is presented as a classifier of concepts. For example, (+**R**+**O**+**I**-**D**) for type, (+**R**-**O**+**I**-**D**) for quasi-type, and (~**R**-**O**+**I**+**D**) for material role where **O** for ownIC, and +**R** and ~**R** are rigidity values: rigid and anti-rigid respectively. For each meta-property, there are three different property values by attaching different symbols: +, -, and ~.

26 Unity is indirectly applied in the meaning of individuals because every individual can be assumed as a whole which is countable and identifiable.

This work was previously published in the International Journal of Intelligent Information Technologies, Vol. 4, Issue 1, edited by V. Sugumaran, pp. 1-30, copyright 2008 by IGI Publishing (an imprint of IGI Global).

Chapter 9
A New Approach for Building a Scalable and Adaptive Vertical Search Engine

H. Arafat Ali
Mansoura University, Egypt

Ali I. El Desouky
Mansoura University, Egypt

Ahmed I. Saleh
Mansoura University, Egypt

ABSTRACT

Search engines are the most important search tools for finding useful and recent information on the Web today. They rely on crawlers that continually crawl the Web for new pages. Meanwhile, focused crawlers have become an attractive area for research in recent years. They suggest a better solution for general-purpose search engine limitations and lead to a new generation of search engines called vertical-search engines. Searching the Web vertically is to divide the Web into smaller regions; each region is related to a specific domain. In addition, one crawler is allowed to search in each domain. The innovation of this article is adding intelligence and adaptation ability to focused crawlers. Such added features will certainly guide the crawler perfectly to retrieve more relevant pages while crawling the Web. The proposed crawler has the ability to estimate the rank of the page before visiting it and adapts itself to any changes in its domain using.

INTRODUCTION

The World Wide Web (WWW) is a huge source of distributed data that is increasingly growing with dynamic nature. Millions of Web pages are added daily and others are deleted. The numerous size and dynamic nature of the Web makes it difficult to search efficiently. Many problems arise when trying to build an information retrieval system on the Web because the data is distributed, unstructured, heterogeneous, as well as, highly volatile with a large volume and poor quality. Today, three search services are available which are directories, meta-search engines, and search engines.

Search directories, also called Web portals or taxonomies, organize Web pages into a tree-like topic hierarchy. General topics can be sub-divided into more specified topics or categories. The tree-like structure of the Web directories allows non-expert users to find useful information easily (Zhdanova & Fensel, 2005). Some of the most popular portals on the Web today are: Yahoo, LookSmart, and Open Directory Project. Directories have two main drawbacks (i) the tax-onomies are manually populated; hence, only a small portion of the Web could be covered and (ii) The directory structure is defined according to the knowledge of the human constructors, which means that different hierarchies could be built for the same page collection by different constructors.

A meta-search engine is a system that sends the user query to a several search engines via a number of interface agents, then collects the results from the different search engines, and present them to the user. Meta-search engines are powerful since

the best search engine covers only about 16% of the Web (Gulli & Signorin, 2005).

Search engines are information retrieval systems that help users to find what they want on the Web. The user sends his query to the search engine in a form of keywords. Then, the search engine searches its database and retrieves the pages relevant to the search query. Finally, the query result is introduced to the user in the form of a ranked list of relevant pages. Most search engines rely on crawlers to traverse the Web to collect pages, pass them to the indexer, and then follow links from one page to another. Web crawlers have the ability to index thousands of pages per day. This overcomes the limitations of the Web portals. They also keep track of changes made to pages visited earlier. No page is added to the search engine database until the crawler visits that page. For the purpose of illustration, the basic components of a typical search engine are shown in Table 1 and Figure 1.

Search engines suffer from many problems such as low precision and recall, freshness problem (Cho & Garcia-Molina, 2000), poor retrieval rate, long list of results which consume user time and effort, a huge amount of rapidly expanded information which causes a storage problem, and finally, a large number of daily hits which means most search engines are not able to provide

Table 1. Search engine components

Component	Description
Crawler	Also called robot, spider, or Web worm; they are used to retrieve Web pages, read them, pass them to the indexer, then follow links to the next page (Marios, Athena, & Loizos, 2005).
Indexer	It receives the pages retrieved by the crawler, analyzes the various elements of each page like title, headings, body text, then extracts the main features of the page, finally dumping the retrieved features into the database (Qiu, Shao, & Zatsman 2003).
Database	Stores information retrieved from each page the indexer analyze.
Query manager	It has four basic functions: (i) it receives the query and reformulates it into a suitable data-base query, (ii) it retrieves relevant pages from a database, (iii) it ranks results according to the user query, and (iv) it performs analysis on the retrieved pages including categorization and text summarization (Jianjun, David, & Yuan, 2000).
User interface	This is the part that the users see. It allows the user to enter his query, sending the query to a database via a query manager and finally displays the search result the user.

enough computational power to satisfy each users' information need (Chau, Zeng, & Chen, 2001). Analysis of search results, such as verifying that the retrieved Web pages still exist or clustering of Web pages into different categories, are not available in most search engines.

To overcome those problems, more specialized search engines to help users locate pertinent information in various domains are proposed. This leads to a new generation of search engines which are called vertical search engines (Michael & Hsinchun, 2004). Many different vertical search engines are available on the Internet, each has its own characteristics, such as LawCrawler that searches for legal information on the Web and BuildingOnline, specialized in searching in the building industry domain on the Web. In contrast to general-purpose search engines, vertical search engines use a special class of crawlers called focused crawlers (Thanh, David, Nick, & Kathleen, 2005), as they crawl the Web for pages with a specific topic or related to a certain domain.

A focused crawler as stated in Padmini, Filippo, and Gautam (2005), can be considered as a special type of crawlers that seeks out pages about a specific topic and guides the search based on both the content and link structure (Gautam & Padmini, 2006). It has a priority queue that is initialized with a number of seed pages (Vinod, Vydiswaran, & Sunita, 2005). The main components of the focused crawler are classifier, distiller, and crawler. The classifier makes relevance judgements on pages to decide on link expansion and the distiller determines centrality of pages to determine visit priorities. The latter is based on connectivity analysis. They discuss harvest ratio which is the rate at which relevant pages are acquired and how effectively irrelevant pages are filtered away. They state that it is desirable to explore out from keyword-based and limited-radius search for resources. Another observation was that the Web graph is rapidly mixing random links related to random topics within an extremely short radius. At the same time, long paths and large subgraphs with topical coherence do exist.

Figure 1. The basic components of a typical search engine

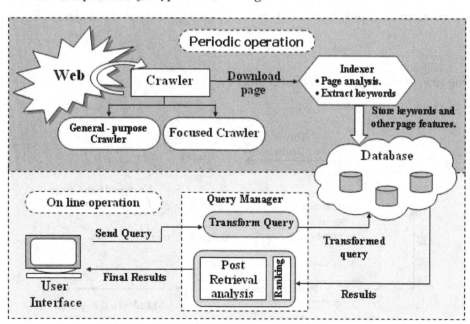

As illustrated in Figure 2, a focused crawler fetches the page that is located on the top of its queue, analyze the page, and assign a score for each link found in the processed page. The links are sorted according to the scores and inserted into the queue; the queue will organize itself in order to place links with higher scores in the queue head so that they will be processed first. This strategy ensures that the crawler moves towards the relevant pages with the assumption that relevant pages tend to be neighbors to each other (Menczer, 2004). The crawler will continue operating as well as its queue has URLs for processing. The key problem in focused crawling research is: What criteria can be used for rating the extracted links? (Chakrabarti, Dom, Gibson, & Kleinberg, 1998)

PREVIOUS WORK IN FOCUSED CRAWLING

Crawlers are a central part of search engines and details on their crawling algorithms are kept as business secrets. Starting with the early breadth first (Najork & Wiener, 2001) and depth first (DeBra & Post, 1994) crawlers, which define the beginnings of research on crawlers, a variety of crawling algorithms has been introduced. Previous work in focused crawling can be classified into three categories: (i) content matching (information retrieval approach), (ii) using relevancy classifier (machine learning approach), and (iii) graph-search techniques.

Content Matching (Information Retrieval Approach)

These approaches are the earliest ones used in focused crawling. They are based on information retrieval (IR) to determine page relevance to the domain of interest. An example of such approaches is the fish search system. In this approach, only those pages that have contents matching a given query as well as their neighbors (pages pointed to by these matched pages) are crawled. When a page is considered similar to the query terms, links extracted from that page is embedded into the queue in the same order those links were extracted with no queue reordering. An improvement for the fish search proposed in Hersovici, Jacovi, Pelleg, and Shtalhaim (1998) is the shark search. Such approach uses perfect weighting methods like term frequency (TF), inverse document frequency (IDF), and cosine measure to determine the page relevancy to the subject of interest. In Cho,

Figure 2. The structure of a typical focused crawler

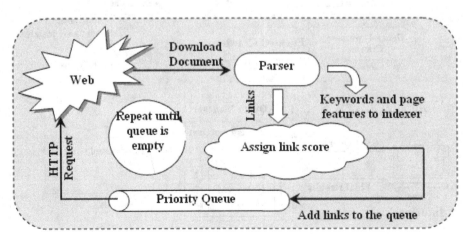

Garcia, and Page (1998), the reordering approach for the crawl queue has been proposed, which is based on the importance of the page containing the link. In such an approach, page importance was computed using various heuristics such as PageRank and the number of links pointing to the page (in-links). The links extracted from the more important pages are placed close to the head of the queue and will be processed first. The major limitation of such an approach is its failure to model tunneling (Altingovde & Ulusoy, 2004). The tunneling principal states that: *a set of off-topic pages may lead to highly relevant pages in the Web graph.*

Relevancy Classifier Crawlers (Machine Learning Approach)

Another set of focused crawling approaches use a relevancy classifier to evaluate the target pages that the current processed page links to for topical relevancy (Chakrabarti, Vander, & Dom, 1999). The user either provides a relevancy classifier in the form of query terms or it can be built from a set of seed pages (Gautam, Kostas, & Judy, 2004). Each link is assigned the score of the target page to which it leads. Each is currently processed and relevant pages gives its relevancy score to all links extracted from it. The page relevancy is determined by the content of the page itself. In some cases, the crawler decisions can be adapted using relevancy feedback, where pages that are marked as relevant by the classifier are also used to update the classifier. However, ensuring flexibility in the classifier, without simultaneously corrupting the classifier, is difficult (Michelangelo, Frans, Lee, & Marco, 2000). An example of crawlers of this category is the soft-focused crawler that was first proposed by Michaelangelo et al. (2000). Crawlers use relevancy classifier share the limitation of IR approaches. Since it is difficult to learn that some sets of off-topic pages lead to highly relevant pages, such crawlers cannot tunnel towards on-topic pages by following a path of off-topic pages (Hongyu, Evangelos, & Jeannette, 2004).

Graph Search Techniques

The Web can be considered as a huge graph by considering pages as nodes and links as edges from one node to the other (Aggarwal, Al-Garawi, & Yu, 2001; Vinod, Vydiswaran, & Sunita, 2005). Focused crawling is designed to traverse a subset of the Web and only gather pages on a specific target topic. A focused crawler aims to identify the promising links that lead to target pages and avoid off-topic branches (Ester, Kriegel, & Schubert, 2004). To establish such aim, some focused crawling techniques employ the Web graph to guide the crawler using a set of heuristic rules collected by the crawler itself about the nature of the Web graph. By tracking the links between pages in the Web graph, the crawler collects useful information about where relevant pages may exist. Such collected experience can be used in future crawling periods to predict whether the currently traversed path is probably useful.

THE PROPOSED INTELLIGENT—ADAPTIVE FOCUSED CRAWLER

Although many focused crawling approaches have been proposed (Michelangelo, Frans, Lee, & Marco, 2000; Hongyu, Evangelos, & Jeannette, 2004; Marios, Dikaiakos, & Loizos, 2005; Liu, Milios, & Janssen, 2004; Menczer, Paint, & Srinivansan, 2004), the area of focused crawling is still open for more research, since more enhancement of the performance is required and many challenges must be considered. The proposed strategy assigns more intelligence to the focused crawler so that it can decide what link to visit next with higher accuracy, based on a new link weight mechanism. Adding more intelligence to the crawler and allowing it to adapt itself to the changes in its domain will certainly lead to a better crawling performance.

The proposed crawler has the ability to estimate the rank of a page before it visits it; also it adapts its performance using a proposed domain oriented probability distribution (DOPD) according to any change in its domain. As depicted in Figure 3, two phases are introduced for the proposed crawler, the first for page content analysis and the second for page link analysis.

Phase 1: Page Content Analysis

The operation of the proposed crawler starts by picking the link in the head of its queue and fetching the corresponding target page. The next step then is to analyze that page to judge its relevancy to the domain of interest. Irrelevant pages will be discarded while relevant pages will be passed to the next phase. Three modules are used in this

Figure 3. The proposed framework components

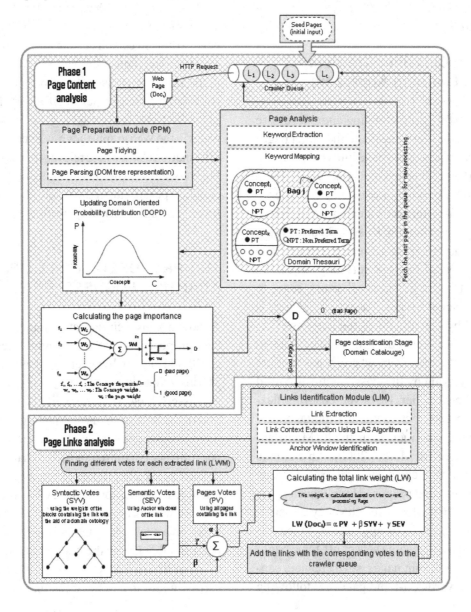

phase, which are: (i) page preparation module (PPM), (ii) page analysis module (PAM), and (iii) page importance module (PIM).

Crawler Queue

The crawler queue (Q) contains pages that are ready-to-process $Q=\{l_1,l_2,l_3, ... , l_n\}$, where l_1, ... , l_n are the (URLs), or simply links, for the ready-to-process pages. Q is a best first queue in which the links are ordered according to the link weight (LW). Links with higher weight are located in the head of Q and will be processed first. *LW* is calculated according to three types of votes. The first is the votes introduced by all pages containing the link (page votes), the second is the votes introduced by all blocks containing the link (syntactic votes), while the last is the one introduced by all anchor windows of the link in the different processed pages (semantic votes).

The ith link in Q is denoted by l_i and is expressed by the following six parameters $\{ID, URL_i, PV_i, SYV_i, SEV_i, LW_i\}$, where URL_i is the uniform resource locators of the target page, PV_i is the page votes for l_i, SYV_i is the syntactic votes for l_i, SEV_i is the semantic votes for l_i, and LW_i is the link weight of li that can be calculated as:

$$LW_i = PV_i + SYV_i + SEV_i$$

Initially, a set of highly ranked pages w.r.t the domain of interest (seed pages) are added to Q, those seeds are processed first (Menczer, Paint, & Srinivansan, 2004). As the crawler starts crawling, more links will be added to Q (with the corresponding votes and total weight). After all seeds are processed, the crawler will start to process the target pages of the added links in order, according to the calculated value of *LW* of each link, hence, links with higher weight will be processed first. The proposed crawler will continue working as well, as its queue has links to process.

Page Preparation Module (PPM)

This module prepares the page for easy processing (tiding and parsing). HTML pages may be mal-formed, since many authors use opening tags without closing them. This may cause problems when parsing the page. To avoid such problems, the proposed crawler relies on Tidy to fix the mal-formed HTML pages.

On the other hand, the aim of page parsing is to represent the Web page in machine readable and easy to process form. The most popular form is the document object model (DOM tree). In such a model, a hierarchical tree of nodes represents the Web page. HtmlAgilityPack was used as an HTML parser. Such parser transforms the page into a navigational DOM tree and permits to navigate easily through the tree nodes in order to extract the inner text of each text node.

Page Analysis Module (PAM)

The objective of this stage is to extract the main features of the page so that it is possible to decide whether the page is related to the domain of interest or not. Page keywords are extracted (from all text nodes of the pages' DOM tree) and then a domain thesauri is used for mapping keywords to the corresponding concepts. A thesaurus is a classification system that combines a set of technical terms with a few basic relations. Hence, it can be considered as a perfect way for knowledge mapping and conceptualization process (Wu & Plamer, 1994). Keyword-concept mapping allows a better page description for two different reasons: (i) the probability of two persons using the same term in describing the same thing is less than 20% (Marcia, 1986). As a result, describing pages using concepts rather that keywords leads to more accurate description and (ii) mapping keywords to concepts simplifying page understanding and analysis since the page keywords could be aggregated into a smaller number of concepts. Such mapping process also eliminates any other terms that are not related to the domain of interest (Maria, Benjamin, Iraklis, & Michalis, 2003).

The proposed domain thesauri divides the domain terms into a set of bags, each bag consists of a set of synonyms and represents a specific concept. For each set, one preferred term (PT) is chosen to represent the underlying concept; the other terms are non-preferred terms (NPT) (instances of the concept). Two basic relations are included; the first is synonymy, while the second is the hierarchical (describes which terms are broader and which ones are narrower). The only considered relation for mapping keywords to concepts is the "synonymy" relation. At the end of this stage, the page Doc_i can be expressed as $Doc_i=\{(C_{i1},f_{i1}), (C_{i2},f_{i2}), \ldots\ldots, (C_{im},f_{im})\}$, where C_{ij} is the jth concept Doc_i, F_{ij} is the frequency of C_{ij}, and m is the number of domain concepts found in Doc_i.

Domain Oriented Probability Distribution (DOPD)

According to information theory, information is strictly defined in terms of the probabilities of events. Therefore, suppose that we have a set of domain concepts $C=\{C_1, C_2, C_3, \ldots C_m\}$ and a set of probabilities for these concepts (probability distribution) $P=\{P_1, P_2, P_3, \ldots P_m\}$. The information gained by the occurrence of concept C_i is calculated as: $I(C_i) = log(1/P_i)$, where $I(C_i)$ is the information gained by the occurrence of concept C_i, and P_i is the occurrence probability of concept C_i. Hence, as the probability of occurrence of the concept increases (the concept is a popular one), the information content in that concept will decrease. This is a reasonable assumption; to narrate confidently, consider the situation that the domain of interest is the "sports" domain. Then, the occurrence of the concept "football" (as an illustrative example) in the processed page does not mean that the page related to the sports domain since the concept "football" is a very popular one. Hence, little information is gained by the

occurrence of such concept inside the processed page. On the other hand, when the concept is a rare one, the occurrence of such a concept in the processed page indicates that the page is strongly related to the domain.

A domain oriented probability distribution (DOPD) is introduced as the source of the probabilities for all domain concepts. In such distribution, horizontal axes represent domain concepts, while vertical axes represent the dynamic concepts probabilities as depicted in Figure 4. If the domain of interest contains U concepts $C=\{C_1, C_2, C_3, \ldots C_u\}$, initially DOPD will be a flat curve with all concepts having the same probability $P_i=1/U$. With time, the probability of each concept will change as a new gets page processed. DOPD has the following properties; (i) *Adaptive*: Since it has the ability to adapt itself continuously as a new page processed, the extracted concepts from the cleaned page will be considered to update DOPD. (ii) *Bell shape:* As any probability distribution, DOPD will have the bell shape by time.

Page Importance Module (PIM)

It is important now to formulate a procedure for estimating the importance of the currently processed page by the occurrence of a number of domain concepts inside such page. The processed page could be either a "good page" (relevant to the domain of interest), or a "bad page" (must be discarded), and then the next URL in the queue should be picked for processing. The good pages will be passed to the higher processing stages. Such decision is taken according to the page importance with respect to the domain of interest.

Calculating the page relevancy to the domain of interest can be represented as a simple Boolean function, that is, 1 for relevant and 0 for irrelevant. A single perceptron can be used to represent such Boolean function since it can be considered as a hyperplane decision surface in the n-dimensional space of features (domain concepts). Each page can be considered as a point in that space and

Figure 4. The of domain oriented probability distribution

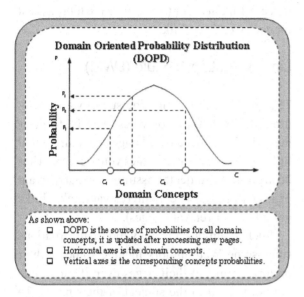

accordingly located in one side of such surface. The proposed perceptron has an input sink for each domain concept and only one output sink to provide its output.

Wd (weight of page) depends on two different factors: (i) the importance of the domain concepts extracted from the page and (ii) the frequency of the domain concepts extracted from the processed page. For illustration, consider the page Doc_i, which contains m domain concepts $\{C_{i1}, C_{i2}, C_{i3}, ..., C_{im}\}$ that occur with frequencies $\{f_{i1}, f_{i2}, f_{i3}, ..., f_{im}\}$. The frequency f_{ij} of concept C_{ij} in Doc_i can be calculated as: $f_{ij} = (f_{concept} + f_{synonyms})|_{C=C_{ij}}$, where $f_{concept}$ is the frequency of occurrence of C_{ij} itself (probably zero), and $f_{synonyms}$ is the frequency of occurrence of all synonyms of C_{ij} (probably zero). Then, Doc_i can be expressed as $Doc_i = \{(C_{i1}, f_{i1}), (C_{i2}, f_{i2}), ..., (C_{im}, f_{im})\}$. So, Wd_i can be determined by following the next steps:

1. The importance of each domain concept (concept weight) found in Doc_i is calculated with the aid of DOPD as $w_{ij} = log (1/P(C_{ij}))$, where w_{ij} is the weight of concept C_{ij}, and

$P(C_{ij})$ is the probability of concept C_{ij} using DOPD. An updated expression of the processed page (after adding the concepts weights) will be $Doc_i = \{(C_{i1}, f_{i1}, w_{i1}), (C_{i2}, f_{i2}, w_{i2}), ..., (C_{im}, f_{im}, w_{im})\}$.

2. The input of such perceptron is the concepts frequencies $\{f_{i1}, f_{i2}, f_{i3}, ...f_{im}\}$. Each input is multiplied by the corresponding concept weight $\{w_{i1}, w_{i2}, w_{i3}, ... w_{im}\}$. Finally, Wd_i can be calculated as:

$$Wd_i = \sum_{j=1}^{m} f_{ij} * w_{ij}$$

3. By using a modeling function Fn, the perceptron can sense whether the processed page is related to the domain of interest or not. Fn is a simple step function that has "zero" value before a critical weight W_c and has a "one" value elsewise. The output signal (D) is the neural network decision, which can be expressed as:

$$D = Fn(Wd_j) = \begin{cases} 0 & \text{(Bad Page)} & Wd_i < Wc \\ 1 & \text{(Good Page)} & \text{Elsewise} \end{cases}$$

4. If the processed page is a bad one (when D=0) the crawler will discard it, then picks the next link in the queue for a new processing. Otherwise (when D=1), the page is labeled as a good one then, two tasks must be performed; the first is to pass such a good page-to-page categorization stage so that it will be categorized according to a predefined categories. The second is to allow the page to continue to the higher processing stages for link extraction and rating.

Phase 2: Page Links Analysis

According to topical locality (pages in the same topic tend to be close to each other in the web graph), as the currently processed page is relevant to the domain of interest, it certainly contains links that point to other relevant pages. In order to compensate the crawler queue with new links, the links found in relevant pages will be extracted, weighted (ranked) according to the domain of interest, and then added to the crawler queue for future analysis. Hence, the tasks performed in this phase are: (i) page links identification, (ii) weight calculation for each extracted link, (iii) injecting all extracted links with the corresponding weights to the queue, and finally (iv) queue re-arrangement so that links with higher weight appear in the head of the queue. These tasks are performed through two modules which are: link identification module (LIM) and link weighting module (LWM).

Link Identification Module (LIM)

In this module, all links found in the relevant page are identified. LIM performs three different tasks for each identified link. These tasks are: (i) extraction of the link URL, hence, the target page can be easily fetched whenever needed. The URL of the link can be extracted from the "HREF" attribute of the anchor tag in the HTML source code of the processed page, (ii) link context extraction using segmentation based on link context extraction, and (iii) anchor window identification for each extracted link. The link anchor window is a window of a fixed number of bytes in the body of the page from both sides of the link anchor tag. Based on the previous efforts, the width of the window is usually set to 50 bytes from both sides of the link anchor tag.

At the end of this stage, the crawler owns a vector $L_i = \{l_{i1}, l_{i2}, ..., l_{ix}\}$, such vector contains all links extracted from the processed page Doc_i, where L_{ij} is the jth link in Doc_i, and x is the number of links extracted from Doc_i. Each link in L_i can be expressed by triple *(URL, anchor window, link context)*. Hence, $L_i = \{(URL_{i1}, AW_{i1}, LC_{i1}), (URL_{i2}, AW_{i2}, LC_{i2}), ..., (URL_{ix}, AW_{ix}, LC_{ix})\}$, where URL_{ij} is the URL of the jth link in Doc_i, AW_{ij} is the anchor window of the jth link in Doc_i, and LC_{ij} is the context of the jth link in Doc_i. Each link in L_i represents another page that will be processed

later. These links will not be added directly to the queue; however, three votes must be calculated for each link in order to calculate the total weight for each extracted link.

Link Weighting Module (LWM)

The proposed link weighting strategy combines three different types of votes. The first one is the votes introduced by all pages containing that link. Such type is called pages votes (PV) and has been proposed under the assumption that relevant pages will certainly contain relevant links (links point to other relevant pages).

Such assumption is not valid in all situations since some Web authors include some of their preferred links in their pages even if such links are not related to the subject of their pages. To compensate such defect, two other types of votes are added to the pre-mentioned one in order to formulate the overall link weighting strategy used in the proposed crawling framework. The two other types of votes are: (i) the votes introduced by all anchor windows of the link (a virtual window of a fixed number of bytes from <A> and </A> tags) in different processed pages, which are called semantic votes (SEV) and (ii) the votes introduced by all visual blocks containing the link, which are called syntactic votes (SYV). After calculating all link votes, it is time to put them together in order to calculate the total link weight (LW). *LW* is proposed to be simply the sum of all previously calculated votes. Hence, $LW_i = PV_i + SYV_i + SEV_i$, where LW_i, PV_i, SYV_i, and SEV_i are the total link weight, pages votes, syntactic votes, and semantic votes of the ith link respectively. The extracted links with the corresponding votes and *LW* will be injected in the crawler queue. The queue will arrange the links so that the links with higher value of *LW* will be located in the head of the queue and will be picked first for processing. The strategies used to calculate each type of votes are explained in the next subsections.

PAGE VOTES (PV) are the votes that are collected from all pages containing that link. It is assumed that each Web page distributes its importance (weight) equally among all links extracted from it; such equal portion is called the vote of that page for any link extracted from it. The page votes (PV) for a specific link is the sum of all votes collected from all pages containining that link. The strategy used for PV calculation combines two different disciplines, namely linking and content structures for the Web. This is simply because the more the popularity of a link, the more pages votes that it will collect and accordingly the more pages votes (PV) it will gain. Consider the page Doc_i that contains m concepts and is represented as:

$$Doc_i = \{(C_{i1}, f_{i1}, W_{i1}), (C_{i2}, f_{i2}, W_{i2}), (C_{i3}, f_{i3}, W_{i3})\}$$

Where $\{C_{i1}, C_{i2}, C_{i3}, \ldots\ldots C_{im}\}$ are the m concepts found in Doc_i, $\{f_{i1}, f_{i2}, f_{i3}, \ldots\ldots f_{im}\}$ are the corresponding frequencies, and $\{W_{i1}, W_{i2}, W_{i3}, \ldots W_{im}\}$ are the calculated weights. The page weight Wd_i (vote of Doc_i) can be calculated using the perceptron in PIM.

It is proposed that Doc_i distributes its weight equally among all links found inside its body. The equal portion of a link l_{ij} (for example) is then multiplied by a page-damping factor (α_{ij}), the result then is called the vote of Doc_i for l_{ij}. The value of α_{ij} changes from link to the other even in the same page. Hence, the vote of Doc_i for l_{ij} is expressed as:

$$\text{Vote}(Doc_i)|_{1ij} = \alpha_{i,j} * Wd_i / x_i = \left[\alpha_{ij} * \sum_{k=1}^{m} W_{ik} * f_{ik}\right] / x_i$$

Where x_i is the number of links extracted from Doc_i, and α_{ij} is the page-damping factor for the jth link in Doc_i. Finally, PV for a link l is the sum of all votes collected from all pages containing l. If the l appears in y pages, PV for l can be calculated as:

$$PV(l) = \sum_{k=1}^{y} \alpha_k(l) * [Wd_k / x_k]$$

Where $PV(l)$ is the pages votes of link l, Wd_k is the weight of Doc_k calculated by the neural network in PIM module, x_k is the number of links in Doc_k, y is the number of pages containing l, and $\alpha_k(l)$ is the page damping factor for the link l in Doc_k.

SEMANTIC VOTES (SEV) are deduced from all anchor windows associated with that link in all previously collected pages as well as the currently processed one. From previous efforts (Chakrabarti & Kleinberg, 1998), the anchor window of the link l can be considered as an excellent prediction for the content of the target page in which l points to. This leads to the assumption that: the more information content in the anchor window for l with width T, the stronger the relevancy of the target page that l points to w.r.t the domain of interest.

Based on that assumption, the semantic votes for a link l can be defined as: "the average information content in all anchor windows with width T associated with the l in all pre-processed pages as well as the current processed one." This type of votes can be calculated as follows: assume that the link l is currently detected in page Doc_i with the anchor window containing n concepts $\{C_1, C_2, \ldots, C_n\}$. The probability of each concept can be found using DOPD as $\{P_1, P_2, \ldots, P_n\}$. The information gained by the occurrence of concept C_k in the anchor window is given by the equation $I(C_k) = log(1/P_k)$, where P_k is the probability of concept C_k. However, if C_k has f_k occurrence (frequency of occurrence) in the anchor window, then, the total information gained by the f_k occurrence of concept C_k in the anchor window with width T is $I_T(C_k) = f_k log(1/P_k)$. Again, as illustrated before, the frequency f_k of concept C_k (in the anchor window) can be calculated as:

$$f_k = (f_{concept} + f_{synonyms})|_{C=C_k}$$

Where f_k is the overall frequency (occurrence) of concept C_k in the anchor window with width T, $f_{concept}$ is the frequency of occurrence of C_k

itself inside the window; $f_{synonyms}$ is the frequency of occurrence of all synonyms of C_k inside the window. Then, the total Information content in the anchor window (I_{AW}) containing the n concepts will be:

$$I_{AW} = \sum_{i=1}^{n} f_i * \log(1/P_i)$$

Where I_{AW} is the total information content in the anchor window of link l in Doc_i. Then, the average information content I_{AV} in the anchor window will be:

$$I_{AV} = \frac{I_{AW}}{\sum_{i=1}^{n} f_i} = \frac{\sum_{i=1}^{n} f_i * \log(1/P_i)}{\sum_{i=1}^{n} f_i}$$

An important question that may arise in the readers' mind is that: Why use the average information content in the anchor window rather than the information content itself? The answer is quite simple; it is believed that having a small number of highly important concepts in the anchor window is better than having large number of low important concepts because the measure here is a semantic measure (i.e., a qualitative measure not quantitative). Finally, the semantic votes for a link l can be calculated as:

$$SEV(l) = \sum_{k=1}^{m} \delta_k(l) * I_{AV_k} = \sum_{k=1}^{m} \delta_k(l) * \left[\frac{\sum_{x=1}^{n_k} f_{kx} * \log(1/P_{kx})}{\sum_{x=1}^{n} f_{kx}} \right]$$

Where $SEV(l)$ is the semantic votes for link l, m is the number of anchor windows associated with l, n_k is the number of concepts found in the kth anchor window, f_{kx} is the frequency of xth concept in the kth anchor window, P_{kx} is the probability of xth concept in the kth anchor window using DOPD, and $\delta_k(l)$ is the window damping factor for the link l in the kth anchor window.

An important criterion that must be considered when calculating the semantic vote of the link in a specific page is the width of the anchor window

T. In Chakrabarti, Dom, Gibson, and Kleinberg (1998), the anchor window width was estimated empirically to be 50 bytes in both sides of the anchor tag. This estimation was proven while treating the page as one solid block. However, the Web page can be portioned into a set of visual blocks. The widths of the anchor window of a specific link will strongly be affected by both the size of the block containing the link and the number of links included inside the block. This assumption is logically valid since the width of the anchor window for a link located in a small block with large number of links should be narrow, also the width of the anchor window for a link located in a large block with a few number of links should be wide. An equation can be formulated for calculating the optimal anchor window width of the jth link in the ith page (T_{ij}), so that, $T_{ij}=F($ Block Width , Number of Block link$s$).

SYNTACTIC VOTES (SEV) These votes will be introduced by all visual blocks containing the link. The block weight is assumed to be its vote. This idea arises with the assumption that, "blocks with height weight must have important links inside them," hence, it will be a good idea to assign the block weight (BW) to all links inside that block. The syntactic votes (SYV) for link l will be the weighted sum of all *BWs* collected from all blocks containing l, which are certainly distributed among different pages. To clarify the idea, consider a link l, which appeared in Z blocks. Such link will gain Z syntactic votes. *SYV* for l can be calculated as:

$$SYV(l) = \sum_{k=1}^{z} \beta_k(l) * BW_k(l)$$

Where $SYV(l)$ is the syntactic votes for link l, z is the number of blocks containing l, $BW_k(l)$: the weight of the kth block that contains l, and $\beta_k(l)$ is the window damping factor for l in the kth visual block. Two important aspects must be considered; the first is how to identify the block that contains l and the second is how to determine the weight of such block.

For identifying the block that contains the link *l*, simply, link aware segmentation (LAS) algorithm is employed to identify the boundaries of the block containing *l*. LAS is a specialized Web page segmentation algorithm that was suggested particularly for link context extraction. The algorithm is applied in two sequential phases (division and merging). Initially, during the division phase, all links were extracted from the processed page and stored in a processing queue. For each link in such queue, the upper and lower boundaries of the block containing the link (anchor block) is detected, the boundaries are simply a set of HTML tags that are considered as containers (e.g., <TABLE>, <TR>, <TD>..), separators (e.g., <HR>, <BR>..), or indicating a new region (e.g., <P>, <OL>, <LI>… etc.). Such tags are called block tags. Whenever one of these tags is detected, a block boundary is recorded. During the merging stage, the task is to measure the similarity among each anchor block and its neighbors, then merge the similar ones to produce bigger blocks whenever possible. Anchor block can be merged with one of its neighbors if both blocks were visually identical and semantically similar.

After identifying the visual block containing the link, all keywords inside the block are available for processing. The key problem now is how to calculate the block weight. Initially, all block keywords were extracted from the block and mapped to concepts using the domain thesauri. It is assumed that, if the concepts extracted from the block were syntactically related, the block must assign a higher weight. The proposed thesauri with its relations (synonym and hierarchical) can be considered as a domain ontology, which will be used to calculate the syntactic relation (similarity) among the block concepts (Resnik, 1999). Such ontology arranges the domain concepts with the corresponding relations between them in a tree like shape (i.e., only simple tree is considered); DAG type is not considered for simplicity. The similarity measure between any two concepts in the ontology can be calculated using (Wu &

Palmer, 1994) equation by the aid of the common parent of both concepts. For example, assume it is needed to calculate the similarity between the two concepts C_1 and C_2 in the tree shown in Figure 5, this can be achieved by calculating the depth of both concepts as well as their common parent C. Similarity between C_1 and C_2 {denoted by $Sim(C_1,C_2)$} could be calculated using "Wu and Palmer" equation as:

$$Sim_{W\&P}(C_1,C_2) = \frac{2*Depth(C)}{Depth(C_1)+Depth(C_2)}$$

By substitution:

$$Sim_{W\&P}(C_1,C_2) = 2*2/(3+4) = 0.57$$

A modification is proposed in the "Wu and Palmer" equation in order to calculate the similarity between the block concepts and accordingly estimating the syntactic relation between block concepts. A new parameter called the parent weight W_p is introduced. It is assumed that, the higher the closeness between the two concepts C_i and C_j (with weights w_i and w_j respectively) to each others in the tree structure, the higher the weight of their parent w.r.t the domain of interest. Hence, it is required to calculate the weight of the parent of C_i and C_j.

As mentioned before, DOPD is used as the source of concepts probabilities and can be used to calculate the amount of information content in each concept. Information content in the concept is considered as the concept weight w.r.t the domain

Figure 5. The ontology as a tree of concepts

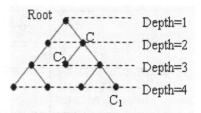

171

of interest. Initially, the "Wu and Palmer" equation is used to calculate the similarity between C_i and C_j. Then, the parent weight {denoted by $W_p(C_i, C_j)$} can be calculated as (where C is the common parent of C_i and C_j in the tree):

$$W_p(C_i, C_j) = \left[W(C_i) + W(C_j)\right] \times Sim_{W\&P}(C_i, C_j) =$$

$$\left[W(C_i) W(C_j)\right] \times \frac{2 * Depth(C)}{Depth(C_i) + Depth(C_j)}$$

Considering Figure 5, the weight of concept C (parent of C_1 and C_2) using the properties shown in Table 2 can be calculated using the "modified Wu and Palmer" equation as:

$$W_p(C_1, C_2) = \left[W(C_1) W + (C_2)\right] \times \frac{2 * Depth(C)}{Depth(C_1) + Depth(C_2)}$$

$$W_p(C_1, C_2) = \left[2.332444 \, 2 + .809584\right] \times \frac{2*2}{6+5} = 1.869828$$

Formulating a criterion for measuring the syntactic relation among all block concepts (and accordingly the block weight) as the algorithm is depicted in Figure 6. The process starts by finding all domain terms found in the block, the used terms are those which are concepts (preferred terms) or their corresponding synonyms. All terms that were found were mapped to the corresponding concepts, and then mapped into the concept tree (domain ontology). The weight of each concept is calculated. The syntactic relation between each two neighboring concepts is calculated to find the weight of their parent using the modified method in (Wu, 1994). The calculations will be repeated recursively with the parents until finding the

weight of the "Most Greatest Parent" (the parent of all block concepts). The block weight (BW) is then the weight of the "Most Greatest Parent" W_{mgp} multiplied by a compensation factor λ as $BW = \lambda W_{mgp}$. The role of λ is to compensate the degradation in the BW as the number of concepts found in the block increases. Finally, the syntactic votes of link l that have been found in z blocks is calculated as:

$$SYV(l) = \sum_{k=1}^{z} \beta_k(l) * BW_k(l) = \sum_{k=1}^{z} \beta_k(l) * \lambda_k * W_{mgp(k)}$$

Where $SYV(l)$ is the syntactic votes for l, $\beta_k(l)$ is the block damping factor for l in the kth block, $BW_k(l)$ is the weight k^{th} block that contains l, λ_k is the compensation factor for the kth block containing l, and $W_{mgp(k)}$ is the weight of the most greatest parent of all domain concepts found in the kth block containing l.

Many possible procedures may be followed to estimate the suitable value of such compensation factor λ. The procedure used in this article is illustrated below (such a procedure provides reasonable results when comparing the resultant block weights with human inspection empirically):

- $\lambda \propto N_B$ (N_B is the number of concepts found in the block)
- $\lambda \propto Import(C_i|Domain) \; \forall \; C_i \in Concepts found in the block$, where $Import(C_i|Domain)$ is the importance of concept C_i w.r.t the domain of interest. *Import* $(C_i|Domain)$ can be represented by the domain information content in C_i. Then,

Table 2. Properties for concepts Ci and Cj for the illustrative example

	Depth in the Tree	Probability in DOPD	Information Contents
C_i	5	0.0046511	2.332444
C_j	6	0.0015503	2.809584
Common Parent (C)	2		

$$\lambda \propto N_B * \sum_{i=1}^{N_B} I(C_i)$$

By substitution,

$$\lambda = \mu * N_B * \sum_{i=1}^{N_B} \log(1/P_i).$$

Where μ is a damping constant, P_i is the probability of concept C_i in DOPD. Using $\mu=1$, the estimated value of λ will be:

$$\lambda = N_B * \sum_{i=1}^{N_B} \log(1/P_i)$$

Calculating The Damping Factors α, β and δ

When the proposed crawler, for each extracted link from that page fetches a new page, three different weights must be calculated. Page vote, block vote, and anchor window vote. Those votes are multiplied by the three damping factors *α, β, and δ respectively*. It is believed that the values of *α, β, and δ* depend on the page, block, and window of the extracted link and their optimal values could be estimated by formulating a set of heuristic rules. According to the closeness to

Figure 6. Block weight calculation algorithm

INPUT

- Domain thesauri (Domain Ontology) contains a set of concepts (with their synonyms) organized in hierarchical manner.
- Input visual block to calculate its weight.
- DOPD (Domain Oriented Probability Distribution) as a source of domain concepts probabilities.

OUTPUT

- BW: Block weight.

STEPS

- o Extract Block Keywords, $B_{keyword}=\{K_1,K_2,...,K_n\}$.
- o Map Block Keywords into concepts $B_{Concept}=\{C_1,C_2,...,C_m\}$.
- o Find Concepts Weights $W(C_1)$, $W(C_2)$ ......, $W(C_m)$, where $W(C_i)=\log(1/p_i)$, p_i is the propability of C_i in DOPD
- o Map block concepts to a domain ontology with the corresponding weights.

    IF   *Concepts_No = 1*   **THEN**   // where "Concept_No" is the number of concepts *extracted from the block*

       BW= λ W(C_1)
    ELSE IF   *Concepts_No = 2*   **THEN**
       BW= λ $\bar{W}_p$(C_1, C_2)   // where "$W_p(C_1, C_2)$" is the weight of the *parent of concepts C_1 and C_2*
    ELSE
       Again:
         IF   *Concepts_No is Odd*   **THEN**   discard the last concept
         Organize concepts into neighboring pairs (C_x,C_y), (C_m,C_n), ... etc.
         IF   *Neighboring_Pairs=1*   **THEN**   GoTo OUT
       FOR   *K=1*   **TO**   *Neighboring_Pairs*
         Find similarity between the current pair, Sim(C_x,C_y) using Wu&Palmer
         Find the parent weight, $W_p(C_i,C_j) = (W(C_i)+W(C_j)) * Sim(C1,C2)$
       NEXT
       The parents as well as their calculated weights will be used as the new block concepts instead of their children.
       IF   *Concepts_No is Odd*   **THEN**   add the previously discard concept
       GoTo Again
       Out:
       Find weight of the most greatest parent W_{mgp}
       Find the block weight BW= λ W_{mgp}

    END IF

the anchor tag that expresses the link, the three damping factors should be ordered as: $\alpha < \beta < \delta$. On the other hand, the value of any of the three weighting factors is not to exceed 1. Hence, the following assumptions are valid:

- Since the value of the window damping factor (δ) is the maximum one, it is assumed to be 1 in all cases ($\delta=1$ for all cases).
- The value of the page damping factor (α) will be found by a set of heuristic rules to get a value between 0 and 1 ($0< \alpha <1$).
- Since the value of β lies between α and δ. It is assumed that it lies in the middle distance between them, that is:

$$\beta = \alpha + \frac{\delta - \alpha}{2} = \frac{\delta + \alpha}{2}$$

ESTIMATING THE VALUE OF α: In order to estimate the proper value of α, the algorithm in Figure 7 is used. Such algorithm uses a set of inter-class (Altingovde & Ulusoy, 2004) rules and is implemented in two phases, namely "training" and "testing". An input domain of interest with C categories is assumed. A set of $C*E$ input Web pages (training examples) related to the domain of interest (E is arbitrary number). During the training phase, the aim is to calculate the probability that a link points to a page that belongs to *Category_X* lies on a page that belongs to *Category_Y*, $\forall$ Category_X, Category_Y $\in$ *Domain Categories*. To establish such aim, all links in training examples for each category is extracted and the corresponding pages are also fetched and classified according to the domain categories or to "none". Then, it will be easy to calculate the required probabilities. Such probabilities can be called the inter-class probabilities; they will be used later during the testing phase to estimate the proper value of α for each extracted link. The inter-class probabilities are expressed as: $Prop(P_{Cat\_A}, L_{Cat\_B})$, which can be defined as the probability that a Page of *Category_A* contains a link with a target page belongs to *Category_B*.

When it is needed to estimate the value of α for a specific link L_{ij} (the jth link in the ith page), the page containing L_{ij} (labeled as Doc_i) is first classified to one of the domain categories using CLNB algorithm. The visual block that contains link is then identified using LAS algorithm. Domain concepts extracted from such block are used to classify the target page of L_{ij} using CLNB. Then, the next simple rule will be used to find the value of α.

- If Doc_i has been classified to *Category_A*, whereas the target page of L_{ij} is being classified to *Category_B*, $\forall$ *Category_A* and *Category_B* $\in$ *Domain Categories,* then $\alpha= Prop(P_{Cat\_A}, L_{Cat\_B})$.
- If the target page of L_{ij} is being classified to "None", then $\alpha= 0$.

After the page-damping factor (α) has been calculated, it will be easy to calculate β and δ using heuristics explained in section 3-2-3.

Calculating the Total Link Weight (LW)

If the link l has not been registered before in the crawler queue, l is then a new one. So, it will be registered by assigning it a new record in the queue with six attributes *{ID, URL, PV, SEV, SYV, LW}*. The value of URL attribute is the value of the "HREF" attribute of the link anchor tag. PV, SEV, and SYV will be initialized by the votes of the current *page*, *window*, and *block* respectively since no old value was stored before. The link weight (LW) is simply the sum of the votes *PV*, *SEV*, and *SYV*. On the other hand, if the link has been already registered before, then attributes *PV*, *SEV*, and *SYV* certainly have old stored values (previously collected votes for the link), such old values will be updated by adding the current *page*, *window*, and *block* votes

Then, the updated value of the link weight will be easily calculated by summing the updated values of *PV*, *SEV*, and *SYV* attributes. Based on

Figure 7. Estimating page damping factor algorithm

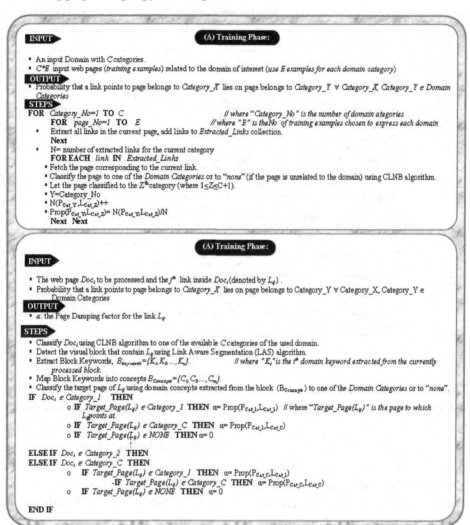

the new value of *LW* of *l*, the link is ordered in its suitable position in the queue. In other words, the queue must be re-ordered to keep the link with the maximum weight in the head of the queue for the next crawling cycle. The general equation for calculating the weight for the link *l* is shown:

$$LW(l) = PV(l) + SYV(l) + SEV(l)$$

By substitution;

$$LW(l) = \sum_{k=1}^{m} \alpha_k(l) * [Wd_k / X_k] +$$

$$\sum_{k=1}^{m} \delta_k(l) * \left[\frac{\sum_{x=1}^{n_k} f_{kx} * \log(1/P_{kx})}{\sum_{x=1}^{n} f_{kx}} \right] +$$

$$\sum_{k=1}^{m} \beta_k(l) * \lambda_k * W_{mgp(k)}$$

The terms used in equation above are defined in Table 3.

Table 3. Terms used in calculating the total link weight

	Description
LW(l)	The overall weight of link l
PV(l)	The pages votes of link l
Wd$_k$	The weight of page Doc$_k$
m	The number of pages, anchor windows, and, blocks containing l
$\alpha_k(l)$	The page damping factor for the link L in Doc$_k$
SEV(l)	The semantic votes for link l
n_k	The number of concepts found in the kth anchor window of link l
f$_{kx}$	The frequency of xth concept in the kth anchor window of link l
P$_{kx}$	The probability of xth concept in the kth anchor window using DOPD
$\delta_k(l)$	The window damping factor for the link L in the kth anchor window
SYV(l)	The syntactic votes for link l
$\beta_k(l)$	The block damping factor for the link L in the kth block
BW$_k$(l)	The weight of the kth block that contains l
λ_k	The compensation factor for the link l in the kth block
W$_{mgp(k)}$	The weight of the "most greatest parent" for concepts that were extracted from the kth block containing the link l.

EVALUATION AND ANALYSIS OF THE PROPOSED CRAWLING STRATEGY

A crawler may be evaluated by measuring its ability to retrieve "good" pages. For a focused crawler, a "good" page is the one that can be considered relevant to the domain of interest. As the value of retrieved and relevant over retrieved and irrelevant pages increases, this indicates the effectiveness of the crawling strategy. Based on Figure 8, the set of pages on the Web is represented by the Web set and denoted by "W," the Web is assumed to contain a set of relevant pages to the domain of interest, this set is called relevant set and denoted by "R." Another set is also considered, which represents the crawled set "C." It is simply noticed that $(R, C) \subset W$. The target of the focused crawling strategy is to maximize the set $R \cap C$, which indicates a large number of good retrieved pages, and minimize the set $X = C - (R \cap C)$. An ideal focused crawler has $R \subset C$ and accordingly

$X = \Phi$. Figure 8 (A) represents the ideal focused crawler, while Figure 8 (B) represents the traditional focused crawler. The target of the focused crawler can be expressed as:

Target (Focused_Crawler) $\equiv$
  $[maximize(C \cap R)][minimize(C - C \cap R)]$
  AND

Parameters Adjustment

The proposed strategy for focused crawling is scalable and flexible. It can be adjusted to work with various domains; also the availability to use variety number of thesaurus makes it scalable. For validating the proposed focused crawling strategy, the "university" is chosen as the domain of interest. Four different categories were assumed to represent the "university" domain, namely, (i) academic and research, (ii) university building and sites tools, (iii) university management and routinism, and (iv) equipments and assistance

Figure 8. Ideal focused crawler versus traditional one

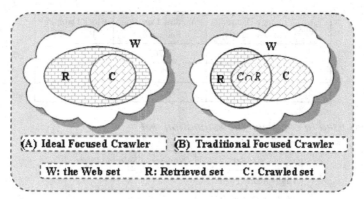

Table 4. Inter-class probabilities obtained

Category of the page that contains the link	Category of the target page {target_Page(Link)}				
	Category1	Category2	Category3	Category4	None
Category1	0.412	0.114	0.081	0.156	0.237
Category2	0.081	0.523	0.107	0.091	0.198
Category3	0.109	0.092	0.602	0.071	0.126
Category4	0.230	0.032	0.048	0.511	0.179

technology. A total of 1100 terms (domain keywords) were collected to represent the domain; these terms were manually mapped to about 215 different concepts.

Damping Factors Adjustment

After applying the training phase for algorithm in Figure 7, inter-class probabilities obtained are illustrated in Table 4. For example, the shaded cell in Table 4 represents the probability that a page of "Category 3" contains a link that refers to a target page of "Category 2", that is, $\text{Prop}(P_{Cat\_3}, L_{Cat\_2}) = 0.092$, and so forth.

Results in Table 4 insure the validity of the "topical locality" property of Web pages. To narrate confidently, consider a page related to university domain and classified to Category2, based on data in Table 5, it is predicted that such page is linked to other pages related to university domain (on average) about 87.4% of the time and linked to pages outside university domain with only 12.6%. Again, based on the inter-class probabilities shown in Table 5, the value of α, and accordingly the values of β and δ, could be estimated easily.

For illustration, consider a page that is related to the university domain and classified to Category2. Three different links (l_1, l_2, and l_3) were extracted from the page. LAS algorithm was applied to detect the visual block containing each one of the three links. Domain keywords were extracted from each block and mapped to domain concepts using the domain thesauri. Based on domain concepts for each extracted link, the three target pages were classified again using CLNB algorithm. If the three target pages were classified to Category 2, 3, and 1 respectively, then the values of α, β and δ for each of l_1, l_2 and l_3 are shown in Table 5.

Table 5. The values of the various damping factors for links L_1, L_2, L_3

Link	Page Damping Factor (α)	Window Damping Factor (δ)	Block Damping Factor (β)
l_1	0.523	0.762	1
l_2	0.107	0.554	1
l_3	0.081	0.541	1

Table 6. The page sets used to construct the estimation_set

Sub-Set	Number of Selected Pages
High Quality Pages	X
Medium Quality Pages	Y
Low Quality Pages	Z

Estimating the Optimal Value of W_c

It is believed that the value of W_c must be balanced (*tuned*) so that relevant pages were passed while the irrelevant were discarded. The value of W_c is dependent on the domain of interest (*change in value from domain to domain*) and can be set empirically by set W_c to an arbitrary (*initial*) value, then such value changed and the corresponding efficiency of PIM calculated. Such process must be continued until a satisfactory level of efficiency has been achieved.

THE INITIAL VALUE OF W_c: can be estimated by following the next steps:

1. An *Estimation_Set* of ($N=X+Y+Z$) relevant pages were selected where such set is manually classified into three different sub-sets according to the relevancy to the domain as shown in Table 6.
    The values of *X, Y, and, Z* can be changed according to the opinion of the domain expert, a suggested values to use $X=Y=Z$.
2. All domain terms were extracted from all pages in the *Estimation_Set* and mapped to the corresponding concepts. The weight of each concept is calculated with the aid of

DOPD (*at its steady state case*) as well as the concept frequency.

Then, the estimated initial value of W_c will be (*assuming m extracted concepts*):

$$W_c(initial) = \frac{(\sum_{k=1}^{1} w_k * f_k)}{N}.$$

Hence, it can be said that the value of W_c will cause PIM to pass high quality pages as well as medium quality pages and reject the low quality ones.

THE OPTIMAL VALUE OF Wc: PIM module can be considered as a simple binary classifier. It distinguishes between relevant and irrelevant pages. Hence, the classification efficiency of such classifier has a great impact on the performance of the proposed focused crawling strategy. In this section, empirical evidence is provided for calculating the proper value of Wc in order to achieve the maximum classification efficiency. An assumption that the optimal value of Wc is the one that gives the higher classification accuracy was considered. A total of 2000 pages are used to measure the efficiency of PIM module. Those pages are divided into two sets. The first set is the relevant pages (1000 pages) and the other set is the irrelevant pages (1000 pages). The initial

Figure 9. Critical weight initialization algorithm

> **INPUT**
> - Domain thesauri with the domain concepts C=(c_1, c_2, c_3, ..., c_n), and their synonyms.
> - A Set of manually selected documents (Estimation_Set), D={d_1, d_2, d_3, ..., d_N}, where, N=X+Y+Z, and, X: number of high quality pages, Y: number of medium quality pages, Z: number of low quality pages w.r.t the domain of interest
> - DOPD (Domain Oriented Probability Distribution) as a source of domain concepts probabilities.
>
> **OUTPUT**
> - The proper initial (tunable) value of Wc [i.e. W_c(initial)].
>
> **STEPS**
>
> **For each document d_j ∈ Estimation_Set do**
> $Words_j$ ← all distinct words found in d_j.
> $Cleaned\_Text_j$ ← clean($Words_j$).   *// Discard words not related to the domain using domain thesauri.* $Concepts_j$ ← Map($Cleaned\_Text_j$)   *// Mapping all words in $Text_j$ into the corresponding concept.* $Estimaion\_Concepts$ += $Concepts_j$ *// add new concepts to Estimaion_Concepts set.*
> **Next**
>
> **For each concept C_j ∈ Estimation_Concepts do**   *// find weight of all found domain concepts*
>   W(C_j)=log (1/P_i)
>   Total_Weight += W(C_j)
>   **Next**
> W_c(initial)= Total_Weight / N.   *// find the initial value of the critical weight.*

Figure 10. PIM accuracy against the critical weight

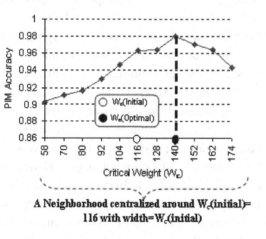

A Neighborhood centralized around W_c(initial)= 116 with width=W_c(initial)

value of the critical weight Wc (initial) was estimated using algorithm in Figure 9, as Wc (initial) = 116 (assuming X=Y=Z=100 pages). In order to calculate the optimal value of Wc, a set of different values of Wc must be used and the optimal critical value is the one, which gives the higher accuracy (the accuracy is the sum of those pages that are assigned correctly and those that are rejected correctly by PIM module over the total number of pages). To establish such task, a neighborhood centralized around Wc (initial) was considered. The width of that neighbor was also made equal to Wc (initial) (i.e., =116). The optimal value for the critical weight within that neighbor is searched for. As shown in Figure 10, the optimal value of Wc was found to be 140, which is the value considered in all the next experiments.

Evaluation Parameters

In this article, three different evaluation parameters, as described in Table 7 are used for measuring the performance of various crawling strategies.

For measuring the performance of various crawlers, human judgment is not preferred for two different reasons. The first is that human judgment is a subjective one. The other is that measuring the efficiency of the crawling strategy requires allowing the crawler to visit and retrieve

Table 7. Parameters used for evaluating various crawling strategies

Evaluation Parameter	Description
Harvest rate (crawling precision)	The parentage of relevant pages to the overall retrieved pages over different time slices of the crawl. $$HR = \frac{n_r}{n}$$ Where n_r is the number of retrieved and relevant pages, and n is the total number of retrieved pages. The page is considered as relevant if its weight equal or exceeds the critical weight measured by PIM module ($W_c = 140$)
Recall (R)	The parentage of relevant pages to the overall retrieved pages over different time slices of the crawl. $$R = \frac{n_r}{n_t}$$ Where n_r is the number of retrieved and relevant pages, and n_t is the total number of relevant pages in the collection.
Average Relevancy (AR)	$$AR = \frac{\sum_{i=1}^{n} Wd_i}{n}$$ Where Wd_i is the weight of the ith retrieved and relevant page by the crawler, and n is the number of retrieved and relevant pages.

very large number of pages. The logical solution is to automate the page-to-domain relevancy calculation, and then it will be simple to summarize performance across a set of crawled pages. To establish such aim, PIM module (using $w_c = 140$) is used to judge the relevancy of the retrieved page to the domain of interest in the following experiments.

Experimental Results

Various crawling strategies are compared against the proposed one. Four different experiments are introduced. The first one introduces a procedure for measuring crawling precision and recall in un-noisy conditions (simulated Web) while the next three experiments measure the performance under noisy conditions (real Web).

Experiment 1: Measuring the Crawling Recall in Un-Noisy Conditions

In this experiment, a decision to use a simulated Web is considered for different reasons. The first

is that, as the Web is very dynamic, crawling simulation is the only way to ensure that all the strategies considered are compared under the same conditions (Ricardo, Carlos, & Andrea, 2005). On the other hand, the number of relevant pages to the university domain on the Web is undetermined which makes determining the crawling recall to be problematic. Another cause is to avoid network congestion and heavy loads on the servers.

The principle simulated Web relies on two basic principels; the first is that the Web is a multi-domain collection of pages. Hence, five different interconnected domains are considered, namely (i) university, (ii) sports, (iii) transports, (iv) tourism, and (v) others. The second principle is that the Web has the shape of a bow-tie. It has four components: a knot, two bows, and a fourth component, which is disconnected from the bow-tie. The knot, which contains slightly less that 30% of the Web, is the fundamental component of the Web graph and is strongly connected, that is, there is a directed path from any node in the knot to any other node in the knot. The left bow contains about 23.4% of the Web and consists of pages that can reach the knot via a directed path but cannot themselves be reached from the knot via a directed path. The right bow, which also contains about 23.4% of the Web, consists of pages that can be reached from the knot via a directed path but cannot themselves reach the knot via a directed path. Finally, the last component, which also contains about 23.4% of the Web, cannot reach or be reached from the bow-tie via a directed or undirected path, that is, it is disconnected from the bow-tie.

In order to verify the above mentioned two principles, 100 undergraduate students in the faculty of engineering of Mansoura University were asked to build the simulated Web. Each student is asked to build at least five interconnected Web sites. Each student is allowed to build at least one site related to each of the five domains (in the case of "others" domain, the student is free to choose the subject for the site). Such technique insures the validation of the first principle since the simulated Web is a collection of multi-domain and linked pages. In order to verify the second principle, all the students are randomly distributed among four different. Then, each student is asked to reformulate his sites to match the characteristics of his category.

The simulated Web consists of 3214 pages, 739 pages of which are relevant to university domain. A total of 20 seeds are chosen as starting points for each of the various crawling strategies. Ten pages are selected from the "knot" while the other ten are chosen randomly from the "left bow" so that there is a chance to access each part of the bow-tie shape illustrated. All crawling strategies are allowed to crawl the simulated Web starting from the same seeds. When the trip of each crawler has been finished, the pages retrieved by each crawler are collected and classified, precision and recall for each crawling strategy is calculated, and results are shown in Table 10.

The performance of various crawling strategies starting from recall level=0.0 until 0.3 are tested, the low measured recall is due to that the simulated Web is not perfectly linked, so that, starting from the used seeds, there is no chance to cover all the simulated Web. This validates the reality that none of the available search engines can cover all the www. In this experiment, the crawler X outperforms another crawler Y, if X provides higher precision and lower crawled pages in the same recall level.

RC and BFC (un-focused crawlers) provide the minimum precision and the maximum crawled pages. They start very well and retrieve relevant pages. However, as they run away from seeds, they achieve a degraded performance. BFC represents better performance than RC especially at low recall levels since the first retrieved pages are the ones very closed to the seeds which will have a high chance to be relevant to the domain of interest.

When comparing both similarity-based crawlers, it is noted that the STDC crawler outperforms the STSC. This is logical since STDC is more general than STSC (STSC performance is restricted to the chosen starting seeds). The more closed strategies to the proposed one are CGC and BC. As illustrated in Figure 11, precision is plotted against recall after each crawled page. In such graphs, precision values are interpolated to a set of standard recall levels (the recall scale starts from 0 to 0.3 in increment of 0.03). In Rila and Hozumi (2000), the particular rule used to interpolate precision at standard recall level I is to use the maximum precision obtained for any actual recall level greater than or equal to I. Although precision is not defined at a recall 0.0, this interpolation rule does define an interpolated value for recall level 0.0.

From Figure 11, it is clear that the proposed crawling strategy (IAC) achieves the higher precision. On the other hand, Figure 12 illustrates the number of visited pages against the same set of recall levels. It is clear that IAC visits the minimum number of pages. Hence, it is believed that IAC outperforms all other traditional strategies

Figure 11. Precision versus recall for the various crawling strategies

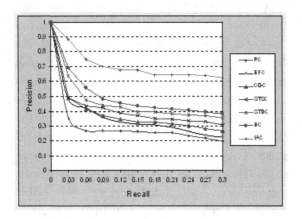

Figure 12. Crawled pages versus recall for the various crawling strategies

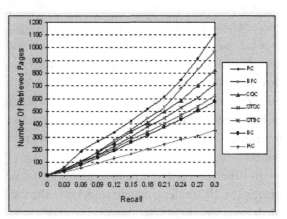

since it achieves the higher precision level while visiting the lower number of pages.

Experiment 2: Measuring the Average Relevancy

In this experiment, the aim is to measure the quality of the pages retrieved by various crawling strategy in noisy conditions (real Web). The quality of the pages retrieved by each crawler can be obtained by calculating the average relevancy (AR) of such pages for each crawling techniques. To establish such aim, the various crawling strategies are allowed to crawl the Web starting from 10 seeds chosen from WebKb Web collection, the relevancy of each page visited by each crawler (page weight) is measured using the PIM module, and then AR for each crawler is calculated. As illustrated in Figure 13, it is noted that: the average relevancy of the un-focused crawlers is the minimum ones. The cause of this is that: since unfocused crawlers have no ability to filter pages related to the domain of interest, hence the relevant pages retrieved by those un-focused crawlers are certainly retrieved by chance. The graph in Figure 13 also reveals that all focused crawlers successfully keep retrieving relevant

pages, but the proposed strategy does better than the others.

Experiment 3: Measuring the Harvest Rate

In this experiment, the harvest rate (HR) is computed at different points during the crawl. HR is considered as a perfect quantitative measure for the crawling performance. High value of HR indicates that the crawler has the ability to retrieve high number of relevant pages. The harvest rate for various crawling strategies can be seen in Figure 14. It shows that un-focused crawlers (BFC and RC) start with a medium HR as they are closer to seeds. However, they have a degraded performance (very low HR) after the first few hundred pages as they run away from seeds. On the other hand, the focused crawlers keep retrieving relevant pages with different abilities. The proposed strategy is the best one, the top competitors are BC, STDC, and CGC.

Experiment 4: Crawling Competition

In this experiment, a new way of evaluating the quality of pages retrieved by various crawlers is formulated. Assume that there are N different

Figure 13. The average relevancy versus the visited pages for various crawling strategy

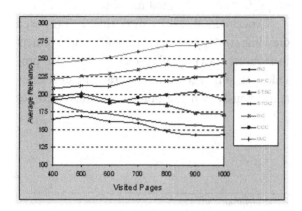

Figure 14. The harvest ratio versus the visited pages for various crawling strategy

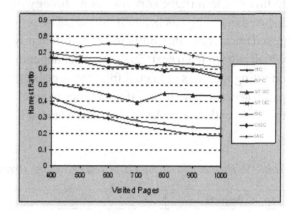

Figure 15. Scores for different crawling strategies

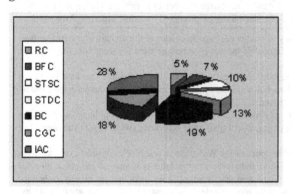

Table 8. Different categories and the corresponding scores

Category ID	Description	Score
1	Very relevant	20
2	Relevant	15
3	Medium	10
4	Related	5
5	Irrelevant	0

crawlers, and that we want to compare them. The *N* different crawlers are started from the same seeds and allowed to run till each crawler gathers a number of *P* pages. The *N*P* pages collected by various crawlers are ranked using human assessor. Then *M* pages are produced (after removing similar pages retrieved by different crawlers); these pages are manually categorized according to five different categories with a corresponding score according to the Table 8.

Then the overall score of each crawler is calculated as:

Score(Crawlerj) =

$$\sum_{i=1}^{P} score\ page_{ji} \bigg/ \sum_{j=1}^{N} \left(\sum_{i=1}^{P} score\ page_{ji} \right)$$

When such evaluation strategy is followed using *P=100, N=7* (the number of crawling strategies compared), a total of 486 distinct pages are collected. Results of the competing crawling strategies are shown in Figure 15. This shows that the proposed strategy achieves the higher score (i.e., high quality of the retrieved pages).

CONCLUSION

In this article, a framework for a new strategy of focused crawling has been introduced. The proposed crawler has the ability to decide efficiently which page to fetch next. Such a crawler depends on rating the links extracted from the processed pages according to three different types of votes; the link with the higher calculated votes will be visited next. It also provides several salient properties that other approaches do not have; such properties are illustrated in Table 9.

Experimental results show that the proposed crawling strategy results in a notable improvement in focused crawling effectiveness, and also provides the ability to boost the crawling efficiency continuously. On the other hand, it overcomes

Table 9. Properties of the proposed crawling strategy

Property	Description
Scalability	One of the challenges faced in this work is the linguistic problems, namely, how to construct a thesaurus that include as much domain terms as possible. The proposed framework uses a domain thesaurus for *"University Domain"* that consists of a set of domain concepts *(215 concepts)* as well as their synonyms. Such a framework can be easily promoted by using a larger thesaurus (large number of concepts). Hence, the proposed framework for focused crawling is a scalable one since it can be promoted by using larger sized thesaurus.
Intelligence	The proposed crawler has an excellent ability to predict the page relevance to the domain of interest without actually visiting it. The source of such intelligence is the novel technique used for weighting the extracted links, in which: • Three different weights are attached to each extracted link. Those weights are extracted from all pages containing the link, all anchor windows of the link in different processed pages, and all visual blocks containing the link found in all processed pages. • The weighting technique is accumulative in nature. It considers the link popularity; hence, as the link appears in more processing pages, it will gain more relevancy (weight) w.r.t the domain of interest. • All traditional crawling approaches consider the Web page as one block; all links extracted from the same page will have the same score with respect to the domain of interest. However, this idea is not usually valid in the Web environment that is full of noisy links that are usually embedded inside the body of Web pages. Also, each block inside the same page (and accordingly the links extracted from that block) may have different importance w.r.t the domain of interest. The proposed technique takes such drawbacks into account; it treats the page as a multi-block structure. The page is divided into a number of blocks (whenever possible) and each block is treated individually.
Self Adaptation	The proposed crawler can adapt itself to any change in its domain by two different methods: ■ using DOPD as a source of concept probabilities ■ using the CLNB algorithm for Web page classification
Flexibility	The proposed framework is also flexible since it can be used for applying focused crawling in any domain. It can be adjusted to operate in any domain after setting its parameters (e.g., W_c, α, β, δ) and choosing the proper domain thesauri.
Performance promotion	Experimental results have shown that the proposed focused crawling strategy demonstrate significant performance improvement (precision and recall) over other traditional focused crawling strategies. Also, it has the ability to enhance its performance with time using the adaptive DOPD.
Self Dependency	No special requirements are needed to build the proposed focused crawling strategy; hence, it achives a high degree of self-dependency. For example, the context focused crawler uses the capability provided by other traditional search engines and the crawler that employs the users' behavior needs a large collection of user sequences, which is not usually easy to achieve.
Simple Implementation	Unlike the other focused crawlers, the proposed one is designed to minimize human effort; hence, it can be easily implemented even in a large scale.
Consistency	Although it may seem that the proposed focused crawler has a complex structure, all its modules are successfully integrated with each other, accordingly, the proposed crawler presents a remarkable performance improvement over other focused crawling strategies.

the various drawbacks of the current crawling approaches.

REFERENCES

Aggarwal, C. F., Al-Garawi, C., & Yu, F. P. (2001, May 1-5). Intelligent crawling on the world wide Web with arbitrary predicates. In *Proceedings of the 10th International World Wide Web Conference (WWW '01)* (pp. 96–105). Hong Kong, China.

Altingovde, I. S., & Ulusoy, Ö. (2004). Exploiting interclass rules for focused crawling. *IEEE Intelligent Systems, 19*(6), 66-73.

Chakrabarti, S., Dom, B., Gibson, P., & Kleinberg, J. (1998). Automatic resource compilation by analyzing hyperlink structure and associated text. In *Proceedings of the 7th Int. World Wide Web Conference (WWW '98)* (pp. 65-74). Brisband, Australia.

Chakrabarti, S., Vander, B., & Dom, M. B. (1999). Focused crawling: a new approach to topic-specific Web resource discovery. In *Proceedings of the 8th International World-Wide Web Conference (WWW '99)* (pp. 545-562). Elsevier Science.

Chau, M., Zeng, D., & Chen, H. (2001, June). Personalized spiders for Web search and analysis. In *Proceedings of ACM/IEEE Joint Conference on Digital Libraries (JCDL '01)* (pp. 79-87). Roanoke, Virginia, USA.

Cho, J., & Garcia, H. M. (2000, May). Synchronizing database to improve freshness. In *Proceedings of the ACM International Conference on Management of Data (SIGMOD '00)* (pp. 117-128). Dallas, Texas, USA.

Cho, J. H., Garcia, M., & Page, L. (1998, April). Efficient crawling through URL ordering. In *Proceedings of the 7th International World Wide Web Conference (WWW '98)* (pp. 161–172). Brisbane, Australia.

DeBra, P., & Post, R. (1994). Information retrieval in the world wide Web: Making client based searching feasible. *Journal on Computer Networks and ISDN Systems, 27,* 183-192.

Donato, D., Leonardi, S., & Millozzi, P. T. (2005). Mining the inner structure of the Web grap. In *Proceedings of the 8th International Workshop on the Web, & Databases (WebDB '05)* (pp. 145-150). Baltimore, Maryland, USA.

Ester, M., Kriegel, H. P., & Schubert, M. (2004). Accurate and efficient crawling for relevant Websites. In *Proceedings of the 30th International Conference on Very Large Databases (VLDB '04)* (pp. 396-407). Toronto, Canada.

Gautam, P., Kostas, T., & Judy, J. (2004, June 7-11). Panorama: extending digital libraries with topical crawlers. In *Proceedings of the 4th ACM/IEEE Joint Conference on Digital Libraries (JCDL '04)* (pp. 203-209), Tucson, Arizona, USA.

Gautam, P., & Padmini, S. (2006). Link contexts in classifier-guided topical crawlers. *IEEE Transactions on Knowledge and Data Engineering, 18*(1), 107-122.

Gulli, A., & Signorin, A. (2005, May 10-14). Building an open source metasearch engine. In *Proceedings of the 14th International World Wide Web Conference (WWW '05)* (pp. 111-119). Chiba, Japan.

Hersovici, M., Jacovi, D., Pelleg, M., & Shtalhaim, S. U. (1998, April). The SHARK SEARCH algorithm—An application: Tailored Web site mappin. In *Proceedings of the 7th International World Wide Web Conference (WWW '98)* (pp. 47-55), Brisbane, Australia.

Hongyu, L., Evangelos, M., & Jeannette, J. (2004, November 12-13). Probabilistic models for focused Web crawling. In *Proceedings of the 6th ACM Int. Workshop on Web Information and Data Management (WIDM'04)* (pp. 167-172). Washington D.C., USA.

Jianjun, C., David, J. D., & Yuan, W. (2000, May). NiagaraCQ: A scalable continuous query system for Internet databases. In *Proceedings of the ACM International Conference on Management of Data (SIGMOD '00)* (pp. 379-390). Dallas, Texas, USA.

Liu, H., Milios, E., & Janssen, J. (2004, September 20-24). Focused crawling by learning HMM from user's topic-specific browsing. In *Proceedings of the IEEE/WIC/ACM Int. Conference on Web Intelligence (WI '04)* (pp. 702-732). IEEE.

Marcia, J. B. (1986). Access in online catalogs: A design model. *American Society for Information Science Journal, Wiley InterScience, 37*(6), 357-376.

Maria, H., Benjamin, N., Iraklis, V., & Michalis, V. (2003). THESUS:Organizing Web document collections based on link semantics. *Int. Journal on Very Large Data Bases, VLDB, 12*, 320-332.

Marios, D., Dikaiakos, A., & Loizos, P. (2005). An investigation of Web crawler behavior: characterization and metrics. *Computer Communications, 28*, 880-897.

Menczer, F. (2004). Lexical and semantic clustering by Web links. *Journal of the American Society for Information Science and Technology (JASIST), Wiley InterScience, 55*(14), 1261-1269.

Menczer, F., Paint, G., & Srinivansan, P. (2004). Topical Web crawlers:Evaluating adaptive algorithms. *ACM Transactions on Internet Technology, ACM, 4*(4), 378-419.

Michael, C., & Hsinchun, C. (2004, December 13-17). Using content-based and link-based analysis in building vertical search engines. In *Proceedings of the 7th Int. Conference on Asian Digital Libraries (ICADL '04)* (pp. 515-518). China.

Michelangelo, D., Frans, C. C., Lee, G., & Marco, G. (2000, September). Focused crawling using context graphs. In *Proceedings of the 26th International Conference on Very Large Databases (VLDB '00)* (pp. 527-534). Cairo, Egypt.

Najork, M., & Wiener, I. N. (2001, May). Breadth-first search crawling yields high-quality pages. In *Proceedings of the 10th International World Wide Web Conference (WWW '01)* (pp. 161-167). Hong Kong.

Padmini, S., Filippo, M., & Gautam, P. (2005). A general evaluation framework for topical crawlers. *Information Retrieval, 8*(3), 417-447.

Qiu, F., Shao, M., & Zatsman, J. (2003, June). *Index structures for querying the deep Web.* Paper presented at the International Workshop on the Web and Databases (WebDB) (pp. 79-86), San Diego, California, USA.

Resnik, P. (1999). Semantic similarity in taxonomy: An information-based measure and its application problems of ambiguity in natural language. *Artificial Intelligence Research Journal, 11*, 95-130.

Ricardo, B., Carlos, C., & Andrea, R. (2005, May 10-14). Crawling a country: Better strategies than breadth first for Web page ordering. In *Proceedings of the 14th Int. World Wide Web Conference (WWW '05)* (pp. 864 - 872) Chiba, Japan.

Rila, M., & Hozumi T. (2000). The exploration and analysis of using multiple thesaurus types for query expansion in information retrieval. *Natural Language Processing Journal, 7*(2), 117-140.

Thanh, T. T., David, H., Nick, C., & Kathleen, G. (2005, October 31-November 5). Focused crawling for both topical relevance and quality of medical information. In *Proceedings of the 14th ACM International Conference on Information and Knowledge Management (CIKM '05)* (pp. 147-154). Bremen, Germany.

Vinod, V., Vydiswaran, G., & Sunita, S. (2005, January 6-8). Learning to extract information from large Websites using sequential models. In *Proceedings of the 11th Int. Conference on*

Management of Data (COMAD '05) (pp. 76-82). Goa, India.

Wu, Z., & Palmer, M. (1994). Verb semantics and lexical selection. In *Proceedings of the 32nd Annual Meetings of the Associations for Computational Linguistics (ACL '94)* (pp. 133–138). Las Cruces, New Mexico.

Zhdanova, A. V., & Fensel, D. (2005, September 19-22). Limitations of community Web portals: A classmates' case study. In *Proceedings of the IEEE/WIC/ACM International Conference on Web Intelligence* (pp. 101-104). Compiegne, France: IEEE Computer Society.

This work was previously published in the International Journal of Intelligent Information Technologies, Vol. 4, Issue 1, edited by V. Sugumaran, pp. 52-79, copyright 2008 by IGI Publishing (an imprint of IGI Global).

Chapter 10

Information Customization using SOMSE:
A Self–Organizing Map Based Approach

Mohamed Salah Hamdi
Ahmed Bin Mohammed Military College, Qatar

ABSTRACT

Information overload on the World-Wide Web is a well recognized problem. Research to subdue this problem and extract maximum benefit from the Internet is still in its infancy. Managing information overload on the Web is a challenge and the need for more precise techniques for assisting the user in finding the most relevant and most useful information is obvious. Search engines are very effective at filtering pages that match explicit queries. Search engines, however, require massive memory resources (to store an index of the Web) and tremendous network bandwidth (to create and continually refresh the index). These systems receive millions of queries per day, and as a result, the CPU cycles devoted to satisfying each individual query are sharply curtailed. There is no time for intelligence which is mandatory for offering ways to combat information overload. What is needed are systems, often referred to as information customization systems, that act on the user's behalf and that can rely on existing information services like search engines that do the resource-intensive part of the work. These systems will be sufficiently lightweight to run on an average PC and serve as personal assistants. Since such an assistant has relatively modest resource requirements it can reside on an individual user's machine. If the assistant resides on the user's machine, there is no need to turn down intelligence. The system can have substantial local intelligence. In an attempt to circumvent the problems of search engines and contribute to resolving the problem of information overload over the Web, the authors propose SOMSE, a system that improves the quality of Web search by combining meta-search and unsupervised learning.

DOI: 10.4018/978-1-60566-970-0.ch005

INTRODUCTION

We live in an age of information abundance. The technology research firm IDC (http://www.idc.com/) determined that the world generated approximately 161 exabytes (i.e., around 161 billion gigabytes) of new information in 2006 (Bergstein, 2007); that's many thousands of times the size of the U.S. Library of Congress. In July 2008, Google announced that it had indexed one trillion (as in 1,000,000,000,000) unique URLs and estimated that the web was growing at a rate of several billion pages per day (Google, 2008).

The plenitude of information, not its scarcity, defines the world we live in now. Historically, more information has almost always been a good thing. However, as the ability to collect information grew, the ability to process that information did not keep up. Today, we have large amounts of available information and a high rate of new information being added, but contradictions in the available information, a low signal-to-noise ratio (proportion of useful information found to all information found), and inefficient methods for comparing and processing different kinds of information characterize the situation. The result is the "information overload" of the user, i.e., users have too much information to make a decision or remain informed about a topic. Seeking to shift between dealing with information scarcity and information abundance is necessary. Locating information is not the problem; locating relevant, reliable information is the real issue.

Information overload on the World-Wide Web is a well recognized problem. Research to subdue this problem and extract maximum benefit from the Internet is still in its infancy. Managing information overload on the Web is a challenge and the need for more precise techniques for assisting the user in finding the most relevant and most useful information is obvious. With largely unstructured pages authored by a massive range of people on a diverse range of topics, simple browsing has given way to filtering as the practical way to manage

Web-based information. Today's online resources are therefore mainly accessible via a panoply of primitive but popular information services such as search engines.

Search engines are very effective at filtering pages that match explicit queries. Search engines, however, require massive memory resources (to store an index of the Web) and tremendous network bandwidth (to create and continually refresh the index). These systems receive millions of queries per day, and as a result, the CPU cycles devoted to satisfying each individual query are sharply curtailed. There is no time for intelligence which is mandatory for offering ways to combat information overload.

Search engines rank the retrieved documents in descending order of relevance to the user's information needs according to certain predetermined criteria. The usual outcome of the ranking process applied by a search engine is a long list of document titles. The main drawback of such an approach is that the user is still required to browse through this long list to select those that are actually considered to be of interest. Another shortcoming is that the resultant list of documents from a search engine does not make distinctions between the different concepts that may be present in the query, as the list inevitably has to be ranked sequentially. The problem lies mainly in the presentation of the list of document titles. These documents are usually listed serially irrespective of the similarity or dissimilarity in their contents - that is, it does not make distinctions between the different concepts. Thus, two documents appearing next to each other in the list may not necessarily be of a similar nature and vice versa. As the list of documents grows longer, the amount of time and effort needed to browse through the list to look for relevant documents increases.

What is needed are systems, often referred to as information customization systems (Hamdi, 2006a, 2006b, 2007a, 2007b, 2008a, 2008b, 2008c), that act on the user's behalf and that can rely on existing information services like search engines that do the resource-intensive part of the work. These systems will be sufficiently lightweight to run on an average PC and serve as personal assistants. Since such an assistant has relatively modest resource requirements it can reside on an individual user's machine. If the assistant resides on the user's machine, there is no need to turn down intelligence. The system can have substantial local intelligence.

In an attempt to circumvent the problems of search engines discussed above and contribute to resolving the problem of information overload over the Web, we propose improving the quality of Web search by combining meta-search and unsupervised learning.

A meta-search engine simultaneously searches multiple search engines and returns a single list of results. The results retrieved by this engine can be highly relevant, since it is usually grabbing the first items from the relevancy-ranked list of hits returned by the individual search engines. The Kohonen Feature Map is then used to construct a self-organizing semantic map such that documents of similar contents are placed close to one another.

The goal is to conceptualize an information retrieval approach which uses traditional search engines as information filters and the semantic map as a browsing aid to support ordering, linking, and browsing information gathered by the filters.

BACKGROUND

Since its advent in the early 1990's, the Worldwide Web has grown to billions of pages today. This huge number of pages is estimated to be several times larger than the number of pages of all the books ever printed since the invention of the printing press over 500 years ago. In fact, the Web is now clearly the most widely used communication medium; the largest source of data and information available anywhere; and the quickest, easiest, and cheapest means of access to valuable content.

The ubiquity of the Internet and Web caused a great deal of search engines to send out new growth and search became the second most popular activity on the Web. In recent years, always more and more innovative and sophisticated search engines have started appearing. These systems index Web sites, images, Usenet news groups, content-based directories, and news sources and allow sophisticated searches, with required and forbidden words, and the ability to restrict results based on a particular language or encoding.

Google, for example, supports a rich query syntax that allows the user to access additional capabilities of the search engine. If, for example, a common word is essential to getting the results the user wants, it can be included by putting a "+" sign in front of it. The user can exclude a word from the search results by putting a minus sign ("-") immediately in front of it. It is possible to search for complete phrases by enclosing them in quotation marks or connecting them with hyphens. Words marked in this way will appear together in all results exactly as entered. Boolean OR search is possible. To retrieve pages that include either word A or word B, an uppercase OR between terms is used. Site restricted search, date restricted search, title search, and a plenty of other options are possible. See (Google, 2006) for details.

Unfortunately, only a small number of web users actually know how to utilize the true power of these engines. Most average web users make searches based on imprecise query keywords or sentences, which return unnecessary, or worse, inaccurate results. The need to accept these queries while overcoming the limitations of their imprecision has given rise to research into ways of improving the retrieval results based on this assumption. A number of research work on automatic keyword and phrase extraction for query expansion and on using user feedback has been reported (e.g. (Xu and Croft, 1996), (Narita and Ogawa, 2000), (Salton and Buckley, 1990)). Recently, however, motivated by the introduction of Web Services of search engines, which allow developers to query the server directly from their application, another class of systems aiming at dealing with these problems and producing search results that are most relevant to user queries have started to emerge. These systems usually adopt "*guided search*" or "*meta-search*" or combinations of them.

GUIDED SEARCH

In guided search, the system helps guide the user's searching sessions and serves as an advanced interface to a given search engine. One example is GuideBeam (http://www.guidebeam.com). GuideBeam has a simple start page, with just a box to type in a keyword or phrase. Clicking the search button results in a list of categories based on the keywords. The user can keep picking categories to target his search. GuideBeam works based on "rational monotonicity". This principle prescribes how the user's current query can be expanded in a way which is consistent with the user's preferences for information. Users can intuitively navigate to the desired query in a context-sensitive manner. This is known as "Query by Navigation". The goal is to elicit a more precise query from the user, which will translate into more relevant documents being returned from the associated search engine (Bruza & van Linder, 1998).

Another example is Google API Proximity Search (GAPS) (http://www.staggernation.com/cgi-bin/gaps.cgi). GAPS is a Perl script that uses the Google API (Google, 2006) to search Google for two search terms that appear within a certain distance from each other on a page. It does this by using a seldom-discussed Google feature: within a quoted phrase, * can be used as a wildcard meaning "any word". So to search for *coppola* within 2 words of *nepotism*, in either order, 6 queries are needed: "coppola nepotism", "coppola * nepotism", "coppola * * nepotism", "nepotism coppola", "nepotism * coppola", and "nepotism * * coppola". The GAPS script simply constructs

these queries, gets the first page of Google results for each query, compiles all the results, and presents them in a specified sort order (Staggernation, 2006). Guided Google (Hoong & Buyya, 2004) is a similar system that performs simple manipulation and automation of existing Google functions. It supports search based on hosts and is also able to generate all combinations of the keywords that appear in the query and search for them.

META-SEARCH

In meta-search (also know as meta-crawling or multi-threading), the user submits keywords in the search box of the system, and the system transmits the search simultaneously to several individual search engines, Web directories and - sometimes - to the so-called Deep Web (Bergman, 2001), a collection of online information not indexed by traditional search engines such as content that resides in searchable databases (dynamically generated sites) and that can only be discovered by a direct query. After collecting the results, the meta-search engine usually removes the duplicate links and, according to its algorithm, combines or ranks the results into a single merged list. Meta-search engines do not own a database of Web pages; they send the search terms to the databases maintained by search engine companies.

The meta-search engine Dogpile (www.dogpile.com), for example, searches Google, Yahoo, LookSmart, Ask.com, MSN Search and others. Sites that have purchased ranking and inclusion are blended in ("Sponsored by..." link below search result). Dogpile accepts Boolean logic, especially in advanced search modes. It also allows the user to see each search engine's results separately in a useful list for comparison. There is also a "domain filter" for filtering generic domain extensions like .com, .gov and .edu and a "search filter" for filtering potentially explicit content from search results.

SurfWax (www.surfwax.com) is another example of a meta-search engine that searches a better than average set of search engines including WiseNut, AllTheWeb, CNN, and LookSmart. It accepts quotes " " and +/- to include and exclude words. Default is AND between words. The results can be sorted by source, relevance, or alphabetically. SurfWax's SiteSnaps (quick summaries of individual results that capture relevant information) and other features help the user dig deeply into results. Clicking on a source link allows viewing complete search results. Clicking on the snap button to the left of a source link allows viewing helpful SiteSnaps extracted from that site in a frame on the right. There are many additional features for probing within a site.

There are plenty of other examples of meta-search engines with different features. See, for example, (Cohen, 2006) to learn more about many of them.

Meta-search engines usually return only a limited number of the documents available to be retrieved from the individual engines they have searched. The cut-off may be determined by the number of documents retrieved, or by the amount of time the meta-search engine spends at the other sites. Some systems give the user a certain degree of control over these factors.

Meta-search engines save searchers a considerable amount of time by sparing them the trouble of running a query in each search engine. Using a meta-search engine can also increase the likely hood of finding relevant information. Results retrieved by meta-search engines can be highly relevant, since they are usually grabbing the first items from the relevancy-ranked list of hits returned by the individual search engines.

As already mentioned, it is estimated that the Web consists of billions of web pages and the number is steadily increasing. Each single search tool such as Google, Yahoo, etc. indexes only a small part of the Web. Moreover, all have different programs that use different criteria to build their databases with the intention to balance number of returns against precision. Every search engine will therefore index different Web pages. As a result, if a user uses only one search engine, he will miss relevant results that can be found in other search engines. Meta-search engines help to fill in the gaps by searching many search engines simultaneously.

Meta-search has also intrinsic advantages that are based on voting. You might be surprised to find that on average only very few of the top ten search engine results are the same. Search engine overlap isn't as great as many would think! (Spink et al, 2006) is just one of the many reports on how little overlap occurs among the top results of regular engines like AltaVista, Google, Yahoo, etc. The overlapping search results are presumably better than the unique hits found by a single engine. When a single search engine is used, these unique hits compete for space and user attention with the consensus-best results, which the user is unable to distinguish from the unique hits.

Meta-search can also be seen to improve on search engines by canceling noise. Search engines adopt several different sources of evidence to rank web pages matching a user query, such as textual content, title of web pages, anchor text information, or the link structure of the web. The use of the latter measure, for example, usually relies on the assumption that a link to a page represents a vote from a user that sustains the quality of that page. However, relying on this assumption may lead to wrong conclusions, especially when the links are intentionally created to artificially boost the rank of some given set of pages. These spam pages (Wu and Davison, 2005), "pay for placement" pages, as well as pages ranked high because of noisy links on the web that are created in a non-intentional way (da Costa Carvalho et al, 2006), are considered as Web noise that negatively affects the results of individual search engines.

Valdes-Perez (2005) holds a viewpoint favoring meta-searching by saying "more heads are better than one" and compares improving the search results using meta-search to performing averaging of noisy signals in electrical engineering, which cancels out random noise and reveals the original noise-free signal. Since Web noise affects regular search engines in different ways, meta-search filters noise by averaging the votes of the underlying engines, revealing the consensus best results.

CLUSTERING OF SEARCH RESULTS

Despite the many advantages of meta-search engines, these systems still suffer from the problems related to the presentation of the list of retrieved documents mentioned earlier. A possible solution to this problem is to (online) cluster search results into different groups, and to enable users to determine at a glance whether the contents of a cluster are of interest. Document clustering has long been proven to be an aid to searchers. If done well, it saves the searcher time and effort in assessing the variety of possible meanings and aspects of a very long list, and provides quick identification of the clusters that best match interests. Document clustering is especially helpful to people who are new to a subject area and don't know the key terms. Additionally, document clustering can disambiguate words that have multiple meanings depending on the context. Jaguar is a classic example. Is that the cat (panthera onca), the car, the club, or the football team?

Clustering works from the premise that closely associated documents tend to be relevant to the same requests (van Rijsbergen, 1999). Close association is determined by analyzing the text for similarity among the documents in words and phrases used. Each cluster can be labeled by a short phrase description derived from the co-occurrence of significant words.

Clustering methods don't require pre-defined categories as in classification methods. Thus, they are more adaptive for various queries. Nevertheless, clustering methods are more challenging than classification methods because they are conducted in a fully unsupervised way.

Most clustering algorithms use the vector space model of information retrieval (Salton and McGill, 1983), in which text documents are represented as a set of points (or term vectors) in a high dimensional vector space. Each direction of the vector space corresponds to a unique term in the document collection, and the component of a document vector along a given direction corresponds to the importance of that term to the document. Similarity between two texts is traditionally measured by the cosine of the angle between their vectors, though Cartesian distance is also used. Documents judged to be similar by this measure are grouped together by the clustering algorithm.

Automatic document clustering is an active and challenging field of research. Recently, researchers have begun to investigate to what extent the pattern recognition power of neural networks can be exploited for this purpose. (Deogun et al., 1991), (Lin et al., 1991), (MacLeod and Robertson, 1991), (Wermter, 1991), (Kohonen, 1997), and (Merkl, 1997) are just some examples.

In general, using these algorithms to cluster a collection of documents represented using term vectors is computationally expensive. This is because of the high dimensionality resulting from the large number of terms in the collection. As the size of the document collection increases, the number of unique words (or terms) also increases. The set of terms in a document increasingly occupy only a small fraction of all the terms in the collection. In other words, the term vector for each document becomes increasingly sparse. There are a number of ways of reducing the high dimensionality of the term vector without necessarily losing its discriminative value. Khan and Khor (2004), for example, used principal component analysis (PCA) (Jolliffe, 1986) to capture the underlying correlation of the terms before using an ART (Adaptive Resonance Theory) neural network (Carpenter and Grossberg, 1988) to build the clusters of documents.

In the case of a meta-search engine, however, the high dimensionality problem does not seem to be a severe issue because the system is usually grabbing only the first few items from the relevancy-ranked list of hits returned by the individual search engines. Hence, the resulting total number of documents returned will be relatively small. The meta-search engine SOMSE described in this paper, for example, returns maximum 60 documents. Additionally, as there is no time to download the original documents off the Web, the system will take short snippets returned by the individual search engines as input for clustering. The resulting vocabulary will therefore be relatively small. Additional operations applied on the vocabulary terms such as stemming, stop word removal, and removal of high and low frequency words will make the vocabulary and hence the dimensionality still smaller. Thus, we can afford some more complex processing, which can possibly let us achieve better results.

We have adopted the Kohonen's self-organizing feature map (Kohonen, 1989) (Kohonen, 1995) for the purpose of clustering the Web search results returned by the meta-searcher. Emphasis on frequencies and distributions of underlying input data, understanding of the computer's role in producing an associative map similar to the feature map in the brain, and projection of a high dimensional space to a two dimensional map are the most distinguishing characteristics of Kohonen's feature map.

Kohonen's self-organizing feature map is very well known as a clustering and dimension reduction tool. Clustering can be used for categorization of input vectors. Dimension reduction can be used for visualization and for reducing information in order to ease search, storage or processing of another kind. The self-organizing feature map algorithm has been widely used in many different engineering and scientific applications such as image recognition, signal processing, and connectionist natural language processing. In addition, it is also widely used in visualization as a dimension (feature) reduction tool. The robustness of the algorithm and its appealing visualization effects have also made it a prime candidate in several large-scale information categorization and visualization projects (e.g., (Honkela et al., 1996), (Chen et al., 1996), (Orwig et al., 1997)).

Figure 1. Architecture of Kohonen's feature map

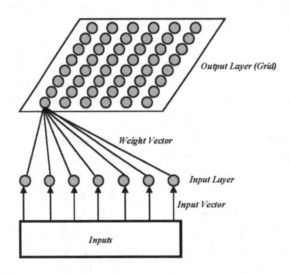

SELF-ORGANIZING SEMANTIC MAPS

Kohonen's feature map is one of the major unsupervised learning methods in the family of artificial neural networks. Kohonen based his neural network on the associative neural properties of the brain (Kohonen, 1989). The topology of the Kohonen self-organizing network is shown in Figure 1.

This network contains two layers of nodes - an input layer and an output (mapping) layer in the shape of a two-dimensional grid. The input layer acts as a distribution layer. The network is fully connected in that every output node is connected to every input node. The number N of nodes in the input layer is equal to the number of features or attributes associated with the input (N-dimensional vector). Each node of the output layer also has the same number of features as there are input nodes (N-dimensional weight vector).

Kohonen's feature map algorithm takes a set of input objects, each represented by a N-dimensional vector, as input and maps them onto nodes of the two-dimensional grid. Initially the components of the weight vectors assigned to nodes of the two-dimensional grid are small random values. They are adjusted through the following learning process:

1. Select an input vector randomly from the set of all input vectors.
2. Find the winning node of the grid, i.e., the node whose weights are closest to the input vector in the N-dimensional space.
3. Adjust the weights of the winning node and the weights of its neighboring nodes in the grid so that they become still closer to the input vector in the N-dimensional space.

This process goes through many iterations (usually hundreds or thousands of repeated presentations: each input vector is presented many times) until it converges, i.e., the adjustments all approach zero. Each input vector is then mapped to a grid node closest to it in the N-dimensional space.

The process corresponds to a projection of the input space onto the two-dimensional grid. The result, called a feature map, should be a spatial organization of the input data organized into clusters of similar (neighboring) regions. Two main properties of such a feature map are (Ritter & Kohonen, 1989): i) The feature map preserves the distance relationships between the input data as faithfully as possible. While some distortion is unavoidable, the mapping preserves the most important neighborhood relationships between the input data, and makes such relationships geographically explicit; ii) The feature map allocates different numbers of nodes to inputs based on their occurrence frequencies. The more frequent input patterns are mapped to larger domains (bigger regions of the 2-dimensional grid) at the expense of the less frequent ones.

It has been demonstrated that the feature map learning algorithm can perform relatively well in noise (Lippmann, 1987). Hence, as already mentioned, its application potential is enormous. Here, in the area of search result clustering, we are faced with a tremendous amount of 'noise' in the input data resulting from the indexing of free-form documents. Document snippets returned by search engines are usually very short and noisy. So we can get broken sentences or useless symbols, numbers or dates on the input.

DETAILS OF THE LEARNING ALGORITHM

The computational algorithm of the feature map consists of two basic procedures, selecting a winning node and updating weights of the winning node and its neighboring nodes. The winning node is defined as that with the smallest Euclidean distance between the weight vector of the node and the input vector. If $X(t) = (x_1(t), x_2(t), ..., x_N(t))$

is the input vector selected at time t and $W^k(t) = (w^k_1(t), w^k_2(t), ..., w^k_N(t))$ is the weight vector for node k at time t, the winning node s is the node that produces the smallest distance d_s:

$$d_s = ||X(t) - W^s(t)|| = min_k ||X(t) - W^k(t)|| \qquad (1)$$

After the winning node s is selected, the weights of s and the weights of the nodes in a defined neighborhood (e.g., all nodes within a square, a diamond, or a circle around the winning node) are adjusted to become more similar to the input vector. In this way, similar input patterns are more likely to select this node again in the future. The adjustment of the weight vectors is achieved as follows:

$$W^k(t+1) = W^k(t) + \eta(t) * (X(t) - W^k(t)) \qquad (2)$$

where $\eta(t)$ is an error-adjusting (learning) coefficient $(0 < \eta(t) < 1)$ that decreases over time and converges to 0. Intuitively, this formula says that if a component of the input vector is greater than the corresponding weight, increase the weight by a small amount; if the input component is smaller than the weight, decrease the weight by a small amount; the larger the difference between the input component and the weight component, the larger the increment (decrement).

Note that the update procedure does not require any external "teaching" signals, so the algorithm is an unsupervised, self-organizing algorithm. To guarantee that the self-organizing algorithm functions properly, two control mechanisms are imposed. The first is to shrink the neighborhood of a node gradually over time. A large neighborhood will achieve ordering and a small neighborhood will help to achieve a stable convergence of the map (Kohonen, 1989). By beginning with a large neighborhood and then gradually reducing it to a very small neighborhood, the feature map achieves both ordering and convergence properties. The second mechanism is the error-adjusting coefficient $\eta(t)$. Since $\eta(t)$ is a slowly decreasing function that

converges to 0, the updating will eventually stop and the map converges (mathematical proof of the convergence of the algorithm as well as additional algorithmic details of neighborhood selection and adjustment can be found in (Kohonen, 1989) and (Lippmann, 1987)).

Kohonen initially defined the coefficient $\eta(t)$ over geographic neighborhoods: at time t, $\eta(t)$ is a small constant within a given neighborhood, and 0 elsewhere. A more recent version of the feature map adapts the Gaussian function to describe the neighborhood and $\eta(t)$. One of the successful stories of current neural network approaches is to apply nonlinear, continuous functions such as the sigmoid function and the Gaussian function to the learning process. The Gaussian function is supposed to describe a more natural mapping so as to help the algorithm converge in a more stable manner. In this paper we adopt a Gaussian function for $\eta(t)$ similar to that used in (Lin et al., 1991):

$$\eta(t,k,s) = A1 \cdot \frac{1}{e^{\frac{t}{A2}}} \cdot \frac{1}{e^{\frac{t \cdot d(k,s)}{A3}}} \qquad (3)$$

where $d(k,s)$ is the Euclidian distance between the node k and the winning node s in the two-dimensional grid. $A1$, $A2$, and $A3$ are three parameters. In the formula, the first Gaussian function controls the weight update speed and the second Gaussian function defines the neighborhood shrinkage. Thus, $\eta(t,k,s)$ unifies learning coefficient and neighborhood definition. Note that $\eta(t,k,s)$ depends on the time t and on the distance of the node k from the winning node s.

MORE INTUITIVE PARAMETERS AND CONVERGENCE

Since, in the context of search result clustering, fast interaction with the user is required, the system should be able achieve convergence within a training period of limited length. It is therefore convenient to assume a training period of a certain given length C, and try to shape the function η appropriately in order to achieve convergence within this period. η should therefore be expressed as a function of C. The best way to do this is through the parameters $A1$, $A2$, and $A3$. We will express these 3 parameters as functions of C and 3 other additional parameters that are more intuitive than $A1$, $A2$, and $A3$, and hence, easier to tune. The 3 new parameters are:

- η_{start}: $0 < \eta_{start} \leq 1$, is the starting value (value at time $t = 0$) for η for the winning node s. Note that the time t goes from 0 to $(C-1)$.

- η_{end}: $0 < \eta_{end} < \eta_{start}$, is the final value (value at time $t = (C-1)$) for η for the winning node s.

- $G2_{end}$: $0 < G2_{end} < 1$, is the final value (value at time $t = (C-1)$) for the second Gaussian function in equation (3) for a node k that is situated at a maximum distance from the winning node s. The maximum distance in the map is the Euclidian distance between two opposite corners. Note that the starting value (value at time $t = 0$) for the second Gaussian function in equation (3) is equal to 1 for any node k.

From equation (3), it is clear that at time $t = 0$, $\eta(0,k,s) = A1$. Hence

$$A1 = \eta_{start} \tag{4}$$

From equation (3), it also follows that

$$\eta((C-1),s,s) = \eta_{end} = A1 \cdot \frac{1}{e^{\frac{(C-1)}{A2}}} \cdot 1$$

Hence,

$$A2 = \frac{(C-1)}{\ln(\frac{\eta_{start}}{\eta_{end}})} \tag{5}$$

According to the definition of $G2_{end}$ we have

$$G2_{end} = \frac{1}{e^{\frac{(C-1) \cdot D_{max}}{A3}}}$$

D_{max} is the maximum distance in the map, i.e., the Euclidian distance between two opposite corners in the map. It is computed as follows

$$D_{max} = \sqrt{(M_r - 1)^2 + (M_c - 1)^2}$$

where M_r is the number of rows in the map and M_c is the number of columns in the map.

Consequently,

$$A3 = \frac{(C-1) \cdot D_{max}}{\ln(\frac{1}{G2_{end}})} \tag{6}$$

With η_{start} and η_{end} it is possible to set the speed with which η decreases within the learning period of length C, and hence, control the weight update speed. Figure 2 shows how the speed, with which the value of η for the winning node decreases, varies from very fast (left) to very slow (right) depending on the value of η_{end}. The curves correspond, from left to right, respectively, to the following values of η_{end}: 10^{-100}, 10^{-50}, 10^{-40}, 10^{-30}, 10^{-20}, 10^{-10}, 10^{-6}, 10^{-5}, 10^{-4}, 10^{-3}, 10^{-2}, 0.1, 0.5, and 0.8. For all these curves the value of η_{start} was equal to 0.9 and the length of the learning period was $C = 5100$ cycles.

With $G2_{end}$ it is possible to set the speed of neighborhood shrinkage within the learning period of length C. Figure 3 shows the neighborhood at many different points in time for different values of $G2_{end}$. The first (left) column of charts in the figure shows a relatively slow neighborhood shrinkage with time for $G2_{end} = 0.5$. The second (middle) column of charts in the figure shows a more quick neighborhood shrinkage with time for $G2_{end} = 0.1$. The third (right) column of charts in the figure shows a relatively quick neighborhood

Figure 2. Influence of η_{end} on the speed with which η for the winning node decreases

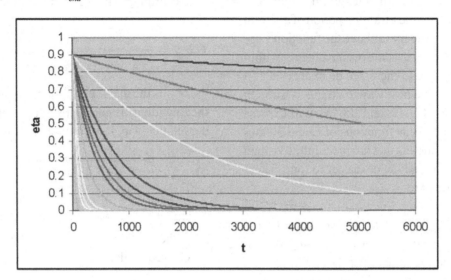

shrinkage with time for $G2_{end}=10^{-4}$. The speed of neighborhood shrinkage grows as $G2_{end}$ becomes smaller. For all charts the other parameter settings were as follows: length of learning period C=5100 cycles; size of map M_rxM_c=10x14; η_{start}=0.9; η_{end}=10^{-6}. Note that at time t = 0, the neighborhood is the whole map, i.e., the value of η is the same for all nodes k in the map. Hence, $G2_{start}$ is always equal to 1.

TIME COMPLEXITY OF THE LEARNING ALGORITHM

The three steps of the learning process are repeated many times for each document and thus account for most of the processing time required. Steps 2 (compute distance to all nodes) and 3 (update weights) require iterations through all coordinates in the input vector. The processing time T for the algorithm is proportional to the number of document presentation cycles and the vector size:

$$T = O(NC) \tag{7}$$

where N is the input vector size and C is the number of document presentation cycles. For textual categorization, input vector size can be as large as the total number of unique terms in the entire collection. The number of unique terms in a collection is typically proportional to the size of a collection (Grefenstette, 1994). Representing the size of a collection as S, we can define N in terms of S as $N=O(S)$. Similarly, because each document is presented multiple times, C can be represented by S as $C = O(S)$. Thus, the total processing time T could be estimated as:

$$T = O(NC) = O(S^2) \tag{8}$$

Given the fact that the size of text collections (i.e., the number of search results or more specifically, the number of snippets) returned by a meta-search engine, as already discussed, is relatively small, the algorithm's time complexity of "square of the size of collection" is still scaleable.

Figure 3. Influence of G2$_{end}$ on the speed of neighborhood shrinkage

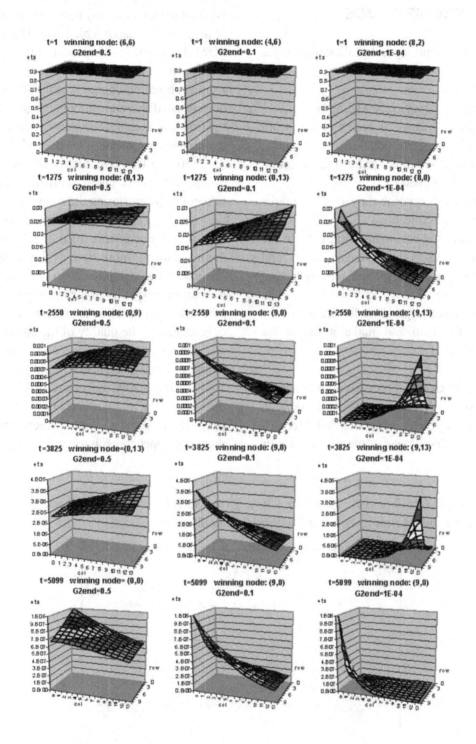

THE SELF-ORGANIZING META-SEARCH ENGINE SOMSE

SOMSE works according to the following general algorithm:

- Get the user query (see Figure 4)
- Get the collection of search results from the underlying individual search engines
- Build an inverted index for this collection (from the snippets)
- Determine the vocabulary (set of unique terms in the collection)
- Represent the documents (snippets) in the collection as N-dimensional vectors and use them as input for the self-organizing feature map
- Train the self-organizing feature map
- Draw the map and make it useful for browsing

SOMSE queries the three most popular search engines Google, Yahoo, and Msn. By default, SOMSE is configured to return the first 20 results from Google (first 2 pages), the first 20 results from Yahoo, and the first 20 results from Msn. It is possible that there may be fewer than 60 results returned by the search. This can also happen when SOMSE automatically removes identical results from the list. This choice for the number of results from each search engine is justified since users do not usually search through pages other than the first few ones, because most of them consider these pages irrelevant to their search.

There are two possible modes of clustering Web search results. The system can either respond in seconds by clustering the snippets returned by the underlying search engines, or it can download the original documents off the Web and cluster them, requiring more time as downloading the documents can be quite slow. On the other hand, the clustering quality of the latter mode is higher since more information is present. However, the degradation in the quality of the clusters is usually moderate when snippets are used instead of the original documents (Zamir and Etzioni, 1998). Additionally, most search engines are well designed to facilitate users' relevance judgment only by the snippet. We can therefore assume that the snippet contents are informative enough.

Figure 4. Using SOMSE to search the Web. Clicking on "Search" will produce a ranked list together with a semantic map. Clicking on "Map" will show only the map.

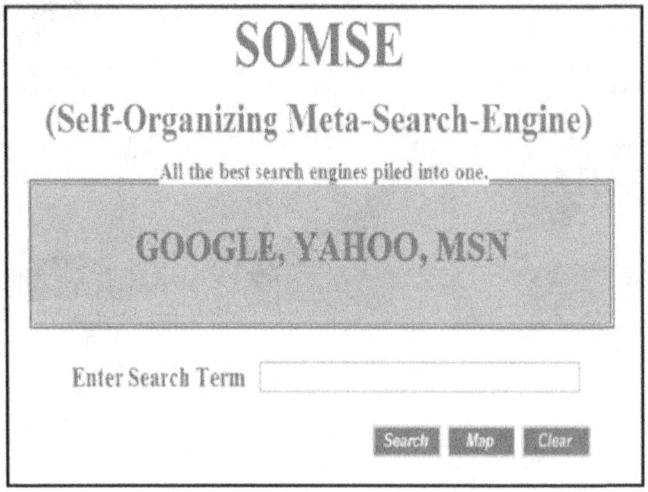

SOMSE therefore performs the clustering on the returned snippets, allowing fast interaction with the user.

First an inverted index of the returned collection of search results is produced. During indexing, stop words are omitted and some basic stemming rules are applied (Porter, 1980). Stop words are words such as "a, the, an, that, so, ...". Stop words have low information content, and therefore have weak discriminating power. They are removed according to a list of common stop words. Stemming reduces morphological variants to the root word. For example, "asks", "asked", and "asking" are all reduced to "ask" after stemming. This relates the same word in different morphological forms and reduces the number of distinctive words.

Additionally, the most frequently occurring words (high frequency words) and the least frequently occurring words (low frequency words) are excluded. High frequency words are words having a document frequency (the document frequency of a word is the number of documents in which it occurs) greater or equal h, where h is a parameter that is computed as follows: $h = p *$ S. In this equation S is the size of the collection, i.e., the number of documents, and p is a threshold percentage. When, for example, $p = 50\%$, all words having a document frequency greater or equal half of the number of documents will be omitted, i.e., not included into the vocabulary. Low frequency words are words appearing no more than l times, where l is a parameter. High frequency words usually occur in most of the documents and have therefore no discriminative value. Rare words are omitted on the argument that they will produce very small clusters. Removing high and low frequency words will also reduce the dimensions of the vector space i.e., the size of input vectors and weight vectors, and hence speed up processing.

The remaining unique terms (stems) are retained and used as the set of indexing words (vocabulary) for the collection of search results. These words and the documents of the collection form a matrix of documents versus indexing words, where each column is a N-dimensional document vector and each row corresponds to a word (stem) of the vocabulary. A document vector contains 1 in a given row if the corresponding word occurs in the document snippet and 0 otherwise.

The document vectors are used as input to train a feature map of N features and a two-dimensional grid of M output nodes (say a 10-by-14 map of 140 nodes). Following the Kohonen's algorithm:

- Each feature corresponds to a selected word.
- Each document is an input vector.
- Each node on the map is associated with a vector of weights which are assigned small random values at the beginning of training.
- During the training process, a document is randomly selected, the node closest to it in N-dimensional vector space according to the Euclidian distance is chosen; the weight of the node and weights of its neighboring nodes are adjusted accordingly;
- The training process proceeds iteratively for a certain number of training cycles. It stops when the map converges.
- When the training process is completed, submit each document as input to the trained network again and assign it to a particular grid node (concept) in the map.

A semantic map of documents that contains very rich information is then constructed (see Figure 5). The map displays on each node a number that indicates the number of documents mapped to that node. These numbers collectively reveal the distribution of the documents on the map. Clicking on a node will cause the corresponding document list to be shown to the user and the user can browse through that cluster (see Figure 6).

As mentioned earlier, it is not enough for a clustering system to create coherent clusters, but the system must also convey the contents of the clusters to the

Figure 5. A 10x14 map generated by SOMSE for the query 'jaguar'

Map	0	1	2	3	4	5	6	7	8	9	10	11	12	13
0	offici 3	offici 0	offici 0	xk 0	xk 0	xj 3	xk 1	world 0	world 1	naia 3	cat 8	cat 2	cat 0	cat 5
1	offici 1	offici 0	offici 0	xk 0	xk 0	xk 0	xk 0	world 0	world 0	inform 0	cat 0	cat 0	cat 0	cat 0
2	car 0	car 0	car 0	car 0	car 0	car 0	car 0	car 0	car 0	inform 0	inform 0	inform 0	inform 0	inform 2
3	car 0	car 0	car 0	car 0	car 0	car 0	car 0	car 0	car 0	inform 0	inform 0	inform 0	inform 0	inform 0
4	car 0	car 0	car 0	car 0	car 0	car 0	car 0	car 0	car 0	car 0	inform 0	inform 0	inform 0	inform 0
5	car 0	car 0	car 0	car 0	car 0	car 0	car 0	car 0	car 0	car 0	car 0	free	free	free
6	car 0	car 0	car 0	car 0	car 0	car 0	car 0	car 0	car 0	car 0	free	free	free	free
7	car 0	car 0	car 0	car 0	car 0	car 0	car 0	car 0	car 0	car 0	free	free	free	free
8	car 0	car 0	car 0	car 0	car 0	car 0	car 0	car 0	car 0	car 0	free	free	free	free
9	car 7	car 0	car 0	car 0	car 0	car 3	car 0	car 0	car 0	car 0	free	free	free	free

users concisely and accurately. The system is most useful when the user can decide at a glance whether the contents of a cluster are of interest.

The map is divided into concept areas (more precisely, word areas) or regions. The area to which a node belongs is determined as follows: compare the node to every unit vector (containing only a single word), and assign to the node the nearest unit vector (or the word it represents). The same effect can also be achieved as follows: assign a word to each node by choosing the one corresponding to the largest weight in the weight vector of the node (winning term).

Neighboring nodes which contain the same winning terms belong to the same concept/topic region (group, area). The resulting map thus represents regions of important terms/concepts with the documents assigned to them. Because of the cooperative feature of the neighboring nodes in the map, the areas are assured of continuity. Therefore, concept regions that are similar (conceptually) appear in the same neighborhood. Similar documents are assigned into same or similar concepts.

The areas could also additionally be labeled as follows: compare each unit vector to every node and label the winning node with the word corresponding to the unit vector. In this way, areas could get longer labels (see Figure 7). For some deeper discussion on the automatic labeling of self-organizing maps we refer to (Rauber and Merkl, 1999).

Figure 6. Cluster of documents associated with node (0,0) of the map of Figure 5

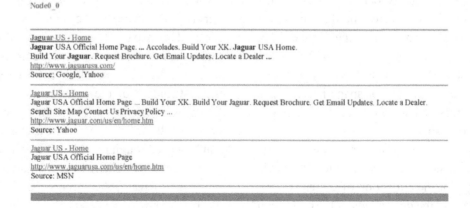

Figure 7. A 10x14 map generated by SOMSE for the query 'world war 2' with longer labels for some nodes. The first and second label are separated by "-".

Map	0	1	2	3	4	5	6	7	8	9	10	11	12	13
0	histori -4	histori -0	histori -2	histori -0	histori -0	histori -0	timelin -0	timelin -0	timelin - 0	timelin - 0	timelin, timelin, 4	timelin ww, 1	timelin -0	hitler - includ,hitler, 5
1	histori - histori, 2	histori -0	histori -0	histori -0	histori -0	histori -0	timelin -0	timelin -0	timelin - 0	timelin - 0	timelin -0	timelin -0	timelin -0	timelin - 0
2	histori -0	histori -0	histori -0	histori -0	histori -0	histori -0	timelin -0	timelin -0	timelin - 0	timelin - 0	timelin -0	timelin -0	timelin -0	timelin -0
3	histori -0	histori -0	histori -0	histori -0	histori -0	histori -0	timelin -0	timelin -0	timelin - 0	timelin - 0	timelin -0	timelin - dai, 0	timelin -0	timelin - 0
4	histori -0	histori -0	histori -0	histori -0	histori -0	histori -0	histori -0	timelin -0	timelin - 0	timelin - 0	timelin -0	timelin -0	inform -0	inform - 0
5	histori -0	histori -0	histori -0	histori -0	histori -0	histori -0	histori -0	timelin -0	timelin - 0	timelin - 0	inform -0	inform -0	inform -0	inform - 0
6	histori -0	histori -0	histori -0	histori -0	histori -0	histori -0	histori -0	timelin -0	timelin - 0	timelin - 0	inform -0	inform -0	inform -0	inform - inform, 4
7	battl -0	battl -0	Battl -0	battl -0	histori -0	histori -0	histori -0	wwii -0	wwii - 0	wwii - 0	inform -0	inform -0	inform -0	inform - 0
8	battl -0	Battl -0	Battl -0	battl -0	battl -0	battl -0	onlin -0	wwii -0	wwii - 0	wwii - 0	wwii -0	site -0	site -0	inform - militari, 1
9	battl - battl, 6	Battl -0	Battl -0	battl -0	battl -0	battl -0	onlin -0	wwii -0	wwii - onlin,wwii, 4	wwii - place,europ, 0	wwii -0	site -0	site - site, 2	site - free,websit,weapon,chess, 11

CHARACTERISTICS OF MAPS GENERATED BY SOMSE

The size of the areas on the map corresponds to the frequencies of occurrence of the words. Usually, the word that appears most often in the collection will have the largest area. The word that appears second most frequently in the collection, will have the second or third largest area, etc. For example, the largest area in the map of Figure 5 is "car", which by frequency counts (document frequency, DF) appears most often in the collection (see Table1). "Inform" appears second most frequently in the collection (DF) and its area is the third largest. However, as the mapping is a nonlinear one, the sizes and the frequencies do not have a linear relationship. In fact, there is a tendency to make "the rich richer, and the poor poorer", that is, the large ones look even larger, and the small ones sometimes simply disappear.

Not only the frequencies of occurrence of the words but also the frequencies of word co-occurrence influence the map. Words that more often co-occur than others will be assigned to neighbor areas. "Car" is next to "free" and "inform" in the map of Figure 5 because it more often co-occurs with these two terms than with any others (see Table 2). "Xj" is next to "xk" for the same reason. Frequency of word co-occurrence visualized on the map by the neighborhood property of areas may compensate for inconsistency and incompleteness in the indexing of documents (see (Lin et al., 1991) (Mozer, 1984) (Belew, 1986)). This is especially helpful because of the problem that originates in the fact that snippets contain little to no redundancy in terms of the information presented in the snippets as well as in the choice of words. Due to their limited length and condensed structure, word repetition and clarification of the most important aspects within the text are usually not present, resulting in less specific vector representations of the documents. Thus using only the snippets provides a somewhat more challenging task than using the complete documents. As there is no time to download the original documents off the Web, the system should produce high quality clusters even when it only has access to the snippets returned by the search engines. This is assured by the above property of the self-organizing map. Additionally, using words representing the areas

Table 1. Vocabulary generated by SOMSE for the query 'jaguar' (corresponds to map of Figure 5). TF is the term frequency: number of occurrences in search result collection. DF is the document frequency: the number of documents in which the stem occurs. SIZE_OF_AREA is the number of nodes on the map that are labeled with the stem.

NO	STEM	TF	DF	SIZE_OF_AREA
0	offici	5	5	6
1	car	17	13	79
2	page	5	5	0
3	home	8	4	0
4	usa	4	3	0
5	build	4	2	0
6	xk	7	6	7
7	dealer	5	5	0
8	amp	6	3	0
9	model	7	7	0
10	price	4	3	0
11	wikipedia	5	5	0
12	free	8	7	19
13	encyclopedia	6	6	0
14	panthera	4	2	0
15	world	4	4	4
16	inform	10	9	15
17	fact	4	4	0
18	big	4	4	0
19	cat	5	5	8
20	new	5	5	0
21	video	7	3	0
22	search	4	4	0
23	latest	4	4	0
24	auto	7	4	0
25	xj	10	4	1
26	type	9	4	0
27	ford	4	3	0
28	naia	4	2	1
29	part	5	2	0

and neighbor areas on the map, the user can look for possible combinations of words to form terms relevant to his request. This allows flexibility and encourages the user to search for terms that best describe his request.

The labels themselves aid in identifying the most important features within every node and thus help to understand the information represented by a particular node. In spite of the little redundancy present in snippets, the labels turn out to be informative in so far as they help the user to understand the map and the set of search results as such. Especially in cases where little to no knowledge on the set of search results itself is available (e.g., when the user is new to a subject area and doesn't know the key terms) the resulting representation can lead to tremendous benefits in understanding the characteristics of the collection of search results.

In summary, the Kohonen's feature map is a practical algorithm based on a profound mathematical analysis. The self-organizing map reveals the frequencies and distributions of underlying data. The self-organizing map achieves this

Table 2. Co-occurrence data for the stems that appear as node labels in the map of Figure 5. The diagonal numbers are document frequencies of each stem.

0	offici	5								
1	car	1	13							
6	xk	2	2	6						
12	free	0	3	0	7					
15	world	0	0	0	1	4				
16	infom	0	4	0	2	0	9			
19	cat	0	0	0	0	1	2	5		
25	xj	1	1	3	0	0	0	0	4	
28	naia	0	0	0	0	0	0	0	0	2
NO	STEM	0	1	6	12	15	16	19	25	28

through the spatial arrangement of nodes on the map. The distance between documents, the nearest neighbors of each word, and the size of each area, are all determined by, and therefore reflect, the internal structure of input data. Additionally, the self-organizing map allows much flexibility. It does not assign links between words specifically. Instead, it shows the tendency of adjacency of words or documents and therefore leaves much space for human recognition and imagination.

SOMSE exploits the obvious advantage of the two dimensional map, namely, the fact that it can be displayed on a screen and uses it as an interface that replaces long lists of ranked documents. Since the map makes underlying structures of the document space visible, the semantic map interface will likely allow more efficient browsing and selection of documents from the document space.

PARAMETER TUNING

The following parameters influence the way SOMSE works and the result it produces:

- $M = M_r \times M_c$: size of the map (the map has M_r rows and M_c columns).
- C: length of the learning period (number of cycles).
- η_{start}: starting value for η (for the winning node).
- η_{end}: final value for η (for the winning node).
- $G2_{end}$: final value for the second Gaussian function in equation (3) (for a node that is situated at a maximum distance from the winning node).
- h: high document frequency threshold.
- l: low term frequency threshold.

Many experiments showed that the size of the map, i.e., the number of rows and columns, does not effect the quality of clustering and the convergence of learning. However, the size of the map influences the appearance of the regions and clusters on it. When the map is large enough, increasing its size will result in just enlarging the individual regions while respecting the proportions. When the map is too small, the larger regions will dominate and the smaller ones will disappear. The size 10x14 looks to be appropriate for arbitrary queries and is therefore the default in SOMSE. However, the user can choose any other size. Of course, increasing the size of the map will results in longer processing times, since many more weight vectors will need to be considered.

As already mentioned, because each document is presented multiple times, the length of the learning period C is represented as $C = a * S$, where a is the average number of presentations per document and S is the number of documents (search results). We experimented with many different values for a and noticed that already with small values for a such as 4 or 5, we can obtain good maps for individual queries by tuning the parameters η_{start}, η_{end}, and $G2_{end}$ appropriately. However, in order to guarantee good results for arbitrary queries and to make the tuning of the other parameters easier, a larger value should be used. We found that, for example, $a = 100$ is an appropriate value that still guarantees an acceptable reaction time of the system (few seconds).

As already discussed, through the parameters η_{start} and η_{end}, we can set the speed with which η decreases, and, through the parameter $G2_{end}$, we can set the speed of neighborhood shrinkage. The speed with which η decreases and the speed of neighborhood shrinkage should be adapted to the length of the learning period, i.e., to the parameter a. We found that the settings $\eta_{start} = 0.9$, $\eta_{end} = 10^{-6}$, and $G2_{end} = 10^{-4}$ in combination with $a = 100$ produce good results for arbitrary queries. However, many other settings are also appropriate. Making η_{end} still smaller in this case will lead to reducing the number of regions on the map. This is because η will decrease very quickly, and hence, the first cycles of the learning period will be the all-dominant in changing the weights and shaping the map. The remaining cycles will not have a lot of effect on the map. Increasing η_{end} will, in contrast, produce more regions, because the weights will keep changing until the end of the learning period and more fine-tuning is performed. Making $G2_{end}$ still smaller in this case will lead to increasing the number of regions on the map. This is because the neighborhood shrinkage will be faster, and consequently, less time is given to the map to achieve more ordering.

All stems having a document frequency greater or equal to the high document frequency threshold h are not included into the vocabulary. As already mentioned, h is computed as $h = p * S$, where S is the number of search results and p a threshold percentage. We experimented with many different values for p such as 25%, 50%, 100%, etc. The value $p = 50\%$ was found to work well for arbitrary queries and produce good clustering results in terms of size and number of regions and clusters. In most of the cases, the query terms that usually appear in all results, are excluded. Additionally, some other high frequency terms may also be discarded which reduces the size of the vocabulary.

All stems having a term frequency smaller or equal to the low term frequency threshold l are not included into the vocabulary. This parameter was set to $l = 3$. This value was found to be reasonable for clustering purposes during many experiments with SOMSE. It also reduces the size of the vocabulary considerably which helps in speeding up processing.

EVALUATION OF SOMSE MAPS

The self-organizing semantic map is a technique for visual display of information that looks to be very suited for an interactive environment like Web search. It represents the document space two dimensionally and provides rich information on the display. It creates a visual effect through geographic features of the areas on the map and

preserves certain structures of the document space. It keeps its simplicity even in the case of a large number of documents.

The map looks to be a good aid to searchers because it enables users to determine at a glance whether the contents of a cluster are of interest. It may save the searcher time and effort in assessing the variety of possible meanings and aspects of a long list of search results, and provide quick identification of the clusters that best match interests. This is especially helpful to people who are new to a subject area and don't know the key terms. Additionally, it seems to succeed in disambiguating words that have multiple meanings depending on the context such as "jaguar" (see Figure 5).

According to Veith (1988), one of the central issues concerning visual display for information retrieval involves creating the ability to spark understanding, insight, imagination, and creativity through the use of graphic representations and arrangements. The semantic maps generated by SOMSE may help create such ability.

The evaluation of a clustering interface is notoriously difficult, particularly in the context of Web search engines, which are used by a heterogeneous user population for a wide variety of tasks: from finding a specific Web document that the user has seen before and can easily describe, to obtaining an overview of an unfamiliar topic, to exhaustively examining a large set of documents on a topic, and more. A clustering system will prove useful only in a subset of these cases.

In a first study, we asked 3 human evaluators to cluster and label the search results returned by SOMSE as ranked lists (before clustering) for 30 queries. We specially selected three types of queries: ambiguous queries, entity names, and general terms, since these queries are more likely to contain multiple sub-topics and will benefit more from clustering search results. All the 30 queries are listed in Table 3. Each evaluator was assigned a different type of queries.

The idea was to consider maps generated by people and compare them to the maps generated

Table 3. The thirty queries used in the preliminary study

Type	Queries
Ambiguous queries	jaguar, apple, Saturn, jobs, jordan, tiger, trec, ups, quotes, matrix
Entity names	susan dumais, clinton, iraq, dell, disney, world war 2, ford
General terms	health, yellow pages, maps, flower, music, chat, games, radio, jokes, graphic design, resume, time zones, travel

by SOMSE. An experiment has been designed to let the 3 evaluators generate semantic maps. Each evaluator is given the same documents (snippets) that are used to train the self-organizing semantic map in SOMSE and a large grid (A1 paper) for each query. Each evaluator is given the task to produce semantic maps for each query of one of the above types of queries. Each snippet is printed on a small card which can be placed in a node on the grid. The task given to evaluators is to put the cards on the grid based on their perceived document similarities. It is emphasized that snippets can be put on any locations of the grid, and that relative distances among documents are more important than the locations. Evaluators are told that the purpose of such a map is to make browsing and selection of documents from the map easier.

From the results of this experiment, it was clear that there are both similarities and differences between the maps generated by SOMSE and the maps generated by the evaluators. There were also some similarities between the processes of map generation.

Other preliminary experimental results demonstrate that we can generate correct clusters with meaningful short (and hopefully more readable) names, that could improve users' browsing efficiency through search results. Also, the time for building the self-organizing is acceptable (few seconds).

To what extent SOMSE produces coherent clusters, and if it actually outperforms, in this respect, other clustering algorithms in the Web search domain is being currently investigated. We will also further investigate several other problems on search result clustering.

FUTURE WORK

We need to make further experiments to gain more insights into the nature of clustering using SOMSE. It may be necessary to develop a model of the user's use of the clustering of results and to create relevance judgments for search results clustering. We believe that through a series of investigations, we should better understand the construction and the properties of the self-organizing semantic map, by which we can produce an interface to make underlying information visible to the user.

When the system is tested thoroughly, a Web-based version of the search tool may be adopted. Many projects have been exploring this path and have made their tools freely available and accessible online.

Another improvement that could be tempted is to speed up the process of building the self-organizing map. This could be reached by reducing the dimensionality of input vectors before doing clustering using, for example, principal component analysis (PCA) to capture the underlying correlation of the terms as adopted by Khan and Khor (2004). Another possible solution is to use a scaleable self-organizing map (SSOM) algorithm, i.e., a data structure and an algorithm that take advantage of the sparsity of coordinates in the document input vectors in order to reduce the self-organizing map computational complexity. Ideas similar to those of Roussinov and Chen (1998) could be adopted.

Another point is related to the fact that the current clustering is still a flat clustering method. We believe a hierarchical structure of search results, i.e., learning a hierarchy of classes that may be present in the input, is necessary for more efficient browsing. For this, we should build hierarchical Kohonen's maps. We produce a hierarchical taxonomy of the clustered documents as well as the concepts discovered in them. We could do it similarly to the way it has been described in (Chen et al., 1996). Documents belonging to the same categories are recursively used to produce smaller maps corresponding to a deeper level in the resulting hierarchy (zoom function). It is easy to see that the concepts are ordered from more general concepts (top) to more narrow ones (bottom).

CONCLUSION

The problems of information overload and vocabulary differences have become more pressing with the emergence of the increasingly more popular Internet services. The main information retrieval mechanisms provided by the prevailing Internet Web software are based on either keyword search (e.g., Google and Yahoo) or hypertext browsing (e.g., Internet Explorer and Netscape). This research aimed to provide an alternative concept-based categorization and search capability based on a combination of meta-search and self-organizing maps. Kohonen's self-organizing map is very well known as a clustering and dimension reduction tool. Clustering can be used for categorization of input vectors. Dimension reduction can be used for visualization and for reducing information in order to ease search, storage or processing of another kind.

SOMSE allows the user to have a different perspective of searching. It gives a lateral way of looking at the results. With the search results obtained and the way they are presented, the users will hopefully get a better idea of what they are searching for, and hence learn to issue more accurate queries.

REFERENCES

Belew, R. K. (1986). *Adaptive information retrieval: machine learning in associative networks* (Doctoral dissertation, University of Michigan, 1986).

Bergman, M. K. (2001). The Deep Web: Surfacing Hidden Value. *The Journal of Electronic Publishing, 7*(1). Retrieved November 17, 2006, from http://www.press.umich.edu/jep/07-01/bergman.html

Bergstein, B. (2007). *So much data, relatively little space.* Retrieved March 28, 2009, from http://www.msnbc.msn.com/id/17472946/

Bruza, P. D., & van Linder, B. (1998). Preferential models of query by navigation. In F. Crestani, M. Lalmas, and C.J. van Rijsbergen (Eds.), *Information retrieval: Uncertainty and logics, volume 4 of The Kluwer International Series on Information Retrieval* (pp. 73-96). Norwell, MA: Kluwer Academic Publishers.

Carpenter, G. A., & Grossberg, S. (1988). The ART of adaptive pattern recognition by a self-organizing neural network. *IEEE Computer, 21*(3), 77–88.

Chen, H., Schuffels, C., & Orwig, R. (1996). Internet categorization and search: A machine learning approach. *Journal of Visual Communication and Image Representation, 7*(1), 88–102. doi:10.1006/jvci.1996.0008

Cohen, L. (2006). Internet Tutorials. Web Support Librarian, University at Albany, SUNY. Retrieved November 11, 2006, from http://www.internet-tutorials.net/

da Costa Carvalho, A. L., Chirita, P., de Moura, E. S., Calado, P., & Nejdl, W. (2006). Site level noise removal for search engines. In *Proceedings of the 15th International Conference on World Wide Web, WWW '06* (pp. 73-82). Edinburgh, Scotland, May 23-26, 2006. New York: ACM Press.

Deogun, J. S., Bhatia, S. K., & Raghavan, V. V. (1991). Automatic Cluster assignment for documents. In *Proceedings of the 7th IEEE Conference on Artificial Intelligence Applications, Miami Beach, Florida, 1991* (pp. 25-27).

Google (2006). *Google SOAP Search API Reference*. Retrieved November 4, 2006, from http://www.google.com/apis/reference.html

Google (2008). *We knew the web was big....* Retrieved March 28, 2009, from http://googleblog.blogspot.com/2008/07/we-knew-web-was-big.html

Grefenstette, G. (1994). *Explorations in automatic thesaurus discovery*. Moston, MA: Kluwer Academic Publishers.

Hamdi, M. S. (2006a). MASACAD: A multi-agent-based approach to information customization. *IEEE Intelligent Systems, 21*(1), 60–67. doi:10.1109/MIS.2006.14

Hamdi, M. S. (2006b). Information overload and information customization. *IEEE Potentials, 25*(5), 9–12. doi:10.1109/MP.2006.1692278

Hamdi, M. S. (2007a). MASACAD: A multi-agent approach to information customization for the purpose of academic advising of students. *Elsevier Applied Soft Computing Journal, 7*, 746–771. doi:10.1016/j.asoc.2006.02.001

Hamdi, M. S. (2007b). Semantic Map Based Web Search Result Visualization. In *Proceedings of the 11th International Conference on Information Visualization (IV07). July 4-6, 2007, ETH, Zurich, Switzerland* (pp. 222-227).

Hamdi, M. S. (2008a). Combating information overload by means of information customization systems. In V. Sugumaran (Ed.), *Intelligent information technologies and applications* (pp. 60-92). Hershey, PA: IGI Global.

Hamdi, M. S. (2008b). Improving the quality of Web search. In C. Calero, M.A. Moraga, and M. Piattini (Eds.), Handbook of research on Web information systems quality (pp. 456-473). Hershey, PA: IGI Global.

Hamdi, M. S. (2008c). SOMSE: A neural network based approach to Web search optimization. *International Journal of Intelligent Information Technologies, 4*(4), 31–54.

Honkela, T., Kaski, S., Lagus, K., & Kohonen, T. (1996). *Newsgroup exploration with WEBSOM method and browsing interface* (In Report A32). Helsinki: University of Technology, January 1996.

Hoong, D., & Buyya, R. (2004). Guided Google: A meta search engine and its implementation using the Google distributed web services. *International Journal of Computers and Applications, 26*(1), 181–187.

Jolliffe, I. T. (1986). *Principal component analysis*. New York: Springer-Verlag.

Khan, S. M., & Khor, S. W. (2004). Web document clustering using a hybrid neural network. *Applied Soft Computing Journal, 4*, 423–432. doi:10.1016/j.asoc.2004.02.003

Kohonen, T. (1989). Self-organization and associative memory (3rd ed.). Berlin: Springer-Verlag.

Kohonen, T. (1995). Self-organization maps. Berlin, Heidelberg: Springer-Verlag.

Kohonen, T. (1997). Exploration of very large databases by self-organizing maps. In . *Proceedings of the IEEE International Conference on Neural Networks, 1*, 1–6.

Lin, S., Soergel, D., & Marchionini, G. (1991). A self-organizing map for information retrieval. In *Proceedings of the 14th Annual ACM SIGIR International Conference on Research and Development in Information Retrieval, Chicago, Illinois* (pp. 262-269).

Lippmann, R. P. (1987). An introduction to computing with neural networks. *IEEE Acoustics Speech and Signal Processing Magazine, 4*(2), 4–22.

MacLeod, K. J., & Robertson, W. (1991). A neural algorithm for document clustering. *Information Processing & Management, 27*(4), 337–346. doi:10.1016/0306-4573(91)90088-4

Merkl, D. (1997). Exploration of text collections with hierarchical feature maps. In *Proceedings of the 20th International ACM SIGIR Conference on Research and Development in Information Retrieval (SIGIR '97)* (pp. 186-195).

Mozer, M.C. (1984, June). *Inductive information retrieval using parallel distributed computation.* Research Report. San Diego, CA: University of California at San Diego.

Narita, M., & Ogawa, Y. (2000). The use of phrases from query texts in information retrieval. In *Proceedings of the 23rd Annual International ACM SIGIR Conference on Research and Development in Information Retrieval, SIGIR 2000, Athens, Greece* (pp. 318-320).

Orwig, R., Chen, H., & Nunamaker, J. F. (1997). A graphical, self-organizing approach to classifying electronic meeting output. *Journal of the American Society for Information Science American Society for Information Science, 48*(2), 157–170. doi:10.1002/(SICI)1097-4571(199702)48:2<157::AID-ASI6>3.0.CO;2-X

Porter, M. F. (1980). An algorithm for suffix stripping. *Program, 14*(3), 130–137.

Rauber, A., & Merkl, D. (1999). Automatic labeling of self-organizing maps: Making a treasure-map reveal its secrets. In *Proceedings of the Pacific-Asia Conference on Knowledge Discovery and Data Mining (PAKDD '99), Beijing, China* (pp. 228-237).

Ritter, H., & Kohonen, T. (1989). Self-organizing semantic maps. *Biological Cybernetics, 61,* 241–254. doi:10.1007/BF00203171

Roussinov, D., & Chen, H. (1998). A scalable self-organizing map algorithm for textual classification: {A} neural network approach to thesaurus generation. *Communication & Cognition, 15*(1-2), 81–112.

Salton, G., & Buckley, C. (1990). Improving retrieval performance by relevance feedback. *J. JASIS, 41*(4), 288–297. doi:10.1002/(SICI)1097-4571(199006)41:4<288::AID-ASI8>3.0.CO;2-H

Salton, G., & McGill, M. J. (1983). *Introduction to modern information retrieval.* New York: McGraw-Hill.

Spink, A., Jansen, J., & Blakely, C. (2006). A study of results overlap and uniqueness among major web search engines. *Information Processing & Management.*

Staggernation (2006). *Google API Proximity Search (GAPS)*. Retrieved November 4, 2006, from http://www.staggernation.com/gaps/readme.php

Valdes-Perez, R. (2005, March 31). Meta-search: More heads better than one? *ZDNet News.* Retrieved November 24, 2006, from http://news.zdnet.com/2100-9588_22-5647280.html van Rijsbergen, C.J. (1999). *Information retrieval* (2nd ed.). Retrieved November 28, 2006, from http://www.dcs.gla.ac.uk/~iain/keith/index.htm

Veith, R. H. (1988). *Visual information systems: The power of graphics and video.* Boston, MA: G.K. Hall.

Wermter, S. (1991). Learning to classify natural language titles in a recurrent connectionist model. In *Proceedings of the 1991 International Conference on Artificial Neural Networks, Vol. 2, Espoo, Finland, 1991* (pp. 1715-1718).

Wu, B., & Davison, B. (2005). Identifying link farm spam pages. In *Proceedings of the 14th World Wide Web Conference, Industrial Track, Chiba, Japan, May 2005* (pp. 820-829).

Xu, J., & Croft, W. B. (1996). Query expansion using local and global document analysis. In *Proceedings of the 19th Annual International ACM SIGIR Conference on Research and Development in Information Retrieval, Zurich Switzerland* (pp. 4-11). New York: ACM Press.

Zamir, O., & Etzioni, O. (1998). Web document clustering: A feasibility demonstration. In *Proceedings of the 19th International ACM SIGIR Conference on Research and Development in Information Retrieval (SIGIR '98)* (pp. 46-54).

Chapter 11
Mining E-Mail Messages:
Uncovering Interaction Patterns and Processes Using E-Mail Logs

Wil M.P. van der Aalst
Eindhoven University of Technology, The Netherlands

Andriy Nikolov
Knowledge Media Institute, The Open University, UK

ABSTRACT

Increasingly information systems log historic information in a systematic way. Workflow management systems, but also ERP, CRM, SCM, and B2B systems often provide a so-called "event log", i.e., a log recording the execution of activities. Thus far, process mining has been mainly focusing on structured event logs resulting in powerful analysis techniques and tools for discovering process, control, data, organizational, and social structures from event logs. Unfortunately, many work processes are not supported by systems providing structured logs. Instead very basic tools such as text editors, spreadsheets, and e-mail are used. This paper explores the application of process mining to e-mail, i.e., unstructured or semi-structured e-mail messages are converted into event logs suitable for application of process mining tools. This paper presents the tool EMailAnalyzer, embedded in the ProM process mining framework, which analyzes and transforms e-mail messages to a format that allows for analysis using our process mining techniques. The main innovative aspect of this work is that, unlike most other work in this area, our analysis is not restricted to social network analysis. Based on e-mail logs we can also discover interaction patterns and processes.

INTRODUCTION

Buzzwords such as BAM (Business Activity Monitoring), BOM (Business Operations Management), BPI (Business Process Intelligence) illustrate the interest in closing the business process management

DOI: 10.4018/978-1-60566-970-0.ch008

loop (van der Aalst and van Hee, 2002; Dumas et al., 2005). This is illustrated by the Figure 1, which shows the increasing level of support for closing the so-called BPM lifecycle.

The lifecycle identifies four different phases: *process design* (i.e., making a workflow schema), *system configuration* (i.e., getting a system to support the designed process), *process enactment*

Figure 1. The level of support is rising - closing the business process management (BPM) cycle

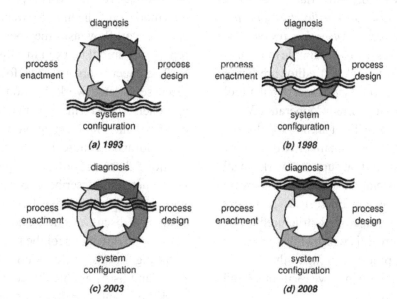

(i.e., the actual execution of the process using the system), and *diagnosis* (i.e., extracting knowledge from the process as it has been executed). BPM technology (e.g., workflow management systems) started with a focus on getting the system to work (i.e., the system configuration phase). Since the early nineties BPM technology matured and more emphasis was put on supporting the process design and process enactment phases in a better way. Now most vendors are trying to close the BPM lifecycle by adding diagnosis functionality.

The diagnosis phase assumes that data is collected in the enactment phase. Most information systems provide some kind of *event log* (also referred to as transaction log or audit trail). Typically such an event log registers the start and/or completion of activities. Every event refers to a *case* (i.e., process instance) and an *activity* (i.e., the step in the process executed), and, in most systems, also a timestamp, a performer, and some additional data. Process mining techniques (van der Aalst et al., 2003; van der Aalst et al., 2004; Agrawal et al., 1998; Cook and Wolf, 1998; Herbst, 2000; de Medeiros et al., 2003; Weijters and van der Aalst, 2003) take an event log as a starting

point to extract knowledge, e.g., a model of the organization or the process. In the context of our ProM tool (van der Aalst et al., 2007) we are able to extract different types of process models (e.g., Petri nets, event-driven process chains, and instance graphs), social networks, organizational models, etc.

Existing techniques for process mining assume an event log to be in place. For many process-aware information systems (Dumas et al., 2005) this assumption is valid. For example, Workflow Management (WFM) systems, Enterprise Resource Planning (ERP) systems, Customer Relationship Management (CRM), Case Handling (CH) and Product Data Management (PDM) systems log information in some transaction log or audit trail. New legislation such as the Sarbanes-Oxley (SOX) Act (Sarbanes and Oxley, 2002) and increased emphasis on corporate governance have triggered the need for improved auditing systems (Hoffman, 2004). To audit an organization, business activities need to be monitored. As enterprises become increasingly automated, a tight coupling between auditing systems and the information systems supporting the operational processes becomes more important. However, *many business processes are not directly supported by some process-aware information system*. For many work processes relatively simple tools such as an e-mail program and text editor are being used. E-mail can be seen as the most popular tool used for Computer Supported Cooperative Work (CSCW) (Ellis, 2000; Ellis et al., 1991; Ellis and Nutt, 1996). The CSCW domain provides a very broad range of systems that support "work" in all its forms. WFM systems and other process-aware information systems can be seen as particular CSCW systems aiming at well-structured office processes. Therefore, it is worthwhile to explore the application of process mining in the broader CSCW domain. In this paper, we focus on e-mail systems and their logs.

E-mail is widely used for communication inside organizations and between organizations. Analysis of e-mail communication (Farnham et al., 2004; Fisher and Dourish, 2004; Nardi et al., 2002) is a popular topic of research in social sciences, in particular sociometry (Bavelas, 1948; Bernard et al., 1990; Burt and Minor, 1983; Feldman, 1987; Freeman, 1977; Freeman, 1979; Moreno, 1934; Nemati and Barko, 2003; Scott, 1992; Wasserman and Faust, 1994). If the tasks in the work processes of the organization involve different employees, then they need to communicate to perform the business process. Assigning tasks, asking for more information, reporting results - all these activities are performed by sending e-mail messages. If it is possible to extract the process-related information from such messages, then they may serve as an event log of the organization. The main problem in this case is extraction of information. Considering the message topic and text can help to make a conclusion about the link between the message and the underlying workflow. Also the sender or recipient can be actively involved in making this link.

This paper describes an approach for extracting process event logs from e-mail logs. Our objective was to investigate the possibility to retrieve the links between the tasks in the process (i.e. the process model) and the links between the employees and the workflow tasks they perform. The paper reports our initial work in this direction.

The paper is organized as follows. Section 2 discusses related work. Section 3 describes the approach proposed in this paper. Section 4 briefly describes the implementation of the EmailAnalyzer tool and illustrates it with a running example. Section 5 discusses how the output of the tool can be evaluated and describes experiments performed with a publicly available Enron e-mail corpus. Section 6 discusses implications of the current system and directions for the future development of the algorithm. Finally, Section 7 concludes the paper and lists possible directions for the future work. For an introduction to process mining issues and approaches we refer to (van der Aalst et al., 2003, van der Aalst et al., 2007).

RELATED WORK

The idea of applying process mining in the context of workflow management was first introduced in (Agrawal et al., 1998). Cook and Wolf have investigated similar issues in the context of software engineering processes using different approaches (Cook and Wolf, 1998). It is impossible to point out the many process mining algorithms proposed in literature. However, we would like to mention the α-algorithm (van der Aalst et al., 2004), which served as a starting point for the ProM framework. For more information on process mining we refer to a special issue of Computers in Industry on process mining (van der Aalst and Weijters, 2004), a survey paper (van der Aalst et al., 2003), and the process mining website (www.processmining.org).

Since the early work of Moreno (Moreno, 1934), sociometry, and Social Network Analysis (SNA) in particular, have been active research domains. There is a vast amount of textbooks, research papers, and tools available in this domain

(Bavelas, 1948; Bernard et al., 1990; Burt and Minor, 1983; Feldman, 1987; Freeman, 1977; Freeman, 1979; Moreno, 1934; Nemati and Barko, 2003; Scott, 1992; Wasserman and Faust, 1994). There have been many studies analyzing organizational activity based on insights from social network analysis. However, some of these studies typically have an ad-hoc character and sociograms are typically constructed based on questionnaires rather than using a structured and automated approach as described in this paper. More structured approaches are often based on the analysis of e-mail interaction and additional electronic sources. Several studies have generated sociograms from e-mail logs in organization (Farnham et al., 2004; Fisher and Dourish, 2004; Nardi et al., 2002) to analyze the communication structure. Such studies have resulted in the identification of relevant, recurrent aspects of interaction in organizational contexts (Begole et al., 2002; Fisher and Dourish, 2004). However, these studies are unable to relate the derived social networks to a particular workflow process, as the analyzed data does not reveal to what activity or case it applies.

Within the data mining community information extraction from e-mails has also been a popular topic of research. The main directions of the studies are the following:

- Social relations extraction, e.g., (Zhou et al., 2005; Culotta et al., 2004).
- Extraction of information about a particular user: organization of folders, ongoing activities, etc., e.g., (Huang et al., 2004; Bekkerman et al., 2004).
- Message categorization and anti-spam filtering, e.g., (Gray and Haahr, 2004; Michelakis et al., 2004).
- Forensic investigation of e-mail mediated cyber crimes, e.g., (Hadjidj et al., 2009).

However, in our study of existing literature on the subject we have not found references to studies which try to mine from e-mail archives information about organization's workflow and relations between people and workflow activities (cases and tasks).

Thus, research performed in the process mining domain so far has not considered organization's e-mail logs as a source of information about the business processes taking place in a given organizational context. In fact, research related to e-mail mining concentrated primarily on extracting information about social interactions between e-mail users, largely ignoring business process-related information. Our approach focuses on extracting this process-related information using e-mail logs as a data source.

E-MAIL LOG ANALYSIS

Process mining techniques allow for a wide variety of analysis. However, not all techniques are applicable for the analysis of e-mail-based logs. The type of e-mail analysis proposed in this paper aims at the following aspects of organizational business processes:

1. *Social networks* expressing communication between people within the organization.
2. *Workflow models* expressing relations between tasks within the workflow.
3. *User involvement diagrams* expressing relations between people and workflow activities.

We have developed techniques to analyze these aspects. First, we explain the approach and then we describe our toolset in more detail.

Mining Social Networks

Based on the set of e-mail messages from all members of the organization, it is possible to

Figure 2. An example of a social network

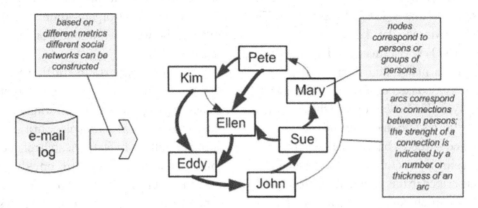

build a sociogram, also known as social network, expressing the frequency of communication between members in the form of a directed graph. Nodes of the graph represent particular users and arcs indicate communication between them. All arcs have weights, which describe the frequency of messages. Each e-mail message from a user A to a user B will increase the weight of the arc from A to B depending on the type of the recipient (direct recipients have greater weights than carbon copy recipients). After processing all messages the weights in the network can be normalized by dividing them by the maximal weight in the network, i.e., $w_{ij}^{norm} = \dfrac{w_{ij}}{w_{max}}$. Figure 2 shows an example of a social network. For details about building such a social network we refer to (van der Aalst and Song, 2004).

Mining Process Logs

While social networks analysis has been in the focus of e-mail mining research for a long time, we consider the extraction of process-related information from e-mail logs to be an interesting new area. Process logs as, e.g., produced by workflow management systems refer to concepts such as tasks (e.g., "Payment processing"), cases (workflow instances) and events (task phases).

The challenge is to translate an e-mail log into a process log assuming that some e-mail messages represent workflow events. We propose to realize a translation of e-mail logs into process logs based on tagging, i.e., explicit references to case and/or task names in message subjects. It is assumed that a message relates to a workflow task if its subject contains a corresponding tag (e.g., a task name or a keyword related to it). Similarly, messages are related to workflow instances (cases) via the subject line or the sender/recipients list. Such correlation is relevant because each case may correspond an individual customer who participates in e-mail communication and different cases should not be mixed.

There are three possible situations:

- The tags (case and task names) are added automatically by a corporative process-aware system in some standard way;
- The user (either the recipient or the sender) is forced (or stimulated) to classify each e-mail message, i.e., the user explicitly tags the message;
- The tags are not added explicitly and the text in the subject field is only intended for the recipient's understanding.

The latter situation means that there is no tagging standard and that the mining algorithm must

Figure 3. Using process mining to extract a process model from an e-mail log

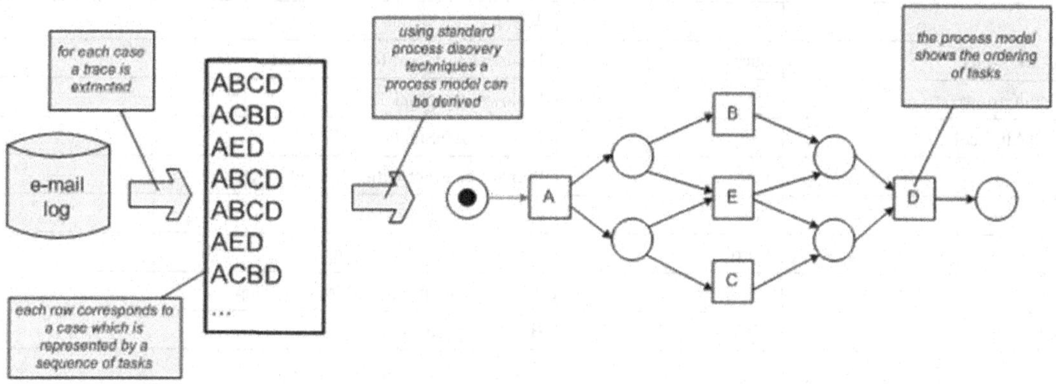

figure out the relations between messages and process cases/tasks. Although we consider the first two scenarios more realistic, we will also show how our tool can deal with the latter situation. The first two scenarios introduce a major limitation related to additional tagging of the messages. Purely manual tagging of the messages will be too inconvenient for the users. Automatic tagging by a corporative system we see as the most realistic case, which would allow tagging messages without introducing any additional workload on the users. However, this limits the area of usability for such an approach making it inapplicable for the organizations which do not use such auxiliary systems. Probably the most promising scenario is the third, which assumes automatic mining of arbitrary messages without any mandatory tags. The current version of EMailAnalyzer tool supports such a scenario but the capabilities of its mining algorithm are still limited. Working with arbitrary messages would require using more advanced (text) mining techniques. Figure 3 sketches the main idea of extracting process models from e-mail logs.

User Involvement Diagrams

Another useful aspect to study involves the links between each member of the organization and the tasks and cases in which (s)he is involved. These

links may help to discover patterns in the users' involvement in the workflow (e.g., whether the same people tend to be involved with the same customer at different stages of the workflow). These links are visualized by *user involvement diagrams*. The *task-person diagram* shows the relations between tasks and users. If a user executes a given task frequently, there is a strong link between both. Similarly the *case-person* diagram displays the relationships between cases and users.

Several events may refer to the same task. We assume that all senders and recipients of all messages related to a task are in some way involved in this task. The task-person diagram shows the links between each employee and the tasks (or cases), in which (s)he was involved. The diagram represents a graph, which has nodes of two types: employees and tasks. The weight of each arc is proportional to the number of times a certain employee was involved in a certain task (or case).

PROTOTYPE IMPLEMENTATION

Software Modules

Our prototype called *EmailAnalyzer* is implemented as a set of plug-in modules for the ProM process mining framework (van der Aalst et al., 2007). The goal of the mining process is to produce

Table 1. A set of messages to handle processing of the example case

From	To	Topic
Mark(UkrAlum)	Sue	Business Proposal for New Plant
Joe(MetalGroup)	John	Business proposal
Michael(AluSteel)	Sue	Proposal AluSteel
Sue	Pete	Prepare contract with AluSteel
John	Pete	Change Conditions AluSteel
John	Carol	Contract with MetalGroup
Mike	Carol	Change Conditions with MetalGroup
Ann(CvetMet)	Mike	Business proposal
Mike	Carol	Contract with CvetMet needed
Sue	Carol	Prepare Contract with UkrAlum
John	Joan	Transfer Payment for UkrAlum
Linda(Sarmat)	Mike	Commercial proposal
Mike	Pete	Cancel Sarmat: No interest
Mike	Carol	Update CvetMet Conditions
Carol	Mike	Cancel CvetMet
Carol	Joe	Conditions of Metalgroup
Carol	George	Transfer payment for MetalGroup
Sarah(Metox)	Sue	Business Proposal for New Plant
Sue	Carol	Prepare Contract with Metox
Mike	Pete	Update AluSteel Conditions
Mike	Pete	Yet another change of AluSteel Conditions
Pete	Mike	AluSteel is Cancelled
Carol	Sue	Cancel Metox

the process log, which can be further analyzed using existing process mining algorithms, from the set of messages stored in the users' inbox folders. In our prototype implementation this process consists of several steps. The first step is to extract e-mail logs from users' e-mail clients. This step depends on the e-mail system used by the organization. Our prototype works with MS Outlook using its COM interfaces. The next step is to pre-process the e-mail log in order to remove ambiguities in recipients' names (e.g., if the same person uses several e-mail addresses referring to the same account) and to exclude irrelevant e-mail messages from the future analysis (e.g., private or spam messages). This extracted e-mail log

can be used to perform social network analysis and to generate the process log using algorithms described above. The process log resulting from such an analysis serves as input for the many mining plug-ins present in ProM. More detailed description of software implementation aspects is provided in (van der Aalst and Nikolov, 2007).

E-Mail Log Processing Example

To illustrate the work of our prototype we will use an example inspired by a real-life case within a metallurgic enterprise. The e-mail log shown in Table 1 represents a set of messages, which reflects processing of six workflow instances, i.e., cases. Note that Table 1 only shows a fragment of a much larger log. Each workflow instance (i.e., case) is related to a potential supplier company. If the sender or the recipient of a message is from an external company, then company's name is given in brackets.

After loading the e-mail log we should add for each external person one additional alias - the name of his/her company and make it his/her main name. Before building a sociogram we can exclude these external users from analysis if we are interested only in communication between employees. The sociogram built on the basis of the e-mail log is shown in Figure 4.

Figure 5 shows the normative model of the example process that we are trying to discover from the log presented in the Table 1. Tasks "Evaluation" and "Quality control" are assumed to be invisible, because these tasks occur but do not result in sending e-mail messages. Other tasks are identified by keywords "proposal", "contract", "condition", "cancel" and "payment" as indicated in Figure 5. Note that this normative model is only given to be able to evaluate the result, i.e.,

in most cases the model is unknown or only partially known.

Using these settings it is possible to generate a process log. Since EMailAnalyzer is embedded in ProM the resulting process log can be stored but also analyzed using one of the many mining algorithms present in ProM. In the remainder of this section, we show the results we obtained by applying the various plug-ins in ProM.

The α-algorithm (van der Aalst et al., 2004) was one of the first process mining techniques able to deal with processes exhibiting concurrency. ProM provides a plug-in for this algorithm and if we apply it to the log generated by EMailAnalyzer we obtain the model shown in Figure 6. The α-algorithm produces a Petri net reflecting only the control-flow in the underlying process. Note that the tasks "Evaluation" and "Quality control" are missing in the Petri net. This makes sense because they are not recorded.

Moreover, instead of three cancellation tasks there is just a single "Cancel". This also makes sense since EMailAnalyzer looks for the keyword "cancel". The α-algorithm has problems dealing

Figure 4. A sociogram built on the basis of the example e-mail log

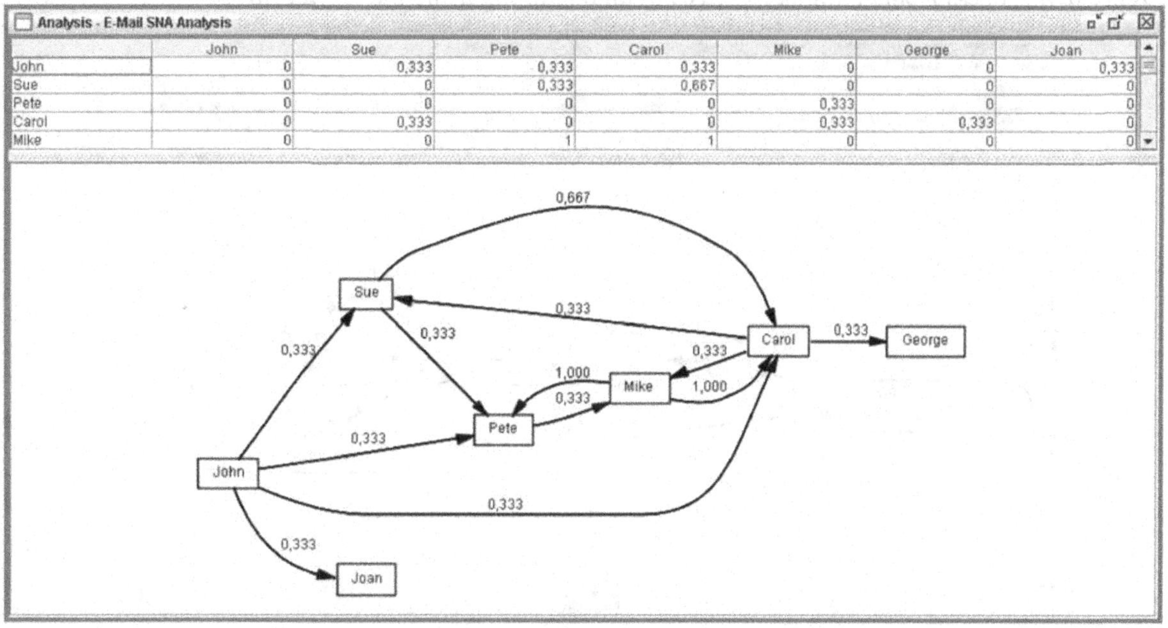

219

with duplicate tasks and as a result the model shown in the Figure 6 is not completely accurate. Results of more powerful mining techniques are shown below.

The multi-phase mining plug-in of ProM is based on so-called instance graphs (van Dongen and van der Aalst, 2004). In contrast to the α-algorithm it does not try to discover the process model in a single step. Instead, it first builds a model (i.e., an instance graph) for every case and only then aggregates these instance graphs into an aggregated instance graph. The result can be visualized in terms of an Event-driven Process Chain (EPC) or a Petri net. Figure 7 shows the result in terms of an EPC. Figure 7 shows that a case can be cancelled at three points in the process. The payment follows after the initial contracting step of after changing the conditions.

As will be discussed below in more detail, logs contain different types of noise. The fact that for

Figure 5. The tasks "Evaluation" and "Quality control" are invisible and the other tasks are characterized by the keyword indicated

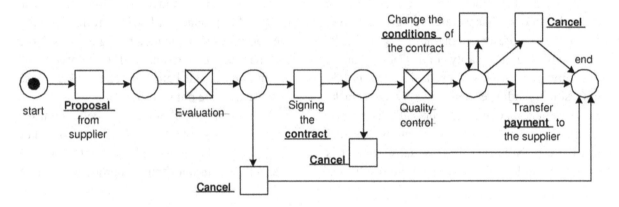

Figure 6. A process model built on the basis of an e-mail log using the α- plug-in

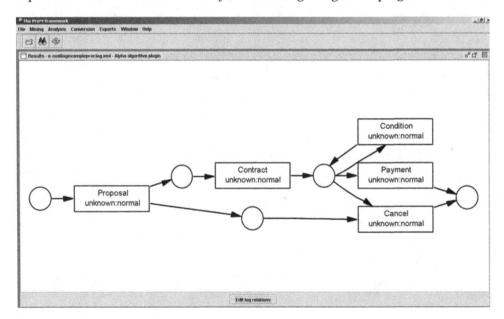

one case a certain path was followed does not necessarily imply that this should be considered as a part of the process model. To tackle these problems there are alternative process mining methods. For example, the genetic mining method uses a genetic algorithm to discover process models. Figure 8 shows the result in terms of a Petri net. The model is behavioral equivalent to the original process model after abstracting from "Evaluation" and "Quality control", and joining the three cancellation tasks into one.

If we compare Figure 5 and Figure 8 we see that the invisible tasks have been removed but that "routing tasks" have been added by the algorithm to reflect choices. For example, after executing task

"Condition" there are three transitions enabled: "t3t3" to again renegotiate the contract, "t3t2" to do the payment, and "t3t2" to cancel after renegotiation. This way the genetic algorithm avoids the problem the α-algorithm could not address (cf. Figure 6).

An example of a task-person diagram based on the process log of the running example is shown in Figure 9 (left). The diagram shows the performers and the tasks and the strength of the relations between both. This allows us to make conclusions about different roles of the performers of these tasks.

A similar diagram can be built for the cases, as shown in Figure 9 (right). The diagram shows

Figure 7. A process model built using the multi-phase plug-in

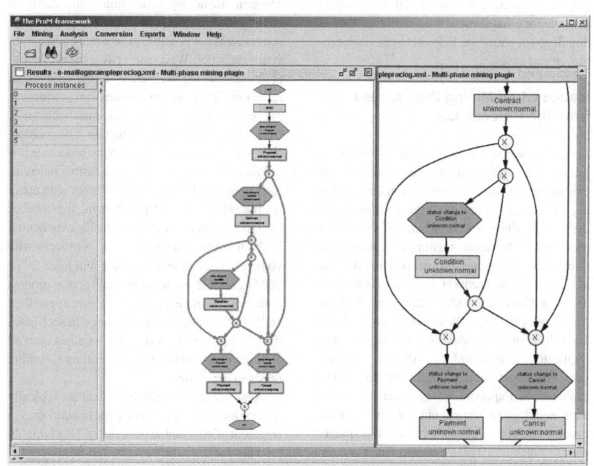

Figure 8. A process model built using the genetic miner plug-in

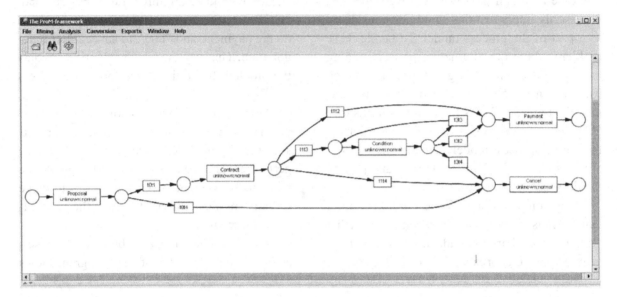

how each employee was involved in each process instance for a fragment of the e-mail log. Arcs in this diagram show the links between each employee and cases.

Issues when Mining the Process from the Process Log

Several algorithms have been proposed for process mining. Many of these algorithms cannot deal with concurrency. (The α-algorithm (van der Aalst et al., 2004) used to construct Figure 6 was among the first to allow for the mining of concurrent processes.) Moreover, existing approaches for mining the process perspective (van der Aalst et al., 2003; van der Aalst et al., 2004; Agrawal et al., 1998; Cook and Wolf, 1998; Herbst, 2000; de Medeiros et al., 2003; Weijters and van der Aalst, 2003) have problems dealing with issues such as duplicate activities, hidden activities, non-free-choice constructs, noise, and incompleteness. The problem with *duplicate activities* occurs when the same activity can occur at multiple places in the process. This is a problem because it is no longer clear to which activity some event refers. The problem with *hidden activities* is that essential routing

decisions are not logged but impact the routing of cases. *Non-free-choice* constructs are problematic because it is not possible to separate choice from synchronization. We consider two sources of *noise*: (1) incorrectly logged events (i.e., the log does not reflect reality) or (2) exceptions (i.e., sequences of events corresponding to "abnormal behavior"). Clearly noise is difficult to handle. The problem of *incompleteness* is that for many processes it is not realistic to assume that all possible behavior is contained in the log. For processes with many alternative routes and parallelism, the number of possible event traces is typically exponential in the number of activities, e.g., a process with 10 binary choices in a sequence will have 2^{10} (= 1024) possible event sequences and a process with 10 activities in parallel will have even 10!(= 3628800) possible event sequences. In such cases it is not realistic to assume that one has seen all combinations and therefore the mining algorithm needs to generalize.

Real-life logs contain noise and are typically incomplete (i.e., the event logs contain only a fragment of all possible behaviors). This is highly relevant for the work presented in this paper because we can expect e-mail logs to be noisy and

Figure 9. Two user involvement diagrams: the task-person diagram (left) and the case-person diagram (right)

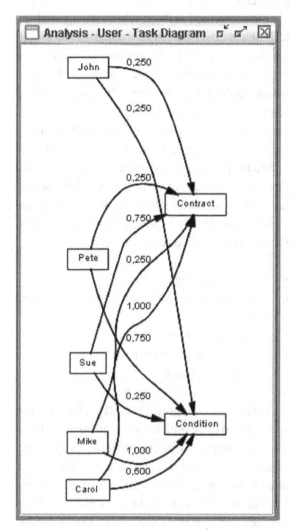
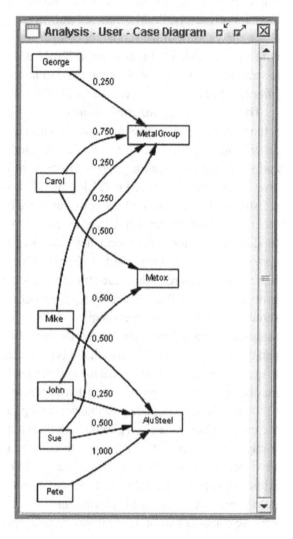

incomplete. Therefore, we developed two ways to address the problem: (1) *heuristics* (Weijters and van der Aalst, 2003), (2) *genetic algorithms* (de Medeiros et al., 2007) and (3) fuzzy algorithms (e.g., the frequency abstraction miner cf. (Günther and van der Aalst 2007).

The discussion on current process mining techniques shows that the mining of e-mail messages can benefit from state-of-the-art approaches for dealing with noise, incompleteness and other issues. This triggers the question: "What is the quality of the discovered model?". This question is addressed in the next section.

VALIDATION

Validation using Conformance Checking

As indicated an event log may contain noise. Moreover, given a log there may be multiple process models that seem appropriate. This makes it important to be able to validate a discovered model. Fortunately, ProM offers several ways to check the validity of the model by comparing it with the log. One of the plug-ins in ProM able to validate a process models is the *Conformance Checker* (Rozinat and van der Aalst, 2006).

The starting point for conformance checking is the presence of both an explicit process model, describing how the process *should be* executed, and some kind of event log, giving insight into how it *was actually* carried out. Clearly, it is interesting to know whether they conform to each other. The Conformance Checker is based on two fundamental notions of conformance: *fitness* and *appropriateness*. An event log and a Petri net "fit" if the Petri net can reproduce each trace in the log. In other words: the Petri net describing the process should be able to "parse" every sequence of e-mail messages observed by in the log. In (Rozinat and van der Aalst, 2006) it is shown that it is possible to quantify fitness, e.g., an event log and Petri net may have a fitness of 0.66 indicating that 66 percent of the events in the log are possible according to the model. Unfortunately, a good fitness does not imply conformance, e.g., it is easy to construct Petri nets that are able to parse any event log. Although such Petri nets have a fitness of 1, they do not provide meaningful information. This is why we consider a second dimension, namely appropriateness. Appropriateness captures the idea of *Occam's razor*: a model is appropriate if it is the "simplest" one, both structurally and behaviorally, explaining the observed behavior.

Experiments with the Enron Corpus

Because of the privacy issues it is hard to present actual examples of e-mail logs of real organizations. Therefore, we resort to a well-known e-mail log that is available in a public domain: the *Enron e-mail corpus* (http://www.cs.cmu.edu/~enron). This corpus has been used in several papers studying the patterns of social relations emerging from e-mail communications (Bekkerman et al., 2004; Zhou et al., 2005).

We performed tests in which we applied the techniques described in this paper to the e-mail messages contained in the corpus. We didn't have the actual description of the workflow of Enron, which made it hard to correctly set the mining settings (i.e. case and task names) and evaluate the results. As the messages were not intentionally tagged, we examined the messages' subject lines to find the process-related information. We found that the customers of Enron were other companies from the energy domain, which interacted with Enron about various kinds of agreements. Examples of such agreements were:

- Gas storage agreement.
- Interconnected Operations Services (IOS) agreement.
- Gas transport agreement.
- Measurement agreement.
- Credit agreement.

Often several agreements of different types were agreed upon with the same customer. Therefore, we interpreted the customer company names as case names and different agreements as task names. In our tests we wanted to find if these agreements represent the tasks of one workflow, in other words, if there were any casual relations between them. We selected a subset of e-mails related to 9 companies (a total of 3828 e-mails) and applied our tool to extract a process log from this subset. We treated a message as related to a particular case and task if the case and task names were appearing in its subject line. During e-mail mining phase each message thread represented one event (i.e. reply messages were discarded).

Based on the processing described above, we first applied the frequency abstraction miner (Günther and van der Aalst 2007). See Figure 10 for the result. This ProM plug-in is particularly suitable for getting some initial insights into the process structure. It shows that *Storage* is the most frequent task (relative frequency of 1) and that IOS has a relatively low frequency (0.267). The numbers on the arcs indicate the relative frequency of taking a branch. It shows that there are a lot of "self loops", i.e., activities following themselves. It also shows that there are causal dependencies between *IOS* and *Transport*, *Transport* and *Storage*, *Storage* and *Measurement*, *Measurement* and *Credit request*, and *Transport* and *Credit request*. Figure 10 shows that the process is quite chaotic, i.e., there is no clear structure in the process.

Using the heuristics miner we focused on the most frequent paths while abstracting from the self loops. The resulting process is shown in the Figure 11. This process model shows the core structure of the process based on the strongest causal dependencies while ignoring the weaker ones. Such a model can be mapped onto several formalisms including the EPCs (see left hand side of Figure 11). However, despite the fact that

ProM is able to build models, it is clear that the process is very unstructured. Using the conformance checker mentioned earlier, we can asses the quality of the idealized model shown in the Figure 11. The conformance checker indicates a fitness of 0.33 percent, i.e., only 33 percent of the behavior of the Enron data is explained by the idealized model constructed by the heuristics miner. We also tested several other mining plugins but they did not achieve a better result. Hence we need to conclude that the process is far from being structured. When checking the e-mail log manually we found that in the actual e-mail log the tasks listed above indeed did not seem to have strong casual relations. The order in which these agreements were agreed upon varied for different customers. One of the few patterns which indeed had stronger support was the fact that an IOS agreement always preceded a transport agreement with the same company.

Figure 10. A process model built from the Enron corpus using the frequency abstraction miner

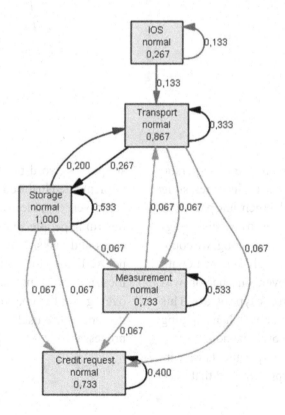

Figure 11. The core structure of the process constructed from the Enron corpus using the heuristics miner

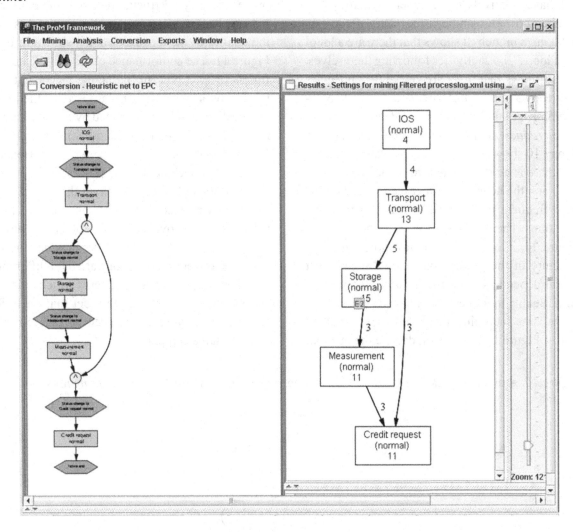

We also built task-person and case-person diagrams and these allowed us to find interesting patterns about people's involvement into particular cases and tasks. Figure 12 is based on a small fragment of the corpus. Generally speaking, we could see that one person is often involved in work with different customers. However, one person was never involved in more than one type of task. This information may appear valuable when studying the working process of the organization.

In general, the results of experiments we performed with the Enron corpus showed that even simple keyword-based techniques, which are implemented in the current version of EMailAnalyzer, were capable to discover interesting patterns regarding people's involvement in processing of cases and tasks. However, these techniques are not sufficient for mining process models if the messages were not tagged intentionally. Moreover, given the chaotic nature of the Enron log, it seems more useful to look at more structured processes.

Figure 12. Two user involvement diagrams based on Enron corpus: the task-person diagram (left) and the case-person diagram (right)

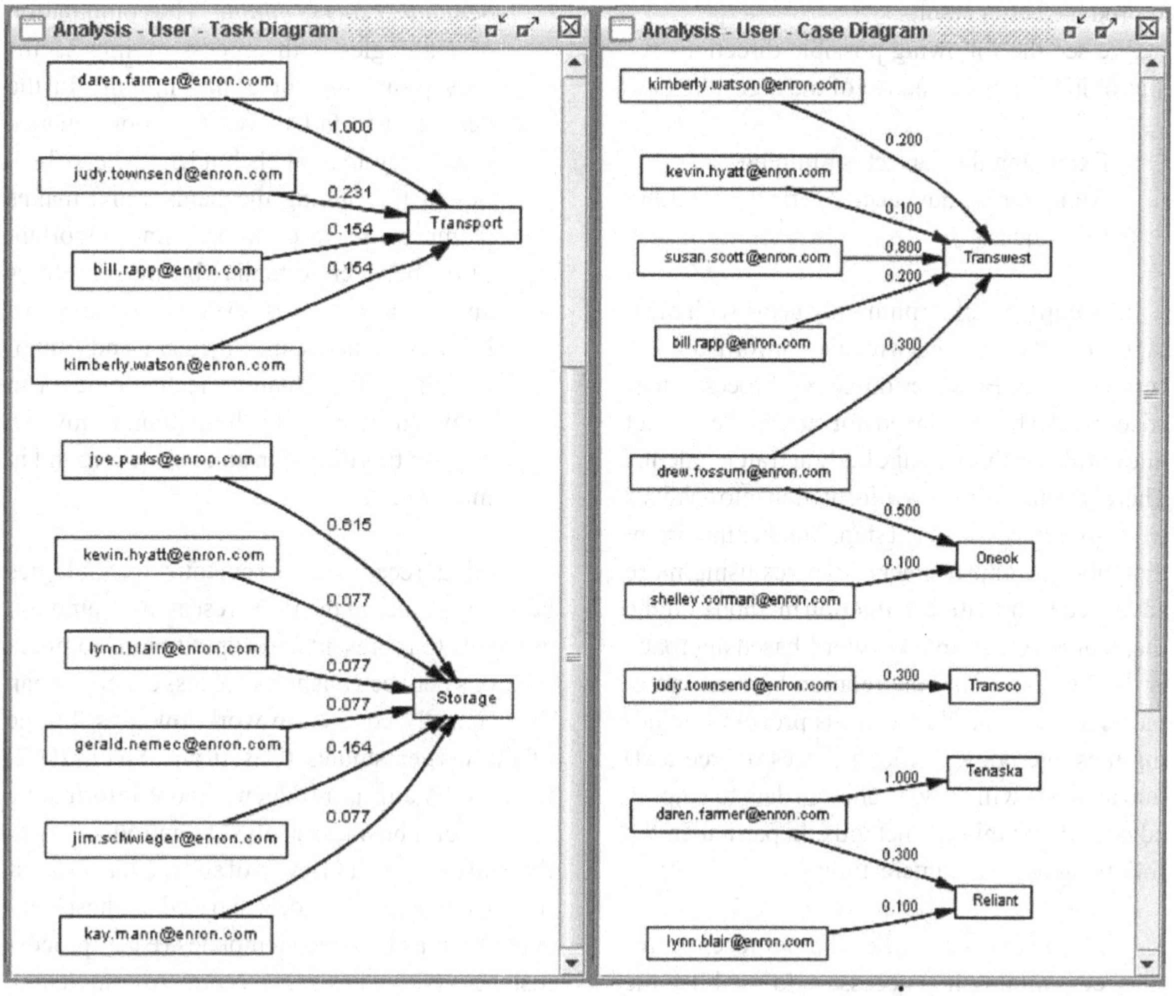

DISCUSSION AND FUTURE WORK

In this work we studied the possibility of using e-mail archives as a source for process mining. Such an approach can provide valuable insights into the business process of an organization in case when a structured event log is not available but e-mail traffic is recorded. The approach can be used, for example, for workflow optimization (by the manager of the organization) and organization auditing.

However, we are aware that the basic algorithm described in the paper suffers from a number of limitations. The algorithm implemented in the course of work was based on finding explicit references to process-related concepts (cases and tasks) in the messages' subjects. While such an approach can be used for process mining if the messages were tagged intentionally, its capabilities when working with arbitrary (i.e., untagged) e-mail messages are still limited. This limits the applicability of the basic approach making it practically impossible to successfully apply process model discovery techniques to an arbitrary e-mail log. We believe that the implementation of more sophisticated text-mining techniques and processing more information (not only subject line but message body and attachments) will allow us to produce better results.

We see the following possible directions for improving the performance of the algorithm:

- Extending the dataset for mining.
- Applying advanced text mining techniques.

Currently the algorithm only deals with message subjects and sender/receiver information to correlate cases. However, obviously, process-related terms can be mentioned not only in the subject line but also in the message body and attachments. Therefore including this information into analysis would be a necessary next step. Another important direction for improvement involves using more advanced information extraction methods. At the moment only a simple keyword-based approach is used to determine the relation between an e-mail message and the business process. Including message body (i.e. long pieces of free text) into analysis will provide enough data to employ advanced text mining methods. In particular, the following areas are interesting:

- *Document search.* For the purpose of process mining it is necessary to establish the relevance between the particular message from one side and the case and the task from the other side. This is similar to the task of determining the relevance between a document and a search query. Therefore the methods developed in this area may be valuable (e.g., tf.idf algorithm (Salton and McGill, 1983) and Latent Semantic Indexing (LSI) (Landauer et al., 1998)).
- *Coreference finding.* In some cases a concept of interest may not be mentioned in the text explicitly (especially in message threads) so the methods, which would identify implicit references to such terms (e.g., using the words like ``they'', ``he'', etc.)

would be valuable (Bagga and Baldwin, 1998).

- *Semantic process mining.* The combination of ontologies with process mining seems very promising for e-mail mining. In the described EMailAnalyzer version reliance on explicit text labels hinders the capabilities of the mining mechanism and makes it impossible to establish some important links between e-mails, business entities and business-process events. Integration of business process management and e-mail mining with semantic technologies can help to overcome this limitation. Below we explain this direction and its background in more detail.

During recent years semantic technologies became popular in the BPM research community as means to represent and exploit more complex relations between business process concepts than those usually covered in workflow logs. In one of the earlier studies (Casati and Shan, 2002) the authors aim at producing more informative reports for a business analyst by introducing additional concepts and levels of abstraction. Process instances can be categorized based on these concepts such as behavior templates (e.g., "process instances taking more than N days to complete"), taxonomies (e.g., classifying process instances by outcomes), process regions (viewing several subtasks as one higher-level unit), etc, although the authors did not use any formal semantic modeling. In (O'Riain and Spyns, 2006) semantics was defined formally using ontologies and used in conjunction with text mining to allow the user to navigate through sets of business argumentation documents. Within the integrated research project SUPER (www.ip-super.org) ontologies were used, in particular, to directly enhance process mining (de Medeiros et al., 2008). Event logs were represented using the SA-MXML format (semantically annotated version of MXML mentioned in this paper) and records in event logs referred to ontological entities rather than syntactic labels. Then ontological reasoning was used to enhance process analysis and infer implicit relations, which were not mentioned directly (e.g., that all *Silver* and *Gold* customer accounts are instances of *SpecialAccount*).

On the other hand, there is a significant research effort focused on the usage of semantic technologies in e-mail management. The concept of Semantic E-Mail was introduced in (McDowell et al., 2004). The authors proposed adding semantic features to e-mails as a way to improve the efficiency of such common tasks as event planning, report generation and organizing auctions. The authors of the X-COSIM framework (Franz et al., 2007) applied semantic technologies for establishing relations between e-mails and other information entities such as files and instant messenger messages. Probably the most relevant for us is implementation of the Semantic E-mail developed as a part of the NEPOMUK project (http://nepomuk.semanticdesktop.org) aimed at creation of a social semantic desktop. In their Semantic E-Mail framework (Scerri et al. 2008) the authors view e-mail threads as "ad-hoc workflows" and propose a formal ontology to model these workflows based on Speech Act Theory (Searle, 1969). E-mail conversation is considered as a sequence of speech acts between the initiator and participants of a thread. The authors distinguish 13 types of speech acts such as "suggest activity", "deliver data", "decline activity", etc., and the Speech Act Process Flow Model (SAPFM), which specifies possible sequences of speech acts. Additionally, in their implementation (http://smile.deri.ie/projects/semanta/) the authors employ text mining to provide the semi-automatic annotation of e-mail content. This text mining service is used to discover relevant keywords and keyphrases from text and tries to associate an e-mail message with one or several speech acts based on its content.

As we can see, there are converging trends in recent developments in both BPM and e-mail

management and analysis research. On the one hand, semantic technologies are used in business process analysis to provide structured view of the process data and apply reasoning to uncover implicit relations between process steps and business entities. On the other hand, semantic technologies are used in conjunction with information extraction algorithms to make explicit the meaning of an e-mail conversation and present it in a formal machine-processable way. The latest studies even apply simple workflow management techniques to handle common e-mail interaction patterns. However, a gap between these two trends still remains: semantic business process mining still primarily uses structured workflow logs, while current research in the Semantic E-Mail considers only very simple and generic workflows. An ad-hoc workflow such as those analyzed in (Scerri et al. 2008) can at best correspond to processing a single task in a complex enterprise business process. This limitation is due to the generic nature of the Semantic E-Mail analysis so far: when an e-mail conversation takes place in the context of an organization-level business process, available domain knowledge about this process is not involved. The approach implemented in the EMailAnalyzer can be "lifted" to a higher level to cover this gap. Its task is to establish links between e-mail messages and threads on the one side and the business process model on the other side. In this scenario a business process model is represented as an ontology, which defines relevant terms: tasks and business process instances (in the described EMailAnalyzer implementation) and potentially richer descriptions such as related contact people, responsible organizational units, standard documents and artifacts involved, etc. While the current EMailAnalyzer implementation uses the MXML format, it is possible to use SA-MXML, which allows for references to ontologies. These terms can allow the e-mail mining module to discover not just a sequence of speech acts in an e-mail thread but also to put this sequence in the context of an upper-level business process.

Potentially such an approach will help to discover e-mail interactions related to organizational workflows with better accuracy than in the original EMailAnalyzer implementation and improve the quality of process models produced by applying process mining to these interactions.

Besides extending our approach in the directions mentioned, the empirical validation of our approach could be strengthened. Because of the privacy issues it is not easy to obtain and use real-world e-mail archives for testing and for those which are available it is hard to verify the existing business process to compare results. Before the tool can be considered applicable on a large scale it will be necessary to some certain technical problems, too. The currently implemented two-step procedure of e-mail logs extraction, which was chosen to cope with possible software heterogeneity, can be inconvenient for the user. This can create significant scalability problems when dealing with e-mail archives of large organizations. One of the necessary steps to improve scalability would be to implement the e-mail log extraction on the server level.

CONCLUSION

This paper presented a tool, named EMailAnalyzer, to mine process logs from e-mail logs. The e-mail log is extracted from the users' inbox folders and translated into the process log according to the settings specified by the user. The resulting process log is saved in a standard format, which can be handled by a variety of process mining tools such as the ones implemented in the context of the ProM framework. We realize that with the current tool a scenario involving arbitrary e-mail messages is not realistic yet. From a practical point of view, we consider the explicit tagging of messages vital.

This paper and the current version of EmailAnalyzer should be considered as a first step towards fully-automated process discovery from e-mail messages. The goal is to extend the functionality of the tool in various directions. The body of the message should be included into the analysis. The mining mechanism itself should be improved by adding text mining techniques and natural language processing heuristics to increase the quality of the mining.

ACKNOWLEDGMENT

The authors would like to thank Boudewijn van Dongen for assisting in embedding the EMailAnalyzer plug-in in the ProM framework. We would also like to thank him and the rest of the "process mining team", in particular Ton Weijters, Boudewijn van Dongen, Minseok Song, Eric Verbeek, Anne Rozinat, Christian Günter, and Peter van den Brand, for their on-going work on process mining techniques.

REFERENCES

Agrawal, R., Gunopulos, D., & Leymann, F. (1998) Mining process models from workflow logs. *6th International Conference on Extending Database Technology*, 469–483.

Bagga, A., & Baldwin, B. (1998). Entity-based cross-document coreferencing using the vector space model. *17th International Conference on Computational Linguistics*, 79–85.

Bavelas, A. A. (1948). A mathematical model for group structures. *Human Organization*, 7, 16–30.

Begole, J., Tang, J., Smith, R., & Yankelovich, N. (2002). Work rhythms: Analyzing visualizations of awareness histories of distributed groups. *ACM conference on Computer Supported Cooperative Work*, 334–343. New York: ACM Press.

Bekkerman, R., McCallum, A., & Huang, G. (2004). Automatic categorization of e-mail into folders: Benchmark experiments on Enron and SRI corpora. *CIIR Technical Report, IR-418.* Amherst: University of Massachusetts.

Bernard, H. R., Killworth, P. D., McCarty, C., Shelley, G. A., & Robinson, S. (1990). Comparing four different methods for measuring personal social networks. *Social Networks, 12,* 179–216. doi:10.1016/0378-8733(90)90005-T

Burt, R. S., & Minor, M. (Eds.). (1983). *Applied network analysis: A methodological introduction.* Newbury Park, CA: Sage.

Casati, F., & Shan, M.-C. (2002). Semantic analysis of business process executions. *8th International Conference on Extending Database Technology (EDBT'02),* 287–296, Berlin: Springer.

Cook, J. E., & Wolf, A. L. (1998). Discovering models of software processes from event-based data. *ACM Transactions on Software Engineering and Methodology, 7*(3), 215–249. doi:10.1145/287000.287001

Culotta, A., Bekkerman, R., & McCallum, A. (2004). Extracting social networks and contact information from e-mail and the web. *1st Conference on Email and Anti-Spam (CEAS).*

de Medeiros, A. K. A., van der Aalst, W. M. P., & Pedrinaci, C. (2008). Semantic process mining tools: Core building blocks. *16th European Conference on Information Systems,* 1953-1964.

de Medeiros, A. K. A., van der Aalst, W. M. P., & Weijters, A. J. M. M. (2003). Workflow mining: Current status and future directions. In Meersman, R., Tari, Z., & Schmidt, D. C., (Editors), *On The Move to Meaningful Internet Systems 2003: CoopIS, DOA, and ODBASE,* 389–406. Berlin: Springer-Verlag.

de Medeiros, A. K. A., Weijters, A. J. M. M., & van der Aalst, W. M. P. (2007). Genetic process mining: An experimental evaluation. *Data Mining and Knowledge Discovery, 14*(2), 245–304. doi:10.1007/s10618-006-0061-7

Dumas, M., van der Aalst, W. M. P., & ter Hofstede, A. H. M. (2005). *Process-aware information systems: Bridging people and software through process technology.* Wiley& Sons.

Ellis, C. A. (2000). An evaluation framework for collaborative systems. *Technical Report, CU-CS-901-00,* Boulder, USA: University of Colorado, Department of Computer Science.

Ellis, C. A., Gibbs, S. J., & Rein, G. (1991). Groupware: Some issues and experiences. *Communications of the ACM, 34*(1), 38–58. doi:10.1145/99977.99987

Ellis, C. A., & Nutt, G. (1996). Workflow: The process spectrum. Sheth, A., (Editor), *NSF Workshop on Workflow and Process Automation in Information Systems,* 140–145.

Farnham, S., Portnoy, W., & Turski, A. (2004). Using e-mail mailing lists to approximate and explore corporate social networks. McDonald, D.W., Farnham, S., & Fisher, D. (Editors), *CSCW'04 Workshop on Social Networks.*

Feldman, M. (1987). Electronic mail and weak ties in organizations. *Office: Technology and People, 3,* 83–101. doi:10.1108/eb022643

Fisher, D., & Dourish, P. (2004). Social and temporal structures in everyday collaboration. Dykstra-Erickson, E., & Tscheligi, M. (Editors), *Conference on Human Factors in Computing Systems (CHI2004),* 551–558. New York: ACM Press.

Franz, T., Staab, S., & Arndt, R. The X-COSIM integration framework for a seamless semantic desktop. *4th International Conference on Knowledge Capture (K-CAP 2007).*, 43–150., New York: ACM Press.

Freeman, L. C. (1977). A set of measures of centrality based on betweenness. *Sociometry, 40,* 35–41. doi:10.2307/3033543

Freeman, L. C. (1979). Centrality in social networks: conceptual clarification. *Social Networks, 1,* 215–239. doi:10.1016/0378-8733(78)90021-7

Gray, A., & Haahr, M. (2004). Personalised, collaborative spam filtering. *1st Conference on Email and Anti-Spam (CEAS).*

Günther, C. W., & van der Aalst, W. M. P. (2007). Fuzzy mining: Adaptive process simplification based on multi-perspective metrics. Alonso, G., Dadam, P., & Rosemann, M. (Editors), *International Conference on Business Process Management (BPM 2007), Lecture Notes in Computer Science, 4714,* 328-343. Berlin: Springer-Verlag.

Hadjidj, R., Debbabi, M., Lounis, H., Iqbal, F., Szporer, A., & Benredjem, D. (2009). Towards an integrated e-mail forensic analysis framework. *Digital Investigation, 5*(3-4), 124–137. doi:10.1016/j.diin.2009.01.004

Herbst, J. (2000). A machine learning approach to workflow management. *11th European Conference on Machine Learning* [Berlin: Springer-Verlag.]. *Lecture Notes in Computer Science, 1810,* 183–194. doi:10.1007/3-540-45164-1_19

Hoffman, T. (2004). Sarbanes-Oxley sparks forensics apps interest: Vendors offer monitoring tools to help identify incidents of financial fraud. *Computerworld, 38,* 14.

Huang, Y., Govindaraju, D., Mitchell, T., Rocha de Carvalho, V., & Cohen, W. W. (2004). Inferring ongoing activities of workstation users by clustering e-mail. *1st Conference on Email and Anti-Spam (CEAS).*

Landauer, T. K., Foltz, P. W., & Laham, D. (1998). Introduction to latent semantic analysis. *Discourse Processes, 25,* 259–284.

McDowell, L., Etzioni, O., Halevy, A., & Levy, H. (2004). Semantic email. *13th international conference on World Wide Web (WWW 2004).*, 244–254, New York: ACM Press.

Michelakis, E., Androutsoppoulos, I., Paliouras, G., & Sakkis, G. (2004). Filtron: A learning-based anti-spam filter. *1st Conference on Email and Anti-Spam (CEAS).*

Moreno, J. L. (1934). *Who shall survive? A new approach to the problem of human interrelations.* Washington, DC: Nervous and Mental Disease Publishing Company.

Nardi, B. A., Whittaker, S., Isaacs, E., Creech, M., Johnson, J., & Hainsworth, J. (2002). Integrating communication and information through ContactMap. *Communications of the ACM, 45*(2), 89–95. doi:10.1145/505248.505251

Nemati, H., & Barko, C. D. (2003). *Organizational data mining: Leveraging enterprise data resources for optimal performance.* Hershey, PA: Idea Group Publishing.

O'Riain, S., & Spyns, P. (2006). Enhancing the business analysis function with semantics. *OTM Conferences, LNCS 4275(1),* 818–835, Springer: Berlin.

Rozinat, A., & van der Aalst, W. M. P. (2006). Conformance testing: Measuring the fit and appropriateness of event logs and process models. Bussler, C. et al. (Editors), *BPM 2005 Workshops (Workshop on Business Process Intelligence), Lecture Notes in Computer Science, 3812*, 163–176. Berlin: Springer-Verlag.

Salton, G., & McGill, M. (1983). *Introduction to modern information retrieval.*, New York, NY: McGraw-Hill.

Sarbanes, P., & Oxley, G. (2002). *Sarbanes-Oxley Act of 2002.*

Scerri, S., Handschuh, S., & Decker, S. Semantic email as a communication medium for the social semantic desktop. *5th European Semantic Web Conference (ESWC2008)*., 124–138, Berlin: Springer.

Scott, J. (1992). *Social network analysis.* Newbury Park, CA: Sage.

Searle, J. (1969). *Speech acts.* Cambridge: Cambridge University Press.

van der Aalst, W. M. P., & Nikolov, A. (2007). EMailAnalyzer: An e-mail mining plug-in for the ProM framework. *BPM Center Report BPM-07-16.* BPMCenter.org.

van der Aalst, W. M. P., & Song, M. (2004). Mining social networks: Uncovering interaction patterns in business processes. Desel, J., Pernici, B., & Weske, M., (Editors), *International Conference on Business Process Management (BPM 2004), Lecture Notes in Computer Science, 3080*, 244–260. Berlin: Springer-Verlag.

van der Aalst, W. M. P., van Dongen, B. F., Günther, C., Mans, R., de Medeiros, A. K. A., Rozinat, A., et al. (2007). ProM 4.0: Comprehensive support for real process analysis. In Kleijn, J., & Yakovlev, A. (Editors), *Application and Theory of Petri Nets 2007, Lecture Notes in Computer Science, 4546*, 484–494. Berlin: Springer-Verlag.

van der Aalst, W. M. P., van Dongen, B. F., Herbst, J., Maruster, L., Schimm, G., & Weijters, A. J. M. M. (2003). Workflow mining: A survey of issues and approaches. *Data & Knowledge Engineering, 47*(2), 237–267. doi:10.1016/S0169-023X(03)00066-1

van der Aalst, W. M. P., & van Hee, K. M. (2002). *Workflow management: Models, methods and systems.* Cambridge, MA: MIT press.

van der Aalst, W. M. P., & Weijters, A. J. M. M. (Eds.). (2004). Process mining, *Special Issue of Computers in Industry, 53(3).* Amsterdam: Elsevier Science Publishers.

van der Aalst, W. M. P., Weijters, A. J. M. M., & Maruster, L. (2004). Workflow mining: Discovering process models from event logs. *IEEE Transactions on Knowledge and Data Engineering, 16*(9), 1128–1142. doi:10.1109/TKDE.2004.47

van Dongen, B. F., & van der Aalst, W. M. P. (2004). Multi-phase process mining: Building instance graphs. In Atzeni, P., Chu, W., Lu, H., Zhou, S., & Ling, T. W. (Editors), *International Conference on Conceptual Modeling (ER 2004), Lecture Notes in Computer Science, 3288*, 362–376. Berlin: Springer-Verlag.

Wasserman, S., & Faust, K. (1994). *Social network analysis: Methods and applications.* Cambridge: Cambridge University Press.

Weijters, A. J. M. M., & van der Aalst, W. M. P. (2003). Rediscovering workflow models from event-based data using Little Thumb. *Integrated Computer-Aided Engineering, 10*(2), 151–162.

Zhou, D., Song, Y., Zhang, Y., & Zha, H. (2005). Towards discovering organizational structure from e-mail corpus. *4th IEEE International Conference on Machine Learning and Applications*, 279–284. Washington, DC: IEEE Computer Society.

Section 3
Decision Support and Modeling

Chapter 12
Semantic Supplier Contract Monitoring and Execution DSS Architecture

A. F. Salam
University of North Carolina at Greensboro, USA

ABSTRACT

This research is motivated by the critical problem of stark incompatibility between the contractual clauses (typically buried in legal documents) and the myriad of performance measures used to evaluate and reward (or penalize) supply participants in the extended enterprise. This difference between what is contractually expected and what is actually performed in addition to the lack of transparency of what is measured and how those measures relate to the contractual obligations make it difficult, error prone and confusing for different partner organizations. To address this critical issue, in this article, we present a supplier performance contract monitoring and execution decision support architecture and its prototype implementation using a business case study. We use the SWRL extension of OWL-DL to represent contract conditions and rules as part of the ontology and then use the Jess Rule Reasoner to execute the contract rules integrating with Service Oriented Computing to provide decision support to managers in the extended enterprise.

INTRODUCTION

Companies are under increasing pressure to transparently integrate and streamline their business activities to increase their service and shorten product delivery times (Weigand & Heuvel, 2002; Chopra & Meindl, 2003). According to Dyer (2000) the fundamental unit of competition is no longer the individual firm but rather the extended enterprise. Extended enterprises comprise collaborative partners typically coordinated by a *focal firm* to jointly create value for the customers in the marketplace (see Figure 1). In an extended enterprise each company is self-organized, while the extended enterprise imposes a federal structure

Figure 1. Extended enterprise focal firm and alliance supply partners

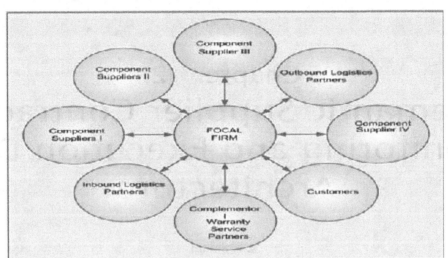

for communication and synchronization between individual enterprises (Bititci and Mendibil, 2005; Ellram, 1990; Fawcett, Stanley & Smith, 1997).

The key to governing and improving performance in an extended enterprise is to create a new set of organizing principles and measures of performance that allow companies to drive performance across their extended enterprise (IBM Executive Brief—http://www.ibm.com). Performance improvement in the extended enterprise should include the correct set of *performance measures* and *incentives (or penalties)* that help motivate the correct set of actions across an extended value chain or network (Dyer, 2000). Business contracts are the key governing mechanisms for inter-organizational collaboration and they are increasingly taking a central role in e-commerce, e-business and extended enterprise governance related to key process integration, exchange of knowledge and information and as drivers for performance (Governatori & Hoang, 2005; Governatori and Milosevic, 2006; Governatori, Milosevic & Sadiq, 2006; Grosof & Poon, 2004; Udupi & Singh, 2006).

Despite the importance of the role of contracts in the extended enterprise, Governatori and Hoang (2005), Governatori, Milosevic and Sadiq (2006) and Nellore (2004) emphasize the limited awareness, among extended enterprise participants, regarding the constraints imposed on business processes and performance by business contracts. The most typical scenario today is in which extended enterprise participants still treat contracts as legal documents typically detached from their governance role for cross-organizational business processes and performance.

It has been recognized in the literature that communication, coordination and other problems arise due to the use of different terms and concepts (and their underlying *lack of common* semantics, meaning or incompatibility) used in the description of the contracts and those terms and concepts used in the description of business processes and performance. These problems obviously lead to the undesired consequences of inability to fulfill organizational obligations (Governatori & Milosevic, 2006; Nellore, 2004) arising out of contractual agreements (Krishna, Karlapalem & Chiu, 2004). This is nowhere more true than in the case of supplier contracts

Figure 2. Sphere of agreed and shared common meaning of supplier performance contract concepts and criteria across the extended enterprise using the extended enterprise supplier performance contract ontology

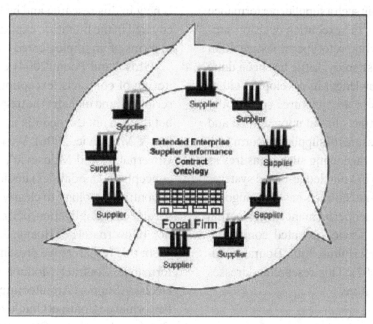

governing supplier performance obligations, as required by the contractual clauses, and the supplier performance criteria used by the focal firm in measuring supplier performance in the extended enterprise (Grosof & Poon, 2004; Governatori & Milosevic, 2006; Nellore, 2004).

This research is *motivated* by this critical problem of stark *incompatibility* between the contractual clauses (typically buried in legal documents) and the myriad of performance measures used to evaluate and reward (or penalize) supply participants in the extended enterprise. This difference between what is *contractually* expected and what is *actually* performed in addition to the lack of transparency of what is measured and how those measures relate to the contractual obligations make it difficult, error prone and confusing for different partner organizations.

If the unit of competition is no longer the individual firm but the extended enterprise (Dyer, 2000; Frazelle, 2002) then it is critical to address

this research issue of developing a contractual mechanism that lays out the contractual obligations of the participating partners as well as direct and transparent measures of performance that are based on the same contractual clauses thus minimizing any ambiguity between what is expected and what is actually performed by business partners (suppliers). Hult, Ketchen, & Slater (2005) point out the need for meaningful knowledge sharing to improve supplier performance. They are basically pointing towards the need for a common ontology for sharing knowledge and information across the supply chain for improving supplier performance, as also has been suggested by Singh and Salam (2006). Ontology is defined as a shared conceptualization of a phenomenon (Guarino, 1995; Welty & Guarino, 2001).

A common supplier performance contract ontology (see Figure 2) based on the widely adopted Supply Chain Operations Reference (SCOR) model (Lockamy III, 2004) can provide a meaningful and effective supplier performance contract monitoring and execution platform (Metzinger & Gallese, 2003; Murthy & Krishnamurthy, 2005). In this article, we present such a supplier performance contract monitoring and execution decision support architecture and its prototype implementation using a business case study. Little has been done (to the author's knowledge) in developing either contract languages or architectures specifically for composing contracts based upon agreed and widely accepted measures of supplier performance such as SCOR and then using such measures as part of information or knowledge-based systems to monitor and execute contracts based on ongoing and real-time supplier performance information through integrated service-oriented computing architecture (Singh & Huhns, 2005; Bouras, Gouvas & Mentzas, 2007). This research addresses this gap in the literature.

CONTRACT LANGUAGES AND ARCHITECTURES

Governatori & Milosevic (2006) proposed the Business Contract Language including notions of deontic concepts of obligation, permission and prohibition. They also included the logic of violation as part of their proposed contract language (Antoniou & Bikakis, 2007; Boella & Torre, 2006). Our research incorporates these important and critical deontic concepts and operationalizes those using the Semantic Web Rules Language (Grosof, Volz, Horrocks, & Decker, 2003) contract rules that are effected should any of the deontic concepts are violated thus implicitly incorporating the notion of violation. Additionally, this research addresses an issue not addressed previously in most contract literature that is the notion of positive incentives or rewards. Typically, the contract literature has mostly focused on remedies related to contract violation but in practice typically in a supply chain scenario, in an extended enterprise, there needs to be incorporation of positive incen-

tives and rewards to address the idea of conforming to obligation and of carrying out that obligation to the satisfaction of the beneficiary. This notion is new in this research and has not been that well covered in the literature explicitly and at least not in terms of an implemented architecture.

Grosof and Poon (2004) considers the monitoring of contracts, exceptions and process descriptions and includes the treatment of violations, but they do not use deontic modalities (Governatori & Milosevic, 2006). We must concede with Governatori and Milosevic (2006) that deontic concepts and modalities should be a required part of contract ontology to clearly set the conceptual parameters of obligation, permission and prohibition (Governatori & Hoang, 2005).

In this research, we present the Supplier Performance Contract Monitoring and Execution Decision Support Architecture using the Supplier Performance Contract Ontology based on the Web Ontology Language (OWL), Description Logics (DL) and extension of OWL DL using SWRL. We demonstrate using a case study approach and a prototype implementation how OWL DL and SWRL can be used for representing Supplier Performance Contract concepts and roles, including deontic concepts of obligation, permission and prohibition. Additionally, we show how the conditions or rules from the contract can be expressed using SWRL. We then present our supplier contract monitoring and execution architecture that uses Jess Rule Reasoner for reasoning with OWL DL concepts and roles and SWRL rules (Grosof & Poon, 2004). According to the author's knowledge, this is one of the first attempts at applying this novel approach to supplier performance within the context of the extended enterprise supply chain and supplier contracts. This research has brought together two disparate worlds: namely, (1) the world of supplier performance measures, supplier selection and supplier retention decisions typically made by supply chain managers and, (2) supply chain contracts that are typically treated as legal (most often hardcopy) documents under the purview of lawyers and legal professionals. But as Governatori and Milosevic (2006) and Nellore (2004) and others have pointed out that these are not to be treated as different worlds but should be treated as an integral component of the same extended enterprise. In the next section, we present an overview of Description Logics and SWRL.

DESCRIPTION LOGICS (DL) AND CONTRACT KNOWLEDGE REPRESENTATION

Description Logics and OWL-DL

Overview of Description Logics Formalism

Description Logics is a family of knowledge representation formalisms that represent the knowledge of an application domain (the "world") by first defining the relevant concepts of the domain (its terminology) and then using these concepts to specify properties objects and individuals occurring in the domain (the world description).

Description Languages

Elementary descriptions are atomic concepts and atomic roles. Complex descriptions can be built from the atomic concepts and roles inductively with concept constructors. Using abstract notation, the letter A and B represent atomic concepts, and the letter R represent atomic roles and the letters C and D represent concept descriptions. Each description language is characterized by its distinguished set of constructors. The language AL (= attributive language) has been introduced as a minimal language that is of practical interest. Other description languages of this family are extensions of AL. The concept descriptions in AL are formed according to the following syntax

rules (Baader, Calvanese, McGuinness, Nardi, and Patel-Schneider, 2003):

$$
\begin{array}{lll}
C, D & \rightarrow A & | \quad \text{(atomic concept)} \\
& \top & | \quad \text{(universal concept)} \\
& \bot & | \quad \text{(bottom concept)} \\
& \neg A & | \quad \text{(atomic negation)} \\
& C \sqcap D & | \quad \text{(intersection)} \\
& \forall R.C & | \quad \text{(value restriction)} \\
& \forall R.\top & | \quad \text{(limited existential quantification)}
\end{array}
$$

In order to define a formal semantics of AL concepts, we consider interpretation I that consists of a non-empty set Δ^I (the domain of interpretation) and an interpretation function which assigns to every atomic concept A a set $A^I \subseteq \Delta^I$ and to every atomic role R a binary relation $R^I \subseteq \Delta^I \times \Delta^I$.

The interpretation function is extended to concept descriptions using the following inductive definitions (Baader, et al, 2003; Borgida, 1995):

$$
\begin{array}{lll}
\top^I & = & \Delta^I \\
\bot^I & = & \varnothing \\
(\neg A) & = & \Delta^I \setminus A^I \\
(C \sqcap D)^I & = & C^I \cap D^I \\
(\forall R.C)^I & = & \{a \in \Delta^I \mid \forall b. (a, b) \in R^I \rightarrow b \in C^I \} \\
(\forall R.\top)^I & = & \{a \in \Delta^I \mid \exists b. (a, b) \in R^I \}
\end{array}
$$

We also say that two concepts C and D are equivalent and write $C \equiv D$ if $C^I = D^I$. Additionally, terminological axioms have the form $C \subseteq D$ or $C \equiv D$ where the axioms of the first kind are inclusions and of the second kind are called equalities. Definitions are used to introduce symbolic names for complex descriptions. An equality whose left-hand side is an atomic concept is called a definition. For example, the axiom

Mother = Woman ⊓ ∃ hasChild.Person

associates the name Mother to the description on the right-hand side. We call a finite set of definitions τ a terminologies or TBox if no symbolic name is defined more than once.

In formal terms, a semantic interpretation is a pair $\mathcal{I} = (\Delta, \cdot^{\mathcal{I}})$, which consists of the domain Δ and the interpretation function $\cdot^{\mathcal{I}}$, which maps every concept to a subset of Δ, every role to a subset of $\Delta \times \Delta$, every individual to an element of Δ. We also assume that different individuals are mapped to different elements of Δ (i.e., $a^{\mathcal{I}} \neq b^{\mathcal{I}}$ for individuals $a \neq b$). This restriction is usually called *Unique Name Assumption* (UNA).

In the context of the extended enterprise supply chain, ComponentTech and AdvancedElectronix are, for example, individual names of companies in the electronics industry. ComponentTech is a supplier of materials to AdvancedElectronix.

This relationship is represented by:

isSupplierOf(ComponentTech, AdvancedElectronix).

This means that ComponentTech is a supplier of AdvancedElectronix and is Role filler for the Role is*SupplierOf.*

Description Logics OWL-DL and Web Ontology Language

Web Ontology Language (OWL) is a W3C recommendation and is a standard for expressing ontologies in the Semantic Web. The OWL recommendation consists of three languages with increasing expressive power. We use OWL DL to construct the supplier performance contract ontology in this research. OWL DL is very expressive but is a decidable fragment of first order logic (Pan & Horrocks, 2007; Brachman & Levesque, 2004). OWL DL corresponds with the SHOIN(D$^+$) fragment of description logics. Following the notation used by Pan and Horrocks (2007), in formal terms, $\mathbf{C}$, $\mathbf{R_I}$, $\mathbf{R_D}$ and $\mathbf{I}$ are the sets that can be used for denoting classes, abstract properties, data type properties, and individuals respectively.

An OWL DL interpretation is a tuple $\mathcal{I} = (\Delta^{\mathcal{I}}, \Delta_D, \cdot^{\mathcal{I}D})$ where the individual domain $\Delta^{\mathcal{I}}$ is a non-empty set of individuals, the data type domain Δ_D

is a non-empty set of data values, $\cdot^{\mathcal{I}}$ is an individual interpretation function that maps:

- each individual name $a \in \mathbf{I}$ to an element of $a^{\mathcal{I}} \in \Delta^{\mathcal{I}}$
- each class name $CN \in \mathbf{C}$ to a subset $CN^{\mathcal{I}} \subseteq \Delta^{\mathcal{I}}$
- each abstract property name $RN \in \mathbf{R_I}$ to a binary relation $RN \subseteq \Delta^{\mathcal{I}} \times \Delta^{\mathcal{I}}$
- each data type property name $TN \in \mathbf{R_D}$ to a binary relation $TN \subseteq \Delta^{\mathcal{I}} \times \Delta_D$

and $\cdot^D$ is a data type interpretation function which can be extended to provide semantics for OWL DL class and property descriptions (Pan & Horrocks, 2007). An OWL DL ontology can be seen as a DL knowledge base (Borgida & Patel-Schneider, 1994; Horrocks, Patel-Schneider & Harmelen, 2003) consisting of a set of axioms, including class axioms, property axioms, and individual axioms (Farrugia, 2003). We use OWL DL in our research.

REPRESENTING CONTRACT ONTOLOGY AND RULES USING OWL DL AND SWRL

Although OWL DL is very expressive, it is a decidable fragment of first-order logic, and thus cannot express arbitrary axioms: the only axioms it can express are of a certain tree structure (Pan & Horrocks, 2007). To overcome this limitation, Horrocks, Patel-Schneider, Bechhofer and Tsarkov (2005) added a new kind of axiom to OWL DL, namely Horn clause rules, extending the OWL abstract syntax and the direct model-theoretic semantics for OWL DL to provide a formal semantics and syntax for OWL ontologies including such rules. This language is known as the Semantic Web Rules Language.

Informally, an atom $C(x)$ holds if x is an instance of the class description C, an atom $P(x, y)$ (resp. $Q(x, z)$) holds if x is related to $y(z)$ by property $P(Q)$, an atom sameAs(*x, y*) holds if *x* is interpreted as the same object as *y*, and an atom differentFrom(*x, y*) holds if *x* and *y* are interpreted as different objects.

In this syntax, a rule has the form:

antecedent ~ consequent.

Using this syntax, a rule asserting that the composition of parent and brother properties implies the uncle property might be written as:

Parent (?a, ?b) $\wedge$ brother (?b, ?c) $\rightarrow$ uncle (?a, ?c)

Using the contract ontology, we can write the following example rule about an Agent and BusinessEnterprise and the employment of the Agent with the BusinessEnterprise.

BusinessEnterprise (?x) $\wedge$ Agent (?y) $\wedge$ isEmployedBy(?y, ?x) $\rightarrow$ isEmployerOf (?x, ?y)

Figure 3 illustrates the above rule in Protégé 3.3.1.

Interested reader is referred to Horrocks, Patel-Schneider, Bechhofer, and Tsarkov (2005) for elaboration on the direct model theoretic semantics of extending OWL DL with rules.

OWL DL Supplier Performance Contract Ontology for the Extended Enterprise

The supplier performance contract ontology presented in this research is based on the Description Logics formalism (Baader, et al, 2003). Contracts are defined as legal agreements between two or more parties (Nellore, 2004). Typically contracts are treated as legal hard copy documents by most businesses. In this research, we are concerned with Electronic Contract Documents and specifically Electronic Extended Enterprise Supply Contract and therefore we conceptualize electronic contracts as being subsumed by the concept *LegalElectronicDocument*, which is subsumed by *ElectronicDocument*. We present

Figure 3.

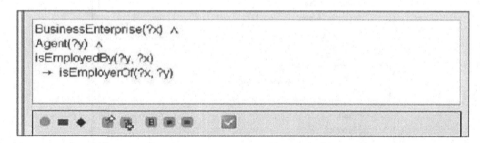

Figure 4. ExtendedEnterpriseSupplyContract concept and its parent and its relationships (Roles) with other concepts in the supplier performance contract ontology

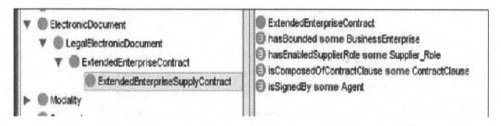

this conceptualization as part of our contract ontology (see Figure 4).

The primary purpose of a contract is to legally bind two or more business enterprises for a set of mutually responsible set of activities. In this context, the *ExtendedEnterpriseSupplyContract* has the *hasBounded* property to bind Individuals of Class *BusinessEnterprise* (see Figure 5 for a snapshot of the Contract Ontology and Figure 6 for the *Agent* Concept).

In Figure 7, we show the definition of the *ContractedSupplierCompany* concept. *ContractedSupplierCompany* is subsumed by the *SupplierCompany* concept. The *ContractedSup-*

Figure 5. Extended enterprise supplier performance contract ontology in Protégé 3.3.1.

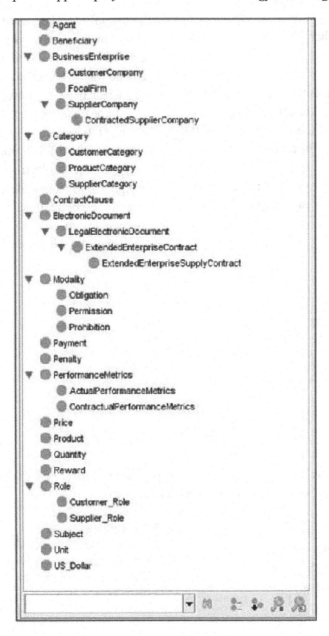

plierCompany has the *hasCustomer* property which has at most one customer that is the FocalFirm. The *ContractedSupplierCompany* also has the *hasSupplierRole* property to enact the *Supplier_Role*.

Contracts are typically composed of Contract Clauses or conditions that parties agree to fulfill as part of their contractual agreement. In this sense, *ContractClause* concept has the *hasComposedContract* property to indicate that some *ExtendedEnterpriseSupply* Contract can be composed using this concept. *ContractClause* concept also has the *hasContractualPerformanceMetrics* property that points to some *ContractualPerformanceMetrics* concept. The *ContractClause* concept and its definition are shown in Figure 8.

The *Supplier_Role* concept (see Figure 9) is central to this contract ontology as it captures and provides the critical performance link between what is contractually obligated what actually

transpires for an entity that takes up this Role. We have two properties of the *Supplier_Role* concept (1) *hasContractualPerformanceMetrics* and (2) *hasActualPerformanceMetrics*. These two properties relate to the Concepts *ContractualPerformance* and *ActualPerformance* respectively in the Contract Ontology (see Figures 5 and 9). In the next section we discuss how SCOR performance criteria can be used as a foundation for developing the supplier performance component of the contract ontology.

SCOR and Supplier Performance Criteria in OWL DL Contract Ontology

Supply Chain Council (SCC) constructed a descriptive framework called the Supply Chain Operations Reference model (Lockamy, 2004). The SCOR model aims to enable companies to

Figure 6. Agent concept in Protégé 3.3.1

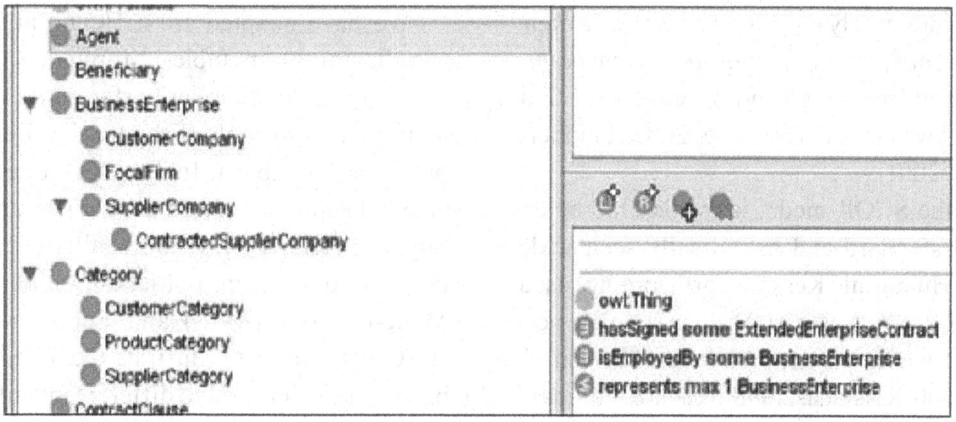

Figure 7. ContractedSupplierCompany concept in Protégé 3.3.1

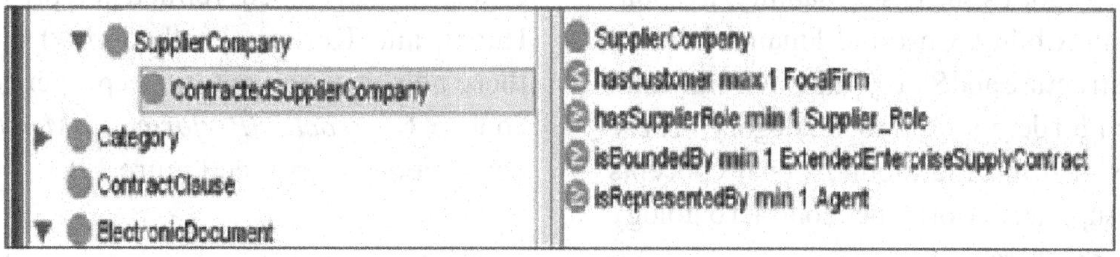

Figure 8. ContractClause Concept in Protégé 3.3.1

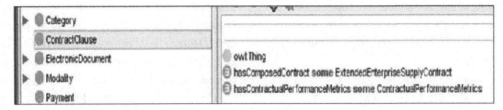

Figure 9. Supplier_Role Concept in Protégé 3.3.1

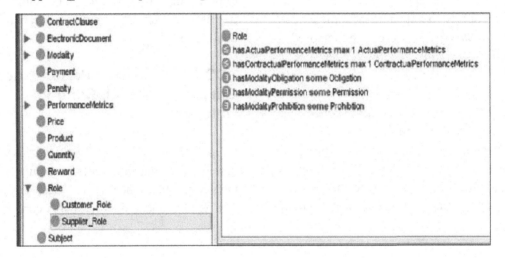

communicate supply chain issues, *measure their performance objectively, identify performance improvement objectives*, and influence future SCM software development (Frazelle, 2002; Lambert & Pohlen, 2001).

Since the SCOR model is intended to be an industrial standard and has already seen wide adoption, Huang and Keskar (Forthcoming) used the SCOR metrics as part of their supplier performance metrics development effort (Petroni & Braglia, 2000; Rolstadås, 1998; Verma & Pullman, 1998; Wang, Huang, & Dismukes, 2004).

Huang and Keskar (Forthcoming) defined five top-level categories such as Reliability, Responsiveness, Flexibility, Cost and Financial, Asset and Infrastructure and Safety and Environmental (see Table 1 for definition of each category). These categories also form the foundational concepts related to supplier performance contract ontology used in our research.

We have adapted from Huang and Keskar (Forthcoming), in Tables 2 through 8, the specific criteria for supplier performance measurement related to each of the top level categories presented in Table 1. In Table 2, we present the adapted supplier performance criteria related to Supplier Reliability. Additionally, the different configurations such as Make-to-Order (MTO), Make-to-Stock (MTS) and Engineer-to-Order (ETO) are shown to illustrate the broad applicability of these criteria to different manufacturing and supply chain concerns.

In this research we have adopted these SCOR criteria as developed, refined and presented by Huang and Keskar (Forthcoming) and made these performance criteria as properties of the concept *ContractualPerformanceMetrics* in our contract ontology (see Figure 10).

Table 1. Definition of top level metric categories

Reliability	Criteria related to the supplier performance in regards to delivering the ordered components to the right place, at the agreed upon time, within the required quality, packaging and quantity
Responsiveness	Criteria related to the velocity at which the supplier provides products to the focal firm
Flexibility	Criteria related to the agility of the supplier to respond to the demand changes of the focal firm
Cost and Financial	Criteria related to the cost and financial aspects of purchasing from the supplier
Asset and Infrastructure	Criteria related to the effectiveness with which the supplier manages assets to support the demands of the focal firm
Safety and Environment	Criteria regarding the supplier's effort related to environmentally friendly production of components for the focal firm

Table 2. Supplier reliability metrics (adapted from Huang and Kesker, forthcoming)

Metrics	Definition	Configuration
1. Percent orders received defect free	Number of orders received defect free by the focal firm divided by the number of orders processed in measurement time	MTS/MTO/ETO
2. Percent orders received complete	Number of orders received complete by the focal firm divided by the total number of orders processed in measurement time	MTS/MTO/ETO
3. Percent orders received on time to required date	Number of orders received on time to required date by the focal firm divided by the total number of orders processed in measurement time	MTS/MTO/ETO
4. Percent Orders received with correct shipping document	Number of orders received with correct shipping document divided by the total number of orders processed in measurement time	MTS/MTO/ETO
5. Fill rate	The percentage of ship-from-stock orders shipped within 24 hours of order receipt by the supplier	MTS/MTO
6. Inventory accuracy	The absolute value of sum of the variance between physical inventory and perpetual inventory	MTS/MTO

Table 3. Supplier responsiveness metrics (adapted from Huang and Kesker, forthcoming)

Metrics	Definition	Configuration
1. Published delivery cycle time	Typical standard lead time after receipt of order currently published to focal firm by the supplier sales organization	MTS/MTO/ETO
2. Order fulfillment lead time	The average actual lead time achieved from order receipt by the supplier to component delivery and receipt by the focal firm	MTS/MTO/ETO
3. Return product velocity	Average time required by the supplier to process returned defective products and reshipping of the correct ordered components to the focal firm	MTS/MTO/ETO
4. Total build cycle	Total build time is the average time for make-to-stock or configure-to-order products from when production beings until product/component is shippable to the focal firm	MTS/MTO/ETO

Similarly, the concept *ActualPerformance* has the same set of SCOR performance measures as they appear as part of *ContractualPerformance* measure as shown in Figures 10 and 11 respectively. Having the same set of widely agreed performance measures in both the *ContractualPerformanceMetrics* and *ActualPerformanceMetrics* allow one to then compare how the *Supplier_Role*

Table 4. Supplier flexibility metrics (adapted from Huang and Kesker, forthcoming)

Metrics	Definition	Configuration
1. Time for expediting delivery and transfer process	Expediting cycle time for delivery and transfer process compared to standard cycle time	MTS/MTO/ETO
2. Upside production flexibility	Number of days required to achieve an unplanned sustainable 20% increase in orders	MTS/MTO/ETO
3. Upside delivery flexibility	Number of days required to achieve an unplanned sustainable 20% increase in deliveries	MTS/MTO/ETO
4. Upside shipment flexibility	Number of days required to achieve an unplanned sustainable 20% increase in shipments	MTS/MTO/ETO

Table 5. Supplier Cost and Financial Metrics (adapted from Huang and Kesker, forthcoming)

Metrics	Definition	Configuration
1. Order fulfillment cost	Total cost incurred by the focal firm in fulfilling order through the supplier	MTS/MTO/ETO
2. Inventory turns	Total cost of goods sold divided by value of inventory carried for components supplied by the supplier in the measurement period	MTS/MTO/ETO
3. Packaging cost	Total packaging cost associated with components delivered by the supplier	MTS/MTO/ETO
4.Inventory carrying cost	Inventory carrying cost associated with components delivered by the supplier	MTS/MTO/ETO

Table 6. Asset and infrastructure metrics (adapted from Huang and Kesker, forthcoming)

Metrics	Definition	Configuration
1. Inventory days of supply	Total gross value of inventory at standard cost	MTS/ETO
2. Designing capabilities	Capabilities regarding design of new components	MTS/MTO/ETO
3. Development capabilities	Capabilities regarding development of manufacturing processes for new component production	MTS/MTO/ETO
4. Customer concentration	Percentage share of sales from the supplier to the focal firm as compared to other buyers of the supplier	MTS/MTO/ETO
5. Quality system certification	Quality certification acquired by the supplier	MTS/MTO/ETO

Table 7. Safety metrics (adapted from Huang and Kesker, forthcoming)

Metrics	Definition	Configuration
1. Number of lost time accidents	Number of accidents per million working hours resulting in lost time	MTS/ETO/ETO
2. Dollars spent on worker compensation	Total dollar amount spent in worker compensation due to work related injury during the measurement period	MTS/MTO/ETO
3. Safety training	Safety training provided by the supplier	MTS/MTO/ETO

Table 8. Environmental metrics (adapted from Huang and Kesker, forthcoming)

Metrics	Definition	Configuration
1. Hazardous/non-hazardous waste	Average volume of hazardous/non-hazardous waste released per day during measurement period	MTS/ETO/ETO
2. Chemical releases	Average volume of chemical releases per day during measurement period	MTS/MTO/ETO
3. Global warming gases	Average volume of global warming gases (carbon dioxide and methane) released per day during measurement period	MTS/MTO/ETO

Figure 10. ContractualPerformanceMetrics and its properties in Protégé 3.3.1 based on SCOR performance measures (Huang and Kesker, Forthcoming) as part of supplier performance contract ontology

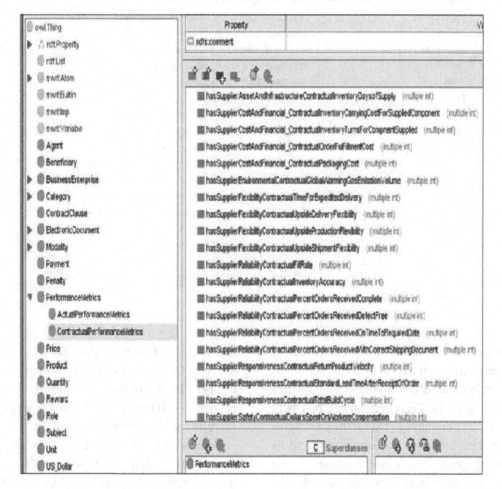

is performing in comparison to what was agreed to and what had actually transpired using the same set of measures. This allows minimization of confusion and reduces the barrier to communication with the suppliers (Prahinski & Benton, 2004) and to all contractual parties in terms of what

is contractually expected and how performance will be measured.

Obligation concept is subsumed by the concept of Modality in Figure 12. Additionally, it has three properties: *hasObligationViolationPenalty*, *hasSubject* and *hasBeneficiary*. If the *Supplier_Role*

Figure 11. ActualPerformanceMetrics and its properties in Protégé 3.3.1 based on SCOR performance metrics (Huang and Kesker, Forthcoming) as part of supplier performance contract ontology

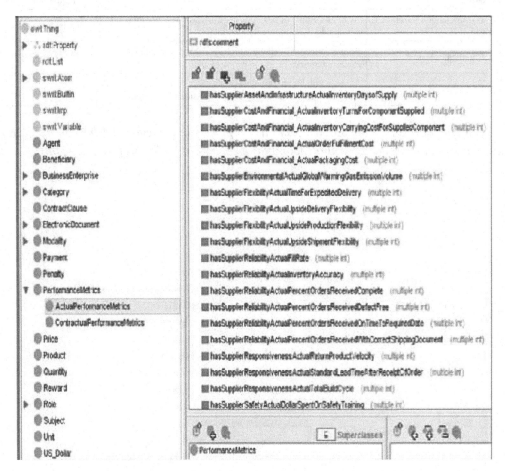

is found to be in violation of any contractually agreed performance measure then this condition will lead to violation of contractual obligation thus resulting in penalty. The violation can be easily determined by comparing value of the contractually agreed performance measure clause and its corresponding actual performance measure for the *Supplier_Role* enacted by a specific Individual of type *ContractedSupplierCompany*.

In our contract ontology we have the *Penalty* concept in Figure 13. The *Penalty* concept has the property *hasPenaltyValue,* which is a OWL DL *DatatypeProperty*.

In addition to *Penalty* concept, we have introduced the concept *ofReward*. The *Reward* concept

has the property *hasRewardValue* of type integer similar to *the hasPenaltyValue* property (see Figure 14). The idea of rewards or positive incentives is not new and have been used in the supply chain literature under various circumstances.

Here we present sample contract rules, based on our case study of an electronics manufacturer, and their corresponding representation in SWRL.

Contract Ontology Based SWRL Business Rules

Example Rule 1- If the Supplier Actual Performance in terms of Standard Lead Time in Hours *exceeds* the Supplier Contractual Performance in

Figure 12. Obligation concept in Protégé 3.3.1

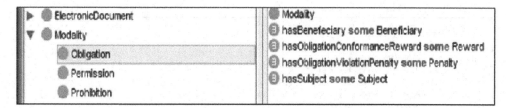

Figure 13.Penalty concept in Protégé 3.3.1

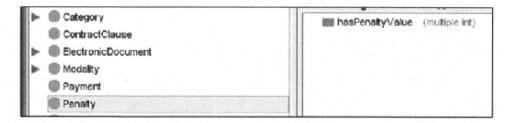

Figure 14. Reward concept in Protégé 3.3.1

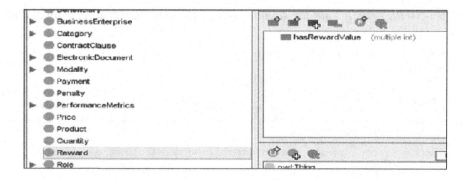

terms of Standard Lead Time then the Supplier will be deemed to be in violation of its Obligation to the Focal Firm and will be subject to the Penalty agreed to by the parties in the Contract (see Figure 15).

Example Rule 2- If the Supplier Actual Performance in terms of Standard Lead Time in Hours **does not** exceed the Supplier Contractual Performance in terms of Standard Lead Time then the Supplier will be deemed to be in conformance to its Obligation to the Focal Firm and will be subject to the Reward agreed to by the parties in the Contract (see Figure 16).

Example Rule 3- If the Supplier Actual Performance in terms of Order Fulfillment Cost in US Dollars *exceeds* the Supplier Contractual Performance in terms of Order Fulfillment Cost then the Supplier will deemed to be in violation of its Obligation to the Focal Firm and will be subject to the Penalty agreed to by the parties in the Contract (see Figure 17).

In the next section, we present the conceptual model of our Supplier Performance Contract Monitoring Execution DSS Architecture to illustrate the different components and their role in the Architecture.

Figure 15. Rule 1-SWRL penalty rule for supplier responsiveness standard lead time after receipt of order

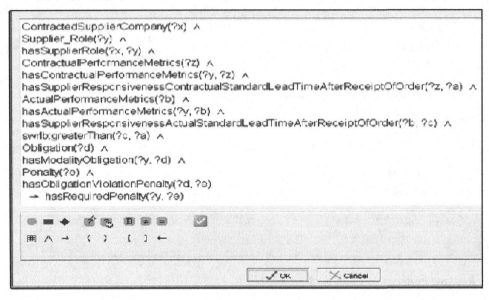

Figure 16. Rule1-SWRL penalty rule for supplier responsiveness standard lead time after receipt of order

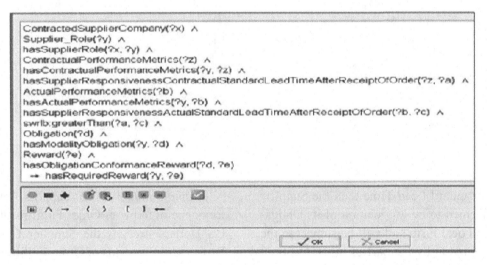

Conceptual Model of the Semantic DSS Execution Architecture

This supplier performance contract ontology including SWRL Rules is translated into Jess Rule Reasoner Representation (see Figure 18). Jess is an open source Java Expert System Shell, which has been successfully tested both with Protégé 3.3.1 and with SWRL for reasoning with OWL DL and SWRL knowledge base after translation through the OWLSWRLJess Translation Bridge API. The Rule Execution Engine then executes the contract rules based on the OWL DL concepts, roles and SWRL rules represented in the knowledge base. In this research, we use a single ontology expressing the contract concepts, roles

Figure 17. SWRL penalty rule for supplier order fulfillment cost

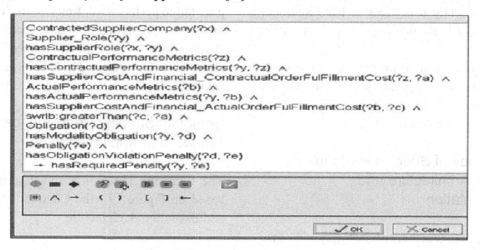

Figure 18. Conceptual architecture for supplier performance contract OWL knowledge base representation and execution

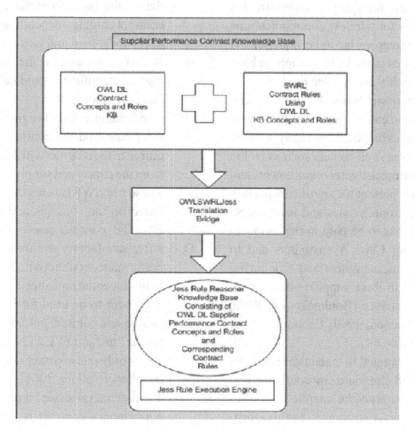

and conditions or rules using OWL DL and SWRL and subsequently using Jess as Rule Reasoner and Contract Execution Engine in the contract architecture.

In the next section, we present a case study and prototype implementation of the supplier performance contract monitoring and execution decision support architecture.

Case Study of Supplier Performance Contract Architecture and Implementation

In order to maintain the confidentiality of the firm utilized in the case illustration, it is referred to as AdvancedElectronix throughout the discussion. AdvancedElectronix designs, develops, manufactures and markets proprietary electronics integrated circuits for wireless communications applications. The company has its headquarter and fabrication facilities in the U. S. Its supplier base is located both within and outside the U.S.

AdvancedElectronix has selected reliability, responsiveness, and cost as the three supplier performance categories based on the widely adopted SCOR model. Class A customers such as Nokia and Ericsson have much tighter requirements and these customers represent the significant portion of AdvancedElectronix's sales and revenue. So special attention has to be paid to the suppliers of components for Class A customers and to the performance measurement and monitoring processes related to these suppliers thus ensuring contract compliance (Boulmakoul & Salle, 2002; Carr & Pearson, 1999; Chapman, 1989; Christopher, 1992).

The company wanted to standardize its contracting process to eliminate any confusion and miscommunication with the suppliers of components for its Class A customers. In this effort, the involved parties developed and agreed upon a set of performance criteria from the categories of responsiveness, reliability and cost (captured using the supplier performance contract ontology)

(Collins, Bilot & Mobasher, 2001). Should a supplier fail to perform over time in this dimension, the supply chain managers at AdvancedElectronix needs to be aware of that fact immediately on a real time basis and be able to take appropriate actions.

Semantic Supplier Performance DSS Architecture Implementation

The following illustration and description are based on Figure 19—the Contract Monitoring and Execution Architecture:

A. Protégé OWL Ontology Editor 3.3.1 to be used by the Semantic KB Designer for creating the initial user interface and select the required set of contract clauses from the contract ontology depending upon the need of the focal firm and its supplier.

B. RacerPro Reasoner is then used for checking the classification and coherency of the contract ontology.

C. The Semantic KB Designer then develops rules based on the contractual clauses required in the contract with the help and input from the concerned supply chain managers. These are SWRL rules that are composed based on the concepts and roles from the OWL DL contract ontology.

D. After satisfactory evaluation, the supplier performance contract ontology is then stored in the accepted repository. This is the OWL document to be used for instantiating any subsequent contract ontology instances using the Protégé-OWL API. The basic premise is that only one contract is used with all the suppliers (Nellore, 2004).

The user interface (see Figure 20) for supplier performance contract is generated by the OWLSupplierPerformanceContractAgent (see Figure 19) and presented to the Supply Chain Manager and the Supplier Representative as they negotiate the specific values of

Figure 19. Supplier performance semantic contract monitoring and execution architecture managed and hosted by the focal firm for the extended enterprise (EE) supply chain

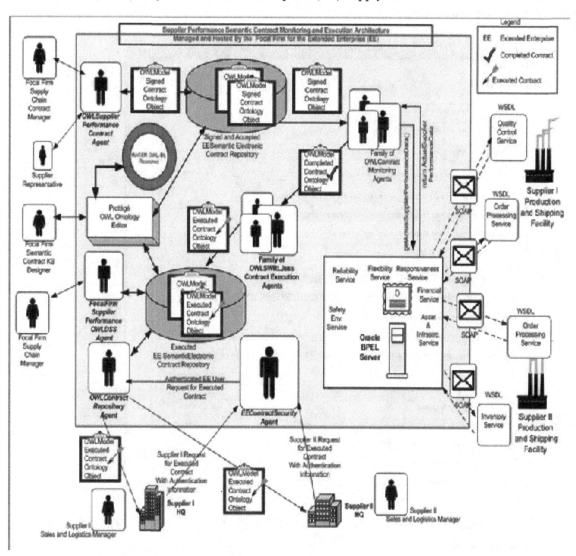

each the Contract Clause. This electronic contract is essentially an OWLModel object generated from the supplier performance contract OWL document. The parameter values entered in the electronic contract essentially set the contractual performance criteria that the parties to the contract are obligated to fulfill. These contractual clauses and corresponding values will be used later by the OWLSWRLJessContractExecution

Software Agents (Figure 19) for executing the contracts using the SWRL rules that apply to the specific contract for a specific supplier Individual.

E. After the values are properly entered and agreed by the parties involved, pressing of the submit contract for execution button on the contract GUI begins the monitoring and execution of this instance of the contract (Figure 20).

Figure 20. Supplier performance contract application user interface presented by the OWL contractagent to the supply chain manager and the supplier agent (human representative) for setting contractual values for each agreed clause

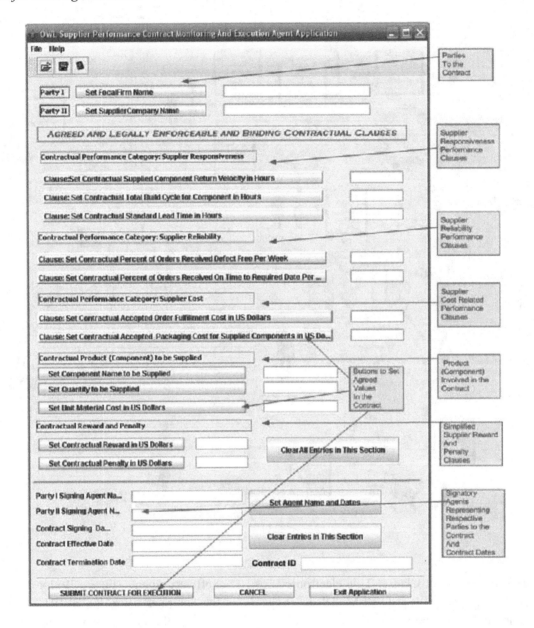

F.   At this stage, the OWLSupplierPerformanceContractAgent stores the OWLModel contract ontology object in the repository and notifies an available OWLContractMonitorningAgent to begin monitoring the contract instance (see Figure 19).

G.   At this stage, the OWLContractMonitorningAgent instantiates the contract based on the contract ID supplied by the OWLSupplierPerformanceContractAgent and invokes the specific Services such as Reliability Service or Cost Service or Responsiveness

Figure 21. SOA component of the semantic DSS architecture

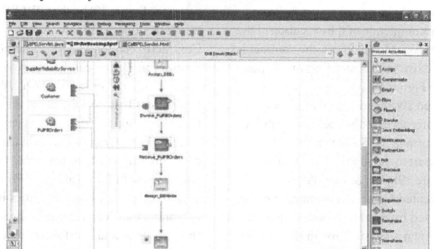

*Figure 22. ContractExecution agent uses the **executeContract** method to execute the **OWLModel com-pleteContract** as part of the contract monitoring and execution DSS architecture implementation*

```
57    public void executeContract( OWLModel completeContract, Rete ruleReasoner, SWRLJessBridge bridge)
58        throws SWRLJessBridgeException, SWRLRuleEngineBridgeException, JessException {
59
60            this.mycontractOntology=completeContract;
61            this.myruleReasoner=ruleReasoner;
62            this.mybridge=bridge;
63
64            mybridge.importSWRLRulesAndOWLKnowledge();
65            mybridge.exportSWRLRulesAndOWLKnowledge();
66            mybridge.resetRuleEngine();;
67            mybridge.runRuleEngine();
68
69    }// End of executeContract Method
```

Service to obtain the necessary actual performance values for the clauses that are part of the signed contract ontology instance. This part of the Architecture provides the connection through Web Services to both internal information systems from the focal firm or with external information systems of the supply partners (Singh & Huhns, 2005; Bouras, et al, 2007) (See Figures 19 and 21 for SOA Part of the Architecture on Oracle BPEL Server).

The OWLContractMonitorningAgent uses similar Java code snippet (see Figure 22) to invoke the Supplier Reliability Service and other similar Services hosted on the Oracle BPEL Server as shown in Figure 21.

H.   Once the OWLContractMonitorningAgent has all of the required parameters related to the actual performance of the supplier, the OWLContractMonitorningAgent then invokes the OWLSWRLJessContractExecution Software Agent and passes the OWLModel object of the completed contract.

I.   The OWLSWRLJessContractExecution Software Agent then executes the received OWLModel object using the executeContract Method as shown in the following Java code snippet.

J.   After the completion of the execution of the contract OWLModel object, the contract is then stored in the Executed Contract Repository (see Figure 19).

K.   The stored Executed Contract objects can then be later accessed by the FocalFirmSupplierPerformancDSS Agent to provide decision support to the supply chain manager(s) (see Figure 19) (Bui & Lee, 1999).

L.   The Executed Contract instances can also be accessed by contracted supply partners for their own analysis through the EEContractSecurityAgent and the OWLContractRepositoryAgent (see Figure 19).

Discussion and Decision Support Features of the Architecture

Once the contracts are executed, the instances of those contracts are stored in the EE Executed Electronic Contract Repository in the Architecture ((see Figure 19) by the OWLSWRLJessContractExecution Software Agent (from now on ContractExecutionAgent). These stored executed contract instances can be analyzed later by the FocalFirmSupplierPerformanceOWLDSSAgent (from now OWLDSSAgent) at the request of the Focal Firm Supply Chain Manager. In the Orders Received On-Time to Date Clause the supplier company HighTech is not doing so well when compared with TransLight (see Figure 23). HighTech has received seven Penalties in violation of its Contractual Performance Obligation by falling short in its Actual Performance in comparison with its Contractually Agreed Performance Obligation (SWRL Rules were used in this type of computation).

On the other hand, HighTech is fairly close in performance with TransLight on the Order Fulfillment Cost Clause (see Figure 24). Both companies received two and four Penalties and 21 and 22 Rewards in relation to their Obligation violation

Figure 23. Weekly report on supplier performance based on orders received on-time to date contract clause

Weekly Extended Enterprise Supplier Performance Report from OWLSuppPerfDSSAgent		
Product: RF Security Chip	Clause: Orders Received on Time to Date	
Supplier Name	HighTech	TransLight
Number of Reward	16	24
Number of Penalty	7	2

Figure 24. Weekly report of supplier performance based on order fulfillment cost contract clause

Weekly Extended Enterprise Supplier Performance Report from OWLSuppPerfDSSAgent		
Product: RF Security Chip	Clause: Order Fulfillment Cost	
Supplier Name	HighTech	TransLight
Number of Reward	21	22
Number of Penalty	2	4

and Obligation Conformance respectively. It is clear that if this trend continues for HighTech then the Focal Firm AdvancedElectronix will have to take some remedial measures as supplier improvement program (Prahinski & Benton, 2004) with HighTech.

Our Contract Architecture has these important features that make it truly an Extended Enterprise Architecture for Decision Support (Karacapilidis & Moraitis, 2001; Krishna, et al, 2004). For example, individual suppliers such as HighTech and TransLight can view their own executed contract instances and can perform their own analysis (Krause, 1997) (see Figures 19 and 25).

Each supplier can request their own aggregate performance report in comparison with other suppliers that supply the same components to the Focal Firm. Figure 25 shows such a report for HighTech generated by the OWLDSSAgent.

CONCLUSION AND FUTURE RESEARCH DIRECTIONS

The integrated decision support illustrated in this research is meaningful because all of the reports related to performances are generated on the basis of agreed and signed contracts using a single agreed upon supplier performance contract ontology for the extended enterprise. This contract ontology provides the foundation for efficient and effective real-time communication between differ-

ent partners in the extended enterprise (Prahinski & Benton, 2004; Bouras, et al, 2007). These are unique features and contributions of this research and of this contract architecture.

In this research, we have adopted a single contract ontology for all of the supply partners. That is, there is one single contract for all of the suppliers. This is not an impractical assumption or application since there are companies that use a single contract for all of their suppliers (Nellore, 2004; Liu, Chen, Liu, & Zhang, 2006). But this limitation needs to be addressed to allow the architecture to incorporate companies that may use different contracts for different suppliers to implement their corporate strategy and policy.

ACKNOWLEDGMENT

The author would like to thank the Editor and the anonymous reviewers for their effort in reviewing this manuscript. This research was partially supported by the UNCG Summer Research Excellence Award 2007.

REFERENCES

Antoniou, G., & Bikakis, A. (2007). DR-Prolog: A system for defeasible reasoning with Rules and ontologies on the Semantic Web. *IEEE Transac-*

Figure 25. Report comparing performance of supplier hightech with another supplier a based on orders received on-time to date contract clause

Weekly Extended Enterprise Supplier Performance Report from OWLSuppPerfDSSAgent		
Product: RF Security Chip	Clause: Orders Received on Time to Date	Extended Enterprise Supplier Comparison
Supplier Name	HighTech	A
Number of Reward	16	24
Number of Penalty	7	2

tions on Knowledge and Data Engineering. *19*(2), 233-245.

Baader, F., Calvanese, D., McGuinness, D., Nardi, D., & Patel-Schneider, P. F., Eds. (2003). *The Description Logic Handbook: Theory, Implementation and Applications*. Cambridge: Cambridge University Press.

Bititci, U. S., and Mendibil, K., Martinez, V., & Albores, P. (2005). Measuring and managing performance in extended enterprises. *International Journal of Operations & Production Management, 25*(4), 333-353.

Boella, G., & Torre, L. (2006). An architecture of a normative system. *AAMAS 2006*, 229-231.

Borgida, A. (1995). Description logics in data management. *IEEE Transactions on Knowledge and Data Engineering, 7*(5), 671–682.

Borgida, A., & Patel-Schneider, P. F. (1994). A semantics and complete algorithm for subsumption in the CLASSIC description logic. *Journal of Artificial Intelligence Research, 1,* 277–308.

Boulmakoul, A., & Salle, M. (2002). Integrated contract management. Online access: http://www.hp.com

Bouras, A., Gouvas, P., & Mentzas, G. (2007). *A semantic service-oriented architecture for business process fusion in semantic web technologies and e-business*. Salam & Stevens (Eds.), London: Idea Group Publishing.

Brachman, R., & Levesque, H. (2004). *Knowledge representation and reasoning*. New York: Morgan Kaufmann.

Bui, L., & Lee, J. (1999). An agent-based framework for building decision support systems. *Decision Support System, 25*(3), 225-237.

Carr, A. S., & Pearson, J. N. (1999). Strategically managed buyer–supplier relationships and performance outcomes. *Journal of Operations Management 17*(5), 497–519.

Chapman, S. N. (1989). Just-in-time supplier inventory: An empirical implementation model. *International Journal of Production Research, 27*(12), 1993-2007.

Chopra, S., & Meindl, P. (2003). *Supply chain management: Strategy, planning, and operation, second ed.* New Jersey: Prentice-Hall.

Christopher, M. (1992). *Logistics and supply chain management: Strategies for reducing costs and improving services*. Financial Times/ Prentice Hall.

Collins, J., Bilot, C., & Mobasher, B. (2001). Decision processes in agent-based automated contracting. *IEEE Internet Computing, 5*(2), 61-72.

Dyer, J. (2000). *Collaborative advantage: Winning through extended enterprise supplier networks*. New York: Oxford University Press.

Ellram, L. M. (1990). The supplier selection decision in strategic partnerships. *Journal of Purchasing and Materials Management, 26*(4), 8–14.

Farrugia, J. (2003). *Model-theoretic semantics for the Web*. May 20-24, 2003, Budapest, Hungary. 29-38. Online access: http://www.ra.ethz.ch/CDstore/www2003/papers/refereed/p277/p277-farrugia.html.

Fawcett, S. E., Stanley, L. L., & Smith, S. R. (1997). Developing a logistics capability to improve the performance of international operations. *Journal of Business Logistics, 18*(2), 101–1 27.

Frazelle, E. (2002). *Supply chain strategy*. New York: McGraw-Hill.

Governatori, G. (2004). Defeasible description logics. *LNCS 3323*, 98-112.

Governatori, G. (2005). Representing business contracts in RuleML. *International Jounal of Cooperative Information Systems, 14*(2-3), 181-216.

Governatori, G., & Hoang, D. (2005). A semantic web based architecture for e-contracts in defeasible logic. *LNCS 3791,* 145-159.

Governatori, G., & Milosevic, Z. (2006). A formal analysis of a business contract language. *International Journal of Cooperative Information Systems,* 1-26.

Governatori, G., Milosevic, Z., & Sadiq, S. (2006). Compliance checking between business processes and business contracts. *EDOC 2006,* 221-232.

Grosof, B. (2004). Representing e-commerce rules via situated courteous logic programs in RuleML. *Electronic Commerce Research and Applications, 3*(1), 2-20.

Grosof, B., & Poon, T. (2004). SweetDeal: Representing agent contracts with exceptions using semantic web rules, ontologies and process descriptions. *International Journal of Electronic Commerce, 8*(4), 61.

Grosof, B., Volz, R., Horrocks, I., & Decker, S. (2003). *Description logic programs: Combining logic programs with description logic.* May 20-24 2003, Budapest, Hungary. 48-57. Online access: http://www.cs.man.ac.uk/~horrocks/Publications/download/2003/p117-grosof.pdf

Guarino, N. (1995). Formal ontology, conceptual analysis and knowledge representation. *International Journal of Human-Computer Studies, 43,* 625-640.

Horrocks, I., Patel-Schneider, P., Bechhofer, S., & Tsarkov, D. (2005). OWL rules: A proposal and prototype implementation. *Journal of Web Semantics, 3,* 23-40.

Horrocks, I., Patel-Schneider, P., & Harmalen, F. (2003). From SHIQ to RDF to OWL: The making of a Web Ontology Language. *Journal of Web Semantics, 1*(1), 7-26.

Huang, S., & Keskar, H. (Forthcoming). Comprehensive and configurable metrics for supplier selection. *International Journal of Production Economics.*

Hult, G., Ketchen, D., & Slater, S. (2004). Information processing, knowledge development, and strategic supply chain performance. *Academy of Management Journal, 47*(2), 241-253.

Karacapilidis, N., & Moraitis, P. (2001). Building an agent-mediated electronic commerce system with decision analysis features. *Decision Support Systems, 32,* 53–69.

Krause, D. R. (1997). Supplier development: current practices and outcomes. *International Journal of Purchasing and Materials Management 33*(2), 12–19.

Krishna, P., Karlapalem, K., & Chiu, D. (2004). An ER^{EC} framework for e-contract modeling, enactment and monitoring. *Data & Knowledge Engineering, 51,* 31-58.

Lambert, D., & Pohlen, T. (2001). Supply chain metrics. *The International Journal of Logistics Management, 12*(1), 1-19.

Linington, F., Milosevic, Z., Cole, J., Gibson, S., Kulkarni, S., & Neal, S. (2004). A unified behavioral model and a contract language for extended enterprise. *Data & Knowledge Engineering, 51*(1), 5-29.

Liu, B., Chen, J., Liu, S., & Zhang, R. (2006). Supply-chain coordination with combined contract for a short life-cycle product. *IEEE Transactions on Systems, Man and Cybernetics-Part A, Vol. 36*(1), 53-61.

Lockamy III, A. (2004). Linking SCOR planning practices to supply chain performance: An exploratory study. *International Journal of Operations & Production Management, 24*(12), 1191-1218.

Metzinger, T., & Gallese, V. (2003). The emergence of a share action ontology: Building blocks for a theory. *Conciousness and Cognition, 12*(4), 549-571.

Murthy, V., & Krishnamurthy, E. (2005). Contextual information management using contract-based workflow. *Conference on Computing Frontiers*, May 4-6, 2005, Ischia, Italy, 236-245.

Nellore, R. (2004). Validating specifications: A contract-based approach. *IEEE Transactions on Engineering Management, 48*(4), 491-504.

Pan, J., & Horrocks, I. (2007). RDFS(FA): Connecting RDF(S) and OWL DL. *IEEE Transactions on Knowledge and Data Engineering, 19*(2), 192-206.

Petroni, A., & M. Braglia. (2000). Vendor selection using principal component analysis. *The Journal of Supply Chain Management, 36*(2), 63-69.

Prahinski, C., & Benton, W. (2004). Supplier evaluations: communication strategies to improve suppler performance. *Journal of Operations Management, 22*(1), 39-62.

Protégé. Protégé-OWL API Programmer's Guide. Online access: http://protege.stanford.edu/plugins/owl/api/guide.html

Rolstadås, A. (1998). Enterprise performance measurement. *International Journal of Operations & Production Management, 18*(9/10), 989-999.

Singh, M., & Huhns, M. (2005). *Service-oriented computing: Semantics, processes, agents*. San Francisco: Wiley.

Singh, R., & Salam, A. F. (2006). Semantic information assurance for secure knowledge management: A business process perspective. *IEEE Transactions on Systems, Man and Cybernetics Part (A),36*(3), 472-486.

Udupi, Y., & Singh M. (2006). Contract enactment in virtual organizations: A commitment-based approach. *American Association for Artificial Intelligence (AAAI)*, Online access: http://www.aaai.org.

Verma, R., & Pullman M. E. (1998). An analysis of the supplier selection process. *Omega, 26*(6), 739-750.

Wang, G., Huang, S. H., & Dismukes, J. P. (2004). Product driven supply chain selection using integrated multi-criteria decision making methodology. *International Journal of Production Economics, 91*(1), 1–15.

Weigand, H., & Heuvel, W. (2002). Cross-organizational workflow integration using contracts. *Decision Support Systems, 33*(3), 247-265.

Welty, C., & Guarino, N. (2001). Supporting ontological analysis of taxonomic relationships. *Data & Knowledge Engineering, 39*, 51-74.

This work was previously published in the International Journal of Intelligent Information Technologies, Vol. 4, Issue 3, edited by V. Sugumaran, pp. 1-26, copyright 2008 by IGI Publishing (an imprint of IGI Global).

Chapter 13
Supporting Structured Group Decision Making through System-Directed User Guidance:
An Experimental Study

Harold J. Lagroue III
University of Louisiana - Lafayette, USA

ABSTRACT

This article addresses an area which holds considerable promise for enhancing the effective utilization of advanced information technologies: the feasibility of using system-directed multi-modal user support for facilitating users of advanced information technologies. An application for automating the information technology facilitation process is used to compare group decision-making effectiveness of human-facilitated groups with groups using virtual facilitation in an experiment employing auditors, accountants, and IT security professionals as participants. The results of the experiment are presented and possible avenues for future research studies are suggested.

INTRODUCTION

Intelligent information technologies have demonstrated considerable potential in helping users more effectively utilize advanced IT applications. Indeed, their widespread use as components of help functions in software applications has made the appropriation process for such software considerably less taxing. On a more complex level, expert systems and other "advice-giving intelligent systems" have proven to be effective in such diverse fields as medicine and finance. Their potential as "explanation facilities" for assisting users in meaningful ways is well documented (Berry & Broadbent 1987; Shortliffe, 1976).

Several researchers have argued that intelligent systems may be the most significant technical contribution to the effective utilization of information technology (Crowston & Malone 1988, Johansen 1988). In the context of group decision making, a number of researchers have claimed that expert systems may hold the potential of transforming group decision support systems (GDSS) from merely "passive agents" that process and present group decision-making information, into "active agents" that enhance group interaction (Aiken, Liu Sheng, & Vogel, 1991, Ellis et al. 1988, Liu Sheng et al. 1989). Aiken, Liu Sheng and Vogel (1991) have asserted that the goal of integrating expert systems with group decision support systems should be in designing systems that facilitate simplified and enhanced group decision-making.

A number of research studies have demonstrated that system-directed user guidance holds the potential of replacing human facilitation for supporting group decision making. Limayem and DeSanctis (2000) found that automated facilitation could result in higher levels of understanding and improved perceptions of the group decision making process. In a follow-up study, Limayem (2003) compared human facilitation with automated facilitation and found that the latter was as effective as human facilitation in improving faithfulness of appropriation.

Wong and Aiken (2003) likewise demonstrated that automated facilitation could be as effective as expert facilitators—and better than novice-human facilitators—for idea generation and ranking tasks. However, their study did not consider the effect of using automated facilitation for providing structured decision-making support, or for affecting satisfaction levels of participants. Likewise, Ho and Antunes (1999) examined the effectiveness of an automated tool for meeting planning, but their results were inconclusive. Chalidabhongse et al. (2002) similarly studied the effects of an intelligent facilitation agent and found that their automated system resulted in greater group participation, more ideas generated, and less group distraction. However, the effects of automated facilitation on intellective tasks were not considered.

Still other studies have proposed integrating expert systems with group support systems but have not empirically tested the effectiveness of such systems. Aiken, Liu Sheng and Vogel (1991) examined potential synergies between intelligent systems and GSS and described a system which would effectively integrate the two technologies, but they did not empirically evaluate their system. Lopez et al. (2002) proposed the possibility of embedding facilitation features in group support systems, but likewise, no empirical study was conducted. Recently, Briggs, DeVreede and Nunamaker (2003) introduced their "thinkLets" concept designed to help systemize the GSS facilitation process, but did not empirically test it.

Because qualified facilitators are not always available or affordable, the need for automated systems that are capable of effectively replicating the human facilitator function is apparent. Moreover, by systemizing the facilitation process and ensuring its consistent replication, the benefits from advanced information technology use can be more predictable (Briggs et al. 2003).

This research addresses an area which holds considerable promise for enhancing the effective utilization of advanced information technologies: the feasibility of using system-directed guidance for facilitating users of advanced information technologies. An application for automating the information technology facilitation process is used to compare decision-making effectiveness of human-facilitated groups with groups using system-directed facilitation in an experiment employing auditors, accountants, and IT security professionals as participants. Comparisons of the two methods of facilitation are made on the basis of brainstorming effectiveness and user satisfaction.

DECISIONAL GUIDANCE

Directly related to the idea of system-directed facilitation is the concept of decisional guidance, or how decision support systems "enlighten or sway users as they structure and execute their decision-making processes" (Silver 1991). As such, decisional guidance can be thought of as one way in which the technology appropriation process is expedited to fully exploit a decision support system's functional capabilities: "Just as a DSS (decision support system) supports the judgments required enroute to making decisions, decisional guidance can support the judgments required in the course of operating the DSS" (Silver 1991, p.106).

The concept of decisional guidance for computer-based decision support was first advanced by Silver (1991) in his explanation of *when and why* decisional guidance should be provided, *how* system designers can build decisional guidance into DSS, and what the *effects* of providing it are. Limayem (1992) defined guidance in a GSS context as "the enrichment of decision models with cues that direct decision makers toward successful structuring and execution of model components." As such, guidance can inform groups as to what to do next (forward guidance), help groups resolve problems from prior activities (backward guidance), or in the case of preventive guidance, prevent disruptions that obstruct progress in group decision-making (Limayem 1992).

Silver asserts that decisional guidance should be provided when users need to make *discretionary judgments*, which is dependent upon how much discretion the system allows its user. Likewise, the decision to provide decisional guidance is primarily based on a desire to create a DSS that is more supportive and that assists users in exercising their judgment as they interact with the decision support system. Thus, the need for decisional guidance is dependent upon both the complexity of the DSS system, as well as the users' perceptions of the decision-making task.

The decision to provide user guidance, however, must be weighed against the possibility of overloading users with information, or in fact making the system more complex with an exces-sive amount of guidance mechanisms. Moreover, the guidance system should avoid directing users to a specific decision, but should instead attempt to influence how users reach a decision (Silver, 1991, pp. 108-109)

DSS design features can be structured to either directly influence how decisions should be made (directed change) or to provide users with a number of alternative capabilities from which to choose in their decision-making activities (non-directed change). A number of design strategies exist for doing so, ranging from highly restrictive DSS, to minimally restrictive DSS. In his earlier study on directed and non-directed change, Silver (1991) presents a broad set of objectives for determining the appropriate level of system restrictiveness.

While Silver established the primary framework for assessing the effectiveness of decisional guidance, he did not empirically examine the efficacy of providing it. Parikh, Fazlollahi, and Verma (2001) conducted an empirical evaluation of the effectiveness of various forms of decisional guidance in four areas: decision quality, user satisfaction, user learning, and decision-making efficiency. The study found that deliberate decisional guidance was more effective in all four areas. Suggestive guidance was found to be more effective in improving decision quality as well as user satisfaction, while informative guidance was determined to be more effective in improving user learning.

EXPERT SYSTEMS

Broadly related to the concept of decisional guidance is the functionality of expert systems, in that each is designed to guide IT users in some fashion. However, while decisional guidance relates to how systems "enlighten or sway" users as they utilize decision support systems (Silver, 1991), expert systems are designed to simulate human experts within a specific domain. As such, expert systems are artificial intelligence tools that support decision making by using a knowledge base and inference techniques. While decisional guidance can provide procedures explaining how to solve problems and why a certain solution is recommended in order to assist groups in their decision-making processes, expert systems attempt to replicate a human adviser (e.g., a group facilitator) and, if effective, can potentially replace them.

Turban and Watson (1986) examined various issues relating to integrating decision support systems and expert systems (ES), and presented two frameworks for integrating DSS and expert systems: ES integration into DSS components; and ES as an additional component of a decision support system. Among the benefits resulting from combining expert systems and decision support systems, are the following, as summarized by Turban and Watson:

- Assistance in selecting decision models
- Providing judgmental elements to models
- Providing heuristics
- Providing explanations
- Providing terms familiar to user
- Acting as a tutor
- Providing intelligent advice
- Adding explanation capabilities
- Expanding computerization of the decision-making process (Turban and Watson. p.124)

By replicating the manager-consultant-computer process, as advocated by Goul and Tonge (1987), an integrated DSS/ES can be designed to query users to determine the general category of a problem, the exact nature of a problem, and finally, suggest an appropriate model for solving the problem. By using expert systems as "consultants" to determine what to do in specific problem-solving situations, the complexity of using GDSS for group decision-making activities can be significantly reduced. Similar applications of integrating DSS and expert systems can include

the provision of explanation capabilities to the DSS that allow users to follow the reasoning behind specific recommendations. By using terms that are familiar to the user as well as by providing tutoring to users, such integrated systems can significantly reduce the cognitive load placed on users of GDSS.

Also related to the concept of decisional guidance and expert systems is the concept of cognitive feedback, or feedback about an individual or collective decision-making process which is "provided interactively as an integral part of the individual and group processes" (Sengupta & Te'eni, 1993). In their study investigating cognitive feedback for improving control and convergence in computer supported group decision-making, cognitive feedback was found to increase cognitive control, resulting in uniformly high levels of cognitive control over time. Additionally, cognitive feedback was found to result in increased levels and degrees of collective control for group decision making. As hypothesized, groups receiving cognitive feedback were found to formulate group decision rules more frequently than groups not receiving cognitive feedback.

Dhaliwal and Benbasat (1996) proposed a model based on cognitive learning theories explaining the reasons and theoretical basis for providing system explanations for facilitating user learning, and a two-part framework and for examining the use of knowledge-based system (KBS) explanations.

Hayes and Reddy (1983) assert that explanations are needed for three principal reasons: explanations *clarify* particular intentions; explanations are intended to *teach*; and explanations are used to *convince*. Although clarifying, teaching and convincing can indeed increase the understanding of information systems users receiving the explanations, the question of whether such explanations actually result in better decision-making remains unclear (Dhaliwal & Benbasat, 1996, p.345).

Dhaliwal and Benbasat contend that only *task information* is effective in promoting learning, and, as such, it forms the "coherent theoretical basis" for the various types of explanations that KBS should provide, including the "explanations provision model" they propose. Moreover, the authors contend that three possible *explanation provision strategies* exist for designing knowledge-based systems: feedforward only, feedback only, or both feedforward and feedback.

Dhaliwal and Benbasat used MYCIN, one of the earliest expert systems developed in the early 1970s at Stanford University, to illustrate the use of feedforward and feedback explanations. For example, "why" explanations in MYCIN were feedforward and presented information explaining why a particular question was being asked of a user. "How" explanations provided information regarding the basis on which a specific conclusion was reached. Although no strategic explanations were provided by MYCIN, later versions (NEOMYCIN) provided such explanations using a combination of feedforward and feedback (Dhaliwal & Benbasat, 1996, p.352).

The automated facilitation application used in the present research provides various feedforward and feedback explanations designed to explain *why* a group decision-making procedure and/ or GSS tool is being used and *how* the previous decision-making activity has influenced the current activity and/or GSS tool. As predicted in the system-directed facilitation model presented in the following, the provision of such explanations should lead to improved user understanding of the decision-making process, resulting in improved user satisfaction, in comparison to groups not receiving such explanations.

As discussed more fully later, the system-directed facilitation application provides explanations to participants who lack significant knowledge regarding the GSS system and the group decision-making processes employed in the experiment. Likewise, by virtue of their audio-based delivery, provision of the explanations is designed to require minimum cognitive effort to assess and assimilate.

FACILITATION

Also broadly related to the concept of decisional guidance is what Dickson, Partridge, and Robinson (1993) originally termed facilitative support, or "the manner in which GDSS users are supported in their utilization of group decision support systems." While decisional guidance is primarily related to how inanimate decision support systems (DSS) advise users as they execute the decision-making processes, facilitative support, and the more general term "facilitation," generally refers to the use of "facilitators" whose function is to direct group members regarding which GDSS features to use, as well as when to use them (Dickson et al., p.173).

Keltner (1990) proposed that the facilitator function is to ensure that all group members are able to fully participate in the decision-making process, and that the process is not dominated by a minority of group members. Ackermann (1990) asserted that external facilitators could help support cognitive processing by providing the group a structure in which to operate. As such, he believed that facilitators could enable the group to match specific modeling techniques to assigned group tasks more easily. Eden, Jones, and Sims (1983) believed that external facilitators could be used to improve a group's cognitive judgment by encouraging discussion of differences in group members' perspectives, reviewing the objectives of a particular task, and identifying inconsistencies among group members' perspectives. Kayser (1990) proposed that facilitators could help the group "free itself from internal obstacles or difficulties so that they more efficiently the effectively pursue the achievement of its desired outcomes (p.12-13).

In an early study of group facilitation, George, Dennis, and Nunamaker (1992) compared facilitated and non-facilitated groups using electronic meeting systems and found no significant differences between the groups in terms of alternatives generated, decision quality, satisfaction levels, or ability to reach consensus.

Anson, Bostrom and Wynne (1995) investigated the effects of human facilitation on group performance, group cohesion, and group interaction processes in group decision-making situations. Their study found that facilitated groups achieved improvements in group performance, interaction processes and group cohesion levels. Moreover, facilitation combined with GSS utilization, were found to enhance the effectiveness of group cohesion and group decision making processes. As such, facilitation was deemed critical in improving GSS effectiveness, especially for first-time users, and in situations where less restrictive GSS tools are used. Moreover, the quality of facilitation is believed to be a significant factor in improving group decision-making outcomes. Indeed, facilitators lacking proper skills may have minimal effects on improving outcomes.

Griffith et al. (1998) describe the facilitator's role as one of "improving a group's communication and information flow…to enhance the manner in which a group makes decisions without making those decisions *for* the group" (p.20). Nunamaker et al. (1997) list four functions normally provided by GSS meeting facilitators:

1. Providing technical support by initiating and terminating specific software tools and functions and guiding the group through the technical aspects necessary to work on the task.
2. Chairing the meeting, maintaining the agenda, and assessing the need for agenda changes.
3. Working with the group to highlight the principal meeting objectives and developing an agenda to accomplish them
4. Providing organizational continuity by setting ground rules for interaction, enforcing protocols and norms, maintaining the group memory repository, and acting as champion/sponsor (p.192-193).

The system-directed facilitation application used in the present study is designed to provide these four facilitator functions in providing GSS fit and appropriation support. As described more fully in the following section, the application is envisioned to provide technical support by offering a simplified tool selection interface, maintaining the agenda, highlighting principal meeting objectives, setting initial ground rules for interaction, and enforcing protocols through both audio and visual messaging.

As previously noted, Limayem and DeSanctis and others (Briggs, De Vreede & Nunamaker, 2003; Chalidabhongse et al. 2002; Ho & Antunes 1999; Lopez et al., 2002; Nunamaker & Zhao 2002; Wong & Aiken 2003) have expanded the concept of facilitation to include the use of "automated facilitation mechanisms" and "intelligent facilitation agents." Indeed, the terms "decisional guidance" and "automated facilitation" are sometimes used interchangeably to describe such software-directed group support and intervention mechanisms (e.g., Limayem, 2003; Limayem & DeSanctis, 2000).

In a survey of 45 experienced GSS facilitators, Bostrom et al. (1996) found that planning and designing a meeting agenda was significantly more important than all other facilitator functions. Other significant contributions of facilitators included matching GSS tools to the assigned task, adapting the meeting agenda is needed, clarifying meeting goals and agenda items; remaining focused on the outcome; and creating an open environment for anticipation. Traditional facilitator functions relating to managing group dynamics, such as building rapport and managing conflict were found to be significantly less important facilitator functions. The system-directed facilitation application used in the present study focuses primarily on planning and directing the meeting agenda, derived principally from Wheeler and Valacich's (1996) multiple activity group decision making heuristic.

In his definitive work on facilitators and their role in developing group effectiveness, Schwarz (1994) describes how facilitators can help improve the way that groups identify and solve problems and make better decisions by improving the manner in which group members work together. As he explains, facilitators can assume one of two roles. In basic facilitation, the facilitator guides the group in reaching an effective decision using the appropriate group process. In developmental facilitation, the facilitator teaches group members how to carry out specific processes for future problem-solving:

Schwarz's approach to facilitation is based on three values: "valid information, free and informed choice, and internal commitment to those choices" (1994, p.8). As opposed to changing group members' behaviors, he argues that the role of facilitators is to provide information to enable group members to decide *whether* to change their behavior, and if they choose to do so, to help them learn *how* to change (p.8). Schwarz asserts that for groups to become more effective, facilitators need to understand which factors contribute to group effectiveness, which factors detract from it, and how such factors can interact, in impacting group effectiveness, using a model built largely on the work of Hackman (1987) and Sundstrom, DeMeuse and Futrell (1990).

While Schwarz does not directly address the role the facilitator in the context of group support systems, his intimate knowledge of the group facilitation process, including his considerable experience in facilitating a number of diverse groups, offers valuable insights into the successful integration of group facilitation theory and practice.

Because the manner in which group members are facilitated during their utilization of a GDSS will have a "profound effect" on the outcome of GDSS use (Dickson et al., p.174) the most effective mode of providing GSS support is of critical importance. Specifically, the need for GDSS facilitation arises from two problems that must

be addressed for groups using a GDSS system for the first time, namely:

1. GDSS users must "overcome the mystique" of using a new and unknown technology,
2. "A sound problem-solving process" used by the group in its GDSS interaction, including the application of the GDSS technology, must be provided (Dickson et al., p. 174).

As discussed in the following section, the automated virtual facilitation application was designed to provide task facilitative support, focusing primarily on which GSS tools to use, in addition to when and how to use them. The research framework is designed to evaluate the effectiveness of groups having such facilitation, in comparison to groups having operational facilitative support (chauffer-driven support) only.

Such "chauffer-driven" support is similar in nature to what Maier (1952) described as *free discussion* techniques, in which a leader poses a problem, then conducts the group discussion "in a permissive manner without making value judgments, but merely helps the group reach agreement on a solution" (p. 320). In comparison, the *developmental* technique for group discussion involves a leader who "breaks the problem into parts so that each part of the problem is discussed separately before the final decision is made" (Dickson, et al, p. 180). Maier found that the "developmental" approach was more effective than the "free" discussion approach in improving decision quality. In contrast, DeSanctis, D'Onofrio, Sambamurthy, and Poole (1989) found that restrictiveness did not lead to improved group consensus, and that excessive restrictiveness may indeed result in groups losing their "sense of ownership and control over the technology," resulting in lower levels of consensus.

As more fully described in the following section, the virtual facilitation application attempts to maintain the meeting agenda without being overly restrictive by requiring all group members to proceed to the next step in the multi-step decision-making process, thus granting each group member a veto power on proceeding to the next step in order to foster a more democratic decision-making process and one which helps ensure greater equality of participation.

METHODOLOGY

The present study examines the effectiveness of system-directed facilitation for supporting structured group decision making through an experiment involving internal auditors, information systems auditors, CPAs, and IT security professionals as participants. Specifically, system-facilitated teams using group decision support systems are compared to human-facilitated teams using GDSS in four areas of decision-making effectiveness: number of problems identified, number of solutions recommended, satisfaction with the decision-making process, and satisfaction with the decision-making outcome).

The number of problems identified and solutions recommended (Hypotheses 1 and 2) was determined by the number of such items submitted by each group for problem identification and solution recommendations. Scores for satisfaction with the meeting process and meeting outcome were calculated by adding the individual item Likert scores in the Briggs et al., (2003) post-session questionnaire, contained in Appendix A.

To distribute unique information among team members, a hidden-profile task was used. Hidden-profile tasks are believed to more accurately simulate real world situations in which relevant information for completing a task is known only by specific group members. In addition, a hidden-profile task does not state the specific problem for the group to solve, as is common with many tasks used in experimental research (Wheeler & Valacich, 1996, p.438).

A hidden-profile task requires all group members to participate and share information in order for the group to identify the pertinent problems and to develop a feasible solution. In a manner similar to the "School of Business Policy Task" used by Wheeler and Mennecke (1992), group members in the current study were required to identify as many IT security-related problems as possible, and to formulate as many recommendations as possible to address those problems. Different information is provided in each of the three case study roles, requiring effective information sharing among team members to successfully complete the assigned tasks.

Participants

Participants in the current study consisted of accountants, auditors, and IT security professionals in government, industry, and public practice, including CPAs, CIAs (certified internal auditors) and CISAs (certified information systems

Table 1. Summary of participants by occupation

Occupation	Percentage of Total Participants
Certified Public Accountants	28%
Certified Internal Auditors/Internal Auditors	48%
IT Security Personnel	12%
Corporate Accountants and Controllers	12%

auditors). Participants received eight hours of continuing professional education (CPE) credit for attending a free day-long seminar entitled "Using COBIT for Complying with the Sarbanes-Oxley Section 404 Provisions" which was designed to cover many of the same IT security issues and information systems control objectives that were pertinent to developing appropriate recommendations for the assigned hidden profile task described in the previous section.

Procedures

In order to balance each set of teams on the basis of information systems audit expertise, participants were assigned to treatment groups based upon their level of previous IS audit experience, as reported during the registration period prior to the seminars. Participants were then randomly assigned to one of the three auditor roles of the hypothetical three-person audit team employed to investigate IT security issues.

Treatment group assignment was based upon the day the seminar was conducted (the first day of the seminars tested GSS-supported groups and the subsequent day tested unsupported groups). After participants were assigned to groups and then randomly assigned to one of the three auditor roles, each day's participants were read an identical series of introductory remarks, and were then read a series of instructions specifically tailored to

each treatment group. They were then each given a specific version of the IT policy case based upon their audit team role

Human facilitated groups were instructed to complete their assigned group decision-making tasks using a prescribed agenda adapted from a group decision-making heuristic by Schwarz (1994) and consisting of problem identification, problem rating, problem drafting, solution brainstorming, solution rating, and solution drafting. Participants were also presented the normal introductory information regarding the GSS software that is typically given to participants before beginning their use of the GSS application.

System-facilitated groups were instructed on the required procedures before beginning the experiment. Participants were informed as to how the automated virtual facilitation application is used (see AVFA section), including the process of clicking an agenda item's hyperlink to hear that agenda item's instructions and subsequently completing the assigned tasks that were explained in the pre-recorded instructions. AVFA-supported groups were also informed that they would not be allowed to ask researchers or other groups for assistance, and that any problems that might occur would need to be resolved within their own group, or by using the user FAQs, or the leader FAQ's that were accessible through the AVFA software's homepage. Participants who had been assigned the "audit partner" role were designated as the

Table 2. Summary of treatment group participants by group size

Treatment Group	Total Participants
Human-Facilitated Groups	23
System-Facilitated Groups	22
Total Participants	47

team leader for each group. As such, they were required to perform the GSS management tasks that are normally carried out by the GroupSystems facilitator or "chauffer" (e.g., initiating GSS tool usage, transferring brainstorming results to the voting tool).

Automated Virtual Facilitation Application

The automated virtual facilitation application (AVFA) is a multi-modal application for prescribing GSS tools to ensure proper task-technology fit, and providing appropriation support for more effectively utilizing the underlying GSS technology. The AVFA application is used in the present research to investigate the effectiveness of virtual facilitation in comparison to conventional facilitation and unsupported group decision-making to determine whether virtual facilitation can be as effective as conventional facilitation in the areas of appropriation, efficiency, and effectiveness.

As previously discussed, the AVFA application is based primarily on operationalizing a multiple-activity group decision-making heuristic, similar to the one utilized by Wheeler and Valacich in their 1996 study. Indeed, the research design described in this chapter is to a large degree adapted from that study, including the incorporation of a hidden-profile task similar to the *School of Business Policy Task* (Wheeler & Mennecke, 1992) utilized in that study. Specifically, the automated facilitation application is intended to guide subjects in faithfully following the structured group decision-making heuristic, the sequence of which provides the basic structure of the AVFA software application. As recommended by the authors, a key extension of the present study is to test an *automated* version of a multiple activity group decision-making heuristic:

The AVFA application was designed to recommend GSS tools for the sequenced activities of the six-step heuristic by operationalizing the GSS fit profiles advocated by Zigurs and Buck-

land (1999) and Dennis and Valacich (1999). The multi-activity group decision-making heuristic used by Wheeler and Valacich (1996) and the problem-solving model presented by Schwarz (1994) incorporate findings from the behavioral literature regarding how heuristic structures can assist groups in overcoming common obstacles to effective decision-making, including separating divergent (idea generation) and convergent (choice) phases of group activity, and writing-out an agreed upon problem statement before working on a solution (Wheeler & Valacich, 1996, p.438). Specifically, the problem-solving model used in the present research incorporates the following two major goals and six sequenced activities:

Hypotheses

As previously noted, the present research was designed to assess the effectiveness of virtual facilitation for supporting structured group decision-making, As illustrated in Figure 1, the virtual facilitation model posits that the assigned task characteristics will dictate established task-technology fit profiles (Dennis & Valacich, 1999; Zigurs & Buckland, 1999) and appropriate group problem-solving models (Briggs et al., 2003). These, in turn, will dictate appropriate GSS tools and group decision-making procedures ("meeting agendas") to be employed in completing assigned group decision-making tasks. Through this process, virtual facilitation is posited to result in efficiency levels, appropriation measures, and decision-making performance metrics that are equal to those achieved through conventional (human) facilitation.

Specifically, the current study posits the following:

H1: *System-facilitated groups will be at least as effective as human-facilitated groups in identifying problems.*

Figure 1. System-directed facilitation model

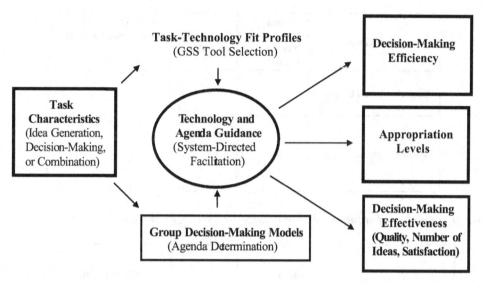

Table 3. Two-step, multiple-activity group decision-making heuristic: Adapted from Schwarz (1994) and Wheeler and Valacich (1996)

Major Goals	Sequenced Activities
(1) Problem identification	Problem statement brainstorming (EB) Problem statement rating (Vote) Problem statement drafting
(2) Solution recommendation	Solution brainstorming (EB) Solution rating (Vote) Solution drafting
GSS Tool Abbreviations: EB = Electronic Brainstorming Tool, Vote = Voting Tool,	

H2: *System-facilitated groups will be at least as effective as human-facilitated groups in recommending solutions.*

H3: *Satisfaction with the meeting process for system-facilitated groups will be at least equal to that of human-facilitated groups.*

H4: *Satisfaction with the meeting outcome for system-facilitated groups will be at least equal to that of human-facilitated groups.*

RESULTS

Hypothesis 1 posited that system-facilitated groups would be at least as effective as human-facilitated groups in identifying problems presented in the case study. As indicated in Table 4, while human-facilitated groups identified more problems and than system-facilitated groups, the difference was not found to be significant. Accordingly, the failure to reject the null hypothesis that system facilitated groups are less effective than human-facilitated groups resulted in the conclusion that

Table 4. Average number of problems identified by treatment group

Treatment Group	Mean Number of Problems Identified	Standard Deviation	Sig. (1-tailed) Human-Facilitated Groups vs. System-Facilitated Groups
Human-Facilitated Groups	15.0	5.95	.063
System-Facilitated Groups	10.6	3.01	

Table 5. Average number of solutions recommended by treatment groups

Treatment Group	Mean Number of Solutions Recommended	Standard Deviation	Sig. (1-tailed) Human-Facilitated Groups vs. System-Facilitated Groups
Human-Facilitated Groups	9.4	3.70	.390
System-Facilitated Groups	8.9	1.58	

system facilitated groups are at least as effective as human facilitated groups in this measure of brainstorming effectiveness.

Likewise, while human-facilitated groups recommended an average of 9.4 solutions per group, system-facilitated groups recommended an average 8.9 solutions, as indicated in Table 5. Accordingly, Hypotheses 2 (system-facilitated groups will recommend at least as many solutions as unsupported groups) was supported by the findings for this measure of brainstorming effectiveness.

Hypotheses 3 and 4 relate to participants' satisfaction with the meeting's process and outcome, positing that system-facilitated groups will be at least as satisfied as human-facilitated groups. Scores for satisfaction with the meeting's

process were calculated by adding the individual item Likert scores in the Briggs et al. post-session questionnaire, as shown in Appendix A.

System-facilitated participants were found to be slightly more satisfied with the meeting's process than human-facilitated participants, as indicated in Table 6. Accordingly, Hypothesis 3 (satisfaction with the meeting process for system-facilitated groups will be at least equal to that of human-facilitated groups) was supported by the data.

Satisfaction with the meeting's outcome was posited in Hypothesis 4. As indicated in Table 7, system-facilitated participants were found to be slightly more satisfied with the meeting's outcome than were human-facilitated participants Accordingly, Hypothesis 4 (satisfaction with the meeting

Table 6. Satisfaction with meeting process

Treatment Group	Mean Satisfaction with Meeting Process Score	Standard Deviation	Sig. (1-tailed) Human-Facilitated Groups vs. System-Facilitated Groups
Human-Facilitated Groups	23.6	6.75	.211
System-Facilitated Groups	25.3	3.82	

Table 7. Satisfaction with meeting outcome

Treatment Group	Mean Satisfaction with Meeting Outcome Score	Standard Deviation	Sig. (1-tailed) Human-Facilitated Groups vs. System-Facilitated Groups
Human-Facilitated Groups	24.3	6.63	.414
System-Facilitated Groups	24.7	7.36	

outcome for system-facilitated groups will be at least equal to that of human-facilitated groups) was supported by the data.

DISCUSSION AND CONCLUSION

This research addresses the feasibility of using system-directed guidance for facilitating users of advanced information technologies in an experiment involving CPAs, internal auditors, and IT security personnel as participants in a simulated information systems audit. Contrary to the study's hypotheses, system-facilitated teams were found to be less effective than human-facilitated groups in completing their assigned tasks. Likewise, satisfaction levels for system-facilitated teams were found to be only slightly higher for system-facilitated teams in comparison to human-facilitated teams.

A significant portion of the lower than expected effectiveness levels of system-facilitated groups can likely be attributed to the complexity of the GDSS application that was used in the experiment and the fairly steep learning curve required to effectively utilize the GDSS software. In a separate post-experiment survey, a significant number of participants commented on various difficulties that were encountered in utilizing the GDSS software.

Moreover, by simplifying the user interface and improving the overall user friendliness of the GDSS application used by audit team members, it is quite likely that audit team performance levels could be significantly improved. Accordingly, future research efforts should focus on utilizing GSS systems such as Microsoft's Live Meeting application which are believed to be significantly easier to utilize and which do not have many of the complexities that participants noted in their evaluations of the GDSS application utilized in the experiment.

REFERENCES

Ackermann, F. (1990). The role of computers in group decision support. In C. Eden & J. Radford (Eds.), tackling strategic problems—the role of group decision support and (pp.132-142).

Aiken, M., Liu Sheng, O., & Vogel, D. (1991). Integrating expert systems with group decision support systems. *ACM Transactions on Information Systems, 9*(1), 75-95.

Anson, R., Bostrom, R., & Wynne, B. (1995). An experiment assessing group support system and facilitator effects on meeting outcomes. *Management Science, 41*(2), 189-208.

Berry, D., & Broadbent, D. The combination of explicit and implicit learning process in task control. *Psychological Research*, 49, 7-15

Briggs, R., DeVreede, G., & Nunamaker, J. (2003). Collaboration engineering with ThinkLets to pursue sustained success with group support systems. *Journal of Management Information System*s, *19*(4), 31-65.

Briggs, R., de Vreede, G., & Reinig, B. (2003). A theory and measurement of meeting satisfaction. In proceedings of the *36th Annual Hawaii International Conference on System Sciences* (HICSS'03) - Track1

Chalidabhongse, J., Chinnan, W., Wechasaethnon, P., & Tantisirithanakorn, A. (2002). **Intelligent facilitation agent for online web-based group discussion system**. *In Proceedings of the 15th*

International Conference on Industrial and Engineering, Applications of Artificial Intelligence and Expert Systems: Developments in Applied Artificial Intelligence, (pp.356-362).

Crowston, K., & Malone, T. W. (1988). Computational agents to support cooperative work. (Working Paper #2008-88). Cambridge, MA: MIT Sloan School of Management.

DeSanctis, G., D'Onofrio, M., Sambamurthy, V., & Poole, M. (1989). Comprehensiveness and restrictiveness in group decision heuristics: Effects of computer support on consensus decision making. *In Proceedings of the Tenth International Conference on Information Systems*, (pp. 131-140).

Dhaliwal, J., & Benbasat, I. (1996). The use and effects of knowledge-based system explanations: Theoretical foundations and a framework for empirical evaluation. *Information Systems Research, 7*(3), 342-363.

Dickson, G., Partridge, J., & Robinson (1993). Exploring modes of facilitative support for GDSS technology. *MIS Quarterly, 17*(2), 173, 22.

Eden, C., Jones, S., & Sims, D. (1983). *Messing about in problems*. Oxford, England: Pergamon Press.

George, J., Dennis, A., & Nunamaker, J. (1992). An experimental investigation of facilitation in an EMS decision room. *Group Decision and Negotiation,* 1(1), 57-70.

Goul, M., & Tonge, F. (1987). Project IPMA: Applying decision support system design principles to building expert-based systems. *Decision Sciences*, 18(3), 448-467.

Griffith, T., Fuller, M., & Northcraft, G. (1998). Facilitator influence in group support systems: Intended and unintended effects. *Information Systems Research*, 9(1), 20-36.

Hayes, P., & Reddy, D. (1983). Steps toward graceful integration in spoken and written man-machine communication. *International journal of man-machine studies, 19*, 231-284.

Ho, T., & Antunes, P. (1999). Developing a tool to assist electronic facilitation of decision-making groups. *Fifth International Workshop on Groupware* (pp. 243-252). IEEE CS Press

Johansen, R. (1988).*Groupware: Computer support for business teams.* New York: Free Press

Keltner, J. (1989) Facilitation: Catalyst for group problem solving. *Management Communication Quarterly, 3*(1), 8-31.

Limayem, M. (2003). *A comparison between human and automated facilitation in the GDSS Context.* Unpublished Manuscript.

Limayem, M.,& DeSanctis, G. (2000). Providing decisional guidance for multicriteria decision making in groups.*Information Systems Research*, 11(4), 386-402.

Lopez, A., Booker, Q., Shkarayeva, N., Briggs, R., & Nunamaker, J. (2002). Embedding Facilitation in Group Support Systems to Manage Distributed Group Behavior, *Proceedings of the 35th Annual Hawaii International Conference on System Sciences (HICSS'02)*-Volume 1-1 table of contents, p.42

Maier, N. (1952). *Principles of human relations.* New York: Wiley.

Parikh, M., Fazlollahi, B., & Verma, S. (2001). The effectiveness of decisional guidance: An empirical evaluation. *Decision Sciences, 32*(2), 303-331.

Schwarz, R.M. (1994). *The skilled facilitator: Practical wisdom for developing effective groups.* San Francisco: Jossey-Bass

Sengupta, K., & Te'eni, D. (1993). Feedback in GDSS: Enhancing control and reducing conflict. *MIS Quarterly, 17*(1), 87-109.

Shortliffe, E. (1976). *Computer-based medical consultation: MYCIN.* New York: Elsevier.

Silver, M. (1991). Decision guidance for computer-based decision support. *MIS Quarterly, March,* 105-122.

Turban, E., & Watson, P. (1986). Integrating expert systems and decision support systems. *MIS Quarterly,*

Wheeler, C., & Mennecke, B. (1992). Modeling group task processes using a hidden profile task: The school of business policy task. *Indiana University School of Business, Working Paper,* number 513,.

Wheeler, B., & Valacich, J. (1996). Facilitation, GSS, and training as sources of process restrictiveness and guidance for structured group decision making: An empirical assessment. *Information Systems Research, 7*(4), 409, 20.

Wong, Z., & Aiken, M. (2003). Automated facilitation of electronic meetings. *Information and Management*, 41(2), table of contents, 125 –134.

Zigurs, I.,& Buckland, B. (1998). A theory of task/technology fit and group support systems effectiveness .*MIS Quarterly*, 22(3), 313-335.

APPENDIX A

Post-Session Questionnaire*

Dependent Variable: Satisfaction with Meeting Process (PROSATIS):

PROSATIS1: I feel satisfied with the way in which today's meeting was conducted.

____ I would strongly disagree	1
____ I would quite disagree	2
____ I would slightly disagree	3
____ I would neither agree nor disagree	4
____ I would slightly agree	5
____ I would quite agree	6
____ I would strongly agree	7

PROSATIS2: I feel good about today's meeting process.

____ I would strongly disagree	1
____ I would quite disagree	2
____ I would slightly disagree	3
____ I would neither agree nor disagree	4
____ I would slightly agree	5
____ I would quite agree	6
____ I would strongly agree	7

PROSATIS3: I liked the way the meeting progressed today.

____ I would strongly disagree	1
____ I would quite disagree	2
____ I would slightly disagree	3
____ I would neither agree nor disagree	4
____ I would slightly agree	5
____ I would quite agree	6
____ I would strongly agree	7

PROSATIS4: I feel satisfied with the procedures used in today's meeting.

____ I would strongly disagree	1
____ I would quite disagree	2
____ I would slightly disagree	3
____ I would neither agree nor disagree	4

___ I would slightly agree	5
___ I would quite agree	6
___ I would strongly agree	7

PROSATIS5: I feel satisfied about the way we carried out the activities in today's meeting.

___ I would strongly disagree	1
___ I would quite disagree	2
___ I would slightly disagree	3
___ I would neither agree nor disagree	4
___ I would slightly agree	5
___ I would quite agree	6
___ I would strongly agree	7

Minimum PROSATIS Score = 5
Maximum PROSATIS Score = 35

Dependent Variable: Satisfaction with Meeting Outcome (OUTSATIS):

OUTSATIS1: I liked the outcome of today's meeting.

___ I would strongly disagree	1
___ I would quite disagree	2
___ I would slightly disagree	3
___ I would neither agree nor disagree	4
___ I would slightly agree	5
___ I would quite agree	6
___ I would strongly agree	7

OUTSATIS2: I feel satisfied with the things we achieved in today's meeting.

___ I would strongly disagree	1
___ I would quite disagree	2
___ I would slightly disagree	3
___ I would neither agree nor disagree	4
___ I would slightly agree	5
___ I would quite agree	6
___ I would strongly agree	7

OUTSATIS3: When the meeting was finally over, I felt satisfied with the results.

____ I would strongly disagree	1
____ I would quite disagree	2
____ I would slightly disagree	3
____ I would neither agree nor disagree	4
____ I would slightly agree	5
____ I would quite agree	6
____ I would strongly agree	7

OUTSATIS4: Our accomplishments today give me a feeling of satisfaction.

____ I would strongly disagree	1
____ I would quite disagree	2
____ I would slightly disagree	3
____ I would neither agree nor disagree	4
____ I would slightly agree	5
____ I would quite agree	6
____ I would strongly agree	7

OUTSATIS5: I am happy with the results of today's meeting.

____ I would strongly disagree	1
____ I would quite disagree	2
____ I would slightly disagree	3
____ I would neither agree nor disagree	4
____ I would slightly agree	5
____ I would quite agree	6
____ I would strongly agree	7

Minimum OUTSATIS Score = 5
Maximum OUTSATIS Score = 35

* Briggs, R., de Vreede, G., & Reinig, B. (2003). A theory and measurement of meeting satisfaction. *In proceedings of 36th Annual Hawaii International Conference on System Sciences* (HICSS'03) - Track1

Chapter 14
Agile Workflow Technology for Long-Term Processes:
Enhanced by Case-Based Change Reuse

Mirjam Minor
University of Trier, Germany

Alexander Tartakovski
University of Trier, Germany

Daniel Schmalen
University of Trier, Germany

Ralph Bergmann
University of Trier, Germany

ABSTRACT

The increasing dynamics of today's work impacts the business processes. Agile workflow technology is a means for the automation of adaptable processes. However, the modification of workflows is a difficult task that is performed by human experts. This chapter discusses the novel approach of agile workflow technology for dynamic, long-term scenarios and on change reuse. First, it introduces new concepts for a workflow modelling language and enactment service, which enable an interlocked modelling and execution of workflows by means of a sophisticated suspension mechanism. Second, it provides new process-oriented methods of case-based reasoning in order to support the reuse of change experience. The results from an experimental evaluation in a real-world scenario highlight the usefulness and the practical impact of this work.

INTRODUCTION

"We could not employ a workflow system that is not adaptable to changes." states a chip design expert from Silicon Image GmbH, Hannover (S.

DOI: 10.4018/978-1-60566-970-0.ch002

Rackow, personal interview, October 25, 2006). Chip designers are used to dealing with the dynamics that result from the evolution of technology as well as from changes in the market. The increasing dynamics of the workflow is a phenomenon that affects the production processes within the high-tech industry: Software developers have to be flexible when the customer requirements change. Healthcare professionals must react to side-effects and to other complications during the treatment of patients. What these examples from various domains have in common is that they cause major deviations from the usual business processes at run time. Furthermore, the ongoing processes need refinement after several weeks or months of running. Workflow technology supports business processes (Workflow Management Coalition, 1999). However, traditional workflow management systems, those described in Leymann and Roller (2000), are not able to deal with adaptable processes. Consequently, there is a need for *agile workflow technology* (Weber & Wild, 2005), that is, a workflow technology that allows the late-modeling and structural adaptation of ongoing workflows. Change reuse is essential to these difficult modeling tasks.

Workflows are "the automation of a business process, in whole or part, during which documents, information or tasks are passed from one participant to another for action, according to a set of procedural rules" (Workflow Management Coalition, 1999). A *workflow management system* "defines, creates and manages the execution of workflows through the use of software, running on one or more workflow engines, which is able to interpret the process definition, interact with workflow participants and, where required, invoke the use of IT tools and applications" (Workflow Management Coalition, 1999). A *workflow enactment service* is "a software service that may consist of one or more workflow engines" (Workflow Management Coalition, 1999).

All agile workflow approaches require the *application of changes concurrently to normal process execution*. In contrast to the existing approaches, *very large process graphs* are dealt with. They require a suspension mechanism in case of *delayed decisions* as they do occur in practise. Due to the highly dynamic environments of the workflows, the approach is *aware of the context of influence factors*. As other agile approaches,

reusing experience from the changes of workflows in the past for the adaptation of an ongoing workflow are aimed at. In contrast to existing change reuse approaches, the retrieval of past workflows should consider the workflows' structure directly rather than solely operating on additional information. In this article, a new approach of agile workflow technology which includes new basic methods for the representation, execution, and partial suspension of adaptable workflows as well as more sophisticated methods for the support of change reuse by means of case-based reasoning is described. It is an extension of previous work described in the literature (Minor, Schmalen, Tartakovsky, & Bergmann, 2008). The following hypothesis that will be investigated empirically in this article is stated: The evaluation of structural differences of workflows provides a good approximation for the usability of past modifications for current change requests. The purpose of our work is to contribute new workflow concepts and methods to solving the practical but difficult problem of handling business processes in very dynamic, long-term scenarios.

LITERATURE REVIEW

The workflows to be interpreted in conventional workflow management systems have a fixed structure. In the literature, a number of approaches exist that aim at making workflows more flexible. Some work on flexible workflows in the broader sense are first discussed and then the literature on agile workflows in the actual sense are briefly reviewed. The latter is closely related to the work. The literature on similarity assessment of workflows is also discussed and the position on context-awareness during change reuse is defined.

Some recent approaches (Luo, Sheth, Kochut, & Arpinar, 2003; Hwang & Tang, 2004; Russell, van der Aalst, & ter Hofstede, 2006; Adams, ter Hofstede, Edmond, & van der Aalst, 2006) deal with exception handling for "deviations from normal execution arising during a business process" (Russell, et al., 2006). Luo et al. (2003) use exception-handling processes for the resolution of conflicts that "primarily arise due to failure of a task in workflow execution" (Luo et al., 2003). For instance, a time out exception may occur for a task and can be handled by a retry, recovery, or compensation process. Russell et al. (2006) and Adams et al. (2006) associate this task-oriented exception handling with a case handling approach (van der Aalst, Weske, & Grünbauer, 2005) that focuses on the whole process and its objectives. This means that the exception handling processes may provide workarounds for larger areas of a workflow than a single task. Both task-oriented and case-oriented exception handling, are not adequate means for the adaptation of very dynamic processes. The mass of nested and overlapping patches that are required to mend different parts of a workflow repeatedly would be quite confusing for the users. Direct changes of the structure of the ongoing workflows are more suitable for very dynamic processes. Nevertheless, exception handling provides a certain amount of flexibility for conventional workflows especially if it "allows the repertoire of actions to be dynamically extended at runtime" (Adams et al., 2006). Emergent workflows (Dourish, Homes, MacLean, Marqvardsen, & Zbyslaw, 1996; Carlsen & Jørgensen, 1998; Meijler, Kessels, Vuijsr, & le Comte, 1998; Hermann, 2001) denote the other extreme of flexible workflows. These approaches learn workflows from sets of loosely coupled tasks. In contrast to process mining approaches (Schimm, van der Aalst, van Dongen, & Herbst, 2003), emergent workflow management systems are able to deal with unfinished process models during runtime.

Agile workflows lie in between exception handling and emergent workflow approaches as they rely on structured processes but allow the incremental modeling as well as structural adaptations of the ongoing processes. The changes may apply to the process templates called *workflow*

definitions as well as to the *workflow instances* that are derived from the workflow definitions. The agile workflow technology can be classified according to three types of structural process changes that can be accomplished at run time:

- Ad-hoc changes of individual workflow instances (Reichert, Rinderle, & Dadam, 2003; Reichert & Dadam, 2009; Weber, Wild, & Breu, 2004; Bassil, Rudolf, Keller, & Kropf, 2004)
- Modifications to a workflow definition that is already in use by instances (Casati, Ceri, Pernici, & Pozzi, 1998; Weske, 1999; Reichert et al., 2003; Reichert & Dadam, 2009)
- Late-modeling and hierarchical decomposition (van Elst, Aschoff, Bernadi, Maus, & Schwarz, 2003; Freßmann, Maximini, & Sauer, 2005).

Typical ad-hoc changes are to re-order some parts of a workflow instance or to insert an additional task. Modifying workflow definitions in the same way leads to the difficult migration task of ongoing instances to the new schema. Late-modelling and hierarchical decomposition mean that a workflow instance can be enacted while it is supposed to be refined later on. The work fits in the first and third classifications. Weber, Reichert, and Rinderle-Ma (2008) propose a fine-granular classification schema for change patterns and change support features. They define a change support feature for "Change Reuse", which also plays a major role in the approach.

The reuse of change requires a similarity measure for agile workflows. Luo et al. (2003) use a building-block similarity that is based on a tree representation of the workflows according to their building blocks (similar to the tree representation for execution purposes that is described in the section on workflow enactment). Madhusudan, Zhao, and Marshall (2004) have developed a similarity flooding approach for the case-based planning of workflows: They compare the task nodes of a workflow initially using a string-oriented similarity measure borrowed from text retrieval. In later steps, they propagate the initial values to neighbouring nodes (similarity flooding). Lu and Sadiq (2006) employ graph reduction techniques in order to match the structure of workflows. Wombacher (2006) considers workflows that are restricted to finite state automata. He investigates different similarity measures for them that use mining conformance algorithms (Rozinat & van der Aalst, 2005) and several n-gram representations for potential execution paths. The building-block similarity, the similarity flooding, the graph reduction, and Wombacher's similarity measures for finite state automata are not suitable for the retrieval of agile workflow instances. Minor changes in the order of workflow elements that are typical for agile workflows, for instance, moving a task to a different block leads to major deviations in the values of the similarity measure.

In the literature, a number of approaches with similarity measures for agile workflows exist that require further information in addition to the workflow structure such as semantic annotations (van Elst et al., 2003; Schwarz, 2003), contextual information (Freßmann et al., 2005), or conversational knowledge (Weber et al., 2004; Rinderle, Weber, Reichert, & Wild, 2005). The approach is context-aware (Kofod-Petersen & Mikalsen, 2005), that is, the contextual information is considered as a part of the similarity assessment of workflows. The *context* of agile workflows in the approach consists of the *influence factors* that have a significant impact on the process. In the chip domain, the influence factors are, for instance, the resources of the design project (persons and tools), the risks, the market situation, and even the part of the requirements for the design artifact and the process that is crucial for change. The target frequency of the chip, for instance, is quite an important requirement and an influence factor for the design process: In case it is missed by a chip module, this may cause the redesign of

other modules. Of course, this leads to changes in the process models of the workflows for the concerned modules. The notion of context differs from Dey's well-known definition (Dey, 2001) of context as "any information that can be used to characterize the situation of an entity". According to this broad definition, further information such as the state of execution of a workflow would belong to the context while the requirements would not. For the purpose of change reuse, the influence factors including the change-relevant requirements are focused on.

However, any contextual information as well as conversational knowledge is not always available and can be processed for the automatic adaptation of workflows only with considerable effort. There is a need for a new similarity measure for workflows that is on the one hand based on the structure of workflows only but on the other hand considers the agility of the workflows in a more adequate way than the similarity measures that we reported earlier. Instead of graph-matching measures which are based on such characteristics as "graph isomorphism" (Babai, Erdös, & Selkow, 1980; Babai & Kucera, 1979), "sub-graph isomorphism" (Ullmann, 1976), and "largest common sub-graph" (Brandstädt, 1994; Mehlhorn, 1984), a graph edit distance measure (Bunke & Messmer, 1993) has been chosen and adapted for similarity assessment in the system.

WORKFLOW MODELING LANGUAGE

Agile workflows should be modelled in a language that balances simplicity with flexibility. Simplicity implies that familiar elements from the traditional workflow languages are integrated as far as possible. Flexibility means that the workflow language supports the application of late-modelling and ad-hoc changes. The workflow modeling language is for the *process model* that describes the control flow structure of tasks and for the *context model* of the workflow. In the following, sample workflows from the chip design domain are used in order to illustrate the concepts in a collaborative, long-term scenario. Figure 1 shows a UML activity diagram of a sample workflow definition that was modelled as a template for new chip design projects. A chip design project is planned and executed by means of a top level workflow. The project units for the design of the particular chip modules have their own workflow instances that are embedded as sub-workflows into the top level workflow. The sub-workflows replace the 'Dummy design unit' in Figure 1 following the template for chip design units given in Figure 2. The process models for the chip domain follow the design flow 'SciWay 2.0', that is, a standardized description of the step by step design process for all digital design projects of our industrial partner Silicon Image GmbH (formerly sci-worx).

Process Model

The language to describe the control flow in a process model is based on the notation of workflow patterns introduced by van der Aalst, ter Hofstede, Kiepuszewski, and Barros (2003).

Workflow patterns "address business requirements in an imperative workflow style expression" (van der Aalst et al., 2003); broadly speaking, they are useful routing constructs within workflows. In terms of van Aalst et al, the process modelling language has the five basic *control flow elements* (workflow patterns) sequence, AND-split, AND-join, XOR-split, and XOR-join, as well as loops. Loops are regarded as structured cycles with one entry point to the loop (the control flow element LOOP-join) and one exit point from the loop (the control flow element LOOP-split). A diamond with an '[L', one incoming and several outgoing arrows with conditions in squared brackets stands for the LOOP-split; a diamond with an 'L]', several incoming and one outgoing arrows stands for the LOOP-join (see Figure 2). For reasons of adaptability, two more control flow elements have been created:

(1) breakpoints are symbolized by stop signs on connections (see Fig. 4);
(2) placeholder tasks for sub-workflows are depicted as rounded boxes with double borders (see 'Dummy design unit' in Figure 1);

Figure 1. The workflow definition of a chip design project following SciWay 2.0

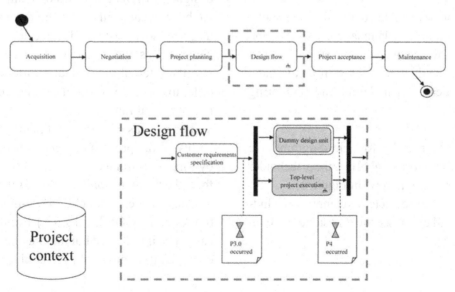

Figure 2. The workflow definition of a chip design unit following SciWay 2.0

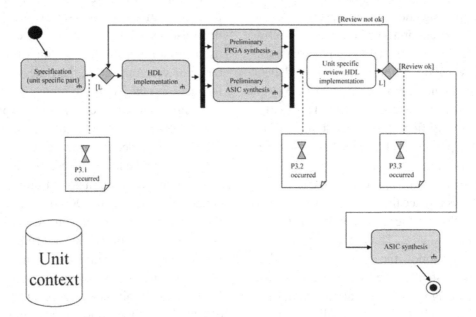

Breakpoints are necessary for the control of modifications in a workflow instance concurrently to the execution. Setting a breakpoint prevents the workflow engine from overrunning tasks that are about to be modified. Placeholder tasks for sub-workflows stand for a reference to another workflow instance. This new control flow element particularly contributes to the systems capability for late-modelling and hierarchical decomposition.

In addition to the nine control flow elements, the process modelling language consists of the usual workflow elements such as tasks, start symbols, and end symbols as well as two new elements dedicated to modelling and monitoring purposes only:

(3) placeholder tasks for sub-diagrams are marked by a fork symbol (see the placeholder task for 'Design flow' in Figure 1);

(4) milestones are depicted as comments including a sand glass (see the milestone 'P3.0' in Figure 1).

Sub-diagrams have only been introduced for reasons of clarity. They allow the user to decompose large workflows into parts which are displayed hierarchically. In contrast to sub-workflows, sub-diagrams do not have their own context or a workflow engine. Milestones are a special kind of comments that encapsulate a certain date for a couple of workflow instances, for example, for the sub-workflows that describe the design of different modules of a chip in parallel. At the moment, neither placeholder tasks for sub-diagrams nor milestones do affect the control flow. Nevertheless, the milestones have been included into the internal representation for execution in order to facilitate an alternative interpretation of milestones in future.

For reasons of clarity and manageability, the agility of the process model has been restricted by three constraints: The control flow elements form the following *building blocks* in the process models: sequence-blocks, AND-blocks, XOR-blocks and LOOP-blocks. (A) Building blocks cannot be interleaved but they can be nested. For example, in Figure 2, the AND-block with 'Preliminary FPGA synthesis' and 'Preliminary ASIC synthesis' is an inner block of a sequence which belongs to the outer LOOP-block. (B) Before a structural adaptation can take place the concerned area of the workflow instance <u>must</u> be suspended from execution by means of a breakpoint. (C) Breakpoints are not allowed for 'the past', that is, in areas of the workflow that have already completed their execution. A process model in the workflow modelling language is *well-formed* if it complies with the constraints (A) to (C).

Configurable, Ontology-Based Context Model

In addition to the process model for the control flow structure, a workflow has a context model (compare Figures 1 and 2). Discussions with chip designers led us to the decision to develop a *configurable* context model. For each type of chip, the context model can be tailored to the appropriate set of context factors. For instance, security aspects play a major role in the automotive area

while factors from the application context like the number of pixels of a camera are more important for consumer products. Furthermore, the analysis of change request documents from the chip domain has yielded several interdependencies between context factors. For instance, the output pins of a chip segment have a direct impact on the input pins of a successor chip. It has been chosen to organize the context in an *ontology-based* model in order to describe interdependencies. Figure 3 shows the top level ontology for the configurable context model. Two areas for the definition and the application of context factors have been distinguished:

(1) 'FactorCategory', 'FactorDefinition', and all its descendant classes ('BooleanFD', 'DateFD', etc.) belong to the pool of context factors. The pool contains the definitions of the factors including the value types and default values.

(2) 'Project', 'ProjectUnit', and 'Factor' with its descendants ('BooleanFactor',

Figure 3. The top-level ontology of the context model

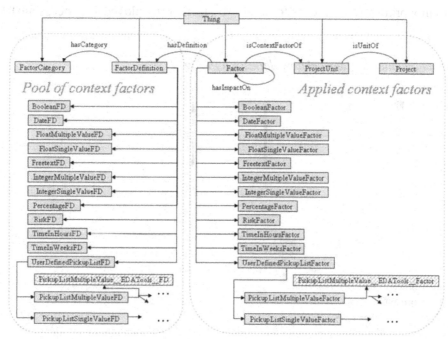

'DateFactor', etc.) are for the assignment of factors to project units and their unit-specific values.

Assigning a context factor to a project unit means to add it to the context of the corresponding workflow. The interdependencies between applied context factors are captured in the 'hasImpactOn' relation. The top level ontology contains general data type classes that are also applicable for other domains as well as user-defined classes that are dedicated to the chip design domain, for instance, the pickup list for the EDA (electronic design automation) tools. The contexts can be specified, updated, and exchanged by means of our context acquisition tool based on Protégé and OWL (Antoniou & van Harmelen, 2004). For further information on the implementation and a user evaluation of the context acquisition tool, the literature is referred to (Minor, 'Schmalen, Koldehoff, & Bergmann, 2007).

WORKFLOW ENACTMENT

The workflow modelling language facilitates the agility within workflows. This leads to new requirements for the workflow execution that can not be met by traditional workflow enactment services. The two additional control flow elements introduced for breakpoints and for sub-workflows need to be handled. Furthermore, the loop blocks require a special treatment since an adaptation of an ongoing loop may lead to different iterations of the same loop. In the following, the concept of states, a tree structure for the processing of the workflows, and the concept of master copies for the loops are introduced.

The *state of processing* are stored for all building blocks and tasks of a workflow instance. Figure 4 shows an ongoing sample workflow instance for a design unit. The placeholder task 'Specification (unit specific part)' and the subsequent loop block have already been completed. The task 'Check whether feature set confirmed' is currently active, that is, it has been assigned to a user's work list who is executing this task. A breakpoint suspends the remainder of the workflow instance from the execution so that it can be edited. In the sample in Figure 4, the new task 'Update implementation specification', the new sub-diagram for 'HDL implementation in addition', and the additional milestone 'P3.5' have been inserted. The following states are employed for processing: READY – the

Figure 4. Sample instance of the workflow definition in Fig. 2

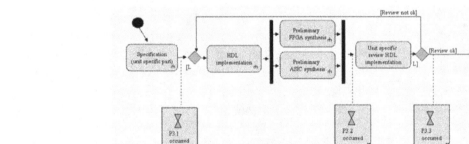

default state for new workflow elements, ACTIVE – currently being executed, COMPLETED - has been executed successfully, FAILED – has been executed unsuccessfully, SKIPPED – has been left out manually, OMITTED – lies in an inactive branch of an XOR, BLOCKED – from a sub-workflow placeholder whose sub-workflow has been suspended, SUSPENDED – is within the scope of a breakpoint. BLOCKED is a special case of SUSPENDED as the workflow area behind a blocked placeholder tasks is suspended for execution but not accessible for modifications as far as the user has not set an additional breakpoint at this workflow's level.

The building block concept allows representing the workflow instances by means of a tree-oriented data structure. The tree consists of different node types for the tasks, the four building blocks, the placeholder tasks for sub-workflows, the milestones, and the breakpoints. Figure 5 shows the tree representation of a very simple sample workflow instance. It has three building blocks: an outer sequence (light grey), a loop block (middle grey), and an inner sequence (dark grey). The tasks 'T1' to 'T3' and the breakpoint form the

leaf nodes. The execution logics of the workflow elements including the states of processing are annotated to the particular node types. Due to this encapsulation, the tree concept is scalable in case the process modelling language is extended, for instance, with new control flow elements for OR-blocks.

The compliance of a new breakpoint with the constraint (C) can be controlled within the tree structure in a straight-forward way by means of the state COMPLETED. The setting of a breakpoint is followed by the propagation of the states SUSPENDED and BLOCKED; the release of a breakpoint causes the propagation of the state READY. The late binding of sub-workflows can be handled within the tree structure as well. A placeholder task is bound to a workflow definition by a special property of the sub-workflow node. Setting this property fires an event for the creation of the new sub-workflow instance.

Loops are prepared for agility with the new concept of *master copies*. The workflow elements that belong to a loop-block are copied during their processing. The master copies form a new sub-tree that is gradually inserted as a sibling of

Figure 5. Block-oriented tree representation of a sample workflow

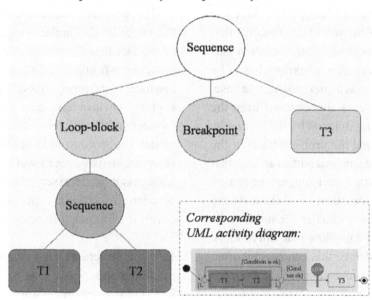

the original sub-tree for the loop-block. In the second and following iterations, the procedure of copying is repeated and leads to the creation of further sub-trees. The current master copies are accessible for the setting of breakpoints and for structural modifications. Modifications are valid for all future iterations but do not affect the past. Nested loops can be modified with restrictions only; due to space limitations, this is not able to be elucidated here in detail.

CASE-BASED ASSISTANCE FOR THE ADAPTATION OF WORKFLOWS

The workflow enactment service can deal with the adaptation of ongoing workflow instances. Case-Based Reasoning (CBR) (Aamodt & Plaza, 1994) is a quite natural approach to support the users in creating the agility of workflows. Experience from the adaptation of workflows in the past can be reused for the adaptation of an ongoing workflow (change reuse). The experience is captured within *cases* and stored in a *case base*. In contrast to a case in workflow terminology (van der Aalst et al., 2005), a case as an experience carrier consists of a pair of subsequent revisions of a workflow instance [X, X']. The previous revision X forms the problem part of the case; X' – the revision of the workflow instance that has already been modified - is the solution part of the case. When a current workflow has to be adapted, it can be used as a *query* to the case base. The best matching cases are *retrieved* from the case base in a ranking induced by the *similarity* between the query and the problem parts of the particular cases. The solution part of a case, that is, the adapted workflow revision, can be reused in order to change the query workflow. At the moment, the user has to transfer the solution for adapting the current workflow manually, but in the future, to what degree this can be supported automatically will be investigated (see the concluding section).

The retrieval of past workflows requires a representation of the workflow instances that is adequate for the similarity assessment. Both parts of a workflow instance need to be represented – the control flow structure and the context. The similarity value for the control flow structure is aggregated with the similarity value for the context to an overall similarity value. The context is represented in a straightforward way by a structural CBR approach (Bergmann, 2002) with attribute-value pairs. The comparison of contexts can be realized according to the local-global-principle of the structural CBR approach. The main challenge is to develop a representation and a similarity measure for the control flow structure. The tree representation according to the building blocks is not suitable for the retrieval of agile workflows (see the discussion of related work). Instead, the idea of a weighted graph edit distance for the similarity assessment of the control flow structures has been chosen. Replaying graph edit sequences in order to adapt workflows does not hurt the modeling language's constraint (A) on building blocks. Edit sequences are only a more fine granular representation of changes that have been made by maintaining the well-formedness. (Reichert & Dadam, 2009) denote this as 'correctness by construction'.

The representation of the control flow structures that underlies the similarity assessment makes use of the fact that the instances are derived from a particular workflow definition (template). As the instances of the process models usually differ only slightly from their templates, they can be described by means of the difference to the particular process model. The process model of a workflow definition is represented as a set of workflow elements with a successor-predecessor relation. The difference between an ongoing instance and its process model covers the following issues:

1. the structural modifications of workflow elements
2. the state of processing

Both can be encoded by the sets of added and deleted workflow elements with respect to the original template. Hereby, completed workflow elements are regarded as deleted. However, this leads to completely different algorithms than those described in the literature.

In the following, the basic idea of graph edit distances are first introduced, then, a very rudimentary representation of the control flow structures is created in order to demonstrate the graph edit distance for the workflows, and, finally, different more sophisticated representations that provide a better approximation of the utility of workflows during change reuse are proposed.

Graph Edit Distances

The measure of Bunke & Messmer (2003) generalizes the string edit distance (Wagner & Bodendiek, 1989). It is defined for attributed directed graphs but can be easily applied in a simplified form to standard graphs as well. Similarity is modelled through a set of edit operations on graphs. Each edit operation e transforms a graph into a successor graph performing a modification of the following kind: insert a new node or a new edge, delete a node or an edge, and change a node or an edge label. Each edit operation has a certain assigned cost $c(e) \in [0, 1]$. A difference can be defined based on the total cost of a sequence of edit operations which transform one graph into the other graph. The cheaper and fewer the operations are that are required to transform a graph x into another graph y the smaller is the difference and hence the higher is the similarity between them. These considerations lead to the following difference function:

$$\delta(x,y) = \min\{\sum_{i=1}^{k} c(e_i) \mid (e_1,...,e_k) \text{ transforms } x \text{ to } y\}$$

The computation of the graph edit distance measure is an NP-complete problem (Bunke & Messmer, 2003) and can be performed by a state-space search, for example, by an A* algorithm. Hence, this similarity measure should be used quite carefully.

Similarity Measure for Restricted Workflows

This section regards similarity assessment for restricted workflows that contain arbitrary tasks as well as control flow elements only of the type "sequence". For the purpose of similarity assessment, an abstract view on workflows will be defined. It includes only tasks, names of tasks, and ordering of tasks, given through control flow elements of the type "sequence". The view can be represented as a directed and attributed graph:

$$View = \langle N, E, name \rangle$$

The nodes N in this graph represent workflows' tasks and the edges E represent the control flow elements of type "sequence". Furthermore, every node is labelled with the name of a respective task:

Name:$N \rightarrow TaskNames$

There are two important characteristics of workflow instances that allow an efficient computation of the graph edit distance $\delta(V_1, V_2)$ between two arbitrary views $V_1 = \langle N_1, E_1, name_1 \rangle$ and $V_2 = \langle N_2, E_2, name_2 \rangle$. The first characteristic is that the name of every task is unique within a single workflow instance. The second characteristic is that two tasks, T_1 from one workflow and T_2 from another workflow, can be seen as identical if and only if their names are equal. This leads to following definitions:

Nodes within V_1 but not within V_2:
$$\hat{N}_1 := N_1 - N_2$$

Nodes within V_2 but not within V_1:
$$\hat{N}_2 := N_2 - N_1$$

Edges within V_1 but not within V_2:
$$\hat{E}_1 := E_1 - E_2$$

Edges within V_2 but not within V_1:
$$\hat{E}_2 := E_2 - E_1$$

Two nodes $n_1 \in N_1$ and $n_2 \in N_2$ are defined to be equal if and only if their labels are equal: $name(n_1) = name(n_2)$. Two edges $e_1 \in E_1$ and $e_2 \in E_2$ are defined to be equal if and only if $name(predecessor(e_1)) = name(predecessor(e_2))$ and $name(successor(e_1)) = name(successor(e_2))$.

The distance can now be defined $\delta(V_1, V_2)$ between the views V_1 and V_2. Suppose, the view V_1 is going to be edited until it is equal to V_2. For this purpose the nodes $\hat{N}_1$ have to be deleted from V_1, since they are not in V_2. The number of edit operations is $| \hat{N}_1 |$. Then, the edges $\hat{E}_1$ have to be deleted for the same reason. The number of edit operations is $| \hat{E}_1 |$. The sets $\hat{N}_2$ and $\hat{E}_2$ have to be added to the view V_1, since the nodes and edges are within V_2 but not within V_1. The number of operations is $| \hat{N}_2 | + | \hat{E}_2 |$. The overall sum of edit operations is $| \hat{N}_1 | + | \hat{E}_1 | + | \hat{N}_2 | + | \hat{E}_2 |$. It can be simply proven that this number of edit operations is minimal. Therefore the distance is set to:

$$\delta(V_1, V_2) = | \hat{N}_1 | + | \hat{E}_1 | + | \hat{N}_2 | + | \hat{E}_2 |$$

It should be mentioned that for this special case, the complexity of the distance assessment is not exponential but quadratic. However, the average complexity could be further improved. The improvement is based on the fact that instances to be compared are created starting from the same workflow definition and differ only slightly from their template (with a view $V_T = \langle N_T, E_T, name_T \rangle$).

Therefore, the respective views V_1 and V_2 can be redefined as follows:

$$V_1 = \langle N_T \cup add.nodes_{V_1} - delete.nodes_{V_1},$$
$$E_T \cup add.edges_{V_1} - delete.edges_{V_1} \rangle$$
$$V_2 = \langle N_T \cup add.nodes_{V_2} - delete.nodes_{V_2},$$
$$E_T \cup add.edges_{V_2} - delete.edges_{V_2} \rangle$$

Hereby, the set $add.nodes_{V_1}$ defines nodes that should be added to the workflow definition in order to get the view V_1. The set of nodes $delete.nodes_{V_1}$ should be deleted from V_T. The sets $add.edges_{V_1}$ and $delete.edges_{V_1}$ have the same semantics but the objects to be altered are edges. The same consideration can be carried out for the view V_2. Now the sets $\hat{N}_1, \hat{N}_2, \hat{E}_1, \hat{E}_2$ can be written as:

$$\hat{N}_1 := \{N_T \cup add.nodes_{V_1} - delete.nodes_{V_1}\}$$
$$- \{N_T \cup add.nodes_{V_2} - delete.nodes_{V_2}\}$$
$$\hat{N}_2 := \{N_T \cup add.nodes_{V_2} - delete.nodes_{V_2}\}$$
$$- \{N_T \cup add.nodes_{V_1} - delete.nodes_{V_1}\}$$
$$\hat{E}_1 := \{E_T \cup add.edges_{E_1} - delete.edges_{E_1}\}$$
$$- \{E_T \cup add.edges_{E_2} - delete.edges_{E_2}\}$$
$$\hat{E}_2 := \{E_T \cup add.edges_{E_2} - delete.edges_{E_2}\}$$
$$- \{E_T \cup add.edges_{E_1} - delete.edges_{E_1}\}$$

Using results of the set theory the edit distance can be transformed to the following formula:

$$\delta(V_1, V_2) = | \hat{N}_1 | + | \hat{E}_1 | + | \hat{N}_2 | + | \hat{E}_2 | =$$
$$| \{delete.nodes_{V_1} \cup delete.nodes_{V_2}\}$$
$$- \{delete.nodes_{V_1} \cap delete.nodes_{V_2}\} | +$$
$$| \{add.nodes_{V_1} \cup add.nodes_{V_2}\}$$
$$- \{add.nodes_{V_1} \cap add.nodes_{V_2}\} | +$$
$$| \{delete.edges_{V_1} \cup delete.edges_{V_2}\}$$
$$- \{delete.edges_{V_1} \cap delete.edges_{V_2}\} | +$$
$$| \{add.edges_{V_1} \cup add.edges_{V_2}\}$$
$$- \{add.edges_{V_1} \cap add.edges_{V_2}\} |$$

Since the sets *add.nodes* and *del.nodes* become available with the construction of instances that starts from templates and since it normally has a low cardinality, the computation time of the edit distance decreases significantly. The sets *add.nodes* and *del.nodes* can be understood as indexes.

Finally, the distance can be normalized and transformed to the compatible similarity measure with a range [0, 1], for example:

$$sim(V_1, V_2) := 1 - \frac{\delta(V_1, V_2)}{\mid N_1 \mid + \mid N_2 \mid + \mid E_1 \mid + \mid E_2 \mid}$$

This similarity measure can be enriched by some weights in order to emphasize particular types of edit operations.

Similarity Measure for Workflows with Control Flow Elements

The distance measure introduced in the previous section does not support other control flow elements than sequences, such as AND-split, AND-join, XOR-split, XOR-join, and so on. However, taking them into consideration improves the approximation of usability (see the following evaluation section). The consideration of the control flow elements in the similarity function entails several challenges. Contrary to tasks, which are unique within workflow instances and which could be identified by unique names, control flow elements do not have unique names and often occur several times within an instance. Because of this circumstance the computation of an exact edit distance becomes computationally more expensive. Therefore, several approximation methods were considered and the usability of the result sets were evaluated empirically.

Approximation Method 1. The first approach supports workflows containing arbitrary control flow elements. However, it does not take into account the semantics of the control flow elements while computing the similarity value. The main idea of this straightforward approach is to represent every control flow element through one or several edges within a view. For this purpose, every two tasks which are directly connected through control flow elements will be transformed to two nodes and one edge between them in the view. The "direct connection" means that there is a path in the workflows' structure connecting these tasks and this path does not contain any further tasks (but one or more control flow elements between them are allowed). For example, consider two paths $(T_1, AND-split, T_2)$ and $(T_1, AND - split, T_3)$ within the workflow snippet $T_1 \rightarrow \begin{vmatrix} \rightarrow T_2 \\ \rightarrow T_3 \end{vmatrix}$.

The tasks T_1, T_2, and T_3 will be converted to nodes n_{T_1}, n_{T_2}, and n_{T_3} in each respective view. The control flow element will be substituted through two edges $e_1 = (n_{T_1}, n_{T_2})$ and $e_2 = (n_{T_1}, n_{T_3})$. The similarity assessment can then be carried out in the same way as presented in the previous section.

Approximation Method 2. The second approach is an extension of the first one. Also, here every control flow element will be represented through one or several edges within a view. The difference is that every edge here is labelled with names of substituted elements. In order to realize this, a view on workflow instances will be extended to the following:

$$View = \langle N, E, name_N, name_E \rangle$$

While $name_N$ is a function providing names (or labels) for nodes, $name_E$ does the same for edges. For two tasks T_1 and T_2 which are directly connected through some path $p = (Task_1, CFElement_1, \ldots, CFElement_n, Task_2)$, the function $name_E(e) = name_E((n_{T_1}, n_{T_2}))$ provides an ordered set of the elements' names: $name(CFElement_1), \ldots, name(CFElement_n)$. For example, consider the workflow instance introduced by the description of approximation method

1. The tasks T_1 and T_2 are directly connected by the path $p = (T_1, AND-split, T_2)$. For the edge $e = (n_{T_1}, n_{T_2})$ the function $name_E$ provides the value "$AND - split$". Now consider two tasks T_1 and T_2 which are directly connected by the path $p = (T_1, AND - split, XOR - split, AND - split, T_2)$. For that setup, the function $name_E$ provides the value "$AND-split,XOR-split,AND-split$". The last thing to do is to redefine the equality of edges. Two edges $e_1 \in E_1$ and $e_2 \in E_2$ are defined to be equal if and only if $name(predecessor(e_1)) = name(predecessor(e_2))$ and $name(successor(e_1)) = name(successor(e_2))$ and $name_E(e_1) = name_E(e_2)$. Using this extended model, the similarity computation can be executed according to the approach presented in the previous section.

Approximation Method 3. The idea of this approximation method is to model the control flow elements of the type "sequence" as edges and the other control flow elements (abbreviated with ¬sequence) as nodes. The only restriction is that for every ¬sequence-control flow element type (e.g. "AND − split") just one node will be introduced in the view, and this is independent from the actual number of the same elements that occurred in a workflow instance. Thus, for all pairs of workflow elements $elem_1$ and $elem_2$, with $elem_2$ being a direct successor of $elem_1$, the following components will be introduced in the view:

- nodes $n_{elem_1}, n_{successor(elem_2)}$ and edge $e = (n_{elem_1}, n_{successor(elem_2)})$ if element $elem_1$ is a task and $elem_2$ is a control flow element of the type "sequence".
- nodes $n_{predecessor(elem_1)}, n_{elem_2}$ and edge $e = (n_{predecessor(elem_1)}, n_{elem_2})$ if element $elem_2$ is a task and $elem_1$ is a control flow element of the type "sequence".
- nodes $n_{elem_1}, n_{type(elem_2)}$ and edge $e = (n_{elem_1}, n_{type(elem_2)})$ if element $elem_1$ is a task and $elem_2$ is a ¬sequence-control flow element.

- nodes $n_{type(elem_1)}, n_{elem_2}$ and edge $e = (n_{type(elem_1)}, n_{elem_2})$ if element $elem_2$ is a task and $elem_1$ is a ¬sequence-control flow element.
- nodes $n_{type(elem_1)}, n_{type(elem_2)}$ and edge $e = (n_{type(elem_1)}, n_{type(elem_2)})$ if the elements are ¬sequence-control flow elements both.

Here, the name of every node $n \in N$ representing a ¬sequence-control flow element is set to the element type: $name_N(n) = type(n)$. For example, the following two parts of one workflow instance $T_1 \rightarrow \begin{vmatrix} \rightarrow T_2 \\ \rightarrow T_3 \end{vmatrix}$ and $T_4 \rightarrow \begin{vmatrix} \rightarrow T_5 \\ \rightarrow T_6 \end{vmatrix}$ will be transformed to the following nodes and edges within a view:

$$
\begin{matrix}
& & & \rightarrow n_{T_2} \\
n_{T_1} & \rightarrow & & \rightarrow n_{T_3} \\
& & n_{AND-split} & \\
n_{T_4} & \rightarrow & & \rightarrow n_{T_5} \\
& & & \rightarrow n_{T_6}
\end{matrix}
$$

Also, in this case the similarity computation is carried out according to the approach presented in the previous section.

The third approximation method could be further improved by counting the recurrent edges within a view. This can be achieved by using bags of edges instead of sets of edges. All operations on sets should then be replaced with operations on bags. The approximation methods 1 and 3 have been selected for the empirical evaluation in order to get first insights whether and to what extent the results differ. In the future, further experiments are required as well as a further extension to the described methods. For instance, the control flow elements could be identified unambiguously by means of a naming function using their succeeding workflow elements.

FORMATIVE EVALUATION

An experimental evaluation of the approximation methods 1 and 3 was conducted. The test case base consists of 37 workflow instances from the chip design domain. They are derived from real change request documents of the industrial partner Silicon Image GmbH (formerly sci-worx). Each of the cases were presented as a query to the remainder of the case base according to the leave-one-out approach. 35 of them have an Empirically Best Matching Case (EBMC) from the remainder of the case base. The EBMC has been selected by a human expert. As a quality criterion for the evaluation, whether the EBMC was in the 10 most similar cases according to approximation methods 1 and 3 was investigated. Method 3 is implemented with the bag approach that was sketched.

Both methods gave excellent results (compare Figure 6 and Figure 7). For 34 of the queries, the EBMC was under the 10 most similar cases for both methods. For 21 of those, the EBMC was among the three most similar cases for both methods. Figure 6 shows the positions of the particular EBMC's in the retrieval result lists. The squared dots stand for the results of method 1 and the diamonds for those of method 3. For

example, for the case number five (x-axis) used as query the EBMC achieved position 3 (y-axis) for method 1 and the best position (position 1) for method 3. The expected position of the EBMC in a result set is with 2.91 for method 1 worse than for method 3 with 2.38. In 17 cases, the two methods gave the identical retrieval results. In 6 cases, method 1 achieved a better result and in 12 cases, method 3 was empirically more successful. In two of those cases, method 3 was significantly better; the EBMC had a difference of 4 positions in the lists of most similar cases.

Figure 7 shows the frequency distribution of the positions of the EBMC's. Method 3 achieved better results than method 1, as the density of the distribution is higher for the better positions (the lower part of the distribution). The representation according to method 1 required less nodes and edges for the same workflow instances. On average, this saved about a third of the size of the graph that was required by method 3.

CONCLUSION

Agile workflow technology is an innovative research area that has a significant practical im-

Figure 6. Position of the empirically best matching case (EBMC) in the retrieval results

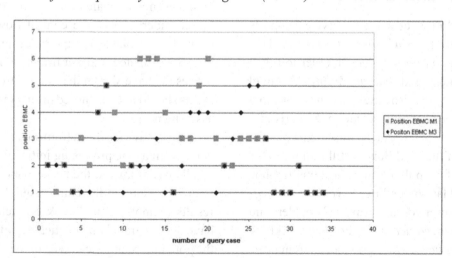

Figure 7. Frequency distribution of the positions of the EBMC's

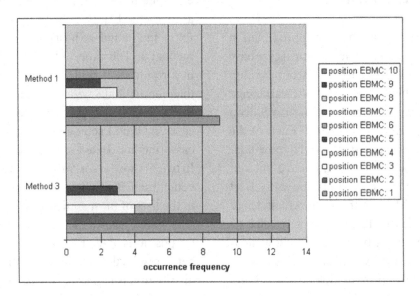

pact. This article contributes to agile workflow technology with a novel approach that enables an interlocked modelling and execution of workflows due to incomplete and inconsistent information in highly dynamic environments. In this approach, late-modelling as well as structural ad-hoc changes of ongoing workflows are supported by means of case-based reasoning.

Some of the challenges for an interlocked modelling and execution of workflows that are derived from a careful analysis of the requirements of the chip design domain have been solved successfully.

The workflow enactment service supports *modifications of workflows at runtime.* This includes both *ad-hoc changes* in order to fulfill change request and *late-modelling.* A novel suspension mechanism prevents the workflow enactment service from executing the parts of a workflow that are about to be modified while the remainder of the workflow is still running. This is a means for applying modifications (ad-hoc changes and late-modelling) to *very large, long-term processes* involving many stakeholders and including *delayed decisions.* For this workflow enactment service, a workflow modelling language

which provides special workflow elements dedicated to agility and supports *context-awareness* was developed.

The modification of workflows is a difficult task that is performed by human experts. The chip design experts of our industrial partner Silicon Image GmbH as well as other experts that have been interviewed highlighted the importance of change reuse. The approach supports the reuse of changes by means of case-based reasoning. A similarity measure is employed in order to retrieve useful experience on workflow modifications. In an experimental evaluation, the hypothesis that the consideration of the control flow structure of workflows plays an important role in this has been investigated and confirmed. Furthermore, the results have shown that the control flow elements should not be ignored during the similarity assessment.

The positive feedback from our industrial partner as well as the promising initial experimental results has prompted the performance of a large scale user study in the chip design domain. The results (Minor, Schmalen, & Koldehoff, 2009) have demonstrated the practical significance and the potential economic impact of the work. In addition, the aim is to extend the approach towards a semi-automatic, interactive modification of agile workflows like the Phala approach (Leake & Morwick, 2008) and the Pegasus/Wings approach (Gil, 2009) apply it for e-science workflows before run time, that is, for non-agile workflows. Furthermore, the focus of the work will be extended to other application domains.

REFERENCES

Aamodt, A., & Plaza, E. (1994). Case-based reasoning: Foundational issues, methodological variations, and system approaches. *AI Communications*, 7(1), 39–59.

Adams, M., ter Hofstede, A. H. M., Edmond, D., & van der Aalst, W. M. P. (2006). Worklets: A service-oriented implementation of dynamic flexibility in workflows. In R. Meersman, Z. Tari et al. (Eds.), *On the move to meaningful Internet systems 2006: CoopIS, DOA, GADA, and OD-BASE, OTM. Proceedings of the Confederated International Conferences, CoopIS, DOA, GADA, and ODBASE 2006, Part I* (LNCS 4275, pp. 291-308). Berlin: Springer.

Antoniou, G., & van Harmelen, F. (2004). Web ontology language: OWL. In S. Staab & R. Studer (Eds.), *Handbook on ontologies* (pp. 29-50). Berlin: Springer.

Babai, L., Erdös, P., & Selkow, S. M. (1980). Random graph isomorphism. *SIAM Journal on Computing*, 9, 628–635. doi:10.1137/0209047

Babai, L., & Kucera, L. (1979). Canonical labelling of graphs in linear average time. In *Proceedings of the 20th Annual IEEE Symposium on Foundations of Computer Science* (pp. 39-46). San Juan, Puerto Rico.

Bassil, S., Rudolf, K., Keller, R. K., & Kropf, P. (2004, June 17-18). A workflow-oriented system architecture for the management of container transportation. In J. Desel, B. Pernici, & M. Weske (Eds.), *Business process management: Proceedings of LNCS 3080, Second International Conference, BPM 2004, Potsdam, Germany* (pp. 116-131). Berlin: Springer.

Bergmann, R. (2002). *Experience management: Foundations, development methodology, and Internet-based applications* (LNAI 2432). Berlin: Springer.

Brandstädt, A. (1994). *Graphen und algorithmen*. Stuttgart: Teubner.

Bunke, H., & Messmer, B. T. (1993, November 1-5). Similarity measures for structured representations. In S. Wess, K.-D. Althoff, & M. M. Richter (Eds.), *Topics in case-based reasoning, first European Workshop, EWCBR-93, Kaiserslautern, Germany, Selected Papers* (LNCS 837, pp. 106-118). Berlin: Springer.

Carlsen, S., & Jørgensen, H. D. (1998, November 14). Emergent workflow: The AIS workware demonstrator. In *Proceedings of the CSCW-98 Workshop: Towards Adaptive Workflow Systems*. Seattle, WA, USA.

Casati, F., Ceri, S., Pernici, B., & Pozzi, G. (1998). Workflow evolution. *Data & Knowledge Engineering*, 24, 211–238. doi:10.1016/S0169-023X(97)00033-5

Dey, A. K. (2001). Understanding and using context. *Personal and Ubiquitous Computing*, 5(1), 4–7. doi:10.1007/s007790170019

Dourish, P., Holmes, J., MacLean, A., Marqvardsen, P., & Zbyslaw, A. (1996, November). Freeflow: Mediating between representation and action in workflow systems. In *Proceedings of the ACM Conference on Computer Supported Cooperative Work CSCW'96* (pp. 190-198). Boston

Freßmann, A., Maximini, K., & Sauer, T. (2005, April 10-13). Towards collaborative agent-based knowledge support for time-critical and business-critical processes. In K.-D. Althoff, A. Dengel, R. Bergmann, M. Nick, & T. Roth-Berghofer (Eds.), *Professional knowledge management: Third Biennial Conference, WM 2005, Kaiserslautern, Germany Revised Selected Papers* (LNAI 3782, pp. 420-430). Berlin: Springer.

Gil, Y. (in press). From data to knowledge to discoveries: Scientific workflows and artificial intelligence. *Science Progress*.

Herrmann, T. (2001). Lernendes workflow. In T. Herrmann, A. W. Scheer, & H. Weber (Eds.), *Verbesserung von Geschäftsprozessen mit flexiblen Workflow-Management-Systemen,* (pp. 143-154). Heidelberg: Physica-Verlag.

Hwang, S. Y., & Tang, J. (2004). Consulting past exceptions to facilitate workflow exception handling. *Decision Support Systems, 37,* 49–69. doi:10.1016/S0167-9236(02)00194-X

Kofod-Petersen, A., & Mikalsen, M. (2005). Context: Representation and reasoning – representing and reasoning about context in a mobile environment. *Revue d'Intelligence Artificielle, 19,* 479–498. doi:10.3166/ria.19.479-498

Leake, D., & Kendall-Morwick, J. (2008, September 1-4). Towards case-based support for e-science workflow generation by mining provenance. In K.-D. Althoff, R. Bergmann, M. Minor, & A. Hanft (Eds.), *Advances in Case-Based Reasoning, 9th European Conference, ECCBR 2008, Trier, Germany* (LNAI 5239, pp. 269-283). Berlin: Springer.

Leymann, F., & Roller, D. (2000). *Production workflow - concepts and techniques.* Upper Saddle River, NJ: Prentice Hall International.

Lu, R., & Sadiq, S. (2006, September 5-7). Managing process variants as an information resource. In S. Dustdar, J. L. P. Fiadeiro, & A. P. Sheth (Eds.), *Business process management, Proceedings of the 4th International Conference, BPM 2006, Vienna, Austria* (LNCS 4102, pp. 426-431). Berlin: Springer.

Luo, Z., Sheth, A., Kochut, K., & Arpinar, B. (2003). Exception handling for conflict resolution in cross-organizational workflows. *Distributed and Parallel Databases, 13,* 271–306. doi:10.1023/A:1022827610371

Madhusudan, T., Zhao, J. L., & Marshall, B. (2004). A case-based reasoning framework for workflow model management. *Data & Knowledge Engineering, 50,* 87–115. doi:10.1016/j.datak.2004.01.005

Mehlhorn, K. (1984). *Data structures and algorithms 2: Graph algorithms and NP completeness,* Berlin: Springer.

Meijler, T. D., Kessels, H., Vuijsr, C., & le Comte, R. (1998, November 14). Realising run-time adaptable workflow by means of reflection in the Baan workflow engine. In *Proceedings of the CSCW-98 Workshop: Towards Adaptive Workflow Systems, Seattle, WA, USA.*

Minor, M., Schmalen, D., & Koldehoff, A. (2009). Fallstudie zum Einsatz agiler, prozessorientierter Methoden in der Chipindustrie. In H. R. Hansen, D. Karagiannis, & H.-G. Fill (Eds.), *Business Services: Konzepte, Technologien, Anwendungen, 9. Internationale Tagung Wirtschaftsinformatik, 25. - 27. Februar 2009, Wien,* volume 1 (pp. 193-201). Oesterreichische Computer Gesellschaft.

Minor, M., Schmalen, D., Koldehoff, A., & Bergmann, R. (2007). Configurable contexts for experience management. In Gronau, N. (Ed.), *4th Conference on Professional Knowledge Management - Experiences and Visions* (Vol. 2), *Potsdam, Univ. of Potsdam* (pp. 119-126). Berlin: GITO-Verlag.

Minor, M., Schmalen, D., Tartakovski, A., & Bergmann, R. (2008). Agile Workflow Technology and Case-Based Change Reuse for Long-Term Processes. *International Journal of Intelligent Information Technologies, 4*(1), 80–98.

Reichert, M., & Dadam, P. (2009). Enabling adaptive process-aware information systems with ADEPT2. In J. Cardoso, & W. van der Aalst (Eds.), *Handbook of research on business process modeling*. Hershey, PA: IGI Global.

Reichert, M., Rinderle, S., & Dadam, P. (2003, June). ADEPT workflow management system: Flexible support for enterprise-wide business processes (tool presentation). In W. M. P. van der Aalst (Ed.), *International Conference on Business Process Management (BPM '03)* (LNAI 2678, pp. 370-379). Berlin: Springer.

Rinderle, S., Weber, B., Reichert, M., & Wild, W. (2005, September 5-8). Integrating process learning and process evolution - A semantics based approach. In W. M. P van der Aalst, B. Benatallah, F. Casati, & F. Curbera (Eds.), *Proceedings of the Business Process Management, 3rd International Conference, BPM 2005, Nancy, France* (LNCS 3649, pp. 252-267). Berlin: Springer.

Rozinat, A., & van der Aalst, W. M. P. (2005, September 5). Conformance testing: Measuring the fit and appropriateness of event logs and process models. In C. Bussler, & A. Haller (Eds.), *Business Process Management Workshops, BPM 2005 International Workshops, BPI, BPD, ENEI, BPRM, WSCOBPM, BPS, Nancy, France. Revised Selected Papers,* (LNCS 3812, pp. 163-176). Berlin: Springer.

Russell, N., van der Aalst, W. M. P., & ter Hofstede, A. H. M. (2006). Workflow exception patterns. In E. Dubois, & K. Pohl (Eds.), *18th International Conference on Advanced Information Systems Engineering (CAiSE '06)* (LNCS 4001, pp. 288-302). Berlin: Springer.

Schimm, G., van der Aalst, W. M. P., van Dongen, B., & Herbst, J. (2003). Workflow mining: A survey of issues and approaches. *Data & Knowledge Engineering, 47,* 237–267. doi:10.1016/S0169-023X(03)00066-1

Schwarz, S. (2003, April 2-4). Task-Konzepte: Struktur und Semantik für Workflows. In U. Reimer, A. Abecker, S. Staab, & G. Stumme (Eds.), *Proceedings of the WM2003: Professionelles Wissensmanagement – Erfahrungen und Visionen, Luzern, Switzerland, LNI P-28* (pp. 351-356), Bonn: Gesellschaft für Informatik.

Ullman, J. R. (1976). An algorithm for subgraph isomorphism. *Journal of the Association for Computing Machinery, 23*(1), 31–42.

van der Aalst, W. M. P., ter Hofstede, A. H. M., Kiepuszewski, B., & Barros, A. P. (2003). Workflow patterns. *Distributed and Parallel Databases, 14,* 5–51. doi:10.1023/A:1022883727209

van der Aalst, W. M. P., Weske, M., & Grünbauer, D. (2005). Case handling: A new paradigm for business process support. *Data & Knowledge Engineering, 53,* 129–162. doi:10.1016/j.datak.2004.07.003

van Elst, L., Aschoff, F. R., Bernardi, A., Maus, H., & Schwarz, S. (2003, June). Weakly-structured workflows for knowledge-intensive tasks: An experimental evaluation. In *Proceedings of the 12th IEEE International Workshops on Enabling Technologies (WETICE 2003), Infrastructure for Collaborative Enterprises, Linz, Austria* (pp. 340-345). Los Alamitos, California: IEEE Computer Society.

Wagner, K., & Bodendiek, R. (1989). *Graphentheorie I*. BI-Wissenschaftsverlag, Mannheim.

Weber, B., Reichert, M., & Rinderle-Ma, S. (2008). Change patterns and change support features - Enhancing flexibility in process-aware information systems . *Data & Knowledge Engineering, 66*, 438–466. doi:10.1016/j.datak.2008.05.001

Weber, B., & Wild, W. (2005, April 10-13). Towards the agile management of business processes. In K.-D. Althoff, A. Dengel, R. Bergmann, M. Nick, & T. Roth-Berghofer (Eds.), *Professional knowledge management, Third Biennial Conference, WM 2005, Kaiserslautern, Germany, Revised Selected Papers* (LNCS 3782, pp. 409-419). Berlin: Springer.

Weber, B., Wild, W., & Breu, R. (2004, August 30-September 2). CBRFlow: Enabling adaptive workflow management through conversational case-based reasoning. In P. Funk, & P. A. Gonzalez-Calero (Eds.), *Advances in case-based reasoning, 7th European Conference, ECCBR 2004, Madrid, Spain* (LNCS 3155, pp. 434-448). Berlin: Springer.

Weske, M. (1999). *Workflow management systems: Formal foundation, conceptual design, implementation aspects*, Habilitation's thesis, University of Münster, Germany.

Wombacher, A. (2006, October 29-November 3). Evaluation of technical measures for workflow similarity based on a pilot study. In R. Meersman, Z. Tari et al. (Eds.), *On the move to meaningful Internet systems 2006: CoopIS, DOA, GADA, and ODBASE, OTM Confederated International Conferences, CoopIS, DOA, GADA, and ODBASE 2006, Montpellier, France, Proceedings, Part I* (LNCS 4275, pp. 255-272). Berlin: Springer.

Workflow Management Coalition. (1999). Workflow management coalition glossary & terminology. Retrieved on May 23, 2007, from http://www.wfmc.org/standards/docs/TC-1011_term_glossary_v3.pdf

Chapter 15
Extending a Conceptual Modeling Language for Adaptive Web Applications

Raoudha Ben Djemaa
MIRACL, Tunisie

Ikram Amous
MIRACL, Tunisie

Abdelmajid Ben Hamadou
MIRACL, Tunisie

ABSTRACT

The complexity of adaptive Web applications (AWA) is increasing almost every day. Besides impacting the implementation phase, this complexity must also be suitably managed while modeling the application. To this end, the paper proposes an approach for AWA called GIWA based on WA-UML (Web Adaptive Unified Modeling Language). This extension defines a set of stereotypes and constraints, which make possible the modeling of AWA. GIWA's target is to facilitate the automatic execution of the design and the automatic generation of adaptable web interface. The GIWA methodology is based on different step: requirement analysis, conceptual design, adaptation design and generation. Using GIWA, designers can specify, at a requirement analysis, the features of web application to be generated. These features are represented, at the conceptual level using WA-UML. At the adaptation level, GIWA acquires all information about users' preferences and their access condition to be used at the generation level. The last level is based on java swing interface to instantiate models which are translated in XML files. GIWA uses then XSL files (user preferences) and RDF files (devices' capability) to generate the HTML page corresponding to the user.

INTRODUCTION

Web applications have become increasingly popular in the last five years as tools for user-driven access to information. By definition, a Web application is a Web system (Web server, network, HTTP, browser) in which user input (navigation and data input) effects the state of the business (Conallen, 2000). This definition attempts to establish that a Web application is a software system with a business state, and that its front end is in large part delivered via a Web system.

However, adaptive Web applications (AWA) is a new direction of research within the area of user-adaptive systems. AWA enhances classic Web application with an intelligent agent which supports the user by adapting the content and the presentation of a Web page to their rights, needs, individual characteristics, and materiel configuration (WAP, browser). AWA avoids the 'incorrect adaptation' problem of classic adaptive systems by providing space for user-driven adaptation. AWA also avoids the 'lost in hyperspace' problem of classic hypermedia systems by providing intelligent guidance. More generally, an AWA is said to be *adaptable* when the user gets the impression that the system has been designed specifically for them.

For these types of applications, the need for adaptation arises from different aspects of the interaction between users and Web applications. User categories, which deal with these systems, are increasingly heterogeneous due to their different interests and preferences. The Web can be accessed through a number of different devices (PC, WebTV, PDA, WAP phone, etc.). Finally, taking into account the user preferences (desired layout, navigation patterns, etc.) and browsing history can lead to a more effective interaction. This leads to the fact that there is a higher need to automate, at least partially, the design process of hypermedia presentation as used in hypermedia and Web applications.

In fact, adaptation can be useful in various Web application fields, such us online advertising, direct Web marketing, electronic commerce, online learning and teaching, and so forth. The number of possible personalization variants seems countless. As with other Web features, a great variety of technologies and systems have been developed and are available in the market, but little or no attention has been paid to the process of modeling and designing AWA.

In AWA, the personalization of presentations and contents (i.e., their adaptation to users' requirements and preferences) is becoming a major requirement. To facilitate the Web engineering of AWA there is an obvious need for a design methodology. This methodology should allow designers to specify applications in an appropriate level of abstraction depending on the different stages of the engineering project (requirements analysis, design, and implementation). As a consequence, adaptive Web engineering represents an active research area. So, developing adaptive Web engineering results in providing a systematic and disciplined approach for designing, implementing and maintaining adaptive Web/hypermedia applications.

For all these reasons, in the last few years, several models and methodologies have been proposed for supporting the development of adaptive Web/hypermedia applications. The main goal of such models is to help designers reason in a structured way on aspects that are specific to hypermedia, such as links, structure, navigation, etc and to express adaptation in the design process. Moreover, they should help engineers to manage the overall complexity of Web development, which requires a variety of activities, such as organizing the structure, choosing the contents, and the presentation modality, some of them involving automated generation of Web pages. So, methodologies usually provide guidelines for performing such activities and suitable models for expressing the results of such operations.

These methodologies and languages should facilitate different aspects of AWA design, such as conceptual design, hypermedia design, presentation design, adaptation design, and so forth.

Some of the works in the hypermedia modeling field only focus on the notation, like the UML extension proposed by Conallen (2000), or the design process, such as OOHDM (Schwabe & Rossi, 1998), UWE (Koch, 2001), OOWS (Fons et al., 2003), KIWIS (Villanova-Oliver et al., 2002), and so forth. The latter use standard notation, like E-R notation, OMT or UML, merely for the conceptual design and define their own notation and graphical techniques for the other steps. In the same vein, in previous works (Djemaa, 2006a, 2006b; Djemaa, 2007), we have presented a user driven method for modeling AWA, called GIWA.

This article addresses the issue by proposing a specific modeling language (WA-UML) as a basis for our design methodology for AWA (called GIWA). GIWA methodology (Djemaa,, 2007) is an audience-driven1 Web application and includes several features in order to provide a better support for an automated design of adaptive Web applications.

The rest of the article is structured as follows. In section 2 we provide an overview of related work. In section 3, we present the GIWA design methodology and discuss the individual steps that are involved in this approach. In sections 4, 5, and 6 we describe the models of WA-UML. We define essentially the use case diagram, the conceptual sequence diagram and the conceptual class diagram. Section 7 presents the process of implementation of GIWA and some examples of interfaces which illustrate the prototype. Finally, section 8 concludes the article and suggests future research directions.

RELATED WORK

Aspects such as adaptation and generation process complicate the design process of Web application and make its complexity beyond the level that is easily handled by a single human developer. Therefore, a strong methodology (supported by a suite of tools) can help to keep the design process at a practical level. Recently, in this context, different approaches for modeling and engineering adaptive hypermedia system have emerged.

Approved hypermedia design principles, such as those defined in OOHDM (object oriented hypermedia methodology design) (Schwabe, 1998) or in RMM (relationship methodology management) (Isakowitz, 1998) have been enhanced with the notions of adaptation and personalization in a further extension of OOHDM (Rossi, Schwabe, & Guimaraes, 2001) or the RMM-based Hera methodology (Frasincar & Houben, 2001; Frasincar, Houben, & Vdovjak, 2002). UWE (UML-based Web engineering) (Koch, 2000, 2001) included a design method for adaptive hypermedia applications (AHDM) and a development process for such applications (AHDP).

In the AMACONT project authors have introduced a component-based XML document format (Fiala, 2003). This project enables to compose adaptive Web applications by the aggregation of reusable document components.

All these methods were originally designed for the adaptive hypermedia application (AHA) and do not deal comfortably with an adaptive Web application (AWA). These methods are very much data-driven or implementation-oriented and do not cover the whole lifecycle of adaptive Web applications. Still, most solutions have been originally developed for a manual hypermedia design process and are not particularly well-suited in the context of automated hypermedia design.

On the other hand, most of the currently-existing methodologies lack a profile model that would allow for the design of truly adaptive Web applications, where adaptation means that the application changes its content based on the user's knowledge or browsing behavior within the application. In fact, this model can play a significant role in such applications: our aim is to include this aspect in the personalization of the hypermedia presentations that get generated.

Generating adaptive presentations require a clean separation of concerns, as advocated in (Frasincar & Houben, 2002).

Finally, the majority of methodologies are based on UML. For example, UWE method (Koch, 2001), OO-HMethod (Gomez, Cachero, & Pastor, 2003) and OOWS method (Fons et al., 2003) offer a modeling process of the AWA, which is based on a set of extended UML diagrams, taking into account the adaptation. Therefore this extension would not be sufficient to capture the relevant semantics of a particular domain or architecture because all these methods do not present a meta-conceptual design defined by a formal language.

To address this purpose, we propose in this article a formal extension mechanism to allow practitioners to extend the semantics of the UML. The new notation, called WA-UML, allows us to define stereotypes, tagged values and constraints that can be applied to model elements. It is specified to provide an adequate notation for the visual representation. It allows for an easy construction of conceptual, presentation and adaptation models, which are part of the proposed methodology.

This work was motivated by the lack of software engineering approaches for adaptive Web application. The GIWA methodology has the following main characteristics. First, it defines a development process that covers the whole lifecycle of adaptive Web applications (Djemaa, 2007). Secondly, it presents a profile model that is visually represented in UML and specified in XML or RDF. Thirdly, it provides a UML extension (WA-UML) for adaptive hypermedia applications. Finally, it integrates a tool which automatically generates adaptive Web interfaces.

GIWA METHODOLOGY

The primary focus of the GIWA is to provide engineering support for adaptive Web applications that automatically generate hypermedia presenta-

tions in response to ad hoc user requirements. The GIWA design methodology guides the designer through the different steps of the design process, each of them yielding a specific model that is being interpreted by the GIWA tools to achieve the objective of automatic presentation generation.

GIWA is an audience-driven methodology which distinguishes several steps to be followed during the design process of a Web application. Each design step produces as its outcome a specification with a certain level of abstraction. The sequence of these steps is depicted in Figure 1.

The requirement analysis step (Djemaa, 2007) is to represent the application domain. This step should express the purpose and the subjects of the Web application through the *functionality model* and define the target audience through the *audience model*. The result of these two models is a set of audience classes together with an informal description of their *functional space*. In GIWA, the functional space is determined by a semi automatic algorithm called AGCA.

In the conceptual design step, the functional space for each audience class is represented using traditional conceptual modeling: use case diagram, sequence diagram, class diagram, and

Figure 1. GIWA design methodology

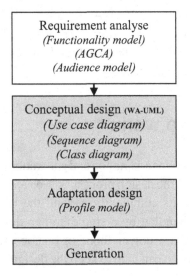

so forth. In GIWA, conceptual models are represented in a specific notation called *Web adaptive unified modeling language* (WA-UML). This new notation increases the expressivity of UML while adding labels and graphic annotations to UML diagrams. This extension of UML defines a set of stereotypes and constraints, which make possible the design of a conceptual model. These models are translated and exported into XML files in the data repository. Within the information system one could distinguish a data repository that contains the data that is available for use in the presentation to be generated: the queries are executed against this repository.

The adaptation design adds adaptation features to the previously defined model. This step defines the user adaptation in the Web application generation process. This level is based on the profile model, which takes into account the user's device capabilities (hardware and software), users' preferences for presentation (desired layout, navigation patterns, etc.) and personal information (e.g., age, sex, language, etc.). In GIWA, we distinguish two kinds of adaptation: adaptability and adaptivity. Adaptability is considered to be static. It is based on information about user preferences for presentation (e.g., font color, page layout, etc.) and user preferences for navigation stored in the profile model before browsing starts. Adaptivity is considered to be dynamic. Our purpose is to provide a system which is able to automatically adapt a given presentation to the user device capabilities (hardware and software configuration). Information about device capabilities are captured from log files and stored in the profile model.

Finally, at the generation level, the designer is invited to instantiate the previous models using the specific interfaces offered by GIWA. Only the aspects related to the first two levels (requirement analysis and conceptual design) are instantiated by the designer. If they are allowed, the user will instantiate information in the profile model (related to the adaptation design), in turn. In GIWA, information related to the devices' capabilities

are dynamically captured by the system (using log files) and then stored in the profile model. At the end of the instantiation step, the GIWA deployment can be launched.

Although requirement analysis is an important phases in the Web engineering life cycle, it is beyond the scope of this article. We primarily concentrate on the steps describing the conceptual level to present the new notation of our modeling language WA-UML and we present a brief description of the adaptation and generation level.

USE CASE DIAGRAM IN WA-UML

The goal of requirements gathering is to elicit the informational and functional requirements of Web application. For our purposes these requirements can be captured using use case diagrams and scenarios. In fact, the use case diagram is used in system analysis to identify, clarify, and organize system requirements.

This diagram is the starting point of our new notation. By analogy to UML, this diagram is represented by the two extended concepts: *Actor* and *Use case*.

Actors in WA-UML

An actor represents something or someone who supplies a stimulus to the system (human user, hardware device or other system). In Web applications, an actor can consult and/or modify the state of the system, by sending and/or receiving messages.

In fact, for Web applications, besides the human user (defined as a physical person) who exploits the Web system; we can distinguish services or functions (roles played by human users) or systems (hardware device, computer systems, Web service).

In this context, and in order to take into account these distinctions, we propose three categories of actors. These actors are classified as follows:

- Physical actor: represents a human user (or a human users' group) who visits the Web application.
- Logical actor: represents a role played by a human user (or a human users' group) to assure the maintenance of Web application.
- System Actor: represents a computer system, device hardware or Web service, and so forth. These systems are generally connected to the application to get information from the system or to update data.

To incorporate adaptation mechanisms in our method we have proposed a profile model. This model translates the different dimensions of adaptation that the user must acquire to execute the functionality in the system. For modeling this, we have extended the actor (notation UML) using a bubble "P"; to designate the concept of profile for each physical and logical actor. We present in Figure 2 the new notation of WA-UML.

Use Case of WA-UML

Generally, we distinguish two kinds of user needs for a Web application that implements an application server, satisfying the users' requests.

The first, called informational, stands for the users' need for information. In our approach, we specify that the information required by the user is either dynamic or static. The former will be represented by dynamic Web pages created at the time of the user's request. The latter will be represented by static Web pages stored in the Web server.

The second type of need, called functional, presents the actions carried out by the user towards the system, and which, after execution, affects the state of the applicative server to modify the set of information accessible by the actors.

Met with the increasing needs of users of Web applications, we distinguish, three types of functionalities: static informational functionality (SIF), dynamic informational functionality (DIF) and professional functionality (PF).

UML does not include a standard notation to distinguish graphically between these three variants of functionalities. To capture these, we have introduced in WA-UML a specific graphical notation for each functionality. Table 1 presents these new notations.

Textual Description of a Use Case

To document use cases, textual description is indispensable, because it permits communication with users easily and precisely. However, the text presents inconveniences since it is difficult to write it and to show stages for each scenario; besides, the maintenance of evolving text often proves to be problematic. To face this limitation, we propose meta-scenarios predefined for every type of use case defined by WA-UML. The latter will be instantiated by the definition of variables list. We present in Table 2 the meta-scenario of a FIS.

In the appendix, we present the meta-scenario of a DIF and the meta-scenario of a PF.

Meta Model of the Use Case Diagram of WA-UML

In Figure 4, we present the meta-model of the use case diagram proposed by WA-UML. To validate our model we propose to add the following OCL (object constraint language) constraints:

[1] A physical actor can have only an association with a use case and this association is binary:

Figure 2. Actors of WA-UML

Physical actor

Logical actor

System actor

Table 1. Use cases of WA-UML

Notation	Description
Name-SIF	**SIF**: Static informational functionality displaying a static Web page related to a specific URL
Name-DIF	**DIF**: Dynamic informational functionality displaying a dynamic Web page building from one (or more than one) "SELECT" server's request. It is a selection of data without affecting the applicative server's state.
Name-PF	**PF**: Profession functionality displaying a dynamic Web page building from one (or more than one) update server request (update, add and delete). The execution of this functionality affects the applicative server's state (information of data base will be modified).

Table 2. Meta scenario of a FIS

Principal actor	«physical actor »
Objective	The user wants to open a static Web page
Preconditions	- The SIF required by the actor belongs to his functional space . - The Web page is available on the application server. - The Web page can be displayed in his context (hardware environment) definite in his Profile "P."
Postconditions	The actor found the page which he looked.

Nominal Scenario	
1.N	The actor clicks on a hypertext or hypermedia link named "name-link" to send to the server a request of research of a static Web page.
2.N	The Web server looks for the "URL" of the Web page required and poster to the user the page result "name_page_res."
3.N	The actor consults the page result "name_page_res."

Alternatives Scenarios	
1.N-A1	The actor did not find the corresponding link to his page.
The actor uses a research form named "name_form_rech" to look for the required page. The system sends back him the link of page "name_link." At this instant, the actor can link on the stage 1.N.	
2.N-A1	The system did not find the page required by the actor.
The system signals the failure to the actor and proposes him to do a new research. The use case started again to the stage 1.N.	
2.N-A2	The system passed the maximum length of research wished by the user to have a result "Time_SIF ."
The system signals the failure to the actor and proposes him to do a new research. The use case started again to the stage 1.N.	
2.N-A3	The actor wanted to interrupt research.
The system abandons research. The use case ends (failure).	

Variables	
Instantiation's Variables of meta-scenario	«Physical actor », « name_link ," « URL », « name_page_res ," « name_form_rech ."
Adaptation's Variables	- Variable of performance: lasted of maximum re-looks for of a static Web page " time_SIF." - Variable of ergonomics: color of the hypertext link (before and after activation), disposition of the hypertext link in the page (depend of the Visibility of the functionality).

```
self.associations->forAll (a | a.connection-
    >size = 2 and
    a.allConnections->exists (r | r.type.
    oclIsKindOf (ActeurPhysique)) anda.
    allConnections->exists (r | r.type.
    oclIsKindOf (UseCase)))
```

[2]   A logical actor can have only an association with a professional functionality use case and this association is binary:

```
self.associations->forAll (a | a.connection-
    >size = 2 and
a.allConnections->exists (r | r.type.ocl-
    IsKindOf (ActeurLogique)) and
```

a.allConnections->exist s(r | r.type.oclIsKin-dOf (CasUtilisationFM)))

[3]   A system actor can have only an association with a professional functionality use case and this association is binary:

```
self.associations->forAll (a | a.connection-
    >size = 2 and
a.allConnections->exists(r | r.type.oc-
    lIsKindOf (ActeurSystème)) and
```

a.allConnections->exists(r | r.type.oclIsKin-dOf (CasUtilisationFM)))

[4]   A use case can have «extends» or « includes » generalizations.

```
self.generalization->forAll   (g
    |g.stereotype.name = 'Extends' or
    g.stereotype.name = 'Includes')
```

The use case diagram and the textual description provide a part of requirements specification. However, this diagram is insufficient to identify IHM classes or those that describe the internals of Web application. This fact will be defined in other diagrams detailed in the following section.

SEQUENCE DIAGRAM OF WA-UML

The goal of the sequence diagram is to present interactions that can exist between the user and the system presented by the different Web pages of the application. This interaction, which is achieved from exchanges of messages, can have parameters in the user's profile.

Figure 3. Meta model of use case diagram proposed by WA-UML

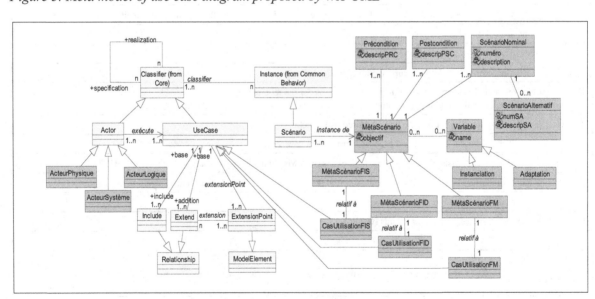

Legend:

NewClass1   meta classes UML

NewClass2   meta classes WA-UML

Concepts of Sequence Diagram

In this diagram, Web pages are presented by the WA-UML objects extended with new icons (cf. Table 3).

In fact, in WA-UML objects are of three types: *server object* (presentation logic, professional rules and behaviors of the system), *client object* (presenting the Web pages which are reached by the user) and *entity object* (presenting objects generated by the application). The latter can be *simple entity objects* (such as the catalog, the basket, the command, etc.) or *user entity objects* presenting the human user of the application (e.g., the customer, the supplier, etc.)

Objects interact while exchanging messages that can be very simple messages (presented by the simple arrows) or profile messages (presented by lozenges arrows carrying the "P" letter). These messages can possess parameters. Figure 4 presents an example of sequence diagram.

Table 3. different Icons of WA-UML Web pages

Type Page	Icons
Static Web page	
Dynamic Web page	
Form	
Frame	
Server Web page	
User Entity	
Simple Entity	

Meta Model of Sequence Diagram

Figure 5 depicts different elements of a sequence diagram in WA-ULM. These elements are defined in the package « Common Behavior » of the semantic UML and they are extended by WA-UML to take into account the different objects and messages.

To validate our model we propose to add the following OCL constraints:

[1]   A client object can only receive messages from other client objects or server objects:
```
self.receiver->forAll (o | o.oclIsKindOf
    (ObjectClient) or o.oclIsKindOf (Ob-
    jetServeur))
```
[2]   A client object can only send messages to other client objects or server objects:
```
self.sender->forAll (o | o.oclIsKindOf
    (ObjectClient) or o.oclIsKindOf (Ob-
    jetServeur))
```
[3]   An entity object can only receive messages from server objects:
```
self.receiver->forAll (o | o.oclIsKindOf
    (ObjetServeur))
```
[4]   An entity object can only send messages to other entity objects:
```
self.sender->forAll (o | o.oclIsKindOf
    (ObjetEntité))
```
[5]   A user entity object can send messages to client objects:
```
self.sender->forAll (o | o.oclIsKindOf
    (ObjetClient))
```
[6]   A server object can receive messages from the client objects or other server objects:
```
self.receiver->forAll (o | o.oclIsKindOf
    (ObjetServeur) or o.oclIsKindOf (Ob-
    jetClient))
```
[7]   A server object can send messages to all types of objects:
```
self.sender->forAll (o | o.oclIsKindOf
    (ObjetServeur) or    o.oclIsKindOf
    (ObjetClient) or o.oclIsKindOf (Ob-
    jetEntité))
```

Figure 4. Example of WA-UML sequence diagram

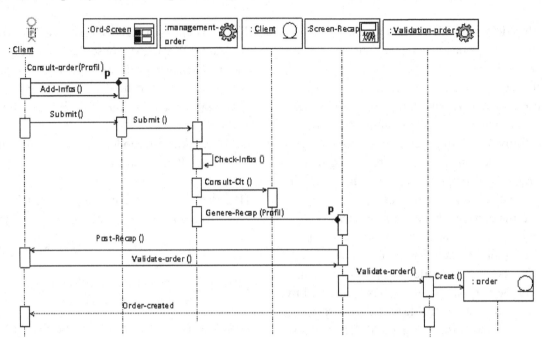

Figure 5. Meta model of sequence diagram

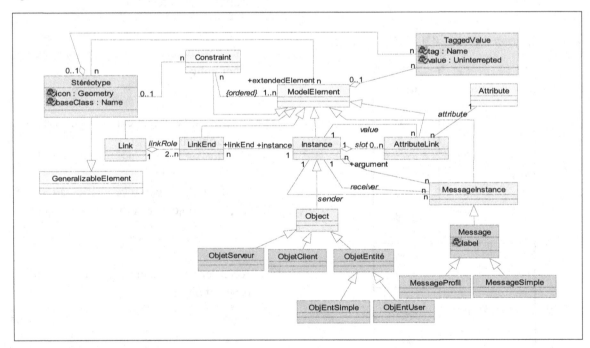

Figure 6. Static and dynamic Web page

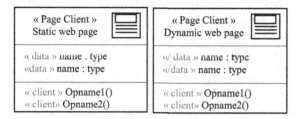

Figure 7. Form Web page

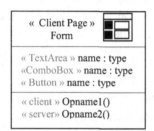

Figure 8. Frameset Web page

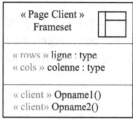

Figure 9. Server Web page

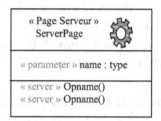

CLASS DIAGRAM OF WA-UML

The goal of class diagram is to model the Web pages of the application defined as objects in the sequence diagram. In WA-UML a class diagram is an illustration of the relationships and source code dependencies among classes. In this context, a class defines the operations and attributes in an object, which is a specific client page or the server page representing the Web application.

Different Classes of WA-UML

In WA-UML, Web pages can be *static Web pages* presenting the static information stored on the server of the application, *dynamic Web pages* presenting a Web page generated dynamically following a user request, *form Web pages* presenting a form that the user must fill and send to the server or *frameset Web pages* presenting a container of other Web pages that can be static Web pages, dynamic Web pages, form Web pages or some other frameset Web pages.

In this step for each type of class, the designer must specify the attributes and operations of classes extended with new icons and stereotypes. Figures 6, 7, 8, and 9 show the different classes proposed by WA-UML.

Figure 6 shows that:

- Attributes stereotyped by "data" to represent data which constitute a static Web page (text, picture, video, etc.).
- Attributes stereotyped by "/data" to distinguish derived data generated by a server script representing the results of a dynamic Web page.
- Operations stereotyped by "client" to specify respectively the client script.

Figure 7 shows that:

- Attributes stereotyped by elements of a HTML form.
- Operations stereotyped by "client" or "server" to specify respectively client script or server script.

Figure 8 shows that:

- Attributes stereotyped by elements of a frame (rows, cols, target, etc.)
- Operations stereotyped by "client" to specify client script.

Figure 9 shows that:

- Attributes stereotyped by "parameter" represent the parameter, which use a server page to execute a script server.
- Operations stereotyped by "server" to specify the server script.

Meta Model of the Class Diagram

Modeling elements of the conceptual class diagram are: the class and the association. In Figure 10, we present the meta model of this class diagram. Associations in this model obey certain rules that we define using OCL:

[1] A client class can be the source of association only for other client classes or server classes:
```
self.source->forAll (o | o.oclIsKindOf
    (ClasseClient) or o.oclIsKindOf
    (ClasseServeur))
```

[2] A client class can be the destination of association only for other client classes or server classes:
```
self.destination->forAll (o | o.oclIsKindOf
    (ClasseClient) oro.oclIsKindOf
    (ClasseServeur))
```

[3] An entity class can be the source of association only with entity classes:
```
self.source->for All (o | o.oclIsKindOf
    (ClasseEntité))
```

Figure 10. Meta model of the conceptual class diagram

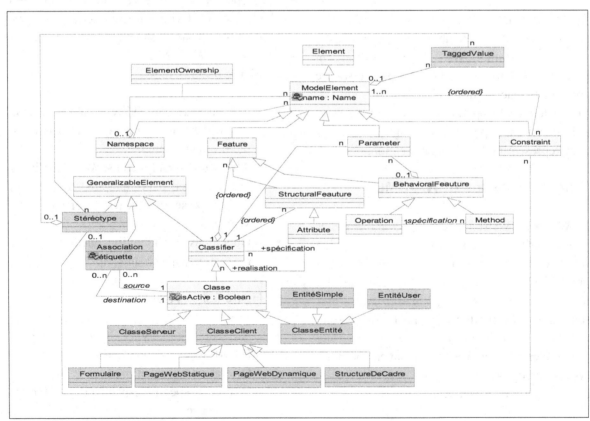

[4] An entity class can be the destination of association only with server classes:

```
self.destination->forAll (o | o.oclIsKindOf
     (ClasseServeur))
```

[5] A user entity can be the source of association with client classes:

```
self.source->for All (o | o.oclIsKindOf
     (ClasseClient))
```

[6] A server class can be the source of association with all types of classes:

```
self.source->for All (o | o.oclIsKindOf
     (ClasseServeur)  or  o.oclIsKindOf
     (ClasseClient)  or  o.oclIsKindOf
     (ClasseEntité))
```

[7] A server class can be the destination of association with client classes or other server classes:

```
self.destination->forAll (o | o.oclIsKindOf
     (ClasseServeur)  or  o.oclIsKindOf
     (ClasseClient))
```

GENERATION LEVEL

The previous sections dealt with the conceptual process of GIWA methodology. This section focuses on the process of generation of adaptive Web applications and describes how the system is dynamically adjusted to varying preferences of users.

The target of this step is to facilitate the automatic execution of the design and the automatic generation of adaptive Web interfaces. It should be possible to program the Web applications in such a way that it can automatically execute the process specified by the design. The tool is based on a collection of engines, which interpret the models provided by the designer during the design process.

GIWA is implemented using Java, according to this architecture (cf. Figure 11).

Architecture of GIWA is split into several layers that each process a different model and thus reflect a different generation step.:

- The semantic level (Djemaa, 2007) instantiates specific data contents of the Web application defined by different semantic model us functionality model, audience model and profile model.

- The conceptual level focuses on the creation of diagrams in WA-UML. In fact, in this level we propose an AGL which supports the new design elements that we proposed. This AGL is based on ArgoUML because it permits to guide the user in the use of the UML notation through a mechanism of critiques and help messages. In addition, the source code of ArgoUML is available on the Web making it possible to analyze its inner workings. Thus, in this extension of ArgoUML, we introduce new types of diagrams to represent the different diagrams of our extension, namely, WA-UML.

- The generation level focuses on the process of Web page generation and describes how the generator GIWA dynamically adjusts to varying user preferences into chosen implementation platform (HTML, WML, SMIL, etc.).

For a designer modeling an adaptive Web application using GIWA, the first step is instantiating the functionalities model. Once instantiated, this model is translated into XML files to be stored in the data repository ❶ and the system executes the algorithm for the generation of audience classes ❷ which builds the audience model. Then this model is validated by a specific process called PVMA ❸. The next step is to translate them into XML file ❹ which contains the functional space for each audience class. At this stage, the content is adapted to each audience class.

So, to adapt the user's presentation preferences, the designer is invited to instantiate the profile model (Djemaa, 2007) using specific interfaces offered by GIWA that treat respectively the following axes:

Figure 11. Architecture of GIWA

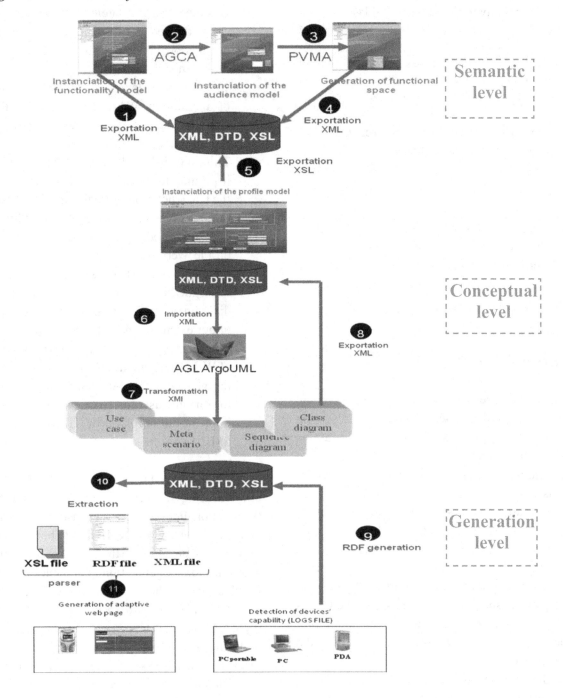

- Personal information about the user such as name, age, sex, language.
- User's presentation preferences defined in terms of Web pages composition and graphi-

cal aspects specified by two charters called composition and graphical charters.

Figure 12. Example of a WA-UML use case diagram

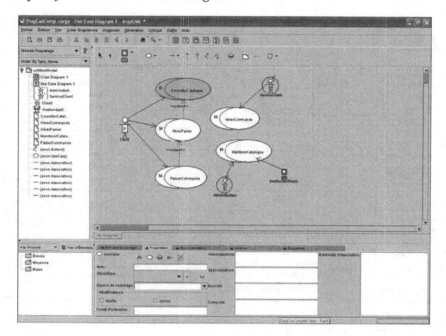

After instantiation, the profile model is exported into XSL files in the data repository ❺. At this stage GIWA treats the aspect of adaptability which appears through the choice of a graphical charter and through the composition of the page after generating users' application. Then XML files are extracted from the data repository ❻ to be imported into the AGL supporting the new design elements that we proposed. This AGL is based on ArgoUML.

So, in our use of ArgoUML, we introduce new types of diagrams to represent the new diagrams of our Extension WA-UML. In these diagrams, the user can add, displace and copy the different design elements as well as replace faces and publish their properties as used in ArgoUML. Our AGL keeps the same compartments of the main window of ArgoUML. However, modifications are brought onto the diagrams to take into account the new notations of our extension. For example, we extended the use case diagram of ArgoUML with new icons of actors and use cases. Figure 12 shows an example of a use case diagram related to the e-commerce application.

All conceptual diagram of WA-UML can be described with the new AGL based on ArgoUML ❼. Figure 13 shows an example of a class diagram.

The last diagram is translated in XML files ❽.

According to the users' device a profile (refers to the aspect of adaptivity) is captured by GIWA using data from *logs files* to be stored on the server according to a RDF vocabulary presented by W3C (W3C, 2002) ❾ and then instantiate the profile model (user/devices profile) by specific capabilities (e.g., bandwidth, display resolution, etc.). Finally, XML, RDF and XSL files are extracted from the data repository ❿ and they are sent to the PARSER in order to publish the HTML page corresponding to the user devices (PC, PDA, cell phone or desktop browse) ⓫.

In Figure 14, we show the interfaces of GIWA used to adapt the presentation of the Web application with two different devices. It shows the

313

Figure 13. Example of a WA-UML class diagram

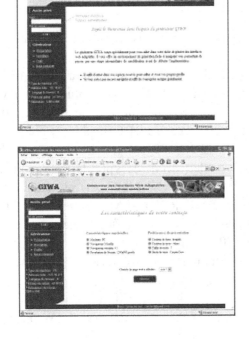

Figure 14. Simulation of GIWA using personnel computer and cell phone (Nokia SDK 5100)

GIWA interfaces presented to user who is connected with, for example, a PC and a user who is connected to the system using a cell phone (Nokia SDK 5100).

CONCLUSION

The research described in this article targets the support of automated modeling and generation of Web interfaces in the context of adaptive Web application (AWA).

In this article, we propose WA-UML (Web adaptive unified modeling language); a UML profile for adaptive Web applications (AWA). It increases the expressivity of UML, while adding labels and graphic annotations to UML diagrams. This extension of UML defines a set of stereotypes and constraints, which make possible the modeling of AWA. These stereotypes and constraints are applied to a number of diagrams represented within the same model and the same diagrams which describe the system. In this article we present the use case diagram of WA-UML as well as its realization by the analysis class diagram.

The new WA-UML language which we have proposed brings answers to mitigate the insufficiencies of the UML language to model adaptive Web applications. In this article we have focused on use case diagram, conceptual sequence diagram and conceptual class diagram. These diagrams make the models capable of adjusting to the features of AWA.

WA-UML is used to develop a methodology for AWA called GIWA supporting both the design and the generation aspects.

The primary focus of the GIWA is to provide engineering support for adaptive Web applications that automatically generate hypermedia presentations in response to each ad hoc user requirement. The GIWA design methodology guides the designer through the different steps

of the design process, each of them yielding a specific model based on WA-UML that is being interpreted by the GIWA tools to achieve the objective of automatic presentation generation. GIWA distinguishes several steps to be followed during the design process of a Web application. First, the requirement analysis step is carried out to organize the data elements at a logical level through two models (functionalities model and audience model) (Djemaa, 2007). Secondly, the conceptual design, which is the scope of this article, presents an extension of the UML language, titled WA-UML. It provides a set of extended UML diagrams (use case and conceptual diagram) taking into account the adaptation. This can be used by any design method of the AWA, which is based on an object oriented approach and using UML. The third level is the adaptation design. It provides adaptation features (users' preferences and devices' capabilities) to the previously created models.

Finally, the generation level is able to automatically adapt a given presentation to the user preferences for presentation and navigation stored in the profile model before browsing starts (adaptability) and the user device capabilities (adaptivity). Information about device capabilities are captured from log files and stored in the profile model. In order to experiment with the proposed methodology, a prototype has been built. The prototype uses XML and RDF to store the data and XSL to specify transformations between consequent steps.

As part of future work, we plan to carry out the following tasks:

- The completion of diagrams of WA-UML to take into account both aspects of presentation and navigation.
- The completion of the implementation of the different diagrams of WA-UML as well as the automatic generation of code.

ACKNOWLEDGMENT

The authors thank Sonda Zghal, masters's student at Sfax University, for his help in the development of a part of this work. Professor Faiez Gargouri for sharing with us his views on the WA-UML.

REFERENCES

Conallen, J. (2000). Concevoir des applications Web avec UML, Editions Eyrolles.

Djemaa, R. B., Amous I., & Ben Hamadou A. (2006b). Design and implementation of adaptive Web application. *In 8th International Conference on Enterprise Information Systems ICEIS'06. 23 - 27, May, Paphos Cyprus.*

Djemaa, R. B., Amous I., & Ben Hamadou A. (2006a). GIWA: A generator for adaptive Web applications. *In ICIW'06, IEEE International conference on Internet and Web Application and Services.*

Djemaa, R. B., Amous I., & Ben Hamadou A. (2007) Adaptable and adaptive web applications: From design to generation. *International Review on Computers and Software (IRECOS)* - May -

Fiala, Z., Hinz M., Meissner K., & Wehneer F. (2003). A component-based component architecture for adaptive dynamic web documents. *Journal of Web engineering, 2*(1&2): 058-073.

Fons, J., Pelechano V., Pastor O., Albert M., & Valderas, P. (2003, May 20-24). *Extending an OO Method to Develop Web Applications.* The Twelfth International World Wide Web Conference. Budapest, Hungary.

Frasincar, F. & Houben G.-J. (2002). Hypermedia presentation adaptation on the semantic web. In P. de Bra, P. Brusilovsky, & R. Conejo R (Eds.), Proceedings of the 2nd International Confer-ence on Adaptive Hypermedia and Adaptive Web-Based Systems (AH 2002), (pp. 133-142). Malaga, Spain.

Frasincar, F., Houben, G.-J., & Vdovjak, R. (2001). An RMM-Based Methodology for Hypermedia Presentation Design. *In Proceedings of the 5th East European Conference on Advances in Databases and Information Systems (ADBIS 2001),* (pp. 323-337). *LNCS 2151,* Vilnius, Lithuania ,

Gómez, J., Cachero, C., & Pastor, O. (2001). Extending a conceptual modeling approach to web application design. *In Proceedings of the 1st International Workshop on Web-Oriented Software Technology,* Valencia, Spain, June 2001.

Isakowitz, T., Stohr, A., & Balasubramanian, E. (1995). RMM: A methodology for structured hypermedia design. *Communications of the ACM 38*(8), 34-44.

Koch, N. (2000). Software Engineering for Adaptative Hypermedia Systems—Reference Model, Modelling Techniques and Development Process, Ph.D Thesis, Fakultät der Mathematik und Informatik, Ludwig-Maximilians Universität München.

Koch, N. (2001). The Authoring Process of the UML-based Web Engineering Approach. 1*st International Workshop on Web-Oriented Software Technology.*

Rossi, G., Schwabe, D., & Guimaraes, R. (2001). Designing personalized Web applications. *In WWW10, The Tenth International Conference on the World Wide Web,* Hong Kong.

Schwabe, D., & Rossi, G. (1998). Developing hypermedia applications using OOHDM. *In Proceedings of Workshop on Hypermedia development Process, Methods and Models,* (pp. 85-94).

Villanova-Oliver, M., Gensel, J., Martin, H., & Erb, C. (2002, April 8-10). *Design and genera-*

tion of adaptable web information systems with KIWIS. In proceedings of the 3rd IEEE Conference on Information Technology ITCC-2002, Las Vegas, USA

World Wide Web Consortium. (2001). eXtensible Stylesheet Language, XSL Specification – version 1.0, W3C Recommendation. Retrieved October 15, 2001 from http://www.w3.org/TR/xsl/

World Wide Web Consortium. (2002). RDF Vocabulary Description Language 1.0: RDF Schema, W3C Working Draft. Retrieved April 30, 2002 from http://www.w3.org/TR/rdf-schemadix

APPENDIX

Meta-Scenario of a DIF

Principal Actor	«physical actor »
Objective	The user wants to find as quickly as possible required information in the data base.
Preconditions	- The FID required by the user belongs to his functional space. - Data of the dynamic Web page is available on the Web server.
Post conditions	The user has found the information which he looked.
Nominal Scenario	
1.N	The actor asks for the execution of this DIF.
2.N	The system displays a research form "name_form_rech" in a Web page "name_page_form ."
3.N	The user execute a research using one or several keys-word "$\{word_1, word_2,..., word_n\}$."
4.N	The system executes the request and displays the page result "name_page_res ."
Alternatives Scenarios	
2.N-A1	The system did not find the research form.
The system signals the failure to the actor and proposes him to renew his demand. The use case started again to the stage 1.N.	
2.N-A2	The system passed the maximum length wished by the user to have a result of research.
The system signals the failure to the actor and proposes him to renew his demand. The use case started again to the stage 1.N.	
3.N-A1	The actor did not well write his request of research.
The system detects this mistake and displays him advices to correct his request. The user does these corrections and can link on the stage 3.N.	
2.N-A2	The actor wanted to interrupt research.
The system abandons research. The use case ends (failure).	
Variables	
Variables instantiation of meta-scenario	"Physical actor," "name_form_rech," "name_page_form ," keys-word: { $word_1$, $word_2$,..., $word_n$}, "name_page_res ."
Adaptation Variables	- Variable of performance: lasted of execution of the select requests for gener-ated a dynamic Web page "time_DIF ." - Variable of ergonomics: disposition of the research form (high of the page, low of the page), disposition of link executing this functionality of research, color of the form, and so forth.

Meta-Scenario of a PF

Principal Actor	"Physical actor" or " logical actor" or " system actor "
Objective	The actor (physical or logical) wants to update data of the system by the execution of a request.
Preconditions	- The actor identified from the system with his login and his password. - The PF required by the actor belongs to his functional space. - Data (or tables) participate in the execution of this PF are available on the Web server.
Post conditions	The actor did the treatment that he or she wanted. Data in the system are updated.
Nominal Scenario	
1.N	The actor asks for the execution of this PF.
2.N	The system displays to the actor a form "nom_form_metier," include in a Web page " name_page_metier."
3.N	The actor seizes the necessary keys word "fields {ch 1, ch 2,…, ch n}" and valid the execution of his request.
4.N	The system treated the demand of the actor and confirms his execution by sending back him a page result "name_page_res."
Alternatives Scenarios	
3.N-A1	The actor annuls his request.
The system comes back to the previous page and the use case ends.	
3.N-A2	The system comes back to the previous page and the use case ends. The actor didn't well seize data of his request (mistake of seizure).
- The system detects this mistake and displays him advices of correction of his request. - The actor does these corrections and can link on the stage 3.N.	
4.N-A1	The system detects a disfunction of update (it could not have executed the user's request).
The system signals the failure for the actor and proposes him to do a new request. The use case started again to the stage 2.N.	
Variables	
Variables instantiation of meta-scenario	"Physical actor" or " logical actor" or " system actor ," « name_form_metier», « name_page_metier », « fields {ch 1,ch 2,…, ch n} ," « name_page_res ."
Adaptation Variables	- Variable of performance: length maximum of execution of PF requests "time_PF." - Variable of ergonomics: disposition of the form of a profession request (highest in the page, lowest in the page).

This work was previously published in the International Journal of Intelligent Information Technologies, Vol. 4, Issue 2, edited by V. Sugumaran, pp. 37-56, copyright 2008 by IGI Publishing (an imprint of IGI Global).

Chapter 16

A QoS Aware, Cognitive Parameters Based Model for the Selection of Semantic Web Services

Sandeep Kumar
Banaras Hindu University (IT-BHU), India

Kuldeep Kumar
Kurukshetra University, India

ABSTRACT

Semantic Web service selection is considered as the one of the most important aspects of semantic web service composition process. The Quality of Service (QoS) and cognitive parameters can be a good basis for this selection process. In this paper, we have presented a hybrid selection model for the selection of Semantic Web services based on their QoS and cognitive parameters. The presented model provides a new approach of measuring the QoS parameters in an accurate way and provides a completely novel and formalized measurement of different cognitive parameters.

INTRODUCTION

Selecting the most appropriate semantic web service is one of the important components of the semantic web service composition process. Most aspects of the Semantic Web Service (SWS) composition process such as automatic discovery, selection, and composition are tightly related to the quality of semantic web services (QoS). QoS can be defined as a part of service description and is an especially important factor for service composition (Zeng et al., 2004). In addition to the QoS, the cognitive parameters of service providers can also prove to be the deciding factors in semantic web service selection and composition. They can be used to decide on a particular SWS to invoke by the user among the numerous services discovered. Various cognitive parameters such as capability, desire, intention, commitment, trust, reputation etc. and a number of QoS parameters such as cost, response time, reliability, accuracy, security feature, execution time, exception handling feature, penalty on breaking service contract etc. have to be considered

DOI: 10.4018/978-1-60566-970-0.ch007

in service selection. To our knowledge, the issue of service selection based on QoS and cognitive parameters has not been thoroughly addressed in the literature till now. This is primarily due to the complexity of QoS metrics and a lack of formal measurement of cognitive parameters. The work by Ermolayev et al. (2004) has presented a method for selection of service provider agents based on some cognitive parameters. But the agent selection model only considers capability and credibility assessment as the base for agent selection and then performs negotiation with each of the capable agent. But assessing these parameters alone may not result in the selection of the best performing agent.

The proposed Hybrid Selection Model (HSM) for service selection can be easily integrated with Multi-Agent based SWS composition process. HSM performs rating of the agents based on their cognitive as well as QoS parameters. Some of the novel features in the model are: providing the formalization and new normalization procedure for QoS parameters, providing the formalization of cognitive parameters, providing a method for measuring the reputation of agent, and providing a dynamic feedback system affecting the reputation of the selected service provider based on the quality of its present service. In support of this work, an evaluation and experimentation is also presented.

The remainder of the paper is organized as follows. Following the introduction section, section 2 describes some similar works. Section 3 provides a description of the hybrid selection model and the details of QoS and cognitive parameters based rating is provided in section 4 and 5 respectively. Section 6 discusses the evaluation of the presented model and some comparison with existing work. The implementation of a system providing service selection based on the proposed model has been discussed in the Section 7. Section 8 provides the conclusion and future work.

RELATED WORKS

In this section, some of the similar works reported in the literature have been discussed. Among others, some of the related works are (Liu et al., 2004), (Mou et al., 2005), (Menasce, 2002), (Wang et al., 2006), (Ermolayev et al., 2004) and (Kumar and Mishra, 2008). However, no work was found dealing with the selection of semantic web services based upon both QoS based and cognitive parameters based rating in hybrid form. Liu et al., (2004) have proposed the QoS parameters based rating of semantic web services. They have proposed an algorithm which is based upon the average ranking. Thus, their algorithm is neglecting the nuances in different quality properties. Further, they have not considered the various cognitive parameters while rating the services. The works by Mou et al. (2005) and Menasce (2002) have also proposed the QoS-based service selection. But, similar to the work by Liu et al. (2004), they have also not considered the cognitive parameters in the service selection process. Further, the works by (Liu et al., 2004), (Mou et al., 2005), (Menasce, 2002) have not considered the user-tendency towards the quality-attributes in the rating process. Wang et al. (2006) have also proposed a QoS parameters based rating of services. Their formulation has provided the proper normalization of various quality parameters and has also considered the user-tendency in the rating process. But, the quality index generated by their model is very discrete in the nature. This work has also not considered the cognitive parameters in the service selection. Kumar and Mishra (2008) have proposed the cognitive parameters based rating of semantic web services. But, they have not considered the QoS parameters based rating in their service selection model. A multi-agent based semantic web service selection and composition model has been proposed by Ermolayev et al. (2004). They have proposed cognitive parameters based rating of semantic web services. But in their model, they have considered the capability and credibility assessments only. They have presented a procedure for maintaining the capability and credibility estimates of agents as well as a formal method for updating these parameters. No discussion on the initialization of these parameters was found.

On the other hand, our proposed model has presented a hybrid selection model which considers both QoS and cognitive parameters in service selection. The proposed model provides a proper normalization of various parameters. The user-tendency towards the quality-attributes has also been considered in the proposed selection model. Further, the index generated by the proposed model is realistic in nature and is not very discrete.

HYBRID SELECTION MODEL

The success of semantic web based system in satisfying a user's request depends highly upon the selection of the most appropriate SWSs. Use of agent based technology in semantic web based systems is one of the emerging and important areas of research. Even in the manifesto by Berners-Lee et al. (2001), the use of software agents in semantic web based systems has been discussed. This approach considers the SWS composition system as a multi-agent system (MAS), in which each component service is considered as an agent capability. Though multi-agent technology has been explored for use in web based systems, little work (Ermolayev et al. 2004; Kungas and Matskin, 2006) has been reported in the literature which directly addresses the agent-based approach inform the semantic web perspective. In MAS based SWS composition systems, the selection of most appropriate SWS seems to be more reliable, because the agents can be characterized by various social, cognitive, and QoS parameters. However, the issue of service selection and composition has been highly discussed in the literature, but the selection of intelligent software agent based on its cognitive and QoS parameters

for a MAS based SWS composition system has not been thoroughly addressed in the literature till now. Ermolayev et al. (2004) have briefly discussed agent selection in SWS composition based on cognitive parameters alone (credibility and capability assessment), where as Wang et al. (2006) have presented a model for the selection of SWSs based on QoS alone. To our knowledge, no work has been reported in the literature, which provides a model for selection of agents acting as SWS providers based on both cognitive and QoS parameters, as well as a formalized method of measuring the various parameters. The model presented in this paper deals with these issues.

HSM calculates an index called Index of Selection (IoS) for the agent based on its cognitive and QoS parameters. The IoS value is then used as the basis for the selection of the best provider agent. HSM can be used by the service requester agent (SRA) for the selection of best performing service provider agent (SPA). A requester agent is any agent that needs services from another agent, called the provider agent. As IoS represents the overall rating of agent based on its cognitive parameters based rating and QoS parameters based rating, it must be the combination of both ratings. However, SRA should be given the freedom to decide the weightage of each rating in overall IoS. Hence, IoS can be defined as the weighted sum of cognitive parameters based rating and QoS based rating of agent.

$$IoS = \beta(QI) + (1 - \beta)(CogI), \qquad \ldots(1)$$

Where $0 \leq QI \leq 1,\ \ 0 \leq CogI \leq 1,\ \ 0 \leq \beta \leq 1,\ \ 0 \leq IoS \leq 1$

In the above equation, QI is the QoS Index, representing the rating of the agent based on its QoS parameters and CogI is the Cognitive Index, representing the rating of the agent based on its cognitive parameters. β is the measure of relative weight given to QoS rating of the agent as compared to cognition based rating of the agent in its selection. The calculation of QI and CogI further depends on a large number of quality and cognitive parameters respectively. The calculation of the QI and CogI values is discussed in the sections below.

QOS PARAMETERS BASED RATING

The QI of an agent can be defined as the weighted arithmetic mean of the quality ratings of different QoS parameters. But the difficulty in the calculation of QI is that the different quality metrics have different value ranges, value types and measurements. The user may have different tendencies towards different quality metrics. For example, for the metrics such as 'Price', 'Execution Time', the user has the tendency of 'lower the better', while for metrics such as 'Reliability', 'Penalty Bearing', the tendency is 'higher the better'. In addition, the metric may even have higher weight in calculation of QI, but its impact may be lowered by its smaller value than other metrics. We have solved these problems by presenting the following normalization of metrics, such that the value of all metrics lie between 0 and 1 and they all are of the tendency 'higher the better'. Now, let $\left\{ Ql_1, Ql_2 \ldots Ql_t, Qh_{t+1}, Qh_{t+2} \ldots Qh_n \right\}$ be the set of published numerical values for n quality attributes to be used in the calculation of QI. Assume that, out of the n attributes, the first t i.e. $\left(Ql_1, Ql_2 \ldots Ql_t \right)$ attributes have the user tendency 'lower the better', while the next (n-t) attributes, i.e. $\left(Qh_{t+1}, Qh_{t+2} \ldots Qh_n \right)$ have the user tendency 'higher the better'.

Consider that $Ql\max_k$ and $Ql\min_k$ be the maximum and minimum numerical values for the attribute Ql_k among all the candidate profiles of agents and Ql'_k be the normalized value for quality attribute Ql_k, where k = 1, 2 ... t. For normalizing Ql_k in the above discussed form, we have to apply normalization for both purposes: normalization to value between 0 and 1 and normalization to user tendency 'higher the better'. The division

by $Ql\max_k$ is enough for first normalization, but for obtaining normalized value according to the second normalization also, the value has to be subtracted from 1. So, Ql'_k will be given as:

$$Ql'_k = 1 - \left(\frac{Ql_k - Ql\min_k}{Ql\max_k + Ql\min_k} \right),$$
$$Where \quad 0 < Ql'_k \leq 1, \qquad \ldots(2)$$

Now further consider that $Qh\max_k$ and $Qh\min_k$ be the maximum and minimum numerical values for the attribute Qh_k among all the candidate profiles of agents and Qh'_k be the normalized value for quality attribute Qh_k, where k = (t+1), (t+2)... n. For normalizing Qh_k in above form, we have to apply normalization to value between 0 and 1 only, as it is already having the user tendency of 'higher the better'. So, Qh'_k will be given as:

$$Qh'_k = \frac{Qh_k}{Qh\max_k},$$
$$Where \quad 0 < Qh'_k \leq 1, \qquad \ldots(3)$$

Thus, all the quality attributes with normalized values $(Ql'_1, Ql'_2 \ldots Ql'_t, Qh'_{t+1}, Qh'_{t+2} \ldots Qh'_n)$ have user tendency of 'higher the better' for their normalized values. Now, if in the calculation of QI, $WQ_1, WQ_2 \ldots WQ_n$ be the quality weights given to set of quality attributes $(Ql'_1, Ql'_2 \ldots Ql'_t, Qh'_{t+1}, Qh'_{t+2} \ldots Qh'_n)$, then as defined initially, QI is the weighted mean of quality ratings of different QoS parameters. Thus, QI will be given as:

$$QI = \frac{\sum_{i=1}^{t} Ql'_i * WQ_i \ + \ \sum_{i=(t+1)}^{n} Qh'_i * WQ_i}{\sum_{i=1}^{n} WQ_i}$$

$$Where \quad 0 < QI \leq 1 \qquad \qquad ...(4)$$

It must be noted that the values here are normalized in such a way that the rating obtained for different quality parameters for different agents are relative to each other. So the QI shows the relative quality index of agent with respect to other competitive agents.

COGNITIVE PARAMETERS BASED RATING

One of the aims of SPA is to provide services to SRAs in such a way that it can create high trustworthiness among the agent community and hence increased acceptance. The SPA creates trustworthiness by providing reliable services and showing good capabilities, strong desire for performing, strong intention, strong commitment to work and other similar features. So, through the cognitive parameters based rating, a SRA will ultimately judge the trustworthiness of SPAs. However, this judgment should not only include the trust from its own point of view but also from other SRA's views. The trust from fellow SRA's view is measured by the reputation of SPA among these SRAs (Barber & Kim, 2001). So, CogI can be defined as the weighted sum of trustworthiness and reputation of agent. These two parameters can further be calculated using other cognitive parameters like capability, commitment, desire, intention etc. So, the CogI parameter is given as:

$$CogI = \chi(TI) + (1 - \chi)(RI) \qquad ...(5)$$

$$Where \quad 0 \leq TI \leq 1, \quad 0 \leq RI \leq 1, \quad 0 \leq \chi \leq 1, \quad 0 \leq CogI \leq 1$$

In the above equation, TI is the Trust Index, representing a value which is the measure of trustworthiness of the agent and RI is the Reputation Index, a measure of the reputation of the agent among other similar requester agents and the given requester agent. χ is the measure of relative weight given to trustworthiness as compared to reputation of the agent. The calculation for TI and RI is discussed in the forthcoming sections. It must be noted that for the calculation of IoS, the relative value of CogI should be used. As we know that QI is calculated as a relative value, so in equation (1), the parameter CogI must also be of relative nature. The relative value of CogI can be calculated as follows:

If $CogI_1$, $CogI_2$ ... $CogI_n$ are the cognitive indexes of different competitive agents, and $CogI_{max}$ is the maximum value of cognitive index among $CogI_1$, $CogI_2$ ... $CogI_n$, then the relative value of a cognitive index $CogI_k$ for k = 1, 2 ... n is given by $(CogI_k/CogI_{max})$.

Trustworthiness of Agent

The trust of an agent on other information source agents is defined as the confidence in the ability and intention of an information source to deliver correct information (Barber & Kim, 2001). We have adapted this definition for the multi-agent based SWS composition system, to define the trust of Service Requester Agent (SRA) on the Service Provider Agent (SPA) as the confidence in the ability and intention of the SPA to deliver the committed services. So TI can be defined as:

$$TI = CI * II \qquad ,$$
$$Where \, 0 \leq CI \leq 1, \quad 0 \leq II \leq 1, \qquad ...(6)$$

where, CI is the Capability Index, representing a value that is a measure of the capability of the agent and II is the Intention Index, a measure of the intention of the agent to deliver the committed service.

Capability of an agent is the ability to react rationally towards achieving a particular goal. An agent can only perform for its committed goal, if it has the capability to do so (Padgham & Lambrix, 2000). It is the measure of both capacity and expertise of an agent. So, capability of an agent can be judged from its past performance towards the accepted tasks and with how much perfection these were performed. So, CI of an agent can be calculated as follows:

The capability of an agent cannot be considered to be only binary i.e. Task Performed or Task Not Performed. We have considered the following multiple scenarios while judging the capability of an agent and these scenarios also indicate the perfection level of the agent:

(i) Task Completed successfully within the committed parameters.
(ii) Task Completed successfully but with some relaxed parameters such as task not performed within the committed time (but acceptable one), with more price, with less quality, with less quantity, etc.
(iii) Task Not Completed.

The first scenario demonstrates the full capability of the agent, while the second shows a little bit lesser capability as compared to the first. The last scenario depicts the inability of an agent and will negatively affect on overall capability. Thus, each scenario affects the capability measure of an agent differently. So, the capability index (CI) of an agent can be determined by the following equation:

$$CI = \frac{WC_C * N_C + WC_{CR} * N_{CR} - WC_{NC} * N_{NC}}{(WC_C + WC_{CR} + WC_{NC}) * N}$$

$$...(7)$$

where, N_C, N_{CR}, N_{NC} are the number of tasks completed successfully with committed parameters, completed successfully with relaxed param-

eters, and not completed, respectively out of a total of N tasks. WC_C, WC_{CR}, WC_{NC} are the capability weights given to the tasks completed successfully, completed successfully but with relaxed parameters, and not completed, respectively.

In addition, the following relations should hold:

1. $N = N_C + N_{CR} + N_{NC} = 100$, as equation (7) takes percentage values for N_C, N_{CR}, N_{NC}.

2. $0 \leq CI \leq 1$, as equation (7) has its value normalized by $(WC_C + WC_{CR} + WC_{NC}) * N$.

3. $WC_C > WC_{CR}$, This will cause greater weight in the capability calculation to the tasks which are completed successfully within committed parameters than the tasks completed successfully but with relaxed parameters.

4. $WC_{NC} > WC_C$, It is clear from equation (7) that W_{NC} is causing the negative effect on the capability of the agent, but this relation will cause an extra penalty over the agent for not completing the accepted task.

5. Values of WC_C, WC_{CR}, WC_{NC} can be taken under any fixed range, but for uniformity, we can take it between 0 and 1.

Intention of an agent relates to the set of plans for the goal it has committed to achieve. Tweedale et al., (2007) have defined intention as "Intention is desire with commitment". Similarly, Cohen and Levesque, (1990) have explained intention as "Intention is choice with commitment". Thus, intention can be defined as the combination of desire and commitment. So the Intention Index (II) of an agent can be calculated as:

$$II = DI * CommI,$$
$$Where\ 0 \leq DI \leq 1, \quad 0 \leq CommI \leq 1 \qquad (8)$$

where, DI is the Desire Index, representing a value which is a measure of the performance of the agent for its desired tasks and CommI is the Commitment Index, representing a value which is a measure of the commitment of the agent towards the accepted work.

Desire of an agent determines its motivation to bring about what it is trying to achieve. It defines the state of the art that needs to be accomplished. It differs from intention in the point of view that, desire defines the motivation towards the work, while intention may be seen as agent's immediate commitment to implementing an action, as is also clear from equation (8) (Pechoucek, 2003). So, if an agent has desire for a task, then ideally it should have performed well with that task. So, measuring the past-performance of an agent for the tasks presently desired by it, can be a good measure of its honesty towards its desire. From this knowledge, a SRA can properly judge how it will react with respect to its present desires. This model is based on the understanding that, if an agent has published its profile for a particular activity (e.g. Flight Booking), then it is obvious that it is desirous of doing that activity. Thus, using the concepts as described in the calculation of CI, the DI of an agent, which is a measure of the performance of an agent for its desired tasks, can be calculated as follows:

$$DI = \frac{WDs_C * N_C + WDs_{CR} * N_{CR} - WDs_{NC} * N_{NC}}{(WDs_C + WDs_{CR} + WDs_{NC}) * N} \quad ...(9)$$

where, WDs_C, WDs_{CR}, WDs_{NC} denote the performance-to-desire weights given to the tasks completed successfully, completed successfully but with relaxed parameters, and not completed, respectively.

In addition to the applicable relations in the calculation of CI, the following relations should also hold:

1. $0 \le DI \le 1$, as equation (9) has its value normalized by $(WDs_C + WDs_{CR} + WDs_{NC}) * N$.

2. $WDs_C > WDs_{CR}$, This will cause greater weight in the DI calculation to the task which is completed successfully within committed parameters, than the tasks completed successfully but with relaxed parameters.

3. $WDs_{NC} > WDs_C$, It is clear from equation (9) that W_{NC} is causing the negative effect on the DI of agent, but this relation will cause an extra penalty over the agent for not completing the accepted task.

4. Values of WDs_C, WDs_{CR}, WDs_{NC} can be taken under any fixed range, but for uniformity, we can take it between 0 and 1.

5. $WDs_C = WC_C$, $WDs_{CR} < WC_{CR}$, $WDs_{NC} > WC_{NC}$, this will work as extra penalty for not performing the task within parameters and not completing the task, even though an agent shows the desire for it.

Commitment of an agent implies some temporal persistence of the intention. The commitment of an agent leads it to make plans for its action based on its intention. It is a conduct-controlling characteristic of an agent, which says that if an agent is committed to do something, then it should not consider the actions which are incompatible with doing so (Tweedale et al., 2007). So, commitment of an agent can be judged from the point of view that how much of its past actions were compatible with its commitments and how much were incompatible. Hence, the CommI of an agent can be given as:

$$CommI = \frac{WCm_C * N_C - WCm_{CR} * N_{CR} - WCm_{NC} * N_{NC}}{(WCm_C + WCm_{CR} + WCm_{NC}) * N} \quad ...(10)$$

where, WCm_C, WCm_{CR}, WCm_{NC} are the commitment weights given to the tasks completed successfully, completed successfully but with relaxed parameters, and not completed, respectively.

In addition to the relations shown in the computation of CI, which can be applicable here, the following relations should also hold:

1. $WCm_C = WC_C, WCm_{NC} > WC_{NC}$, to assign the penalty of not completing the committed task, as it is due to the reason that some actions incompatible to the commitment must have occurred.

2. $WCm_{CR} \leq WC_{CR}$, the negation for WCm_{CR} in equation (10) must be noted. It is to assign penalty for not doing the task within committed parameters, ultimately due to the reason that some actions incompatible to the commitment must have occurred.

3. Values of WCm_C, WCm_{CR}, WCm_{NC} can be taken under any fixed range, but for uniformity, we can take it between 0 and 1.

The values corresponding to N_C, N_{CR}, N_{NC} in the profiles are updated after utilizing the services of the selected SPA.

Measuring Reputation of Agent

Using TI, the SRA tries to judge the trustworthiness of agent using various cognitive parameters. However, the trustworthiness of agent from the view of other similar SRAs is not judged by the TI. Hence, it should be one of the important parameters for the selection of SPA. This is accomplished by the RI, which is the measure of reputation of an agent. We have adapted the definition of reputation for information source presented in (Barber & Kim, 2001), for the multi-agent based SWS composition system under consideration. Reputation is the amount of trust a SPA has created for itself through interactions with different SRAs. If a SPA consistently meets the expectations of SRAs, then it will increase its reputation and likewise, not satisfying expectation of SRAs due to either incompetence or maliciousness will

decrease its reputation. Checking the reputation of an agent also serves as social law, mandating the SPA to stay trustworthy to all SRAs. However, in the computation of TI, the SPA may publish unreliable information, if it is not controlled by any central body, but now, the agent will risk the reputation it has been building among the SRAs. The agent with consistently low reputation can become isolated from the SRA community (Barber & Kim, 2001).

The reputation of an agent can be calculated using either of the following mechanisms:

1. A central controller exists, which has the reputation indexes for all the published SPAs.

2. Each of the SRA maintains a separate Reputation Table (RT) in its service profile, which has reputation indexes of SPAs from its own point of view.

The Reputation Table (RT) is a data structure which is maintained by the SRA and holds reputation indexes of all those SPAs from which the given SRA has used services in past. An example structure for RT is shown in Table 1. Each entry

Table 1. A reputation table

P	$RI_{R \to P}$
p_3	0.65
p_5	0.72
p_1	0.80
. . .	. . .
p_7	0.78

in the shown RT for requester agent R contains following elements:

i) The Service Provider Agent identifier (P).

ii) The reputation index from requester agent R for the provider agent P ($RI_{R \to P}$).

A given SRA may not consider the reputation feedback from all the similar SRAs equally. The reputation feedback from some of the SRAs may be more effective or reliable for the given SRA than the other ones. So, the overall RI of SPA will be the weighted arithmetic mean of the reputation indexes from all the SRAs including the given SRA itself. Thus, the RI parameter is computed as follows:

$$RI = \frac{\sum_{i=1}^{n} RI_i * WR_i}{\sum_{i=1}^{n} WR_i},$$

$$Where \quad 0 \leq RI_i \leq 1, \qquad \ldots(11)$$

where, RI_i is the reputation index from any service requester agent R_i for the concerned SPA for the required task and WR_i is the weight given by the SRA to the reputation feedback of R_i. One definition for WR_i can be as follows:

$$WR_i = \begin{cases} = 1 & \text{If } R_i \text{ is the given reference SRA} \\ > 0, \leq 1 & \text{If } R_i \text{ is any other SRA} \end{cases}$$

$$\ldots(12)$$

There is also the provision to update the RI of a selected SPA after using its services by the given SRA in its local RT. So, if q is the quality rating given by the reference SRA to the reference SPA based on its services and RI' is the existing reputation index of this SPA in the RT of given SRA, then the updated RI can be calculated as:

$$RI = \varepsilon * RI' + (1 - \varepsilon) * q,$$

$$Where \quad 0 \leq \varepsilon \leq 1, \quad 0 \leq q \leq 1 \qquad \ldots(13)$$

Where, ε is the relative weight given to the past reputation of SPA as compared to its present quality rating.

This feedback system will not only cause the selection process of SPA to be dynamic, but also affect its chances of selection in the future by any of the SRAs. Hence it will compel the SPA to consistently perform well to maintain its established reputation.

EVALUATION

Our proposed Hybrid Selection Model mainly focuses on the computation of IoS based on QoS and cognitive parameters. The model can be used for the selection of the best SPA in the multi-agent based SWS composition process. To our knowledge, no such formalized model considering both cognitive and QoS parameters for SPA selection in multi-agent based SWS composition has been reported in the literature. So, we will evaluate QoS parameters based rating and cognitive parameters based rating individually.

Similar to the presented QoS based rating, the work by (Liu et al., 2004), (Mou et al., 2005), (Menasce, 2002) and (Wang et al., 2006) have proposed QoS-based service selection. However, the works by (Liu et al., 2004), (Mou et al., 2005), (Menasce, 2002) do not seem to provide fair and effective evaluation algorithms. The algorithm by (Liu et al., 2004) uses average ranking, neglecting the nuances in different quality properties. The normalization approach presented in these works cannot make a fair evaluation of all the qualities, because all quality metrics do not have the same range. So, the real impact of a metric may get decreased, i.e., it may really have a high impact but has less numerical value than others with low impact but high numerical value. Also, these methods do not take into consideration the user's tendency towards the quality metrics. For example, these methods rate the metrics with a tendency of 'higher the better', but some metrics like cost have the tendency of 'lower the better'. Our algorithm for QI calculation solves these problems by normalizing each quality metrics into a value between 0 and 1 and generating the value such that it has the tendency of 'higher the better' irrespective of the actual tendency of that quality metric. The work by (Wang et al., 2006) has also presented an algorithm which handles these problems. But our algorithm is better because of the following reasons:

1. Our algorithm generates a relative index for a quality metric, by generating a more than zero value of the index for even the smallest value of the metric. So the generated index can be used independently in other calculations as well, for the respective metric.
2. The indexes generated are relative to each other and the resulting values of the indexes are such that they can give a clue of the nearest relative value and the difference in the actual values of the metric. However, the indexes generated by Wang et al. (2006) are very discrete.
3. In the absence of actual values of parameters, the index generated by the proposed model can easily reveal the actual values of the metric, if some standard value is known.

But the index generated by the algorithm in (Wang et al., 2006), can not properly reveal the values.

These facts can be easily verified from the following calculation.

For comparison purposes, we have adopted test data (see table 1) from (Wang et al., 2006) and (Liu et al., 2004). In their experiment, Liu et al. (2004), have implemented a hypothetical phone service registry, which provides various phone services such as long distance, local, wireless, and broadband. 600 users have been simulated to collect the experimental data. They have shown the seven quality criteria for four phone services, but have assigned quality weight equal to zero for two of them, so they are not affecting the overall quality index calculation. Hence, in our experiment we have used the other five quality criteria only and they have the same quality weights as used in (Wang et al., 2006), i.e., 4, 2, 1, 1, 2 for price, compensation rate, penalty rate, execution time, and reputation respectively. The attributes, price and execution time has the user tendency 'lower the better' and all other have 'higher the better'. So, if $Q_p', Q_c', Q_{pr}', Q_e', Q_r'$ are the normalized values for quality attributes price, compensation rate, penalty rate, execution time, and reputation respectively, then their values as calculated in (Wang et al., 2006), corresponding to values in table 2, are as shown in table 3. Using the proposed normalization method and applying equation (2) for price and execution duration and equation (3) for compensation rate, penalty rate,

Table 2. Test data adopted from (Wang et al., 2006)

SPA	Price (in $)	Compensation Rate (in percent)	Penalty Rate (in percent)	Execution Duration (in microsecond)	Reputation (rank value in 0 to 5)
ABC	25	0.5	0.5	100	2.0
BTT	40	0.8	0.1	40	2.5
A_1	28	0.2	0.8	200	3.0
A_2	55	0.6	0.4	170	4.0

Table 3. Normalized quality indexes from (Wang et al., 2006)

SPA	Q'_p	Q'_c	Q'_{pr}	Q'_e	Q'_r
ABC	1	0.5	0.571	0.625	0
BTT	0.5	1	0	1	0.250
A_1	0.9	0	1	0	0.5
A_2	0	0.667	0.429	0.188	1

and reputation, we compute the normalized values as shown in table 4.

Table 4 shows that the resulting values are consistent with the results from (Wang et al., 2006) (table 3). Further, it can be observed that the nature of variation among the normalized values of a quality attribute is more similar to the nature of corresponding actual values, in the case when values are calculated by the proposed model. Now, consider that one only knows the calculated indexes of SPAs (but not the index calculation algorithm) for the attribute price and that the general public opinion for the price of the above mentioned phone service is an average value of $37. Then, an approximate value for the parameter should be obtained by multiplying the general public opinion value and the index if the

user tendency of the index and the actual value are matching and by dividing the general public opinion value by the index if the user tendency of index and the actual value are opposite. As tables 3 and 4 show the indexing of SPAs for the above mentioned service, the price corresponding to ABC, BTT, A_1, A_2 will be $37/1 = 37$, $37/0.5 = 74$, $37/0.9 = 41.11$, $37/0 =$ undefined, respectively when indexes by (Wang et al., 2006) is known and will be $37/1 = 37$, $37/0.8125 = 45.54$, $37/0.9625 = 38.44$, $37/0.625 = 59.2$ respectively when indexes by our proposed model is known. These results show that a guess for the actual price from the indexes is nearer to the actual when indexes are calculated using the proposed method than the case when indexes are calculated by the method provided in (Wang et al., 2006). Figure 1 shows

Figure 1. Price prediction comparison

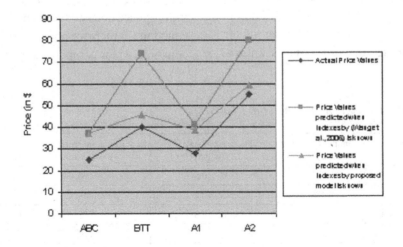

Table 4. Normalized quality indexes calculated using our proposed method

SPA	Q'_p	Q'_c	Q'_{pr}	Q'_e	Q'_r
ABC	1	0.625	0.625	0.75	0.5
BTT	0.8125	1	0.125	1	0.625
A_1	0.9625	0.25	1	0.333	0.75
A_2	0.625	0.75	0.5	0.4583	1

that price prediction from indexes by the proposed model is much near to the actual values than prediction from indexes by (Wang et al., 2006).

Wang et al. (2006) show that the overall quality index of ABC, BTT, A_1, A_2 calculates to 6.196, 5.500, 5.600, 3.951 respectively. On applying equation (4) of the proposed method on normalized values of table 3, the overall quality index of ABC, BTT, A_1, A_2 calculates to 0.7625, 0.7625, 0.7183, 0.6958. So, the obtained results are consistent with (Wang et al., 2006) and ABC has the highest quality index by both approaches. However, it is to be noted that the results of the proposed model differ from the model by (Wang et al., 2006) in the sense that it has quality index of BTT equal to the index of ABC and greater than the index of A_1. It is due to the fact that for the lowest value of each quality attribute, the corresponding normalized value comes out to be zero, which causes the overall quality index calculation of its corresponding service to be zero independent of the quality weight assigned to it. So, the index calculation in the proposed method is more appropriately taking the different quality attributes into consideration, which is in line with human intuition.

Similar to the presented work, Kumar and Mishra (2008) have presented a cognition based rating of semantic web services. But, they have not considered the QoS parameters in the rating process. In their work on agent-enabled semantic web service composition, Ermolayev et al. (2004) have presented a cognition based rating, but it only considers capability and credibility assessment of the SPA. They have presented a procedure

for maintaining the capability and credibility estimates of agents as well as a formal method for updating these parameters. However, they have not discussed the methods for their initial measurements. The relations for both capability estimation and credibility assessment presented by them are of recursive nature, with no discussion on their initial measurement. So, these can only be used for updating the capability and credibility values. Where as, the proposed cognition based rating not only considers more cognitive parameters like trust, reputation, capability, desire, intention etc. but also presents a formal method of measuring each using different basic parameters which depends upon the general task performances of SPAs. A distributed approach of measuring the reputation of SPA among the agent community has also been presented by the model. In contrast to the centralized way of maintaining the reputation record, this approach will be faster, as it will enable parallel requests to SRAs for their feedback about reputation of a SPA. Further, the distributed approach is also in line with the distributed nature of semantic web. Hence, the presented cognition based rating will result in more reliable results.

IMPLEMENTATION

We have implemented a semantic web service composition system which uses HSM for service selection. This system uses OWL (Web Ontology Language) (McGuinness & Harmelen, 2008) based service profiles developed using Jena (HP Labs Semantic Web Programme, 2008). The Jena based reasoning (Jena's OWLReasoner) and querying support, which uses SPARQL (Prudhommeaux & Seaborne, 2008) internally, is also used. The negotiation and communication in the system can be maintained using FIPA Contract Net Protocol (Smith & Davis, 2008) and FIPA-ACL (FIPA Architecture Board, 2008) respectively. Figure 2 shows the results of selecting a SPA using HSM.

Specifically, Figure 2 shows the results of applying the model to a semantic web service composition system for education planning. Education planning is the problem of planning the complete process of securing admission in some higher education program, which may involve various activities such as counseling and preparation for entrance examination, choosing the appropriate institute, getting funds, completing admission

formalities, and arranging the transportation to join. The selection of agents providing services for each of the mentioned activities has been carried out using HSM.

The service profiles of different agents are maintained in OWL using Jena Ontology APIs (HP Labs Semantic Web Programme, 2008). The ontology corresponding to the, 'Universal Admissions' agent that provides admission consultancy services, developed using Jena and observed in Altova SemanticWorks (Altova, 2008) at the RDF/OWL level is shown in Figure 3. The process starts with gathering user input for education planning. The input request is composed of some essential parameters like course in which admission is sought, session of admission, qualifying examination score etc. and some constraints and preferences such as constraints on travel class, budget etc. The input ontologies derived on the basis of input parameters are used in the pro-

Figure 2. HSM based SPA selection

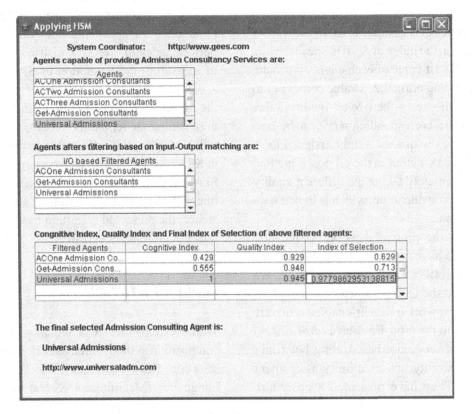

cess of mapping the input request into possible simple tasks. Then, these input ontologies are used to discover the matching SWSs for each task. As shown in Figure 2, 'ACOne Admission Consultants (http://www.aconeac.com)', 'Get-Admission Consultants (http://www.getadmission.com)' 'Universal Admissions (http://www.universaladm.com)' are the various discovered agents which can perform admission consultancy in fulfilling the admission formalities in education planning. For these admission consulting agents, the HSM is applied to calculate the IoS and the agent with maximum IoS i.e. 'Universal Admissions (http://www.universaladm.com)' is selected as the Admission Consultant.

Before reaching the final selection based on IoS (as shown in Figure 2), various steps are performed, as shown in Figure 4. The first table in Figure 4 shows various quality attributes and past performance (percentage of tasks completed, completed with relaxation, and returned) of discovered agents. These parameters are maintained

in the service profiles of respective agents. Using the performance values, the capability, intention, desire, and commitment based ratings of agents are calculated using equations (7), (8), (9), and (10) respectively, as shown in the second table of Figure 4. The third table in Figure 4 shows the extracts from reputation tables of different SRAs, and the final cognition based ratings and corresponding normalized ratings of the discovered agents are shown in the fourth table. The fifth table in Figure 4 shows the normalized values of different quality attributes. These normalized values are calculated using equations (2) and (3), as previously discussed. This table also shows the resulting quality indexes of agents. The calculation of final hybrid index of selection using equation (1) is shown in the last table of Figure 4. The agent with the highest score of index of selection (IoS) is finally selected.

Figure 3. Ontology of a SPA

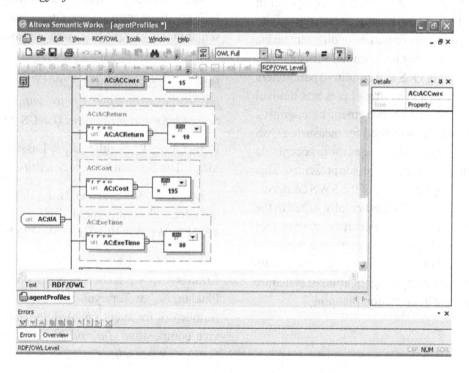

Figure 4. Calculation of various indexes

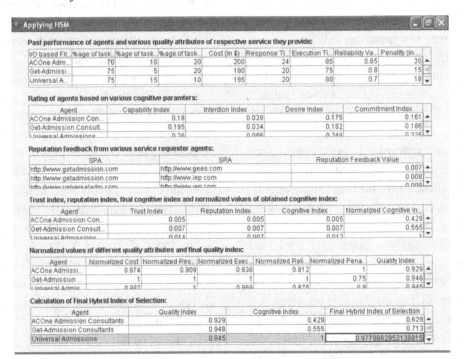

CONCLUSION

This paper has presented a service selection model, HSM, which can be used in the SWS composition process for the selection of the most appropriate semantic web service provider for different tasks. The model is based on the computation of an Index of Selection using QoS and cognitive parameters of service provider. The model presents a novel approach for formal measurement of cognitive parameters and a new method for measuring QoS parameters. The model provides more acceptable results as shown by the comparison presented. This model can be applied to any of the SWS composition process; however it is especially suited to the multi-agent based SWS composition process. Our future work will involve further enhancing the presented model to provide more reliable selection, and further exploring the application of semantic web technology in education planning.

REFERENCES

Altova (n.d.). SemanticWorks Semantic Web tool - Visual RDF and OWL editor. Retrieved March 1, 2008 from http://www.altova.com/products/semanticworks/semantic_web_rdf_owl_editor.html

Barber, K. S., & Kim, J. (2001). *Belief revision process based on trust: Agents evaluating reputation of information sources* (LNCS 2246).

Berner-Lee, T., Hendler, J., & Lassila, O. (2001, May). The Semantic Web. *Scientific American*.

Cohen, P. R., & Levesque, H. J. (1990). Intention is choice with commitment. *Artificial Intelligence*, *42*, 213–261. doi:10.1016/0004-3702(90)90055-5

Ermolayev, V., Keberle, N., Kononenko, O., Plaksin, S., & Terziyan, V. (2004). Towards a framework for agent-enabled Semantic Web service composition. *International Journal of Web Services Research*, *1*(3), 63–87.

FIPA Architecture Board. (n.d.). Foundation for intelligent physical agents, FIPA Communicative act library specification. Retrieved February 12, 2008 from http://www.fipa.org/specs/fipa00037/SC00037J.html.

Foundation for Intelligent Physical Agents. (n.d.). *FIPA contract net interaction protocol specification*. Retrieved February 12, 2008 from http://www.fipa.org/specs/fipa00029/SC00029H.html

Kumar, S., & Mishra, R. B. (2008). A framework towards Semantic Web service composition based on multi-agent system. *International Journal of Information Technology and Web Engineering*, *3*(4), 59–81.

Kungas, P., & Matskin, M. (2006). *Semantic Web service composition through a P2P-based multi-agent environment* (. LNCS, *4118*, 106–119.

Labs Semantic Web Programme, H. P. (n.d.). Jena-A Semantic Web Framework for Java. Retrieved March 1, 2008 from http://jena.sourceforge.net/

Liu, Y., Ngu, A. H. H., & Zeng, L. (2003). QoS computation and policing in dynamic Web service selection. In *Proceedings of the 13th International Conference World Wide Web*. McGuinness, D.L, & Harmelen, F.V. (n.d.). OWL Web ontology language overview. Retrieved February 13, 2008 from http://www.w3.org/TR/owl-features/

Menasce, D. A. (2002). QoS Issues in Web services. *IEEE Internet Computing*, *6*(6). doi:10.1109/MIC.2002.1067740

Mou, Y., Cao, J., Zhang, S.S., & Zhang, J.H. (2005). Interactive Web service choice-making based on extended QoS model. *CIT*, 1130-1134.

Padgham, L., & Lambrix, P. (2000). Agent capabilities: Extending BDI theory. *American Association for Artificial Intelligence*. Retrieved from www.aaai.org

Pechoucek, M. (2003). Formal representation for multi-agent systems. *Gerstner Laboratory, Czech Technical University in Prague*. Retrieved from http://agents.felk.cvut.cz/teaching/33ui2/bdi.pdf

Prudhommeaux, E., & Seaborne, A. (2008). SPARQL Query Language for RDF, Retrieved from http://www.w3.org/TR/2008/REC-rdf-sparql-query-20080115/

Tweedale, J., Ichalkaranje, N., Sioutis, C., Jarvis, B., Consoli, A., & Phillips-Wren, G. (2007). Innovations in multi-agent systems. *Journal of Network and Computer Applications, Elsevier*, *30*(3), 1089–1115. doi:10.1016/j.jnca.2006.04.005

Wang, X., Vitvar, T., Kerrigan, M., & Toma, I. (2006). *A QoS-aware selection model for Semantic Web Services* (LNCS 4294, pp. 390-401).

Zeng, L. Z., Benatallah, B., Anne, H. H. N., Dumas, M., Kalagnanam, J., & Chang, H. (2004). QoS-Aware middleware for Web service composition. *IEEE Transactions on Software Engineering*, *30*(5), 311–327. doi:10.1109/TSE.2004.11

Compilation of References

Aamodt, A., & Plaza, E. (1994). Case-based reasoning: Foundational issues, methodological variations, and system approaches. *AI Communications, 7*(1), 39–59.

Ackermann, F. (1990). The role of computers in group decision support. In C. Eden & J. Radford (Eds.), tackling strategic problems—the role of group decision support and (pp.132-142).

Adams, M., ter Hofstede, A. H. M., Edmond, D., & van der Aalst, W. M. P. (2006). Worklets: A service-oriented implementation of dynamic flexibility in workflows. In R. Meersman, Z. Tari et al. (Eds.), *On the move to meaningful Internet systems 2006: CoopIS, DOA, GADA, and ODBASE, OTM. Proceedings of the Confederated International Conferences, CoopIS, DOA, GADA, and ODBASE 2006, Part I* (LNCS 4275, pp. 291-308). Berlin: Springer.

Aggarwal, C. F., Al-Garawi, C., & Yu, F. P. (2001, May 1-5). Intelligent crawling on the world wide Web with arbitrary predicates. In *Proceedings of the 10th International World Wide Web Conference (WWW '01)* (pp. 96–105). Hong Kong, China.

Agrawal, R., Gunopulos, D., & Leymann, F. (1998) Mining process models from workflow logs. *6th International Conference on Extending Database Technology*, 469–483.

Aiken, M., Liu Sheng, O., & Vogel, D. (1991). Integrating expert systems with group decision support systems. *ACM Transactions on Information Systems, 9*(1), 75-95.

Altingovde, I. S., & Ulusoy, Ö. (2004). Exploiting interclass rules for focused crawling. *IEEE Intelligent Systems, 19*(6), 66-73.

Altova (n.d.). SemanticWorks Semantic Web tool - Visual RDF and OWL editor. Retrieved March 1, 2008 from http://www.altova.com/products/semanticworks/semantic_web_rdf_owl_editor.html

Ambler, S. (1998). *Process patterns: Building large-scale systems using object technology*. Cambridge University Press.

Anderson, L. W., & Krathwohl, D. R. (2001). A Taxonomy for Learning, Teaching, and Assessing: A Revision of Bloom's Taxonomy of Educational Objectives. New York: Longman.

Annoni, A., Friis-Christensen, A., Lucchi, R., & Lutz, M. (2008). Requirements and challenges for building a European spatial information infrastructure: INSPIRE. In P. v. Oosterom & S. Zlatanova (Eds.), *Creating spatial information infrastructures: Towards the spatial Semantic Web* (pp. 216). CRC.

Anson, R., Bostrom, R., & Wynne, B. (1995). An experiment assessing group support system and facilitator effects on meeting outcomes. *Management Science, 41*(2), 189-208.

Antoniou, G., & Bikakis, A. (2007). DR-Prolog: A system for defeasible reasoning with Rules and ontologies on the Semantic Web. *IEEE Transactions on Knowledge and Data Engineering. 19*(2), 233-245.

Antoniou, G., & van Harmelen, F. (2004). Web ontology language: OWL. In S. Staab & R. Studer (Eds.), *Handbook on ontologies* (pp. 29-50). Berlin: Springer.

Aridor, Y., & Lange, D. B. (1998). Agent design patterns: Elements of agent application design. In *Proc. of* the 2nd Int. Conf. on Autonomous Agents, Agents'98, Minneapolis, USA (pp.108-115).

Baader, F., Calvanese, D., McGuinness, D., Nardi, D., & Patel-Schneider, P. F., Eds. (2003). *The Description Logic Handbook: Theory, Implementation and Applications.* Cambridge: Cambridge University Press.

Babai, L., & Kucera, L. (1979). Canonical labelling of graphs in linear average time. In *Proceedings of the 20th Annual IEEE Symposium on Foundations of Computer Science* (pp. 39-46). San Juan, Puerto Rico.

Babai, L., Erdös, P., & Selkow, S. M. (1980). Random graph isomorphism. *SIAM Journal on Computing, 9,* 628–635. doi:10.1137/0209047

Baddeley, A. (1990). Human memory. Boston: Allyn & Bacon.

Bagga, A., & Baldwin, B. (1998). Entity-based cross-document coreferencing using the vector space model. *17th International Conference on Computational Linguistics,* 79–85.

Baker, P.G., Brass, A., Bechhoferb, S., Goble, C., Paton, N., & Stevens, R. (1998). TAMBIS-Transparent Access to Multiple Bioinformatics Information Sources. In *Proceedings of the 6th International Conference on Intelligent Systems for Molecular Biology, AAAI Press,* (pp. 25-34).

Ball, G., & Breese, J. (2000). Emotion and personality in a conversational agent. *Embodied Conversational Agents* (pp. 189-218). Cambridge, MA: MIT Press.

Barber, K. S., & Kim, J. (2001). *Belief revision process based on trust: Agents evaluating reputation of information sources* (LNCS 2246).

Basili, V. (1992). The experimental paradigm in software engineering. *Lecture Notes In Computer Science, 706,* 3-12. London: Springer-Verlag.

Bassil, S., Rudolf, K., Keller, R. K., & Kropf, P. (2004, June 17-18). A workflow-oriented system architecture for the management of container transportation. In J. Desel, B. Pernici, & M. Weske (Eds.), *Business process management: Proceedings of LNCS 3080, Second In-* ternational Conference, BPM 2004, Potsdam, Germany (pp. 116-131). Berlin: Springer.

Bauer, B., Muller, J. P., & Odell, J. (2001). Agent UML: A formalism for specifying multiagent interaction. In *Proc. of the 1st Int. Workshop on Agent-Oriented Software Engineering, AOSE'00, Limerick, Ireland* (pp. 91-103).

Bavelas, A. A. (1948). A mathematical model for group structures. *Human Organization, 7,* 16–30.

Beck, K., & Cunningham, W. (1987). Using pattern languages for object-oriented programs. *Workshop on the Specification and Design for Object-Oriented Programming (OOPSLA'87).*

Begole, J., Tang, J., Smith, R., & Yankelovich, N. (2002). Work rhythms: Analyzing visualizations of awareness histories of distributed groups. *ACM conference on Computer Supported Cooperative Work,* 334–343. New York: ACM Press.

Beierle, C. (1992). An Order-sorted logic for knowledge representation systems. *Artificial Intelligence, 55,* 149–191.

Bekkerman, R., McCallum, A., & Huang, G. (2004). Automatic categorization of e-mail into folders: Benchmark experiments on Enron and SRI corpora. *CIIR Technical Report, IR-418.* Amherst: University of Massachusetts.

Belardinelli, F. (2006). *Quantified modal logic and ontology of physical objects.* PhD Thesis, Scuola Normale Superiore (SNS) in Pisa.

Belew, R. K. (1986). *Adaptive information retrieval: machine learning in associative networks* (Doctoral dissertation, University of Michigan, 1986).

Bellifemine, F., Poggi A., Rimassa, G. (2001). Developing multi-agent systems with a FIPA-compliant agent framework. *Software Pract Experience 2001, 31*(2),103–28.

Bellifemine, F., Poggi, A., & Rimassa, G. (2000). *Developing multi-agent systems with JADE.* Proceedings of the Seventh International Workshop on Agent Theories, Architectures and Languages (ATAL 2000), Boston, MA.

Bergman, M. K. (2001). The Deep Web: Surfacing Hidden Value. *The Journal of Electronic Publishing, 7*(1). Retrieved November 17, 2006, from http://www.press.umich.edu/jep/07-01/bergman.html

Bergmann, R. (2002). *Experience management: Foundations, development methodology, and Internet-based applications* (LNAI 2432). Berlin: Springer.

Bergstein, B. (2007). *So much data, relatively little space.* Retrieved March 28, 2009, from http://www.msnbc.msn.com/id/17472946/

Bernard, H. R., Killworth, P. D., McCarty, C., Shelley, G. A., & Robinson, S. (1990). Comparing four different methods for measuring personal social networks. *Social Networks, 12*, 179–216. doi:10.1016/0378-8733(90)90005-T

Berner-Lee, T., Hendler, J., & Lassila, O. (2001, May). The Semantic Web. *Scientific American.*

Berry, D., & Broadbent, D. The combination of explicit and implicit learning process in task control. *Psychological Research, 49*, 7-15

Biggs, J. (1996). Enhancing Teaching through Constructive Alignment, Higher Education, 32, 347-364.

Bigus, J. P., & Bigus, J. (1997). *Constructing intelligent agents with Java: A programmer's guide to smarter applications.* New Jersey: Wiley.

Bititci, U. S., and Mendibil, K., Martinez, V., & Albores, P. (2005). Measuring and managing performance in extended enterprises. *International Journal of Operations & Production Management, 25*(4), 333-353.

Bloom, B., Englehart, M. Furst, E., Hill, W., & Krathwohl, D. (1956). Taxonomy of educational objectives: The classification of educational goals. Handbook I: Cognitive domain. New York, Toronto: Longmans, Green.

Boella, G., & Torre, L. (2006). An architecture of a normative system. *AAMAS 2006*, 229-231.

Borgida, A. (1995). Description logics in data management. *IEEE Trans Knowledge and Data Engineering, 7*(5), 671–782.

Borgida, A., & Patel-Schneider, P. F. (1994). A semantics and complete algorithm for subsumption in the CLASSIC description logic. *Journal of Artificial Intelligence Research, 1*, 277–308.

Borland Together (2007). Retrieved August 16, 2007 from http://www.borland.com/downloads/download_together.html

Bosch, J. (1998). Design patterns as language constructs. *JOOP Journal of Object-Oriented Programming, 11*(2), 18–32.

Boulmakoul, A., & Salle, M. (2002). Integrated contract management. Online access: http://www.hp.com

Bouras, A., Gouvas, P., & Mentzas, G. (2007). *A semantic service-oriented architecture for business process fusion in semantic web technologies and e-business.* Salam & Stevens (Eds.), London: Idea Group Publishing.

Bowers, S., & Delcambre, L. (2000). *Representing and transforming model-based information.* Paper presented at the Workshop on the Semantic Web at the Fourth European Conference on Digital Libraries.

Brachman, R., & Levesque, H. (2004). *Knowledge representation and reasoning.* New York: Morgan Kaufmann.

Bradshaw, J. M. (1997). An Introduction to Software Agents. In Bradshaw J. M., *Software Agents*, Cambridge, MA: MIT Press, 3- 46.

Brandstädt, A. (1994). *Graphen und algorithmen.* Stuttgart: Teubner.

Briggs, R., de Vreede, G., & Reinig, B. (2003). A theory and measurement of meeting satisfaction. In proceedings of the *36th Annual Hawaii International Conference on System Sciences* (HICSS'03) - Track1

Briggs, R., DeVreede, G., & Nunamaker, J. (2003). Collaboration engineering with ThinkLets to pursue sustained success with group support systems. *Journal of Management Information System*s, *19*(4), 31-65.

Brooks, R. A. (1986). A robust layered control system for a mobile robot. *IEEE Journal of Robotics and Automation, 2*(1), 14-23.

Brown, W. J., Malveau, R. C., Hays, W., McCormick Iii, H., & Mowbray, T. J. (1998). *AntiPatterns: refactoring software, architectures, and projects in crisis.* John Wiley & Sons.

Brugali, D., & Sycara, K. (2000). Towards agent-oriented application frameworks. ACM Computing Surveys (CSUR), *ACM Press 32*(21).

Bruza, P. D., & van Linder, B. (1998). Preferential models of query by navigation. In F. Crestani, M. Lalmas, and C.J. van Rijsbergen (Eds.), *Information retrieval: Uncertainty and logics, volume 4 of The Kluwer International Series on Information Retrieval* (pp. 73-96). Norwell, MA: Kluwer Academic Publishers.

Bui, L., & Lee, J. (1999). An agent-based framework for building decision support systems. *Decision Support System, 25*(3), 225-237.

Bunke, H., & Messmer, B. T. (1993, November 1-5). Similarity measures for structured representations. In S. Wess, K.-D. Althoff, & M. M. Richter (Eds.), *Topics in case-based reasoning, first European Workshop, EWCBR-93, Kaiserslautern, Germany, Selected Papers* (LNCS 837, pp. 106-118). Berlin: Springer.

Burt, R. S., & Minor, M. (Eds.). (1983). *Applied network analysis: A methodological introduction.* Newbury Park, CA: Sage.

Buschmann, F., Meunier, R., Rohnert, H., Sommerlad, P., & Stal, M. (1996). *Pattern-oriented software architecture - A system of patterns.* John Wiley & Sons.

Caire, J. & al. (2002). Agent-oriented analysis using MESSAGE/UML. In *Proceedings of the 2nd Int. Workshop on Agent-Oriented Software Engineering* (LNCS 2222, pp. 119-135).

Cali, A., Calvanese, D., Colucci, S., Noia, T. D., & Donini, F. M. (2004). *A description logic based approach for matching user profiles.* Unpublished manuscript.

Carlsen, S., & Jørgensen, H. D. (1998, November 14). Emergent workflow: The AIS workware demonstrator. In *Proceedings of the CSCW-98 Workshop: Towards Adaptive Workflow Systems.* Seattle, WA, USA.

Carpenter, G. A., & Grossberg, S. (1988). The ART of adaptive pattern recognition by a self-organizing neural network. *IEEE Computer, 21*(3), 77–88.

Carr, A. S., & Pearson, J. N. (1999). Strategically managed buyer–supplier relationships and performance outcomes. *Journal of Operations Management 17*(5), 497–519.

Carver, C.A., Howard, R.A., & Lane, W.D. (1999). Enhancing Student Learning Through Hypermedia Courseware and Incorporation of Student Learning Styles, IEEE Transactions on Education, 42(1), pp. 33-38.

Casati, F., & Shan, M.-C. (2002). Semantic analysis of business process executions. *8th International Conference on Extending Database Technology (EDBT'02),* 287–296, Berlin: Springer.

Casati, F., Ceri, S., Pernici, B., & Pozzi, G. (1998). Workflow evolution. *Data & Knowledge Engineering, 24,* 211–238. doi:10.1016/S0169-023X(97)00033-5

Castro, J., Kolp, M., & Mylopoulos, J. (2002). Towards requirements-driven information systems engineering: The Tropos project. *Information Systems, 27*(6), 365–389. doi:10.1016/S0306-4379(02)00012-1

CEC. (2003). *Linking up Europe: The Importance of interoperability for e-government services- Commission of the European communities- Commission staff working paper* (No. 801): Commission of the European Communities & Interchange of Data between Administrations (IDA).

CEC. (2006). *European interoperability framework for pan-European e-government services-communication from the commission to the council and the European parliament.* Brussels: Commission of the European Communities.

Ceri, S., & Widom, J. (1993). Managing semantic heterogeneity with production rules and persistent queues. In *Proceedings of the 19th VLDB Conference* (pp. 108–119). Dublin, Ireland.

Chakrabarti, S., Dom, B., Gibson, P., & Kleinberg, J. (1998). Automatic resource compilation by analyzing hyperlink structure and associated text. In *Proceedings* of the *7th Int. World Wide Web Conference (WWW '98)* (pp. 65-74). Brisband, Australia.

Chakrabarti, S., Vander, B., & Dom, M. B. (1999). Focused crawling: a new approach to topic-specific Web resource discovery. In *Proceedings of the 8th International World-Wide Web Conference (WWW '99)* (pp. 545-562). Elsevier Science.

Chalidabhongse, J., Chinnan, W., Wechasaethnon, P., & Tantisirithanakorn, A. (2002). **Intelligent facilitation agent for online web-based group discussion system**. *In Proceedings of the 15th International Conference on Industrial and Engineering, Applications of Artificial Intelligence and Expert Systems: Developments in Applied Artificial Intelligence,* (pp.356-362).

Chalupsky, H. (2000). A translation system for symbolic logic. In Proceedings of the *Principles of Knowledge Representation and Reasoning (KR2000)* (pp. 471–482).

Champagne, A. & Bunce, D (1991). Learning-theory-based science teaching. In The Psychology of learning science, (Eds.) S.M. Glynn, R.H. Yeany, B.K. Britton, Hillsdale, NJ, Lawrence Erlbaum Associates.

Chang, M.K., & Cheung, W. (2001). Determinants of the intention to use Internet/WWW at work: a confirmatory study. Information & Management 29(1) 1-4.

Chapman, S. N. (1989). Just-in-time supplier inventory: An empirical implementation model. *International Journal of Production Research, 27*(12), 1993-2007.

Chau, M., Zeng, D., & Chen, H. (2001, June). Personalized spiders for Web search and analysis. In *Proceedings of ACM/IEEE Joint Conference on Digital Libraries (JCDL '01)* (pp. 79-87). Roanoke, Virginia, USA.

Chen, H., Schuffels, C., & Orwig, R. (1996). Internet categorization and search: A machine learning approach. *Journal of Visual Communication and Image Representation, 7*(1), 88–102. doi:10.1006/jvci.1996.0008

Chidamber, & S.R, Kemerer, C.F. (1994). A metrics suite for object-oriented design. *IEEE Transactions on Software Engineering, 20*(6), 476-493.

Cho, J. H., Garcia, M., & Page, L. (1998, April). Efficient crawling through URL ordering. In *Proceedings of the 7th International World Wide Web Conference (WWW '98)* (pp. 161–172). Brisbane, Australia.

Cho, J., & Garcia, H. M. (2000, May). Synchronizing database to improve freshness. In *Proceedings of the ACM International Conference on Management of Data (SIGMOD '00)* (pp. 117-128). Dallas, Texas, USA.

Chopra, S., & Meindl, P. (2003). *Supply chain management: Strategy, planning, and operation, second ed.* New Jersey: Prentice-Hall.

Christopher, M. (1992). *Logistics and supply chain management: Strategies for reducing costs and improving services.* Financial Times/Prentice Hall.

Cockburn, A. (1996). The interaction of social issues and software architecture. *Communications of the ACM, 39*(10), 40–49. doi:10.1145/236156.236165

Cohen, I., Garg, A., & Huang, T. S. (2000). *Emotion recognition from facial expressions using multilevel-HMM.* Paper presented at the 2000 NIPS Workshop on Affective Computing. Denver, Colorado.

Cohen, L. (2006). Internet Tutorials. Web Support Librarian, University at Albany, SUNY. Retrieved November 11, 2006, from http://www.internettutorials.net/

Cohen, P. R., & Levesque, H. J. (1990). Intention is choice with commitment. *Artificial Intelligence, 42,* 213–261. doi:10.1016/0004-3702(90)90055-5

Collins, J., Bilot, C., & Mobasher, B. (2001). Decision processes in agent-based automated contracting. *IEEE Internet Computing, 5*(2), 61-72.

Conallen, J. (2000). Concevoir des applications Web avec UML, Editions Eyrolles.

Conati, C. (2002). Probabilistic assessment of user's emotions in educational games. *Applied Artificial Intelligence, 16*(7-8), 555–575. doi:10.1080/08839510290030390

Connell, T. A. (2000). A simplistic approach to internationalization: Design considerations for an autonomous intelligent agent. In *Proceedings of the 6th ERCIM Workshop on User Interfaces for All,* Italy.

Cook, J. E., & Wolf, A. L. (1998). Discovering models of software processes from event-based data. *ACM Transactions on Software Engineering and Methodology, 7*(3), 215–249. doi:10.1145/287000.287001

Coplien, J., & Schmidt, D. (1995). *Pattern languages of program design*. Addison-Wesley.

Coplien, O. (1991). *Advanced C++ programming styles and idioms*. Addison-Wesley International.

Corsi, G. (2002). A unified completeness theorem for quantified modal logics. *Journal of Symbolic Logic, 67*, 1483-1510.

Craglla, M., & Signoretta, P. (2000). From global to local: The development of local geographic information strategies in the United Kingdom. *Environment and Planning, B*(27), 777–788.

Cresswell, M. J. (2001). *A Blackwell guide to philosophical logic*.

Crowston, K., & Malone, T. W. (1988). Computational agents to support cooperative work. (Working Paper #2008-88). Cambridge, MA: MIT Sloan School of Management.

Culotta, A., Bekkerman, R., & McCallum, A. (2004). Extracting social networks and contact information from e-mail and the web. *1st Conference on Email and Anti-Spam (CEAS)*.

da Costa Carvalho, A. L., Chirita, P., de Moura, E. S., Calado, P., & Nejdl, W. (2006). Site level noise removal for search engines. In *Proceedings of the 15th International Conference on World Wide Web, WWW '06* (pp. 73-82). Edinburgh, Scotland, May 23-26, 2006. New York: ACM Press.

Davidson, S.B., Overton ,C., Tannen, V., & Wong, L.(1997). BioKleisli: a. digital library for biomedical researchers. *International Journal on Digital Libraries, 1*(1), 36-53.

Davis, A. (1995). *201 principles of software development*. McGraw-Hill.

de Medeiros, A. K. A., van der Aalst, W. M. P., & Pedrinaci, C. (2008). Semantic process mining tools: Core building blocks. *16th European Conference on Information Systems*, 1953-1964.

de Medeiros, A. K. A., van der Aalst, W. M. P., & Weijters, A. J. M. M. (2003). Workflow mining: Current status and future directions. In Meersman, R., Tari, Z., & Schmidt, D. C., (Editors), *On The Move to Meaningful Internet Systems 2003: CoopIS, DOA, and ODBASE*, 389–406. Berlin: Springer-Verlag.

de Medeiros, A. K. A., Weijters, A. J. M. M., & van der Aalst, W. M. P. (2007). Genetic process mining: An experimental evaluation. *Data Mining and Knowledge Discovery, 14*(2), 245–304. doi:10.1007/s10618-006-0061-7

DeBra, P., & Post, R. (1994). Information retrieval in the world wide Web: Making client based searching feasible. *Journal on Computer Networks and ISDN Systems, 27*, 183-192.

Deogun, J. S., Bhatia, S. K., & Raghavan, V. V. (1991). Automatic Cluster assignment for documents. In *Proceedings of the 7th IEEE Conference on Artificial Intelligence Applications, Miami Beach, Florida, 1991* (pp. 25-27).

DeSanctis, G., D'Onofrio, M., Sambamurthy, V., & Poole, M. (1989). Comprehensiveness and restrictiveness in group decision heuristics: Effects of computer support on consensus decision making. *In Proceedings of the Tenth International Conference on Information Systems*, (pp. 131-140).

Deugo, D., Oppacher, F., Kuester, J., & Otte, I. V. (1999). Patterns as a means for intelligent software engineering. In *Proceedings of the Int. Conf. on Artificial Intelligence, IC-AI'99, Las Vegas, Nevada, USA* (pp. 605-611).

Dey, A. K. (2001). Understanding and using context. *Personal and Ubiquitous Computing, 5*(1), 4–7. doi:10.1007/s007790170019

Dhaliwal, J., & Benbasat, I. (1996). The use and effects of knowledge-based system explanations: Theoretical foundations and a framework for empirical evaluation. *Information Systems Research, 7*(3), 342-363.

DHS. (2009). DHS Geospatial Data Model, version 2.7 [Electronic Version]. Retrieved March, 2009 from http://www.fgdc.gov/participation/working-groups-subcommittees/hswg/dhs-gdm/

Dickson, G., Partridge, J., & Robinson (1993). Exploring modes of facilitative support for GDSS technology. *MIS Quarterly, 17*(2), 173, 22.

Djemaa, R. B., Amous I., & Ben Hamadou A. (2006). GIWA: A generator for adaptive Web applications. *In ICIW'06, IEEE International conference on Internet and Web Application and Services.*

Djemaa, R. B., Amous I., & Ben Hamadou A. (2006). Design and implementation of adaptive Web application. *In 8th International Conference on Enterprise Information Systems ICEIS'06. 23 - 27, May, Paphos Cyprus.*

Djemaa, R. B., Amous I., & Ben Hamadou A. (2007) Adaptable and adaptive web applications: From design to generation. *International Review on Computers and Software (IRECOS).*

Do, T. T., Faulkner, S., & Kolp, M. (2003). organizational multi-agent architectures for information systems. In *Proceedings of the 5th International Conference on Enterprise Information Systems, ICEIS 2003* (pp. 89-96).

Do, T. T., Kolp, M., Hang Hoang, T. T., & Pirotte, A. (2003). A framework for design patterns for Tropos. In *Proceedings of the 17th Brazilian Symposium on Software Engineering, SBES 2003.*

Doan, A., Madhavan, J., Domingos, P., & Halevy, A. (2002). Learning to map between ontologies on the semantic Web. In *Proceedings of the World Wide Web Consortium 2002,* ACM.

Donato, D., Leonardi, S., & Millozzi, P. T. (2005). Mining the inner structure of the Web grap. In *Proceedings of the 8th International Workshop on the Web , & Databases (WebDB '05)* (pp. 145-150). Baltimore, Maryland, USA.

Dourish, P., Holmes, J., MacLean, A., Marqvardsen, P., & Zbyslaw, A. (1996, November). Freeflow: Mediating between representation and action in workflow systems.

In *Proceedings of the ACM Conference on Computer Supported Cooperative Work CSCW'96* (pp. 190-198). Boston

Dumas, M., van der Aalst, W. M. P., & ter Hofstede, A. H. M. (2005). *Process-aware information systems: Bridging people and software through process technology.* Wiley& Sons.

Duric, Z., Gray, W., Heishman, R., Li, F., Rosenfield, A., & Schoelles, M. J. (2002). Integrating perceptual and cognitive modeling for adaptive and intelligent human-computer interaction. *Proceedings of the IEEE, 90*(7), 1272–1289. doi:10.1109/JPROC.2002.801449

Dussauge, P., & Garrette, B. (1999). *Cooperative strategy: Competing successfully through strategic alliances.* Wiley and Sons.

Dyer, J. (2000). *Collaborative advantage: Winning through extended enterprise supplier networks.* New York: Oxford University Press.

Eden, C., Jones, S., & Sims, D. (1983). *Messing about in problems.* Oxford, England: Pergamon Press.

Egenhofer, M., & Mark, D. (1995). *Naive geography.* Paper presented at the International Conference COSIT '95 (LNCS).

Ehrig, M., & Stabb, S. (2004). *Qom-quick ontology mapping.* Technical report, University of Karlsruhe, Institute of AIFB.

Ellis, C. A. (2000). An evaluation framework for collaborative systems. *Technical Report, CU-CS-901-00,* Boulder, USA: University of Colorado, Department of Computer Science.

Ellis, C. A., & Nutt, G. (1996). Workflow: The process spectrum. Sheth, A., (Editor), *NSF Workshop on Workflow and Process Automation in Information Systems,* 140–145.

Ellis, C. A., Gibbs, S. J., & Rein, G. (1991). Groupware: Some issues and experiences. *Communications of the ACM, 34*(1), 38–58. doi:10.1145/99977.99987

Ellram, L. M. (1990). The supplier selection decision in strategic partnerships. *Journal of Purchasing and Materials Management, 26*(4), 8–14.

Ermolayev, V., Keberle, N., Kononenko, O., Plaksin, S., & Terziyan, V. (2004). Towards a framework for agent-enabled Semantic Web service composition. *International Journal of Web Services Research, 1*(3), 63–87.

Ester, M., Kriegel, H. P., & Schubert, M. (2004). Accurate and efficient crawling for relevant Websites. In *Proceedings of the 30th International Conference on Very Large Databases (VLDB '04)* (pp. 396-407). Toronto, Canada.

Etzioni, O., & Weld, D. S. (1995). Intelligent agents on the Internet: Fact, fiction, and forecast. *IEEE Expert, 104*(4), 44-49.

Fallahia, G. R., Frankb, A. U., Mesgaria, M. S., & Rajabi-fardc, A. (2008). An ontological structure for semantic interoperability of GIS and environmental modeling . *International Journal of Applied Earth Observation and Geoinformation, 10*(3), 342–357. doi:10.1016/j.jag.2008.01.001

Farnham, S., Portnoy, W., & Turski, A. (2004). Using e-mail mailing lists to approximate and explore corporate social networks. McDonald, D.W., Farnham, S., & Fisher, D. (Editors), *CSCW'04 Workshop on Social Networks.*

Farquhar, A., Fikes, R., & Rice, J. (1996). *The Ontolingua Server: A Tool for collaborative ontology construction.* Stanford, CA: Knowledge Systems Laboratory- Stanford University.

Farrugia, J. (2003). *Model-theoretic semantics for the Web.* May 20-24, 2003, Budapest, Hungary. 29-38. Online access: http://www.ra.ethz.ch/CDstore/www2003/papers/refereed/p277/p277-farrugia.html.

Fawcett, S. E., Stanley, L. L., & Smith, S. R. (1997). Developing a logistics capability to improve the performance of international operations. *Journal of Business Logistics, 18*(2), 101–1 27.

Felder, R. M. (1996). Matters of Styles. ASEE Prism, 6(4), 18-23.

Feldman, M. (1987). Electronic mail and weak ties in organizations. *Office: Technology and People, 3,* 83–101. doi:10.1108/eb022643

Ferber, J. (1999). *Multi-agent systems: An introduction to distributed artificial intelligence.* Addison Wesley.

Fernandez, E. B., & Pan, R. (2001). A pattern language for security models. In *Proceedings of the 8th Conference on Pattern Language of Programs, PLoP 2001.*

FGDC. (2009). Content Standard for Digital Geospatial Metadata (CSDGM), Vers. 2 (FGDC-STD-001-1998) Retrieved March 2009 from http://www.fgdc.gov/metadata/geospatial-metadata-standards

Fiala, Z., Hinz M., Meissner K., & Wehneer F. (2003). A component-based component architecture for adaptive dynamic web documents. *Journal of Web engineering, 2*(1&2): 058-073.

Finin, T., Weber, J., Wiederhold, G., Genesereth, M., Fritzson, R., & McGuire, J. (1993). *Specification of the KQML agent communication language.* Technical Report, DARPA knowledge sharing initiative, External Interfaces Working Group.

FIPA Architecture Board. (n.d.). Foundation for intelligent physical agents, FIPA Communicative act library specification. Retrieved February 12, 2008 from http://www.fipa.org/specs/fipa00037/SC00037J.html.

FIPA. (2006). The foundation for intelligent physical agents. Retrieved May, 2006, from http://www.fipa.org/

FIPA. (2007). *The Foundation for Intelligent Physical Agent (FIPA).* Retrieved from http://www.fipa.org

Fisher, D., & Dourish, P. (2004). Social and temporal structures in everyday collaboration. Dykstra-Erickson, E., & Tscheligi, M. (Editors), *Conference on Human Factors in Computing Systems (CHI2004),* 551–558. New York: ACM Press.

Fitting, M., & Mendelsohn, R. L. (1998). *First-order modal logic.*

Fons, J., Pelechano V., Pastor O., Albert M., & Valderas, P. (2003, May 20-24). *Extending an OO Method to Develop Web Applications*. The Twelfth International World Wide Web Conference. Budapest, Hungary.

Fonseca, F., & Egenhofer, M. (1999). Ontology-driven geographic information systems. In C. B. Medeiros (Ed.), *7th ACM Symposium on Advances in Geographic Information Systems* (pp. 14-19). Kansas City: ACM Press.

Foundation for Intelligent Physical Agents. (n.d.). *FIPA contract net interaction protocol specification*. Retrieved February 12, 2008 from http://www.fipa.org/specs/fipa00029/SC00029H.html

Fowler, M. (1997). *Analysis patterns: Reusable object models*. Addison-Wesley.

Franklin, S., & Graesser, A. (1996). Is it an agent or just a program? A taxonomy for autonomous agents. In *Proceedings of the Third International Workshop on Agent Theories, Architectures, and Languages*, New York: Springer Verlag.

Franz, T., Staab, S., & Arndt, R. The X-COSIM integration framework for a seamless semantic desktop. *4th International Conference on Knowledge Capture (K-CAP2007).*, 43–150., New York: ACM Press.

Frasincar, F. & Houben G.-J. (2002). Hypermedia presentation adaptation on the semantic web. In P. de Bra, P. Brusilovsky, & R. Conejo R (Eds.), Proceedings of the 2nd International Conference on Adaptive Hypermedia and Adaptive Web-Based Systems (AH 2002), (pp. 133-142). Malaga, Spain.

Frasincar, F., Houben, G.-J., & Vdovjak, R. (2001). An RMM-Based Methodology for Hypermedia Presentation Design. *In Proceedings of the 5th East European Conference on Advances in Databases and Information Systems (ADBIS 2001),* (pp. 323-337). *LNCS 2151,* Vilnius, Lithuania ,

Frazelle, E. (2002). *Supply chain strategy*. New York: McGraw-Hill.

Freeman, L. C. (1977). A set of measures of centrality based on betweenness. *Sociometry, 40,* 35–41. doi:10.2307/3033543

Freeman, L. C. (1979). Centrality in social networks: conceptual clarification. *Social Networks, 1,* 215–239. doi:10.1016/0378-8733(78)90021-7

Freßmann, A., Maximini, K., & Sauer, T. (2005, April 10-13). Towards collaborative agent-based knowledge support for time-critical and business-critical processes. In K.-D. Althoff, A. Dengel, R. Bergmann, M. Nick, & T. Roth-Berghofer (Eds.), *Professional knowledge management: Third Biennial Conference, WM 2005, Kaiserslautern, Germany Revised Selected Papers* (LNAI 3782, pp. 420-430). Berlin: Springer.

Fuxman, A., Pistore, M., Mylopoulos, J., & Traverso, P. (2001). Model checking early requirements specifications in Tropos. In *Proc. of the 5th IEEE Int. Symposium on Requirements Engineering, RE'01* (pp. 174-181).

Gamma, E., Helm, R., Johnson, R., & Vlissides, J. (1995). *Design patterns: Elements of reusable object-oriented software*. Addison-Wesley.

GAO. (2003). *Geographic information systems: Challenges to effective data sharing* (Testimony Before the Subcommittee on Technology, Information Policy, Intergovernmental Relations and the Census, Committee on Government Reform, House of Representatives No. GAO-03-874T): United States General Accounting Office.

Gautam, P., & Padmini, S. (2006). Link contexts in classifier-guided topical crawlers. *IEEE Transactions on Knowledge and Data Engineering, 18*(1), 107-122.

Gautam, P., Kostas, T., & Judy, J. (2004, June 7-11). Panorama: extending digital libraries with topical crawlers. In *Proceedings of the 4th ACM/IEEE Joint Conference on Digital Libraries (JCDL '04)* (pp. 203-209), Tucson, Arizona, USA.

Genesereth, M., & Fikes, R. (1992). Knowledge Interchange Format, *Version 3.0 Reference Manual*. Technical Report 92-1. Computer Science Department. Stanford University.

George, J., Dennis, A., & Nunamaker, J. (1992). An experimental investigation of facilitation in an EMS decision room. *Group Decision and Negotiation, 1*(1), 57-70.

Gil, Y. (in press). From data to knowledge to discoveries: Scientific workflows and artificial intelligence. *Science Progress*.

Gilbert, J.E. & Han, C.Y. (1999). Adapting Instruction in Search of "A Significance Difference". Journal of Networking and Computing Applications, 22, 3.

Göktürk, E. & Akkok, N. (2004). Paradigm and software engineering. *Proceedings of Impact of Software Process on Quality*.

Gómez, J., Cachero, C., & Pastor, O. (2001). Extending a conceptual modeling approach to web application design. *In Proceedings of the 1st International Workshop on Web-Oriented Software Technology*, Valencia, Spain, June 2001.

Google (2006). *Google SOAP Search API Reference*. Retrieved November 4, 2006, from http://www.google.com/apis/reference.html

Google (2008). *We knew the web was big....* Retrieved March 28, 2009, from http://googleblog.blogspot.com/2008/07/we-knew-web-was-big.html

Goul, M., & Tonge, F. (1987). Project IPMA: Applying decision support system design principles to building expert-based systems. *Decision Sciences*, 18(3), 448-467.

Governatori, G. (2004). Defeasible description logics. *LNCS 3323*, 98-112.

Governatori, G. (2005). Representing business contracts in RuleML. *International Jounal of Cooperative Information Systems, 14*(2-3), 181-216.

Governatori, G., & Hoang, D. (2005). A semantic web based architecture for e-contracts in defeasible logic. *LNCS 3791,* 145-159.

Governatori, G., & Milosevic, Z. (2006). A formal analysis of a business contract language. *International Journal of Cooperative Information Systems,* 1-26.

Governatori, G., Milosevic, Z., & Sadiq, S. (2006). Compliance checking between business processes and business contracts. *EDOC 2006,* 221-232.

Gray, A., & Haahr, M. (2004). Personalised, collaborative spam filtering. *1st Conference on Email and Anti-Spam (CEAS)*.

Gredler, M. E. (1997). Learning and instruction: Theory into practice (3rd ed). Upper Saddle River, NJ: Prentice-Hall. Kelly, D., & Tangney, B. (2002), Incorporating Learning Characteristics into an Intelligent Tutor, Proceedings of the 6th International Conference on Intelligent Tutoring Systems, p.729-738, June 02-07.

Grefenstette, G. (1994). *Explorations in automatic thesaurus discovery.* Moston, MA: Kluwer Academic Publishers.

Griffith, T., Fuller, M., & Northcraft, G. (1998). Facilitator influence in group support systems: Intended and unintended effects. *Information Systems Research*, 9(1), 20-36.

Grosof, B. (2004). Representing e-commerce rules via situated courteous logic programs in RuleML. *Electronic Commerce Research and Applications, 3*(1), 2-20.

Grosof, B., & Poon, T. (2004). SweetDeal: Representing agent contracts with exceptions using semantic web rules, ontologies and process descriptions. *International Journal of Electronic Commerce, 8*(4), 61.

Grosof, B., Volz, R., Horrocks, I., & Decker, S. (2003). *Description logic programs: Combining logic programs with description logic.* May 20-24 2003, Budapest, Hungary. 48-57. Online access: http://www.cs.man.ac.uk/~horrocks/Publications/download/2003/p117-grosof.pdf

Gruber, T. R. (1993). A translation approach to portable ontology specifications. *Knowledge Acquisition*, 5(2). doi:10.1006/knac.1993.1008

Guarino, N. (1995). Formal ontology, conceptual analysis and knowledge representation. *International Journal of Human-Computer Studies, 43*, 625-640.

Guarino, N. (1997). Semantic matching: Formal Ontological distinctions for information organization, extraction, and integration. In M. Pazienza (Ed.), *Information extraction: A multidisciplinary approach to an emerging information technology* (pp. 139-170). Frascati, Italy: International Summer School.

Guarino, N., & Giaretta, P. (1995). Ontologies and knowledge bases: Towards a terminological clarification. In N. Mars (Ed.), *Towards Very large knowledge bases: Knowledge building and knowledge sharing* (pp. 25-32).

Guarino, N., & Welty, C. (2001), Supporting ontological analysis of taxonomic relationships. *Data and Knowledge Engineering, 39*, 51–74.

Günther, C. W., & van der Aalst, W. M. P. (2007). Fuzzy mining: Adaptive process simplification based on multi-perspective metrics. Alonso, G., Dadam, P., & Rosemann, M. (Editors), *International Conference on Business Process Management (BPM 2007), Lecture Notes in Computer Science, 4714*, 328-343. Berlin: Springer-Verlag.

Guizzardi, G., Wagner, G., & Sinderen, M. (2004). A formal theory of conceptual modeling universals. In *Proceedings of the Workshop on Philosophy and Informatics (WSPI)*.

Gulli, A., & Signorin, A. (2005, May 10-14). Building an open source metasearch engine. In *Proceedings of the 14th International World Wide Web Conference (WWW '05)* (pp. 111-119). Chiba, Japan.

Hadjidj, R., Debbabi, M., Lounis, H., Iqbal, F., Szporer, A., & Benredjem, D. (2009). Towards an integrated e-mail forensic analysis framework. *Digital Investigation, 5*(3-4), 124–137. doi:10.1016/j.diin.2009.01.004

Hall, D. L., & McMullen, A. H. (2004). *Mathematical techniques in multisensor data fusion*. Norwood, MA: Artech House.

Hamdi, M. S. (2006). MASACAD: A multiagent-based approach to information customization. *IEEE Intelligent Systems, 21*(1), 60–67. doi:10.1109/MIS.2006.14

Hamdi, M. S. (2006). Information overload and information customization. *IEEE Potentials, 25*(5), 9–12. doi:10.1109/MP.2006.1692278

Hamdi, M. S. (2007). MASACAD: A multi-agent approach to information customization for the purpose of academic advising of students. *Elsevier Applied Soft Computing Journal, 7*, 746–771. doi:10.1016/j.asoc.2006.02.001

Hamdi, M. S. (2007). Semantic Map Based Web Search Result Visualization. In *Proceedings of the 11th International Conference on Information Visualization (IV07). July 4-6, 2007, ETH, Zurich, Switzerland* (pp. 222-227).

Hamdi, M. S. (2008). Combating information overload by means of information customization systems. In V. Sugumaran (Ed.), *Intelligent information technologies and applications* (pp. 60-92). Hershey, PA: IGI Global.

Hamdi, M. S. (2008). Improving the quality of Web search. In C. Calero, M.A. Moraga, and M. Piattini (Eds.), Handbook of research on Web information systems quality (pp. 456-473). Hershey, PA: IGI Global.

Hamdi, M. S. (2008). SOMSE: A neural network based approach to Web search optimization. *International Journal of Intelligent Information Technologies, 4*(4), 31–54.

Hayden, S., Carrick, C., & Yang, Q. (1999). Architectural design patterns for multiagent coordination. In *Proceedings of the 3rd Int. Conf. on Agent Systems, Agents'99, Seattle, USA*.

Hayes, P., & Reddy, D. (1983). Steps toward graceful integration in spoken and written man-machine communication. *International journal of man-machine studies, 19*, 231-284.

Haynes, K. A., & Fotheringham, A. S. (1984). *Gravity and spatial interaction models*. Beverly Hills, CA: Sage Publications.

Heckerman, D., Breese, J., & Rommels, K. (1996). Decision-theoretic: Troubleshooting. *Communications of the ACM, 38*(3), 49–57. doi:10.1145/203330.203341

Herbst, J. (2000). A machine learning approach to workflow management. *11th European Conference on Machine Learning* [Berlin: Springer-Verlag.]. *Lecture*

Notes in Computer Science, 1810, 183–194. doi:10.1007/3-540-45164-1_19

Hernandez, T., & Kambhampati, S. (2004). Integration of biological sources: current systems and challenges ahead. ACM SIGMOD Record, *ACM Press, 33*(3), 51 – 60.

Herrmann, T. (2001). Lernendes workflow. In T. Herrmann, A. W. Scheer, & H. Weber (Eds.), *Verbesserung von Geschäftsprozessen mit flexiblen Workflow-Management-Systemen,* (pp. 143-154). Heidelberg: Physica-Verlag.

Hersovici, M., Jacovi, D., Pelleg, M., & Shtalhaim, S. U. (1998, April). The SHARK SEARCH algorithm—An application: Tailored Web site mappin. In *Proceedings of the 7ᵗʰ International World Wide Web Conference (WWW '98)* (pp. 47-55), Brisbane, Australia.

Ho, T., & Antunes, P. (1999). Developing a tool to assist electronic facilitation of decision-making groups. *Fifth International Workshop on Groupware* (pp. 243-252). IEEE CS Press

Hoffman, T. (2004). Sarbanes-Oxley sparks forensics apps interest: Vendors offer monitoring tools to help identify incidents of financial fraud. *Computerworld, 38,* 14.

Hokyin Lai, Huaiqing Wang, & Minhong Wang (2007). Agent-oriented e-learning Process Modeling, Proceedings of Americas Conference on Information Systems (AMCIS 2007), Colorado, USA, August 2007.

Hongyu, L., Evangelos, M., & Jeannette, J. (2004, November 12-13). Probabilistic models for focused Web crawling. In *Proceedings of the 6ᵗʰ ACM Int. Workshop on Web Information and Data Management (WIDM'04)* (pp. 167-172).Washington D.C., USA.

Honkela, T., Kaski, S., Lagus, K., & Kohonen, T. (1996). *Newsgroup exploration with WEBSOM method and browsing interface* (In Report A32). Helsinki: University of Technology, January 1996.

Hoong, D., & Buyya, R. (2004). Guided Google: A meta search engine and its implementation using the Google distributed web services. *International Journal of Computers and Applications, 26*(1), 181–187.

Horrocks, I. (1998, May 5-8). *The FaCT system.* Paper presented at the TABLEAUX '98, In Automated Reasoning with Analytic Tableaux and Related Method, International Conference Proceedings, Oisterwijk, The Netherlands.

Horrocks, I., Patel-Schneider, P. F., & Harmelen, F. v. (2003). From SHIQ and RDF to OWL: The making of a Web ontology language. *Journal of Web Semantics, 1*(1), 7–26. doi:10.1016/j.websem.2003.07.001

Horrocks, I., Patel-Schneider, P., Bechhofer, S., & Tsarkov, D. (2005). OWL rules: A proposal and prototype implementation. *Journal of Web Semantics, 3,* 23-40.

Horvitz, E., & Paek, T. (1999). A computational architecture for conversation. In *Proc. of the Seventh International Conference on User Modeling* (pp. 201-210). New York: Springer-Verlag.

Horvitz, E., & Paek, T. (2000). *DeepListener: Harnessing expected utility to guide clarification dialog in spoken language systems.* Paper presented at the 6th International Conference on Spoken Language Processing, Beijing.

Horvitz, E., Breese, J., Heckerman, D., Hovel, D., & Rommelse, K. (1998). The Lumiere Project: Bayesian user modeling for inferring the goals and needs of software users. In *Proceedings of the Fourteenth Conference on Uncertainty in Artificial Intelligence* (pp. 256-265). San Francisco: Morgan Kaufmann.

Huang, E., Haft, R., & Hsu, J. (2000). Developing a roadmap for software internationalization. Retrieved from www.symbio-group.com/knowledge_center.html

Huang, S., & Keskar, H. (Forthcoming). Comprehensive and configurable metrics for supplier selection. *International Journal of Production Economics.*

Huang, Y., Govindaraju, D., Mitchell, T., Rocha de Carvalho, V., & Cohen, W. W. (2004). Inferring ongoing activities of workstation users by clustering e-mail. *1st Conference on Email and Anti-Spam (CEAS).*

Hudlicka, E., & McNeese, M. D. (2002). Assessment of user affective and belief states for interface adaptation: Application to an Air Force pilot task. *User*

Modeling and User-Adapted Interaction, 12, 1–47. doi:10.1023/A:1013337427135

Hughes, G. E., & Cresswell, M. J. (2003). *A new introduction to modal logic* (3rd ed.). Routledge.

Hult, G., Ketchen, D., & Slater, S. (2004). Information processing, knowledge development, and strategic supply chain performance. *Academy of Management Journal, 47*(2), 241-253.

Hwang, S. Y., & Tang, J. (2004). Consulting past exceptions to facilitate workflow exception handling. *Decision Support Systems, 37,* 49–69. doi:10.1016/S0167-9236(02)00194-X

Isakowitz, T., Stohr, A., & Balasubramanian, E. (1995). RMM: A methodology for structured hypermedia design. *Communications of the ACM 38*(8), 34-44.

Islam, A. S., Bermudez, L., Beran, B., Fellah, S., & Piasecki, M. (2006). Ontology for geographic information - Metadata (ISO 19115:2003). Retrieved May 2006, from http://loki.cae.drexel.edu/~wbs/ontology/iso-19115.htm

JACK Intelligent Agents (2006). Retrieved on January, 1st, 2008 from http://www.agent-software.com.

JADEX BDI Agent System (2007). Retrieved on January, 1st, 2008 from http://vsis-www.informatik.uni-hamburg.de/projects/jadex/

Jakoniene, V., & Lambrix. (2005). Ontology-based integration for bioinformatics. Proceedings of the VLDB Workshop on Ontologies-based techniques for DataBases and Information Systems—ODBIS, (pp. 55-58).

Jameson, A. (1996). Numerical uncertainty management in user and student modeling: An overview of systems and issues. *User Modeling and User-Adapted Interaction, 5,* 193–251. doi:10.1007/BF01126111

Jennings, N. R., & Wooldridge, M. (2001). Agent-oriented software engineering. In *Handbook of Agent Technology.* AAAI/ MIT Press.

Jensen, F. V. (2001). *Bayesian networks and decision graphs.* New York: Springer.

Jianjun, C., David, J. D., & Yuan, W. (2000, May). NiagaraCQ: A scalable continuous query system for Internet databases. In *Proceedings of the ACM International Conference on Management of Data (SIGMOD '00)* (pp. 379-390). Dallas, Texas, USA.

Johansen, R. (1988). *Groupware: Computer support for business teams.* New York: Free Press

Jolliffe, I. T. (1986). *Principal component analysis.* New York: Springer-Verlag.

Jurafsky, D., & Martin, J. H. (2000). Dialogue and conversational agents. In *Speech and language processing: An introduction to natural language processing, computational linguistics, and speech recognition,* Prentice Hall.

Kaisler, S.H. (2005). *Software paradigms.* New Jersey: Wiley.

Kalfoglou, Y., & Schorlemmer, M. (2002), If-map: An ontology mapping method based on information-flow theory. In *Proceedings of the 1st International Conference on Ontologies, Databases and Applications of Semantics (ODBASE'02).*

Kalfoglou, Y., & Schorlemmer, M. (2005). Ontology mapping: The state of the art. *Journal of Semantic Interoperability and Integration,*

Kaneiwa, K., & Mizoguchi, R. (2005). An order-sorted quantified modal logic for meta-ontology. In *Proceedings of the International Conference on Automated Reasoning with Analytic Tableaux and Related Methods (TABLEAUX 2005), LNCS 3702.*

Kaplan, A. N. (2001). Towards a consistent logical framework for ontological analysis. In *Proceedings of the International Conference on Formal Ontology in Information Systems* (pp. 244–255). ACM Press.

Karacapilidis, N., & Moraitis, P. (2001). Building an agent-mediated electronic commerce system with decision analysis features. *Decision Support Systems, 32,* 53–69.

Karasavvas, K. A., Baldock, R., & Burgera, A. (2004). Bioinformatics integration and agent technology. Journal of Biomedical Informatics, *Elsevier Science, 37*(3), 205 – 219.

Kashyap, V., & Sheth, A. (1996). Semantic heterogeneity in global information system: The role of metadata, context and ontologies. In M. Papazoglou & G. Schlageter (Eds.), *Cooperative information systems: Current trends and directions* (Vol. London, pp. 139-178). Academic Press.

Keltner, J. (1989) Facilitation: Catalyst for group problem solving. *Management Communication Quarterly, 3*(1), 8-31.

Khan, S. M., & Khor, S. W. (2004). Web document clustering using a hybrid neural network. *Applied Soft Computing Journal, 4*, 423–432. doi:10.1016/j.asoc.2004.02.003

Klein, L.A. (2004). *Sensor and data fusion: A tool for information assessment and decision making.* SPIE Press Monograph, PM138.

Koch, N. (2000). Software Engineering for Adaptative Hypermedia Systems—Reference Model, Modelling Techniques and Development Process, Ph.D Thesis, Fakultät der Mathematik und Informatik, Ludwig-Maximilians Universität München.

Koch, N. (2001). The Authoring Process of the UML-based Web Engineering Approach. *1st International Workshop on Web-Oriented Software Technology.*

Kofod-Petersen, A., & Mikalsen, M. (2005). Context: Representation and reasoning – representing and reasoning about context in a mobile environment. *Revue d'Intelligence Artificielle, 19*, 479–498. doi:10.3166/ria.19.479-498

Köhler, J., Philippi, S., Lange, M.(2003). SEMEDA: ontology based semantic integration of biological databases. *Bioinformatics, 19*(18), 2420-2427.

Kohonen, T. (1989). Self-organization and associative memory (3rd ed.). Berlin: Springer-Verlag.

Kohonen, T. (1997). Exploration of very large databases by self-organizing maps. In . *Proceedings of the IEEE International Conference on Neural Networks, 1*, 1–6.

Kolp, M., Faulkner, S., & Wautelet, Y. (2007). Social-centric design of multi-agent architectures. In P. Giorgini, N. Maiden, J. Mylopoulos, E. Yu (Eds.), *Social modeling for requirements engineering.* MIT Press.

Kolp, M., Giorgini, P., & Mylopoulos, J. (2002). Information systems development through social structures. In *Proceedings of the 14th Int. Conference on Software Engineering and Knowledge Engineering, SEKE'02, 27* (pp. 183-190).

Krause, D. R. (1997). Supplier development: current practices and outcomes. *International Journal of Purchasing and Materials Management 33*(2), 12–19.

Kripke, S. (1971). Identity and necessity. In M. Munitz (Ed.), *Identity and individuation* (pp. 135–164).

Krishna, P., Karlapalem, K., & Chiu, D. (2004). An ER[EC] framework for e-contract modeling, enactment and monitoring. *Data & Knowledge Engineering, 51*, 31-58.

Kruchten, P. (2003). *The rational unified process: An introduction (3rd Ed.).* Addison-Wesley.

Kuhn, T. (1996). *The structure of scientific revolutions (3rd Ed.).* University of Chicago Press.

Kuhn, W. (2005). Geospatial semantics: Why, of what, and how. *Journal on Data Semantics, 2*, 1–24.

Kumar, S., & Mishra, R. B. (2008). A framework towards Semantic Web service composition based on multi-agent system. *International Journal of Information Technology and Web Engineering, 3*(4), 59–81.

Kungas, P., & Matskin, M. (2006). *Semantic Web service composition through a P2P-based multi-agent environment* (. *LNCS, 4118*, 106–119.

Labs Semantic Web Programme, H. P. (n.d.). Jena- A Semantic Web Framework for Java. Retrieved March 1, 2008 from http://jena.sourceforge.net/

Lambert, D., & Pohlen, T. (2001). Supply chain metrics. *The International Journal of Logistics Management, 12*(1), 1-19.

Landauer, T. K., Foltz, P. W., & Laham, D. (1998). Introduction to latent semantic analysis. *Discourse Processes, 25*, 259–284.

Langseth, H., & Jensen, F. V. (2003). Decision theoretic troubleshooting of coherent systems. *Reliability Engineering & System Safety, 80*(1), 49–61. doi:10.1016/S0951-8320(02)00202-8

Lassila, O., & Swick, R. (2004). Resource description framework (RDF) model and syntax specification. *W3C (World-Wide Web Consortium)*. Retrieved from http://www.w3.org/TR/REC-rdf-syntax/

Leake, D., & Kendall-Morwick, J. (2008, September 1-4). Towards case-based support for e-science workflow generation by mining provenance. In K.-D. Althoff, R. Bergmann, M. Minor, & A. Hanft (Eds.), *Advances in Case-Based Reasoning, 9th European Conference, EC-CBR 2008, Trier, Germany* (LNAI 5239, pp.269-283). Berlin: Springer.

Leymann, F., & Roller, D. (2000). *Production workflow - concepts and techniques*. Upper Saddle River, NJ: Prentice Hall International.

Li, X., & Chandra, C. (2008). Toward a secure supply chain: A system's perspective. *Human Systems Management, 27*(1), 73–86.

Li, X., & Ji, Q. (2005). Active affective state detection and user assistance with dynamic Bayesian networks. *IEEE Transactions on Systems, Man, and Cybernetics-Part A, 35*(1), 93–105. doi:10.1109/TSMCA.2004.838454

Li, X., Chandra, C., & Shiau, J.-Y. (2009). Developing security taxonomy and model for security centric supply chain management. *International Journal of Manufacturing Technology and Management, 17*(1/2), 184–212. doi:10.1504/IJMTM.2009.023785

Li, Y. (2004). Task type and a faceted classification of tasks. In Schamber, L., & Barry, C. L. (Eds.), *ASIST 2004: proceedings of the 67th ASIS&T Annual Meeting, volume 41 of Proceedings of the ASIST Annual Meeting*, Medford, NJ: Information Today.

Limayem, M. (2003). *A comparison between human and automated facilitation in the GDSS Context*. Unpublished Manuscript.

Limayem, M.,& DeSanctis, G. (2000). Providing decisional guidance for multicriteria decision making in groups. *Information Systems Research, 11*(4), 386-402.

Lin, S., Soergel, D., & Marchionini, G. (1991). A self-organizing map for information retrieval. In *Proceedings of the 14th Annual ACM SIGIR International Conference on Research and Development in Information Retrieval, Chicago, Illinois* (pp. 262-269).

Linington, F., Milosevic, Z., Cole, J., Gibson, S., Kulkarni, S., & Neal, S. (2004). A unified behavioral model and a contract language for extended enterprise. *Data & Knowledge Engineering, 51*(1), 5-29.

Lippmann, R. P. (1987). An introduction to computing with neural networks. *IEEE Acoustics Speech and Signal Processing Magazine, 4*(2), 4–22.

Liu, B., Chen, J., Liu, S., & Zhang, R. (2006). Supply-chain coordination with combined contract for a short life-cycle product. *IEEE Transactions on Systems, Man and Cybernetics-Part A, Vol. 36*(1), 53-61.

Liu, H., Milios, E., & Janssen, J. (2004, September 20-24). Focused crawling by learning HMM from user's topic-specific browsing. In *Proceedings of the IEEE/WIC/ACM Int. Conference on Web Intelligence (WI '04)* (pp. 702-732). IEEE.

Liu, Y., Ngu, A. H. H., & Zeng, L. (2003). QoS computation and policing in dynamic Web service selection. In *Proceedings of the 13th International Conference World WideWeb*. McGuinness, D.L, & Harmelen, F.V. (n.d.). OWL Web ontology language overview. Retrieved February 13, 2008 from http://www.w3.org/TR/owl-features/

Lockamy III, A. (2004). Linking SCOR planning practices to supply chain performance: An exploratory study. *International Journal of Operations & Production Management, 24*(12), 1191-1218.

Lopez, A., Booker, Q., Shkarayeva, N., Briggs, R., & Nunamaker, J. (2002). Embedding Facilitation in Group Support Systems to Manage Distributed Group Behavior, *Proceedings of the 35th Annual Hawaii International Conference on System Sciences (HICSS'02)*-Volume 1-1 table of contents, p.42

Love, T. (1997). *Object lessons*. Cambridge University Press.

Lu, R., & Sadiq, S. (2006, September 5-7). Managing process variants as an information resource. In S. Dustdar, J. L. P. Fiadeiro, & A. P. Sheth (Eds.), *Business process management, Proceedings of the 4th International Conference, BPM 2006, Vienna, Austria* (LNCS 4102, pp. 426-431). Berlin: Springer.

Luo, Z., Sheth, A., Kochut, K., & Arpinar, B. (2003). Exception handling for conflict resolution in cross-organizational workflows. *Distributed and Parallel Databases, 13*, 271–306. doi:10.1023/A:1022827610371

Mackay, D. (2003). *Information theory, inference, and learning algorithms*. Cambridge, UK: Cambridge University Press.

MacLeod, K. J., & Robertson, W. (1991). A neural algorithm for document clustering. *Information Processing & Management, 27*(4), 337–346. doi:10.1016/0306-4573(91)90088-4

Madhusudan, T., Zhao, J. L., & Marshall, B. (2004). A case-based reasoning framework for workflow model management. *Data & Knowledge Engineering, 50*, 87–115. doi:10.1016/j.datak.2004.01.005

Maedche, A., Motik, B., Silva, N., & Volz, R. (2003). *MAFRA—an ontology mapping framework in the context of the semantic Web*.

Maes, P. (1994). Agents that reduce work and information overload. *Communications of the ACM, 37*(7), 30-40.

Maier, N. (1952). *Principles of human relations*. New York: Wiley.

Malucelli, A., Palzer, D., & Oliveira, E. (2006). Ontology-based Services to help solving the heterogeneity problem in e-commerce negotiations. *Electronic Commerce Research and Applications, 5*, 29–43. doi:10.1016/j.elerap.2005.08.002

March, S. T. (1990). Heterogeneous databases [Special issue]. *ACM Computing Surveys, 22*(3).

Marcia, J. B. (1986). Access in online catalogs: A design model. *American Society for Information Science Journal, Wiley InterScience, 37*(6), 357-376.

Maria, H., Benjamin, N., Iraklis, V., & Michalis, V. (2003). THESUS: Organizing Web document collections based on link semantics. *Int. Journal on Very Large Data Bases, VLDB, 12*, 320-332.

Marios, D., Dikaiakos, A., & Loizos, P. (2005). An investigation of Web crawler behavior: characterization and metrics. *Computer Communications, 28*, 880-897.

Marjanovic, O. (2005). Towards A Web-Based Handbook of Generic, Process-Oriented Learning Designs, *Educational Technology and Society, 8*(2), 66-82.

Marjanovic, O. (2007). Using Process-oriented, Sequencing Educational Technologies: Some Important Pedagogical Issues, *Computers in Human Behavior, 23*, 2742-2759.

Masterman, M. (1970). The nature of paradigm. In Lakatos I., & Musgrave A., *Criticism and the Growth of Knowledge*, Cambridge University Press.

Mataric, M. (1992). Integration of representation into goal-driven behavior-based robots. *IEEE Transactions on Robotics and Automation, 8*(3), 304-312.

McDowell, L., Etzioni, O., Halevy, A., & Levy, H. (2004). Semantic email. *13th international conference on World Wide Web (WWW 2004).*, 244–254, New York: ACM Press.

McTear, M. F. (2002). Spoken dialogue technology: Enabling the conversational user interface. *ACM Computing Surveys (CSUR), 34*(1).

Mehlhorn, K. (1984). *Data structures and algorithms 2: Graph algorithms and NPcompleteness*, Berlin: Springer.

Meijler, T. D., Kessels, H., Vuijsr, C., & le Comte, R. (1998, November 14). Realising run-time adaptable workflow by means of reflection in the Baan workflow engine. In *Proceedings of the CSCW-98 Workshop: Towards Adaptive Workflow Systems, Seattle, WA, USA.*

Menasce, D. A. (2002). QoS Issues in Web services. *IEEE Internet Computing, 6*(6). doi:10.1109/MIC.2002.1067740

Menczer, F. (2004). Lexical and semantic clustering by Web links. *Journal of the American Society for Information Science and Technology (JASIST), Wiley InterScience, 55*(14), 1261-1269.

Menczer, F., Paint, G., & Srinivansan, P. (2004). Topical Web crawlers:Evaluating adaptive algorithms. *ACM Transactions on Internet Technology, ACM, 4*(4), 378-419.

Merkl, D. (1997). Exploration of text collections with hierarchical feature maps. In *Proceedings of the 20th International ACM SIGIR Conference on Research and Development in Information Retrieval (SIGIR'97)* (pp. 186-195).

Metzinger, T., & Gallese, V. (2003). The emergence of a share action ontology: Building blocks for a theory. *Conciousness and Cognition, 12*(4), 549-571.

Meyer, B. (1997). *Object-oriented software construction (2nd Ed.).* Prentice Hall.

Michael, C., & Hsinchun, C. (2004, December 13-17). Using content-based and link-based analysis in building vertical search engines. In *Proceedings of the 7th Int. Conference on Asian Digital Libraries (ICADL '04)* (pp. 515-518). China.

Michelakis, E., Androutsoppoulos, I., Paliouras, G., & Sakkis, G. (2004). Filtron: A learning-based anti-spam filter. *1st Conference on Email and Anti-Spam (CEAS).*

Michelangelo, D., Frans, C. C., Lee, G., & Marco, G. (2000, September). Focused crawling using context graphs. In *Proceedings of the 26th International Conference on Very Large Databases (VLDB '00)* (pp. 527–534). Cairo, Egypt.

Miled, Z. B., Webster, Y.W., & Liu,Y. (2003). An ontology for semantic integration of life science web Databases. *International Journal of Cooperative Information Systems, 12*(2), 275-294.

Miled, Z.B., Li, N., & Bukhres, O. (2005). BACIIS: Biological and chemical information integration system. *Journal of Database Management, 16*(3), 72-85.

Miller, B. (1987). "Exists" and existence. *Review of Metaphysics, 40*, 237–270.

Minor, M., Schmalen, D., & Koldehoff, A. (2009). Fallstudie zum Einsatz agiler, prozessorientierter Methoden in der Chipindustrie. In H. R. Hansen, D. Karagiannis, & H.-G. Fill (Eds.), *Business Services: Konzepte, Technologien, Anwendungen, 9. Internationale Tagung Wirtschaftsinformatik, 25. - 27. Februar 2009, Wien,* volume 1 (pp. 193-201). Oesterreichische Computer Gesellschaft.

Minor, M., Schmalen, D., Koldehoff, A., & Bergmann, R. (2007). Configurable contexts for experience management. In Gronau, N. (Ed.), *4th Conference on Professional Knowledge Management - Experiences and Visions* (Vol. 2), *Potsdam, Univ. of Potsdam* (pp. 119- 126). Berlin: GITO-Verlag.

Minor, M., Schmalen, D., Tartakovski, A., & Bergmann, R. (2008). Agile Workflow Technology and Case-Based Change Reuse for Long-Term Processes. *International Journal of Intelligent Information Technologies, 4*(1), 80–98.

Mintzberg, H. (1992). Structure in fives: Designing effective organizations. Prentice-Hall.

Mitra, P., & Wiederhold, G. (2002). Resolving terminology heterogeneity in ontologies. In *Proceedings of ECAI'02 Workshop on Ontologies and Semantic Interoperability.*

Morabito, J., Sack, I., & Bhate, A. (1999). Organization modeling: Innovative architectures for the 21st century. Prentice Hall.

Moreno, J. L. (1934). *Who shall survive? A new approach to the problem of human interrelations.* Washington, DC: Nervous and Mental Disease Publishing Company.

Mou, Y., Cao, J., Zhang, S.S., & Zhang, J.H. (2005). Interactive Web service choice-making based on extended QoS model. *CIT*, 1130-1134.

Mouratidis, H., Giorgini, P., & Manson, G. (2003). Modelling secure multiagent systems. In *Proceedings of the 2nd International Joint Conference on Autonomous Agents and Multiagent Systems* (pp. 859-866). ACM Press.

Mozer, M.C. (1984, June). *Inductive information retrieval using parallel distributed computation.* Research Report. San Diego, CA: University of California at San Diego.

Muller, J. P., & Pischel, M. (1994). Modeling interacting agents. In Dynamic environments, in *Proceedings of the Eleventh European Conference on Artificial Intelligence (ECAI-94),* (pp. 709-713), The Netherlands.

Muller, J. P., Pischel, M., & Thiel, M. (1994). A pragmatic approach to modeling autonomous interacting systems. In Wooldridge, M., & Jennings, N. R. (Eds.), *Pre-proceedings of the 1994 Workshop on Agent Theories, Architectures, and Languages,* Netherlands, 226-240.

Murphy, K. (2001) The Bayes Net Toolbox for Matlab. *Computing Science and Statistics, 33.*

Murthy, V., & Krishnamurthy, E. (2005). Contextual information management using contract-based workflow. *Conference on Computing Frontiers,* May 4-6, 2005, Ischia, Italy, 236-245.

Najork, M., & Wiener, I. N. (2001, May). Breadth-first search crawling yields high-quality pages. In *Proceedings of the 10th International World Wide Web Conference (WWW '01)* (pp. 161-167). Hong Kong.

Nardi, B. A., Whittaker, S., Isaacs, E., Creech, M., Johnson, J., & Hainsworth, J. (2002). Integrating communication and information through ContactMap. *Communications of the ACM, 45*(2), 89–95. doi:10.1145/505248.505251

Narita, M., & Ogawa, Y. (2000). The use of phrases from query texts in information retrieval. In *Proceedings of the 23rd Annual International ACM SIGIR Conference on Research and Development in Information Retrieval, SIGIR 2000, Athens, Greece* (pp. 318-320).

Nedovic-Budic, Z., & Pinto, J. K. (1999). Interorganizational GIS: Issues and prospects. *The Annals of Regional Science, 33,* 183–195. doi:10.1007/s001680050100

Negroponte, N. (1997). Agents: From direct manipulation to delegation. In J. M. Bradshaw (Ed.), *Software Agents,* Cambridge: MIT Press, 57-66.

Nellore, R. (2004). Validating specifications: A contract-based approach. *IEEE Transactions on Engineering Management, 48*(4), 491-504.

Nemati, H., & Barko, C. D. (2003). *Organizational data mining: Leveraging enterprise data resources for optimal performance.* Hershey, PA: Idea Group Publishing.

Norman, D. A. (1997). How might people interact with agents. In J. M. Bradshaw, (Ed.), *Software Agents,* Cambridge: MIT Press, 49-55.

Noy, N. F., & Musen, M. A. (2002). Evaluating ontology-mapping tools: Requirements and experience. In *Proceedings of the Workshop on Evaluation of Ontology Tools at EKAW'02.*

Noy, N. F., & Musen, M. A. (2003). The prompt suite: Interactive tools for ontology merging and mapping. *International Journal of Human-Computer Studies, 59,* 983–1024.

O'Riain, S., & Spyns, P. (2006). Enhancing the business analysis function with semantics. *OTM Conferences, LNCS 4275(1),* 818–835, Springer: Berlin.

Odell, J. J. (2002). Objects and agents compared. *Journal of Object Technology, 1*(1), 41-53.

OMG, 2005. *The software process engineering metamodel specification.* Version 1.1.

Opdyke, W. F. (1992). *Refactoring object-oriented frameworks.* PhD Thesis, University of Illinois at Urbana-Champaign.

OpenCyc. (2006). OpenCyc 1.0. Retrieved May 2006, from http://www.cyc.com/cyc/opencyc/

Orlich, D.C., Harder, R.J., Callahan, R.C., Trevisan, M.S., & Brown, A.B. (2004). Teaching Strategies, a guide to effective instruction. (7th Ed.), Boston: Houghton Mifflin Company.

Orwig, R., Chen, H., & Nunamaker, J. F. (1997). A graphical, self-organizing approach to classifying electronic meeting output. *Journal of the American Society for Information Science American Society for Information Science, 48*(2), 157–170. doi:10.1002/(SICI)1097-4571(199702)48:2<157::AID-ASI6>3.0.CO;2-X

Osman, H., & El-Diraby, T. E. (2006, June 14-16). *Interoperable decision support model for routing buried urban infrastructure.* Paper presented at the Joint International Conference on Computing & Decision Making in Civil and Building Engineering, Montreal.

Padgham, L., & Lambrix, P. (2000). Agent capabilities: Extending BDI theory. *American Association for Artificial Intelligence.* Retrieved from www.aaai.org

Padmini, S., Filippo, M., & Gautam, P. (2005). A general evaluation framework for topical crawlers. *Information Retrieval, 8*(3), 417-447.

Pan, J., & Horrocks, I. (2007). RDFS(FA): Connecting RDF(S) and OWL DL. *IEEE Transactions on Knowledge and Data Engineering, 19*(2), 192-206.

Parikh, M., Fazlollahi, B., & Verma, S. (2001). The effectiveness of decisional guidance: An empirical evaluation. *Decision Sciences, 32*(2), 303-331.

Parunak, V. (1997). Go to the ant: Engineering principles from natural agent systems. *Annals of Operations Research, 75,* 69–101. doi:10.1023/A:1018980001403

Pazienza, M. T., Stellato, A., Henriksen, L., Paggio, P., & Zanzotto F. M. (2005). Ontology mapping to support multilingual ontology-based question answering. In *Proceedings of the 4th International Semantic Web Conference,* Galway, Ireland.

Pearl, J. (1988). *Probabilistic reasoning in intelligent systems: Networks of plausible inference.* San Mateo, CA: Morgan Kaufmann.

Pechoucek, M. (2003). Formal representation for multi-agent systems. *Gerstner Laboratory, Czech Technical University in Prague.* Retrieved from http://agents.felk.cvut.cz/teaching/33ui2/bdi.pdf

Peng, Y., Finin, T., Labrou, Y., Chu, B., Long, J., Tolone, W. J. et al. (1998). A multi-agent system for enterprise integration. International Journal of Agile Manufacturing, *UMBC eBiquity, 1*(2), 213-229.

Peng, Z. R., & Tsou, M. H. (2003). *Internet GIS: Distributed Geographic information services for the Internet and wireless networks.* John Wiley.

Petroni, A., & M. Braglia. (2000). Vendor selection using principal component analysis. *The Journal of Supply Chain Management, 36*(2), 63-69.

Picard, R. (1997). *Affective computing.* Cambridge, MA: MIT Press.

Porter, M. F. (1980). An algorithm for suffix stripping. *Program, 14*(3), 130–137.

Prahinski, C., & Benton, W. (2004). Supplier evaluations: communication strategies to improve supper performance. *Journal of Operations Management, 22*(1), 39-62.

Prawat, R.S., & Floden, R.E. (1994). Philosophical-perspectives on Constructivist Views of Learning, Educational Psychologist 29(1): 37-48, WIN 1994.

Pree, W. (1994). *Design patterns for object oriented development.* Addison Wesley.

Protégé. Protégé-OWL API Programmer's Guide. Online access: http://protege.stanford.edu/plugins/owl/api/guide.html

Prudhommeaux, E., & Seaborne, A. (2008). SPARQL Query Language for RDF, Retrieved from http://www.w3.org/TR/2008/REC-rdf-sparql-query-20080115/

Qiu, F., Shao, M., & Zatsman, J. (2003, June). *Index structures for querying the deep Web.* Paper presented at the International Workshop on the Web and Databases (WebDB) (pp. 79-86), San Diego, California, USA.

Rao, A. S., & Georgeff, M. P. (1991). Modeling rational agents within a BDI architecture. In Fikes, R. & Sandewall, E. (Eds.), *Proceedings of knowledge representation and reasoning (KR&R 91)*, San Mateo, CA: Morgan Kaufmann Publihsers.

Rational Rose, I. B. M. (2007). Retrieved August 16, 2007 from http://www-306.ibm.com/software/rational

Rauber, A., & Merkl, D. (1999). Automatic labeling of self-organizing maps: Making a treasure-map reveal its secrets. In *Proceedings of the Pacific-Asia Conference on Knowledge Discovery and Data Mining (PAKDD'99), Beijing, China* (pp. 228-237).

Reichert, M., & Dadam, P. (2009). Enabling adaptive process-aware information systems with ADEPT2. In J. Cardoso, & W. van der Aalst (Eds.), *Handbook of research on business process modeling.* Hershey, PA: IGI Global.

Reichert, M., Rinderle, S., & Dadam, P. (2003, June). ADEPT workflow management system: Flexible support for enterprise-wide business processes (tool presentation). In W. M. P. van der Aalst (Ed.), *International Conference on Business Process Management (BPM '03)* (LNAI 2678, pp. 370-379). Berlin: Springer.

Ren, F. & Shi, H. (2000). A general ontology based multilingual multi-function multi-media intelligent system. In *Proceedings of the IEEE International Conference on Systems, Cybernetics,* (pp. 2362-2368), Nashville.

Resnik, P. (1999). Semantic similarity in taxonomy: An information-based measure and its application problems of ambiguity in natural language. *Artificial Intelligence Research Journal, 11,* 95-130.

Reynolds, R., Caley, L., & Mason, R. (2002). How do People Learn? London: CIPD.

Rhodes, L.K., & Bellamy, G.T. (1999). Choices and Consequences in the Renewal of Teacher Education. Journal of Teacher Education, 50(1), 17.

Ricardo, B., Carlos, C., & Andrea, R. (2005, May 10-14). Crawling a country: Better strategies than breadth first for Web page ordering. In *Proceedings of the 14th Int.*

World Wide Web Conference (WWW '05) (pp. 864 - 872) Chiba, Japan.

Rich, E. (1989). Stereotypes and user modeling. In A. Kobsa & W. Wahlster (Eds.), *User models in dialog systems.* Springer.

Riehle, D., & Züllighoven, H. (1996). Understanding and using patterns in software development. *Theory and Practice of Object Systems, 2*(1), 3–13. doi:10.1002/(SICI)1096-9942(1996)2:1<3::AID-TAPO1>3.0.CO;2-#

Rila, M., & Hozumi T. (2000). The exploration and analysis of using multiple thesaurus types for query expansion in information retrieval. *Natural Language Processing Journal, 7*(2), 117-140.

Rinderle, S., Weber, B., Reichert, M., & Wild, W. (2005, September 5-8). Integrating process learning and process evolution - A semantics based approach. In W. M. P van der Aalst, B. Benatallah, F. Casati, & F. Curbera (Eds.), *Proceedings of the Business Process Management, 3rd International Conference, BPM 2005, Nancy, France* (LNCS 3649, pp. 252-267). Berlin: Springer.

Ritter, H., & Kohonen, T. (1989). Self-organizing semantic maps. *Biological Cybernetics, 61,* 241–254. doi:10.1007/BF00203171

Ritter, M., Meier, U., Yang, J., & Waibel, A. (1999). Face translation: A multimodal translation agent. In *Proceedings of Auditory Visual Speech Processing.*

Rolstadås, A. (1998). Enterprise performance measurement. *International Journal of Operations & Production Management, 18*(9/10), 989-999.

Rossi, G., Schwabe, D., & Guimaraes, R. (2001). Designing personalized Web applications. *In WWW10, The Tenth International Conference on the World Wide Web,* Hong Kong.

Roussinov, D., & Chen, H. (1998). A scalable self-organizing map algorithm for textual classification: {A} neural network approach to thesaurus generation. *Communication & Cognition, 15*(1-2), 81–112.

Rozinat, A., & van der Aalst, W. M. P. (2006). Conformance testing: Measuring the fit and appropriateness of event logs and process models. Bussler, C. et al. (Editors), *BPM 2005 Workshops (Workshop on Business Process Intelligence), Lecture Notes in Computer Science, 3812*, 163–176. Berlin: Springer-Verlag.

Russel, S., & Norvig, P. (1995). *Artificial intelligence: A modern approach*. New Jersey: Printice Hall Inc.

Russell, N., van der Aalst, W. M. P., & ter Hofstede, A. H. M. (2006). Workflow exception patterns. In E. Dubois, & K. Pohl (Eds.), *18th International Conference on Advanced Information Systems Engineering (CAiSE'06)* (LNCS 4001, pp. 288-302). Berlin: Springer.

Salton, G., & Buckley, C. (1990). Improving retrieval performance by relevance feedback. *J. JASIS, 41*(4), 288–297. doi:10.1002/(SICI)1097-4571(199006)41:4<288::AID-ASI8>3.0.CO;2-H

Salton, G., & McGill, M. (1983). *Introduction to modern information retrieval.*, New York, NY: McGraw-Hill.

Salvucci, D. D., Boer, E. R., & Liu, A. (2001). Toward an integrated model of driver behavior in a cognitive architecture. *Transportation Research Record*, 1779.

Sankey, H. (1994). *The incommensurability thesis*. Ashgate.

Sarbanes, P., & Oxley, G. (2002). *Sarbanes-Oxley Act of 2002*.

Scerri, S., Handschuh, S., & Decker, S. Semantic email as a communication medium for the social semantic desktop. *5th European Semantic Web Conference (ESWC2008).*, 124–138, Berlin: Springer.

Schimm, G., van der Aalst, W. M. P., van Dongen, B., & Herbst, J. (2003). Workflow mining: A survey of issues and approaches. *Data & Knowledge Engineering, 47*, 237–267. doi:10.1016/S0169-023X(03)00066-1

Schwabe, D., & Rossi, G. (1998). Developing hypermedia applications using OOHDM. *In Proceedings of Workshop on Hypermedia development Process, Methods and Models*, (pp. 85-94).

Schwarz, R.M. (1994). *The skilled facilitator: Practical wisdom for developing effective groups*. San Francisco: Jossey-Bass

Schwarz, S. (2003, April 2-4). Task-Konzepte: Struktur und Semantik für Workflows. In U. Reimer, A. Abecker, S. Staab, & G. Stumme (Eds.), *Proceedings of the WM2003: Professionelles Wissensmanagement – Erfahrungen und Visionen, Luzern, Switzerland, LNI P-28* (pp. 351-356), Bonn: Gesellschaft für Informatik.

Scott, J. (1992). *Social network analysis*. Newbury Park, CA: Sage.

Scott, W. R. (1998). *Organizations: Rational, natural, and open systems*. Prentice Hall.

Searle, J. (1969). *Speech acts*. Cambridge: Cambridge University Press.

Segil, L. (1996). Intelligent business alliances: How to profit using today's most important strategic tool. *Times Business*.

Sengupta, K., & Te'eni, D. (1993). Feedback in GDSS: Enhancing control and reducing conflict. *MIS Quarterly, 17*(1), 87-109.

Shawn M. Glynn, Russell H. Yeany, & Bruce K. Britton. A Constructive View of learning Science. The Psychology of learning science. LEA Publishers, 1991

Shortliffe, E. (1976). *Computer-based medical consultation: MYCIN*. New York: Elsevier.

Shute, Valerie & Towle, Brendon (2003). Adaptive E-Learning, Educational Psychologist, 38(2), 105-114.

Silver, M. (1991). Decision guidance for computer-based decision support. *MIS Quarterly, March*, 105-122.

Singh, M., & Huhns, M. (2005). *Service-oriented computing: Semantics, processes, agents*. San Francisco: Wiley.

Singh, R., & Salam, A. F. (2006). Semantic information assurance for secure knowledge management: A business process perspective. *IEEE Transactions on Systems, Man and Cybernetics Part (A), 36*(3), 472-486.

Skarmeas, N. (1999). *Agents as objects with knowledge base state*. Imperial College Press.

Smith, B. (1996). Mereotopology: A theory of parts and boundaries. *Data & Knowledge Engineering, 20,* 287–303. doi:10.1016/S0169-023X(96)00015-8

Sobia, S., & Nirmala, P. (2007), Context-based travel planning agent. (Tech. Rpt. No.) Pondicherry: Pondicherry University, Department of Computer Science.

Sommerville, I. (1992). *Software engineering (4th Ed.).* Addison-Wesley.

Spink, A., Jansen, J., & Blakely, C. (2006). A study of results overlap and uniqueness among major web search engines. *Information Processing & Management.*

Staggernation (2006). *Google API Proximity Search (GAPS).* Retrieved November 4, 2006, from http://www. staggernation.com/gaps/readme.php

Sterling, L., & Shapiro, E. (1986). *The art of prolog.* Cambridge, MA: MIT Press

Stevens, R., Goble, C.A., Paton, N.W., Bechhofer, S., Ng, G., Baker, P. et al. (1999). Complex Query Formulation Over Diverse Information Sources Using an Ontology. Workshop on Computation of Biochemical Pathways and Genetic Networks, European Media Lab (EML), (pp. 83–88).

Tanasescu, V. (2007). Spatial semantics in difference spaces. In *Spatial Information Theory* (Vol. 4736/2007, pp. 96-115). Berlin / Heidelberg: Springer.

Tang, J., Li, J., Liang, B., Huang, X., Li, Y., & Wang, K. (2006). Using Bayesian decision for ontology mapping. *Journal of Web Semantics,*

Tennenhouse, D. (2000). Embedding the Internet: Proactive computing. Communications of the ACM, 43(5).

Thanh, T. T., David, H., Nick, C., & Kathleen, G. (2005, October 31-November 5). Focused crawling for both topical relevance and quality of medical information. In *Proceedings of the 14th ACM International Conference on Information and Knowledge Management (CIKM '05)* (pp. 147-154). Bremen, Germany.

Tun, N. N., & Tojo, S. (2005). IC-based ontology expansion in devouring accessibility. In *Proceedings of the*

Australian Ontology Workshop (AOW 2005) (Vol. 58, pp. 99–106). Australian Computer Society.

Turban, E., & Watson, P. (1986). Integrating expert systems and decision support systems. *MIS Quarterly,*

Turunen, M., & Hakulinen, J. (2000). Jaspis: A framework for multilingual adaptive speech applications. In *Proceedings of the 6th International Conference of Spoken Language Processing.*

Tweedale, J., Ichalkaranje, N., Sioutis, C., Jarvis, B., Consoli, A., & Phillips-Wren, G. (2007). Innovations in multi-agent systems. *Journal of Network and Computer Applications, Elsevier, 30*(3), 1089–1115. doi:10.1016/j. jnca.2006.04.005

Udupi, Y., & Singh M. (2006). Contract enactment in virtual organizations: A commitment-based approach. *American Association for Artificial Intelligence (AAAI),* Online access: http://www.aaai.org.

Ullman, J. R. (1976). An algorithm for subgraph isomorphism. *Journal of the Association for Computing Machinery, 23*(1), 31–42.

Vakkari, P. (2003). Task-based information searching. *Annual Review of Information Science and Technology, 37,* 13-464.

Valdes-Perez, R. (2005, March 31). Meta-search: More heads better than one? *ZDNet News.* Retrieved November 24, 2006, from http://news.zdnet.com/2100-9588_22-5647280.html van Rijsbergen, C.J. (1999). *Information retrieval* (2nd ed.). Retrieved November 28, 2006, from http://www.dcs.gla.ac.uk/~iain/keith/index.htm

van der Aalst, W. M. P., & Nikolov, A. (2007). EMail Analyzer: An e-mail mining plug-in for the ProM framework. *BPM Center Report BPM-07-16.* BPMCenter.org.

van der Aalst, W. M. P., & Song, M. (2004). Mining social networks: Uncovering interaction patterns in business processes. Desel, J., Pernici, B., & Weske, M., (Editors), *International Conference on Business Process Management (BPM 2004), Lecture Notes in Computer Science, 3080,* 244–260. Berlin: Springer-Verlag.

van der Aalst, W. M. P., & van Hee, K. M. (2002). *Workflow management: Models, methods and systems.* Cambridge, MA: MIT press.

van der Aalst, W. M. P., & Weijters, A. J. M. M. (Eds.). (2004). Process mining, *Special Issue of Computers in Industry, 53(3).* Amsterdam: Elsevier Science Publishers.

van der Aalst, W. M. P., ter Hofstede, A. H. M., Kiepuszewski, B., & Barros, A. P. (2003). Workflow patterns. *Distributed and Parallel Databases, 14,* 5–51. doi:10.1023/A:1022883727209

van der Aalst, W. M. P., van Dongen, B. F., Günther, C., Mans, R., de Medeiros, A. K. A., Rozinat, A., et al. (2007). ProM 4.0: Comprehensive support for real process analysis. In Kleijn, J., & Yakovlev, A. (Editors), *Application and Theory of Petri Nets 2007, Lecture Notes in Computer Science, 4546,* 484–494. Berlin: Springer-Verlag.

van der Aalst, W. M. P., van Dongen, B. F., Herbst, J., Maruster, L., Schimm, G., & Weijters, A. J. M. M. (2003). Workflow mining: A survey of issues and approaches. *Data & Knowledge Engineering, 47*(2), 237–267. doi:10.1016/S0169-023X(03)00066-1

van der Aalst, W. M. P., Weijters, A. J. M. M., & Maruster, L. (2004). Workflow mining: Discovering process models from event logs. *IEEE Transactions on Knowledge and Data Engineering, 16*(9), 1128–1142. doi:10.1109/TKDE.2004.47

van der Aalst, W. M. P., Weske, M., & Grünbauer, D. (2005). Case handling: A new paradigm for business process support. *Data & Knowledge Engineering, 53,* 129–162. doi:10.1016/j.datak.2004.07.003

van Dongen, B. F., & van der Aalst, W. M. P. (2004). Multi-phase process mining: Building instance graphs. In Atzeni, P., Chu, W., Lu, H., Zhou, S., & Ling, T. W. (Editors), *International Conference on Conceptual Modeling (ER 2004), Lecture Notes in Computer Science, 3288,* 362–376. Berlin: Springer-Verlag.

van Elst, L., Aschoff, F. R., Bernardi, A., Maus, H., & Schwarz, S. (2003, June). Weakly-structured workflows for knowledge-intensive tasks: An experimental evaluation. In *Proceedings of the 12th IEEE International Workshops on Enabling Technologies (WETICE 2003), Infrastructure for Collaborative Enterprises, Linz, Austria* (pp. 340-345). Los Alamitos, California: IEEE Computer Society.

Veith, R. H. (1988). *Visual information systems: The power of graphics and video.* Boston, MA: G.K. Hall.

Verma, R., & Pullman M. E. (1998). An analysis of the supplier selection process. *Omega, 26*(6), 739-750.

Villanova-Oliver, M., Gensel, J., Martin, H., & Erb, C. (2002, April 8-10). *Design and generation of adaptable web information systems with KIWIS.* In proceedings of the 3rd IEEE Conference on Information Technology ITCC-2002, Las Vegas, USA

Vinod, V., Vydiswaran, G., & Sunita, S. (2005, January 6-8). Learning to extract information from large Websites using sequential models.In *Proceedings of the 11ᵗʰ Int. Conference on Management of Data (COMAD '05)* (pp. 76-82). Goa, India.

Visser, P. R. S., Jones, D. M. R., Bench-Capon, T. J. M., & Shave, M. J. R. (1997). Assessing heterogeneity by classifying ontology mismatches. In *Proceedings of AAAI'97 Spring Symposium on Ontological Engineering,* Stanford University, USA.

Von Glasersfeld, E.(1989) Constructvism in education. 162-163. In Husen, T., & Postlethwaite, T.N(eds). The international encyclopedia of education, \AS;supplementary volume one\AS;, Pergamon Press plc.

Vygotsky, L. S. (1978). Mind in society: The development of higher psychological processes. Cambridge, MA: Harvard University Press. Published originally in Russian in 1930.

Wagner, K., & Bodendiek, R. (1989). *Graphentheorie I.* BI-Wissenschaftsverlag, Mannheim.

Wang, G., Huang, S. H., & Dismukes, J. P. (2004). Product driven supply chain selection using integrated multi-criteria decision making methodology. *International Journal of Production Economics, 91*(1), 1–15.

Wang, M. H., & Wang, H. Q. (2006). From Process Logic to Business Logic – A Cognitive Approach to Business Process Management, Information and Management, 43, 179-193.

Wang, X., Vitvar, T., Kerrigan, M., & Toma, I. (2006). *A QoS-aware selection model for Semantic Web Services* (LNCS 4294, pp. 390-401).

Warnecke, L., Beattie, J., Cheryl, K., & Lyday, W. (1998). *Geographic information technology in cities and counties: A nationwide assessment.* Washington, DC: American Forests.

Wasserman, S., & Faust, K. (1994). *Social network analysis: Methods and applications.* Cambridge: Cambridge University Press.

Wautelet, Y., Achbany, Y., Kiv, S., & Kolp, M. (2009). A service-oriented framework for component-based software development: An i* driven approach. In *Proceedings of the 11th International Conference on Enterprise Information Systems, ICEIS '09, Milan.*

Wautelet, Y., Kolp, M., & Achbany, Y. (2006). *I-Tropos: An iterative SPEM-centric software project management process* (Technical Report IAG Working paper 06/01). IAG/ISYS Information Systems Research Unit, Catholic University of Louvain, Belgium. Retrieved from http://www.iag.ucl.ac.be/wp

Wayne, L. (2005). *Metadata in action: Expanding the utility of geospatial metadata.* Federal Geographic Data Committee.

Weber, B., & Wild, W. (2005, April 10-13). Towards the agile management of business processes. In K.-D. Althoff, A. Dengel, R. Bergmann, M. Nick, & T. Roth-Berghofer (Eds.), *Professional knowledge management, Third Biennial Conference, WM 2005, Kaiserslautern, Germany, Revised Selected Papers* (LNCS 3782, pp. 409-419). Berlin: Springer.

Weber, B., Reichert, M., & Rinderle-Ma, S. (2008). Change patterns and change support features - Enhancing flexibility in process-aware information systems . *Data & Knowledge Engineering, 66*, 438–466. doi:10.1016/j.datak.2008.05.001

Weber, B., Wild, W., & Breu, R. (2004, August 30-September 2). CBRFlow: Enabling adaptive workflow management through conversational case-based reasoning. In P. Funk, & P. A. Gonzalez-Calero (Eds.), *Advances in case-based reasoning, 7th European Conference, ECCBR 2004, Madrid, Spain* (LNCS 3155, pp. 434-448). Berlin: Springer.

Webster, B. F. (1995). *Pitfalls of object oriented development.* John Wiley & Sons Inc.

Weigand, H., & Heuvel, W. (2002). Cross-organizational workflow integration using contracts. *Decision Support Systems, 33*(3), 247-265.

Weijters, A. J. M. M., & van der Aalst, W. M. P. (2003). Rediscovering workflow models from event-based data using Little Thumb. *Integrated Computer-Aided Engineering, 10*(2), 151–162.

Weld, D. (1994). An introduction to least commitment planning. *AI Mag, 15*(4), 27–61.

Weld, D. (1999). Recent advances in AI planning. *AI Mag, 20*(2), 93- 123.

Welty, C., & Guarino, N. (2000). A formal ontology of properties. In *Proceedings of EKAW-2000: The Conference on Conceptual Modeling.*

Welty, C., & Guarino, N. (2000). Identity, unity and individuality: Towards a formal toolkit for ontological analysis. In *Proceedings of ECAI-2000.*

Welty, C., & Guarino, N. (2001). Supporting ontological analysis of taxonomic relationships. *Data & Knowledge Engineering, 39*, 51-74.

Welty, N., & Andersen, W. (2005). Towards OntoClean 2.0: A framework for rigidity. *Journal of Applied Ontology,*

Wermter, S. (1991). Learning to classify natural language titles in a recurrent connectionist model. In *Proceedings of the 1991 International Conference on Artificial Neural Networks, Vol. 2, Espoo, Finland, 1991*(pp. 1715-1718).

Wertsch, J.V. (1985). Vygotsky and the social formation of mind. Cambridge, Mass.: Harvard University Press.

Weske, M. (1999). *Workflow management systems: Formal foundation, conceptual design, implementation aspects*, Habilitation's thesis, University of Münster, Germany.

Wheeler, B., & Valacich, J. (1996). Facilitation, GSS, and training as sources of process restrictiveness and guidance for structured group decision making: An empirical assessment. *Information Systems Research, 7*(4), 409, 20.

Wheeler, C., & Mennecke, B. (1992). Modeling group task processes using a hidden profile task: The school of business policy task. *Indiana University School of Business, Working Paper,* number 513,.

Widom, J. (1995). Research problems in data warehousing. In *Proceedings of the Fourth Int. Conf. on Information and Knowledge Management* (pp. 25-30). ACM Press.

Wolf, C. (2002). iWeaver: Towards an interactive web-based adaptive learning environment to address individual learning styles. European Journal of Open and Distance Learning.

Wombacher, A. (2006, October 29-November 3). Evaluation of technical measures for workflow similarity based on a pilot study. In R. Meersman, Z. Tari et al. (Eds.), *On the move to meaningful Internet systems 2006: CoopIS, DOA, GADA, and ODBASE, OTM Confederated International Conferences, CoopIS, DOA, GADA, and ODBASE 2006, Montpellier, France, Proceedings, Part I* (LNCS 4275, pp. 255-272). Berlin: Springer.

Wong, K. (2003). *Rigid designation, existence and semantics for quantified modal logic* (Tech. Rep.), Department of Philosophy, The Chinese University of Hong Kong.

Wong, Z., & Aiken, M. (2003). Automated facilitation of electronic meetings. *Information and Management, 41*(2), table of contents, 125 –134.

Wood, M., DeLoach, S. A., & Sparkman, C. (2001). Multi-agent system engineering. *International Journal of Software Engineering and Knowledge Engineering, 11*(3), 231–258. doi:10.1142/S0218194001000542

Woodridge, M., & Jennings, N. R. (1995). Intelligent agents: Theory and practice. *The Knowledge Engineering Review, 10*(2), 115-152.

Woodridge, M., Jennings, N. R., & Kinny, D. (2000). The Gaia methodology for agent-oriented analysis and design. *Autonomous Agents and Multi-Agent Systems, 3*(3), 285–312. doi:10.1023/A:1010071910869

Wooldridge, M. & Jennings, N.R. (1995). Agent theories, architectures and languages: a survey. In: Wooldridge, M. and Jennings, N.R. (eds) Intelligent Agents, Lecture Notes in AI, Vol. 890, pp. 1-39, Springer-Verlag.

Wooldridge, M. (1999). Intelligent agents. In Weiss, G. (Ed.), *Multiagent systems: A modern approach to distributed artificial intelligence*, MIT Press, 27-77.

Wooldridge, M. (2000). *Reasoning about rational agents.* MIT Press.

Wooldridge, M., & Jennings, N. R. (1995). Intelligent agents, theory and practice. *Knowledge Engineering Review, 10*(2).

Workflow Management Coalition. (1999). Workflow management coalition glossary & terminology. Retrieved on May 23, 2007, from http://www.wfmc.org/standards/docs/TC-1011_term_glossary_v3.pdf

World Wide Web Consortium. (2001). eXtensible Stylesheet Language, XSL Specification – version 1.0, W3C Recommendation. Retrieved October 15, 2001 from http://www.w3.org/TR/xsl/

World Wide Web Consortium. (2002). RDF Vocabulary Description Language 1.0: RDF Schema, W3C Working Draft. Retrieved April 30, 2002 from http://www.w3.org/TR/rdf-schemadix

Wu, B., & Davison, B. (2005). Identifying link farm spam pages. In *Proceedings of the 14th World Wide Web Conference, Industrial Track, Chiba, Japan, May 2005* (pp. 820-829).

Wu, Z., & Palmer, M. (1994). Verb semantics and lexical selection. In *Proceedings of the 32nd Annual Meetings of the Associations for Computational Linguistics (ACL '94)* (pp. 133–138). Las Cruces, New Mexico.

Xu, D. M., & Wang, H. Q. (2006). Intelligent Agent Supported Personalization for Virtual Learning Environments, Decision Support Systems, 42(2), 825-843.

Xu, J., & Croft, W. B. (1996). Query expansion using local and global document analysis. In *Proceedings of the 19th Annual International ACM SIGIR Conference on Research and Development in Information Retrieval, Zurich Switzerland* (pp. 4-11). New York: ACM Press.

Yoshino, M. Y., & Srinivasa Rangan, U. (1995). *Strategic alliances: An entrepreneurial approach to globalization.* Harvard Business School Press.

Yu, E. (1995). *Modeling strategic relationships for process reengineering.* PhD thesis, University of Toronto, Department of Computer Science.

Yule, G. (1996). The study of language. Cambridge: Cambridge University Press.

Zambonelli, F., Jennings, N. R., & Wooldridge, M. (2000). Organizational abstractions for the analysis and design of multi-agent systems. In *Proceedings of the 1st International Workshop on Agent-Oriented Software Engineering* (pp. 243-252).

Zambonelli, F., Jennings, N. R., Omicini, A., & Wooldridge, M. (2000). Agent-oriented software engineering for Internet applications. In *Coordination of Internet Agents: Models, Technologies and Applications* (pp. 326-346). Springer Verlag.

Zambonelli, F., Jennings, N.R., & Wooldridge, M. (2000). Organizational abstractions for the analysis and design of multi-agent systems. In *Proceedings of the 1st international workshop on agent-oriented software engineering,* (pp. 243-252).

Zamir, O., & Etzioni, O. (1998). Web document clustering: A feasibility demonstration. In *Proceedings of the 19th International ACM SIGIR Conference on Research and Development in Information Retrieval (SIGIR'98)* (pp. 46-54).

Zeng, L. Z., Benatallah, B., Anne, H. H. N., Dumas, M., Kalagnanam, J., & Chang, H. (2004). QoS-Aware middleware for Web service composition. *IEEE Transactions on Software Engineering, 30*(5), 311–327. doi:10.1109/TSE.2004.11

Zhdanova, A. V., & Fensel, D. (2005, September 19-22). Limitations of community Web portals: A classmates' case study. In *Proceedings of the IEEE/WIC/ACM International Conference on Web Intelligence* (pp. 101-104). Compiegne, France: IEEE Computer Society.

Zhou, D., Song, Y., Zhang, Y., & Zha, H. (2005). Towards discovering organizational structure from e-mail corpus. *4th IEEE International Conference on Machine Learning and Applications,* 279–284. Washington, DC: IEEE Computer Society.

Zigurs, I, & Buckland, B. (1998). A theory of task/technology fit and group support systems effectiveness. *MIS Quarterly,* 22(3), 313-335.

Zimmerman, B. J. (1989). A social cognitive view of self-regulated academic learning. Journal of educational psychology, 81(3), 329-339.

About the Contributors

Vijayan Sugumaran is Professor of Management Information Systems in the department of Decision and Information Sciences at Oakland University, Rochester, Michigan, USA. His research interests are in the areas of Ontologies and Semantic Web, Intelligent Agent and Multi-Agent Systems, Component Based Software Development, Knowledge-Based Systems, and Data & Information Modeling. His most recent publications have appeared in *Information systems Research*, *ACM Transactions on Database Systems*, *IEEE Transactions on Engineering Management*, *Communications of the ACM*, *Healthcare Management Science*, and *Data and Knowledge Engineering*. Dr. Sugumaran is the **editor-in-chief** of the *International Journal of Intelligent Information Technologies* and also serves on the editorial board of seven other journals. He was the program co-chair for the *13th International Conference on Applications of Natural Language to Information Systems* (NLDB 2008). In addition, he has served as the chair of the *Intelligent Agent and Multi-Agent Systems* mini-track for Americas Conference on Information Systems (AMCIS 1999 - 2009) and *Intelligent Information Systems* track for the Information Resources Management Association International Conference (IRMA 2001, 2002, 2005 - 2007). He served as Chair of the E-Commerce track for Decision Science Institute's Annual Conference, 2004. He is the Information Technology Coordinator for the Decision Sciences Institute. He also regularly serves as a program committee member for numerous national and international conferences.

* * *

H. Arafat Ali, received a BSc in electrical engineering (electronics), and MSc and PhD in computer engineering and automatic control from the Faculty of Engineering, Mansoura University, in 1987, 1991 and 1997, respectively. He was assistant professor at the University of Mansoura, Faculty of Computer Science, from 1997 to 1999. From January 2000 up to September 2001, he joined as a post doctor at the Department of Computer Science, University of Connecticut, Storrs. From 2002 up to 2004 he was the vice dean for student affairs in the computer science and information department at University of Mansoura. Since 2004 he has been an associate professor in the computer engineering department, Faculty of Engineering, University of Mansoura. His interests are in the areas of network security, mobile agent, pattern recognition, databases, and performance analysis.

Ikram Amous Ben Amor received her bachelor's degree in business data processing from Sfax University, Tunisia, in 1998 and her master's degree in data processing from Paul Sabatier University (UPS), Frence, in 1999. She received her Doctorate in Informatics from the UPS University in December 2002. She is currently an Assistant professor in the Electronic and Communication Institute of Sfax in Tunisia. She is also a member of the MIRACL laboratory of Sfax University, Tunisia. Her research interests include multimedia document personalization, multimedia document annotation and querying, approaches for adaptive web applications. She has participated in several program committees of National and International conferences.

Ralph Bergmann is full professor at the University of Trier and is directing a research group on business information systems. He studied computer science at the University of Kaiserslautern and finished his doctoral dissertation on hierarchical case-based planning in 1996. In 2001 he received the postdoctoral degree (Habilitation) with a thesis on experience management and became full professor at the University of Hildesheim. In 2004 he accepted an offer for a professorship position at the University of Trier. His main interests include experience management, particularly case-based reasoning and semantic search, machine learning and knowledge discovery, as well as knowledge representation and processing.

T. Chithralekha is a doctoral candidate and a research scholar in the Dept. of Computer Science, Pondicherry University, Pondicherry, India. She has completed her bachelor's and master's degree in computer science & engg. from Pondicherry University. Her research area pertains to software agents and languagebased systems. She has carried out many research projects in this area. She is also a reader in the Dept. of Banking Technology of the same University. Prior to this, she has been working as lecturer in the Dept. of Computer Science, Pondicherry University and also as Lecturer in the Dept. of Computer Science & Engg. in Pondicherry Engineering College, Pondicherry. She has twelve years of post-graduate teaching and research experience. Her other areas of interest include distributed systems, object-oriented systems, computer networks and algorithms.

A.I. El-Dousky is a full-time professor at the computer and control department, Mansoura University. He received the BSc degree in electrical engineering from the Faculty of Engineering, Mansoura University, Egypt. He received his MSc and PhD degrees in computer science and control from the Departments of Electronics and Electrical Engineering, University of Glasgow, Glasgow, UK. From 1984–2002 he was the manager of the computer center of Mansoura University. He has many publications in computer network, software engineering, AI, and distributed systems. His interests are in the areas of network security, mobile agent, pattern recognition, databases, and performance analysis.

Hossam M. Faheem received the MSc degree in computer engineering and science from the faculty of electronic engineering, Egypt, in 1995 and the PhD degree in computer and systems engineering from the faculty of engineering, Ain Shams University, Egypt, 2000. He is currently an associate professor of computer systems in the faculty of computer and information sciences, Ain Shams University, Egypt. He is the Director of Egyptian Universities Network EUN. His research interests include multi agent-based systems, data security, vulnerability assessment, parallel processing architectures, and pattern recognition. He has published more than 20 papers on these topics, most of them have been published in IEEE conferences and magazines.

Zaki Taha Fayed is an associate professor of computer science in the faculty of computer and information sciences, Ain shams University. He received his PhD degree in communications and electronics from the faculty of engineering, Ain shams University in 1998. His research interests include multiagent-based systems, speech recognition, and data mining.

Abdelmajid Ben Hamadou received his PhD in computer sciences from the Orsay University of Paris,(France) in 1979 and his "Doctorat d'Etat" in computer sciences from University of Tunis in 1993. Currently he is a full Professor at the High Institute of Computer Sciences and Multimedia, Sfax (Tunisia) and he is also the Director of the research laboratory MIRACL. He has published 20 papers in refereed journals and Lecture notes and about 100 papers in conference proceeding. His research areas include software engineering, object oriented software development and natural language processing.

Mohamed Salah Hamdi received a Diploma degree in Computer Science from the Technical University of Munich (Germany) in 1993 and a Ph.D. degree in Computer Science from the University of Hamburg (Germany) in 1999. From 1994 to 1999 he was a lecturer in the Department of Computer Science at the University of Hamburg. From 1999 to 2001 he was an assistant professor in the National Institute of Applied Sciences and Technology at the University of Tunis. From 2001 to 2005 he was an assistant professor in the Department of Mathematics and Computer Science at the United Arab Emirates University in Al Ain. From 2005 to 2008 he was an assistant professor in the Department of Computer Science and Engineering at Qatar University in Doha. Since September 2008 he is teaching at Ahmed Bin Mohammed Military College, Doha, Qatar. His research interests are in information customization, data mining, web mining, information retrieval, intelligent agents, machine learning, and artificial intelligence in general.

Raoudha Ben Djemaa Hamza received her bachelor's degree in business data processing from Sfax University, Tunisia, in 1998 and her master's degree in information system and new technology from Sfax University, Tunisia, in 2002. She is currently working as an research assistant at the Higher Institute of Sciences Applied and Technology of Sousse in Tunisia. She is also a member of the MIRACL (Multimedia, Information Systems and Advanced Computing) laboratory of Sfax University, Tunisia. Her research interests include software engineering, web application development and approaches for adaptive web applications. She has participated in several National and International conferences.

Jingwen He is currently an MPhil candidate at the Department of Information Systems, City University of Hong Kong. Her research interests are in the areas of multi-agent systems development, commonsense knowledge management, and multi-agent supported financial applications.

Sodany Kiv is a research assistant in Information Systems at theUniversité Catholique de Louvain (UCL), Belgium. In 2004, she got an engineering degree in Computer Science from Institute of Technology of Cambodia (ITC). She got a French government scholarship to study at Institut National des Sciences Appliquées (INSA) de Rennes, France for her fifth year from 2003 to 2004. Sodany Kiv worked as a lecturer in Computer Science at ITC from 2004 to 2006. In 2007, she got a master degree in computer science from Faculté Polytechnique de Mons, Belgium. She has been preparing a PhD degree in the field of Management Information Systems (MIS) at UCL since October 2007. Her research interests include enterprise application integration, ERP II system, software project management methodologies, and commercial off-the-shelf component-based software development.

Manuel Kolp is a professor in Information Systems at the Université catholique de Louvain, Belgium where he is also head of the Information Systems Research Unit and Academic Secretary of Research for the Louvain School of Management. Dr. Kolp is also invited professor with the Universitary Faculties St. Louis of Brussels. His research work deals with agent-oriented and socio-technical architectures for e-business and ERP II systems. He was previously a Post Doctoral Fellow and an adjunct professor at the University of Toronto. He has been involved in the organization committee of international conferences and has chaired different workshops. His publications include more than 70 international refereed journals or periodicals and proceedings papers as well as three books.

S. Kuppuswami is the director of studies, educational innovation and rural reconstruction of Pondicherry University, Pondicherry, India. Prior to this, he has served as Dean of the Ramanujan School of Mathematics & Computer Science, Pondicherry University, head of the Department of Computer Science, Pondicherry University, head of the Dept. of Computer Science & Engg. of Pondicherry Engineering College, Pondicherry, Lecturer in the Dept. of Computer Science & Engg, Guindy College of Engineering, Chennai. He has completed his Doctorate in Computer Science & Engg. from the University of Rennes I, France. He supervises research works pertaining to the areas of multilingual systems, software agents, bioinformatics, object-oriented systems and software engineering.

Kuldeep Kumar is with Department of Computer Science and Engineering, University Institute of Engineering and Technology (UIET), Kurukshetra University, Kurukshetra, India-136118. He has also worked as the summer trainee in the Department of Computer Engineering, Institute of Technology, Banaras Hindu University (IT-BHU), Varanasi, India-221005. His current areas of interest include Semantic Web, Automata Theory, Compiler Design, and Statistical Models.

Sandeep Kumar is with Department of Computer Engineering, Institute of Technology, Banaras Hindu University (IT-BHU), Varanasi, India-221005. He has done his BTech in information technology (Hons) and Gold Medal of the university and has completed his PhD course work in computer engineering with the best grade point from IT-BHU. He has many years of experience as a software engineer as well as teaching staff. He has published several papers on national and international levels and has also authored multiple of books. He is the member of review and editorial committee of various international publications such as WASET, WSEAS, and ORS. His current areas of interest include Semantic Web, Web-based systems, multi-agent systems, knowledge-based systems, and software engineering.

Harold J. Lagroue III received a Bachelor's of Arts degree in political science from the Tulane University College of Arts and Sciences in 1974, and a Master of Business Administration degree from the Tulane University Graduate School of Business Administration in 1976. He later received a Master's of Science degree in information systems and decision sciences from Louisiana State University in 2002 and successfully defended his doctoral dissertation in the Department of Information Systems and Decision Sciences in 2006. Since 1980 he has practiced as a certified public accountant in Lafayette, Louisiana. He currently serves as a Visiting Lecturer in the Departments of Accounting and Business Systems Analysis and Technology in the B.I. Moody III College of Business Administration at the University of Louisiana at Lafayette, and as a board member of The Moody Company.

Hokyin Lai is currently a MPhil candidate at the Department of Information Systems at the City University of Hong Kong. Her research interests are in the areas of e-learning systems development, multi-agent supported financial applications, and commonsense knowledge management.

Xiangyang Li is Assistant Professor with the Department of Industrial and Manufacturing Systems Engineering of the University of Michigan – Dearborn. He received a Ph.D. degree with research in information security from Arizona State University, a M.S. degree with research in systems simulation from the Chinese Academy of Aerospace Administration, and a B.S. in automatic control from Northeastern University, China. Dr. Li is the member of IEEE, the Association for Computing Machinery, the Chinese Association for Systems Simulation, the senior member of Institute of Industrial Engineering, and Academic Advocate to the Information Systems Audit and Control Association (ISACA). His research interests include quality and security of enterprise and information systems, heath system engineering, knowledge discovery and engineering, human machine studies, and system modeling and simulation. Dr. Li has published extensively in peer-reviewed books, journals, and conferences.

Faheema Maghraby is a Master student in the computer system department at Faculty of Computer & Information Science, Ain Shams University. She gained her BSc in information systems from Ain Shams University. Her research interests are in the areas of Bioinformatics, and Multiagent technology.

Mirjam Minor is a postdoc at the University of Trier, Germany, in the research group on business information systems. She studied computer science at the Humboldt University Berlin, Germany, and received her Ph.D. degree there in 2006. Her main research interests are in agile workflow technology, case-based reasoning, experience & knowledge management, and multiagent systems.

Santosh K. Misra is a Professor of computer and information science at Cleveland State University (CSU) in Cleveland, Ohio, does extensive research work in information systems and its applications to international business. He has been a member of the Department of Computer and Information Science in the University's College of Business Administration since 1984. Misra received a Doctorate of Business Administration from Kent State University in Kent, Ohio. He is currently the chair of the department.

Andriy Nikolov is a PhD student at the Knowledge Media Institute, The Open University, UK. He received his MSc degree from the Vrije Universiteit Amsterdam in 2004. His research interests include ontologies and Semantic Web, machine learning, data mining and information extraction. Currently his research focuses on data integration for the semantic Web.

A. F. Salam is an associate professor in the ISOM Department in the Bryan School of Business Economics at UNCG. His research interests include semantic Web technologies and e-business, strategic role of IS, services science and, trust and ecommerce. Dr. Salam has over 50 refereed articles published in various journals and conferences. His research has been published in the CACM, IEEET SMC, Information & Management, CAIS, Information Systems Journal, Information Systems Management, IJSWIS and eService Journal. He has recently co-edited the book titled, Semantic Web Technologies and E-Business: Toward the Integrated Virtual Organization and Business Process Automation published in 2007.

A. I. Saleh holds a BSc degree in computers and systems engineering with an excellent grade. He received his master's degree in the area of mobile agent ad computing. He is currently a PhD student in the computer engineering and systems department, Mansoura University, Mansoura, Egypt. He possesses an excellent knowledge of Networks Hardware and Software. Currently he is working as a teaching assistant with the faculty of engineering, Mansoura University. His research interests are in the areas of programming languages, networks and system administration, and database.

Christophe Schinckus is a postdoc fellow at the Facultés universitaires Saint-Louis in Brussels, Belgium. He completed his PhD in financial economics at the University of Paris I Panthéon-Sorbonne. Economist and philosopher of science, Dr. Schinckus works on epistemological analysis of financial theory and philosophy of economic knowledge. He has also a BSc in computer science and is interested in software engineering processes.

Daniel Schmalen studied Business Informatics at the University of Trier, Germany. Since 2005 he is member of the research group on business information systems led by Prof. Dr. Ralph Bergmann. His main research interests are in adaptive workflow management systems and exception handling of workflows.

Iftikhar U. Sikder is an assistant professor of computer and information science at Cleveland State University. He holds a PhD in computer information systems from the University of Maryland, Baltimore. His research interests include spatial database, data mining, intelligent systems and soft computing. He has authored numerous journal articles, book chapters and presented papers in many national and international conferences.

Taysir Soliman is a lecturer and a researcher in the Department of information systems, Faculty of Computer and Information, Asuit University, Egypt. She received her PhD from Ain Shams University in April 2004. Her research interests are in the areas of data mining, including clustering, graph, sequential, and tree mining, global gene expression, 3D protein structure prediction and phylogenetic trees.

Alexander Tartakovski studied Computer Science at the Universities of Braunschweig and of Kaiserslautern, Germany. 2002-2004 he had a full time researcher position in the research group "Data and Knowledge Management" of Prof. Dr. Ralph Bergmann at the University of Hildesheim, Germany. 2004-2008 he was working in the research group on business information systems led by Prof. Dr. Ralph Bergmann at the University of Trier, Germany. Since 2008, he is working at Piterion GmbH. His interests include case-based reasoning, machine learning, as well as design of algorithms.

Vi Tran is a PhD researcher in Information Systems at the Université catholique de Louvain, Belgium. She is completing a PhD thesis on agent based approach for model driven engineering of user interface. Before that, she was a software engineer at FCG, working in web services technologies.

Satoshi Tojo received the Bachelor's of Engineering, Master' of Engineering, and Doctor of Engineering degrees from University of Tokyo, Tokyo, Japan. He joined Mitsubishi Research Institute, Inc., Tokyo, Japan from 1983 to 1995, and JAIST (Japan Advanced Institute of Science and Technology), Ishikawa, Japan, as associate professor from 1995 to 2000 and professor from 2000. His research interests are in logic in artificial intelligence, including knowledge representation of artificial agent and formal semantics of natural language. In addition, he is interested in language evolution and language model of music.

Nwe Ni Tun received her PhD (information science) from Japan Advanced Institute of Science and Technology (JAIST) in March 2007. Her research was sponsored by the Graduate Research Program (GRP) of JAIST through the Special Coordination Funds for Promoting Science and Technology by the Ministry of Education, Culture, Sports, Science and Technology (MEXT), Japan. Dr. Tun is conducting research in the areas of formal ontology, Semantic Web, knowledge representation and intelligent systems. In her PhD research, she developed a semantic enrichment technique to deal with semantic heterogeneity in ontologies and ontology mapping. She received her BCSc (Computer Science) and MCSc (Computer Science) degrees from University of Computer Studies, Yangon (UCSY), Myanmar. Her current academic affiliation is a research fellow at National University of Singapore (NUS). She is a lso a member of American Association of Artificial Intelligence (AAAI) and Australian Computer Society (ACS).

Wil van der Aalst is a full professor of information systems at the Technische Universiteit Eindhoven (TU/e). Currently he is also an adjunct professor at Queensland University of Technology (QUT) working within the BPM group there. His research interests include workflow management, process mining, Petri nets, business process management, process modeling, and process analysis. Wil van der Aalst has published more than 80 journal papers, 12 books (as author or editor), 200 refereed conference publications, and 25 book chapters. Many of his papers are highly cited and his ideas have influenced researchers, software developers, and standardization committees working on process support.

Huaiqing Wang is a professor at the Department of Information Systems, City University of Hong Kong. He specializes in research and development of business intelligence systems, intelligent agents and their applications (such as nulti-agent supported financial information systems, virtual learning systems, KM systems, and conceptual modeling). He received his PhD in computer science from the University of Manchester in 1987.

Minhong Wang is an assistant professor of the Faculty of Education, The University of Hong Kong. She received her PhD in information systems from City University of Hong Kong in 2005. Her research interests include e-learning systems development, business process management, KM, and AI.

Yves Wautelet is an IT project manager and a postdoc fellow at the Université catholique de Louvain, Belgium. He completed a PhD thesis focusing on project and risk management issues in large enterprise software design. Dr. Wautelet also holds a bachelor and master in management sciences as well as a master in Information Systems. His research interests include aspects of software engineering such as requirements engineering, project management, software development life cycles, component-based development, epistemological foundations of SE and CASE-Tools but also information systems strategy.

Index

A

active agents 262
adaptive Web applications (AWA)
    299, 300, 301, 302, 315
agent-based e-learning process model
    78, 79, 88
agent-orientation (AO) 44, 45, 46, 47, 48,
    49, 50, 51, 52, 53, 54
agent-oriented 83
agent oriented programming (AOO) 40
agent-oriented software 1, 4, 25, 55
agent platform security manager (APSM)
    114, 117
agent types 36
agile workflow 279, 280, 281, 282, 294
anti-pattern 25
architectural description language (ADL) 20
architectural design
    1, 3, 5, 7, 17, 20, 22, 26
assessment answers 84, 87
atomic actual existence formula 131
atomic formula 131
atomic identity formula 131
automated virtual facilitation application
    (AVFA) 269, 270
autonomous agents 1, 25, 26
average relevancy (AR) 180, 182

B

BACIIS 31, 33, 34, 40, 42
Barcan formula (BF) 131
Bayesian network 92, 93, 94, 95, 97
behavior context 65, 68, 69, 70, 71, 74
belief-desire-intention (BDI) 13, 16, 49, 54,
    63, 64, 66, 68, 74, 75, 76

belief revision function (BRF) 63
belief, task and behavior (BTB) 56, 57, 58,
    65, 68, 69, 72, 73, 74
bioinformatics 32, 33, 41
biological data 30, 31, 32, 34, 36, 39, 40
biological domain ontology
    30, 32, 34, 39, 40, 41
biological queries 30, 32, 40, 41
Blackboard 88
block weight 170, 171, 172
Bloom's taxonomy 79, 80, 89
boundary ontology 113
business activity monitoring (BAM) 212
business operations management (BOM) 212
business process intelligence (BPI) 212

C

C3I systems 92
call-for-proposals pattern (CFP) 15, 16
case-based adaptation 279
case-based reasoning (CBR) 288
case handling (CH) 213
centralized planning 36
chain of values 18
cognitive parameters 320, 321, 322, 323, 32
    4, 327, 328, 331, 334
collaborative natural language interaction
    (CNLI) 56, 57, 59, 60, 61, 72, 73, 75
common constraint (CC) 136, 137, 138,
    139, 149, 151, 153, 155
common value attribute (CVA) 136, 137, 138,
    139, 140, 148, 149, 151, 155
communicational dimension 10, 15
computer supported cooperative work (CSCW)
    214, 231